Tom Yawkey

Tom Yawkey

Patriarch of the Boston Red Sox

BILL NOWLIN

UNIVERSITY OF NEBRASKA PRESS · LINCOLN & LONDON

Library of Congress Cataloging-in-Publication Data
Names: Nowlin, Bill, 1945– author.
Title: Tom Yawkey: patriarch of the Boston Red
Sox / Bill Nowlin.
Description: Lincoln: University of Nebraska Press, 2018.
Includes bibliographical references and index.
Identifiers: LCCN 2017017421 (print)
LCCN 2017047250 (ebook)
ISBN 9781496204394 (epub)
ISBN 9781496204400 (mobi)
ISBN 9781496204417 (pdf)
ISBN 9780803296831 (hardback: alk. paper)
Subjects: LCSH: Yawkey, Thomas A., 1903–1976.
Baseball team owners—United States—Biography.
Boston Red Sox (Baseball team)—History—20th century.
BISAC: BIOGRAPHY & AUTOBIOGRAPHY / Sports.
SPORTS & RECREATION / Baseball / History.
Classification: LCC GV865.Y38 (ebook)
LCC GV865.Y38 N68 2018 (print)
DDC 796.357092 [B]—dc23
LC record available at
https://lccn.loc.gov/2017017421

Set in Lyon Text by E. Cuddy.

Contents

Introduction

AS I BEGAN to write a biography of Tom Yawkey, I was surprised to learn how little had ever been written about him. He was, after all, sole owner of the Boston Red Sox from 1933 to his death in 1976, and his widow Jean and her trust continued to own the team into 2002—a span covering some sixty-nine years. Yawkey was also a prominent philanthropist; his name now graces many buildings and organizations. Yet one of the lengthiest pieces about him heretofore was a 3,949-word biography written by Mark Armour in 2009 for the Society for American Baseball Research (SABR) BioProject.[1] Length aside, there are few pieces written about either Tom or Jean Yawkey.[2]

The Yawkeys put their stamp on Boston baseball. Their charitable legacy lives on, in terms of both the billion dollars or so that they will ultimately have donated to worthy causes and the thirty-one square miles of conservation land they have given to the state of South Carolina. Dick Johnson of the Sports Museum of New England has said, "If they had a Hall of Fame for philanthropy, [Tom] and Jean Yawkey would be charter members of that institution."[3]

Tom Yawkey

1

A Baseball Santa, Tom Yawkey in 1933

TOM YAWKEY SEEMED to come out of nowhere when he bought the Boston Red Sox on February 25, 1933. By the end of that year, he was being called a "baseball Santa" for the largesse he was lavishing on the team and, by extension, its fans. There was even a newspaper headline reading "Boston Baseball Fans Think of Erecting a Monument to Honor Tom Yawkey."[1]

From the day he was born (February 21, 1903, in Detroit) to the day he purchased the team, Yawkey shows up not once in a comprehensive online search of the *Boston Globe*'s archives, neither as Tom Yawkey nor as Thomas Yawkey nor as Thomas Austin, which was his name at birth. Even Tom's uncle, William Hoover "Bill" Yawkey (one-time owner of the Detroit Tigers), got little press in Boston. The situation was the same with the *Boston Herald*: there was not one mention of Tom.[2]

Unknown he may have been, but Yawkey burst on Boston big-time when he became the owner of the Red Sox, the team sold him by J. A. Robert "Bob" Quinn, who had purchased the Red Sox from Harry Frazee in 1923.

The team Yawkey bought needed help badly. The Sox had finished in eighth place (last place in the eight-team league) in 1922, and they finished last again in 1923. Unfortunately the Red Sox dwelt in the American League cellar for most of the decade: they finished seventh in 1924 but then last again in 1925, 1926, 1927, 1928, 1929, and 1930. A glimmer of hope arose in 1931, when the Sox finished sixth, but they reverted to last place once more in 1932.

It was hard to believe that this was the same team that had won four World Series championships in 1912, 1915, 1916, and 1918. But Frazee had sold Babe Ruth—and any number of other Red Sox players—to the Yankees, starting in December 1919. And Quinn was severely undercapitalized. There were decent arguments to be made in favor of Frazee's selling off the disruptive Ruth, but when the player sales went on and on and the team became more deeply mired in the standings, there was some rejoicing in Boston when Quinn purchased the Red Sox from Frazee. A correspondent for *The Sporting News* even speculated, tongue in cheek, in a subtitle, "Hub May Make Date of Red Sox Sale New Holiday." Wanting a competitive ball team in Boston, American League president Ban Johnson was said to be "elated that Frazee finally is out of baseball."[3]

It can take money to build, or rebuild, a competitive ball club, and within a relatively short period Palmer Winslow, the main finance man in the Quinn group, took ill and died in April 1927. And a couple of years later, the country was plunged into the beginning of what became the Great Depression. Quinn's Red Sox couldn't even play baseball on Sundays. The overall prohibition against playing the game on the Lord's Day was overturned by a statewide referendum in November 1928, taking effect before the 1929 season, but there was a prohibition on playing within one hundred yards of a house of worship, and Fenway Park was fewer than one hundred yards from the Church of the Disciples, at the corner of Peterborough and Jersey Streets. Perhaps it was feared that the distractions of the national pastime might cause worshippers to divert to the ballpark while on their way to church.

After the referendum the Boston Braves were permitted to play on Sundays at Braves Field, less than a mile and a half from Fenway, but the Red Sox couldn't play in their own home park. The Braves welcomed the Sox to play baseball at Braves Field on Sundays beginning on April 28, 1929, but they quite naturally had to share the revenues. On February 25, 1929—four years to the day before the Yawkey purchase—Quinn was reportedly contemplating selling Fenway Park and working out a deal to play Red Sox home games at Braves Field, in an arrangement similar to one in St. Louis, where the Cardinals and Browns shared Sportsman's Park as their common home field.

An exasperated John S. Dooley (a longtime baseball fan who had helped Boston's American League franchise become established in 1901) spoke up, and at his indirect behest, Lt. Gov. Leverett Saltonstall approached the minister of the Church of the Disciples, Abraham Rihbany, and simply asked if the minister had any objection to the Sox playing on Sundays. Not at all, was the reply, given that Red Sox games started at 1:00 p.m. and the church service was over by noon. The first Sunday game at Fenway Park was played on July 3, 1932. The Yankees beat the Red Sox, 13–2. From that time forward, Sunday baseball has been played at Fenway.[4] But times remained just too tough for Bob Quinn. Had he not found a willing buyer, he might have been forced to declare bankruptcy.[5] Indeed the burden of debt he'd been bearing "would make most men jump out of a fourteenth-story window," he once said.[6]

Finally Quinn just couldn't hack it any longer and—rather than jump—he sold the Red Sox for a reported $1.5 million to young Tom Yawkey. Yawkey had just turned thirty. "He's just a kid," wrote Boston sportswriter Joe Cashman.[7]

2

Tom Yawkey and Eddie Collins Buy the Red Sox

THE SALE OF the Red Sox, of course, was front-page news in Boston. "Yawkey and Collins Buy the Red Sox," blared the February 26, 1933, *Boston Globe*. Though the money was all Yawkey's, it was not just Tom Yawkey who would front the club. He named himself president but wisely brought in a baseball man—Eddie Collins. Collins had been a star player with a twenty-five-year career for the Philadelphia Athletics and Chicago White Sox, and he had been out of the game for only a very few years. He sported a lifetime .333 batting average and was such a star that he was inducted into the Hall of Fame in 1939, just three years after the hall's first induction ceremony in 1936.

Yawkey declared he wouldn't have bought the team without Collins's coming on board. There had been other opportunities for the young millionaire, in both the Minor and the Major Leagues. But he hadn't wanted to be a minority owner or even a co-owner; he wanted to be in charge. And he hadn't wanted to be in charge of a Minor League ball club. He'd waited until he could own a Major League team.

Yawkey had plenty of money. It's true that a fortune left him by his adoptive father, his uncle William Yawkey, had become his only four days earlier, on his thirtieth birthday. But he had had millions before that. He'd inherited a large sum from his mother in September 1918 and then yet more in March 1919. On his thirtieth birthday he came into $3,408,650—twice as much as he needed to acquire the club.[1] And buying a baseball club was something he'd been thinking about. Young he was, though an earlier owner of the franchise—John I. Taylor—had been just twenty-nine when he became the team's leader in the winter of 1903–4.

The *New York Times* reported that Tom Yawkey "was always anxious to get into baseball" and that there had been a couple of possibilities, both for teams in New York, where Yawkey lived. Both the Brooklyn Dodgers and the New York Giants had offered opportunities for him to get into the game. With the Dodgers, "one half of the club could be bought, but Mr. Yawkey didn't want a half." And he may have been one of those who had bid for the Giants. ("That has never been denied," reported the *Times*.) The *Times* also wrote, "Some time ago Mr. Yawkey was urged to go into a minor league club; he could have had one of very good standing for almost nothing, but he told those interested that he wanted a big league outfit or nothing—that his father had been a big leaguer, had helped form the American League with the late Byron Bancroft Johnson and that he would not take anything that seemed small in comparison to the Tigers."[2]

Why the Red Sox, "a losing team with a crumbling 21-year-old park"? Yawkey's answer: "I don't see how any man can get any real satisfaction out of taking a success and merely running it along. That's like landing a fish that somebody else hooked. The big kick comes from taking something that's down and seeing if you can put it up and across. That's what my daddy did. I want to see if I'm as good a man as he was."[3]

How long Yawkey had been talking with Quinn is not something that can be pinned down with certainty, but it preceded his most recent inheritance, likely in anticipation. The *Springfield Republican* reported on March 2 that "the club was offered to him several months ago."[4] He had, however, "delayed buying it until he could secure the consent of Eddie Collins to become his general manager." "General manager" (GM) was a newly created position, customized for Collins. Yawkey told the *New York World-Telegram*, "I knew if I could get him, I wouldn't have anything to worry about."[5] Why hadn't he made an offer for the Giants? "I'm an American Leaguer. I wouldn't buy a National League ball club."[6]

A story that came out late in 1934 noted that it was Elise Yawkey, Tom's wife, who first talked about Tom's buying a ball club. The

Associated Press (AP) ran a story in December that year that told of a gathering with Collins and Connie Mack at Yawkey's apartment in 1932. The A's had lost, and Collins, Mack, and Yawkey were commiserating, recounting the game inning by inning, when Mrs. Yawkey spoke up during a momentary lull: "Tom, why don't you buy a club of your own and be done with it?" "Say, maybe I will," he responded. It was after they left that Mack asked Collins if Yawkey were serious and told Collins that he knew Quinn was ready to sell and that American League president William Harridge wanted to see a deal made for the betterment of the league.[7]

Tom Yawkey looked up to two men: first of all, his uncle Bill Yawkey, who had owned the Tigers, an American League club, and second, Eddie Collins, whom Yawkey had admired as a player and who, young Yawkey was well aware, had graduated (as Tom had) from the Irving School in Tarrytown. Collins was already a major baseball star by the time Tom enrolled at Irving in 1912. In 1914, the year Yawkey turned eleven, Collins won the Chalmers Award, given to the most valuable player in the American League. He was a hero to all the boys at Irving.

(Another baseball man attended Irving as well: Ryan Ellis, who was principal owner of the Cleveland Indians from 1949 to 1952.)[8]

Tom Yawkey was apparently a good athlete at Irving. After his passing, the *Boston Herald* wrote that he had won the school's Edward T. Collins medal for "all-around athletic proficiency."[9] It was actually Tom's roommate who had won the award.[10] But Yawkey came close; twice he placed second for the medal.

Yawkey first met Collins in 1928, when Ty Cobb brought Collins to a dinner at the Alamac Hotel in New York so that Collins could "meet a good friend [of Cobb's], a young fellow who is keenly interested in baseball." They talked for a couple of hours, "got along famously," and Collins learned that Yawkey had also attended the Irving School.[11]

Cobb and Yawkey had long known each other. As a boy, Tom even played pepper with Ty Cobb, Sam Crawford, and other Tigers greats. It was part of the reason that he wanted to own his own club.[12] But it was more than playing pepper. Cobb had visited Yawkey's adoptive father in South Carolina, and Tom had gone hunting with him.[13]

And Bill Yawkey had invited Cobb and others to his summer home in Sandwich, Ontario, across the river from Detroit. Cobb would hit grounders to Tom, and Bill "would be out there yelling at me because I wasn't handling the grounders well enough to suit him."[14]

Yawkey also showed a sense of democratic values and—perhaps—a shrewd sense of what it might take to reestablish a strong following for his new ball club in Boston. "I believe the real, genuine interest in baseball lies in the bleachers. I may be mistaken, but I think the grandstand fan is a casual—he comes to the game in much the same mood and manner that the theatergoer goes to a popular hit. Over in Boston we are going to encourage the bleacher fan," he told the *Boston Globe*.[15] The *Globe* story ran under the headline "More Bleacher Seats at Sox Park Planned," and indeed Yawkey had already begun to think of renovations to Fenway Park. First, however, he moved to renovate the team.

The announcement of the purchase in the *Boston Globe* introduced Thomas A. Yawkey as a "New York millionaire business man, with general investments in national resources." At the end of a lengthy story on the sale, the paper's James C. O'Leary added of the new owner, "He is at present connected financially with and is active in the manufacturing of various mining, manufacturing, lumbering, and paper mill companies, both in the United States and Canada." He was a member of a considerable number of private clubs. "Mr. Yawkey said he could not take up a residence in Boston. Even New York, he said, was hardly a satisfactory headquarters from which to conduct his various and widespread interests, but it was better than anywhere else."[16]

The February 25, 1933, deal had been consummated shortly after 11:00 a.m. in the Fenway Park offices, but it was not announced until four hours later at a luncheon that Quinn hosted at the Copley Plaza Hotel, attended by Quinn, Yawkey, Collins, Will Harridge, Boston newspapermen, and some other guests. A photograph of Collins and Yawkey flanking Quinn ran on page one. There was no comment on the price paid. It was understood that Collins was awarded a partial share in ownership, perhaps as much as 10 percent.[17] This was quite a gesture on Yawkey's part; he was noted for always wanting to own 100 percent of anything he did own. It may have been a necessary element in enticing Collins, or it may have reflected Yawkey's reverence of Collins.

Quinn had also been offered an ongoing slice of ownership—so the story said—but he declined, saying he'd had his shot and felt it was best to give the new owners complete control. Part of his reason to decline may have been the state of his finances; he admitted, "In case of another bad season, I could not stand any further losses."[18] He did agree to stay on for a while as an adviser, but Yawkey became the president and Collins the vice president (VP) and GM. New York attorney Frederick DeFoe became club secretary. DeFoe had been the executor of William Yawkey's will and served as Tom Yawkey's legal adviser. The two remained close for the rest of DeFoe's life.

After the luncheon, Yawkey expressed polite regrets that Quinn couldn't see his way to staying on. "He said the new organization would do its utmost to give Boston a winning club, and he believed it would eventually be successful if hard work, desire and the expenditure of money could bring about such a result."[19]

Collins had introduced Yawkey and Quinn about eight months earlier, but there were no discussions of a possible sale until a very few weeks before it occurred. Collins said it all had developed "so quickly that it was a shock to him." He added, "Of course we cannot be expected to build up a ball club in a day or a week or a year."[20] Yawkey said almost the same thing: "It will not change in a day, a month or even a season. It is going to be a long, hard job, but we are going through to the end and eventually we will put the Red Sox back on their rightful heights."[21]

They got to work almost at once. Marty McManus was kept on as manager for the 1933 season. There wasn't time to make a change at this point, and McManus hadn't been responsible for the state the team was in. He'd taken over only partway through the 1932 season.

After the announcement luncheon, Harridge, Yawkey, and Collins paid a courtesy call to Judge Emil Fuchs, the owner of the Boston Braves. Just four days later, the Red Sox party from Boston set off for spring training in Sarasota, Florida.

The transition from Quinn to Yawkey was complete. There remained one final transaction, which would enable Tom Yawkey to take full ownership of Fenway Park. The Yankee owners held a mortgage on the park, dating back to their acquisition of Babe Ruth. It led to speculation that the Yankees actually owned part of the team. The AP succinctly wrote of Frazee's ownership of the Red Sox: "He wrecked it by selling Babe Ruth, Everett Scott, Ernie Shore, Dutch Leonard, Joe Bush, Stuffy McInnis, Sad Sam Jones, Harry Hooper, Duffy Lewis, Herb Pennock, Joe Dugan, Waite Hoyt, and a host of lesser lights."[22] *The Sporting News* wasn't any less kind: "He wrecked the Boston team whenever occasion arose to make a deal for money profit; he practically killed baseball in Boston."[23]

The franchise hadn't done better under Quinn. We noted in chapter 1 that there was something approaching euphoria when his group bought the Red Sox, but after Quinn's financial angel died, he never had the funds to seriously compete in putting first-rate talent on the field. As early as July 1923, there had been an editorial in *The Sporting News* that reported, but then challenged as likely spurious, a published story that Bob Quinn and the new owners of the Red Sox had issued an appeal to the other ball clubs to help out the Red Sox by sending them surplus players in order that Boston could become more competitive. For his part, Quinn had confessed back in November 1928 that he hadn't even dared trade with the Yankees after all the ill will engendered by Frazee's repeated dealings with the New York rivals.

Quinn's financial shortcomings led to speculation about one incident. In 1926 some small fires broke out during the May 7 ballgame and were doused by fans, but on the evening of May 8 a three-alarm blaze "wiped out the third-base bleachers [and] damaged the western end of the grandstand."[24] Glenn Stout and Richard A. Johnson suggest that "the circumstances appear suspicious," given that Quinn pocketed the insurance proceeds and elected not to rebuild that part of the ballpark.[25] It fell to Tom Yawkey to do so years later, after he had purchased the team.

Quinn dashed the thought that there had been a Yankees' ownership interest:

Now that the Red Sox have passed out of my hands, I want to kill a rumor that has persisted for many years. The New York Yankees have not, and never have had, any financial interest in the Red Sox. I have been carrying for many years a load that would make most men jump out of a fourteenth-story window. I tried and spent plenty of money to build up the Red Sox. I failed and I apologize to the Boston public. Now I am turning that over to new owners who are eager to do everything required to put Boston back on the baseball map. I want to assure the Boston public that Mr. Yawkey and Mr. Collins are well equipped to build up the Red Sox.[26]

The following day, the *Globe* wished Quinn well: "Against great handicaps he made a game fight to get the Red Sox into the race. That he failed was due to conditions beyond his control." Yawkey was acknowledged as "the son of an ex–major league magnate," and it was said he "knows his baseball."[27] The *Hartford Courant*'s well-connected sports editor, Albert W. Keane, wrote, "[Yawkey] has always wanted to follow the footsteps of his foster father in both business and baseball."[28] And the *Boston Herald* noted that the new owner "was raised in baseball" and "has money and enthusiasm."[29] AL president Harridge said, "We are thoroughly delighted about the transaction and the American League is fortunate to have two men like Collins and Yawkey among its magnates. They have their pep, ambition, and, what is more important, the finances to carry on and bring Boston back to its former high place in baseball."[30]

Had Yawkey also fully freed Fenway Park from the grip of the Yankees? The *Boston Herald*'s Tim Horgan notes that Yawkey used to enjoy telling the story of how, on buying the team, he learned that, indeed, the Yankees' Jacob Ruppert still held a mortgage on Fenway Park dating back to the deal with Frazee for Babe Ruth. He reportedly asked Ruppert if he (Ruppert) could hold onto the mortgage for one more year, and Ruppert replied, "Of course. We're happy to have you in the league." But, Horgan adds, there reportedly followed a series in which the Sox swept New York and Ruppert got so angry that his lawyer called the Red Sox the day after and demanded Yawkey pay off the mortgage at once. "I sent the s.o.b. a check the next day," laughed Yawkey every time he told the story.[31]

3

The First Season

BUILDING UP THE Red Sox was indeed the mission. Yawkey and Collins spent most of February 27, 1933, meeting with Quinn and Marty McManus at Fenway Park, working on the transition. The AP reported that Yawkey had budgeted $250,000 for immediate use in rebuilding the ball club. The new owners looked over Fenway Park itself—the field was covered in snow at the time—and "did not miss a thing in the whole layout."[1] They specified some changes they'd like in the layout of the offices. But given that it was late February, the business of preparing for the season was already under way. Clubhouse man Moe Gottlieb had already departed for Sarasota along with the trunks containing player equipment. On March 1 traveling secretary Phil Troy and a dozen others—including a few newspapermen—departed from Boston for spring training. The veteran Hugh Duffy went along to help coach the team.

As soon as he returned to his office in New York, Tom Yawkey apparently read of rumors that Babe Ruth had been offered the position of manager. Confused, he telephoned Quinn in Boston but was reassured by Quinn's response: "Don't worry about things like that. You'll get plenty of the same sort of shocks while you are in baseball, and you might as well start in not allowing things like that to get under your skin."[2]

Yawkey arrived in Sarasota on the morning of March 8, with Eddie Collins and Mrs. Collins, for his first visit to the spring training site of his new team.

Back in Boston a little over a week later, there was a fire at or near Fenway Park, as reflected in the fire record of March 17. At 3:25 p.m.

there was a fire in a "tar kettle" on Jersey Street. Thomas Yawkey was listed as the owner of the property there. The loss was reported to be $10.[3] As we shall see in looking at 1934, it was not the last fire to take place at Fenway Park.

After everyone had settled in and the exhibition games were under way, Collins sat on the terrace of the team hotel at Sarasota and told John Kieran of the *New York Times* how the sale of the Sox had come to fruition:

> It all started with a dinner at Tom Yawkey's home on Fifth Avenue, in New York. That was on one of the trips of the Athletics to New York some time ago. You see, Ty Cobb introduced me to Tom some seven or eight years ago. Ty knew him through his father, who once owned the Detroit club. Well, I got to know Tom Yawkey pretty well. We have gone to the same school . . . though I was there before he was. So we saw one another fairly often; used to go shooting together, and so forth. We became good friends.[4]

Collins told Yawkey that the Red Sox might be available, and Collins arranged and attended a luncheon with Quinn and Yawkey, but at the time Quinn wasn't ready to sell. At the winter meetings at the end of 1932, though, Quinn asked Collins if Yawkey might still be interested. Collins continued: "I had been down in North Carolina shooting ducks with Tom. I told Bob I'd write him, and I did. Tom wrote back that he'd be North as soon as the ducking season was over and he'd be glad to see Bob Quinn and go over his proposition. He came up in January and they met in Tom's office." They asked Collins to sit with them, and, Collins told Kieran, "they more or less came to terms."[5]

A while later the headmaster of the Irving School died, and both Yawkey and Collins attended his funeral. On the train on the way back to the city, Yawkey asked Collins if his contract with the Athletics was one that would allow him to leave. Collins said he talked to Athletics owner Connie Mack the next day, telling him that something had come up. "I know what's come up," Mack said. "Yawkey wants you to go to Boston with him. You run right along with him. You can't miss."[6] The story took on more drama in subsequent telling. "One of the toughest decisions I've had to make in my life,"

Collins later said, "was when Tom Yawkey asked me if I would go with him as general manager if he bought the Red Sox. I had come to regard Mr. Mack as I would my own father and even the thoughts of leaving him were terrifying. But, after I had a terrible time breaking the news to Mr. Mack and asking him what I should do, he put me at ease by saying, 'Eddie, if you don't take the job, I'll fire you.'"[7]

Only five weeks after Yawkey bought the Red Sox and even before the new owner had seen his team play a regular-season game, the team itself came close to being wiped out. On April 2, as the team made its way north to Boston, there was a deadly train wreck. The "Cavalier"—the Pennsylvania Railroad's Norfolk–to–New York express train carrying the Red Sox—was traveling at about fifty miles per hour when it hit an open switch and crashed around 3:12 a.m. in the town of Wyoming, Delaware (five miles south of Dover), derailing the engine and eight of the train's twelve cars, including two of the three sleeper cars containing the Red Sox team, and tossing the players about. Both the engineer and fireman were killed, but the Red Sox escaped serious injury. *Boston Globe* reporter Mel Webb was on board and provided a graphic account of the twisted wreckage. Doc Woods, the Red Sox trainer, helped minister to some of the wounded passengers on board. Outfielder Tom Oliver tried to extricate the engineer but gave up when he realized the man was dead. Only pitcher Bob Kline felt possible effects, to his shoulder, later in the day. Four of the Sox trunks were destroyed, but not even one bat was cracked. Players were naturally relieved at their narrow escape.[8]

The 1933 season got under way with back-to-back losses on the road in New York on April 13 and 14. The team was 4-11 in April and never got higher than fifth place. On May 9, with the Red Sox in seventh place, both Yawkey and Collins attended the annual spring meeting of American League owners in Cleveland. They made their first big move by packaging $50,000 of Yawkey's fortune with backup catcher Merv Shea to St. Louis. Shea had been in the Minor Leagues for the past three seasons. In exchange the Sox secured left-handed pitcher Lloyd Brown and catcher Rick Ferrell, who later became a Hall of Famer.

It was Yawkey's inaugural spring meeting and according to the

Boston Globe, "Mr. Yawkey entered the conference with his checkbook out and wasted little time going into a huddle with Phil Ball, owner of the St. Louis Browns, who has been losing considerable money this season by playing to empty stands."[9] The cash was key, said Collins: "The deal for Ferrell and Brown was to a large extent a cash transaction, although we also gave the Browns Mervyn Shea."[10]

Yawkey also conferred with Cleveland GM Billy Evans, making an offer for outfielder Joe Vosmik. On May 15 the Sox acquired outfielder Dusty Cooke from the Yankees.

To the newspapermen, Yawkey said, "Boston is a good baseball town and deserves a winning team. I am in the market for good players and will buy any that are available. I do not intend to stop until the Red Sox are strong enough to compete with any club in the league on even terms." Collins added that he was talking with the Yankees about shortstop Lyn Lary.[11]

Three days after acquiring Brown and Ferrell, the Red Sox purchased both pitcher George Pipgras and infielder Billy Werber from the Yankees in a straight cash deal.[12] The tables had turned from the Frazee days; now the Sox were buying players from the Yanks.

Yawkey had gone out on the road with the team at the beginning of June, but he stayed behind in New York to attend to some business matters before rejoining the ball club on June 9 in Boston. He seemed to express a little frustration that he hadn't found more willing sellers after his initial acquisitions. "We are trying to make some deals, either by trade or by purchase, but they are pretty much up in the air at present. I find it rather difficult to get anywhere. . . . We will, you may be sure, keep on trying."[13]

The *Courant*'s Keane wrote that the Yawkey–Collins combo had ignited a fresh and fervent revival of interest in the Red Sox in Boston. The purchase of Brown and Ferrell, he wrote, was "the first of what Boston expects will be a new era in its baseball. It was the first time since 1918 . . . that the Red Sox have purchased stars from other American League clubs." He added, "Since that time, the Red Sox have done all the selling and no buying."[14]

On July 2 Tom's adoptive mother, Margaret A. Yawkey, died of pneumonia at the age of fifty-six.[15] Yet more wealth came Tom's way through inheritance. Four days later Eddie Collins was back in uniform for a day as third-base coach for the AL team managed by Connie Mack at the very first All-Star Game, on July 6, played at Chicago's Comiskey Park.

Tom Yawkey spent time in Boston during the summer, hosting AL president Harridge in his box on July 23, when the Red Sox took two from the White Sox, 6–2 and 7–2. Judge Fuchs of the Braves visited Yawkey's box during the day too.

The Red Sox made other moves to reposition the organization for the future. On July 31 they purchased the Reading, Pennsylvania, ball club (New York–Pennsylvania League) from Bob Quinn. Baseball teams at the time had working relationships with some clubs but only rarely had what we know as farm clubs today. The AP assessed, "Although Collins will not admit it—he would be overwhelmed by every club willing to unload if he did—Reading will soon go down in baseball history as the start of the modern Red Sox farm system."[16]

Collins foresaw future moves. "Taking over Reading as a farm is all right as a starter, but the Red Sox need contacts with the double-A leagues. I think a youngster should get at least a year's experience in the International, American Association or Pacific Coast League before getting into the majors."[17] The Red Sox also implemented some form of arrangement with Montreal (International League).

The August 9 *Globe* reported a "red hot rumor in Philadelphia . . . that owner Tom Yawkey and vice-president Eddie Collins had made an offer of $100,000 to Connie Mack for Jimmie Foxx. Of course there was nothing but denials."

On September 7 the Sox purchased the contract of Baltimore's slugging outfielder Julius Solters. The following day the Red Sox had a doubleheader combining both Ladies' Day and Shriners' Day celebrations.

Throughout August and September, the Red Sox inhabited seventh place in the league standings. Their only month with a winning record had been July (16–10), but a nine-game losing streak in August seemingly put paid to any hope of their rising further in the ranks. Seventh place was an improvement on last place, but it wasn't where Yawkey (and Sox fans) had hoped they would be. There had been giddy thoughts before the season began of the Sox's reaching the first division, maybe even as high as third place. But they finished seventh at 63-86, 34½ games behind the first-place Senators. The White Sox were 31 games back. Only the Browns were worse, 43½ games behind Washington.

The Red Sox finished the season in New York with a 6–5 loss to—of all people—Babe Ruth, who threw a complete game in the last game he ever pitched. Since coming to the Yankees, Ruth had pitched in five games and was an undefeated 5-0. He'd also homered in the game, his thirty-fourth of the season.

The last Red Sox home game was on September 24. Attendance had climbed from 182,150 in 1932 to 268,715, a 47.5 percent increase despite the fact that the Great Depression had truly taken hold and settled in to stay. It was well below the 396,000 average that Fenway had drawn in the years 1928–31, but it was a major increase over 1932, in a year when average AL attendance had dropped 6.6 percent. In 1934 Fenway Park attendance doubled.

Just getting out of last place constituted a successful start to Yawkey's ownership. The Red Sox had finished last in nine of the preceding eleven seasons. That they had won twenty more games in 1933 than in 1932 provided some hope for Red Sox fans. Tom Yawkey never saw his team finish last; there were only four more times a Red Sox team ever finished last—1992, 2012, 2014, and 2015.

A little less than a week before the end of the home season, the Red Sox announced that Yawkey and Collins had met for several days with representatives of Osborn Engineering of Cleveland— the firm that had designed Fenway back in 1912—and that it would embark on a substantial renovation of the facility while the Sox were wrapping up the season on the road. All in all, the budget was estimated to be in the $300,000–$400,000 range and perhaps as high as half a million dollars. "It certainly will mean work for a large number of men," observed the *Globe*; it was a major project to launch during the Depression.[18]

Yawkey himself was well aware of the impact the construction would have, and he was making a mark as a very good citizen in the city of Boston. "Unemployment was rife," he told *Baseball Magazine*, "and Mayor Curley of Boston urged us, if possible, to elaborate our plans so as to give employment to more men. This, I may say, had a considerable influence on our plans. . . . During the months of January, February and March there were over a thousand laborers on our payroll. The net result was that instead of two hundred thousand dollars we planned to spend, we have already spent well over a million."[19]

Eighty years later, Dick Johnson of the Sports Museum of New England said the following of Tom Yawkey:

"There are really two reasons I think he's remained a hero in Boston. The first is that during the depths of the Depression, the rebuilding of Fenway Park was the second-largest construction project in the city after the building of the Mystic River (Tobin) Bridge. And he hired union help when he didn't have to. He put food on people's tables at a time when it was very important to the community. The second thing, of course, is his stewardship after the Braves moved out of town—his stewardship and the Red Sox stewardship of the Jimmy Fund. The lasting legacy is the philanthropy of the Yawkey Foundation, which is a superb legacy to have left in town."[20]

The improvements would increase Fenway's capacity by about ten thousand seats, enlarging the grandstand in both length and breadth:

A left wing will be added to it that will extend to the left field corner, and there will also be an extension of the right wing into the pavilion. The center field stand will be moved back and a concrete wall will be erected, and there will be no more "Duffy" Lewis cliff in the outfield. All the wooden structures in the present plant will be removed, except the roof of the grandstand, and only steel and concrete will be used in the reconstruction work. About all that will remain of the present grandstand will be the roof, the south side wall and the foundation. There are to be exits from the new extensions on Lansdowne and Ipswich Streets.[21]

One can visit Fenway Park in the early twenty-first century and see how current sections 28–33 reflect the left-field extension and sections 1–8 embrace the extension of the right wing. Fenway Park celebrated its one hundredth anniversary in 2012, and the renovations done under the John W. Henry/Tom Werner/Larry Lucchino ownership in the decade from 2003 through 2011 have given it a life that foresees at least another thirty years. As Dick Johnson said in 2014, "The current ownership was wise enough to realize that Fenway Park is sort of the essence of the team. . . . The new Fenway Park was possible because of the '33–'34 reconstruction. And that's entirely Tom Yawkey."[22]

Duffy's Cliff was an earthen incline on the field that butted up against and helped support the left-field wall. With its removal, left fielders would now have to rely on a warning track to let them know they were approaching the wall, rather than finding the grade rise and having to run uphill to catch a ball in front of the wall. From this construction forward (the 1934 renovation is still acknowledged by a plaque affixed to the exterior of Fenway Park on Jersey Street, now Yawkey Way), the left-field wall would loom even higher than it had before and become evermore the most distinctive feature of Fenway. It would not become what was later dubbed the "Green Monster" until 1947, however, when Yawkey saw to the removal of all the advertising that covered the wall, making it a very good hitter's backdrop. Even then it was decades before the wall picked up the "Green Monster" moniker.

Before they left town in 1933 for their final four games on the road, the Red Sox played the Boston Braves in a charity game to benefit the unemployed. The game was held at Braves Field, but the Fenway Park ticket office was also open for sales. The price was $1.00 per ticket, and $16,000 was raised for charity. The Braves beat the Red Sox, 2–1.

4

The First Offseason

THE DAY AFTER the 1933 season ended, the Red Sox released Marty McManus as field manager after Collins and the new Red Sox owner had huddled at Yawkey's suite in the Hotel Commodore in New York. No replacement was announced. Yawkey lounged against a door jamb while Collins fielded questions from the press. The Red Sox executives uttered nothing in the way of criticism of McManus, but—wrote Victor O. Jones of the *Boston Globe*—"It was evident from their replies to a machine gun salvo of questions that one of the outs about Marty had been his independence, or that at least, was the way I interpreted several of the answers."[1]

The first move in player personnel came on October 12, when the club traded for middle infielder Chalmer "Bill" Cissell, sending to Cleveland pitcher Lloyd Brown, who'd performed adequately but filled a need for the Indians. Cissell was "regarded as a star of the first magnitude" in the eyes of James C. O'Leary of the *Globe*.[2] Less than two weeks later, after a brief hunting trip, Tom Yawkey announced that the Red Sox had traded Tom Winsett and Johnny Michaels to obtain left-handed pitcher Fritz Ostermueller.[3]

The big news came the following day. On October 26 the Red Sox were said to have purchased Lefty Grove from the Philadelphia Athletics for an estimated $200,000.[4] The actual announcement didn't come until mid-December, but the word was out, if it had not been before, that Tom Yawkey was willing to do what it took to make the Red Sox contenders once more. Ticket sales in Philadelphia had dropped significantly (Philadelphia was still without Sunday baseball), and Connie Mack needed revenue, even if it meant selling off a player whom the *Washington Post* called a "superstar," adding, "Grove has long been recognized as the most effective of all big league pitchers during the past decade."[5] He'd been 31-4 as recently as 1931 and 24-8 in 1933. His record for the Athletics was 125-79, with a 2.88 ERA; he'd led the American League in ERA from 1929 through 1932.

Yawkey, it was said, was planning to invest a million dollars in his ball club before the start of the 1934 campaign. Half of that would be available for renovating Fenway, but he "announced he had $500,000 more in cold cash ready to purchase playing material from either the American or the National Leagues."[6]

Eddie Collins must have felt he'd found a dream job. He was reported to be "determined that next season his club [would] finish in the first division of the American League. . . . Yawkey, the man with the bankroll and baseball enthusiasm, is with Collins one hundred per cent in this viewpoint."[7]

On October 27 rumors again emerged from New York that Babe Ruth would be named manager—and that Tom Yawkey was in favor of the idea.[8] Two days later, those rumors were finally put to bed when Stanley "Bucky" Harris was named manager at a buffet luncheon for the press at Fenway Park. Harris was given a one-year contract. Yawkey and Collins had "assured him they would provide him with plenty of additional strength." Yawkey himself said, "We intend to do everything possible to strengthen the club."[9] The next day, Yawkey was in New York watching Fordham play Alabama at football.

More rumors were flying to the effect that Connie Mack was going to break up the Athletics and that players were for sale. Collins visited Mack in early November and then returned to Boston, reporting that Philadelphia had approved the playing of Sunday baseball and that this could alleviate Mack's financial straits. In mid-month Collins went south, first to Minor League meetings at Galveston and then, with his wife and Mr. and Mrs. Harris, for a visit to Tom Yawkey's place in South Carolina.

The group spent a couple of weeks hunting birds and deer on Yawkey's approximately twenty-thousand-acre estate on South Island, near Georgetown. Red Sox players George Pipgras and Hank

Johnson were among the party. They arranged a shipment of duck, quail, and venison to Fenway Park that arrived on December 1. A letter from Eddie Collins explained, "Tom is the best shot I ever saw—better, I think, than Chief Bender, whom we used to think had no peer; and Mrs. Yawkey is pretty near as good as her husband. It has been a wonderful outing."[10]

Collins and Yawkey both returned to Boston on December 5, and Collins told reporters that the weather had been good the whole time; that the party had gotten the "bag limit [on] quail, wild turkey, deer, etc."; and that Pipgras had gotten two wild turkeys on Thanksgiving morning. In the meantime, the renovation of Fenway was well under way. Six to eight jackhammers were pounding away at the concrete in portions of the park being demolished, while new concrete footings were already in place in other areas. *Globe* reporter O'Leary wrote, "It is rather a weird looking place just now, but a hive of industry."[11]

During the winter meetings in Chicago on December 12, the Athletics traded pitchers Lefty Grove and Rube Walberg and infielder Max Bishop to the Red Sox in exchange for Bob Kline, Rabbit Warstler, and a sum of money believed to have been $125,000. O'Leary called it "the greatest deal put over, from a Boston viewpoint, since Harry Frazee sold Babe Ruth to the Yankees, but that one was in the reverse."[12] (Mack had also sold Mickey Cochrane to the Tigers and George Earnshaw to the White Sox.)

On December 14 a column in the *Globe* led with a note: "Tom Yawkey waved his magic wand again yesterday and Carl Reynolds, a fast, hard-hitting outfielder, landed in the Red Sox fold. His acquisition should help." The Red Sox traded pitcher Ivy Andrews, outfielder Smead Jolley, and cash to get Reynolds. The Sox also announced a new working agreement with the Kansas City ball club.

A week and a half before Christmas, Cy Peterman wrote a story out of Chicago that painted a picture of stockings hung by the chimney with care: "Mr. Yawkey is the smiling young man with the $1,000,000 check book. He . . . has gone to great expense in providing a complete and fancy line of new Sox for Boston's Christmas. Indeed, the row of Red Sox that Mr. Yawkey can now hang out, will quite outdo anything by Santa Claus. To Boston, Mr. Yawkey becomes a fair-haired Santy himself." Collins responded, "We're almost through for the moment. No, not all through." Tongue in cheek, Peterman wrote, "Yes, the Red Sox are set. They are sitting so well that just about all American Leaguers are willing to concede them 1934's pennant."[13]

Of course, as the *Washington Post's* Shirley Povich pointed out, "It is hardly conceivable, however, that [the Yankees' Jacob] Ruppert will stand by idly if Owner Tom Yawkey of the Red Sox wishes to make the 1934 campaign strictly a battle of check books. The Yankee owner has quite a corpulent checking account of his own, and what with his brew now legalized [thanks to the end of Prohibition], is probably in the market for some outstanding talent."[14]

After the winter meetings Eddie Collins remarked, "I never enjoyed the mid-winter big league meetings as much as I did at Chicago. Tom Yawkey had a great time. He's primarily in baseball for the kick he gets out of it. His other business interests are greater, materially, than his baseball venture, but he's the type who wants to be successful in everything, even in his avocations."[15]

5

Tom Yawkey's Past

WHERE HAD TOM Yawkey come from? On the day he was introduced to the Boston press, the *Boston Globe* wrote, "He traces his ancestry to the early settlers of America who came from England and Holland."[1] The paper noted that he was born in Detroit on February 21, 1903, the son of William Hoover Yawkey and Margaret Alice Williams Yawkey. The paper was wrong.

Margaret Alice Williams Yawkey had been born in Grass Lake, Michigan, to Mr. and Mrs. Charles Williams. She attended the University of Michigan for two years. As noted in chapter 3, she died on July 2, 1933, at the age of fifty-six. Her husband William had died in 1919, and she had inherited $10 million.

At the age of twenty-eight, William Yawkey had himself inherited a $10 million lumber fortune from his father, and he had a strong interest in baseball. On January 22, 1904, he bought out Samuel F. Angus's interest in the Detroit Tigers. Angus had become wealthy in railroad and insurance and headed a syndicate that had purchased the team only a little more than two years earlier, in November 1901, but his business ventures had begun to falter and he needed to seek a buyer. His bookkeeper, Frank Navin, arranged the $50,000 sale.[2] Yawkey has been described as a "playboy boss [who] regarded his ownership of the Tigers as a lark, occasionally treating his players to a drunken night on the town to break a slump, or slipping a hundred-dollar bill into a favorite's pocket to recognize a job well done. He left most of the day-to-day details of the business to Navin."[3]

William Hoover Yawkey was also "the richest man in baseball" according to an article by Hugh C. Weir in *Baseball Magazine*. Weir describes him as "a constant avoider of the limelight, a shrinker from publicity," adding that one would search in vain at the executive offices of the Tigers for any sign of his ownership of the team. He was said to be rich enough that he could have written a check to buy up every one of the other franchises, in both the American and National Leagues. Weir describes Bill's father, William Clyman Yawkey, as a "German prospector" who was primarily interested in lumber but then found that under the lumber he had cut was the immense mineral wealth of the Mesabi Range.[4]

William Yawkey allowed Navin to buy up stock in the Tigers, even loaning him the money to buy a half-interest in the team in September 1907, a purchase that eventually made Navin a decent fortune.[5] Weir states that Yawkey had promised Navin a half-interest in the team if Navin could win a pennant.[6] After Yawkey moved to New York, Navin effectively ran the club until Yawkey's death in 1919, though Yawkey invested capital to help build the $300,000 ballpark that became Navin Field in 1912.[7]

Tom Yawkey thus grew up in a baseball family, his adoptive father owning the Tigers before Tom was a year old. However, the *Globe* was wrong about Tom Yawkey's parents. He had been adopted by the Yawkeys. Bill Yawkey was not truly his father, though Tom considered him as such while growing up. Bill Yawkey was his uncle.

William Clyman Yawkey (Bill's father) and his wife had two children, Bill and Augusta Lydia Yawkey. Augusta married an insurance man named Thomas J. Austin, and they had two children themselves—Emma Marie Austin and the subject of this book, Thomas Yawkey Austin.

There's an interesting, if bizarre, story about Thomas J. Austin from 1896, one of the few stories found about him in a detailed search of online newspaper databases. In November, Austin and John S. Rankin had gone to survey timber on Ontario's Fitzwilliam Island, off the northern shore of Lake Huron. The captain of the tug *Seaman* dropped them off with a guide. When the captain returned a week later, "on entering the shanty occupied by the men [he] found the body of Rankin in a box standing against a wall. His face was covered with bruises. Pinned to the dead man's breast was a note stating that his comrade and guide had left for Tobermoray." Rankin's death was said to have been an accident.[8] Austin survived, but one wonders what truly occurred.

Thomas J. Austin died of pneumonia on September 18, 1903, in Bruce, Ontario, when the infant Tom was not quite seven months old. (Born on March 20, 1894, Emma was nine years older than Tom.) Augusta Austin seems to have raised Tom and perhaps looked after Emma for a few years, but by 1906 she had entrusted them to her brother. Bill Yawkey was unmarried at the time (his first wife, Emma Noyes of Vermont, had died in 1892), but he had the children looked after. As Glenn Stout and Richard A. Johnson have speculated, the children "grew up in a fantasy world in a posh apartment at 12 East 87th Street in New York catered to by maids, nannies, and servants."[9]

Bill Yawkey married Margaret Draper in 1910. She had reportedly come from a modest background, growing up in an apartment over a Detroit plumbing store. She was a "cloak model" and salesgirl in a Woodward Avenue shop.[10] Margaret and Bill had first met some years before their marriage. After they met, he fell in love and "installed her" in a flat. "Master of millions, he would not spend money on her. Yet he spoke always of his deep affection for her. There were those who said that he was testing her love for him by making her live in such surroundings. Whatever the reason, he changed suddenly. He slipped away to New York with her and married her there and settled upon her a private fortune. She blossomed forth as a charming hostess in New York after almost ten years of near poverty in her loft above a Detroit bakeshop."[11] In any event, Bill and Margaret tied the knot about four years after Augusta Austin had transferred Emma and Tom to Bill Yawkey's care. Margaret Yawkey later explained that Tom "was taken into the family because his own mother was ailing, and it was felt that it would be better for him to be brought up under his uncle's direction."[12] Thomas Yawkey Austin took on the Yawkey surname around 1917, and it was conferred upon him legally when Augusta Austin died in September 1918.[13]

Bill Yawkey seemed to be—perhaps reflective of his social class and the times—a man who preferred the company of men. How much time he spent with Margaret is not known. As it happens, Bill and Margaret seem to have had a child of their own—Elizabeth, born out of wedlock in July 1906—but not one they acknowledged.[14] Their apartment on East Eighty-Seventh Street was indeed well staffed. The New York State census of 1915 listed the two of them as residents, with six servants: two butlers, two maids, one house-man, and one cook.

It's not clear how much contact Emma and Tom had with each other. It is notable that they shared the same financial adviser in later life, but that was business. Whether there was warmth between them, we do not know. Census records in 1910, four years after Augusta reportedly entrusted the children to her brother, show Augusta Austin living in New York on Central Park West with Tom and a servant, Mary Mead. The 1915 New York State census shows Thomas Y. Austin, age twelve, living on Central Park West with his mother, Augusta Austin, and three servants: Mary Brooks, a cook; Alberta Bright, a maid; and Mamie Smith, a housekeeper. There was clearly some ongoing relationship between mother and son. Though Tom was listed with his mother in both censuses, he was by 1915 a student at the Irving School in Tarrytown, where he boarded from the age of nine until he graduated at seventeen.

Augusta Austin died in New York of influenza on September 5, 1918. Stout and Johnson report that her estate was worth about $4 million and that Tom was the sole heir.[15] Perhaps the inheritance simply reflected primogeniture. Bill and Margaret Yawkey adopted Tom and changed his name around: he became Thomas Austin Yawkey rather than Thomas Yawkey Austin.

Emma Austin married attorney Leland Gardner. Their first child, William A. Gardner, was born in Toledo in June 1920. Robert Gardner was born in 1922, and Jane, in 1926. In 1930, however, Emma and Leland divorced in Volusia County, Florida. Emma and the children lived on Park Avenue in New York—with seven servants. She later married Gilmore Ouerbacker (1892–1984) of Louisville.

The idea that the Austin side of the family may have been trace-able to the "early settlers of America" (as mentioned in the *Globe* article cited above) is questionable because the 1900 census indicates that both of Thomas J. Austin's parents had emigrated from

England in the nineteenth century. He himself was born in Michigan, although the Clyman and Noyes families had a deeper American background.

The Yawkey side, through Augusta Yawkey, had other roots. Stout and Johnson note that Tom Yawkey's great-great-great-grandfather was Johann Georg Jäky, who had come to Philadelphia from Germany in 1736. Jäky became Yaky and then Yockey and then Yawkey.[16] Anyone dating back to 1736 could fairly be described as an early settler. National boundaries have always been somewhat fluid, and since there was no Germany until 1871, it's possible that Johann Georg Jäky came from rather close to what we would now call the Netherlands. He may well have come from the area around Aachen or Enschede or Gronau.

Bill Yawkey lived only a little more than six months after his sister Augusta died. He died of illness thought to be bronchopneumonia in Augusta, Georgia, on March 5, 1919. Margaret and Tom were both with him at the time.[17] They were on their way to the Detroit Tigers training camp.[18] Bill Yawkey's will divided his estate (estimated at $40 million) among Margaret, Emma, and some others, with a full 50 percent going to young Tom, sixteen at the time. Tom got $500,000 up front, and the rest was to be held in trust for him until he turned thirty. Emma received $500,000, to be held for her until she was thirty. Tom said his ambition was to become a businessman like Bill Yawkey, whom he called "my dad."[19]

As is only natural, and perhaps especially so with a parent who was as outgoing as Bill Yawkey, Tom wanted to emulate his father. It turned out, also perhaps not surprisingly, that Tom became as shy as Bill Yawkey had been boisterous. Nearly twenty years after his death, a King Features Syndicate article described William Hoover Yawkey as follows: "A combination of shrewd businessman, spendthrift playboy, ardent sportsman and baseball fan, Bill Yawkey was a glamorous figure in his day." He would sometimes get such a thrill out of seeing his team win that he would inadvertently undermine its consistent effectiveness: "He'd take the whole team out on a party, rendering [the players] useless for work the next day."[20] One could well make the argument—and some have—that Tom spent much of his life trying to measure up to the image he held of Bill Yawkey.

Bill became very friendly with some of the Tigers, Ty Cobb in particular. Star baseball players were perhaps even greater celebrities in those days than they are today, and there is every reason to believe that the young Tom was enthralled with the glimpses of life his colorful uncle showed him when he was home from boarding school. Bill Yawkey bought a couple of expansive estates near Georgetown, on the coast of South Carolina. (Georgetown itself was first laid out in 1729, and many of the downtown streets, as well as the name of the town itself, reflect homage to British royalty. Five rivers flow into Winyah Bay and the Atlantic Ocean.) Bill would relocate to one of his properties, South Island—as Tom did too in later years—to hunt and fish and enjoy life. Tom followed the same pattern, taking hunting trips to far-off locales like Wyoming, but he always returned to South Carolina. The neighbors there were the Vanderbilts and the Baruchs—some of the wealthiest figures from the world of New York business—dubbed by the Georgetown County Museum as the "second Yankee invasion."[21] Other neighbors included Isaac Emerson, Archer M. Huntington, Dr. Henry Horris, Jesse Metcalf, Thomas G. Samworth, Walker Inman, and Herbert Pulitzer. Historian George C. Rogers Jr. wrote, "By 1931 there was scarcely a plantation left in the hands of native South Carolinians."[22]

Bernard Baruch himself was a native of Camden, South Carolina. His family moved to New York, where he was schooled and amassed a fortune. His purchase of Hobcaw Barony was not a random act but was rooted in his own family background. There was a significant Jewish presence in Georgetown as well.[23] It seems that a visit by President Grover Cleveland to South Island in December 1894 sparked an interest among some of the rich Northerners to move to the region. Tom Yawkey ultimately felt most at home at South Island.

While Bill Yawkey may have hobnobbed with the elite, Tom kept much more to himself. He would often entertain a small party—a Cobb or a Lefty Grove with a couple of friends—but he rarely interacted with the titans of finance on the other estates.

There may have been a rupture in Tom's relationship with Cobb, though. Carl Yastrzemski reports that Yawkey told him of a time he and Cobb went hunting in the Rocky Mountains for mountain goats with some friends, one of whom had cancer. All agreed that the man, likely on his last hunt, would get the first shot of the trip, but when they spotted a ram the very next day, the hypercompetitive Cobb shot the animal. "Mr. Yawkey got so mad that he jumped all over Cobb and they wrestled right there on the side of the mountain. Mr. Yawkey said he never spoke to Cobb again." How did the fight come out? "Cobb kicked the crap out of me," Yawkey admitted.[24]

Tom Yawkey may have been a little more effervescent as a young man than the reserved and almost hermitic man he became. Stout and Johnson note that "a classmate once told a reporter that Yawkey's years at Yale were 'a life of fast cars, pretty girls, drinks and laughs.' He spent freely, invited friends along for the ride, and showered them with money. Behind the wheel of a sleek sedan with a slew of companions in tow, bolting from one speakeasy to another or nipping from a flask, Yawkey was the center of the party. He found it easy to attract women. He was clearly a catch."[25]

On the subject of fast cars, when he was a sophomore, Tom was arrested at his Yale residence for a hit-and-run accident on May 19, 1922. The *New Haven Journal-Courier* reported, "Yawkey is alleged to have run into a machine on College Street, damaging it somewhat but not stopping to ascertain what had taken place." A three-hour search led to his arrest. He was released on a $500 bond.[26]

Tom was arrested again a little more than two years later. The charges were reckless driving, operating a motor vehicle while under the influence of liquor, and resisting an officer. He seems to have gotten off lightly. He was "fined $134 and forced to pay for an officer's uniform after being found guilty on three counts." Two others were charged, one of them fined $5 for obstructing the sidewalk. The news story described the incident: "Yawkey was arrested Friday night while driving a car on Ocean Avenue at a fast rate of speed. He was told to stop, but paid no attention to the command, but later when he arrived at Savin Rock he was arrested for speeding by another officer and taken to headquarters. While being booked he started a dispute with an officer and assaulted him, the police say. The dispute was over almost as soon as it started but the officer's uniform was ruined."[27]

In 1924 Yawkey reported that his estimated expenses for his junior year were $3,000.[28] That sum offered the same buying power as a little over $40,000 in 2014.[29] This is not to say that he hadn't been taught the virtues of humility at an early age. A widely published story told of how his adoptive mother once sat him down after he'd seen stories calling him the "world's richest boy." Mrs. Yawkey "arranged a series of saucers on the table with varying heaps of beans, graded according to the wealth of the Rockefellers, Vanderbilts, Morgans and others, and in the last saucer placed one bean to represent the Yawkey millions. This, according to the young man, was a lesson he never forgot."[30]

Bill Yawkey had taught him something else too, and Tom put it into practice, applying the lesson even after Bill Yawkey was gone. "The Yawkeys had the idea that the only way to learn a business was from the bottom," Tom told Roger Birtwell of the *Boston Globe*. Thus Tom Yawkey spent some time working in a deep copper mine, about three thousand feet below ground. "I worked a regular shift. It was in the middle of a desert—about 65 miles northwest of Phoenix—and nobody then had ever heard of Scottsdale." He also spent time working underground in a family-owned coal mine in West Virginia. At what age and for how long he worked at the two jobs is unknown. While at Yale, he worked about four weeks of each summer at one of the Yawkey logging camps in Wisconsin. "I learned a little about lumber," he said, "and it was great for getting in condition."[31]

A fraternity brother wrote a piece on Yawkey in 1933, just after he had purchased the Red Sox. It could hardly have been more flowery. He recalled "Tim" as "the sort that is accustomed to knock out homers no matter what Fate has on the ball," and he added, "He is possessed of a disposition that would make the ordinary sunny day of metaphor seem like a fog-filled midnight in a London coal cellar by comparison. If anyone had ever seen Tim when he didn't have a grin spread all over his face, the news has not yet spread."[32]

Tom Yawkey always enjoyed driving. Stories for years afterward recorded how speedily he drove south to spring training—driving himself, not with a driver. Those who worked with him on South

Island still remember that he drove around the roads there almost with abandon. Jim Sargent, who sometimes served as his driver, recalls, "He had a special car, a dark green 1956 Ford Fairline. I could drive that car to the airport to pick him up . . . but he was going to get on the wheel coming back. You'd see that thing going one hundred miles an hour and he's talking to me or he's talking to his wife, and I'm sitting there looking at the speedometer. . . . We'd take a trip, like to go to Mt. Pleasant. I'd have Mrs. Yawkey in the station wagon and he's in that '56 Ford. He's going one way and I'm going another way, each seeing who could beat the other." Yawkey always drove Fords, "straight stick and overdrive."[33]

Until Yawkey gave it up, alcohol was a reliable companion. Some rumors had it that he drank as much as a bottle of whiskey a day.[34] Seagram's VO was a favorite, and with it he sometimes said things he later regretted or sloughed off. Red Sox executive Joe Cronin's daughter Maureen remembered the following:

My father was fiercely protective of Tom, and he would fend off all newspaper reporters and writers who wanted interviews. From what I've been told, specifically by Curt Gowdy, Tom was a difficult boss who would fire my father regularly after a few drinks. I think he was tough on my dad. I think everybody thought that my dad was running the show—but he wasn't. He covered for Tom a lot of the time. He tried to . . . keep Tom's name out of the newspapers, and he took the brunt of most of what came down. I think he thought that was his job. Dad never once complained about Tom; in fact, he was very fond of him as a man. I asked about Tom once: "Dad, he's kind of a quiet person. What's he like?" He said he [Tom] was one of those guys who likes to have two people working for him. I think he was trying to tell me he was one of those bosses who would pit you against someone else in hopes that you would perform better. That was the impression my dad gave me.[35]

Tom Yawkey gave up alcohol not for medical reasons but sometime in his fifties, says wildlife biologist Phil Wilkinson, who lived on South Island and worked for Yawkey for the last ten years of Yawkey's life. "He told me that when he drank, his personality changed . . . to be unpleasantly aggressive. He didn't like himself, whatever went on there. He felt that the best thing for him was to just not to fool with it. He said he couldn't drink it moderately very easily. If he had a drink, he wanted another one."[36] Columnist Bud Collins said of Yawkey in Boston, "They kept him under wraps, I think."[37] Yawkey later developed diabetes.

Tom Yawkey and women—and children—were another matter, a complicated story to which we shall return. We can present an assessment here, offered by Judge Alex Sanders of South Carolina: "If I had to describe Mr. Yawkey's personality, I would say he was a simple person. He wasn't a complicated person. In fact, he was almost childlike. I always thought that stemmed from the fact—this is an amateur appraisal on my part—that he probably didn't have control of his money all his life, until he was much older. If you go your whole life until you're thirty years old without making any decisions or doing anything that isn't okayed by someone else, that would tend to make you immature. A late starter."[38]

At the Irving School, Tom impressed Headmaster John M. Furman:

> Tom is one of my best boys. He is absolutely loyal. I have never found him to do one mean thing. He is just a natural boy with simple tastes. He joined the First Reformed Church in November. He is straightforward in everything, has a level head, and I know he is going in the right way. He is one of my best students. While in the lower school he won the scholarship for standing highest in the school for four years and is at present at the head of his class. He rooms with Allen [sic] MacMartin, who is the same age. They have been chums ever since they have been in the school.[39]

Yawkey was described in a *Baltimore Sun* article as "a fair lad, of good physique, a blond, with two dimples that add much to the attractiveness of his smile." The article noted that MacMartin was said to be worth $12 million. Headmaster Furman continued praising his charge: "You'd never know Tom was a millionaire if you were to see him playing the game in old shoes and an old shirt. He is no boy for the streets. He prefers to be in school and to study. If he has any time he devotes it to sports." Furman said he had taught Tom the value of money. He used to give him a quarter a week so that he could buy some penny candy or whatever in the town, and Tom always gave him an accounting of how he had spent the money.[40]

In an article about his inheritance, the sixteen-year-old Tom told a *New York Tribune* reporter, "Do you know I've never had more than one dollar in my pocket at any one time? That is my allowance—one dollar a week."[41]

At the time the *Baltimore Sun* reporter talked with Tom about inheriting so much money at such a young age, Yawkey wasn't wearing old clothes—though in later life, he clearly preferred to do so. "He wore a blue suit with a small stripe in it, a soft collar and a black necktie striped with green. On his watch chain hung a miniature football of gold, which he had won for excellence in that sport." Tom called football his favorite sport to play. He was an end on the Irving team.[42]

Tom was naturally sad to lose his father (the second loss of a father, we might remind ourselves). "I knew I was going to be very rich some day but I never expected 'my dad' to die. I thought he would live on, and when I finished college I could go into business with him and he could guide me right. Now I've got to go it alone."[43]

6

Yawkey at Yale

TOM YAWKEY GRADUATED from the Irving School in 1920 and entered Yale, where he studied at the university's Sheffield Scientific School. The *Boston Globe* notes that while he was there, he "specialized in mining and chemistry in preparation for his life work."[1] Later in 1933, in an article about Yawkey's acquisition of the Red Sox, the *Tampa Tribune* wrote that he "played second base for dear old Yale."[2]

As a freshman in the Class of 1924, Thomas Yawkey was assigned dormitory room 334W.[3] He did not sign a pledge form and therefore was not rushed for a fraternity. At Sheffield he became a member of Phi Gamma Delta. By virtue of entering the Sheffield Scientific School, he became a member of '25 S., the Class of 1925. Yawkey was active in sports at Yale, a fact first mentioned in the *Yale Daily News* on April 16, 1923, when he and a classmate named Talbot were given charge of the traps for the Gun Club.

Yawkey was one of sixteen "Sheff Men" on the '25 S. baseball team; this was not the Yale varsity but a Sheffield team from his class. They played games against other Sheffield classes.[4] "I'd say I was a mediocre ballplayer in those days," he said years later. "I didn't work too hard at it. I was mostly a second baseman. I hit the ball pretty good but my fielding probably wasn't anything too sharp."[5] More than fifty years later, the *Boston Globe*'s Ray Fitzgerald wrote—based on we know not what—that Yawkey's "biggest accomplishment on a ball field was completing an unassisted triple play while holding down third base at Yale."[6]

Tom was also one of nine nominated for the '25 S. track team and one of eleven on the class's basketball team.

He wasn't called "Tom" at Yale; he was called "Tim." A profile in a 1925 class publication notes the following:

Tim prepared for college at the Irving School and took the general science course at Sheff. Before entering our Class at the beginning of Sophomore year, he was a member of the Class of 1924. He was on the Freshman Baseball Squad, Dr. Bull's Squad in Sophomore year, and the Class Baseball and Basketball teams for three years, and has his numerals. He is a member of Mory's Association and Phi Gamma Delta and Vernon Hall. He roomed with A. A. MacMartin, *ex-*'24 S., in 1921–1922, with L. V. Bogart, ex-'24 S., in Sophomore year, with E. Ohnell, Jr., '24 S., in Junior year, and with Tony McDevitt in Senior year. He expects to devote his time to mining and lumbering after graduation. His permanent address is Suite 840, 200 Fifth Avenue, New York City.[7]

For the Junior Promenade, his guest was Miss Kathryn Warren.

Tom's adoptive mother, Margaret Yawkey, was noted only once during his time at Yale, when she served as one of the patronesses for the Vernon Hall tea dance on November 21, 1924.

The only other time Tom Yawkey turns up in the *Yale Daily News* is in the issue of May 18, 1934, when Mr. and Mrs. T. A. Yawkey are listed among the six couples of patrons and patronesses of the President's Ball; university president and Mrs. James Rowland Angell were among the others.

So Tom played class sports but not university varsity sports and kept a low profile, graduating with the Class of 1925. For the '25 S. Class Book, he completed a form listing, among other items, the most likely to succeed (Tom said it was John C. Newsome). He described himself as a Congregationalist, said that his favorite sport—both to play and to watch—was football, and offered a number of other favorites:

Favorite character in fiction: Falstaff
Favorite novel: *The Pride of Palomar*
Favorite prose author: Peter B. Kyne

Favorite poem: "Crossing the Bar"

Favorite poet: Robert W. Service

Favorite actor: Bill Hart

Favorite actress: Patrice Clark

Most valuable subject: Business Law

Hardest subject: Physics

Favorite political party: Republican

Favorite world figure: Paavo Nurmi[8]

Fellow "Fiji" (Phi Gamma Delta member) James McKeldin had noted Yawkey as a gamer, with some shortcomings as an athlete: "He was one of those notorious human sacrifices known as a second-string football man, one of the queer chaps who persist in going out for the game even after it is obvious that they haven't the remotest chance of ever making that touchdown in the last six seconds and thereby figuring largely in the Sunday morning papers—one of those fellows who are forever being matched against bigger, better teams, and who get nothing out of the perpetual pummeling they take except a funny thing they don't talk about, called sport."[9]

Yawkey, for his part, submitted thoughts for his Senior Class Book. He was already engaged to be married, he reported, but focused on athletics when he wrote, "My chief regret to my college course is that I did not go in for more athletics and take them more seriously." He also offered some "advice to Freshmen": "Pay less attention to your clothes, New Haven girls, and New York timetables, and more to your books and thus profit greatly. I supposed we must all have one fling, but why do it all at once—spread it out over a little longer period."[10]

Yawkey kept in touch with his freshman year roommate Allan A. MacMartin, who had come with him from the Irving School. A note sent to Yale by another Fiji (F. H. Diebold) in November 1932 informed that MacMartin and "Brother Yawkey" had just returned from a two-month hunting trip to Alaska, where they had both killed their limit of Alaska brown bear and black bear—two of each. "Brother Yawkey reports that they also had excellent fishing of various kinds, including trout and salmon, did some whaling and porpoise harpooning, and killed all kinds of ducks and geese."[11]

Yawkey had been treasurer of his fraternity house at Yale and perhaps helped it survive the Depression, providing "continued interest and generosity toward the House during the past years of financial troubles."[12] Some of the animals he killed while hunting adorned the front hall of Vernon Hall in 1938. At the time, he routinely visited on Alumni Day. He often attended Yale football games as well.

At the time Yawkey purchased the Red Sox, the *Boston Globe* reported he was deeply involved with business and "active in the management of various mining, manufacturing, lumbering, and paper mill companies, both in the United States and Canada. His clubs include the New York Athletic, the Detroit Athletic, the Congressional Country Club of Washington D.C., the Sleepy Hollow Country Club and the Rockwood Hall, also Yale Club."[13]

It was while at Yale that Tom became engaged to Elise Sparrow. He graduated from Yale in June 1925, and they got married on June 18. There was no notice of his marriage in the *New York Times* or other papers of the day. His chosen bride was no New York debutante or high society woman, and Tom had no parents fussing over him. The November 2, 1924, *Times* noted his engagement, the news provided by his future mother-in-law from Birmingham, Alabama, though her name was given as Mrs. Starrow Aiken and her daughter's name as Miss Elise Starrow. The *New York Herald Tribune* wrote that her parents were named Akin. The family names were Sparrow and Akins, and Elise's mother's name was Stella. James L. L. Akins was her stepfather.

Elise Sparrow was a very attractive woman. Born in Birmingham in 1899, she grew up in modest circumstances. Her father, William Sparrow, was a railroad conductor. Her stepfather worked at a fire station as assistant chief. There was no "Miss Alabama" in 1922, but Miss Sparrow competed as "Miss Birmingham" in Atlantic City that September in the Pageant of Beauty. Mary Catherine Campbell of Columbus, Ohio, won the competition, but in 1925 *The Mirror*, the yearbook of Phillips High School (where Elise went to school), connected Elise to one of the most noted illustrators of the day: "Elise Sparrow, the first Miss Birmingham, has made quite a hit in New York, and because of her unusual talents has been adopted by Howard Chandler Christy." Christy was noted for portraits of the

"Christy Girl."[14] While touring with a dance troupe, Elise is said to have caught Tom Yawkey's eye.[15] Apparently he used to enjoy calling her "the fire chief's daughter."[16] In Birmingham, she was called "the Cinderella girl."[17]

The best man at Tom and Elise's wedding was John Newsome. Attending the wedding, held at Margaret Yawkey's East Eighty-Seventh Street home, were Mr. and Mrs. Howard Chandler Christy, Senator T. Coleman DuPont, Frank Hitchcock, and Will Hays.[18] The newlyweds were to sail on the *Mauretania* on June 24 and spend the summer abroad.[19]

7

The First Full Season of the Yawkey Era, 1934

NO ONE EXPECTED the Red Sox to lay immediate claim to the 1934 pennant, but there was a strong feeling of optimism as the year got under way, the first full year of Yawkey ownership. The team hadn't finished 64 games out of first place, as it had in 1932. It had finished only 34½ games back. It had won 20 more games than in 1932, and it had climbed out of the cellar, to seventh place. Fans knew Yawkey was bringing new hope to the ball club. There was hope that a first-division finish might be attainable in 1934.

Several newspapers ran photographs of new manager Bucky Harris, GM Eddie Collins, and Tom Yawkey, posed with some of the game they had killed while hunting in South Carolina. Collins met with some Boston writers on January 3 and passed out some wild duck that Yawkey had shipped up from South Carolina. He told them that Yawkey's goal was to build up the ball club and become more competitive, to "give the Boston fans a run for their money" and to create "a club which should be in the running all the time; one which will be able to hold its own against all comers."[1]

The renovation of Fenway Park was well under way, with work going on day and night. The pouring of cement for the center-field bleachers was expected to be completed within a day or two, and the pouring of the cement for the new right-field pavilion was pretty much ready. Costs had already gone well over original estimates, and when Yawkey was told that some other changes he'd suggested would cost even more, he is quoted as having said, "Hang the money. What is the use of having money unless you do something with it?"[2]

The year had started with Yawkey's shock upon learning of the suicide of a relative, nineteen-year-old Cyrus Yawkey Woodson, a Deerfield College student and the only male heir of his grandfather, Wisconsin lumberman and financier Cyrus Yawkey.[3] There had once been a Yawkey Park baseball field, in Wausau, which hosted its first games in May 1911. It was the home of the Wausau Lumberjacks and was named after Cyrus Yawkey. The park's name was later changed to Recreation Park and finally to Athletic Park; Minor League baseball was played in Athletic Park until 1990.

In the depths of the Great Depression, 1932 and 1933 were the worst years of all, with GDP declining a staggering 13.4 percent in 1932 alone. Forty percent of the nation's banks had failed, and industrial stock prices were down 80 percent. With the launch of the New Deal in 1934, the plunging GDP was slowed to 2.1 percent, but unemployment was 24.9 percent. In the morning edition of the January 5, 1934, *Boston Globe* it was briefly noted that Yawkey "appears to be doing more than his share in aiding the cause of recovery. Keeping a force of men at work through the Winter on his $700,000 improvement project at Fenway Park certainly is a real contribution to the public welfare."

Around 1:00 p.m. that very afternoon, a massive general-alarm fire broke out in the bleachers at Fenway, causing an estimated one-quarter of a million dollars of damage to the park and five nearby buildings. The fire had even leapt across Lansdowne Street and completely gutted at least two brick buildings there. The fire was blamed on a salamander.

It wasn't an amphibious, lizard-like creature that was being blamed. "Salamander" was the name given to a heating unit, in effect a stove, used to dry wet concrete. One apparently had become overheated and ignited some heavy tarpaulins that were being used to shield the concrete under the bleachers from the weather outside. The fire spread with remarkable rapidity. The concrete supports were still encased in the wooden molds into which the concrete had been poured as recently as twelve hours earlier. A lot of scaffolding and lumber on the ground had caught fire as well as the oil-soaked tarps. Intense heat cracked windows in the Checker Cab Garage across the street and scorched many of the automobiles inside. Thousands of automobile tires at the Seiberling Building were destroyed as well, adding to the thick black smoke billowing out of the area. The smoke hung so heavily in the winter air that rail travel behind the buildings across Lansdowne (where the Massachusetts Turnpike is today) was suspended for a while and proceeded very slowly after that.

Telling reporters that the Sox still planned to open the season on time, Eddie Collins declared, "If we have to rebuild sections of the bleachers . . . we'll look on it as just another construction job, and hire additional men."[4] There had been 766 men employed before the fire, and the number was expected to increase to over 1,000.[5]

Suspicion that arson may have been involved cropped up only later, when another fire broke out in mid-February.

Tom Yawkey paid a couple of days' visit to Boston on January 24, looked over the damage, and checked on the renewed reconstruction before leaving for New York to attend to what were reported as his "20-odd other business enterprises."[6] Though it's not evident anyone believed him, he stated, "We are all through buying and trading for this year. We've got enough baseball stock on hand to land in the .500 class and that will give us a nice start."[7] He told Burt Whitman of the *Boston Herald*, "I'll be tickled if the Red Sox finish in the first division this year."[8]

Only a few days earlier, the team had begun to make some modest moves. After pitcher Herb Pennock was released by the Yankees in the first week of the year, the Red Sox signed him, prepared to use him as a pitcher if the forty-year-old still had it in him but would be glad to have him as a pitching coach if not. There had been significant turnover in Yawkey's first twelve months in charge. Only six players who'd begun 1933 with the team were still there by Opening Day 1934: Roy Johnson, Bob Seeds, and pitchers Hank Johnson, Gordon Rhodes, Bob Weiland, and Johnny Welch.

Yawkey was among those attending the baseball writers' dinner on February 4 at the Hotel Commodore in New York. Red Sox pitcher Mickey McDermott later said that Tom Yawkey owned the Commodore.[9]

On February 27 Yawkey was among those who paid their respects to John McGraw in his Pelham Manor, New York, home, where his body lay in state. Yawkey was one of the youngest of owners, and McGraw was a long-time veteran of the game.

The March 1 papers quoted Yawkey on another visit to Boston: "One cannot build a pennant-winning club in one year. Of course, if we finish in the first division, the higher up we are, the better we will be pleased." Would the Sox allow any games to be broadcast over the radio in 1934? It was too early to say, Collins answered.[10]

As noted in chapter 3, the Red Sox were building a farm system, owning the Class A Reading club and with working agreements with four others: Kansas City and Jersey City (both in Double A), Columbia (Class B, Piedmont League), and Joplin (Class C, Western Association).

The March 18 game against Detroit at Sarasota was the "first game of ball ever played on Florida soil between two American League clubs" and also the first Red Sox preseason game anywhere against an American League opponent.[11]

In a reflection of his breakneck driving style, Yawkey reportedly drove the six hundred miles from South Carolina to Sarasota in under twelve hours (quite an accomplishment on the roads of the day), arriving on March 20 to take in some spring training and meet some of the new players. He was "in good trim" from playing handball, and he threw the ball around some; a day later he suited up in a Red Sox uniform, did a little catching, and hit some fungos.[12] In the game on March 22, Branch Rickey sat with Yawkey and Collins and saw the St. Louis Cardinals beat the Red Sox, 9–7. On March 25 Elise Yawkey saw her first game. The following day, Tom failed to attend the game at St. Petersburg due to a sprained ankle that kept him in his room. He and Mrs. Yawkey drove to a game in Fort Myers a few days later. On March 30 the Yawkeys both sat in the bleachers for an exhibition game at Payne Park in Sarasota against the Boston Braves. Both Collins and Yawkey headed back north on March 31, but Yawkey took the train rather than driving due to his ailing ankle. He shipped his automobile on the train.

The Boston City Council had taken a moment on March 26 to express its gratification to Tom Yawkey for his efforts to build a championship club and for his investment in the renovation of the ballpark.

Yawkey had made his wife's nephew happy, having a Red Sox uniform made up for little Jimmy Sparrow. Jimmy took in the Red Sox exhibition games against the University of Alabama at Tuscaloosa on April 6 and in his hometown of Birmingham on the April 7. Mrs. Yawkey was an alumna of the university and had arranged for the game in Tuscaloosa.[13] The eleven-year-old Jimmy came to visit his aunt Elise in Boston in June and saw the Sox win five straight, sitting on the Red Sox bench as a mascot in four of them.[14]

The telephone helped Tom Yawkey keep in touch with the club from New York. He was said to have called traveling secretary Phil Troy an average of five times a day.[15] When the Sox played in nearby Newark on April 12, Yawkey came to attend the game. And he naturally traveled to Boston for the 3:05 p.m. game start on April 17, when New Fenway Park (as it was very briefly called) opened.[16] The ticket takers and ushers had brand-new uniforms. Governor Joseph B. Ely threw out the first pitch and bounced it as numerous political and baseball dignitaries looked on. The game drew a record Opening Day crowd for a Boston baseball game. Groundskeeper Tommy O'Neil was reported to have done a good job, but expectations were perhaps different at that time than today: "In the outfield the grass has not started to appear, but you could spot signs of its coming out in a few scattered places."[17]

Under new manager Bucky Harris, the Red Sox lost to the Senators in 11 innings, 6–5. They lost the next game too but then took both games of a Patriot's Day doubleheader. They were 76-76 at season's end but 42-35 at home.

Yawkey was in Boston for the first home stand, though when the team went to Washington, he returned to New York. Mel Webb of the *Globe* noted, "He has mines and ships, rubber wares and lumber, zinc and iron, and lots of other things to keep him in New York."[18] In later years, Yawkey would not come north to Boston until May or even June, and he also would hardly ever attend spring training.

Yawkey took in the April 22 game against the Yankees, which drew the biggest crowd in Red Sox history at Fenway (44,631); it was an 8–1 loss. It was, wrote the *Christian Science Monitor*, the first time that would-be spectators had been turned away from a game at Fenway.[19] Even that crowd—thousands over capacity, penned on the field of play itself behind ropes and watched over by mounted police—would be topped in August. The new park was a hit, and Yawkey's willingness to pour money into getting prime players had kindled the optimism of the fan base. Some of that investment was reflected in better ticket sales.

On April 29 the Massachusetts State Building Trades Council unanimously passed a resolution to commend Tom Yawkey for his fairness to organized labor, offering "working and wage conditions never better in the history of this city."[20]

On May 2 more than eight hundred people attended a testimonial banquet for Tom Yawkey at Boston's Copley Plaza Hotel. Mayor Frederick Mansfield was there, as was former mayor James Michael Curley. The governors of Maine and Rhode Island were there, and so was Connie Mack. Baseball coaches from Harvard, Holy Cross, Boston College, and Tufts were present, as was an array of business people from Boston and New England, representatives of the Catholic Church and other clergy, and Judge Emil Fuchs of the Boston Braves.

The younger Yawkey was often out on the town for athletic events and some civic affairs during his first couple of years in Boston. Despite all the banquets and honors that began to come his way, there is every indication that he remained a very modest, even shy, man. A syndicated story that ran in several newspapers in June claimed, "Tom A. Yawkey, Boston sportsman, blushes meeting strangers." "No one loves baseball better or hates the spotlight more," wrote Grantland Rice about Tom Yawkey in December 1947.[21]

Yawkey remained shy, avoiding the limelight more as the years passed. Some fifty years later longtime Red Sox broadcaster Curt Gowdy told the *Boston Herald*'s Mike Shalin, "Mr. Yawkey was a man who stayed in the background—but he came to the front when you needed him."[22]

In early May, Yawkey came up with a bonus plan for his Red Sox players if they came in first, second, or third in the American League standings. The plan would give them a certain percentage increase of their salary for a third-place finish, double the increase for a second-place finish, and triple the increase for first place. It was not promoted as an incentive (of course it was expected that they would be playing hard all the time) but as a way of sharing in the prosperity of the club, should the club do well. *New York Times* writer John Kieran reported that for his part, Eddie Collins—a devout philatelist—had suggested to the postmaster general that the U.S. Post Office begin to ready some postage stamps to honor the rise of the Red Sox.[23]

There hadn't been that many transactions before the season got under way. The only two deals of real significance were both completed in May. On May 15 the Sox acquired Lyn Lary from GM Ed Barrow of the Yankees for Freddie Muller and $20,000. And on May 25, after Yawkey and Collins met in Cleveland with Indians president Alva Bradley and GM Billy Evans, the Red Sox acquired pitcher Wes Ferrell and outfielder Dick Porter for Bob Weiland, Bob Seeds, and $25,000. The left-handed Ferrell came with a 102-62 career record and was now united with his catcher brother, Rick Ferrell.

On June 11, the same day Sox pitcher George Pipgras went on the voluntarily retired list, Yawkey and Collins, with Herb Pennock, Hugh Duffy, and Tom Daly, were among the 4,500 or so who went to the Heights but saw Boston College lose a ten-inning game to Holy Cross. After Mrs. Yawkey came to town for the Yawkeys' ninth anniversary, she joined Tom at a number of events. The Red Sox climbed into third place on June 22 with an 11–1 win over the White Sox. They were in and out of third place for a full month and again for another five days in mid-August. There was such a demand for tickets to Fenway that scalpers emerged. On the Fourth of July Boston police arrested nine people outside the park as "ticket speculators."

In early July, Lefty Grove had his tonsils removed. He was 4-4 at the time, on his way to an 8-8 season that matched the team's .500 record for the year—after seven consecutive seasons of 20 or more wins, with an average of 24½ wins a year. His work was a severe disappointment, and clearly his tonsils were not the reason.

On July 10 Yawkey treated the team and the entire Red Sox office staff to a trip to the Polo Grounds in New York to take in the All-Star Game, the second one ever held.

It would be called tampering today, but in late July Yawkey said he'd like to buy Jimmie Foxx from the Athletics. A week before the season ended and the St. Louis Cardinals headed to the World

Series, he said he'd like to buy both of the Dean brothers, Dizzy and Paul, from the Cardinals.[24]

Even the expanded Fenway Park couldn't handle some of the crowds that turned out for games. Somehow the team managed to cram in a reported 46,766 paying customers for the August 12 doubleheader against the Yankees, and another 15,000 fans "stormed and fumed in the streets because they could get no nearer to the scene."[25] Several thousand patrons were accommodated by being let out onto the field itself from right to center field. Clearly fire regulations were different (or nonexistent) at the time.

Collins and Yawkey were out hunting for more pitching, and they went to a game in Rochester, home of the Double A Red Wings, on August 13, an off day. On August 15 the two came to a working agreement with the Syracuse Chiefs, making the team a farm club for the Red Sox.[26]

On August 20 the Sox traveled to Springfield, Massachusetts, and played the Milton Bradley Toymakers company team, raising thousands of dollars in a benefit game for the Shriners Hospital for Crippled Children. The Sox played nine in-season exhibition games during 1934; they had a perfect 9-0 record in such games. It's too bad they had to play regular-season games against such teams as the Detroit Tigers and the Cleveland Indians.

The team finished 76-76, as noted. Winding up with a .500 record may not seem that impressive, but the last time the Sox had won even half their games was in 1918. They finished fourth, out of the money in terms of the promised player bonuses, but a first-division finish nonetheless. Fans had flocked to Fenway, with the larger-capacity and fully renovated park a draw in itself, in addition to the stars that Yawkey and Collins had brought in. Attendance figures were more than triple the 1932 total of 182,150 and more than double the 1933 total of 268,715: 610,640 paying patrons. Yawkey's investment in the team and ballpark was at least attracting significantly greater revenues.

Yawkey and Collins took in the World Series games in Detroit, Yawkey rooting for the Tigers, of course. He personally ran the football pool at Fenway Park after baseball was done for the year.[27]

A couple of weeks after the season ended, the Red Sox made

a bold move by acquiring Joe Cronin from the Washington Senators for Lyn Lary and the huge cash sum of $225,000—"the biggest proffer in baseball history."[28] The largest prior deal had been for $139,000, the amount that the Yankees reportedly paid to get Babe Ruth from the Red Sox. Cronin was a star shortstop but would do double duty as player-manager for the Red Sox. The cash sum was an astonishing amount of money at the time, "an amount greater than the entire player payroll of fourteen of the sixteen teams."[29] The player personnel salary total for the Red Sox had been $145,896 in 1933.

Yawkey had asked Collins if he wanted a particular player or manager, and Collins replied that "there was only one player in the entire American League who could do as much for Boston as Mickey Cochrane did in 1934 for Detroit": Joe Cronin.[30] Yawkey reportedly went to Washington and personally visited team owner Clark Griffith and made an offer Griffith ultimately could not refuse—despite the fact that Cronin was married to Griffith's daughter Mildred. He did refuse the offer the first time around. And he hung up on Yawkey, exploding, "To Hell with you!" when the Red Sox owner called him a couple of weeks later to follow up on his initial offer. Better judgment prevailed; Griffith was in debt to a bank for $124,000, and he also knew Cronin would always be subject to "that son-in-law guff" if he remained with Washington. So he agreed to sit down with Yawkey and then agreed to terms—so long as Yawkey sent Lyn Lary to the Senators. "'Lary, too?' Yawkey shouted. I replied, 'Yes, Lary, too, because I need somebody to replace Joe."[31]

Griffith sold his son-in-law to Tom Yawkey, and Yawkey signed Cronin to a multiyear contract. "I regard him as the greatest shortstop in the game today," said Collins. "And don't think the price paid was exorbitant. Just realize we get two great stars for the one price— Cronin the player and Cronin the manager."[32] The sum expended brought the total spent by the "boyish millionaire" on the team and the renovations of Fenway to over $3 million since "TAY" had taken over ownership.[33] Several years later Yawkey said that the deal for Cronin was the only one he had personally engineered.[34]

If we judge by figures from a U. S. House of Representatives Judiciary Committee report, the $3 million figure more or less matches the total of all team salaries for all sixteen Major League clubs added together.[35]

Joe Cronin spent time at the Red Sox offices in early December and then went with Eddie Collins to the winter meetings in New York. As a new owner, Yawkey spoke little. There were discussions on barnstorming, bonuses, the scheduling of doubleheaders, and broadcasting, but the only subject on which he spoke was Babe Ruth, who was leaving the Yankees and wanting to find another position. In the end, he came to the Boston Braves. Ruth's first choice, Yawkey said, had been the Red Sox, and "there was a lot of pressure brought to bear [to hire Ruth], and that really was an appealing idea"—he realized it might have drawn five hundred thousand more fans for a year or maybe two—but "it was our idea to build an organization and put everything we could into it, and for that reason we did not consider him."[36]

The team made no moves at the winter meetings, but the Red Sox reshuffled their farm system near the end of the year, dropping Reading and purchasing Charlotte in the Carolina League. They held working agreements with Syracuse and Knoxville. Yawkey seemed to indicate disappointment at not having been able to add some new men to the team at the meetings. It seemed as though a number of clubs dangled players in front of him to see what kind of price they might attract, but then they pulled them back. The *Globe* reported that Yawkey was "disgusted" with some of the business methods he had encountered, saying, "If a player is not for sale, why the kidding?"[37] Among the player he had wanted was Oscar "Ski" Melillo from the Browns. He offered $50,000, but Rogers Hornsby, the Browns' player/manager, needed more than money. "I can't use dollar bills out there in the infield," he said. "I gotta have somebody to get in front of those balls."[38]

Not everyone associated with the game was pleased at the sums Yawkey and a few others were so freely spending. "Baseball has gotten to be a millionaire's plaything," grumbled Casey Stengel of the Dodgers. "I'm not a Communist, either. I've just been stuck with the job of jerking a seventh place ball club out of the salt mines and I find I'm bucking fellows who laugh at $50,000 cash."[39]

8

Settling in as Red Sox Owner, 1935–1938

FOR ALL THE attention paid to the Red Sox and race in later years, it's noteworthy that the Sox in 1933, 1934, and 1935 had Native American Roy Johnson often playing left field and Mexican-born Mel Almada playing center. Their inclusion on the team did not represent any explicit commitment to diversity but reflected an openness in signings that later might have theoretically been extended to other players of color.

Under new skipper Joe Cronin, the 1935 Red Sox won two more games than in 1934. They remained in the first division, staying in fourth place, with a record of 78-75. Though winning just two more games than the year before, they achieved a milestone of sorts: they broke .500 for the first time since 1918.

The team got off to a good start but then sank to where it spent pretty much stayed the whole season—third, fourth, or fifth place. After April 26 it never saw second place again, but never once did it drop as low as sixth.

Cronin's 95 RBIs led the team. He hit .295 and had a .370 on-base percentage. Lefty Grove reverted to form and won 20 games (he was 20-12 with a 2.70 ERA), and Wes Ferrell was 25-14, with a 3.52 ERA.

In December 1934 and January 1935 there were stories that Braves Field would be turned into a dog-racing track and that the Braves would play their home games at Fenway; it did not come to pass. Braves Field was indeed leased by the company that controlled the field, and at least technically the Braves were "homeless," but Tom Yawkey wasn't prepared to share Fenway Park with them. He wanted it for his own exclusive use, just as he had told the Braves

when they'd offered to let him lease Braves Field before he renovated Fenway. If it were an emergency, such as one occasioned by
a fire, he'd work something out. But "Fenway Park is not available
as a place of refuge," he said. The Braves had brought this problem on themselves.[1] The National League didn't want to run as a
seven-team league and lose one of its charter franchises. Matters
were worked out. The year even saw Babe Ruth call Braves Field
his home; in 1935, Ruth's final year of play, he played for the Boston Braves.

Yawkey realized his buying spree had driven up asking prices
across the board. He declared in early February, "I am through buying; now let the market drop." Yawkey said he and Collins had enough
players. But he added, "We're perfectly willing to do a little trading
if the boys will just forget that we're supposed to be philanthropists
and come down to earth in the dickering." He hadn't regretted a
penny he'd spent, he said; the Red Sox "are a business and pleasure
with me," and he expected his investments would reap dividends.[2]
One of the reasons he'd resisted the Braves' overture was that he
hadn't wanted to encourage dog racing as competition to baseball.

Yawkey had shown an interest in the players' investments as well.
An unidentified June 1935 newspaper clipping reported, "Not long
ago on bench he felt out some of the boys as to whether they were
saving money and making right kind of investments. . . . Several players had placed dough in a large insurance investment service. . . .
They asked their boss what he thought of the company. . . . 'I'll look
it up and let you know,' he said. . . . A few days later, boys received
letter, assuring them that company was sound and responsible."[3]

Yawkey perhaps palled around with the players more than some
owners felt seemly. At the time it was said that he often entertained
players at his homes in Boston and New York and that some players
had come to his South Carolina estate to go hunting. A newspaper
column reported that while that sort of camaraderie had been common enough during the 1890s, it had become quite rare. Yawkey,
however, "refused to follow other present-days owners by building
a stern social wall between himself and his players."[4]

When the train from Boston to Sarasota stopped at Penn Station on February 26, 1936, Yawkey was there to greet those of the

Red Sox party aboard before they continued on to Florida while he remained in New York. His digs in New York were comfortable; an earlier article in the *Cleveland Plain Dealer* noted that his penthouse contained fourteen rooms and five baths.[5]

The Sox stopped in Birmingham again in early April (as they had the previous year) as they headed north from Sarasota, and again they played to small crowds—this time, one paper cracked, "before an audience composed mainly of Mrs. Yawkey's sisters, her cousins and her aunts."[6] (Elise Yawkey seems to have come from a somewhat sizable family; she herself had as many as three siblings, and her mother picked up four stepchildren when she remarried.)

The season started on time, and Wes Ferrell opened it with a two-hitter, winning 1–0 over the Yankees in New York, and the Sox were 6-1 after the first week. With the season launched, the Yawkeys and the DeFoes traveled to Ketchikan, Alaska, where they chartered the yacht *Westward* for a month of hunting and cruising in the area. While stopping in Seattle on the way to Alaska, Yawkey told the *Seattle Daily Times* that owning a Major League ball club was "the biggest and most complicated business I ever ran into. . . . Baseball is a year-round job for a club owner. He spends the winter making connections with the minor leagues, buying players. . . . I work in the winter. So now I'm going hunting. Collins and Joe Cronin will probably run the club better now, if I'm away. People think it's funny when someone in baseball goes off to get away from baseball worries. But that's why I like hunting. I can forget everything else, and I like the exercise."[7] (He was hoping to bag a brown bear.) On May 1 the Red Sox purchased backup infielder Dib Williams from Connie Mack.

Yawkey was still in Alaska as of May 23, 1936, and his party had shot eight black bears, but the brown ones had proven elusive. Elise Yawkey herself shot a bear in Alaska in 1935.[8] Mrs. Yawkey, it turns out, shot two black bears and two brown bears—one of them weighing one thousand pounds—the first brown bear on Chichagof Island off Peril Strait and the second on Baranof Island. "She's intensely interested in shooting," said her husband, "and is always striving to improve."[9]

The search for bear kept Yawkey from attending the second marriage of his sister, Emma Austin Gardner, who married Gilmore Ouerbacker on May 26. Gardner offspring remained in the Yawkey family, of course, and we see in 1969 that Emma's son, William A. Gardner, became the owner of the Red Sox farm team in Louisville.

It was just as well that Tom was not in town during June, since a sordid story of murder and party girls unfolded elsewhere. An Elizabeth Carmichael Witherspoon came forward to claim that she was the daughter of Tom's adoptive parents (William H. and Margaret D. Yawkey), that she had been born a few years before they were married, and that she had been adopted by one of William's closest friends, real estate man James Carmichael. She said she had no idea she was the Yawkeys' daughter until after they had both died, when she received a posthumous message with the information. Carmichael had died by then too. The law firm that handled the Yawkey estate assigned attorney Howard Carter Dickinson to the case. Dickinson was a nephew of Chief Justice Charles Evans Hughes of the U. S. Supreme Court. He was gathering depositions and researching the case, according to a story in the June 28, 1936, *Chicago Tribune.* Two days later Dickinson was murdered. His body was found in a Detroit park.

Dickinson, who had telegrammed his wife the day before that he had "a large amount of money" on him, was shot once in the head and once in the chest and had been thrown from a moving car.[10] Very shortly police had the culprits: William Lee Ferris (alias William Schweitzer) and three "party girls" who had made a practice of getting seemingly wealthy men drunk and then rolling them. They believed Dickinson had a large sum with him, but since he knew a couple of them, Ferris decided to kill him. They found out Dickinson had only $134 on his body.[11] That August all four were convicted of first-degree murder.

Witherspoon's claim may have had some merit. A *Detroit News* story in April 1936 mentioned that she had been paid a reported $250,000 by way of settlement, a large figure at the time to make a case "go away" if the case were purely without merit.[12]

Tom Yawkey saw his first game of the season on June 15, in Cleveland. The Indians scored six times in the bottom of the first, but the Red Sox had scored once in the first and once in the fifth and then added five in the top of the sixth to take a 7–6 lead—and Yawkey "nearly jumped out on the field and performed a war dance on his own account."[13] The Indians won the game, 9–7.

Yawkey chartered a plane from Chicago to get to Philadelphia in time to see the A's host the June 28 game and crush the Red Sox, 14–2. He left for New York at 6:30 the next morning, a man on the move.

Yawkey arrived in Boston on July 5. The Red Sox were in fifth place, eight games out of first. A brief human interest story showed the soft side of the Red Sox owner. Mickey Cochrane's young daughter Joan was the guest of Elise Yawkey in her box on the Fenway roof. She was "playing bride" and enjoying herself while the game was going on, but then the shrill whistles of third base coach Al Schacht caught her ear. She asked Tom Yawkey, "Can you whistle like that?" He said he could, but when she asked him to, he replied, "Can't do that, my dear. If I whistled, your daddy, who is down there catching, would come right up and put me out of the box." "Well, you own the ball park, don't you?" she asked. "Guess I do." "Then I don't see why you can't whistle if you want to." Tom tried to do so but was unable.[14]

Yawkey did allow his park to be used for other events, as had other owners before him. In 1932 the park was booked on fifty-two different days for a variety of activities, including lacrosse, wrestling, boxing, and a large number of high school football games. On July 9, 1935, the Boston Department of Public Welfare hosted a field day, a summer carnival with bands and choruses, and wrestling. There were some high school football games and a pair of wrestling matches, both won by local favorite Dan O'Mahoney. The National Football League's Boston Redskins won their first and last home games of the 1935 season at Fenway Park, though they lost the five games in between. The NFL played at Fenway through the 1938 season, pro football returning in the 1960s with the Boston Patriots of the American Football League.

Being the owner of the ballpark put Yawkey in a position to occasionally pull a string or two. Wes Ferrell hit a solo home run in the bottom of the ninth in the July 22 game against the visiting Browns, winning it 2–1. Yawkey said, "I've seen hundreds of balls hit over that fence, but that's the longest yet. A couple of feet more and it would have lit in the B&A tracks." He found that a Ralph Amoroso retrieved the ball from his assigned parking space in the Lansdowne Street garage, so he dickered with Amoroso for the ball and then presented it to Ferrell.[15]

Other than take some batting practice or play pepper, did Tom ever actually play baseball at Fenway Park? The baseball writers annually played a ballgame against the Fenway front office nine. The writers won the September 23, 1935, game, 16–3. A newspaper description of the game showed that good fun was had by all and that two women from the front office—Mary Cadigan and Peg Healy—prevented the game from being a total rout. Afterward the Fenwayites claimed that the absence of Tom Yawkey and Eddie Collins "weakened their lineup immeasurably," and there was talk of another game. The question remains whether Yawkey ever got himself into a game at Fenway.[16]

About forty-nine thousand packed the park for a game against the Yankees on September 22, 1935, eclipsing the prior year's attendance record. About ten thousand were turned away. The fans had been hoping to see Wes Ferrell win his twenty-fifth game, but New York won, 6–4.

As the season approached its end, Yawkey was already gearing up for 1936. He joined Collins and Cronin for a long meeting with Connie Mack at Boston's Hotel Touraine on September 24, and the next day's *Boston Globe* subhead read, "Foxx, Higgins, Cramer Are Men Reported Sought." Foxx had a career .339 average at the end of 1935, with 302 homers; he had been a Triple Crown winner in 1933 and the Most Valuable Player (MVP) in both '32 and '33.

For a while it didn't look like the A's players could be added. On October 1 Yawkey complained, "I would have to rob a bank to pay for those players." (A rumor had him buying Foxx and five other Philadelphia players.) Sure, he could get maybe one or two, but in general Yawkey said he was no longer going to spend "big money" for "big names." Cronin said the Red Sox were not interested in Foxx and that they would rather spend money on younger players.[17] Some fans in Boston urged Yawkey to go after pitchers, not sluggers.

Yawkey and Collins went hunting in Maine in late October, returning in time to see the Yale-Dartmouth football game in New Haven on November 2. Eddie Collins Jr. was a freshman at Yale, though his older brother Dave was a Dartmouth grad.

Frank Navin of the Tigers died in November. He'd run the Detroit ball club for thirty-two years. Yawkey attended his November 16 funeral in Detroit. About ten days later, Collins traveled to South Carolina to do some more hunting with Yawkey. The two men obviously enjoyed each other's company.

At the winter meetings, held at the Palmer House in Chicago, the Red Sox made their move, purchasing Jimmie Foxx on December 10 for an estimated $200,000, pitcher Dusty Rhodes, and a minor leaguer. Yawkey also acquired outfielder Doc Cramer, pitcher Johnny Marcum, and infielder Eric McNair. Foxx was signed to a three-year deal. Cramer and McNair were not announced at first, but it was understood at the time that their deals would be announced the following January. The *New York Times* initially reported the overall price as $350,000; it may have been $400,000. The total Tom Yawkey had spent for the purchase of new players had now passed the million dollar mark. The *Literary Digest* reported the late 1935 deal as "the largest cash transaction in the history of baseball."[18]

Years later Foxx recalled his first encounter with Tom Yawkey:

I had a two-year contract running for $18,000. All Mr. Yawkey had to do was sit tight and I would have been forced to play for that figure here. When I first went to see Yawkey, I mentioned that I had no kick coming but that it was costing me something to move to Boston. Tom looked at me a minute and said, 'What salary do you think you should get?' I swallowed hard and said, 'I think I should get about $25,000.' Tom didn't bat an eye. He said, 'I think so, too.' And with that he tore up the signed contract he was holding in his hand.[19]

League officials recognized Yawkey's growing influence in a relatively short period of time; he was one of four owners named to the American League board of directors.

At the 1935 winter meetings, Yawkey proposed creating a farm system for umpires so that former players could receive appropriate training to become umpires without being thrust immediately into a Major League game, while umpires in the Minor Leagues couldn't survive on the pay without getting other employment. He suggested the American League hire umpires but then farm them out to the Minors to gain experience and cover their expenses during spring training. The motion carried. Boston GM Eddie Collins was present as well, and he and Yawkey also talked about better ways to get more young boys to come to the ballpark. The executives present agreed on setting a price of twenty-five cents for admission to the bleachers.

A reading of the minutes of the 1935 meetings—some 155 pages of them—reveals one moment of note regarding race that reflected the small group of white men meeting privately as magnates of the game. In a discussion of how to limit postseason barnstorming, Clark Griffith of the Washington Senators grumbled, "They go around playing these nigger teams."[20] The owners voted to limit barnstorming to ten days after the end of the American League schedule. No other owner remarked on Griffith's wording or commented regarding race matters during the meeting. Minutes taken in later years were never as detailed, generally consisting of summaries of actions and running a very few pages. It is unfortunate that we can't read what owners discussed in the years closer to integration.

Immediately after the winter meetings, Yawkey returned to Georgetown, where he hosted Lefty Grove, Bing Miller, and both Rick and Wes Ferrell for more hunting.

While there, the dealing didn't stop. On December 17 the Red Sox traded Roy Johnson and Carl Reynolds straight up to Washington for Heinie Manush. It was, at this point, the rare Red Sox deal where cash was not a prominent part of the transaction.

When the official year-end league statistics were released on December 19, Yawkey added a new hat to his holdings, thanks to a friendly wager he had made with Collins. Lefty Grove had led the AL in ERA, with a 2.70 mark.[21]

The following year, 1936, might have been one of the more frustrating ones for Tom Yawkey. Lefty Grove had the best ERA in the league again, and Jimmie Foxx hit 41 homers and drove in 143 runs. Wes Ferrell won 20 games. Before the season got under way, a lot of people around baseball were talking pennant, but not seasoned veterans like Rogers Hornsby and Walter Johnson. (Incidentally, Walter Johnson was rumored to have been very close to purchasing the Red Sox at the time that Yawkey received his inheritance and unexpectedly burst onto the scene.)[22] It's easier in retrospect to see that standout individual performances don't necessarily win games. The Sox had only one other pitcher who won as many as 10 games; they finished 74-80, a losing record, and in sixth place. All that money poured into the team and the Red Sox seemed to have lost whatever ground they had gained.

Doc Cramer and Eric McNair did indeed join the team, as anticipated, on January 4, with Hank Johnson, Al Niemiec, and cash said to be $75,000 sent to the Athletics. There were no other significant trades or purchases. Yawkey said he was through spending money. How were the Red Sox going to fare? "That's for Cronin to figure out. He has the ball players. Now, he'll have to figure out what to do with them."[23] The team had not been pleased with its experience in Charlotte and moved the franchise to Rocky Mount, North Carolina. The team had working agreements with Syracuse, Little Rock, and Memphis, and on February 24 Billy Evans was appointed as head of scouting and the Sox Minor League system. The team seemed to be moving in the direction of trying to develop its own players through a robust farm system.

Fenway Park added four thousand more seats. Attendance, which had dipped in 1935, increased to a new all-time high. But it was how his team did on the field that interested Yawkey more than ballpark revenue. Phil Troy told of a phone call in the summer of 1935, when Yawkey had called in the early evening after a doubleheader. "I told him we had had over 48,000 people that day and that we had to turn about 8,000 away. 'I don't give a da—mn about the crowd,' Mr. Yawkey said. 'What I want to know is how did the games come out?'"[24]

On March 3 Tom Yawkey was guest of honor at the New York Sportsmen's Show. Joe Cronin predicted a pennant (he later denied it on the eve of the season opener), and Yawkey added, "I think I have a winner. I really do. But I've seen too much baseball to count us 'in.' Too many things can happen. I won't hold Cronin responsible if we don't finish on top. If Joe gets my ball team up there and makes a fight out of it, I'll be satisfied."[25]

With so much money having been spent on the Red Sox, there was resentment of course, some derisively calling the Sox the "Millionaires" and "the little Lord Fauntleroys of the league." John Kieran of the *New York Times* gave voice to those who asked, "Did they wear velvet suits with Eton collars and put up their hair in curls?"[26]

It wasn't only his ball club on which Tom lavished money. After Mrs. Yawkey checked out of the hotel in Charlotte, on April 7, 1936, she realized while on a train heading north that she'd left a knitting bag behind. It contained a million dollars' worth of jewelry. The hotel located the bag, jewelry untouched by the maid who had turned it in, and she returned to collect her belongings.[27]

Yawkey drove himself from South Island to Sarasota, traveling entirely alone and making the 604-mile drive in nine hours and twenty-four minutes. He'd lost a bet he could do it in nine hours.[28] Even in the twenty-first century, former employees recalled how fast Yawkey would drive.

When the Sox were in Birmingham, Mrs. Yawkey's sister and brother-in-law, Dr. Lewis E. Sorrell, had the team over for dinner. The good doctor looked over new acquisition Johnny Marcum and urged him to have his tonsils removed, the same advice he'd given Lefty Grove two years earlier.[29]

Tom griped a bit about all the attention paid to his spending. He acknowledged that two or three officials from rival clubs had complained. A *Christian Science Monitor* headline read, "Tom Yawkey Would Like to Spend Money Without So Much Criticism."[30] It wasn't a subject he particularly liked to talk about. At the very beginning of 1936, when Burt Whitman of the *Boston Herald* asked him if it were true that he'd now spent over $4 million on the team, "He merely grunted."[31]

Yawkey still enjoyed activities with his players. On April 14 he went to see Jack Sharkey box at the Boston Garden, attending with Foxx, Grove, both Ferrells, and Joe Cronin, and the men were all introduced by the emcee after the semifinal bout of the evening.

In the second game of the season, on April 16, Joe Cronin fractured his thumb. "One broken thumb isn't going to beat us in this pennant race," Yawkey said, and the team did have solid infield backups in McNair and Billy Werber.[32] But Cronin was out more than the originally expected three weeks. He missed nearly twice that time and got into only eighty-one games in 1936. Even though Grove, Manush, and Rick Ferrell also suffered early-season injuries, it was later in the year that the Sox played most poorly, winning only 37 percent of their games (20-34) in August and September. They were 1-10 in extra-inning games.

The "husky, moon-faced" magnate was a true fan. He'd said he hoped to see one hundred games in 1936. Though business often took him away (to New York for a while in May, to help cover for the ailing DeFoe), he nonetheless was described in an early June United Press (UP) feature as follows:

> [He is one who] travels more with his club than any other owner, and watches more games. And he doesn't merely watch the games. Being slightly nutty on the subject of baseball, he plays in all of them—from his box seat—almost as strenuously as his athletes on the field. He keeps up a running fire of comment, to himself or to anyone who would listen, as the game progresses. He actually talks more during a game than his utility outfielder, Bing Miller. And Lefty Grove says "that Miller talks so much during a game that he disgusts himself and tells himself to shut up—or else." Peculiarly enough, Yawkey admitted, "usually I don't really enjoy watching my club play because I work so hard in the pinches."[33]

In later years, while in South Carolina, Yawkey would listen to the Boston radio broadcasts on Boston radio—by asking the Fenway Park receptionist to turn on the radio and have it play over the telephone to him. One could well say that qualifies him as "slightly nutty on the subject." One could also well admire that sort of passion for the game. Haywood Sullivan said that in later years Yawkey would have two televisions and two radios on, all at the same time, following ballgames.[34] It was even said that he would often sit in the Fenway Park bleachers eating peanuts, disguised by virtue of wearing a gym shirt, and thus able to get a good idea of what Red Sox fans really thought of the team.[35]

Yawkey was much more out in the public eye in the 1930s and

more ready to expound upon his love for the game and his desire to build up his team. He wasn't the wealthiest owner in baseball, however. That honor probably belonged to Jacob Ruppert of the Yankees, whose wealth expanded exponentially after Prohibition ended. Ruppert just didn't wear his heart on his sleeve and ran his team more like a business than a hobby. An AP story out of New York said that Ruppert's "fortune towers above that of Tom Yawkey" but that he was more reluctant to pay hefty prices for big-name players.[36]

The *Christian Science Monitor*'s Ed Rumill wrote a column in midseason giving voice to the growing sense that "trying to buy an American League pennant is risky as well as costly business." Yawkey had spent over $4 million in player acquisitions and at least another million renovating his ballpark. Those weren't the only expenditures, though, nor was the bonus plan from early 1934. When he brought his newly acquired players to Boston, Rumill continues,

> Yawkey rewarded them with handsome salaries. In his enthusiasm to win a pennant, he offered his stars contracts in double figures. [Most players made well under $5,000 in the mid-1930s. He had bumped Foxx's salary up from $18,000 a year to $25,000. That didn't mean he was always a pushover for money. The difference of $1,000 made Billy Werber a holdout in 1936, and in the end it was Werber who blinked, not Yawkey.] He believed that money would be an inducement and encourage the boys to go out and win. But the enthusiastic young Red Sox president is discovering that money isn't everything. He has what is probably one of the most expensive ball clubs in the history of the sport, yet it is getting nowhere. And as this is written, it appears that his present club never will get anywhere.[37]

Injuries were one thing, but Rumill also said that "certain members of the present Boston outfit are taking advantage of Tom Yawkey's good nature. They have accepted his money, but haven't given their best baseball in return. Several of the so-called 'stars' have enjoyed life immensely since coming to Boston. Unfortunately, however, pennants are won in ballparks by well-conditioned and serious-minded athletes, and not by a lot of individuals who figure that a wealthy and good-natured club owner is a Santa Claus."[38] The day before Rumill's column ran, the Red Sox were 10½ games out of first place, nowhere near the league-leading Yankees.

Others began to refer to the team as the Gold Sox and the like, but Yawkey—perhaps just putting on a good face—said he was satisfied with the team. "We made no pennant claims at the start of the 1936 season. Perhaps we will not win this year, but look out for us next year or the year after. So far as criticism on the way my money is being spent—that's my business—and my money. I figure I have received value for every penny that I have spent."[39] If he was indeed satisfied, perhaps that was a root of the problem.

On July 10 Tom and Elise Yawkey got "nine or ten pounds of heaven": they adopted a child. The Cradle of Evanston, Illinois, was able to entrust them with an eight- or nine-week-old girl, whom they named Julia Austin Yawkey. (The Cradle was apparently noted as a source for affluent hopefuls seeking to adopt and had previously served both New York mayor Jimmy Walker and entertainer Al Jolson. Yawkey himself had been adopted, of course, albeit by a family member.)[40] It was a three-day process; in the meantime, a nursery was being prepared in the Yawkeys' Fifth Avenue penthouse in New York.

Why was Julia given that name? The "Julia" came from a Chicago friend of Mrs. Yawkey's, Mrs. O'Neill Ryan Jr. "Austin" was Tom Yawkey's middle name and his original surname, but Elise Yawkey said it was bestowed in recognition of Austin King, a friend from Danville, Illinois. The Yawkeys engaged a nurse who traveled with them to bring their new daughter back to New York. Ralph E. Batten, counsel for the Cradle, couldn't help but crack, "One thing's certain; your child will never be a ball player." Mrs. Yawkey said with a smile, "Yes, if it were a boy, I'd be in constant fear Tom might trade him."[41]

Handball was Yawkey's sport. He played at the New York Athletic Club and excelled. At the end of January, he'd exulted to Eddie Collins that he and his partner had just beaten St. Louis Cardinals manager Frankie Frisch and his partner. Outplaying a National Leaguer gave Yawkey an extra thrill. He played almost every day "and undoubtedly is the best handball player of this era among big league baseball men, which include the major league players as well as owners, managers and business men."[42]

The Red Sox became the first team to travel by air—all on the same airplane—on July 30, when they flew from St. Louis to Chicago on an American Airlines plane. They'd just dropped three out of four to the Browns but were able to eat dinner during the ninety-minute flight and "get a good night's rest in hotel beds instead of a rolling sleeper," said Joe Cronin.[43] Yawkey traveled with Pennock and Grove in a different plane. The Sox won the game after their good night's rest but then lost seven in a row.

The team was known for staying at the best hotels, and at least a generation or two of Red Sox players felt very positively about the way Tom Yawkey treated them, to the point of near worship in numerous cases. Johnny Pesky, Ted Williams, and Carl Yastrzemski all offered nothing but glowing appreciation of Mr. Yawkey. In 1936 Wes Ferrell—who had had strong disagreements with ownership in Cleveland—told the UP that Yawkey was "the perfect man to work for and that all the players feel the same way."[44] And there were those such as Dizzy Dean, who on March 5 had said, "Tell Yawkey I think he's the greatest sport in baseball and that if he will be so kind as to buy me, I will guarantee him a pennant."[45]

In the background the team was investing in developing players. In early August the Red Sox bought the contract of outfielder Buster Mills from Rochester, with delivery planned for 1937. On August 9 Eddie Collins was in Portland, Oregon, to look over second baseman Bobby Doerr of the Pacific Coast League (PCL) San Diego Padres, with an eye to buying an option on his contract from the Padres' Bill Lane. Collins took options on Doerr and catcher Gene Desautels, but Lane was unsuccessful in selling an option on shortstop George Myatt. Collins inquired, though, about the right fielder who'd played in the doubleheader that day: Teddy Williams. When Lane told Collins the boy was only seventeen, Collins asked Lane instead for his word that the Red Sox would get first crack at Williams before San Diego ever sold his contract. Collins couldn't have known it at the time, but with that verbal commitment from

Lane—which Lane honored come December 1937—he had made deals to sign two future Hall of Famers in one day.

Everyone had warned the Red Sox that Wes Ferrell could be temperamental. During the August 21 game against the Yankees, after Albie Pearson's sixth-inning single had cleared the bases, Wes simply walked off the mound—and into the Yankees' dugout and out of the park. He was fined $1,000 by an irate Cronin. Ferrell later explained that he had seen Cronin gesture from the Boston dugout and thought he had been waved out of the game in favor of a reliever and had made the mistake of not looking around and realizing that Cronin was not making a move. The Yanks' dugout was on the way to the Red Sox clubhouse. When he first learned of the fine, Ferrell said some harsh things about Cronin, "but that was all forgotten when I talked with Joe and Tom Yawkey later. We parted friends."[46] Yawkey said, "I think it is the best thing that could have happened to Wes. I think it will go a long way toward making Ferrell the pitcher he is capable of being. I gave him a good going over last night and I believe Wes will be a changed person."[47]

Later in August the *Sunday Worker* asked National League president Ford Frick if there was anything to prevent a Major League owner from hiring a Negro as a player. There was not, Frick replied. The newspaper inquired of a number of team owners on the subject. Tom Yawkey wired his response: "Have never given any thought to the matter. This would be something for the big leagues as a whole to decide, therefore, feel that any expression should come from baseball in general and not from individuals like myself." Other owners who chose to reply did so in a similar vein. Ed Benson of the *Chicago Defender*, one of the country's leading African American newspapers, ended his story, "The buck thus passes from side to side. It's a hot potato."[48]

After their sixth-place finish, it was learned that Yawkey had promised a $1,000 bonus to each member of the Red Sox had the team finished first or second in the standings.[49] It was yet another reminder that it required more than individual financial incentives to forge a first-place team.

Buying established stars wasn't the only answer. "[Yankees owner

Jacob] Ruppert bought some pennants, when he was able to reach into the Red Sox for players," Yawkey reportedly told Collins and Cronin. "But, it doesn't seem to work for us when we buy Mack's old champions. So we've got to try something else and raise our own. We've got to build up a farm system such as Rickey has built up for Breadon in St. Louis and Barrow and Weiss for Ruppert in New York. That's the only way we can catch the Yankees."[50]

Despite their poor showing, Yawkey said that the team made a small profit in 1936. "We've broken somewhat better than even," he explained to the AP.[51] He also pretty much confessed that he'd returned the $1,000 fine that Cronin had levied on Wes Ferrell.[52] He said he wasn't going to spend any more money on buying players for 1937, though. (The club's financial statement became public in April 1937 and showed a loss of $804,560. Whether creative accounting was involved to engineer a loss, we do not know.)[53] Continuing the "Santa" theme, the *New Haven Register* wrote in December of the "young owner of the Red Flops, who dropped $800,000 down a pair of chimneys the last three years, thereby making those holidays very happy ones for Connie Mack and Clark Griffith."[54]

Mack had made out well. Economic circumstances had forced him to dismantle the Philadelphia Athletics team that had won the pennant in 1929, 1930, and 1931. And it was Yawkey who took most advantage of the opportunity. A look at the Athletics roster in the 1931 World Series shows the following members with the Boston Red Sox just a few years later: Max Bishop, Doc Cramer, Jimmie Foxx, Lefty Grove, Eric McNair, Bing Miller, Rube Walberg, and Dib Williams.

Yawkey, Collins, Mickey Cochrane, Tris Speaker, Bing Miller, and Rube Walberg all spent some time hunting antelope, elk, and deer and shooting pheasant and ducks in Cody, Wyoming, in October and into November.[55] Yawkey's 1976 obituary in the *New York Times* noted that friends considered him "an expert shot, an avid fisherman, and a competitive squash and handball player," adding, "He hunted grizzly bears in Wyoming and other game all over North America."[56] In 1937 Yawkey took along Jimmie Foxx, Lefty Grove, and Mike "Pinky" Higgins. It wasn't necessarily true "roughing it": "The Yawkey hunting expedition is no slight thing. It involves a string of about 30 horses, and the necessary men to handle and feed them, guides, cooks, and others. It is quite a posse when it leaves Cody."[57] Such a collection of ballplayers constituted quite a coterie. As Wyoming's Lew Freedman wrote, "That's not a hunting party, it's an All-Star team."[58] Indeed, Cochrane, Collins, Foxx, Grove, and Speaker were all future Hall of Famers.

Before the year was out Yawkey spent money to forge deals with six Minor League clubs: renewals with Louisville, Canton, and Danville and the signing of new deals with Minneapolis, Hazelton, and Clarksdale to build up the farm system under Billy Evans and develop the Sox's own players. The Red Sox exercised their option on Bobby Doerr, and they traded Bill Werber to the Athletics for Pinky Higgins on December 9. There were rumors that Yawkey was interested in buying a pro football club, but they were strenuously denied, and he never became involved in any professional sport but baseball.

How were Tom Yawkey's other enterprises faring at this point during the Depression? We have no way of knowing, and when his New York office at the Graybar Building closed following his death forty years later, almost none of the older business records were shipped to Boston. The office in New York had specialists who were experts in lumber, oil, and minerals, but the management of assets changed once the office was relocated.

Something else happened in 1935–36 that is worth note and precedes by almost a decade the now notorious time when the Red Sox had an opportunity to sign Jackie Robinson in 1945. In a reflection of interscholastic baseball in 1935, a Somerville High School slugger named Joe Zagami was apparently given an opportunity that Francis "Frannie" Matthews of Cambridge's Rindge Tech was not. Zagami was a "white" athlete and Matthews was "black." This difference in opportunity prompted something of a protest by the *Afro-American* newspaper of Baltimore. In February 1936 the paper ran a story headlined "Boston Boy Sees Inferior Get Trial with Red Sox." The lead paragraph read, "Francis Matthews, captain of the 1935 edition of the Rindge Tech nine, must sit idly by and watch Joseph Zagami, white, get a trial with the Boston Red Sox"[59]—despite the fact that it was Matthews, not Zagami, who was selected as the all-state and all-scholastic first baseman for 1935.[60] The *Boston Globe* singled out Matthews and Somerville second baseman Walter Berry for extra praise and compared Matthews to Zagami (without noting the race of either one): "Matthews' record speaks for itself. He compiled a batting average of .515, striking out only three times during the season, and made only one error. . . . Joe Zagami of Somerville might have won the position in an ordinary year. He's extraordinarily capable in all departments, but doesn't hit quite as often as Matthews and hasn't quite the class of the Rindge boy afield."[61]

Somerville High became the state champion in 1935, winning three June games at Fenway Park. (During the championships, Zagami hit a long home run into Fenway Park's center-field bleachers, a feat that at the time only Jimmie Foxx and Billy Rogell had accomplished.)[62] The championship games would have afforded Red Sox scouts more of an opportunity to see Zagami than Matthews since the Rindge team did not play in the finals at Fenway. Moreover, some Somerville High alumni had made the Majors (including Danny MacFayden with the Red Sox and Hod Ford and Shanty Hogan with the Boston Braves, all of whom had played in the early 1930s), so scouts surely had their eyes on Somerville High. But they had their eyes on baseball in Greater Boston generally.

Zagami never made the Majors, but he did play at least eight seasons of Minor League ball. Matthews played semipro ball and then signed with the Newark Giants in the Negro Leagues and in 1941 played with the Royal Giant All-Stars in a postseason exhibition game in San Diego against an all-star team that fielded both Foxx and Ted Williams. On August 12, 1943, he subbed for Buck O'Neil and played first base for the Kansas City Monarchs. Matthews doubled off the base of the wall in right field. There he was, playing at Fenway, but Matthews never got his own tryout with the Red Sox.[63]

Tom Yawkey wasn't as much in the news in 1937 as he'd been in prior years. He hadn't lost his perpetual optimism, though. Dubbed "the happiest sixth place club owner in the business," he hadn't lost faith in Joe Cronin, though part of his evaluation—characteristically—appears to have been based on personal friendship: "I think the purchase of Joe Cronin is the best deal I've made and I'd make the deal again tomorrow at twice the figure! He's one of the greatest guys I ever saw."[64]

Dizzy Dean had an early February trade to recommend: "I'm trying to trade Branch Rickey for Tom Yawkey, and I'll give Rickey my next year's pay to boot."[65]

Spring training opened with optimism, with every hope the Red Sox would reestablish themselves in the first division. Player-manager Cronin said of himself, "I'm just another fellow trying to make the team."[66] He foresaw Pinky Higgins as contributing and believed that Bobby Doerr was ready to play second base in the big leagues. Naturally he hoped the team wouldn't suffer as many injuries as in 1936, which had begun with Cronin's broken thumb. The best the *Globe*'s Hy Hurwitz could divine was that Yawkey himself thought his team might finish fifth.[67] If so, he was spot on.

Yawkey stuck with his stance of building a farm system, though not a "chain system" of ball clubs owned by Boston on the model established by Branch Rickey with the St. Louis Cardinals. Rather, farm director Billy Evans argued, it should be a system comprised of working agreements with other clubs that could help feed players to the Red Sox without an additional investment. The Red Sox entered into agreements with as many as eleven clubs, giving them first call on the clubs' players: Little Rock, Hazleton, Rocky Mount, Brockville, Clarksdale, Canton, Danville, Elizabethton, Opelousas, Moultrie, and Mansfield.[68]

Yawkey enjoyed making a number of small wagers with people. Mickey Cochrane bet him $100 he'd play in at least ninety games for the Tigers (Cochrane lost), and Clark Griffith bet him $50 that Shanty Hogan could beat Rick Ferrell in a fifty-yard dash (neither player was known for speed). Griffith instead traded for Ferrell in mid-June, doing a deal on June 11 to get both Ferrells (Rick and Wes) for Washington, along with Mel Almada, in exchange for Ben Chapman and Bobo Newsom. Between them, Hogan and Rick Ferrell stole one base for the Senators in 1937 (it was Ferrell's steal). Yawkey then bet a sportswriter $5 that Newsom would beat Wes Ferrell the first time the two faced each other. Yawkey paid off on that one after the 6–4 Washington win on June 30.

There was a discussion about radio at a league meeting in July. The first broadcast of a baseball game had occurred in Pittsburgh in 1921. Some club owners feared that giving the games away for free on radio would result in declining revenues at the turnstiles. Ed Barrow of the Yankees suggested banning radio altogether for a year—a moratorium—after which he believed stations would bid to pay a large sum (maybe $100,000) for radio rights. Yawkey suggested forming a special centralized radio office. He'd conducted his own study and found one club that had sold broadcast rights for $15,000 and then found the station had sold sponsorship rights for $75,000.[69] The first Red Sox radio broadcast had been in 1926, but it was just for Opening Day. By 1929 there was a six-state network comprising twenty-two stations that broadcast such Sox games as were available for radio.

The Sox put together a six-game winning streak in mid-June, their longest streak in the Yawkey era—but then doubled that by winning twelve in a row starting on July 28 (if one elects not to count a 2–2 tie in the second game of the August 2 doubleheader; after all, it wasn't a loss). They reached as high as second place during those early August days but then came back to earth. And Yawkey went hunting again in early September, returning to Cody. Foxx joined him in Wyoming on another trip, in late October, as did Pinky Higgins and Lefty Grove. Each one shot an elk.

Yawkey retained sentiment for Cody. Gabby Barrus was an assistant to Yawkey party guide Max Wilde. His son Mick said that after World War II, "the Cody town team ran into financial trouble, but when an appeal was made, Yawkey sent bats, balls and old Red Sox uniforms. For years after that the Cody team was called the Cody Red Sox." There was another time that Yawkey generosity was evidenced. Mick Barrus was coaching Little League in the early 1960s at Fort Ord in California. Barrus told Lew Freedman that Tom Yawkey donated playing equipment for the whole league.[70]

The Yankees' Ed Barrow and author Damon Runyon went hunting with Yawkey in November. Though he traveled to other parts of the land to hunt, Yawkey preferred hunting small game on his own lands in South Carolina—"ducks, shore birds, woodcock, quail, turkey, and deer—all of which abound on my preserve near Georgetown."[71]

The team had won six more games than in 1936, finishing with a winning 80-72 record (with two ties), but it was only good enough for a fifth-place finish. Progress though that was, it was still shy of the first division that the Sox had reached in 1934 and 1935. The respected Gordon Cobbledick of the *Cleveland Plain Dealer* reported that Yawkey may have borne a few cracks in his perpetual optimism, calling him "disillusioned and slightly embittered"—and also ready to deal anyone on the team save Cronin, Lefty Grove, and pitcher Jack Wilson, who'd won sixteen games in 1937, just one less than Lefty.[72] Yawkey may have come to the conclusion that one couldn't buy a pennant. He did, however, trade for Joe Vosmik. On December 2 the Sox sent Bobo Newsom, Red Kress, and Buster Mills to the St. Louis Browns to get him.

During the winter meetings in Chicago, the Red Sox acquired Ted Williams from San Diego. Bill Lane had promised Eddie Collins an option and sent word that it was time. Other teams were now bidding for Williams, who'd finished his second season with the San Diego Padres, and he'd graduated from high school too. Lane held everybody off while he waited to hear from Collins, who now needed to close the deal. Collins had to get Yawkey and Cronin on board.

> And suddenly Yawkey balked. He'd decided to invest in building a farm system rather than buying players from other teams. Collins had to argue for Williams, while telling Yawkey that he fully supported commitment to the farm system. "But this happens to be the one time in 100 that we should break our rule," he argued. It wasn't an easy argument, but Cronin apparently chimed in his support and though the discussion dragged on, in the end Yawkey yielded. And not a moment too soon. Lane had been waiting without word, and he was about to pull the trigger on a pending offer.[73]

Collins rushed down to the lobby of the Palmer House and emerged from the elevator just as Lane was heading upstairs to work on a deal with the unnamed other club. With fifteen minutes to spare before Lane's midnight deadline, the deal was done. "The Kid" became a member of the Boston Red Sox.

The year 1938 started out with some ribbing dealt out to Yawkey (among many others) at the New York Baseball Writers dinner; a skit accused the Red Sox owner of "buying every dummy Eddie Collins recommends."[74] Joe Vosmik joined Yawkey (and Bob Quinn, who now headed the Boston Bees, as the Braves were known at the time) at the Boston writers' dinner.

A *Globe* headline reported, "Yawkey Promises Pennant," but a look at his actual remarks makes it clear he didn't say when. He told the group at the Boston writers' dinner that he had "full intentions of bringing a pennant to this city" and that he was determined to do so if it "takes 1,000 years."[75] That kind of wait may not have been what most fans had hoped, but the determination probably sounded good. It was Yawkey's first appearance at the Boston dinner.

Yawkey later spoke along lines: "I never did think I could go in the market and buy a championship team. I realize that could upset the general opinion but it's honest truth. What I knew had to be done was to restore the faith of Boston fans in the Red Sox. I believe I have done that even if we haven't won a flag. That will come later."[76]

In 1937 four players held out—McNair, Marcum, Archie McKain, and Doc Cramer. All but Cramer were gone before the end of the year, though not necessarily for punitive reasons, even though Yawkey had said, "I'm through paying unnecessarily large salaries. The players who are looking for more dough will either sign their present contracts or stay out of baseball."[77]

Yawkey paid his first visit of the year to Sarasota on March 14 (and admitted on arrival he'd sweetened his offer to McNair). This time he'd made the trip south averaging seventy miles per hour.

The Red Sox owner first saw Ted Williams bat in a March 17 exhibition game against the Boston Bees; Ted pinch-hit in the fifth and made an out. Williams was sent down from Major League camp on March 21 to join the Minneapolis Millers. On the same day, Mrs. Yawkey joined several player wives in a softball game on the Payne Park field.

There is no indication that Yawkey made any comment about

Williams in the week that they were both in Sarasota at the same time. After the Kid's pinch-hit out on March 17, the team played three out-of-town games. Ted was 0-for-1 in late-inning work on March 19, and the last time Tom Yawkey would have seen him was an 0-for-1 performance on March 21, coming in for Chapman in the late innings.

The Red Sox kicked off the regular season nicely, winning four of their first five games. All three outfielders had played in the 1935 All-Star Game: Vosmik, Cramer, and Chapman. And Jimmie Foxx came back from a subpar 1937. At the very end of the 1937 season, Tom Yawkey encountered Foxx in a "Broadway hot spot" and told him, "Jimmie, no one likes a party more than I do. But I am paying you to win ballgames and you can't do that and give this night life the play you have been giving it all summer."[78] Foxx took the advice to heart; he led the league with a .349 batting average, hit 50 homers in 1938, and drove in what remains a franchise-record 175 runs (and this in a 154-game season). He'd won the Triple Crown back in 1933 and would have won another in 1938 had Hank Greenberg not hit 58 homers.

After the May 5 game, Yawkey chartered a plane and flew with Joe Cronin to Washington so Joe could be there in time for the birth of his child. A few days later, on May 10, both Yawkey and Eddie Collins spoke to the Yale Club of Boston, with Yawkey expressing his hopes about bringing a pennant to town in the near future.

There was an early eight-game winning streak in May, and Yawkey showed a bit of baseball superstition, according to pitcher Charlie Wagner: "In 1938, no one wanted to interrupt a streak, so you did the same things exactly the same way to keep a streak going. We went on an eight-game winning streak and Red Sox owner Tom Yawkey gave us lamb chops for eight straight days so as not to break the streak; Joe Cronin chewed the same gum for eight days; and I was on prune juice for eight straight days. I'm glad we lost."[79]

There were comings and goings, signings and releases, during 1938. Deals involving Pat Malone, Roy Parmelee, Bob Daughters, Chief Hogsett, and Phil Weintraub got little attention. On August 1 the Sox sold Joe Gonzales to the Indians and bought Joe Heving from them, though the two transactions were not characterized as a trade. The next day they traded $20,000 to Buffalo (with Johnny Marcum) to acquire pitcher Bill Harris, who was 5-5, and then sold him to the Giants at the end of the year.

From August 23 on, the Red Sox were in sole possession of second place. The team's batting average was .299. The shortcoming was in pitching. Wins leaders were Jim Bagby Jr. and Jack Wilson, but each won only fifteen. The team ERA was 4.49. Had Lefty Grove (14-4) not twice missed three or more weeks, hospitalized for arm treatment, they might have finished closer than the 9½ games behind New York in the standings. Still, second place was a true accomplishment. They hadn't been closer than fourth since 1918.

On September 8 the Red Sox bought the Louisville club in the American Association, its players (including Pee Wee Reese), and its ballpark. Tom Yawkey even had ball clubs he didn't know he had; a story in late June said that his Pacific Coast scout, Ernie Johnson, had learned that the Silverton, Oregon, team was sponsored by the Silver Falls Timber Company, in which Yawkey owned a controlling interest.[80] As it happens, a young Portland boy named Johnny Pesky played for Silverton in 1938 and 1939. Johnny signed with Johnson and the Red Sox in early August.[81]

Ted Williams excelled in Minneapolis, winning the American Association Triple Crown; he hit for a .366 batting average, homered 46 times, and drove in 142 runs. There was no denying him a promotion to the Majors.

On December 15 the Sox traded Ben Chapman to the Indians for Denny Galehouse and Tommy Irwin; they thought Ted Williams could handle right field. It was the same day they sold Bill Harris. A busy day indeed. They also traded Pinky Higgins to Detroit and got Elden Auker, Whistlin' Jake Wade, and Chet Morgan in return. Six days later, they traded Eric McNair to the White Sox for Boze Berger.

9

The Kid Makes the Big Leagues, 1939

IT WAS IN 1939 that the Kid broke into big league baseball. Ted Williams made his debut with the Boston Red Sox, and he did so setting a record that has never been equaled: he drove in 145 runs as a rookie. Williams defined charisma; from the day he arrived in Boston, fans followed his every move.

The first time Tom Yawkey met him, Williams was his usual irreverent self. In later years, Williams usually called him "Mr. Yawkey" when speaking about the Red Sox owner—as did almost everyone— but when they first met, the Kid said, "Don't look so worried, Tom. Foxx and me will take care of everything."[1] Veteran St. Louis newspaperman Bob Broeg told of how Yawkey may have achieved an early camaraderie with his young star. Broeg said that the Kid "saw the 36-year-old club owner talking with 52-year-old General Manager Eddie Collins. 'Good morning, Mr. Collins,' said Williams. 'Hi, Tom.'"[2]

The man who signed Williams—Red Sox GM Eddie Collins—was named to the Baseball Hall of Fame in January 1939.

The first business of 1939 was to take care of Jimmie Foxx. He had taken a $5,000 pay cut for 1938 after a disappointing 1937 season. But he'd excelled in 1938 and been named MVP of the league. He wanted a dramatic salary increase, and he let it be known. He got a good one; though not perhaps as much as he would have wanted, it still was a very good paycheck, and he led the league in home runs (35) and on-base percentage (.464) in '39, hitting for a higher batting average than he had in 1938—.360. Many years later, Tom Yawkey said he really didn't believe in pay cuts. He'd rather trade a player than cut his pay and leave him unhappy.[3] One wonders if Yawkey may have made up the difference to Foxx after the season. It wouldn't at all have been out of character.

Things were coming together nicely. Bobby Doerr continued to excel in his third year in the Majors, and rookies Jim Tabor and Ted Williams both played first-rate ball (third baseman Tabor had 95 RBIs). From April 29 on, the Red Sox never dropped lower than second place. They were behind the Yankees, the two teams 1–2 from May 9 on, New York capturing the flag and Boston firmly fixed in second.

Yawkey had driven to Sarasota once more, but he was in the news less frequently again, perhaps as much as anything because the story of the "rich sportsman with the common touch" was not as novel any more. He'd spent a lot of money, yes, but placing second was not the same as being fifth or sixth.

Yawkey got to see Ted Williams in the spring of 1939, and his first published comment about Williams that I could find was from April 2: "That Ted Williams has the most remarkable eye I ever saw. He never bites at a bad ball, and has an uncanny instinct for judging it as soon as it leaves the pitcher's hand. He could hit in any league."[4]

April 30 was Lou Gehrig's final game in baseball, but he traveled with the Yankees some in the weeks that followed. During the July 2 doubleheader in Boston, as Lou Gehrig brought out the lineups to the home-plate umpire before the second game, Tom Yawkey walked onto the field at Fenway and shook Gehrig's hand, earning a big cheer from the day's large crowd.

On May 30, with the Yanks in town again, there was a huge overflow crowd again, and some fifteen thousand were turned away. Yawkey declined to allow the crowd to be fully packed, in order that those who had paid for seats would not have their view blocked by those standing on the field.[5]

A most unusual occurrence in early July: the Red Sox went to Yankee Stadium and swept a five-game series from New York, one game on July 7 and then back-to-back doubleheaders on July 8 and 9.

After the game on May 9, the Red Sox chartered two airplanes to fly them from St. Louis to Chicago, and "several American League owners . . . objected." AL president William Harridge "officially frowned" on the practice and put the kibosh on future charters—even though the Red Sox had flown as far back as 1936.[6] Perhaps the other owners thought Yawkey was treating his players too well. The next time the team traveled from St. Louis to Chicago, after the June 9 doubleheader, Yawkey chartered a special train instead.

Yawkey rarely ever traveled with the team. One time a few years earlier, though, infielder and practical joker Billy Werber got him. Al Hirshberg wrote of Werber:

> He was never without a firecracker, an electric buzzer to shake hands with, a stink bomb or any other weapon of that kind on which he could lay his hands. He once put a possum in the room of Johnny Orlando, the clubhouse boy and assistant trainer, and Orlando spent half the night cringing in a corner of his room, thinking the beast was a wolf. On another occasion, Werber sneaked open the door of Yawkey's bedroom on a train and exploded a stink bomb, which drove his boss into the corridor, but not in time to catch the perpetrator of the stunt.[7]

Yawkey had a mischievous streak too. Mike Seidel writes that after the August 29 game in Cleveland, when Williams had hit his twenty-first homer and the Sox had won, 7–4, Yawkey and secretary Tom Dowd were in the Lake Shore Hotel in a room above Ted's. They called out to him, and when Ted stuck his head out the window, "Yawkey, a kid himself at heart, let go with a pitcher of water."[8]

The year 1939 was deemed baseball's centennial, and over fifty former players came to Fenway Park on July 11 for an old-timers' game, including the great Red Sox outfield of Duffy Lewis, Tris Speaker, and Harry Hooper.

A July 19 Grantland Rice column, titled "A Lady Calls the Turn," showed Elise Yawkey's awareness of the game, quoting her at length just before (and somewhat predicting) a twelve-game Sox win streak from July 4 through July 16 that included four doubleheader sweeps. He called her "the No. One feminine fan" in America.[9]

Yawkey traveled to Chicago for the funeral of White Sox owner J. Louis Comiskey on July 22. Around that time he was asked his opinion regarding night baseball. His reply put the fans first: "I don't like it and I know the players don't, but if the fans of Boston want it they shall have it."[10] Earlier in the month, he'd said he'd watch how night ball went over in Chicago, Cleveland, and Philadelphia; he thought the weather in Boston was probably the least conducive to playing at night, but they would conduct a study. If the Sox were to install lights, however, he'd want to play enough games—maybe fourteen a season—to earn back the investment. He'd want to vary the schedule between day games and night games and not play every game at night during the warmest months.[11] "If night baseball is to be a success," he said, "it would be a mistake to make it monotonous."[12]

Yawkey kept up with technology and was frequently spotted bringing a portable radio to games so that he could listen to other contests being played; the first truly portable radios had only been developed by the U.S. military in 1938.[13]

On September 24 Yawkey announced that the right-field stands would be brought in twenty feet closer to the plate beginning with the 1940 season. He said it was to provide a place for pitchers to warm up (that is, to create enclosed bullpens). The earlier expansion of the right-field grandstand had taken the place where pitchers had previously gotten loose. Everyone knew, however, that the reason for the change was to help Ted Williams hit more home runs to right field. Earlier in the year, Yawkey had said he wouldn't do it, but he had apparently come around. There had been talk of a second deck for Fenway Park too, but Yawkey didn't believe he'd recoup such an investment.

A little before the end of the season, Yawkey signed Joe Cronin to a new five-year contract. He also signed up Doerr, Foxx, Tabor, and Williams to their 1940 contracts, removing the possibility of contract problems during the wintertime. Three days after the season was over, Yawkey had an operation in Boston to remove cartilage in his left knee. With an 89-62 record the Red Sox had enjoyed a very good season, but the dominant Yankees (106-45) finished a full 17 games ahead of them in first place. All the team truly needed was a strong catcher, Yawkey felt, to better contend in 1940.

Elise Yawkey cropped up in the society columns from time to time. Tom may or may not have appreciated her getting extra attention; some have suggested it may have contributed to their eventual divorce. On the last day of the year the "Gossip and Smart Talk: Chatterbox" column in the *Los Angeles Times* read, in part, as follows:

Glamorous Elise Yawkey, whose name appears frequently in the smarter columns, had invaded local circles much to everyone's delight. This luscious blonde, whose e-n-o-r-m-o-u-s diamonds are as famous as her Husband Tom (owner of the Boston Red Sox) flew into town for the opening of the races yesterday. She'll have a try at Santa Anita, then set sail for the romantic Hawaiian Islands sometime in January. And you may take it from us, she'll keep the place in table talk after she lands. Is a friend of Dan Topping (who also flew into town) and Dan, as you know, knows everyone on the Islands from debs to "Internationals." While visiting here, you'll find this charmer seeing the sights under the guidance of the Russell Havenstripes and Avery Wrights.[14]

10

Before the War, 1940–1941

IN NOVEMBER 1939 the Red Sox had purchased the contract of Dominic DiMaggio from the San Francisco Seals. They had also done deals to acquire Herb Hash, Bill Butland, and a few other players who are today of lesser note because they never made the Majors with the team. The Sox continued to invest in Minor League talent, often outbidding other teams to get their man. Dom cost them over $50,000. A story came out a couple of years later that Larry Woodall was playing with the Seals when Heinie Groh came to scout Dom, but Groh felt Dom was too small and wore glasses and couldn't hit a curveball. Joe Cronin inquired of a friend, Bert Dunn, what he thought of young DiMaggio and was told, "He can do everything on the ball field better than Joe except hit." Woodall, by this time a Red Sox scout, signed him after Tom Yawkey told him, "If he's that good and you don't get him, you better stay out on the Coast."[1]

The Sox were confident enough in Dom that they sold Joe Vosmik in mid-February 1940. And Dom hit .301, scored 81 runs, and drove in 46 in his rookie year. Ted Williams was moved to left field because it was easier to field than Fenway's vaster right field; also, right field was the "sun field," and the team wanted to reduce any strain on their young star's eyes.[2]

Elise Yawkey spent the winter in the west and began to crop up more frequently in the Los Angeles society pages. In January 1940 there was a "gay evening at the Beverly Hills Hotel when the Walt Disneys entertained . . . Elise Yawkey—whose fame sparkles brightly from coast-to-coast (and we do mean brightly). Her enormous diamonds are the few not eclipsed by those of Pauline MacMartin. Elise won the champagne dancing contest—Avery Wright leading the intricate steps."[3] Elise apparently took up residence at the Beverly Hills Hotel, as was reported a week later. In February: "Horatio Luro—handsome chap from Buenos Aires—was the cynosure of feminine eyes at Ciro's the other night as he waltzed pretty Elise Yawkey's kid sister about. But from where we sat it was Elise, not baby sis, who had captured the young man's fancy."[4] A note in the April 14 *Los Angeles Times* had her still out west and getting attention by doing nothing: "From Honolulu comes absolutely NO news of Mrs. Hattie Haggerty and Elise Yawkey. The girls are having such a whirl they haven't had time to write. And do you wonder?"[5]

One does wonder what Tom Yawkey may have felt about all this. In 1944 it was learned that Elise and Tom had been separated since 1939. The Yawkeys had reunited—at least for a while—by the summer of 1940, however. They rented Mrs. Ring Lardner's house on Apaquogue Road in East Hampton during June. In August they were in another East Hampton house on Lily Pond Lane. In May, Yawkey leased an apartment at the swanky Hotel Pierre, at Fifth Avenue and Sixty-First Street in Manhattan.

Tom Yawkey could take some kidding, at least about baseball matters. During the early February baseball writers' dinner in New York, Ken Smith of the *New York Mirror* dressed up like Commissioner Landis and declared Babe Ruth (out of baseball since 1935) a free agent, then "freed 104 Boston Red Sox players, padlocked Fenway Park for six months, and fined Tom Yawkey $189,675.25."[6]

The Sox owner continued to be irritated at people talking about how much money he'd spent on his team. "What the hell business is it of anyone how I spend my money? Other people indulge in hobbies. Why shriek about it, if I spend my money on something I like?"[7] AP writer Steve O'Leary described Yawkey as a "stocky, broad-shouldered fellow, whose round, cherubic face is lighted by an almost perpetual grin, is jovial, frank, and democratic, possessing a rare modesty which belies his wealth and financial interests in timber, mining, and manufacturing." O'Leary pointed out that "his Red Sox investment probably represents the smallest portion of his vast financial interests."[8]

Baseball was indeed what Yawkey loved. At least one newspaper proclaimed that no other owner traveled with his team on the road, and Yawkey did it often. In 1940, near the beginning of spring training, Tom Yawkey was again in Sarasota; on March 11 he, Cronin, and Billy Evans drove to Arcadia to look over the prospects training with the Louisville club. While there, Evans's assistant, Herb Pennock, pitched to Yawkey during the afternoon workout—and struck him out six times. Three days later, a brief note in the *Globe* simply said, "Tom Yawkey works out with the boys and gets quite a kick out of it."[9]

Five of the Yankees' first ten games were postponed due to rain. Walter Briggs of the Detroit Tigers suggested starting the season on May 1 and playing a 140-game schedule. Yawkey didn't like the idea and pointed out that lopping more than 10 percent of the games off the schedule might well dictate a 10 percent reduction in salaries from club executives to players to groundskeepers.[10]

Yawkey helped host a "Lefty Grove Day" banquet in early June at the Copley Plaza Hotel.

The Sox were in first place for most of April and May and the first half of June, but by June 22 they had dropped to third place, where they stayed for almost two months before slipping one rung lower. Near the middle of August, Ted Williams spouted off that he didn't like Boston and wanted to be traded to New York. He told the *Boston American*'s Austen Lake, "I've asked Yawkey and Cronin to trade me away from Boston. I don't like the town. I don't like the people, and the newspapermen have been on my back all year."[11]

"Don't make me laugh," said Yankees manager Joe McCarthy. Yawkey said, "He'll just have to stick to his playing ball and learn to curb his temperament." Boston newspapermen said Ted's chief peeve was with them. A darling of the press in 1939, Williams had soured at the Boston writers; it was a feud that lasted the rest of his days. Williams reportedly even "blasted" Yawkey for underpaying other players on the team.[12] Numerous explanations for his attitude have been advanced (and we cannot explore them here), but this was just the first of a number of incidents over the years. As long as he was producing and not "using bad language in talking back to the fans in the stands," Yawkey—who said he had already spoken about the situation to Ted once before—decided to let Williams work it out on his own.[13] On another occasion Yawkey elaborated: "The reason I feel sorry for Williams is that he is only hurting himself. He had everybody with him a year ago and now is tossing all that away. I made that clear to him the one time I discussed the matter with him. I pointed out to him that when a situation got so that everybody was out of step but him it was high time he took stock to find out if maybe the real trouble lay within himself."[14] The *Globe* allowed that Ted Williams was Yawkey's "problem child."

Williams led the American League in on-base percentage and runs scored, but (despite the new bullpens installed in right field) his homers in 1940 were down from 31 to 23, and only 9 of the 23 were hit at home. Of those, only 4 went into "Williamsburg"—the area created by the bullpens.[15]

The Red Sox finished in fourth place, 82-72. Team ERA had declined to a very disappointing 4.89. Lefty Grove, now forty, won only 7 games, and no starter won more than 10 (Joe Heving and Jack Wilson each won a dozen, but only 4 of Heving's wins and 8 of Wilson's came in starts.)

Yawkey had said he didn't plan any major changes looking ahead to 1941, but on September 5 the Red Sox traded for both shortstop Skeeter Newsome and pitcher Mike Ryba; sold a few players; and then were particularly busy on December 12, buying Pete Fox from the Tigers, trading Doc Cramer to the Senators for Gee Walker, and then turning around and trading Walker (with Jim Bagby and Gene Desautels) to the Indians for catcher Frankie Pytlak, Odell Hale, and Joe Dobson.

In 1941 the Red Sox reclaimed second place, though they finished nowhere near the first-place Yankees. After a season in which not one Sox pitcher had won more than twelve games, it was clear that pitching was the team's greatest shortcoming. The team acquired Dick Newsome from the PCL, and the thirty-one-year-old "rookie" finished 19-10, though his 4.13 ERA was not that special. The season's most notable event was the hitting for average of Ted Williams. Williams hit .406; more than seventy years later he remains the last batter to hit .400 over the course of a season.

GM Collins, manager Cronin, and secretary Hi Mason all met

in January in New York for their "annual business meeting" but also to take in the Armstrong-Zivic prize fight.[16] Tom Yawkey came up from South Island to meet with them. The previous December Lefty Grove had visited Yawkey in South Carolina—one of the few ballplayers to do so. As he was departing after some days of hunting, his foot literally on the starter, Yawkey reportedly exclaimed, "Hey Mose, what about the contract?" Grove asked where it was. Yawkey grabbed a form, Grove took it from him, scrawled his signature on it, and started up the car. "But what about the money? How much?" "Put in anything," Grove said as he drove off. He had signed a blank contract, fully trusting that Yawkey would put in an acceptable figure for him.[17]

The team's approach to contracts may have been a bit unorthodox; Ted Williams, one of their bigger stars, had reportedly not even been sent a contract as of early January, when the more routine contracts began to come back to the office in the mail.[18] At the time, Yawkey himself tended to personally sit down and sign contracts with his two or three bigger stars—Foxx, Grove, and Williams in 1941.[19] For someone who hated to fire people and would often absent himself from Fenway for several days before, say, a manager was to be fired, Yawkey seemed to enjoy signing up his star players, at least when he could give out raises and good news.

The occasional letter to the editor in the Boston newspapers complained that Yawkey was too "soft-hearted" in palling around with men like Cronin and Collins, who the correspondents felt were not up to snuff. "Yawkey is loyal, but that doesn't get us fans anywhere," wrote one, complaining that Yawkey was always ready to go hunting with his cronies, "but that doesn't win ballgames."[20] There would be echoes of Yawkey and his unfortunate penchant for cronyism in years to come. There may have been a hint from John Kieran later in the springtime that Yawkey was a little too collegial, lacking, say, the fighting spirit that in later years characterized a George Steinbrenner. "Uncle Tom Yawkey of the Fenway Millionaires is a fan and he has plenty to say about the handling of his own club, but who ever heard Uncle Tom fire a blast at a rival magnate or an enemy ball club? When he gets his gun, it's to go hunting in North Carolina or Alaska."[21]

Bobby Doerr had his appendix removed in January. After training camp was already under way, Ted Williams phoned Collins on March 1 to say he'd been out of touch while hunting wolves in Minnesota. Since he hadn't signed his contract, he hadn't been sent an invitation (and expenses) to come to spring training. Collins told Yawkey, and Yawkey told Cronin. The Kid got his invitation.

Papers filed with the Massachusetts Department of Corporations and Taxation showed that Yawkey had lost an average of $173,014 over his years of ownership of the Red Sox through 1940.[22] He was said to have invested over $4,280,000 in the club but lost over $1,000,000. Connie Mack biographer Norman L. Macht says that through the first three years of Yawkey's ownership he lost more money every year than Mack had as his entire annual budget.[23]

On March 6 Yawkey "about 40 pounds overweight," arrived in Sarasota to help Lefty Grove celebrate his forty-first birthday.[24] Ted Williams arrived the next day, and on March 8 he signed his contract on the terms offered him.

Yawkey worked out himself, putting on a Red Sox uniform to do so, but only after the games had ended and the Payne Field fans had departed. He was a dead pull hitter and was said to wear out the third baseman and left fielder when he took batting practice.[25] The bat he used, at least in later years, was a Ted Williams model.[26] When he took fielding practice, he liked to play second base, the position he'd played at Yale.[27] Of course, there's every reason to believe that he had favored treatment and was maybe even thrown special, livelier balls ("Phillips 99 balls, they were called") that would travel further.[28]

A group of fans from New England, precursors of today's BoSox Club, was dubbed the "Royal Rooters" in a nod to tradition. They held a New England boiled dinner in Long Beach, near Sarasota, and Yawkey, Cronin, and others attended. The Red Sox were prepared to go to Havana to play exhibition games against Cincinnati there, but the promoters in Cuba took a while to send the guarantee money. The Sox and Reds did play four games there in late March, staying at the Hotel Nacional. As Burt Whitman had noted as the trip was being planned, "Tom Yawkey insists that his club stop at the best available hotels on the road, and that, of course, adds to the overhead of spring training. [At the Nacional] the rate per man, in late March, is about three times what a ball club has to pay at top rate hotels during the American League season."[29]

Early in training, Ted Williams hurt his ankle sliding into second base. It was downplayed at first, but it turned out to be more serious—a minor fracture, confirmed by Dr. Sorrell, an expert with X-rays who ran a large hospital in Birmingham and (as noted in chapter 8) just happened to be Tom Yawkey's brother-in-law.[30] The injury kept Williams out for a few weeks and affected him all year long, though it paradoxically may have helped him in the end, forcing him to hold back on his swing a split second longer before committing and giving him that little bit longer of a look at the pitch. Before he was able to return to playing regularly, he worked hard taking batting practice with pitcher Joe Dobson, insisting that Dobson throw him tough pitches—including his curveball—and not just batting practice fastballs so that he'd be better ready to face league pitching.[31]

Yawkey visited with Judge Landis, the commissioner of baseball, on March 22 and hosted AL president Will Harridge on March 23, while rooting for his Louisville farm club to beat the Red Sox. Louisville fell just short, 5–4.

Interviewed on April 1, Yawkey was optimistic about the season, perhaps overly so, reminding writers that even Walter Johnson had been unheralded once but then blossomed. It was noted as unusual, but Yawkey took in a preseason City Series game in Boston and saw the Red Sox beat the Boston Braves on April 12 at Braves Field, 11–6. The injured Ted Williams sat with Yawkey in the "royal box" atop the grandstand at Fenway to take in Opening Day.[32]

Sox fans may have sensed that Cronin wasn't performing at a high enough level. The respected Shirley Povich of the *Washington Post* wrote that "matters are not at all serene" at headquarters, that Cronin was thought to mishandle pitchers, and that "they're thinking of firing Joe Cronin. . . . They don't want him to play shortstop because they think he can't do the job justice," and "Yawkey and Collins feel the need of a bold step."[33] Even players like Jimmie Foxx said, after they'd left the team, "If Cronin had handled our pitchers properly, we might have won several pennants. Our hitting was always good, but the pitching didn't hold up. It wasn't the fault of the pitchers, either. They could have won if Cronin had used more judgment in picking their spots. Didn't every one of them turn out to be winners after they got away from Boston?"[34] Foxx also said that Yawkey was too friendly with players on the ball club and that he may thereby have hurt the team inadvertently. He admitted that he himself was one of those players, "but I'm still sticking to my story."[35]

If such was the storm brewing, Cronin weathered it well—though 1941 was his last full season as a player. Winning the first five games of the season helped. Just a few days later, Yawkey responded to the Cronin story—"denied with some heat"—and stated, "Those stories are not only untrue but they are offensive to Cronin, one of the finest personalities in baseball. Never have I considered releasing Cronin."[36] Another newspaper quoted him in a statement that seemed to represent the sort of loyal relationships that characterized Yawkey throughout his life: "There will always be room for Cronin on the Red Sox as long as I am connected with the team."[37] Again, though, we have perhaps a bit of an insight into how Yawkey appraised the men closest to him: he remarked on Cronin's personality rather than his managerial talent.

Cronin had a very good season in 1941. He ultimately played in 143 games, his .311 average was second only to that of Ted Williams, and his 95 RBIs—though fourth on the club—were clearly excellent for a shortstop of the era.

Some labor-management issues arose in May when a picket line went up at Fenway. The Building Service Employees Union charged that Yawkey had refused to collectively bargain with the ground crew. He was quoted as saying that the workers' representative did not reflect the park workers' views; a spokesman said that some of the workers had reached out to the union local but had then withdrawn their request for recognition.[38] Organizer Luke Taylor said that twenty-one members of the union had been forced to resign from the union; hence the picket.

Ted Williams had an early twenty-three-game hitting streak, from May 15 through June 7. He was hitting .431 at the time, about 30 percent of the way through the season. On July 8 Tom Yawkey was thrilled to be present at the All-Star Game in Detroit when the Kid hit a ninth-inning come-from-behind game-winning three-run home run to propel the American League to victory. "When Ted hit that home run," he said, "I jumped out of my seat and started jumping up and down and clapping my hands. Because I was watching Ted, who was doing the exact same thing as he ran around the bases."[39]

Grantland Rice wrote a column complimentary of Yawkey, calling him "one of the keenest baseball followers anyone ever saw" and saying that despite being a "genial, liberal citizen . . . baseball to him is no idle plaything. . . . On the inside, he is a tough loser, no matter what the competition."[40] Yawkey's interest in improving the ball club sometimes took remarkable forms; in late June or early July, he brought the Cleveland groundskeeper to Boston to redo the pitcher's mound at Fenway Park.[41]

The Red Sox were in Cleveland a week or so later, and so was Tom Yawkey, and again he had a guest who sat with him in his box during the game: Ted Williams. Williams's ankle had just been freshly treated before the day's doubleheader, and he sat it out, taking in the game with TAY.

Ted was off his feet for only a couple of days before he resumed hitting; from July 25 to the end of the season his average dipped below .400 only once, on the next-to-last day of the schedule, when it fell to .39955. Rounded up, it would be .400, but rounding up wasn't the way the Kid wanted to go into the record books. He played in both games of the September 28 doubleheader, went 6-for-8, and erased any notion of just squeaking by, finishing the year with a .406 batting average.[42] No batter has hit .400 since. Williams's on-base percentage was .553; in other words, more than half the time he came up to bat, he got on base. Williams repeated such a high figure in 1954 (.513) and 1957 (.526). Twice, in 1942 and 1947, he finished at .499.

Yawkey was there the day before: "I went to Philadelphia to watch the games, but left after the game on Saturday. Ted went 1-for-4, so I thought I was a jinx. I went to New York after the game and left instructions for Phil Troy to keep in touch with me the next day about how Ted was doing."[43]

Although the Red Sox finished second (up from fourth in 1940), they were a full seventeen games behind the Yankees. Yawkey said he stopped looking at the standings around the end of August. "They make me sick. They just start out with New York, and then there's a big blank space. It's just like the rest of us were in another league."[44] The third-place White Sox were twenty-four games out, seven games behind Boston. In that sense, it was a comfortable second place, but comfort wasn't where Yawkey yearned to be. He wanted a pennant.

There had been rumors in mid-August that Yawkey was so frustrated that he was going to break up the ball club, but he responded to these rumors with what Bill Cunningham of the *Herald* called "the longest telegram I ever received"; he printed it in his August 23 column.

Genial Yawkey may have been, but there was a darker side too. As noted in chapter 8, Billy Evans had been hired in 1937 to build up a farm system for the Red Sox. Over the next four years he built an excellent one, and on August 10, 1941, Yawkey asked Evans to move to Louisville to oversee the new franchise he had helped the Sox acquire. The Louisville team owned the contract of shortstop Pee Wee Reese. Joe Cronin did not welcome the possibility of a threat to his position at shortstop. Only a few weeks later, on September 6, Yawkey called Evans and asked for his resignation. Evans claimed Yawkey was drunk at the time, and it was just his misfortune to have been home at the time of the call.[45]

In early December, Shirley Povich outlined Yawkey's dilemma: "What has stumped Yawkey for the past several years . . . is the reluctance of other clubowners to sell for cash. . . . The club owner who sells for cash these days must go into hiding and hope that the storm will blow over."[46] Although money wasn't everything, writers sure enjoyed writing about it. Whitney Martin offered one of the more colorful phrases, dubbing Tom Yawkey "the genial young bulgy-pockets of the Boston Red Sox."[47] Even if the other owners were willing to sell players to Boston for cash, there was no guarantee that a pennant would follow. "You need more than a group of fancy sluggers to win a pennant," wrote W. T. Lee.[48] Pitching, as noted, was the problem.

Lefty Grove had apparently been contemplating playing another season, Yawkey revealed over a dozen years later. In a 1954 interview with George C. Carens of the *Boston Traveler*, he said that

"Mose came down to visit me in South Carolina before the following season [1942] and allowed that he had an urge to keep fogging them in. He and I chinned on the subject for a few days while we hunted for game down there in the south. Then he decided to stay retired. It was the correct decision, too."[49]

Overshadowing everything, baseball and beyond, was the outbreak of war. Just ten weeks to the day from the final game of the baseball season, Japanese warplanes attacked the American forces at Pearl Harbor, Hawaii, killing more than 2,400 on December 7. The very next day, the U.S. Congress declared war on Japan. Three days after that, Germany and Italy—allies of Japan—declared war on the United States. America was plunged into war both in the Pacific and in Europe. It was uncertain whether professional sports such as baseball would close down operations for the duration.

11

The War Years, 1942–1945

IN HIS AUTOBIOGRAPHY Ted Williams wrote of the 1941 season: "Tom Yawkey got into the act. He said he didn't think it would be smart for me to come to spring training."[1] What? The owner of the Red Sox urging his biggest star, his .400 hitter, not to join the team for spring training? Ted reacted stubbornly. "That was the *first* mistake the Red Sox made with me. I made up my mind that I was going to go anyway."[2]

There was, of course, a story behind Ted's actions. It was wartime, though on January 15, 1942, President Franklin Roosevelt had written Commissioner Landis that he felt it was "best for the country to keep baseball going," largely for purposes of recreation and morale. Roosevelt also spoke favorably of extending night baseball so that workers on the day shift could take in a game in the evening. Neither the Boston Red Sox nor the Boston Braves had made any move toward installing lighting, though during 1941 Yawkey had visited other ballparks that had lights and had gathered information on the subject. The Sox began to contemplate playing twilight games. Yawkey took under advisement the idea of putting lights in Fenway Park but finally decided in the spring of 1944 to consider the matter only after the war was over.[3] He had strong opinions on the subject; he really didn't want lights.[4]

Ted Williams was in the midst of a controversy over his military draft status. As sole support of his mother, he had been granted a III-A deferment and by pure coincidence a story to that effect had run in numerous papers, including the *New York Times,* on the morning of December 7, 1941. Later that day, pretty much everyone in the country knew that America had been plunged into war. The timing was far from ideal. A few weeks later, in January, Williams was reclassified I-A, subject to immediate conscription. An appeal was filed on Williams's behalf, and on February 27 he was restored to III-A status.

When the press learned of the restored status, there was a negative reaction—indeed, a firestorm (in some cases, apparently, fanned by columnists who themselves had exemptions).[5] Dave Egan—Williams's biggest antagonist among the Boston writers—came to his defense, however. Deferments and appeals were there for a reason, he wrote. Williams had a right, like any citizen, to appeal, and in this case the president had agreed with his appeal. But it just looked bad for the reigning batting champion to be excused from service while other young men had to go. The Red Sox saw it as a public relations (PR) nightmare.[6]

Yawkey told the press that he had no right to tell someone whether or not to enlist but that he had urged Ted to think over the ramifications and that he might face unfriendly crowds.[7] Quaker Oats canceled an endorsement deal with Ted, and his own business manager advised him that it would be unwise to seek deferment. Stubborn as always, Williams reported to spring training. (He got rousing ovations from servicemen in the crowds at spring training games, as well as from other fans, a response that more or less sealed the controversy.) On May 22, having made his point and committed to play out the 1942 season, Williams went and enlisted in the navy. Yawkey was back in Georgetown at the time but expressed his pleasure.

American League president Will Harridge had called Ted, who said he "told me to keep my chin up, that I wouldn't have been deferred in the first place if I wasn't in the right."[8] But that hadn't been Cronin's or Yawkey's reaction. Cronin had actually arranged for Williams to visit the Great Lakes naval base in early March; that backfired when Mickey Cochrane, head of athletics at the base, told Ted that he'd be booed unmercifully if he played baseball. That got Ted's back up. Somewhat later, Yawkey reportedly placed a call to Williams to ask him to see Cochrane again.[9] That didn't happen, and Yawkey came around, noting that there had been over two thousand similar appeals to the appeals board, eighty-seven of them rejected, and only one appeal had occasioned public comment: Ted's.[10]

Yawkey said, "He's making his own decision about his immediate future. He's always been a pretty good boy thus far, and whatever step he takes now I know it will be the honest one."[11] On March 15 over 1,750 midshipmen saw the Sox play an exhibition game in Tampa, and not one boo was heard.

It wasn't clear how the year would shape up. Lefty Grove had retired. Rookie Johnny Pesky—the American Association MVP—looked good to take over at shortstop, leaving Cronin to focus more on managing.[12] It was thought Jimmie Foxx might retire (he played the first six weeks or so but was then offered on waivers and taken by the Cubs). In a way, it was like a changing of the guard as the "three musketeers" that had constituted Yawkey's biggest acquisitions began to move on. Of course the demands of the war left everyone uncertain as to whether those who were back could play out the season or not.

In mid-March it was announced that Tom Yawkey (he was then thirty-nine years old) would be taking a captain's commission in the U. S. Army. A few weeks later, however, Yawkey said he wasn't going into the service just yet. For one thing, his businesses were supplying materiel for the war effort. "My business interests outside of baseball are busy right now helping furnish tools and equipment for the armed forces. I consider that just as important a war effort as toting a gun."[13] Also, he said he wanted to be sure that when he went in, he would be doing something for which he was suited; he mentioned a friend of his who had volunteered for a dollar-a-year job but then found he was assigned a job for which he had no experience.[14] In fact Yawkey did not enter the army. In the spirit of the time he said he'd begun a program of physical fitness playing handball every day and had never been in better shape.

On April 4 Yawkey donated five ambulances to the American Red Cross that would be shipped to the Middle East. Five days later, catcher Frankie Pytlak signed up for the navy. This was the first year Yawkey had not visited the team during spring training. Traveling secretary Troy routinely sent him a one-hundred-word telegram, starting with "win" or "lose" and then detailing a game.[15] At the end of August Yawkey gave the American Field Service a $10,000 check.

Also lending her service was Elise Yawkey, who became head of the Civilian Defense Volunteer Office (CDVO) blood donors service in New York.[16] In August she even played some baseball—in the second annual ladies' baseball game at the Maidstone Club in East Hampton.[17] Each year she showed up as one of the committee for events such as the White Elephant Sale at the Stork Club. She was also part of a syndicate (including Grantland Rice and golfer Bobby Jones) that financed "colored lightweight" boxer Beau Jack of Augusta, Georgia.[18]

The baseball season got under way, and there was no further controversy involving Ted Williams's status. (He homered in a 3-for-5 Opening Day and drove in five runs.) His signing up for the navy in May removed any issue that might have lingered.

Forty thousand fans turned out for the April 26 game against the visiting Yankees, and another twenty thousand were turned away. Yawkey flew to town in time to take in a series with the Tigers that started on April 28. Fans were doing their part for the war effort, returning every foul ball hit into the stands. The team collected these balls in baskets along the first- and third-base stands.

The year had begun with UP columnist George Kirksey writing, "Tom Yawkey must have a hoodoo hanging over him. He tries harder and makes less progress than any major-league owner."[19] Of course, with the war looming large, one didn't know which men might be drafted into or sign up for the service. Planning for 1943 and later—building a team for the future—was going to be exceptionally difficult. Yawkey did keep all five farm clubs in the system active in 1942. Both the Braves and Red Sox announced that servicemen stationed in New England would be admitted free to any game all season long. They had only to obtain their tickets through the morale or recreation officer of their branch of service. As a further part of the war effort, the Red Sox announced later in the season that anyone who brought ten pounds of scrap metal to Fenway Park would earn free admission to the game.[20]

How much did Yawkey love to follow the Red Sox? He wasn't around them nearly as much in 1942 as in earlier years, but he kept in touch. Phil Troy said he'd phoned from New York during the May 31 game, for instance, to hear how the game was going. Troy also told of a time a couple of years earlier when Yawkey called from Alaska:

> I told him we were behind 2–1 going into the last of the ninth and he said he'd hang on while I told him what happened in the ninth. Our first hitter in the ninth drew a walk, and Mr. Yawkey got all excited. Bobby Doerr was up next and I gave him the full count of balls and strikes on Doerr and then had to tell him Doerr popped up. I heard him moan, but he asked, "Who's up next?" I told him Foxx was up and he wanted to know what was happening on every pitch. Foxx fanned for the second out, and when I told him that I heard the phone click, and I knew Mr. Yawkey had hung up in disgust.[21]

It was a rare time that he gave up too soon; two weeks later, Yawkey learned that Joe Cronin had hit the first pitch he saw for a home run that won the game.

At the end of July, a somewhat surprising discussion arose about integration in baseball—at least in some circles. Philadelphia Phillies owner Gerry Nugent said that his manager, Hans Lobert, had given a tryout to Roy Campanella and then added that Campanella was "the son of an Italian father and a colored mother." Campanella "also received a letter from the Boston Red Sox, according to ballplayers, who said they read it last week."[22]

The 1942 Red Sox won nine more games than in 1941, finishing 93-59. They were in second place, more than 10½ games ahead of third-place St. Louis, but nine games behind the Yankees. That was a lot better than the 17 games behind New York they'd been in 1941 but still nothing in the way of a pennant race.

Johnny Pesky in particular had enjoyed a spectacular rookie season, with a league-leading 205 base hits and a .331 batting average, second in the league only to Ted Williams. He came in third in MVP voting.[23]

During the World Series there were a number of broadcast appeals for blood donations. They were arranged by Elise Yawkey.[24]

The war was on in full swing, but some could enjoy life as usual. After the World Series, Yankees president Ed Barrow traveled to South Carolina for two weeks of hunting on Yawkey's game preserve.

Looking ahead to the 1943 season, no one knew what to expect. Was Roosevelt's "green light" still on? Yawkey believed that it was, but he didn't see it as a time to be wheeling and dealing and picking up players from other teams. He was willing to take pot luck and just see how it all worked out.[25] He said, "We intend to play ball with what we have. Teams are talking about what may be their nucleus. That's what gets me. The Red Sox can't be said to have any nucleus with Williams, DiMaggio, and Pesky in the service. . . . All we can do is check up on what material we may have available in March, and then figure out from there."[26]

When Pesky left to go into the service, with Williams, he had had just one year in a Boston uniform. Yawkey saw to it that he was not disadvantaged by the loss of the income he otherwise would have anticipated. In the last week of the season, Johnny found a note on his chair asking him to report to Eddie Collins. Collins handed him an envelope that contained a check for $5,000. (His salary that year had been just $4,000.) It was enough to pay for a new house for Johnny's parents on Overton Street in Portland— and earn Tom Yawkey loyalty for life. "It has stayed with me," Pesky said, more than sixty years later, "what Mr. Yawkey did. That's why I have always loved the Red Sox—with Mr. Yawkey— because of what he did not only for me but for my family. They were so darn nice."[27]

The Boston Red Sox held 1943 spring training in Greater Boston—at Tufts University in Medford, all of eight miles from Fenway Park. During wartime all of the big league teams trained closer to home to cut down on rail travel so that trains could be freed up for the transport of troops and essential goods. One columnist suggested that the Red Sox could train on Yawkey's South Carolina plantation and maybe put in a little extra time working the rice fields.[28] The Red Sox were the first Major League team to announce they would train at home.[29]

Yawkey also supplied the Red Sox with individual trunks so that players could carry their own luggage—again, a modest contribution intended to help with the war effort. One less porter who did not have to perform nonessential duties for the railroad could be one more soldier or one more worker who could help load the trains with supplies.

Good questions arose as to whether the team could truly be competitive; many felt that the Red Sox had lost more of their key players to military service and defense work than any other team in baseball. Outfielder Lou Finney, for instance, was farming in Alabama, food being—of course—essential to sustenance for both the citizenry and those in service.

The team experimented with a 10:30 a.m. game on May 27 so that workers on the 3:00–11:00 p.m. shift could take in a game. It was a split-admission doubleheader, with the second game starting at 3:00 p.m. Attendance was light for both, a little lighter for the morning game.

The Sox also had no way of knowing what ballpark attendance figures might be. In 1941 it had increased significantly at Fenway Park, from a record 716,234 in 1940 to an even higher 918,497. It reverted in 1942 to 730,340, but in 1943 it fell by more than 50 percent to 358,275. There had been fears of such a decline, and that was one of the reasons the Red Sox made very few moves of significance. Yawkey's total payroll had declined from a high in 1940 and remained lower until 1946.

On April 10 and 11 the Red Sox played two exhibition games in New York against the New York Giants. It is amusing that at the Polo Grounds, Tom Yawkey made his way to a seat in the stands "in spite of an officious usher who wanted to see his seat check."[30] All of the proceeds from the Braves–Red Sox City Series game, played later in April, were donated to the American Red Cross. Throughout the offseason Joe Cronin had worked in Washington at the offices of the Red Cross and then toured overseas locations on behalf of that organization.

The Sox got off to a terrible start, 4-10 over the first fourteen games. With so many of their key players off to war, from the second game to the end of the season the highest they were able to achieve was third place for about ten days at the end of June. The first five games, which Yawkey himself attended, were all losses. Bemoaning Yawkey's otherwise rare appearances, *Boston Globe* columnist Victor O. Jones noted that Tom Yawkey "has, or had, homes in Detroit, New York, and South Carolina, but never more than a couple of hotel rooms here in Boston."[31]

From July 5 on, the Red Sox were never higher than fifth place. From early August to September 11, they were in sixth place, and from September 12 on they were in seventh. Only 714 people turned out for the September 27 game; it was the smallest attendance figure of any game since Tom Yawkey had purchased the team.

The Yankees finished first again; the Philadelphia Athletics finished last. The Red Sox were 68-84, twenty-nine games out of first place but still twenty games ahead of Philadelphia. In just one season there had been a drop of twenty-five games.

An AP story that ran in November suggested that perhaps Yawkey had miscalculated in not having made more moves before the season. The story added that he "is not going to be caught napping again if the majors go to a third wartime season. A year ago the Red Sox owner was certain that baseball would be declared out for the duration. When he became convinced to the contrary, it was much too late to strengthen his war-riddled club with any last-minute shopping."[32] A UP story pointed out that the Red Sox had been "left with one of the most depleted rosters in the major leagues."[33]

Near the end of the year, the Phillies—with Yawkey's permission—hired Red Sox director of Minor League operations Herb Pennock as general manager. In Pennock's place, the Sox promoted George "Specs" Toporcer, who had been with the team since 1935 as a scout and Minor League manager.

Not all of Yawkey's relationships with other clubs were as amicable. Though he often came across as Mr. Congeniality, it was Yawkey who called off a trade with the Indians because he learned that the Indians were planning to trade Jeff Heath and Jim Bagby to the Red Sox for several players but were then going to trade two of the players they received to a third club. Though such trades happened with some regularity, perhaps the etiquette was that a club was supposed to disclose such intentions beforehand. Yawkey was miffed enough that news reports called it a "sudden feud . . . nothing but hard feelings between the two clubs."[34] There was some history, apparently. Yawkey felt he had been "had" a couple of times in his earlier years. He may have overreacted due to his sensitivity on related issues.

Yawkey was ready to buy ballplayers when the opportunity presented itself. In early 1944 he acquired "Indian Bob" Johnson from the Athletics in a cash deal. Johnson had a superb year in 1944 and was a key element in what became a perhaps surprising run for the pennant. Stories as late as April 1944, however, foresaw the possibility of the Sox ending up in the cellar.

With the nation focused on war, the press paid less attention to Tom Yawkey. Perhaps he was keeping a lower profile (too many society events could appear unseemly, though even in his younger days he never seemed to be attracted to high society), or he was simply busier with his other enterprises (which were likely quite profitable due to the additional demand for materiel). He did his part on a personal level, donating ambulances and contributing money, as noted, but he was also spotted ducking into a blood donor center on Boylston Street in Boston on May 23 to donate a pint.

In April 1944 Boston city councilor Isadore Muchnick wrote to both Yawkey and Bob Quinn protesting the ongoing discrimination "against the employment of colored people as ball players"; and although the city granted both teams the requisite license for playing baseball on Sundays, there had been a "spirited debate" on the council on the subject of discrimination.[35]

The Red Sox did not have employees of color anywhere in the organization. Whatever Tom Yawkey's feelings on race, an interesting glimpse into Elise Yawkey's sheltered views on the subject cropped up in a society column written by Alice Hughes in the "Women's Magazine and Amusement Section" of the July 4, 1943, *Cleveland Plain Dealer*. Hughes and three other women had dined with a fifth person at a penthouse terrace in New York; the four of them were, as she put it, "career women," which "simply means we have jobs which we treat importantly." They expected a serious discussion. Hughes continued:

> Then the Fifth Lady moved into the picture. She was a pretty, extremely blond Southern girl, whose husband owns the Boston American base-

ball club. He is so lavish in buying ball players that irreverent sports writers call it "the rich Red Sox." . . . Mrs. Elise, wearing pale blue gabardine slacks and a white printed blouse, took over completely. Her subject was the Yawkey estate in one of the Carolinas—its colored retainers, its church socials, its weddings and its babies. We four "careerists" were stopped dead as Mrs. Yawkey filled her continued story with southern charm and warmth. It came from a world we know nothing of. So the lush evening ended with little settled about our "serious discussion." We had enjoyed ourselves, projected into the sunny South. What wound the party up was a reference to the national tragedy of colored racial troubles which have been raging. That was a world Mrs. Yawkey didn't know. So we ambled on home.

As to Tom Yawkey, a perhaps somewhat flippant comment at the baseball meetings in December demonstrated some awareness on his part of demographics. "I'm in the market for a good Jewish ball player. I'm now convinced that's the only way I'm ever going to win over the South Boston trade."[36] Even though Fenway Park had hosted the occasional Negro League game (for instance, an exhibition game featuring the Homestead Grays against a shipyard team on May 26), courting ticket sales from Boston's small African American community by signing a black ballplayer wasn't a market Yawkey sought to tap.

There was still some wheeling and dealing to improve the ball club; in a straight-up deal on May 6, the Red Sox traded outfielder Ford Garrison to the Athletics for catcher Hal Wagner. At the end of June the club sent Vic Johnson down to Louisville and reinstated Lou Finney. Yawkey was said to have been heard musing, "Finney! There's a player I've always liked. I'll take a hustler like him ahead of a so-called star who loafs."[37]

As the season progressed, the teams were fairly well bunched in the standings into June. As late as June 7, only 5½ games separated first place from last place. The Sox were in the second division until then but were suddenly in second place on June 11 and were in second place—sometimes third—right until the end of August. It was ironic, wrote Ed Rumill of the *Christian Science Monitor*, that the team was doing so well with players the Red Sox had either developed (like Bobby Doerr, Tex Hughson, and Jim Tabor, among others Rumill mentioned) or acquired relatively inexpensively (like Bob Johnson).[38] Yawkey knew he'd spent a lot of money on players in years past and obviously wished one of his teams had won a pennant, "but I'm not crying because they didn't. You can't be a cry baby and be in the baseball business." Baseball in Boston had "needed a kick in the pants. And one of the quickest and surest ways to bring it back, of course, was to go out and buy well-known ballplayers and talk about pennants." Yawkey, Rumill assessed, was "one of the greatest fans in the game, cheering and rooting for Cronin and his mates from his box atop the grandstand roof."[39]

On July 9 there was a benefit game for the War Relief and Service Fund, one of several held games throughout the war years from which Yawkey donated the day's receipts. Everyone—even the players!—paid for admission to the game. Yawkey himself purchased 497 tickets for servicemen to attend.[40] In July also, Fenway Park was selected as the site for the 1945 All-Star Game.

There was some controversy when Jimmie Foxx called out Cronin for the way he handled pitchers (Yawkey said, "Cronin is OK with me" and said he thought it was poor taste on Foxx's part to express such a sour attitude other than directly to Cronin himself).[41] At month's end, Yawkey extended Cronin's contract through 1947. "Joe can manage any ball club I own as long as he likes."[42] Yawkey also put up the money to bring in pitchers Rex Cecil and Clem Dreisewerd, hoping they would help in the stretch.

The team lost ace pitcher Tex Hughson after he had won his eighteenth game on August 9; he was 18-5, with about a third of the season yet to come, when he left to join the army air force. Catcher Hal Wagner was called to service on August 27. Bobby Doerr's last game came on September 3. He was batting .325 and leading the league in hitting, but he was called to service in the army. It was inopportune timing.

On September 1, despite winning that day's game, the Red Sox slipped to fourth place (though only 2½ games out of first, very much still in contention). They remained in fourth the rest of the year, thanks in large part to a ten-game losing streak that began on September 17.

The Sox finished the season dead even at .500: 77 wins, 77 losses. They'd been 1½ games out on September 2 but went 8-16 in September and found themselves twelve games behind when the season ended a month later.[43]

Perhaps in part because of how well the season had gone until the final month, attendance was up from 358,275 to 506,975. There was also increased optimism about the war coming to a close. In 1945 attendance increased once more, though it was not quite up to 1942 standards: the Red Sox drew 603,794 to Fenway.

After the season, Yankees president Ed Barrow joined Yawkey in Georgetown for twenty-three days of hunting and fishing. Perhaps they commiserated with each other; the St. Louis Browns had won the pennant, and the Yankees had finished third. Spending more than three weeks together must have reflected some true friendship between the two magnates.

Yawkey was one of the four owners in Major League Baseball's leadership group. The group had met in February 1944 to discuss postwar planning. In December of that year Yawkey became part of a joint committee of American and National League owners that would formulate plans to replace late commissioner Landis. The *New York Times* reported a rumor that Tom Yawkey was planning to sell the Red Sox and buy the Yankees.[44] The next day, GM Collins said there had never been any basis for such a yarn.

Elise Yawkey hadn't been around. She'd filed for divorce and had been living at the Tumbling D-W Dude Ranch at Reno, Nevada, under the name Elise Young for the six weeks it took to attain legal residency. Her petition noted that she and Tom had been separated since September 1939. When granted the divorce on November 13, she asked for and was awarded custody of their adopted eight-year-old daughter, Julia. Some have speculated that Tom and Elise had hoped that adopting a child would bind them closer together, but it did not. The agreement as to property rights was sealed.

Why the separation? Phil Wilkinson, the wildlife biologist who worked for Yawkey on South Island from 1966 to 1977 (through Tom Yawkey's death in 1976), presents an interesting possibility. Wilkinson and Yawkey lived a couple of hundred feet from each other on the property, a brick path leading through some live oaks from one residence to the other, and the two men talked often. "I don't know anything about his relationship with the first Mrs. Yawkey," Wilkinson admits, and continues:

She was Miss Alabama, so she was obviously beautiful. From the information I got from the crew and other people in Georgetown that knew her, they just adored her. She was just totally adored. She apparently had the kind of personality that attracted adulation. I think that burned him [Tom] a little bit. I think that might have been what was the trouble. You know, he felt like he was the big name, and if people gave her all the attention, somehow maybe subconsciously he might not have liked that too much. It might have been subconscious. . . . He'd talk about her sometimes, and I got the idea that he thought she was really good looking, but he might have been a little jealous of that part about her being so adored.[45]

A motivating factor in the divorce was no doubt reflected in Elise's December 2, 1944, marriage to widower Harry Dorsey Watts of East End Avenue, New York. She had found someone else. Watts headed an engineering and building company, James Stewart Construction. The company had built Grand Central Terminal and the New York post office on Eighth Avenue. Watts was also described as a wealthy sportsman.

Stout and Johnson suggest that as Yawkey's marriage began to disintegrate, Tom Yawkey sought some solace in alcohol. He was now older than most of his players and "increasingly felt like a stranger in their midst. Now when Yawkey came to Boston he stayed in seclusion in a suite he kept on the 16th floor of the Ritz. He even took meals in his room, usually venturing out only to go to Fenway Park. He'd arrive early in the morning at Fenway Park, and instead of working out with the players as he once had, he now paid batboys and other employees to throw him batting practice."[46] No doubt it was something of a command performance, but Yawkey compensated them well for the work.

Yawkey really didn't roam all over Boston. His long-time secretary Mary Trank told the *Globe*'s Stan Grossfeld, "He'd go right from his office, right down the ramp, into the wagon they had for him, and then right to the [Ritz-Carlton] hotel. You wouldn't see him till the morning. He never went out in the hotel to dinner; he always had dinner brought to his suite."[47] The Newbury Street door attendant at the Ritz, Norman Pashoian, remembered, "He wasn't a flamboyant person. He was very conservative. He wore a brown suit all the time, but he probably had about a dozen of them. I never spoke with him other than to say 'Good morning' and that's it. . . . He had dinner in his suite. He'd come back from the park, and if there was a night game, he wouldn't be back until late. But he had dinner in his suite. Sometimes he had dinner with Joe Cronin. With Pinky Higgins, I think, one time. I saw that Ted Williams went up there a few times."[48]

Tom Carroll worked eighteen years on the bell staff at the Ritz. He remembers the Yawkeys' place. It was on the top floor of the hotel that had rooms: "He lived in Room 1619. It was a two-bedroom suite, with a large living room in between. It was the last one all the way around. Our manager, [William] Ebersol at the time, lived one floor below him. It looked over the Charles River and into Cambridge. If you looked out the other way, you could actually see Fenway Park." Carroll added, "If you were to go up to the floor now and went to the end of the hallway—the 19 room would be to your right—you'd be looking to the west, right at Fenway Park." Carroll agreed that one wouldn't see Tom Yawkey in the hotel restaurant. "You never saw him in the Café. Never. And Mrs. Yawkey was very quiet. They kept to themselves."[49]

Dick Johnson of the Sports Museum of New England summed up: "[Yawkey] was an eccentric to the core. It's amazing to think that a guy with that much money comes to Boston and is so isolated. He basically lives this sort of weird monastic existence here, going back and forth from his hotel room to the ballpark. And nowhere else."[50] James S. Kunen once dubbed him "the Phantom of Fenway Park."[51]

Before he'd taken the suite at the Ritz, Yawkey had stayed at the Somerset Hotel at 400 Commonwealth Avenue, just a half mile from Fenway. Arthur D'Angelo, proprietor of Twins Enterprises ("The Souvenir Store" on Yawkey Way), used to sell the *Daily Record* and the *Boston American* on the street when he and his twin brother Henry first arrived in Boston from Italy in 1938. The papers sold for two cents. "I met him in 1938, actually. I was selling newspapers. He used to stay at the Somerset, and he used to walk by here and I used to give him the newspapers." Even in those days, D'Angelo said, Yawkey pretty much kept to himself. "He was a loner. I mean, he didn't associate with anybody. He conversed with people a little bit but very, very little. We had a short conversation but never any long conversations. He never, never dressed up. He was not a fancy guy. A very casual guy, but he was a loner. He was a decent guy, but he kept to himself."[52]

Mel Parnell recalled, "Whenever we went away on a road trip, [Yawkey]'d work out at Fenway with Vince Orlando and take batting practice, and the kids around the neighborhood would wait for Mr. Yawkey to come out and go out and shag flies for him while he was taking batting practice. Then after he was finished he'd give them all a $20 bill. The kids loved that. They'd gather around waiting for him to come out. He sent a lot of our batboys to college and one of them (John Donovan) came back to be our team lawyer."[53] Ticket taker Larry Corea remembered, "We'd all get our turn to hit. If he wasn't hitting, he'd feed the pitcher the balls to throw in to the batter. It wasn't what it is now, but we had a batting cage. We didn't have any protection as far as the pitcher goes, though. You had to be alert."[54]

David Halberstam wrote, "Those times when he actually appeared in the Ritz dining room were rare indeed."[55] Maureen Cronin added, regarding her father Joe, "My father was very closely tied to Tom on a daily basis, especially during the baseball season, and would spend many many hours at the ballpark with him. [Tom] never came to the house for dinner that I can remember, and our family never joined Jean and Tom for dinner in Boston."[56]

In any event, Tom didn't waste a lot of time after the divorce and Elise's remarriage. He took out a marriage license on December 22, and on Christmas Eve, December 24, Tom Yawkey married Mrs. Jean R. Hiller of New York in the living room of friends Leila and Ralph Ford, who owned the C. L. Ford Grocery Store in downtown Georgetown. The *Boston Globe*'s Susan Trausch writes that at their wedding they were dressed in "their hunting clothes, casual pants and tops, much more like L. L. Bean than Jay Thorpe."[57]

Jay Thorpe was an upscale women's clothing store at 24 West Fifty-Seventh Street at Fifth Avenue in Manhattan, and Jean had been working as a saleswoman and model when, apparently, she caught Tom Yawkey's eye one day when he was shopping there with Elise.[58] *Time* magazine described Jean as a "onetime Saks Fifth Avenue model."[59] Jean Hiller's entry in the 1940 U.S. census perhaps reflected her wanting to suit her upscale surroundings. Rather than "saleswoman in a women's clothing store," she described herself as a "vendeuse" and the industry as "couture." She lived at 1026 First Avenue, between Fifty-Sixth and Fifty-Seventh Streets, at Sutton Place.

William Oppenheim's father, Charles J. Oppenheim Jr., was the founder of Jay Thorpe. It was a sizable ladies' specialty store, à la Bergdorf Goodman, with branches in resort areas such as Palm Beach, Florida, and Newport, Rhode Island.[60] Oppenheim was about ten years younger than Jean but remembered her as "most attractive, quite tall.... She modeled ready to wear dresses." These weren't agency models; they were permanent store employees. They worked 9:00 to 5:30, Oppenheim said. The store had fifteen models, and they did fashion shows all the time. "When we sold a dress," he said, "We always had it modeled with accessories."[61]

Tom and Jean had apparently met sometime in the late 1930s. The Fords' son, Ralph Jr., said that "Tom refused to marry again as long as Elise was not married, but Jean lived with Tom five years before their marriage, and even brought her mother to South Island. Such things were almost unheard of in those days."[62]

Jean Hiller had been born in Brooklyn on January 24, 1909, as Jean Remington Hollander, but she grew up on Rosedale Avenue in Freeport, Long Island. Her father was in the parquet floor business. Her classmate Sidney Shebar recalled she had a brother who played football and was known as "Blub." The family was considered "well-to-do" and "looked upon with regard."[63] In 1926 Jean graduated from Freeport High School. For a woman who seemed so reticent to the media, it's interesting that in her senior year she and classmate James Staros won the annual public speaking contest. (She and Staros were each awarded $10 for their winning speeches.) And she served as editor of the school newspaper, the *Student*, in her senior year. She was a member of the Glee Club for three years (1922–24) and by senior year was also active in the Science Club, French Club, Dramatic Club, and Gavel Club. In both her junior and senior years she served on the Dance Committee. She was a member of the casts of both *The Touchdown* and *Bab*. The *Student* reported that Jean's "crush" was "Charlie," her future occupation was to be "actress," and her distinguishing characteristic was "haircut."

After graduation Jean Hollander married a fellow 1926 graduate, Charlie Hiller, her high school sweetheart and for three years a school basketball player. Their marriage did not last long. Perhaps he was a little too self-centered? The *Student* reported his "crush" as "Jean, also Charlie," and his present and future occupations were listed as "slinging it" and "same, only more of it." How was he distinguished? The school newspaper offered: "7th Regiment—my soldier boy." He appeared in the same two dramatic productions as Jean and was also active in the glee, French, science, and dramatic clubs. He was also a cheerleader for the school in his junior and senior years. Charlie went on to NYU. He later worked in a store, as did his mother. His father had been a merchant. At the time of his enlistment in the army in 1943, Hiller was working as a foreman in a manufacturing concern. Little more is known about his life.[64]

Jean Yawkey and Tom remained married until Tom's death in 1976.

In 1945, the third year of wartime baseball, Red Sox spring training was set for Pleasantville, New Jersey. There was reason for optimism if one looked ahead; the war was going well for the Allies in both the European and the Pacific theaters. Yawkey first visited the team on March 31 in a game at Atlantic City. A bizarre news item resulted, quoted here in its entirety: "Tom Yawkey, millionaire owner of the Boston Red Sox, swore Sunday that he would never spend more than the $7500 waiver price for any player."[65] What prompted this particular expression of parsimony, we do not know. We do know he didn't hold to the purported resolve.

Political figures stepped up pressure on the Red Sox regarding racial discrimination. Pursuing his mission to secure a commitment from the Red Sox to equal opportunity in hiring, Boston city councilor Muchnick had the backing of the new acting mayor of Boston, John E. Kerrigan, who as a councilor had voted with Muchnick in 1944 to deny the Red Sox the requisite license to play baseball on Sundays. Muchnick asked the Massachusetts Commission against Discrimination (MCAD) to investigate hiring practices on the ball club, among the staff as well as uniformed personnel. The Red Sox typically drew their biggest crowds on Sundays, and to lose the license would have been financially disastrous.

No team in baseball had yet fielded a "Negro" ballplayer. Yet African American soldiers were fighting in the war. They were subject to military conscription and asked to possibly give their lives for their country, yet in many states they were unable to vote, and many fields of endeavor—such as Major League baseball—were closed to them. Muchnick wanted to press the Red Sox to demonstrate their willingness to sign a black ballplayer. Columnist Wendell Smith of the *Pittsburgh Courier*, one of the country's leading black newspapers, was prepared to bring two or three prime candidates to try out. The Red Sox agreed, though not without some hiccups—scheduling, canceling, rescheduling. Smith brought three players to Fenway Park on April 16 for what was said to be a tryout: Sam Jethroe, Jackie Robinson, and Marvin Williams. The pressure had built for years; now Muchnick had pretty much forced the issue, and the tryout was held.

FBI files later revealed that "agents monitoring a meeting in Boston of the Communist Party of the United States filed an internal memo that cited a participant advocating racially integrating Major League Baseball with Negro leagues stars such as Jackie Robinson and Satchel Paige."[66] A few months after the tryout, on July 21, 1945, the Communist Party held a regional meeting at a perhaps incongruous venue: New England Mutual Life Hall in Boston. The FBI report noted that one participant, Nat Garfield, "mentioned that Satchel Paige and Jackie Robinson were to appear in Boston and said that these two negroes would be of great help to either the Boston Red Sox or the Boston Braves."[67] Indeed the Kansas City Monarchs did play a game against a team from the Charlestown Navy Yard at Braves Field on August 13 (and won, 13–1).

The Red Sox had a historic opportunity to become the first team in the Majors to desegregate. Instead, as it happens, they bear the shame of being the last. It was not until 1959, fourteen years after the 1945 tryout, that the Red Sox fielded a black ballplayer—Elijah "Pumpsie" Green. In retrospect, it is clear how badly the Red Sox missed out.

The story of Jackie Robinson's April 16 tryout (it was, of course, a tryout for all three players) has been told from many angles. Inspired by the fiftieth anniversary of Pumpsie Green's joining the Red Sox, eight authors contributed essays to *Pumpsie and Progress: The Red Sox, Race, and Redemption* in 2010.[68] The book presents differing looks at the tryout, and we will not attempt to retell the whole story here. No one truly knows what happened that day or why, but after an apparently impressive tryout, no one in the visiting party ever heard from the Red Sox again. Many years later sportswriter Clif Keane recounted that someone from the front office shouted, "Get those niggers off the field!" Keane claimed that no one knew who uttered the words. Historian Glenn Stout noted that no one else who was there ever mentioned such an outburst, but he added that Keane told sportswriter Larry Whiteside that it was either Yawkey, Cronin, or Collins. (The Red Sox had a very small front office at the time.) Stout later wrote, "A lot of people don't give that the greatest credibility. Is it apocryphal? It might be. If it is apocryphal, it might also be true figuratively."[69]

Joe Cronin reportedly watched from the stands, so he wasn't a likely candidate. Some have speculated that it was Tom Yawkey himself, though no evidence has ever surfaced in that regard. Some have wondered whether indeed the words were actually uttered. *Globe* writer John Powers in 2014: "It seemed unlikely. Clif Keane? Oh, sure. Yeah. He might have made it up."[70]

Boston media figure Tom Shaer said that Keane told three different versions of the story:

In 1979, Keane told the *Globe*'s Larry Whiteside he didn't know who gave that racist order. He is quoted in Dan Shaughnessy's 1990 book, *The Curse of the Bambino*, as saying it did *not* come from Tom Yawkey and, finally, Howard Bryant's book, *Shut Out* . . . reported Keane "believed" it *was* Yawkey. Bryant's book also identifies Keane as a regular user of the N-word. . . . Accepting without proof the "belief" of someone like Keane that it was Yawkey who yelled such a disgusting command is not sound journalism. The late Boston sports writer and broadcaster Larry Claflin was my friend and coworker. Before partnering with Keane, Larry's progressive credentials included a personal letter from Jackie Robinson lauding his pro-integration writing about the Red Sox and race. On numerous occasions, Larry railed to me about the racism of [Pinky] Higgins and others, but he never said Yawkey was like them.[71]

Television reporter Clark Booth doubted that Keane had fabricated the remark:

Clif swore to me, and actually I have a tape of him saying that he was there. Willy McDonough [of the *Boston Globe*], to his dying day, insisted that Clif wasn't at the ballpark that day. Now who do you believe? Willy hated Clif, for God knows what reason. Here were two guys who could hate. . . . They were world-class haters, each in a different way. When you got on Willy's shit list, man, . . . it was worse than being on Whitey's hit list, and it was the same with Cliffie. If he wrote you off, man, that was it. You were done. And they hated each other. Jesus, every time that thing came up, Willy would go bananas about how Clif was making up all that shit, but Clif insists he was there. . . . Clif swore it was Yawkey—although he did not say he saw him. He heard him. But he always swore it was Yawkey. Clif was a lot of things, but he really was a good reporter. He was colorful, eccentric, and a character at times, but, man, you didn't last if you made shit up in those days. They policed themselves much more rigorously than they do today."[72]

McDonough, Booth explained, came from a different place: "Willy was a pro-Yawkey guy. Willy liked him a lot. Mainly because Willy was tied in with Cronin. Willy's cousin married Maureen Cronin. Hank. He's a good guy, a Holy Cross guy. There was a real tie there. So Willy was on the Cronin dance card. Cronin had a big place down on the Cape. Willy could have blind spots."[73]

Joe Cronin was at the tryout, and Eddie Collins was there. So were Larry Woodall, Hugh Duffy, and Otey Clark, who threw batting practice to the trio of Negro Leagues players. Tom Yawkey was in town. Could it have been Eddie Collins? Booth said, "They used to call [Collins] a black Irishman. He was a Protestant Irish. He allegedly was bitterly anti-Semitic as well as anti-Catholic. It was quite a crowd."[74] But Rick Huhn in his excellent biography, *Eddie Collins*, devotes a few pages to the question of Collins's possible prejudices and finds no evidence one way or the other.[75]

Opportunities to sign black ballplayers were not new. In chapter 8, we noted the story of Frannie Matthews and Joe Zagami. And occasional Negro League games were played at Fenway Park—for instance, the Philadelphia Stars against the Baltimore Elite Giants on September 8, 1942. Games in 1943 featured the New York Black Yankees, Cuban All-Stars, Kansas City Monarchs, and Birmingham Black Barons. In 1944 the Homestead Grays played the Fore River Shipyard team. Moreover, it's not as though there wasn't an established history of black baseball in the Boston area—documented in the work of (among others) Boston sportswriter Mabray "Doc" Kountze, himself an African American who wrote for "colored" newspapers such as the *Boston Chronicle*. Indeed a number of black teams frequently played at Fraser Field in nearby Lynn, and in 1946 the Lynn team was a Minor League affiliate of the Red Sox.[76]

Opportunities went way back before Frannie Matthews, of course. Another player named Matthews—William Clarence Matthews— might have signed as far back as 1905.[77] He was a Harvard player who'd hit .400 in his senior year and stolen 25 bases in the short college season. That summer he was playing in Burlington, Vermont, in the Northern League, which in six years claimed one hundred Major Leaguers to its credit.[78] It was not unusual at the time for talented collegiate players to head straight to the Majors. The *Boston Traveler* reported that Matthews might be signed by Fred Tenney of the Boston Braves, himself an Ivy Leaguer who had attended Brown. Harvard graduate Matthews did not shy from the issue of race, declaring, "A negro is just as good as a white man and had just as much right to play ball. . . . This negro question on the diamond might as well be settled now as any time."[79] Indeed the question was settled but not in the way Matthews would have hoped.[80]

There were plenty of other opportunities, needless to say. The Red Sox had Hispanic players in their first decade—Frank Arellanes (1908-10) and Charlie Hall (1909-13). They had a Cuban player briefly in 1918, Eusebio Gonzalez. They had Harry Wolter (1909) and Ed Hearne (1910), both of mixed Latino background. In 1925 and 1926 they had Havana-born Ramon "Mike" Herrera. Bizarre as it may seem, Herrera came to the Red Sox after playing in the Negro Leagues and returned to the Negro Leagues after playing in Boston—more than twenty years before Jackie Robinson. His ethnicity is uncertain, but he clearly was not seen as "black" or—in the parlance of the day—Negro. It wasn't as though he had to "pass for black" to get into the Negro Leagues; it was Major League Baseball that discriminated on the basis of skin color, not the Negro Leagues.

According to Kountze, there had been stories that Babe Ruth, who broke in with the Red Sox in 1914, "had Negro relatives." Kountze wrote: "In fact my late and eldest sister Barbara, who lived in New York, told me she had met Colored people claiming kinship to the famous Home Run King, who came up from Maryland."[81] He added, "And some old-time fans recall they used to refer to baseball star Edmund 'Bing' Miller as 'Colored Folks,' and he played in Boston, too."[82]

The Red Sox also fielded the first Mexican-born player in Major League history—Mel Almada (1933-37, the first five Yawkey years). The Red Sox could have fielded a black ballplayer too— not without controversy, of course, but they could have done so, and they certainly could have taken advantage of Jackie Robinson when he was made available to them.

Yawkey has always come under some suspicion as a racist by those who identified him as South Carolinian, apparently unaware that he was born in Detroit and grew up in New York. Jackie Robinson himself believed that Yawkey was a racist, in 1967 calling him "probably one of the most bigoted guys in organized baseball."[83] Or at least Robinson came to believe that. Other Robinson comments, some of which follow, were more moderate.

For almost thirty years (1946–76), Mary Trank worked at Fenway Park as an executive secretary, Tom Yawkey's secretary for much of the time. She says she never heard Tom Yawkey say a racist thing: "I wouldn't say he never made a remark about it but he wouldn't do it in front of me. . . . Maybe he was careful in things he said to me, but I never heard him say, 'Don't get that guy because he's black.' He never did interfere with anything. He would say [to his general manager], 'If you think that's what we need, do it.'" Many of Yawkey's critics felt he should have asserted himself more, rather than relying on the men around him. One thing he never did, Trank told Stan Grossfeld of the *Globe*, was to make a deal for the sake of making a deal. "Some guys tried to be big deals to make an impression. He was never like that."[84]

Perhaps Yawkey was not personally racist. Regardless of how one looks at the issue, however, whatever the Red Sox decided, through action or inaction, during the Yawkey years was ultimately his responsibility. Because he was sole owner of the team, the buck stopped at his desk. He had the power to see that the team was integrated. Excuses there may have been—it was often suggested by team executives that the Red Sox had simply been unable to find a good enough black ballplayer. Jackie Robinson was the Rookie of the Year two years after the tryout, in 1947. Sam Jethroe, one of the others to try out at Fenway, became Rookie of the Year three years after that, in 1950—for the Boston Braves. And somehow, in the years between the April 1945 tryout and Pumpsie Green's joining the Red Sox during the 1959 season, other teams were able to find black or Latino ballplayers who won nine Rookie of the Year awards and eight MVPs.

In an effort to help break the color barrier in Boston, Doc Kountze met personally with President Bob Quinn of the Boston Braves and was cordially received. Quinn wished the barrier could be broken and "told me quietly" that he was well aware of the abilities of colored athletes at the time, having played with and against some of them in his younger days. He said he "wished he could have sepia stars like [Will] Jackman and [Burlin] White and [Satchel] Paige and others on his club. . . . [Quinn] left no doubt in my mind he would have voted to remove the Major League color line in 1938. But be told me, at that time, the other club owners would have 'voted him down.'"[85] Quinn had come to Boston from Brooklyn and predicted that the Brooklyn Dodgers would be the first team to field a black ballplayer.[86]

What was Joe Cronin's explanation for not pursuing any of the three men who tried out? Years later he told the *Globe*'s Larry Whiteside the following:

> I remember the tryout very well. But after it, we told them our only farm club was in Louisville, Ky. and we didn't think they'd be interested in going there because of the racial feelings at the time. Besides, this was after the season had started and we didn't sign players off tryouts in those days to play in the big leagues. I was in no position to offer them a job. The general manager did the hiring and there was an unwritten rule at that time against hiring black players. I was just the manager.[87]

Cronin shunted some of the blame to Eddie Collins. He also seems to come across as serving up too many excuses too rapidly.

In 1946 the Montreal Royals (with Jackie Robinson, who led the International League [IL] in batting average and runs scored) won the IL pennant and then beat Boston's Triple A affiliate, the Louisville Colonels of the American Association, in that year's Little World Series. Robinson was greeted in Louisville with "a chorus of Bronx cheers, but the Royals' star took the jeering in stride. With the demand for seats by his Negro followers greater than the supply, members of his race crowded the roofs of buildings adjacent to Parkway Field." There was one arrest due to "a slight disturbance."[88]

Referring not only to the racial question, Charlie Pierce commented in 1988: "All the encomiums relentlessly thrown in the direction of the late Tom Yawkey—you know, how he really *deserved* a world champion—ignore the fact that the man clearly didn't know how to run a baseball team. Being the last team to integrate wasn't merely morally reprehensible, it was also pragmatically stupid. There was no denying that Red Sox fans would've been infinitely better off had Yawkey peddled the team in 1948 to people who knew what they were doing."[89]

Perhaps far too naively, Yawkey trusted others to do the right thing for him. That trust was sometimes misplaced. It's not that Yawkey believed in passing the buck. Sports editor Bart Fisher of the *Bristol Press* recalled how the Sox owner had first approached him: "He'd seen me around the ballpark every once in a while and one day he just walked up, stuck his hand out, and introduced himself. He asked me where I was from and how I was being treated by the press people. When I told him I was treated just fine, he told me, 'That's good, but if you have any complaints you know who to go to.' I said, no, who do I go to and without hesitating a second, he just pointed to himself and said, 'You're looking at him.'"[90]

Dick Johnson also suggested that Yawkey trusted others to do the right thing:

> It was unforgivable. It was stupidity and bad management. That was the "Crony Island" group, as I call them, with Joe Cronin and Higgins and the backroom guys they had. It was only years afterward when Neil Mahoney and Dick O'Connell and Ed Kenney and the really good, intelligent, colorblind (for the most part) staffers they had were allowed to have a say and to have a little bit of control over things [that things changed]. Things changed, and they changed dramatically. Never with a social agenda but just with a baseball agenda. The social took care of itself.[91]

At the time, Jackie Robinson was diplomatic about the whole affair, as he wrote in 1947 and early 1948 for the *Pittsburgh Courier*. In various "Jackie Robinson Says" columns, he praised Boston columnist Dave Egan for his support. He also expressed appreciation to the *Courier* and Wendell Smith for bringing him to the tryout. "We never got very far with that particular experiment," he wrote, "but it helped a lot because soon after the Dodgers signed me to play with Montreal."[92] He called out no one person for complaint. As indicated by his later "bigoted" comment, Robinson became quite bitter about Tom Yawkey, though it may not have been due to anything he specifically experienced in 1945. His embitterment may instead be attributed to the fact that the Red Sox took longer than any other team in the Majors to integrate. Robinson did seem to accuse Yawkey of personal racism and did not just condemn him for a failure to desegregate earlier.

The regular 1945 season began in New York the day after the tryout, on April 17. Joe Cronin fractured his leg stumbling into second base in the third game of the year, still in New York, and Yawkey put him up at the Hotel Pierre, where he himself resided. Though he had his own home in South Carolina, Yawkey lived for years in private apartments at the Hotel Pierre in New York and at the Ritz Carlton in Boston. (In the early years of the twenty-first century, both the Pierre and the Ritz Carlton had become part of the Taj Group, owned by Indian Hotels Company Limited.)

On April 24 the baseball owners named U.S. senator (and former governor of Kentucky) Albert B. "Happy" Chandler as commissioner of baseball. And as we shall see below, Yawkey was one of four club owners on a committee formed to look into the issues facing baseball, one of which was the "race question."

The standout performance of the year for the Red Sox—and probably for the league as a whole—was that of right-hander Boo Ferriss. His first start was a five-hitter, a 2-0 shutout of the Athletics on April 29. He and Yawkey had never met in person, but they were introduced to each other by telephone. Yawkey, in his New York office, told Ferriss, "Glad to know you, Ferriss. If you can throw a few more five-hitters like that we'll be the best of friends."[93] Ferriss's next start was a shutout too, against the Yankees. Starting one's career with back-to-back shutouts was rare enough that Ferriss was only the third pitcher to have ever done so. Ferriss won his first eight decisions, four of them shutouts. He finished the season 21-10, with a 2.96 ERA. Unfortunately no other Red Sox pitcher won more than eight games.

Ferriss's salary for the Red Sox was $750 per month. He'd received a $3,000 bonus when he'd first signed as a prospect in 1942, and his father had successfully talked the Sox into including a clause that he would get a bonus of $6,000 if he should make the team and stay with the Red Sox for thirty days. In the intervening three years, Ferriss's father had died, and Boo himself had spent time in the service. When the bonus check arrived, it was a total surprise; he'd totally forgotten about the possibility. Then, according to Ferriss, another event came to pass: "Mr. Yawkey called me in near the end of the season and gave me a check for $10,000. I thought I was really rich. You hear so many old-timers complain about how stingy the owners were, but I always thought Tom Yawkey took care of his players, and I know he took care of me."[94]

The All-Star Game planned for Fenway Park in 1945 was postponed due to the war. Fenway got the game in 1946 instead.

In midseason it had seemed that the Red Sox had a shot. They'd been in last place for the first nine games and as late at May 20. Climbing quickly, they were in third place for almost all of June. They came as close to first place as 2½ games in mid-July, and on July 26 Yawkey, "who always has been long on cash and short on talk, thinks his team has a chance to win the pennant this year . . . [and] unloaded one of his longest speeches as follows: 'Washington comes here tomorrow for a series that could mark the turning point for our club. Although they haven't added much strength, they are only three games behind the Tigers and the Sox are close enough to be in second place by Saturday night. If our club can realize its potentialities, I'm satisfied its chances for the pennant are as good as any club in the league.'"[95] The Sox took two of three from the Senators but then lost five of six during a visit to Washington in early August. The team was seven games behind and in fifth place by the time it left Washington. It kept slipping and wound up in seventh place, 17½ games behind Detroit.

During the off-season rumors pop up all the time. On November 30 GM Eddie Collins denied that Yawkey was selling the Red Sox to entertainer Bing Crosby. The story had some legs, as Crosby was known to be a fervent fan who had tried in the past to buy himself a ball club.[96]

The war was indeed over, millions of men had already been mustered out of military service, and 1946 was shaping up to be an interesting season with the return of so many of the stars that had populated the Red Sox back in 1942—Williams, Pesky, DiMaggio, Doerr. If they were matched with Hughson and Ferriss, the Sox could have the nucleus of a very strong team.

In this period Yawkey turned his interests to health care for the underserved. In 1945 Georgetown resident Ralph Ford approached Yawkey and asked him to help support a campaign to improve medical care in the county. Ford was hoping to fund a hospital—no small undertaking. Yawkey kicked off the effort with a $100,000 gift. Prior to the establishment of Georgetown Hospital, area residents had to travel all the way to Charleston to go to a hospital, and the roads were far from good before the national dedication to building better roads in the postwar period and the implementation of the interstate highway system. Jim Healey of the Yawkey Foundations says, "Jeep Ford was the recent past chairman of the hospital, and he told me the story. Jeep's father and uncle and a couple of other people approached Tom Yawkey. They went to Tom, and Tom said, 'Well, how much is it?' They said it was $350,000, and Tom said, 'Well, I'll do that.' Pop DeFoe was there, and he said, 'Wait a minute, Tom. Let's talk about this.' They talked a little bit, and then Tom said, 'OK, I'll do it, but I'll pay you over three years.' So the original little hospital, he built. That was added on twenty times over the years."[97]

The endowment committee brought together many of the wealthier landowners in the area: Thomas A. Yawkey was chairman, and Bernard M. Baruch was vice chairman. Among those on the committee were Frederick W. DeFoe, Eugene DuPont, Archer M. Huntington, Walker P. Inman, and George Vanderbilt. Georgetown Hospital opened in 1950.

Having a hospital in the area made a huge difference to families in the region, as did Tom Yawkey's commitment to medical care for his own employees. Jim Sargent's father worked for Yawkey, and Jim grew up on South Island with his five brothers. "I was told that we had five or six sisters, but they died. I think the oldest girl lived to about eight or nine years. All of them died early. All the girls. . . . Back then we didn't have hospitals."[98]

Other than summer work or work during school breaks, Jim started working for Yawkey a year or two after his father finished, in 1954: "First job I had after high school." Tom Yawkey took a paternal interest in those who lived and worked on South Island. "He took care of all our medical expenses. Medical and dental."[99] Jim's wife Mary Sargent also worked for Jean Yawkey.

Yawkey's funding of the hospital continued in later years, including a $65,000 donation to the building fund in 1978–79 and $50,000 toward the children's wing in 1986.[100]

There's an amusing story behind the first Yawkey donation, involving the county's largest business. The region was dominated in the nineteenth century by rice production, and the Georgetown area produced nearly one-half of the total rice crop of the United States; the port exported more rice than any port in the world.[101] The cultivation of rice benefited from the institution of slavery, and after the Civil War, when the slaves were freed, this source of very inexpensive labor was no more. Hence cultivation fell off dramatically. Competition from elsewhere and a series of hurricanes combined to render rice production unprofitable. Into the void stepped the Atlantic Coast Lumber Company, which by 1914 had established the largest lumber-producing plant on the East Coast. Tom Yawkey's adoptive father was among the lumbermen in the area. The company struggled during the early Depression and went bankrupt in 1932. Four years later International Paper Company built a plant, and within six years it was the "largest kraft paper mill in the world." The plant is an imposing one that greets visitors coming north from Charleston.[102]

Naturally International Paper wanted to present itself well in the community. As by far the largest employer in town, it wanted to kick off the hospital fund-raising. Phil Wilkinson recalled what happened next:

> The International Paper Company said that they would match any individual's donation. Ralph Ford was my godfather, and he was the person in charge of raising the donations, so he knew Mrs. [Elise] Yawkey. He ran a grocery store and a hardware [store] down on Front Street. So he went down to see Mr. Yawkey, to sort of see how he felt about going up against International. He [Yawkey] said, 'Well, let's see if they'll put their money where their mouth is.' He offered up $100,000—which was a lot of money in those days. A lot of money. International folded on that one. They wound up donating $10,000. They didn't want to go that high. They thought nobody in Georgetown would [contribute so much]. . . . They didn't know that someone out in the countryside would challenge them there. So [Yawkey] was one of the major donors. The only major donor.

Wilkinson said of Yawkey, "He tells that with a big grin on his face."

12

Postwar and the Pennant, 1946

FINALLY IN 1946 everything came together. The stars returned home—and they were indeed stars. Naturally no one could know how well they might do, rusty from all the time off from pro ball. Rookie Johnny Pesky, for instance, had hit a league-leading and franchise-record 205 base hits in 1942, his one and only year in the big leagues. Who could know if he had a chance to approach that success? Ted Williams had won baseball's Triple Crown in 1942, leading the league in homers, batting average, and RBIS. That is such a rare accomplishment that no one would dream he could do it again after more than three years out of the game.

The Sox had the best crop of players returning from the war, but they weren't counting on that alone. With Pesky and Doerr coming back, shortstop Eddie Lake, who had done well in 1945, was traded to the Tigers on January 3 for first baseman Rudy York, who'd led the AL in both homers and RBIS in 1943; but the Tigers had Hank Greenberg coming back. It was later said that Cronin had lobbied hard for York, over the opposition of the rest of the front office—including Yawkey.[1] As early as January 14, the AP's Whitney Martin named the Red Sox as "probable winner of the American League pennant."[2] It could be Yawkey's year.

The Mexican League posed a threat to all the teams in baseball. Jorge Pasquel and his four brothers were extremely wealthy and wanted to build up La Liga Mexicana, of which Jorge was president. The Pasquels made salary offers to a number of Major Leaguers, wanting to bring them to Mexico to play. Among the players they approached in Havana, when the Red Sox played two exhibition games there against the Washington Senators at the beginning of March, were Johnny Pesky, Ted Williams, Joe DiMaggio, and Bob Feller. Feller recalled Pasquel's offers to him, Ted, and DiMaggio as "$125,000 a year, all the money up front, for a three year deal."[3] All three, as well as Johnny Pesky, turned him down, though some other players did not. Among them were Max Lanier, Mickey Owen, and Vern Stephens. As early as 1942, Pasquel had hired Negro Leagues players. At the time, he represented a double threat to Major League Baseball: he was a competitor with a great deal of money who could drive up salaries in the American baseball market, and he was willing to present integrated baseball teams at a time when Major League teams were still excluding players of color. Among the Negro Leagues players who worked for Pasquel were future Baseball Hall of Famers Cool Papa Bell, Ray Dandridge, Leon Day, Martin Dihigo, Josh Gibson, Monte Irvin, Satchel Paige, and Willie Wells.[4]

Both Pesky and Williams felt a strong loyalty to Tom Yawkey, and they continued to express it in the more than twenty-five years they each outlived him. No doubt there were other considerations in their thinking as well, but the Sox team remained intact.

Some Sox-specific controversy arose deep in spring training when Boston writer Harold Kaese's article "What's the Matter with the Red Sox?" was published in the March 23 *Saturday Evening Post*. Kaese said the magazine changed his title from "Star Rich, Pennant Poor" to the more provocative one, a move he regretted because it seemed to put more pressure on Cronin—though the new title did indeed encapsulate his theme. The *Boston Globe* reprinted the story in full on March 31, along with comments that the story had evoked.

Kaese also faulted Yawkey of course, recalling that Yawkey had fired farm director Billy Evans back in 1941 since Yawkey as a rule favored Cronin; he "idolized Cronin as a player; Yawkey is stubborn, wealthy, and loyal." To a fault. Kaese noted that Yawkey was back to spending again and had recently paid out extremely large bonuses to prospects such as Dick Callahan and Ted del Guercio. Neither of them ever made the Majors. Ed Rumill had noted in the *Christian Science Monitor* back in 1944 that the Red Sox were doing at least as well with players they had developed on their own. Kaese returned to the theme in May with a story headlined "Yawkey's Farm System Produces Better Than His Loaded Bankroll."[5]

Yawkey never looked in on the 1946 club during the springtime, nor did he do so in Boston until the home opener on April 20. There was an amusing incident the following weekend. The Braves had applied a fresh coat of green paint to the seats at Braves Field, but it hadn't quite dried when patrons began sitting down. They had to deal with some aggrieved fans, but Yawkey and Collins granted the Braves rent-free use of Fenway Park for the three days the Red Sox went on the road while the paint dried.

The Sox got off to the best start in franchise history and never looked back during the regular season; for just one day they weren't in first place—April 24. The next day they launched a fifteen-game winning streak. Jean Yawkey did her part, in line with baseball tradition. Once they started winning, she would not vary her routine, sitting in a separate section of the press box from Tom every game and carrying her own cushion.[6] In later May, when Johnny Pesky began to slump a bit, Jean contributed another way. Hy Hurwitz wrote, "He broke out in St. Louis, where Mrs. Yawkey expectorated (spit is a horrid word for a lady) on his bat each time he came up. What a fan she has become."[7] She was traveling with Tom and the team on the road trip.

On May 2 the Sox announced that they would install lighting for the 1947 season. Just three months later, they held "Bobby Doerr Day" on August 2. The event was organized by Tom Kenney, one of the Red Sox employees, but with the full cooperation of Tom Yawkey. One of the special gifts Doerr received was a "power plant"—a 5,000-watt electric generator, directly from Yawkey. Bobby's son Don Doerr says, "Because of their close relationship, Mr. Yawkey knew that Dad did not have electricity at his home on the Rogue River in southern Oregon."[8] So Tom Yawkey's gift brought light.

On May 31 Cronin officially retired as a player—he was reportedly talked out of playing by Yawkey—but was given a new contract extending through 1947; it made him the highest-paid manager in the game. On June 12 Yawkey took additional care of the players, giving each and every one of them a life insurance policy for $5,000, with the proceeds payable to whomever they listed as beneficiary.[9]

Yawkey was never just a playboy simply living on the proceeds of a trust fund. He took an active role in running his enterprises. "Business pressure kept him in New York" during all but two games of the team's second major winning streak, from May 29 through June 11. "The best he could do was to arrange each day's schedule so he was fairly free after 3 o'clock and could watch the baseball ticker in his office or call Fenway Park for a play-by-play report from Eddie Collins, who had a telephone handy in the owner's box."[10] During one recounting of the game, Collins told Yawkey there were runners on second and third with one out and York at the plate. "There's a fly that will score one run anyhow. It's going out. . . ." And then there was clattering, and a minute or two passed before Collins got back on and said he'd dropped the phone and then it got all tangled up. "But what about York's fly?" "Oh, that. It went over the fence. It was a home run." Yawkey hung up on him.[11]

Yawkey was generous not just to players, offering rookie bonuses to Pesky in 1942 and to Ferriss in 1945, but he sometimes bestowed gifts—"sometimes of automobiles"—on his office staff.[12] It is no wonder that he engendered such fierce loyalty from most who worked for him. When the team was in New York, it wasn't unusual for the whole coaching staff to be invited to his place for dinner. In earlier years, when Larry Woodall was present with the team, he would address the boss as "Mr. Yawkey" but was told, "Larry, the name is Tom."[13]

An excess display of wealth may have turned many people off, but Yawkey seems to have carried himself with sufficient humility and showed an abiding love of the game. People around baseball wished him well. Rogers Hornsby was no exception: "I'd like to see the Red Sox win it because of Tom Yawkey, who has proved himself a real sportsman from the time he bought the club. . . . Moreover, I'd like to see Boston fans enjoy a World Series after many disappointing seasons. . . . They really deserve it."[14] (The AP's Joe Reichler saw the Red Sox, despite Yawkey's million-dollar spending, as perennial underdogs.)[15]

Not everyone was a Yawkey acolyte, however. Gordon Cobbledick in the *Cleveland Plain Dealer* reported, "Yawkey, the multimillionaire owner, has made himself unpopular in certain influential circles." Cobbledick added that a Boston writer had claimed "the Hearst clique is out to get Williams and Yawkey."[16] Cobbledick's wasn't the only negative voice. Veteran Portland, Oregon, newspaperman L. H. Gregory claimed that the Boston writers didn't like the Red Sox organization. "From Tom Yawkey and Eddie Collins on down through the list we just don't take to them," he was told.[17]

On July 8 Fenway Park hosted its first All-Star Game. As it happened, the Red Sox were riding so high that almost one-third of the team—eight different players—made the AL All-Star squad: Dom DiMaggio, Bobby Doerr, Boo Ferriss, Mickey Harris, Johnny Pesky, Hal Wagner, Ted Williams, and Rudy York. The AL won the game, 12–0. Ted Williams hit two homers and drove in five of the runs. That evening Tom Yawkey held a "grand dinner with all the fixin's" for all the groundskeepers and park employees to show his appreciation for the work they had done.[18] He also gave out wrist watches to front office staff.

It was announced at the game that the Red Sox had purchased the contract of infielder Don Gutteridge to bolster the team. They were, after all, only 7½ games ahead of everyone else. "Well, it looks like the panic is on," joked someone.[19] Yawkey was, in that peculiar way that still afflicts many Red Sox fans, not at all relaxed but was worried that things could go wrong, waiting for the other shoe to drop. Victory was starting to get close enough to taste, but things can and do sometimes go wrong. Near the end of July, the Red Sox picked up Wally Moses as outfield insurance. Yawkey, wrote Grantland Rice, was "as nervous as a cat on a hot stove."[20]

There was some other hunting at Fenway on July 15. Not for the first time, Ted Williams brought a shotgun and, firing away from inside the right-field bullpen, "knocked over several score [pigeons]." With Ted was his own wife, Doris, and Jean Yawkey.[21]

Because of the perceived threat of the Mexican League and other considerations, such as an effort to head off unionization, a joint committee of the National and American Leagues recommended the adoption of a new and uniform player contract and invited player input. As mentioned, Yawkey was one of four owners on the committee.[22] An initial and harmonious meeting with player representatives was held in early August. Before the season was over, they had agreed to a $5,000 per year minimum salary, a provision that no salary could be cut more than 25 percent, an increase in expenses, moving costs in the event of trade, and a number of specified deadlines for (among other things) the mailing of contracts and the starting date of spring training.[23]

As early as mid-August, the Red Sox were already announcing plans for World Series ticketing.

Bob Feller announced his postseason plans to stage a tour of exhibition games with top players. Ted Williams was to take part and was promised $1,000 a game for ten games. Tom Yawkey—not wanting his biggest star to subject himself to unnecessary risk— offered Williams $10,000 *not* to play in the Feller-organized games. Unfortunately this offer left a few other Sox players out in the cold because Feller huffed he wouldn't extend invitations to any other Red Sox players.[24] "Mr. Yawkey was certainly never frugal around me," Williams acknowledged.[25]

The Red Sox won eight games in a row from August 30 through September 5. At that point, all they needed to do was win one more game to clinch at least a tie for the pennant. Yawkey joined the team in Washington and arranged for champagne to be on hand for the anticipated celebration. The Sox lost the September 6 game. They traveled to Philadelphia to play the Athletics, so the crates of champagne were loaded on board the team's train. Philadelphia won both games on September 7 and 8. The team, the champagne, and Tom Yawkey all boarded the train to Detroit. They played two games there, losing to the Tigers both times. The champagne was logging some serious traveling time. And then the Sox lost the first game in Cleveland.

Finally, on September 13, after the Sox had lost six games in a row, Ted Williams took matters into his own hands in the very first inning. Facing the "Williams shift," with almost every defender shifted over to the right side of the diamond, he hit the ball hard to left field. Cleveland left fielder Pat Seerey had no chance to get it, as he was playing behind the shortstop position. Ted ran all the way around the bases and scored, for the only inside-the-park home run of his career. Tex Hughson threw a three-hit shutout, and the first-inning score stood after nine full: 1–0 Red Sox. It was time to celebrate.

But to clinch sole possession that day required a little more patience. Not only did the Red Sox have to win, but they also had to wait to hear if the Yankees beat the Tigers, thus eliminating Detroit as a contender. Cronin joined Yawkey in Yawkey's hotel room at the Statler to get inning-by-inning updates. Around 5:30 (the Red Sox game had ended just before 3:00), they learned they'd won the pennant.[26]

Williams wasn't at the postgame celebration, though. What was up with that? The front page of the September 14 *Globe* had a seven-column headline: "Ted Ducks Party to Visit Dying Vet." Yawkey himself credited Cronin: "I want to say again that that guy there has done the best job ever seen in baseball. He's justified my high praise in him, hasn't he?"[27]

The Red Sox actually hosted two celebrations after clinching the pennant. In contravention of the usual practice at the time, there was one celebration for the team and another for the traveling press writers, who felt they'd been banished to a back room. "The food and liquor were good," wrote Al Hirshberg, "but our mood was nasty indeed." Then Yawkey, "possibly trying to make up for what he knew had been a ridiculous blunder, came to fraternize." Instead he got into "a shouting match" with Austen Lake that "nearly erupted into a fist fight."[28]

Yawkey's Red Sox won 104 games during the regular season and their first pennant under Yawkey, the first one for the team since 1918, and they went all the way to the seventh game of the World Series. Attendance had more than doubled, from 603,794 to 1,416,944. It was almost double any prior attendance figure in franchise history.

Jordan Marsh, one of Boston's biggest department stores, took out a newspaper ad with the headline, "Thank you SanT.A. Yawkey"; it showed Yawkey in a Santa Claus cap.[29]

There was such a massive demand for World Series tickets that a limit was announced: two tickets for one game. Even at that, hundreds of thousands of orders arrived, so many that the team had to spend an estimated $15,000 (in 1946 dollars) to return all the unopened letters that flooded in.[30]

On the eve of the World Series a rumor resurfaced that Ted Williams was going to be traded after the season. Despite the denials, there may have been some basis to the possibility.[31] Williams himself was quoted in the *Boston Traveler* as expecting a trade to occur.[32] The *Globe*'s Kaese noted that Cronin wanted to trade Ted but Yawkey wanted to keep him.[33] Moreover, a group from California was reportedly offering to buy the Red Sox.[34] It seemed as though the team couldn't just play in peace with all these rumors swirling around.

Because the Red Sox had clinched so early—despite having to wait a week for the pleasure of popping the corks—and because the Cardinals and Dodgers had tied for first place and required a best-of-three playoff series to determine the National League winner, the Sox had to do something to keep up their skills, so they worked out at Fenway in an exhibition game against a group of American League All-Stars (including Joe DiMaggio) imported for the occasion. A pitch got away from Senators pitcher Mickey Haefner in the fifth inning, and it hit Ted Williams on the right elbow. Williams suffered a "severe contusion." It was the first time in his career that Ted had been forced out of the lineup after being hit with a ball; it had immediately raised a knot "about the size of an egg."[35] X-rays proved negative for any chip, but the injury was serious and raised doubts as to whether Williams could play in the World Series. He did, but he was subpar throughout.

The Red Sox had been favored going in, but the long timespan between their clinching and the first game of the Series (twenty-three days) may have robbed them of their edge, while the Cardinals (who had won the playoff with the Dodgers) necessarily had to stay in fighting trim right to the end.

On the eve of the series, in St. Louis, Yawkey was overwhelmed by a gift presented him: a sterling silver plaque with the facsimile signatures of every player on the 1946 pennant-winning Red Sox.

There was a robbery during the Series. Just before Game Three, when Tom Yawkey's sister Emma Ouerbacker and her family had joined Tom to watch the Red Sox shut out the Cardinals from his box at Fenway Park, Emma had reported to police that a $2,500 emerald and diamond ring and some other valuables had been stolen from her Boston hotel room.[36]

The Sox lost the World Series late in the seventh game, when Enos

Slaughter made his famous "mad dash" from first base all the way around third to home on an innocent, loopy fly ball to left-center that Leon Culberson fielded kind of casually and then threw to Johnny Pesky, who had no idea that Slaughter was blowing through his own coach's "stop" signal at third and streaking for the plate. Slaughter scored the go-ahead run, and Pesky was unjustly accused of having held the ball. The Red Sox failed to score in the top of the ninth, and the world championship went to St. Louis. Through the window of the train as the Red Sox left town, Williams was seen crying before someone pulled down the shade for privacy.

The powerful Red Sox offense—and in particular the physically hampered Ted Williams—had been held down. Ted had swung hard at one pitch in Game Two and lost his grip on the bat and could have decapitated his boss. The bat went "right over the head of Red Sox owner Tom Yawkey who sat in the first row of the temporary field seats."[37] It went sailing into the Red Sox dugout. Good pitching can stop good hitting, and Harry Brecheen in particular was spectacular—3-0 with an ERA of 0.45. Williams hit .200 in the Series, with no extra-base hits and just one RBI. Yawkey was understanding: "Hitting is not like a faucet. Nobody can go up there and make a hit whenever he wants to."[38]

Yawkey, "trying to smother his feelings" (in the words of Hy Hurwitz), was fatalistic: "If that's the way it had to be, there's nothing we could have done about it."[39] He paid a visit to the Cardinals' clubhouse after the game. Yawkey had won his first pennant, but that was understandably little consolation in the aftermath of a losing World Series. Al Wolf of the *Los Angeles Times* described him after the game as a "grey, sagging figure, pitiful to behold."[40]

Early in the season, the Red Sox boss was said to have offered bonuses if players won the pennant, but Commissioner Landis had scotched that plan.[41] A couple of days after the Series, though, Yawkey gave out around $100,000 in checks, a percentage of each man's salary. "I did not give the boys bonuses," he said. "It was just a salary increase."[42] Red Sox players netted a little more than the winning Cardinals. The extra money was not limited to the players; others, such as trainer Win Green, earned a little more too. Yawkey also assured Ted Williams that he would be with the Red

Sox in 1947, adding that he hadn't wanted to dignify the rumors that had been out there.

A couple of days later, Boo Ferriss and perhaps a couple of others stuck around to see the Yanks play at Fenway on October 20—that is, the Boston Yanks pro football team, hosting the Washington Redskins.

Even though the Sox lost the World Series, other accolades followed. Ted Williams was named the 1946 American League's MVP. On December 28 *The Sporting News* named Tom Yawkey the Major League executive of the year.

The future looked good. The Red Sox team that had been assembled had exceptional success for five consecutive postwar seasons, 1946 through 1950.

13

Strong Seasons, 1947–1950

WHAT BETTER WAY, Tom Yawkey may have thought, to work one's way into a new baseball season than a couple of weeks of duck hunting? He invited Joe Cronin to South Island for the middle two weeks of February before the Sox started for Sarasota on February 24.

The contracts were coming in earlier in the year. Bob Klinger said he'd never been treated better by any organization. "That goes from Mr. Yawkey right down to the clubhouse boys."[1] Johnny Pesky was back; he'd not only come back from three years in military service, but he'd also hit even more in 1946 than in his 1942 rookie season, collecting 208 base hits, making the All-Star team, and coming in fourth in the MVP voting. "I sure have been treated just fine," he said regarding his contract.[2] On February 1 Commissioner Chandler issued a ruling that any team handing out bonuses would be fined. A player pension plan was also introduced.

Yawkey let the players know about the pension plan in a team meeting he convened. Boo Ferriss said, "He seldom came to the clubhouse in those days, so that was a surprise. He told us Major League Baseball was going to start a pension fund and that we would all profit from it. They wanted each player to invest money from every paycheck into the fund. Mr. Yawkey said we should do it, but if anyone couldn't, 'I'll put it in,' he said. 'The Red Sox will be 100 percent behind the plan because it is important for you and your families."[3]

Some other executives grumbled about Yawkey's driving up salaries, at one point drawing a rebuke from Collins. "I'm sick and tired of hearing the bleats of Pennock, Griffith, and Breadon that salary boosts threaten to shake the financial structure of the major leagues. We're paying Williams' salary; they're not. . . . We are paying Williams what we think he is worth at the gate." Noting the Red Sox had drawn around 1.5 million at Fenway, he asked rhetorically, "Did people at Fenway and other parks in the league come out to see a lot of Humpty-Dumpties? They did not. They came out, in our case, to see Williams."[4] And the Red Sox had turned a profit of $491,000 in 1946—but the cost of installing the new lights and other improvements was likely to be just a bit more than that. One improvement, though at a loss of revenue, would be the removal of advertising from the left-field fence. It was a policy Yawkey would have implemented earlier were it not for the long-standing relationships with many of the advertisers, but before the '47 season and in tandem with the installation of lighting, he had the ads removed. Now, he said, fans would better be able to tell where a ball hit when it struck the wall.[5] Yawkey had considered adding a second deck but found the expense was far too great (more than a million dollars) for the additional twelve thousand or so seats it would provide.

A new press box was installed on the roof at a total cost of $175,000. The old press box was made into a private area for the Yawkeys. The Yankees' Red Patterson griped, "It may be a beautiful press room, but all you can get to eat is a ham and cheese sandwich or a hot dog. At the Stadium Club you can get roast beef."[6] The Yawkeys would sometimes host corned beef and cabbage dinners in their "entertainment quarters."[7] Yawkey also had his own sports ticker there, the best technology of the day to keep up with the scores of other games around baseball.

While removing the advertising from the left-field wall, Tom Yawkey, in a romantic touch, had his and his wife's initials—TAY and JRY—rendered vertically in Morse code on the scoreboard. Tom Yawkey loved his ballpark, and Dick Bresciani of the Red Sox later said of Jean Yawkey, "She used to tell us how she and her husband used to come down here all by themselves with lunch and a blanket when the team was on the road, and have a picnic in center field."[8] In another touch of the romantic, Maureen Cronin says that when Tom put on his Red Sox uniform, his jersey bore the number "44," the year he and Jean married.[9] Sportswriter Clif Keane saw how much Tom cared about his ballpark. In the earlier years, when he was in Boston before the season began, Yawkey would walk the park and check every seat and even check the bathrooms.[10]

Yawkey came to Boston before the '47 season began and said that due to the illness that had begun to affect Eddie Collins since around the time of the World Series, "I expect to spend more time in the office this season. . . . I'll put in more time and the office staff will pitch in to take care of the work Collins is unable to perform."[11] There had been rumors before the season began that Yawkey was considering hiring former Yankees manager Joe McCarthy to handle the team on the field and bring Cronin upstairs in place of Collins. A little later in the season there were rumors that Lou Boudreau was being considered, as well as Birdie Tebbetts and Steve O'Neill. For his part, Cronin's answer was simple: "What do they say about having to cut your uniform off? Well, that's the way I feel."[12]

For several decades, the only advertising in Fenway Park was a graphic promoting the charity with which both the Red Sox and the Yawkeys are most associated: the "Jimmy Fund" of the Boston-based Children's Cancer Research Foundation (now the Dana-Farber Cancer Institute). The fund was launched in 1948. It was at Boston Children's Hospital that Dr. Sidney Farber did his pioneering work with chemotherapy and achieved the first remissions of leukemia in children. One of those children was given the name "Jimmy," and in 1948 a number of Boston Braves players appeared on the nationwide Ralph Edwards radio program, which launched the effort. In April 1947, about a year before the Jimmy Fund was formally launched under that name, Tom Yawkey and the Red Sox made a substantial early donation of $5,000 to the Boston Children's Hospital Medical Center campaign.[13] The long-term involvement of the Red Sox came later, at the time the Braves left Boston.

Jean Yawkey accompanied Tom to many an event, from the opening of the New England League season in Lynn in April to Fenway Park on the evening of June 10, 1947, to follow the Red Sox game via ticker tape. The Sox were in Cleveland, playing the Indians. But the Yawkeys wanted to know how the team was doing. The image of them at an otherwise empty Fenway, watching details of the game come across the transmitter used to convey updates, is compelling. So is a detail offered by Harold Kaese. Boston had a 2-0 lead in the seventh inning, but Eddie Robinson of the Indians hit a two-run homer off Joe Dobson. Yawkey showed some of the passion he never vented in public. He "picked up a chair and threw it across the room, breaking the back."[14] Doerr singled in Pesky in the eighth, and the Red Sox won, 3-2.

Though the Yawkeys traveled to many games together, they typically did not sit together. Joseph Dinneen explained in a 1948 *Boston Globe* story: "Ever notice that Tom Yawkey and his wife do not generally sit in the same penthouse box at Fenway Park? That's because Tom gets so wrapped up in the game that he's bad company."[15] Of Jean Yawkey, one "longtime friend" said, "She was a good scout, but she was a very very lonely person. When Tom was alive, she said very little. [Dick] O'Connell recalls that when she tried to assert her opinions about the Red Sox, her husband would tell her: 'Now, Mother, you mind the household. I'll mind the baseball.'"[16]

Baseball games were broadcast in the local market on radio, and in June it was reported that Yawkey began bringing a portable radio to his roof box so he could listen to the reporting of the scores of other games; in between games of a doubleheader, he might also go down to the office to read the ticker.[17]

The team didn't fare as well in 1947, finishing in third place and a full 16 games behind the Yankees. As mid-September approached, one smart aleck said, "Yawkey gave the Sox bonuses for not winning the World Series, and maybe they think that now he'll give 'em bonuses for not winning the pennant."[18] Ferriss won 12 games, fewer than half the 25 he'd won in 1946. Hughson won 12 too; he'd won 20 in 1946. Joe Dobson (18-8, 2.97 ERA) was the best pitcher. For the third year in a row, Johnny Pesky collected over 200 hits. And Ted Williams won the Triple Crown again, his 32 homers, 114 RBIs, and .343 batting average all leading the league. Once again, he fell short to a Yankee in the MVP voting, this time by one point (201 to Joe DiMaggio's 202) because two of the voting writers refused to consider Williams one of the top players in the league, presumably out of some sort of spite. Had Williams won the award under spiteful circumstances, there's a good chance he would have refused to accept it and would have presented it to DiMaggio.

At least one Red Sox staffer got a big bonus: Yawkey gave bat-boy Tommy Kelly a new Ford automobile. Kelly had been teaching his mother how to drive, and he totaled the family car. "This is for you, and be more careful," Yawkey said on presenting Kelly with the keys.[19] (On Yawkey's death, one club employee who'd worked with the Red Sox for forty-five years said, "He was class, class. All that money he gave to the Jimmy Fund. I believe it was $10 million. And he sent all the bat boys to college—he paid for their scholarships.")[20]

The day after the season ended, Joe McCarthy was hired as manager for 1948, with Cronin named GM and Collins retaining the position of vice president. McCarthy admitted that he'd been offered the job a year earlier but had declined. Some felt that taking over a pennant winner may have presented too much pressure from the start; managing a third-place team back toward success might prove more rewarding. McCarthy and Yawkey met briefly in the Washington airport, first sitting down to spend time together in New York in early December.

Building for 1948, on back-to-back days in November the Sox dealt with the Browns. First, they acquired slugging infielder Vern Stephens and pitcher Jack Kramer in a November 17 trade; they gave up seven lesser players and some cash—as much as $300,000, enough to bring the Browns out of the red.[21] (Yawkey may have written another sizable check the same day, investing $200,000 to buy the Scranton ball club.) The very next day, they acquired Ellis Kinder and Billy Hitchcock for three players and another $65,000.

The PCL requested that it be granted status as a third major league. This request was sent to committee and was rejected on a 2–2 vote, Yawkey and Larry MacPhail voting for it and Walter Briggs and Phil Wrigley of the Cubs voting against it.[22] Had the PCL been recognized as a third major league, much of the westward franchise shifting in the NL and AL that began in the 1950s would not have occurred.

On December 10, the Sox traded Leon Culberson and Al Kozar to the Senators for outfielder Stan Spence. All this activity showed a determination to get back in the race for 1948. Stating the obvious, Whitney Martin wrote, "It becomes more and more apparent the Red Sox are going to make a strong bid for the flag in 1948. Tom

Yawkey has the money and is willing to spend it, and McCarthy and Joe Cronin will see that it is spent most advantageously. While other clubs are building, Boston is setting up a prefabricated house. Complete with push buttons, no less."[23]

At the beginning of January 1948, Ted Williams signed on for another season. His contract was understood to be the richest in baseball, topping even Joe DiMaggio's. Williams had always been paid more than Joe DiMaggio, Ed Linn wrote: "Not because Ted wanted it that way, but because Tom Yawkey did. In 1948, immediately after the Yankees had made DiMaggio the first $100,000 player, a pack of writers caught Yawkey on the way up to his office. He had just sent Williams his contract, Yawkey told them, and it was going to be for more than DiMaggio's. 'It may be only $1,000 more . . . but Ted Williams will always get more money than anybody else.'"[24]

There is an oft-told story that Tom Yawkey and Yankees co-owner Dan Topping had once, around 1948 or 1949, traded Ted Williams for Joe DiMaggio straight up, only to call it off perhaps six hours later. George Weiss of the Yankees explained:

> It started as a fanning bee. What would Williams, a left-hander, hit if he played in Yankee Stadium? What would DiMaggio, a right-hander, hit if he played in Fenway Park? By the whim of the draw, so to speak, Williams and DiMaggio had wound up in the wrong parks. I mean, Yankee Stadium with its low rightfield barrier was made to order for a left-handed power hitter, just as Fenway Park, with its close left-field wall, was a beckoning target for a right-handed power hitter. The press box had found this an intriguing subject and had gotten a good deal of mileage out of it. Now, as the night lengthened, and the more Yawkey and Topping explored the possibilities, the better they liked it.[25]

One understands that beverages were being consumed throughout as the evening wore on. Finally, Weiss continues, Yawkey said, "Okay, it's a deal," but he thought better of it in the morning. "We hit the hay around 2 a.m., and at 8 a.m. or so the next morning, Yawkey called it off."[26]

Joe McCarthy had won eight pennants and seven world championships for the Yankees. Now, after a year and a half out of the game, he was back to try for Boston. There was a general feeling that the Sox were going to bounce back, regardless of the manager, due to the flurry of acquisitions after the '47 season and the feeling that they couldn't suffer as many injuries as they had borne before. Cleveland Indians president Bill Veeck said, however, "If Tom Yawkey had done nothing more than land McCarthy, he would have improved his club at least 20 percent."[27]

It turned out to be a year when the Boston Red Sox and the Boston Braves came as close as can be to an all-Hub World Series.

In April, during the City Series, Lou Perini and John Quinn of the Braves had a luncheon with Yawkey and Cronin and began to discuss the possibility of televising baseball games. A week or so later, on April 23, the Red Sox played the Yankees in New York, and the Yawkeys and Joe Cronin were among several hundred in a large room at Boston's Parker House who watched the game on television. It was the first time a baseball game was broadcast in Boston. "The reception was very clear," reported the *Globe*, "and the spectators were able to follow the flight of the ball and the progress of the game, with a running commentary, very easily."[28] Even better: the Red Sox won, Mickey Harris shutting out New York, 4–0. For the first time, viewers in Boston saw a televised Ted Williams home run. "A great roar went up from the Parker House select group when Ted Williams connected for his first home run of the season."[29]

Both teams gave free video rights to the sponsors who were advertising on the radio broadcasts. Both channels WBZ and WNAC were given television rights, and both could show the games.[30] Yawkey didn't believe that televising games would hurt attendance, and he considered that it might help. "It will be just like it was with radio, more people will turn out for games after they see the broadcasts."[31]

Night games at Fenway were not frequent—fourteen were scheduled in 1948—but they were well attended. The first time attendance dipped below thirty thousand in a night game was on July 8. Later in July, the Red Sox rewarded twenty-five-year-employee Mary C. Lynch with a gift of a European trip with a party to Rome and Lourdes that included Richard Cardinal Cushing. She had served as a secretary to Yawkey, Collins, and Cronin.[32]

The 1948 Sox got off to a poor start, falling as far back as 11½ games out of first place before the end of May and not getting even a game above .500 until June 20. A thirteen-game winning streak in July propelled them into a tie for first place by June 25. For a solid month, August 26 to September 25, they were in first place but then slipped into second, behind the Indians. A 6-7 road trip in mid-to-late September showed that the club had fallen into some doldrums. Even before the end of the season, on September 29, traveling secretary Phil Troy—who had been with the Red Sox since 1930—was informed by Tom Yawkey that he did not fit in the club's plans for the future. His firing was ascribed by the *Boston Herald* to "the demoralized situation . . . which necessitated the presence of Joe Cronin in the west on the club's last tour."[33] A few days after the season, Yawkey relieved coach Del Baker and farm director Specs Toporcer of their duties. Tom Dowd succeeded Troy, and Johnny Murphy succeeded Toporcer. Kiki Cuyler replaced Baker.

The Sox won the final four games on the schedule and found themselves tied with Cleveland, necessitating a single-game playoff, at Fenway Park, on October 4. Pitching had been Boston's weakness. For whatever reason—it has been debated for decades—Joe McCarthy gave Denny Galehouse the starting assignment rather than the statistically better Kinder, on regular rest, or Mel Parnell. (Galehouse had pitched very well against the Indians in late July, though he'd been bombed when he faced them at the end of August.) Gene Bearden pitched for Cleveland on one day's rest and was very effective. The Sox lost, 8-3.

"I have a story from 1948 that Mary Walsh used to tell," remembered office staffer Mary Jane Ryan. "The playoff game. There was only a handful of people in the office in those days. All the girls came down with long faces after the game. They were all feeling miserable. And who's banging on the door trying to get in but a florist? The poor guy couldn't get up the street before the game. He had corsages for all the girls. And Mary said, 'Here we are with our long faces, and the poor guy was trying to get the flowers delivered.'"[34]

The team wasn't as despondent as it had been in 1946, though batboy Don Fitzpatrick later told Yastrzemski he'd shed tears, only to have the boss come over and say, "Now, Donald, hang in there."[35]

Yawkey himself put a good face on, looking ahead to 1949. "There's one way to prevent losing in a playoff," he said. "That's to win by 20 games the way I hope we'll do it next year."[36] Little could he know how close the Red Sox would come again in 1949.

In Boston the Yawkeys, Cronins, and McCarthys all had front-row box seats for the first game of the 1948 World Series—at Braves Field.

Fenway that fall hosted four more Boston Yanks football games and three for Boston University (BU).

Yawkey's attempt to "buy the pennant" with the infusion of cash he'd pumped into the team before the 1948 season had fallen just short. In 1949 he was back to emphasizing the farm system and wanting to grow his own players. For instance, he hadn't joined the bidding for pitcher Jack Sanford, who signed with the Yankees for $100,000.

Internally Joe Cronin was named treasurer of the Red Sox in March, augmenting his duties as GM and relieving Eddie Collins of more responsibilities. Collins worked as more of an adviser due to his declining health. On March 23 a *Wall Street Journal* story prompted Tom Yawkey to deny that he was planning to sell the Red Sox.

The Red Sox opened an advance ticket office at 72 Brookline Avenue, between Lansdowne and Jersey Streets—more or less where it is in the early twenty-first century. Before 1949 advance tickets had been sold at outlets other than at the park itself. Some additional box seating was added atop the roof on the right-field side.[37]

On May 5 the Red Sox spent a reported $125,000 (and Stan Spence) to acquire Al Zarilla from the Browns. A little later in May, Red Sox prospect Chuck Koney, twenty-two, an infielder with Louisville who might have succeeded Bobby Doerr at second base, suffered horrible burns when a water heater exploded in his home. His leg had to be amputated. Tom Yawkey promised him lifetime employment with the Red Sox as a scout. Subsequent history shows he was true to his word.[38] This was another example of the generosity to those in his employ that engendered intense loyalty to Tom Yawkey in response. There was a downside, though. It wasn't just that Yawkey was generous to those in need or players who had enjoyed a good season or (in later years) players who had thrown a no-hitter or the like. It was that he believed in the people he hired and could seemingly never bring himself to let them go. It was a weakness that, on occasion, he readily confessed. For instance, in 1959 he commented to George Carens that what he liked least about being an owner was dealing with changes in management personnel.[39]

Perhaps in a sense Yawkey lucked out in his choice of Eddie Collins to run things in the first decade or so of Yawkey ownership. Al Hirshberg wrote the following:

> But even if Collins hadn't had executive ability, he would have been general manager indefinitely, because Yawkey liked and admired him so much. This was also true of Cronin. When the ailing Collins could no longer function as boss of the organization, Yawkey replaced him with another man he had admired as a ballplayer and liked as a friend. Yawkey knew as little about Cronin's executive abilities as he had about Collins's qualifications. It was pure lucky accident that Collins turned out to be a good general manager, and pure unlucky accident that Cronin turned out to be a poor one. [By the time it was clear Collins had to be replaced, Yawkey] should have gone outside the organization, if necessary, to find someone as well qualified as Collins. But that would have meant hurting a friend, which Yawkey couldn't do. Cronin was a poor choice because he too surrounded himself with friends in key jobs, and the club suffered.[40]

Attendance was slightly off in the early going, though a new city permit allowed the club to sell as many as two thousand standing-room tickets, so capacity was up. By the end of the year, attendance was up, even though most clubs in the league showed declines.

On June 13 the Sox were in fourth place and 6½ games out of first. They wanted to bolster their pitching staff and sent Mickey Harris and Sam Mele (and maybe some money) to Washington for Walt Masterson. It might have looked good on paper, but Masterson was only 3-4 after coming to the Red Sox. On the June 17 Tom and Jean Yawkey were present to see Mickey McDermott get his first Major League win, 10-8 against the White Sox.

After dropping both games of the Independence Day doubleheader, the Red Sox lost eight in a row (the longest losing streak they'd had since Yawkey bought the team), and they were twelve games out of first place. There were rumors that Joe McCarthy would be replaced, but the word was put out that McCarthy would be welcome to stay on as manager for as many years as he might want.

Harold Kaese's July 15 story was headlined "Is Tom Yawkey Losing Interest in Red Sox?" The story noted that Yawkey "seldom sees the Red Sox play at Fenway Park now" and that he "spends less and less time here during the season." Kaese pretty much admitted that there was no basis for his speculation, but he said the feeling persisted that Yawkey might sell the team. He said that "considering all he has done for Boston baseball in 17 years, his departure would be a sports calamity." He later wrote that Yawkey would miss the times he worked out at the ballpark. Yawkey, for his part, said he wondered where such stories came from.[41] For the next several weeks, the owner was around the park. A Boston-based group expressed interest in the Sox should Yawkey decide to sell; it was headed by former ambassador Joseph Kennedy, father of Congressman John F. Kennedy.[42]

The day after the Sox ended their losing streak, they started a winning streak that also ran for eight games. A seven-game winning streak in mid-August took them from 6 games out to just 2½. Slugger Johnny Mize came on the market, and even though the Yankees didn't have a need, they outbid the Red Sox for his services in order to keep him from the Sox.[43] On August 12 the Sox had taken second place. Yawkey seemed to have settled in for the duration.

An eleven-game winning streak that kicked off on September 13 carried the Sox into first place on September 25, and they stayed there through the end of the month. Yawkey thought he had it. Around September 20, he said, "Those darn palookas of mine are going to be the champs."[44]

The Sox were in first place when they headed to New York for the final two games on the schedule. If they won either game, they would win the pennant. The Yawkeys paid their first 1949 visit to Yankee Stadium on October 1 but saw the Yankees overcome an early 4-0 Red Sox lead and win, 5-4. It came down to the last day of the season. This time it was the Yanks who took the lead, 1-0 through seven innings, adding four in the eighth to make it 5-0.

The Red Sox put a scare in them, scoring three times in the top of the ninth, but they couldn't quite make it. For the second year in a row, they'd lost the last game of the year and were without the pennant. Yawkey said, "If we can't win one out of two, we don't deserve it."[45] In leaving the stadium, one of the Boston sportswriters walked along with Yawkey "down the long, cold ramps," but he didn't dare speak because "Yawkey was fighting back tears."[46]

Years later New York's Tommy Henrich told Bobby Doerr why he thought the Yanks had won. "You had a great ball club," he told Doerr. "We were always afraid of you." So why didn't the Red Sox win? "Because you didn't have to and we had to. We needed the extra money from the World Series check. That was our extra salary. You guys were all making more money than us because of Yawkey."[47]

McCarthy's contract ended with the end of the season, but Yawkey said he was "thoroughly satisfied" with McCarthy's work.[48] The Sox had played .711 ball for the whole second half. If they'd only gotten off to a better start, they would have easily captured the flag. Or if they'd won a few more games on the road—really, just one more— they'd have won it too. The 1949 team played .792 at Fenway but only .455 away from home. Rumors quickly popped up that McCarthy wouldn't be coming back, so two days later Yawkey gave an exclusive interview to the *Globe*: "I'd rather finish second with Joe McCarthy than have anyone else managing the Red Sox. . . . McCarthy is the best manager in baseball. I hope he returns."[49] On November 1 McCarthy signed on for another two years.

Ted Williams was named the American League MVP. Ted said, "I don't believe anybody could ask for a better club owner than Tom Yawkey. He's spent more money and had worse luck than anybody in the business. . . . Maybe next season will be our year."[50]

On December 30 the "Sox are being sold" rumor cropped up again, this time from a part-owner of the Washington Senators who said Yawkey wanted to sell the club but wanted to sell it to Joe Cronin. The rumors continued into early 1950. Cronin pointed out a few reasons why it was good to have a well-fixed sole owner: "There is no board of directors to satisfy. There is no dual ownership. There are no differences of opinion among a group of stockholders."[51] When sale rumors had come up during the summer, Cronin had commented, "Some of the people spreading the rumor should genuflect every time Tom Yawkey comes to Boston."[52]

It has been noted that Tom Yawkey used to like to work out with clubhouse kids and grounds crew personnel. George Sullivan, in later years the PR director for the team, offers a detailed memory of the first time he met the boss and gives some insight into why Yawkey was so beloved by so many employees:

> I was fifteen years old, and I was the visiting team batboy. That was 1949. I had joined midway through the season. John Donovan, who had been the visiting team batboy, moved over to home team batboy and that left a vacancy, and I was fortunate enough to become the visiting team batboy. [For] the clubhouse kids—especially under the Orlandos—the ballgame was like your coffee break. You worked these long hours before the game and after the game. For $2 a day. The home batboy got $2.50 a game. Of course, we looked forward to doubleheaders; you got $4.
>
> The first ten days I was working there, the team was on the road. The batboys and clubhouse kids had to report to work every day. Mr. Yawkey was very friendly; he was unbelievable. He made sure all the kids got their at-bats, not just him. He would not leave the field until all of us had hit. Of course, he got more time in the cage than we did, but we got good time. He wanted to make sure we all got in.
>
> That shows what kind of a guy he was. He came down to the clubhouse, and he suited up—not a full uniform but the baseball pants and the white sanitaries and the sort of undershirt that baseball players wore underneath, with the colored sleeves and the gray in front, and a cap. The word was we were all going to work out.
>
> He was pretty impressive. Of course, the ball was being grooved for him, but still he didn't look bad in the batting cage. I know he hit the wall. I don't remember if he put one over or not, but he was good. We'd be out shagging, and then, one by one, he'd make sure we all got our chance. It was me and John Donovan and one or two of the clubhouse kids.
>
> He came in; Vince Orlando had done the pitching to him that particular day. Sometimes Johnny Pohlmeyer.(Wonderful guy, by the way; he had been a farmhand for the Red Sox and blew his arm out.

I don't know how he came together with Mr. Yawkey, but he sort of became Mr. Yawkey's Man Friday. Often, he would pitch.)

[Yawkey] had a portable chair taken out from the locker room and put near the batting cage. As a kid from Cambridge, I'd never seen one before, but he had a high-powered radio—the team was in Detroit, as I recall; it was a day game—and he had that radio playing the whole time we worked out. He was standing in the batting cage or shagging for us. He had it turned up, and he could hear how the team was going.

Even before I worked there, I had a favorable impression of him from what I read in the newspapers and heard on radio. But, gee, to be working out with this guy! He was just like one of us kids. The only thing to differentiate him was that he got a little more time in the batting cage than we did. But we got plenty.

I know I was surprised that he hit the ball so well. I don't care if this was Little League pitching; he was hitting the ball sharply.

I remember when I stepped in, wow, there's the greatest target in the history of baseball, looming up there. I had played at Cambridge a little bit. Anyway, I hit a ball to right field—and I was a right-handed hitter—that hit the wall in front of the Red Sox bullpen. I remember a lot of people, including Mr. Yawkey, said, "Wow." But damned if I could hit a ball off the left-field wall. Of course, my intention was to hit a ball over it. Maybe that's what affects a lot of hitters; they try too hard.

When we came in, [Yawkey] got on the rubbing table in the trainer's room, and Vince Orlando gave him a rubdown. I was working near that area, and I heard him say something about "the new kid" and "What's his name?" and I heard Orlando say it was Sullivan. He got a shower and got dressed and as he was leaving, I was toward the other end of the locker room. As he passed by, he said he enjoyed working out with me and it was nice to meet. Welcome aboard. That type of stuff. Then he said, "Oh, by the way, my secretary will have something for you. Why don't you drop by tomorrow?"

I did, and it was a plain Red Sox envelope with my name on it. As soon as I got on the stairs leading down to the ballpark, I opened it up, and it was a crisp $10 bill—which in 1949 was a lot of money. To be paid for something that was probably my biggest thrill at that point in my life . . . .

Sometimes when we worked out, a player who was maybe on the disabled list like Boo Ferriss [that is, a player who had been left behind]—he had a lot of problems that year with sore arms—would take part in those workouts too.

[Yawkey] knew us all by name, including me after we met that first time. It was "Sully" this and "Sully" that."[53]

On the first day of the 1950s, the *Globe*'s Roger Birtwell made the point that in seventeen seasons the Yawkey-run Red Sox had often been the bridesmaid but never the bride and that the one World Series they played, they lost—the first time a Boston team had ever lost a Series after six championships between 1903 and 1918. "The Red Sox of the Yawkey era," he wrote, "will be remembered for their stats rather than their successes."[54]

In January the Sox signed former Indians and Tigers manager Steve O'Neill to scout for them in the central states. Some felt that it was a wise move to have the experienced O'Neill in the organization should Joe McCarthy decide to resign. When coach Kiki Cuyler died just before the season, O'Neill was slotted in as third base coach.

Ted Williams signed on, as always without any controversy and without holding out. It was thought he was being paid somewhere around $100,000 and maybe even as much as $125,000. An AP story imagined the salary discussion:

YAWKEY: "Hello, Ted." How are you?"

WILLIAMS: "Fine, Mr. Yawkey. Just caught a five-pound catfish."

YAWKEY: "How about 100 again this year?"

WILLIAMS: "Okay. See you at Sarasota March 1."[55]

Whatever he was paid, it prompted Williams to say, "There was no dickering. There never has been. As I've told you many times, the luckiest break I ever received in my life was that I was bought by the Red Sox. Throughout my career, everybody in the Red Sox organization has treated me swell. Tom Yawkey is the most generous owner in baseball."[56] The only holdout in 1950 was Vern Stephens. He was said to have been the first holdout under Yawkey since Billy Werber in the mid-1930s.

Other interests did present their demands on Tom Yawkey. Ed Rumill acknowledged that they took priority over baseball—though it's not clear how often throughout Yawkey's life business interests truly claimed such priority. Rumill's comment was one of the very few times I could find such a suggestion. When Yawkey arrived in Boston on April 10, Rumill wrote that his absence from spring training should not give credence to rumors he'd lost interest in the team. "Those close to the Red Sox are aware that Yawkey's lumber business kept him far too busy through March and early April to allow even a flying trip to Sarasota. He still considers baseball his chief 'outside interest' and will be rooting from his private box adjoining the Fenway Park press box in the months ahead."[57]

The Yawkeys arrived by train from New York even before the team got to town, and they were greeted by hundreds of students from Cathedral High in Boston, some bearing placards with greetings such as "Welcome Home Tom," "Good Luck Tom," and "Baseball's No. 1 Man." The *Boston Globe* ran a photograph on its front page. One wonders who orchestrated the reception.

As the season began, Yawkey realized, "Someone asked me the other day how long I'd been in baseball, and when I began to figure it out, I suddenly realized I'm getting to be a veteran club owner."[58] For the third year in a row, many picked the Red Sox to win the pennant.

The 1950 Red Sox were a hard-hitting team. They scored 1,027 runs. (They allowed only 804 runs.) It was the only time in franchise history they had cracked the one-thousand-run mark, and they did it in the days of the 154-game schedule.[59]

The biggest concern was whether or not the Sox could play better on the road. By season's end, they had a 55-22 record at home and had a winning record on the road too—but only by one game (39-38). It took until the thirteenth game of the season before they had a winning record at all (7-6). The next day, April 30, they beat the Athletics in the first game of two by a score of 19–0, and Harold Kaese wrote that they could have won the game "with Tom Yawkey playing second base and batting cleanup."[60] That one game certainly helped the run differential. So did the 11–1 win on May 6. It was in early June that they really exploded.

First, there was another visit from Tempestuous Ted. On May 11 the Sox lost both games of a doubleheader. Williams made two errors during one game in May, got booed, and made inappropriate gestures toward the fans. After a talk with Tom Yawkey the next day, Ted "requested that this announcement be made to the fans. 'Ted is sorry for his impulsive actions on the field yesterday and wishes to apologize to any and all whom he may have offended.'"[61] Five policemen were stationed in the left-field corner seats for the next day's game. A lengthy story in the May 13 *Globe* quoted Yawkey as saying he had not fined Williams and believed Ted truly regretted his actions. Clif Keane noted that in all the years Yawkey had owned the team, it was "the first time that Yawkey, who happened to be in Boston, has taken personal charge."[62] The *Boston American* was not assuaged; its editorial suggested that Williams "had removed himself from the ranks of decent sportsmen" and called him "a dirty little man."[63] The *Globe*'s Jerry Nason, noting the phrasing "wishes to apologize" envisioned lines of fans queuing up at the park so that Ted could offer his apologies.[64]

Williams denied stories suggesting there might be a rift. "I don't want to play baseball anywhere except in Boston, and I don't want to play for anybody except Tom Yawkey."[65]

The Red Sox did restrict press access to the clubhouse, however. It is now closed to the media for forty-five minutes prior to games and for a brief period after. (Williams had tried to have the media banned entirely following games.) In his autobiography, Birdie Tebbetts gives an insider's view of the story. He realized how horrific some of the sensationalism was and how "foul" and "cruel" a couple of the writers were who focused on Williams's private life. He also understood how important publicity could be to other ballplayers. Yawkey sympathized with Williams but in the end pressed for a compromise that gave his players a thirty-minute media-free cooling-off period after games.[66]

From May 27 the Red Sox ranked no higher than third. The batters got in their licks on June 7 and 8 with back-to-back slaughters of the St. Louis Browns, 20–4 and 29–4. Yawkey didn't get to see those games, though. He was in South Carolina, listening to the "Game of the Week" on radio. And he didn't get to hear it all, either. Radio reception was interrupted, so he had to telephone Joe Cronin to get a play-by-play description.[67]

Later in June Joe McCarthy left the team. And he took a swing at a cameraman when he arrived at the airport in Buffalo. He hadn't been fired. He hadn't quit. He had pleurisy, his wife said. Soon, however, it was said that he was tired and weary; he didn't think it was fair to Mr. Yawkey for him to continue with him being so physically exhausted, so he had resigned. "I've had enough baseball," he told the AP.[68] With a little over a week left on the schedule, the Red Sox signed Steve O'Neill to a 1951 contract.

Disaster struck at Comiskey Park during the 1950 All-Star Game. Fielding a ball in left field, Ted Williams badly chipped a bone in his elbow, and he missed the next two months of the season, from July 9 to September 7. He was on the way to his most productive season. He already had 25 homers before the All-Star Game and 83 RBIs. Yawkey visited Williams in the hospital, and they watched a ballgame together on TV.

Williams resumed full-time action only on September 15, adding 3 more homers and 14 RBIs in what remained of the month. The team played well without him but bobbed back and forth between third and fourth place, winding up in third, four games out of first. The standings were bunched, though, and as late as September 19 the Sox were only a half-game out of first. There were those who decried Ted and said the Sox were a better team without him. The team had indeed reeled off an eleven-game winning streak between August 15 and 25, interrupting Yawkey's schedule a bit. He'd been in Boston as it unwound, intending to leave around August 21, but he hadn't dared leave with the streak still in progress.[69] With two more months of Ted Williams—who typically hit better in the later months—they might have made a tighter race of it or even prevailed.

Tom Yawkey wasn't above taking the team bus from the hotel to the ballpark. It was a surprise to Ted, though, when he saw the owner get on board. "Are you bussing it?" he asked, and Yawkey replied, "Why, sure. I took the bus out to the park in Chicago and we won."[70]

The 1950 Red Sox had a team batting average of .302. They scored

6.67 runs per game. They'd scored 113 more runs than the next-closest club, the Yankees. Rookie Walt Dropo drove in 144 runs, tying him with Vern Stephens for the lead, just one RBI less than the record Ted Williams had set back in 1939—and which still stands in the twenty-first century. Billy Goodman won the AL batting crown, despite the fact that he had no regular position; he'd played all four infield positions (mostly third and first base) and filled in for Williams in left field. The Sox still wound up short—another painfully close finish. From 1946 through 1950, they'd come so close four out of five times.

Birdie Tebbetts blamed the shortcoming on internal dissension—feuds in the clubhouse and what he called "a couple of juvenile delinquents and moronic malcontents" on the pitching staff. And he wasn't referring to Mickey McDermott since McDermott was in the audience for his remarks.[71] In December 1950 Tebbetts was shuffled out of town, sold to the Cleveland Indians—according to Tebbetts, for the price of $1.00.[72] Actually Tebbetts tells a version of his departure that makes it sound like other than retribution. He says that Indians GM Hank Greenberg was sitting in a booth at Toots Shor's in New York with Tom Yawkey, and they were talking about trading Ted Williams for a couple of Cleveland's best pitchers and some other players. Yawkey was drinking Johnny Walker Black Label. There were offers and counteroffers back and forth, and each time Greenberg added, "And I get Birdie Tebbetts." Finally Tebbetts says, "Yawkey got so goddamn mad hearing my name he said, 'I'll tell you what, Greenberg. You want Tebbetts? Well, you can have the son-of-a-bitch. As a matter of fact, you can have him for nothing.' And that's how I was sold to Cleveland for $1."[73]

Headlines suggested that there would be a showdown between Ted Williams and Tom Yawkey after Ted said he'd condition himself and play when he felt like it. O'Neill responded that Ted wasn't bigger than baseball and he'd play in the spring training games he was asked to play. The mid-November flap almost seemed to come out of nowhere. "Ted has often said, and sincerely too, that he hopes to end his playing career working for Tom Yawkey. Yawkey has treated Ted like he was his own son. The Kid could do no wrong." But there were signs, argued Hy Hurwitz, that Yawkey might be souring on Ted, as he had soured on Jimmie Foxx and Joe McCarthy.[74]

Later in November the Red Sox signed Lou Boudreau to play shortstop. Who would get traded? Pesky? Stephens? Neither, as it turned out, and both played more than Boudreau in the infield. Boudreau got into eighty-two games in 1951. The Indians wanted to go another direction, and a reported $60,000 of Yawkey cash enticed Boudreau to give up working as Tribe manager and begin playing in Boston under his former skipper, O'Neill. Indians GM Hank Greenberg said in December that Boudreau was paid $150,000 for two years.[75]

Was Yawkey done yet? The question was asked on the eve of his arrival at the winter meetings at St. Petersburg, the first time in a dozen years that he'd attended winter meetings held in a locale other than Chicago or New York. The Red Sox and White Sox made a trade on December 10, with Boston getting Ray Scarborough and Bill Wight for Joe Dobson, Dick Littlefield, and Al Zarilla.

At the winter meetings, the owners voted to find a new commissioner of baseball to replace Happy Chandler, but they did not buy out the remaining time on his contract (until the end of April 1952), nor did Chandler resign. Yawkey declined to say how he'd voted, though it was reported that he and John Galbreath of the Pirates "stormed out" of the meeting at one point and came back with Chandler in tow.[76] Later reports said it was the "pillars of the major leagues" that had wanted to retain Chandler—Clark Griffith, Connie Mack, Walter Briggs, Phil Wrigley, and Tom Yawkey.[77] It was perhaps not so much that they were enthralled with Chandler but that they harbored some bitterness toward a newer group of owners that had decided to oust the commissioner.[78] The December 13, 1950, *Herald* noted, "There is no question that owner Tom Yawkey of the Red Sox was in Chandler's corner all the way." Nonetheless, there were insufficient votes to confirm Chandler for another term.

As one of the "pillars of the major leagues," of course, Yawkey might have had some leeway to lead in racial matters, though acting in 1950 to integrate the Red Sox would hardly have placed him in the vanguard. The Red Sox signed their first "Negro player" in 1950: Lorenzo "Piper" Davis. He was from Birmingham, a Negro

League veteran, and player-manager of the pennant-winning Birmingham Black Barons in 1948. When Sox scout Larry Woodall passed up the opportunity to sign a young Baron named Willie Mays, he signed Davis instead. Davis had hit .382 in 1947 and .354 in 1948. The Red Sox did indeed have an exceptionally strong ball club from 1948 through 1950, and one can understand that Davis might not have been brought to the big leagues, but the way he was let go struck a false note.

Davis trained in Florida, having to room separately from the rest of the team—literally in servant's quarters. He was assigned to Scranton, and if he'd stuck with the team until May 15, he would have been due an additional $7,500 in salary. He played in fifteen games at Scranton and was batting .333 when he was released. When he was called into the office, he thought he was being promoted. Instead Howard Bryant writes in *Shut Out*, "On May 13, with Davis leading the club in home runs, batting average, RBIs, and stolen bases, manager Jack Burns told Davis the club was releasing him from his contract."[79] He was told he was being released "for economic reasons."[80] Burns was apparently incensed about it but powerless, says historian Jules Tygiel.[81] Davis later told Peter Golenbock, "Tom Yawkey had as much money as anyone on the East Coast. I don't talk about it that much. It wouldn't help. Sometimes I just sit here and a tear drops from my eye. I wonder why it all had to happen, why we have to have so much hate."[82]

The Red Sox weren't moving rapidly to desegregate, but after the 1950 season Yawkey decided he wanted a change in the team's approach to radio. Difficult as it may be to understand today, only home games were broadcast on radio. Because the Red Sox and Braves schedules were planned so that both teams were not home at the same time, one man—Jim Britt—could broadcast the home games of both teams. Yawkey decided he wanted to have Red Sox road games broadcast to the home audience in New England. Lou Perini of the Braves was not pleased, but that's the way it was to be. Yawkey saw to it that Curt Gowdy was hired away from New York radio.

In *Seasons to Remember*, Curt Gowdy and coauthor John Powers recount that Yawkey felt that Gowdy was more than capable and that he'd be a good fit in Boston as long as he played it straight with the knowledgeable Boston listeners. Yawkey warned Gowdy, "These are real fans up here. . . . They're going to give you hell for a while, but eventually you'll be accepted. There's no town in America that knows big-league baseball better than Boston does. . . . You're not going to kid them. So don't make any pop flies into line drives. And don't make excuses for the ballplayers. Just give 'em the ball game."[83]

Powers recounts the following:

There was one anecdote about Curt that he didn't want me to put into the book, so I didn't. When he was the number two guy to Mel Allen, it was the first year that the Yankees were going on TV. He said for the first couple of innings of the first game, Mel was doing it as if it were a radio broadcast. "Finally, after the third inning," he said, "I turned to Mel and said, 'Mel, they can see the guy.'"

That was how Yawkey got him. Gowdy knew he was going to be number two to Mel Allen.

One reason why Yawkey liked Gowdy was the outdoors aspect. Gowdy said he went up to see Yawkey after the first set of games, and Yawkey said, "I like you very much, but I'll tell you what, which way was the wind blowing?" "It was blowing left to right." "That's something that I need to know." It struck him just how much of a fan Yawkey was.[84]

In fact, Yawkey had been more specific: "Don't tell me it's blowing from east to west. Tell me it's blowing from first to third or from centerfield in."[85]

14

The Early 1950s

ARTHUR SAMPSON SCORED an interview with Joe McCarthy that ran in *The Sporting News*. McCarthy distinguished between his Yankees clubs and the Red Sox he'd managed by emphasizing that the Yankees teams weren't as one-dimensional. Yes, both teams had a lot of offense and power, but the Yankees teams had several key players (he named Frankie Crosetti) whose primary contributions were on-base percentage, advancing the runner, and defense. "A strong defensive team can sometimes win a pennant with very little punch," he said.[1]

Hartford Courant sports editor Bill Lee wrote, "Tom Yawkey in his early years of lavish spending either made the personal mistake of building in the wrong way or else was badly advised. He had big names, great sluggers but all too few defensive stalwarts.... Even in recent years the Red Sox have been out of balance, with too much power and too little defense. Perhaps now that they have bolstered their pitching quite some, the Red Sox will have a better chance, but there are still defensive and spiritual weaknesses about the organization that makes this doubtful."[2] Lee likely had the additions of pitchers Scarborough and Wight in mind.

One would like to have heard more about the "spiritual weaknesses." Surely Lee wasn't getting all mystical. He may simply have been alluding to the notion of a team that was coddled by an owner who was perhaps too generous with his money and the demands (or lack of demands) he placed on his executives. David Halberstam wrote in *Summer of '49* that "Tom Yawkey ... was second to none in coddling."[3] There were intimations as well that a star such as Ted Williams could simply go around the manager or the GM if he had any problems and go straight to Yawkey.[4] The headline on a Harold Kaese column in March exemplified the sense that the Red Sox were run differently than other ball clubs: "Sox Pay Top Prices, Other Ball Clubs Run Like Business Firms."[5] However much money Yawkey may have pumped into the ball club, a *Wall Street Journal* report at the end of 1951 mentioned that the Red Sox had turned a profit of over $100,000 in 1950.[6]

The Red Sox decided, for the first time, to broadcast all 154 games—home and away. This was an aggressive departure from the détente they'd had with the Boston Braves.[7]

Early in '51 the situation with Commissioner Chandler got more complicated. Senator Virgil Chapman of Kentucky was killed in an automobile accident. His death opened up the possibility that should Chandler leave the commissioner's post a year before his contract was up, he might be appointed by the governor to serve out Chapman's term. With the support of only seven (Yawkey and the old guard—Yawkey was now part of the "old guard") of the sixteen owners, Chandler's days were likely numbered. It is interesting that most of the ballplayers were disposed to like Chandler and felt he'd been good to the players; they said they would petition for a role in selecting his replacement, a proposal destined to go nowhere.[8]

Though it seemed to drag on forever, Chandler finally agreed in late June to resign on July 15. When the annual player representative and club owner meeting was held on July 9, there does not appear to have been any request for players to take part in selecting commissioners, and the players from both leagues even endorsed the reserve clause as a necessary element of the game.[9]

After Chandler resigned, baseball's executive committee ran the game. The committee was composed of the two league presidents (Ford Frick and Will Harridge), Tom Yawkey, and GM Warren Giles of the Cincinnati Reds. Yawkey himself cared about the game as a whole, not just his own parochial or personal interests. He served many years on the executive committee; in the early 1970s he told his assistant PR man, Dick Bresciani, who joined the Red Sox in May 1972, "We're just part of Major League Baseball. There are 24 teams [after the expansion in 1969], and they have to work together for the good of everyone. No team can exist by itself. That's what bothers me sometimes when some owners don't see the benefit of a compromise when it might not be in their own best interests."[10]

Manager Steve O'Neill—who'd managed the Tigers with a staff built around Hal Newhouser, Virgil Trucks, and Dizzy Trout—was very pleased with the depth of the staff the Red Sox had assembled. "We have nine pitchers capable of starting," he said. The Yankees maybe had a better top three or four, but O'Neill felt that Boston had the most depth in the league. "If I have to take a pitcher out I'll be able to replace him with a man just as good."[11] He had Parnell, Scarborough, Willard Nixon, McDermott, Wight, Chuck Stobbs, and Harry Taylor, and he could have Masterson and Kinder in the bullpen.

Bobby Doerr felt it was the best Red Sox team he'd been on since he'd first joined the team in 1937.[12] Grantland Rice couldn't foresee a way the Red Sox could lose: "It would take a master mind or a set of master minds to figure a way to lose this time. But it could happen."[13] Just after the season got under way, Rice added, "Yawkey has now supplied the Red Sox with everything except two corps of Marines, plus the Air Corps."[14]

In the meantime, Ted Williams got booed by some fans in Sarasota, hit a home run his next time up, and made a rude gesture to the fans. Some things hadn't changed.

The team had to feel good about getting Lou Boudreau to help with infield work, and observers used to the Red Sox overbidding for talent may have been surprised to learn that he'd agreed to play for Boston for $10,000 less than the $50,000 he'd been offered by the Senators. He thought the Red Sox had a better chance at the pennant and that he might have a better chance to manage again if he were with Boston.[15]

Eddie Collins, who had been in and out of hospitals since suffering a brain hemorrhage in August 1950, died on March 25. It may have seemed as though he was a grand old man of baseball, but he was only sixty-three. Tom Yawkey was among the pallbearers at his funeral.

Yawkey himself was honored. The Boston City Council voted unanimously to present him with a plaque "in appreciation of his splendid sportsmanship over a long period of years."[16] Any idea that he might dispose of the team may have faded. Jean Yawkey had "become an ardent baseball enthusiast," wrote the *Boston Traveler*, "so if her husband ever had any notion of closing up shop at Fenway Park, it no longer exists."[17]

On May 15 the team hosted a fiftieth reunion of the 1901 Boston Americans (now the Red Sox) and welcomed other figures from the era such as Connie Mack. Two days later the team traded Matt Batts for Les Moss of the Browns. A couple of other players were sent to St. Louis too, along with $100,000. Batts was a little bitter and griped that the Red Sox would never win anything if they didn't learn to hustle a little. Among other things, he said their lack of hustle put too much pressure on Ted Williams. Mack was not shy about stating a preference for the Red Sox because he felt Yawkey had done a lot of good for the game: "I'm rooting for Mr. Yawkey to win the pennant."[18]

For whatever reason, the team was slow to start. After the first two dozen games, the Red Sox stood at 12-12. Their record improved as the days got warmer, and on July 12 they reached first place after sweeping a doubleheader from the White Sox. The Red Sox hung in first for a couple of weeks, then dropped to second place by the end of the month. Though just a half-game out of first as late as August 3, they dropped to third place the following day and stayed there for the remainder of the season—even with a nine-game losing streak that ended their year.

Boudreau's broken hand cost him a month—most of August. Walt Dropo, such a star in 1950, dropped more than eighty points in hitting, from .322 to .239, and saw his RBIs drop from 144 to 57—a decline of 87. Bobby Doerr's production was off too, and he'd told reporters in August that back problems might well prevent him from returning in 1952. He'd averaged over 110 RBIs for five years running, but now they had dropped to 89. Vern Stephens had been hurt. So had Mickey McDermott. Williams led the team with 30 homers, 126 RBIs, and a (for him subpar) .318 average. He still led the league in on-base percentage and slugging.

Even as August ended, there were "persistent reports" out of Boston that suggested Yawkey would trade Pesky, Stephens, and/or Dom

DiMaggio (but not Williams) should the Sox fail to win the flag in 1951 and that he'd probably replace O'Neill as manager with Boudreau.[19] Yawkey himself wasn't giving any indication, with the *Washington Post* noting, "Yawkey is the most inaccessible of club owners anyway, and traditionally keeps to himself the thoughts with which other owners rush into print. He has given no sign that he is even displeased with the present state of affairs." The team was becoming older too, the *Post* observed.[20]

The *Springfield Union* wrote, "It could be, as many suggest, that Yawkey made the tragic mistake of paying his stars too much and thus robbed them of their ambition."[21] That comment is in line with what Tommy Henrich later told Bobby Doerr. "How Much Longer Will Tom Yawkey Tolerate Failures of His Red Sox Club?" asked Ed Rumill. It was a philosophical question. He had no answers. Williams himself said he was worried he'd be traded so that the Red Sox could get someone like pitcher Ned Garver, who'd won seventeen games for the last-place Browns. He hoped not, he said, repeating his mantra, "I couldn't work for a better guy than Tom Yawkey."[22]

On September 20 Ford Frick was elected as the new commissioner of baseball. Yawkey had taken the lead in promoting his candidacy following Chandler's departure.

The subhead on Kaese's September 30 column in the *Globe* read, "Owner hires executives because they're capable, not because he likes them." Near the end of a fairly long article about the Yankees' continued success, Kaese wrote, "The Red Sox are a hobby for which Tom Yawkey repeatedly makes up deficits. The difference in the success of the Yankees and Red Sox may be attributed to the fact that Ruppert hired his executive because they were capable, whereas Yawkey has hired his because he liked them. The Yankees have been run on a systematic, the Red Sox on a sentimental basis. The difference? See the American League standings."[23]

The city was awash in rumors even before the World Series got under way. One story reported that Williams had been offered to any and all, though no team would confirm it. Another story claimed that Ted would quit if he were traded. On October 22 Boudreau signed as manager of the Red Sox and said he'd trade anybody.

"There are no untouchables on this team. We'll trade Williams or anyone else if it'll add to the team."[24]

That may have been true, but no one was offering value for Williams, and on December 8 Boudreau said he was taking Ted off the market. At least one report stated that Yawkey had become irked at the press coverage about a potential trade and ordered Boudreau to make that December announcement.[25] Ted's two MVP awards were not ones he would take with him; they graced the walls of Tom Yawkey's office.[26]

In 1952 Ted Williams was lost to the Red Sox yet again, this time for most of two years. This time it wasn't a broken elbow, though. Rather, he was recalled to military service in the year he turned thirty-four. That wasn't anything anyone had expected, and he wasn't pleased at the prospect. But he was in the Marine Corps Reserve, and the force needed pilots for the war in Korea. Though he might easily have avoided combat by offering to perform morale-boosting and public relations duties for the corps, Ted felt that if the Marines wanted him back, he was going to see action. And he did.

Ted got in all of twelve plate appearances in 1952—though he took advantage of them, batting .400 (with a .500 on-base percentage) and hitting a tie-breaking, game-winning homer on April 30 in his final at-bat.

At least the team learned the news well before spring training began. It was January 9 when his recall was announced. He said the right things for public consumption: "If Uncle Sam wants me, I'm ready. I'm no different from the next fellow."[27] Joe Cronin said they'd had no warning the recall was coming.

Cronin visited Yawkey in South Carolina not that many days later. It was understood that Yawkey would probably pay Williams's full salary during the time he was away and that Williams would train with the team until his April 2 physical and then more or less play it by ear. Assuming he passed the physical, he would play until given a date to report.

Did Williams ever visit Yawkey on South Island? Improbable stories abound in Georgetown. Jim Sargent says that Williams came just once and he picked him up at the airport. "And that was long after he was in baseball. I picked him up at the Charleston Airport. He brought his shotgun. They were going bird hunting. Can you imagine coming into the airport with a shotgun now?"[28]

A questionable anecdote in the January 21, 1952, *Globe* repeated a story from *Ducks Unlimited Quarterly*. It claimed that Ted had visited South Island the preceding autumn and was placed in a duck blind on Yawkey's preserve "with a dowager of Yawkey's acquaintance." That alone should have raised the skepticism quotient. Purportedly a flock of ducks came in to land, and the woman raised her shotgun to shoot, prompting Ted to tell her not to shoot as they arrived but only as they departed so as to give the ducks a better chance. "Young man, when I shoot, they always have a chance," was her reported rejoinder.[29]

Bobby Doerr had retired, and now Ted Williams's status was uncertain, so Boudreau likely had two major holes to fill, not to mention the perennial need for pitching. He also acknowledged a problem he might face with motivation. In an article that appeared in the *Saturday Evening Post*, he remarked that Tom Yawkey was "unusually generous" and more or less intimated that he was paying his players more than they deserved. "The net result, Boudreau concluded, was that the Red Sox players were lazy or didn't play to their abilities because of these large salaries."[30]

Yawkey was in Boston before the season began and enjoyed taking in the first annual "spring training camp" held at Fenway Park for some five thousand high school and local club boys for an event jointly hosted by the Red Sox and Braves.[31]

Williams had passed his Marine Corps physical and was told to report on May 2. During a farewell sendoff on "Ted Williams Day," April 30, players from both teams held hands in a line that spread across the field from dugout to dugout as "Auld Lang Syne" was sung; in his roof box seat, Tom Yawkey held hands with Mildred Cronin on one side and her husband Joe on the other side.[32] Yawkey expressed some concern that an older Williams might not have as quick reflexes as it would take to fly the faster jet aircraft, particularly after six years away from flying, but he quickly added, "I'd hate to have anyone think I want to add words that sound like a eulogy for a friend who has died."[33]

A couple of days after "Ted Williams Day," Jean Yawkey wrote an article for the *Boston Herald*, as told to Jack McCarthy, on the greatest game she'd ever seen. She selected the seventeen-inning 5-4 win over the White Sox on July 12, 1951. "Tom and I were the only Boston fans there," she said, "which makes it all the more thrilling because you root harder to offset the enemy cheers."[34]

The season had gotten off to a very strong start; the Sox had won six of the first seven games, and with the Williams home run on April 30, they had a 10-2 start for the first month. They lost the lead but had just regained first place the day before a major trade was announced, a nine-player deal, a blockbuster. Johnny Pesky and Walt Dropo were traded to the Tigers, with Fred Hatfield, Don Lenhardt, and Bill Wight, in exchange for Hoot Evers, George Kell, Johnny Lipon, and Dizzy Trout.

Stocking the farm system wasn't paying off, but that didn't stop Yawkey from trying. Joe Cashman of the *Boston Record* wrote that in nearly twenty years the Red Sox had developed just one great pitcher through the farm system—Tex Hughson—and one better-than-average pitcher—Mel Parnell.[35]

"Yawkey Still Spending" was a headline in the *Monitor*. Ed Rumill estimated Yawkey had invested $450,000 in June: somewhere around $100,000 for pitching prospect Frank Baumann, perhaps around the same for Marty Keough, $50,000 for Haywood Sullivan, and other sums for players who never made it: Larry Isbell, Edward Urness, and Jerry Zimmerman.[36] Joe Cronin claimed the figures reported were exaggerated but that advances of that nature were business as usual. "It's Only Money" read the headline on Arthur Daley's June 29, 1952, column in the *New York Times*.

The team signed up seventeen bonus babies, and Yawkey revealed at one point that he'd outbid the Yankees in thirteen instances.[37] His signing spree had prompted calls to cap bonuses that could be paid. Accused in September 1951 of running the team like a hobby, he acknowledged the accusation early in 1952, in so many words: "I do not look upon baseball as a business. Baseball is my hobby. It may be that I won't make any money out of the Red Sox. Even so, I find it a distinct pleasure to be connected with the game."[38]

On June 27 Elise Sparrow Yawkey's husband, Harry Dorsey Watts, died at age sixty-seven.

During the summer the on-field antics of rookie outfielder Jimmy Piersall led to a great deal of anguish and uncertainty. It was learned that he suffered from mental illness, the story of which he later told so movingly in his book, *Fear Strikes Out*. Among Boston sports columnists, Dave Egan—"the Colonel," who had built a following decrying Ted Williams—was highly complimentary of the way the matter was handled, the Sox removing Piersall from the glare of the spotlight. "I tell Jimmy Piersall that he was fortunate indeed to fall into the good hands of such a person as Tom Yawkey and that the longer he lives, the more he will realize that the world knows few men who would have done for him what this man has done for him."[39] On July 23 the *Boston Herald* wrote an editorial along similar lines. It was later written that "when Piersall was hospitalized, Yawkey took care of everything for him."[40]

Care for Piersall continued after he was released from the mental health facility. From the days they had both worked in media in Chicago, Piersall was very friendly with Tom Shaer, and Shaer says that after Piersall finished his treatment, Tom Yawkey sent him, along with his wife and children, to Sarasota for the wintertime to work out with Red Sox coach George Susce. He had paid Piersall's full baseball salary not only during the time he was institutionalized, but over that winter as well so that he wouldn't have to worry about offseason employment, could have his family with him, and could concentrate to see if he could get baseball-ready and back in the game.[41]

Dave Egan wrote a blistering column targeting players who took advantage of Yawkey's "gravy train" just a few months later. He commented that the "Red Flops" played so poorly on the road because they slacked off, performing well only in front of Yawkey in Boston. Yawkey was too indulgent and let them get away with trying to "flim-flam Tom Yawkey out of as much money as possible," whereas a GM such as Branch Rickey felt a hungry ballplayer made for a better ballplayer. He concluded: "Unfortunately parasites have clustered around Tom Yawkey."[42] The crusty columnist kept up the drumbeat; a week later he called the Sox "far lower than professional pickpockets."[43]

The Red Sox finished the 1952 season with a record of 76-78, not even at .500, and they were nineteen games out of first, solidly in sixth place. It was their worst season since 1945. "Not in modern Tom Yawkey times . . . have the Red Sox ended in such a shambles as this year," wrote the *Boston Traveler*'s Arthur Siegel.[44]

Attendance was down about 15 percent, and the *Wall Street Journal* calculated that Yawkey had lost money in twenty of the twenty-nine seasons he'd owned the team. The best year had been 1946, when the team earned a $720,000 profit.[45] All in all, there was no doubt that Yawkey was out to the tune of several million dollars overall.

Earl Brown of the *New York Amsterdam News* was one of the first to advance the argument in print that the failure of the Red Sox to win more pennants was due to racism on the part of Tom Yawkey. He wrote, "Yawkey, owner of the Red Sox, won't think of hiring a Negro player. Remember, he had a chance back in 1945 to hire [Jackie] Robinson, who tried out with the Red Sox as a kind of unwanted and uninvited guest. It is easy to see the huge price Yawkey has paid for his prejudice. If he had hired Jackie in '45 or '46, the Red Sox inevitably would have won practically every pennant since then."[46] Dave Egan called Brown's remarks "twaddle" and wrote, "If Cleveland ever put Larry Doby up for auction, Tom Yawkey would bid sky-high in an effort to get him."[47]

The year 1953 was meant to be the second year in what was characterized as a "youth movement" under Lou Boudreau. He'd given players such as Sammy White, Jimmy Piersall, Ted Lepcio, and Faye Throneberry a real shot, "far more opportunity than any of his predecessors [had given]."[48] The Red Sox had signed Harry Agganis in November 1952 and continued to add bonus babies, notably Billy Consolo on February 2. New rules regarding bonus signings had been adopted on November 4, 1952. (The Agganis signing came one day before the new rules went into effect, a foresightful move by the Red Sox administration.) Perhaps trying to save Yawkey from himself, the clubs voted to institute a curb on unlimited player bonuses. Now a team that wanted to sign a player badly enough to pay an amount exceeding $4,000 had to keep the "bonus baby" on the Major League roster for two years. Doing so would eat up a roster spot, thus discouraging the shoveling out of large sums of money on prime but untested prospects. Unfortunately as a result of the rule, numerous players were kept on the bench, to keep them from other teams, but in the process they did not get the development experience that could make them better ballplayers. The two wealthiest owners were Yawkey and Bob Carpenter of the Phillies. They both supported the new rule.

There were rather few players on the 1953 club who had been with the team in 1951, particularly if one counted neither Ted Williams, who was in the Marines, nor Dom DiMaggio, who retired on May 12, before the season was a month old.

Even before spring training truly got under way, two major stories grabbed headlines in baseball. First, the biggest star of the Red Sox, Ted Williams, arrived in Korea with Marine jet squadron VMF-311, and on his third combat mission, on February 16, his plane was hit by enemy ground fire. He had to crash-land his aircraft, barely escaping with his life. Less than twenty-four hours later, Captain Williams set out on yet another mission the following morning. Williams flew thirty-nine combat missions in all—some of them with squadron mate John Glenn. As the war wound down, he was mustered out of the service and returned to baseball in early August.[49]

Second, the Boston Braves left town and relocated to Milwaukee—on such short notice that tickets had already been printed for the home games at Braves Field in Boston. The Braves had been in Boston since 1876, twenty-five years longer than the Red Sox, and they had been to the World Series more recently than the Red Sox (1948), but they weren't attracting anywhere near the attendance the Sox did. Boston was now a one-team city. The Red Sox were the only game in town.

There was a sense that Boston newspapers gave better coverage to the Red Sox while belittling the Braves. Shortly after their 1948 pennant-winning season, Braves owner Lou Perini had tried to work out a deal whereby the Braves would use Fenway Park for their home games, but Tom Yawkey preferred to keep his park exclusively for the use of the Red Sox and declined to make it available. When Perini and Yawkey met, the day before the Braves' stunning announcement, Yawkey told him he could use Fenway Park, but

Perini replied, "I asked for the use of the park four years ago and was turned down. I don't want it now."[50] He added, "I have nothing against Boston and the baseball fans. Maybe some day Tom Yawkey will want to sell the Red Sox. If he ever does, I'll buy."[51]

Dave Egan of the *Boston Record* was over the top as usual, writing about how "garish" and "filthy" Braves Field had become, dubbing the owner "Perini the Plunderer" (and commenting that his leaving Boston would be "one fewer rat"), and suggesting that Yawkey be made commissioner of baseball.[52] It wasn't the reserve clause that bound Red Sox players to the "Yawkey plantation"; it was loyalty, wrote Egan.[53] Fenway Park offered water fountains while Braves Field lacked them—and the hot dogs were larger.[54]

The Red Sox constructed a new clubhouse under the third base stands with a tunnel leading directly to the visitors' dugout. The two teams had previously dressed in side-by-side quarters under the first base stands; at a cost of about $100,000, the home team now enjoyed a larger clubhouse.

The last games the Braves played in Boston (until a Jimmy Fund benefit game in June 1957) were two City Series games at Fenway on April 11 and 12. The *Globe*'s Kaese noted that Perini—perhaps courageously—was seated in a box next to the visitors' dugout. Sitting inconspicuously on the roof, in his box, alone save for a couple of friends, was Tom Yawkey. "Not for him the place in the spotlight, the prominent headline, or the pictorial layout. Not for him any desire to advertise himself," wrote Kaese. "Many men with his opportunity would have thrust themselves on the Boston scene. Yawkey had thrust nothing upon us but the Red Sox, and $10,000 gifts to charity that he has tried to keep quiet."[55] One observer said to another, "He has given us the most and we know him the least."[56] Though after his death the Yawkey name appears on numerous buildings and centers, it was not always that way, and it was not so during his lifetime. One of his $10,000 gifts was to Children's Hospital, and when Yawkey was told a plaque would be placed on the ward he had funded, he asked that the plaque honor Bobby Doerr.[57]

Doerr was, of course, one of the very first new signings to make the Majors under Yawkey's ownership, and Yawkey always held a special fondness for him. Don Doerr talked to his father about Tom

Yawkey in July 2014 and reports, "Dad had been invited to Tom's apartment in New York a few times. Dad felt that Mrs. Yawkey had a special liking for him because Dad was a team player and because of Dad's commitment to the Red Sox. Dad wasn't aware that many players had been invited to their private apartment."[58] Indeed none of the extensive research for this book turned up any other instance of ballplayers ever visiting Tom or Jean Yawkey in New York.

Yawkey lamented the departure of the Braves, saying he felt bad about the loss of a Boston institution. He also felt that the Braves' leaving could hurt attendance at Red Sox games because it would remove some of the daily interest in baseball. "You need continuous performance to keep people baseball-minded. . . . The Braves' departure will hurt attendance in Boston." His prediction proved accurate in that attendance at Fenway Park declined, though of course the quality of Red Sox offerings may have had a lot to do with that. More successful Sox teams in the 1950s might have made a big difference.[59] To replace some of the anticipated slacking off of attendance, Yawkey began to think of televising all Red Sox road games beginning in 1954 while perhaps blacking out home games.[60]

In July, looking to protect Jimmy Piersall from the fierce riding he was taking, Yawkey was said to have "asked Allie Reynolds, the American League player representative, to see 'if the other clubs' more savage bench jockeys would discard their whips.' It was the first favor Yawkey ever asked of a ballplayer. According to Piersall, the riding died down afterward."[61]

The prior year had been costly; the Red Sox had lost $1,700,000. Yawkey had a little trouble with the IRS as well, owing a little over $95,000 more in 1944 taxes and $105 more for 1945 due to a "deficiency in gift taxes growing out of a divorce settlement."[62]

Back from Korea, Marine captain T. S. Williams attended the 1953 All-Star Game with Yawkey and Joe Cronin and was asked to throw out the first ball. After being checked out at Walter Reed and being discharged from the service, he traveled on to Fenway Park, signing a 1953 contract with Yawkey and Cronin on July 29. His bat could come in handy; the very next day, the White Sox slaughtered the Red Sox, 17–1.

Ted had come by Fenway on July 28, recalled George Sullivan, and Yawkey cajoled him into hitting some balls on the field. Ted hadn't played ball for more than sixteen months. Sullivan told how Ted and Tom went back and forth about Ted's hitting or not hitting. "They were like two little kids," Sullivan said. "Yawkey was really excited. He really wanted to see Ted hit. . . . You knew [Ted] wanted to do it, but he had to be talked into it. They went back and forth." Ted went down and dressed. Paul Schreiber threw to him. He swung at a very few pitches and then—boom—he hit nine in a row out of the park.[63]

No longer a batboy or an usher, Sullivan had graduated high school and was a student at Boston University in 1953. He had just begun writing a column for the *Cambridge Chronicle* titled "I Was a Big League Bat Boy." One of his first columns ran on April 30 and retold the 1949 story of when the fifteen-year-old Sullivan first met Tom Yawkey. After the story ran, he heard from the boss:

I got a handwritten letter back from South Carolina, from Mr. T. A. Yawkey. It was on Red Sox stationery but it was handwritten and I still have it. He just about said I was going to be the next Red Smith, you know, to encourage me. Just a nice, nice letter. I think it was in the late winter or early spring, because he asked if I would come up and see him in the coming season. "Call my secretary when you're available."

I called her around June and we set up a date during the season. It was in July. A few days beforehand, I saw that Ted Williams had come back from Korea and was going to throw out the first pitch at the All-Star Game. He'd probably be back in town on Friday. It was the same day I was coming in to see Mr. Yawkey.[64]

Sullivan offered to postpone his visit, but he was told to come in. Williams arrived as he was talking with Yawkey.

Yawkey said, "Ted, do you want to hit a couple?" He said, "No, jeez, I haven't even touched a bat for a year." Ted liked to be coaxed. I left and made a beeline for the field. They went down to the clubhouse, and I went down to the batting cage.

I always said it was one of the greatest things I ever saw, how many balls he hit out of the ballpark. My nose was up almost to that batting cage. I noticed during the end of it that there was blood streaming down Ted's hands. Just superficial, from his hands not being calloused from hitting a baseball.

A "Welcome Home" dinner for Ted Williams raised $125,000 for the Jimmy Fund, Ted's chosen charity and one that had been adopted by the Boston Braves. With the Braves leaving town, Lou Perini paid a visit to Tom Yawkey and asked if he could pass him the baton. Yawkey didn't hesitate, and the Red Sox themselves adopted the Jimmy Fund as the team's official charity. (We will recall that in 1947 Yawkey had removed all advertising from the inside of Fenway Park. From 1953 and for nearly fifty years afterward, the only "advertisement" inside Fenway was for the Jimmy Fund.) At the "Welcome Home" dinner Yawkey bought tables for twelve paraplegic veterans from Cushing Hospital.[65] In September both Tom Yawkey and Joe Cronin were named to the board of trustees of the Jimmy Fund Research Foundation.[66]

Jim Healey of the Yawkey Foundations summarized:

[Yawkey] made [the Jimmy Fund] the official charity of the Red Sox. This is back when baseball teams just didn't do that. Every sports team now has its own foundation. They raise money and they give money to everybody, but back then this was really the model for that sort of thing. They both [Tom and Jean] became part of it personally. Tom was on the board for a number of years and was president of the institute and chairman of the board. Jean later became president and chairman. I remember being at the Red Sox. We would go over there as a group every now and then, every few years, and sit down and listen to them talk about the progress in cancer research and what they were doing. We were always having Jimmy Fund kids at Fenway. It was something Tom and Jean were very big on, bringing the kids over and treating them. In the early years, most of the kids didn't survive. In later years, they did, but still we'd take them in and bring them around, down to the dugout to meet the players, the clubhouse, the whole nine yards. Some of those kids wouldn't last long after that.[67]

The Yawkeys had seen the patients—and their families—firsthand, and Tom Yawkey once said, "A man wouldn't be very much if he saw those kids and came away without wanting to do everything he could to help them."[68]

More than sixty years later, Dick Johnson of the Sports Museum of New England added, "I would say that [Yawkey's] legacy from a charitable standpoint is even more significant than any championships they might have won. How do you put a value on getting the Jimmy Fund . . . not off the ground, but getting it into the position to which it has come? It's probably the greatest sports-related charitable enterprise on the planet, and the Yawkey name is all over it. . . . [The Yawkeys] were great citizens."[69]

Despite a decent 84-69 record, the 1953 Red Sox wound up in fourth place. On September 27, after the final game of the year, Lou Boudreau had dinner with the GM and the owner, and he was rehired for two more years.

The Red Sox had played only .500 ball at Fenway (38-38) and had played much better on the road (46-31). They'd been outscored in their home park. That's one of the reasons they traded to get right-handed slugger Jackie Jensen. With Williams gone, no Red Sox batter had more than the 67 RBIs that Dick Gernert had in 1952 or the 73 runs George Kell pushed across in 1953. On December 9 the Red Sox traded Mickey McDermott and Tom Umphlett to the Senators for Jensen, who came through with more than 100 RBIs in five of the next six seasons.[70]

After Williams got into playing shape, he appeared in 37 games—and drove in 34 runs. He hit .407 (37 for 91, with a .509 on-base percentage) and had 13 homers.[71]

Players continued to organize, even if only in baby steps and despite counterintuitive notions such as praising the reserve clause. Attorney J. Norman Lewis had been retained by player representatives to provide legal advice, and in December Yawkey let it be known that during the summer Lewis had threatened owners with the possibility of a players' strike and lawsuit in behind-the-scenes wrangling over the player pension fund. Yawkey bristled. He was hurt and said, "It was Larry MacPhail and myself back in 1946 who were instrumental in putting the pension plan across. I got hell then from some of the owners. Now, I'm getting it from the players." He had taken offense at the aggressive stance Lewis had assumed: "He started out by telling us what to do and talking about strikes and suits if we don't."[72]

Yawkey added that he'd be willing to sell his team to the players for a fair price and let them worry about funding the ball club going forward. "The players might change their attitudes if it was their own millions they were spending and not that of the club owners."[73] And later he added, "We gave them a plan they could not have got in any other way, and now they say they don't like it. What do they expect?"[74]

At the winter meetings Yawkey was reelected to the executive council. And there was apparently a time when Yawkey sat down with Frank "Trader" Lane of the White Sox and they talked about trading Ted Williams to the White Sox, at least a little facetiously. Yawkey wrote "Ted Williams" on one side of his napkin. On the other side, he wrote down Minnie Minoso, Billy Pierce, Nellie Fox, and Chico Carrasquel, and he kept on adding others.[75]

Something novel occurred as the 1954 season approached: the Red Sox raised ticket prices. For twenty-first-century patrons used to annual increases, it no doubt seems remarkable that it was the first ticket price increase since Tom Yawkey purchased the Red Sox in 1933. It was a stretch of twenty-two years without a raise in ticket prices. Ticket prices for children under twelve remained the same. It was noted at the time that Red Sox management had hosted 112,000 children without charge during the 1953 season—school and church groups, Little League and other children's baseball leagues, Boy Scouts, and the like.

Then on April 3 the team announced it was instead *lowering* prices because a 20 percent amusement luxury tax had been halved by Congress. The Red Sox stood ready to process refunds for about one hundred thousand advance tickets sold, but they recommended that patrons support the Jimmy Fund by designating their overpayment to go to the team's favored charity.[76]

The team experimented with its first Saturday night game.

In the spring manager Boudreau made an announcement that had to bother traditional baseball fans and no doubt still would sixty years later: "Williams will play when he comes to me and says he wants to play. He will be on his own.... He may not play in any exhibition games on the road."[77] In other words, Ted Williams could set his own schedule and train in whatever way he saw fit. Boudreau justified the decision by noting how well Williams had played, without the benefit of spring training or any "tune-up" games, after returning from the Marines in the latter half of 1953.

Three days later, only fifteen minutes into the very first day of spring training, Williams stumbled in the outfield, fell, and broke his collarbone. With the break, he was not expected to be able to play until well into May. Though he'd talked of retiring after 1954, now he said he might owe it to Tom Yawkey to come back in 1955. Trainer Jack Fadden added, "Ted is a very sentimental fellow. Just sentimentality alone may make him change his plan—if he thinks Tom Yawkey or Joe Cronin need him and that he can help them by staying around."[78]

On March 12 Bob Quinn died in Providence, the man who had sold the Red Sox to Yawkey. He'd later been president of the Boston Braves.

An April 15 dinner was planned by the Boston Sports Lodge of B'nai Brith to honor Tom Yawkey. It was the first dinner held in Boston to honor Yawkey since he had bought the team. Lefty Grove, Jimmie Foxx, Bobby Doerr, and Dom DiMaggio were among the former players to attend. Ted Williams presented him with a silver cigarette box on behalf of the 1946 Red Sox All-Stars. He stated, "I'm honored to be associated with Mr. Yawkey, a big man in all ways, especially in his heart. He is the best owner in baseball."[79]

The Red Sox loaned Fenway Park out to host the Mayor's Field Day, which attracted more than twenty-five thousand. Archbishop Cushing said that Tom Yawkey was one of Boston's greatest benefactors.[80] Yawkey not only provided the park each year but also paid for the ushers and assumed all associated expenses.

In meetings in July, Cleveland GM Hank Greenberg suggested that baseball consider thirty-two games of interleague play during the season. Five veteran owners or GMs came out against it, but Yawkey's public comment was that he was "open-minded and willing to listen."[81] He said he'd come around to agreeing with Greenberg and believed that most in the AL would support the concept but knew the NL would not.[82]

The Red Sox season was a discouraging one, with the team in sixth place more than in any other slot. They'd been stuck in last place for twenty-four days as late as July 9. There had even been some question as to whether they were surrendering when they traded third baseman George Kell to the White Sox for Grady Hatton and $100,000 near the end of May. (Disposing of Kell turned out to be a good enough deal; he had only one more good season.) Cronin commented, "The offer was so good that we couldn't turn it down. For a change the money comes to Tom Yawkey instead of him giving it up."[83]

The team never finished last under Yawkey, and it did not do so until 1992. On July 13 Yawkey said, "You can't expect miracles. Not when you have a bunch of kids like we have. I'll be happy if we can finish fourth after the start we made and all the troubles we've had."[84]

They did finish in fourth. With a 69-85 record, it was a very disappointing season, the worst showing for the team since the anomalous 68-84 war year of 1943. The Red Sox were forty-two games behind the Indians and just a game ahead of the fifth-place Tigers.

Williams missed the first month of the year due to the broken clavicle, getting into his first game on May 15. He played well when he did return, recording a .345 batting average and leading the league in walks with 136. He homered 29 times and drove in 89. Even though he hit four points higher than anyone else in the league, the batting title went to Bobby Avila because Ted had finished with only 386 at-bats, 14 below the 400 to qualify. With all the walks he had drawn, he had 526 plate appearances, and from that time forward the qualifications were changed to reflect plate appearances instead of just at-bats.

Jackie Jensen led the Sox with 117 RBIs. Frank Sullivan (15-12, 3.14 ERA) led the team in pitching.

Writers from afar said Yawkey suffered what Jack Murphy of the *San Diego Union* called "the most atrocious run of luck in the history of the game."[85] With Williams breaking his collarbone—and then losing another couple of weeks in June due to pneumonia—the team never got off to the start it could have.

Globe columnist Victor O. Jones didn't think it was just bad luck; the Red Sox had put themselves at a disadvantage: "Big league teams who think they can afford the luxury of keeping their lineups all white are giving away something like maybe 25 percent" of the potential they could achieve if they opened themselves to all talent. "Nobody argues," he wrote, "that a major league owner, Yawkey, for instance, can't run his ball club, including the color line, any way he wants to. All I'm saying is that he's handicapping himself.... The days are past when either an American or National League team will win the World Series in the great American pastime without a Negro on the roster."[86]

In December, Brooklyn Dodgers VP Buzzy Bavasi said that the Red Sox had tried to purchase rights to "Negro second-baseman" Charley Neal. It was "the highest offer ever made for a minor league ballplayer—more than $100,000."[87] Louisville Colonels manager Pinky Higgins was said to regard Neal as one of the best prospects in the American Association.

On October 11 the Red Sox hired Pinky Higgins to manage the team in 1955. It was thought to be the first year Yawkey had had to "buy up" a contract—Boudreau's—but it turned out the Red Sox held an option for Boudreau's second year and not an obligation. Yawkey made the final decision on the October 10; the next day Cronin made the call to inform Boudreau.[88]

Ted Williams later wrote that he'd been offered the position by Cronin and Yawkey during the 1954 season, but he had told them, "No, hell no, I don't want to manage. I'm a ballplayer. I can still hit in this league. If I stick around, it's going to be as a player. There's a big transition from player to manager. I'm not trained. I don't have the desire.... I don't even know how to make out the lineup card. I don't know enough about the subtle things." Cronin said he would get Ted all the help he needed. More time passed with the ball club going nowhere, and the owner asked Williams whom he'd like to see as manager. Ted's response: "Mr. Yawkey, you've got a guy in Louisville who's been fighting his way up from the minor leagues. He deserves it. I think Pinky Higgins deserves a chance to manage the club."[89]

Higgins had managed successfully in Louisville and won the "Lit-

tle World Series" (the champions of the American Association playing the champions of the International League), and other teams
were asking for permission to speak with him. At least one newspaper headlined a story "Red Sox Keep Pinky in Clan."[90] Later students
of the Red Sox have metaphorically linked Pinky to a different Klan.

In a descriptive phrase Red Sox fans would later find inapt, Higgins was said to be a "quiet, studious type."[91] He had, of course, hit
.292 in his fourteen years as a third baseman. He'd played for the
Red Sox in 1936 and 1937 and again in 1946. He was said to be a personal favorite of Yawkey's. He was seen as a "builder" and someone who would take better advantage of the younger players such
as Consolo and Agganis, who were underutilized under Boudreau.[92]

In November, Julia Yawkey was among the twenty-five young
ladies presented at the International Debutante Ball at the Plaza
Hotel in New York. The proceeds were devoted to "a national non-
sectarian movement to assist in rebuilding the spiritual basis of
the struggle against communism."[93] The New York Junior League
debuted forty-eight young ladies, including her, on November 24.
A photograph of her at the reception was published in the November 26 *Globe*. Her name appeared in several other stories over the
active debutante season. A December 20 event at the Waldorf-
Astoria appears to have wound up the year, save for Laura Rocke-
feller's debut a couple of days later.

At the winter meetings, Tom Yawkey was elected to baseball's
executive council for the fifth year in a row. Sox GM Joe Cronin
acknowledged that the Red Sox had been studying the San Francisco market, oddly saying, "Mr. Yawkey has never talked about
such a move, but if he turns around some day and asks me about
San Francisco, I've got the answer."[94]

As Yawkey had predicted when the Braves left town, Red Sox
attendance did fall off—dramatically. Sportswriter Red Smith blamed
it on a failure of marketing of baseball in Boston.[95] But the lower
figures didn't mean the Red Sox were likely to move—to San Francisco or to Montpelier, Vermont (population 8,559 in 1950). And yet
such rumors still surfaced from time to time. In July, even though
Joe Cronin had already felt compelled to deny that the team was
being sold to a wealthy Montpelier insurance broker, a reporter

called and perhaps woke up Tom Yawkey at the Ritz-Carlton. The response: "Who? What did you say his name was? I never heard of him."[96] On the next-to-last day of the year, Cronin said from his office at Fenway, "Yawkey continues to feel Boston is excellent baseball territory, and will go his utmost to give Red Sox fans the best possible baseball."[97]

Dave Egan, who had taken such vitriolic pleasure in lambasting Ted Williams, continued as a Yawkey booster. "Tom Yawkey is probably right when he says that some other man might have won more pennants with the Red Sox over the span of years, but Boston and New England prefer a Tom Yawkey, losing every year while winning friends, to a Del Webb and a Dan Topping, winning every year while losing friends. Yawkey can be accused only of kindness and generosity. He can be found guilty only of placing a higher importance on people than on pennants, and on decency than on dollars."[98] Boston writers generally, though (and that would include Egan), never seem to have gotten close to Yawkey, who indeed spent most of his time in New York or South Carolina.

Egan also did not believe Yawkey was racist. "Nor can I bring myself to believe that Tom Yawkey would discriminate against anybody for any reason that is based in bigotry. He wants to build a baseball empire, not turn back the tides. He has done too much in too many directions for too many years to be accused of littleness. He will use colored ballplayers in his own good time, exactly as the Yankees will, but he will not hire them simply because of the color of their skin, any more than he would repudiate them for the same reason. He will sign them because they will be players of major-league promise, and that's the way it should be."[99]

It was Egan who had beat the drums for integration louder than most ten years earlier. Now, however, eight big league seasons had passed since Jackie Robinson—at whom the Red Sox had had first shot—had broken in and become the 1947 Rookie of the Year, and Robinson had already been an All-Star six times. Ted Williams was the 1949 MVP in the American League, and Robinson was the 1949 MVP in the National League. Three other MVPs had been "colored ballplayers," and for five years in a row, from 1949 through 1953, a "Negro" ballplayer was named Rookie of the Year; one of them was in Boston even: Sam Jethroe of the Boston Braves in 1950. One could reasonably conclude—if nothing else—that there were obstacles in the Red Sox farm system to signing and developing players of color.

Would Ted Williams be back in 1955? It was a conversation that threaded through 1954, from his April 10, 1954, *Saturday Evening Post* article "This Is My Last Year in Baseball" right to the end of the year. Tom Yawkey, reached in Georgetown on the final day of the 1954 season, had said, "So, he said he was through, huh? Well, ever since he came back from Korea, I've let him make his own decisions on when and if he wanted to play. So we'll just let things rock along for a little while and maybe we'll be hearing differently."[100]

Maybe Williams meant it after all. In early January it was revealed that he had signed a couple of contracts to compete in fishing exhibitions in May and June.[101]

When the Red Sox equipment truck left for Sarasota in mid-February, Joe Cronin left for Georgetown to visit Yawkey. Spring training started without Williams in the fold, though he had not officially retired. The deadline for announcing retirement was May 12, the thirty-first day of the season.

What did Yawkey know, and when did he know it? We will almost certainly never know for sure. We do know that the divorce initiated by Doris Soule Williams against her husband Ted was resolved on May 9. The setting of alimony was deferred by the judge to the following day. The whole thing cost Ted $122,000.[102] Less than twenty-four hours later, it was announced that Ted would rejoin the Red Sox (and sign a new contract in the range of $80,000–$100,000, an asset that Ted did not have on the date of the divorce). Could it have seemed any more obvious that Williams was waiting for the final settlement before he suddenly decided to return to baseball?

What was the relationship between Williams and Yawkey truly like? We will never know that either. It was "much closer than a boss-player relationship," wrote the *Boston Daily Record*. "Ted respects and trusts Yawkey, probably more than he does any man living. He credits Yawkey with his transcendent success in baseball. He has always sought Yawkey's advice and counsel in his myriad problems. Yawkey has a mutual admiration for Williams, personally and professionally."[103]

As noted above, both Cronin and Yawkey had pitched Williams on becoming manager after 1954, but Ted turned them down, "saying he knew it would be a disaster. He'd get into one kerfuffle after another with the writers, and before long he'd be fired."[104] Ted later managed the Washington Senators for three years and—after the franchise moved to the Dallas area—the Texas Rangers for their first year, but he apparently always felt some disappointment that Yawkey had never offered the post to him after he retired in 1960. Perhaps it never would have worked, but it might have been nice to be asked. There may simply have been an awkwardness, Ted Williams having become such a huge star and Tom Yawkey not knowing quite how to handle him when the Kid's playing days were done.

Yawkey had been in Boston for the home opener on April 15, 1955, an 8-4 win over the Yankees. "Any game the Red Sox win leaves me in a happy frame of mind," he was quoted as saying. The *Globe* observed that Yawkey "rarely has much to say publicly about his club."[105] He had chatted with Governor Christian A. Herter of Massachusetts and Boston mayor John Hynes before the game. It was unusual for him to be in town so early in the season, but then he was away from Boston for more than two months, returning only after the first week of July.

Yawkey was enjoying the play of shortstop Billy Klaus, twenty-six, in his first full season in the Majors, and thirty-one-year-old pitcher Tom Hurd. He explained: "Maybe it is because Klaus and Hurd are small men. Maybe it is because they were sort of kicked around, kept in the bushes so long. Yet they have courage and enthusiasm. They never lost faith in themselves while being shunted around. Now they're showing what they can do as real big leaguers."[106]

When the Red Sox beat the Yankees on April 24 at Yankee Stadium (Willard Nixon throwing a two-hitter), the game was televised in the Boston area and may have drawn as well in the market as any prior World Series game. Growing TV audiences could make up, at least to some extent, for the loss of gate attractions such as Ted Williams.

It seems the Red Sox had access to some embryonic sabermetrics fifteen years before SABR was founded. Reference was made to a "postseason compendium by Roy Mumpton that contains more facts than the book of knowledge. Such facts as chances to drive in runs, advancing runners, etc. are in there."[107]

The team got off to a rough start, 9-17, and was in seventh place before the announcement of Williams's return. The now divorced Kid worked to get in shape and first played in a game on May 28. The Sox were in fifth place (17-24) the day before his return.

On June 1 and 2 Williams and Harry Agganis played in the same games, but June 2 was Agganis's last game. He took sick on the road. Mel Parnell remembered it: "That illness set in on him, and I remember we were in KC. The team doctor was with us, and they sent Harry to the hospital. The team doctor contacted Mr. Yawkey, and Mr. Yawkey said, 'Get him back to Boston ASAP—charter a plane if you have to but get him back.' I recall that our team doctor told us later: 'Mel, he'll never get out of the hospital.' And he didn't. He probably could have been our first baseman for years to come."[108] A number of players visited Harry in the hospital, including his roommate, Ted Lepcio.

Agganis died on June 27, only twenty-six years old. Over the years questions have been raised about the treatment he received. Clark Booth, writer and narrator of a DVD film on Harry Agganis, notes, "The baffling circumstances of his subsequent demise began to be muddled with the mystery of it all never to be fully fathomed. It begins with questions about the hospital itself."[109] Harry was treated, as all Red Sox players were for many years, at Sancta Maria Hospital in Cambridge, at the time located at 350 Memorial Drive. It was what Booth calls "a modest infirmary across the river." Journalist Ken Hartnett was among many over the years who have sought answers. Hartnett says in the *Agganis* film, "Why it was Sancta Maria Hospital when MGH was five minutes away is beyond me. You have the foremost centers for trauma care in the world five minutes away. Why wouldn't you send the patient there?"

Booth continues:

Even in its heyday, Sancta Maria had little stature and was mainly known only as the Red Sox' own private little infirmary. The team used it because it was convenient. Only a couple of miles from the ballpark across the Charles River, and simple—a place the team could control, where they would be totally deferred to. It was adequate for the players having ordinary bumps and bruises or the occasional sniffle, but why they kept Agganis there once his medical issues became complex remains difficult to accept, nor have the Red Sox officially ever tried to explain it. Nearly six decades later, the question still cries out to be answered.

On the staff at the hospital at the time was Dr. Panos Dukakis (father to Massachusetts governor Michael S. Dukakis). Clark Booth later interviewed Governor Dukakis, who responded as follows:

> I don't remember my father ever, ever being critical of another doctor. He was very respectful of other people in the profession. But after Harry died, I remember driving with him someplace and asking him, what was this thing, and how do you get a clot? Agganis was in fabulous physical condition, took care of himself and stuff. And he [Dr. Dukakis] had been at the staff meeting, at the Sancta Maria, apparently shortly after Agganis died. And he said to me, . . .—I can't quote you his exact language—but, in effect, "Mistakes were made." That's all he said. And when I tried to kind of probe him, he said, "That's all I'm going to tell you." But I've never forgotten that, obviously. . . . All I can tell you is what my sainted father said to me. And he didn't say much. But if Panos Dukakis said that, based on what he had heard, mistakes were made, mistakes were made.[110]

Booth says, "When hospitalized in mid-May, Agganis was under the care of 39-year-old Dr. Tim Lamphier." Lamphier was the team physician at the time, but Booth asserts he was at some odds with Joe Cronin and quotes Lamphier as saying—in the *Agganis* DVD but not necessarily in specific regard to Harry Agganis—"I was the doctor in name only. They did as they pleased. I used to kiddingly call them Dr. Cronin and Dr. Yawkey."

Thousands upon thousands attended Agganis's wake in Lynn, but Booth notes, "Owner Yawkey, who always abhorred any association with death, stayed away."[111] In October it was Yawkey's $25,000 gift that launched the Harry Agganis Foundation.

From the second game on June 5 through July 10, the Red Sox went 28-6. On July 13 Yawkey—seeing his team in fourth place at 48-36—said, "The way the team has been going so far, I wouldn't be surprised if it went all the way this season."[112] Hundreds of fans turned out at the airport to greet the team when it returned from a road trip on July 25. Jean Yawkey had made the trip with the team, as had Mrs. Eddie Collins. Tom was ill with a sinus infection, and he kept in touch with the team by listening on the radio and through both his wife and the team's traveling secretary. "Between Mrs. Y and Dowd, I was filled in on all the details that may have escaped me in the radio broadcast. . . . She was still raving about the game young George Susce pitched against the Athletics."[113]

On July 28 Bobby-Jo Williams, Ted's seven-year-old daughter, first saw him play in a Major League game. She was the guest of Jean Yawkey and watched from Mrs. Yawkey's box. Ted was 1-for-4 and the Sox won, 6-2. For the first time, there was public talk about whether Yawkey might offer Ted Williams an executive role of some sort after his playing days were over. Such a post was "likely," wrote Hy Hurwitz.[114]

The Sox had been 20-9 in June and 21-8 in July. Despite their poor start, they finished July with a record of 60-43. They were in fourth place—though only three games out of first. "I guess it just wasn't our year to win it," lamented the Sox owner in mid-September after seeing his team go 14-13 in August and play about .500 ball for the first half of September.[115] The AP voted Mike Higgins as manager of the year, edging out New York's Casey Stengel—the first time a fourth-place manager had ever been so honored.

On November 28 the Red Sox purchased the San Francisco Seals franchise of the PCL—and it became clear why Yawkey had wanted to learn more about baseball in the Bay Area. There was now a viable "ax hanging over the heads" of Red Sox fans. If attendance continued to fall below 1 million at Fenway, the lure of moving the team to the West Coast might become too attractive. Joe Cronin, a San Francisco native, took pains to say that the Red Sox had not purchased the Seals for that reason. He also said that Yawkey had had "two chances to move his club other places not long ago, but wants to stay in Boston."[116] However, the purchase meant that any other team that wanted to move into the San Francisco area would have to consult with the Red Sox. More broadly Yawkey once said it was a move "to protect baseball and protect the American League."[117]

At the winter meetings in Chicago in December, Tom Yawkey was elected VP of the American League. He took over the position previously held by Clark Griffith.

Also in December the Red Sox placed forty-year-old Ellis Kinder on waivers. He'd served eight years with the Sox, and some stories suggested the team might have been a bit heartless. Dave Egan wrote in sarcastic response, "When Yawkey's heart was of melted butter and he himself was a hero-worshipper of the famous men who played for him, the cry of complacency went up and it was said that the Red Sox team was composed of petted and pampered country-clubbers. Now that he has steeled himself to sanction the unpleasant moves that are necessary if a pennant is to be won, I somehow get the impression that he and Cronin are unfeeling and ungrateful brutes, casting a bare-footed Kinder into the blizzard that howls outside the door."[118]

15

Doldrums Descend, the Latter 1950s

EARLY IN 1956, not only did the Boston baseball writers honor Tom Yawkey, but also in February the New York chapter of the Baseball Writers' Association of America (BBWAA) presented him with its Slocum Award "for long and meritorious service to baseball." Prior winners included Branch Rickey, Walter Johnson, and Kenesaw Mountain Landis. There were three different dinners within a five-day period—the first was the February 1 Junior Good Will Dinner in Boston organized by the Massachusetts Committee of Catholics, Protestants, and Jews. There were "tremendous cheers" for Yawkey from the 1,400 at the New York dinner.[1]

Ed Rumill offered a nice appreciation of Yawkey, noting that it would be shortsighted to suggest that all he had to show for twenty years and $5 million invested in the Red Sox was one pennant in 1946. In baseball, Rumill wrote, you meet people who come from varied backgrounds, and some are among the finest you would ever meet. "Yawkey has never been one to invade the privacy of the clubhouse, but many of the boys who signed his contracts and played for him have been his good friends, and after the ball season he has often joined them on hunting and fishing trips into the northwest or deep south. You can be sure Yawkey treasures these friendships, as much as he would treasure pennants or World Series victories. Perhaps he treasures them more."[2]

"He may be the No. 1 fan in all baseball history," wrote Harold Kaese. "Whatever it takes to be a champion fan, Yawkey has it." Kaese cited Yawkey's loyalty, endurance, optimism, generosity, and love of the game. And he recounted how Yawkey would call Fenway

Park when he was out of town and either have someone give him a personal play-by-play or have the phone placed next to the radio so he could listen to Curt Gowdy's broadcast. Yawkey's secretary, Barbara A. Tyler (he called her "BAT"), said he enjoyed having fun in the office, but "of course he's more fun when we win than when we lose." And he would still suit up and take batting practice at the ballpark. Kaese said that he could occasionally hit the left-field wall "using lively balls from the Texas League."[3]

In the 1960s Carl Yastrzemski wrote that Yawkey liked to play pepper, to work on his infield practice. "Mr. Yawkey's rules were that he had to catch twenty in a row. What the heck, it was his bat, his ball, his glove, his park. His rules. Fitzie [clubbie Don Fitzpatrick] would hit him eighteen, and he could field them flawlessly, but if he dropped the nineteenth—watch out. He'd throw his glove on the ground and shout, 'Goddam it!' Fitz would have to start all over again."[4] At least in those later years, Yaz never saw him hit the wall, but Yawkey would have Vince Orlando move the batting cage to the outfield and throw to him, and he would have "a hell of a time enjoying it when he hit one into the stands."[5]

PR assistant Donna Mountain recalled, "There were times I'd have my lunch in the stands. What a nice place to be sitting in the middle of the city, with all this grass, and he'd be out there playing pepper with Carl Yastrzemski."[6] Batboy Paul Needham (1959–60) remembers the following:

> He liked to play pepper behind home plate, and then after that, he liked to hit. We'd shag the balls in the outfield. And he made sure that everyone who shagged the balls got a chance to hit from home plate—even the clubhouse guys. He had his own batting practice pitcher, if you will. John Pohlmeyer. He was sort of a right-hand man, like an assistant to Tom.
>
> I don't think there were special balls. He didn't hit with power, but I remember him getting his hits. He'd hit sort of the base of the wall. He'd hit flairs to the outfield, mostly to the left side, but he sprayed the ball a little.
>
> He liked ginger ale, so we made sure there was ginger ale in the cooler. I don't remember him having his own locker. We would come

in early, to make sure that we were there for his workouts when the team was on the road. It was on the early side.[7]

Jim Lonborg first joined the team in 1965; he recalls: "I'd come into the ballpark early sometimes and find Mr. Yawkey in his sweatpants and sweatshirt. He might have just been coming off the field playing pepper or screen ball. We used to hit baseballs up on the screen behind home plate, and then the ball would come zooming down the screen and bounce back on all kinds of different angles, and then you'd have to try and hit it back up on the screen again. He would play that game all the time with the batboys and the clubhouse people."[8]

Pohlmeyer was Yawkey's "chauffeur, bartender, jack-of-all-trades," wrote Curt Gowdy. "What Yawkey liked about him was that he kept his mouth shut. 'I can talk about the most intimate details of my life in front of Pohlmeyer,' Yawkey would say. 'And nobody will ever know about it.'"[9] That was the sort of loyalty and discretion Yawkey prized.

Barbara Tyler was sometimes asked to send telegraphic accounts of the game to Yawkey "including how a player looked when he was relieved, because the Red Sox owner wasn't satisfied with newspaper accounts."[10] Tyler even got drafted to play ball more than once. As a young girl, her father gave her a bat and glove, and she played in school. In 1958 Jenny Nourse of the *Boston Globe* recounted the following about Tyler:

> Years ago, she would don her playing togs and work out with [Yawkey] in the Park. Oftentimes, when the team was on the road, an impromptu game would take place between the Clubhouse Boys and the Office Group. One day, [when] the Clubhouse (Yawkey's group) was short a player, Barbara was recruited to complete the roster.
>
> "I was playing second [says Barbara]. Yawkey pitched. Vince Orlando was covering first with a man on. The next batter up connected. Vince caught the ball, threw to me for a 3-4-3 double play. I tagged second, all set to throw to first, when I was plowed into and knocked flat on my sit-down area! Still clutching the ball, I sat there momentarily stunned.

"In his raucous voice, Yawkey yelled, 'Hey, are you all right?' When I dazedly nodded an assent (I might add not one gentleman came to my rescue), he commanded, 'For crying out loud, then get up and throw the ball!'

"That ended my baseball career. I put myself on the voluntarily retired list."[11]

PR secretary Mary Jane Ryan told two anecdotes that showed some of Yawkey's simple sense of humor:

There was one day that we came back from lunch; there was a sale on at Lechmere [a department store]. I always got back in an hour. That's the way it was. I didn't go out for two-hour lunches. Ruth [a co-worker] and I were hurrying back, running practically, and we bumped into Mr. Yawkey. He said, "What are you girls doing?" We were all out of breath, and we said, "Mr. Yawkey, we just came . . . we just came . . . we had to buy some slow cookers." A crockpot, when they first came out. He said, "Slow cookers? What you need are fast cookers!" We all thought he was a peachy guy, just a wonderful man, and we loved him.

He kind of had nicknames for everybody. My boss was Bill Crowley. Mr. Yawkey would call me up first thing in the morning: "Is Crawl there?" I'd be nervous, and I'd say, "No, Mr. Yawkey. He isn't here right now. I think he had to do an errand on his way in." He'd say, "Yeah—stop and play nine?" That was him. He wasn't mad. He got a big kick out of it.[12]

Yawkey himself had never been any more interested in gourmet meals than he had been in fine tailoring. "Fenway was more than an office for him," wrote Curt Gowdy. "It was his social club, his playground, his sanctum. He'd arrive there around ten in the morning and talk with Joe Cronin, his general manager. Then he'd roam around the offices, make calls to the other owners, and have lunch. Nothing fancy, just good old American food. T. A. wasn't much of a gourmet."[13]

An amusing note emerged years later when Peter Gelzinis contributed a memory of Tom Yawkey to the *Herald*: "Few people actually laid eyes on him in the light of day. I did, because I once worked in the bowels of Fenway, and saw the wrinkled face of a multimillionaire. I hid in the tunnel one morning, between the first base boxes, and watched Mr. Yawkey tap the ball back to Dave More-head. It was like peeking at Bela Lugosi. You see, there was a rule among us lowly employees at Harry M. Stevens Concessions. We were never . . . *ever* to stare at Mr. Yawkey! Something about going blind, I think."[14]

Rico Picardi of Harry M. Stevens later said, "Mr. Yawkey said if it wasn't for the Stevens family, there would be a lot of franchises in baseball today that wouldn't be there. They didn't have the income and the Stevens company used to just give them a loan to make the payroll at the end of the year, to pay off the players. Otherwise, they wouldn't have no franchise. They did that with a lot of them. Mr. Yawkey used to say that."[15]

Pinky Higgins was given a three-year contract as Red Sox man-ager, through 1958. Ted Williams signed early, on February 3, as he arrived in Boston for a nine-day engagement at the annual Sports-men's Show at Mechanics Hall. Also primed for his rookie year in 1956 was Don Buddin—the seventh different shortstop the Red Sox had started on consecutive Opening Days.

In the farm system Louisville was stocked with bonus babies. "The big prices [Yawkey] used to pay for established stars, he has been paying for rookies. The result is that the Red Sox have spent more on bonuses than any other team, but they also have the most good rookies. The team that gives the most bonuses should come out on top simply as a matter of percentage. The Red Sox have the odds going for them. What Yawkey wants, Yawkey gets. That's the way he is." So said Cincinnati Reds manager Birdie Tebbetts.[16] Yawkey, wrote Kaese, "used his bankroll to steamroller the oppo-sition." The only time he was ever outbid was when he yielded to Bob Carpenter of the Phillies in the bidding for Curt Simmons.[17]

For fourteen years Yawkey had not visited spring training.[18] He was present for Opening Day in Boston. "I think it is going to be a close fight."[19]

Rocky Marciano brought his father along when he watched the June 14 ballgame from Tom Yawkey's box. Later in June, Ted Wil-liams was named general chairman of the Jimmy Fund. He said the record he hoped to break in 1956 was the fund-raising total from the prior year.

In a thrilling game at Fenway on July 14 Marvelous Mel Parnell threw a 4-0 no-hitter against the White Sox. Yawkey was "grinning ear to ear" according to the AP.[20] The *Chicago Tribune* wrote that he "busted into the clubhouse and handed the veteran southpaw a $500 check. 'You'll have to sign a new contract with a $500 raise to make it legal,' said Yawkey."[21] Parnell was a Red Sox lifer, in the tenth and final year of his tenure with the team. It was the first no-hitter at Fenway since Howard Ehmke's in 1923. More than forty years later, Parnell remembered the moment with Tom Yawkey: "A nice and generous man. Treated us like family but didn't spoil us like the press alleged. That was untrue. When I pitched my no-hitter, when I got to the clubhouse, he was the first man to greet me, and he had a new contract and a pen in his hand. He said, 'Sign this!' I said, 'Mr. Yawkey, you pay me to do this kind of thing.' He said, 'Sign this already.' How many owners would do that? Not many."[22]

He would help out with a loan now and again too. Infielder John Kennedy recalled, years later, "He was a very generous man. As a matter of fact, I even took out a loan through [the Red Sox] to buy a house. Joe Cummiskey was the treasurer; I went through him. I'm sure it had to be OK'd by Mr. Yawkey. There was no problem. Within days, they said OK. He was nice that way. He was just a nice guy."[23]

Bob Montgomery had a similar experience:

After '75, when we were involved in the World Series, I'd been looking for a house to buy in Florida, and I'd gone there and found a house. You don't get your World Series check until sometime around the first week of December. I called Dick O'Connell, who was then the general manager, and asked him if I could get a $10,000 advance. I thought that was about what we were going to get in our World Series check. He didn't ask me what I wanted it for. He didn't ask me when I was going to pay it back. He says, "Where do you want me to send it?" He would have to have done that knowing that Mr. Yawkey would have approved that with no problem.

To carry this story a little bit farther, they did not charge me one nickel of interest. [O'Connell] did not ask me for the money back when the World Series checks were distributed. They simply took it out of my check on a per paycheck basis through the next summer. Not one dime of interest. Nothing. Terrific. And I'm sure they would have done that for any player.[24]

Dick Johnson, who has heard a lot as the curator of the Sports Museum of New England since its founding in 1977, marvels, "I never heard anyone say a bad word about him personally. And there are not many people in Boston sports you can say that about."[25]

"Red Sox Eager to Sign Negro Players" read a *Globe* headline on July 15, 1956. *Globe* writer Bob Holbrook noted that the team was one of only three in the Majors that didn't have a black player on its roster. "Pigment of the skin means nothing to us," asserted Cronin, but he added, "We will not be pressured into signing a player merely because he is a Negro." The idea that Yawkey discriminated against black players because he was from South Carolina was a "canard": "Yawkey is not a Southerner unless you consider Detroit south."[26] Stody Ward of Cambridge led a program organized by the *Boston Guardian* to bring about better racial relations and "also was [the] first [man from the African American community] to meet, and even talk with, [the] not easily reachable Tom Yawkey."[27]

Though perhaps unappreciated at the time is the fact that the area around Georgetown was rather heavily African American. Because of the labor-intensive rice production there prior to the Civil War, the area had "the highest slave ratio anywhere in the United States"; the 1860 census showed Georgetown's population as 85 percent black and 15 percent white. Reflecting the franchise awarded the freed people, before Reconstruction took hold, it is notable that the first African American to serve in the U. S. Congress was Joseph Hayne Rainey, a Georgetown native. He served in the House of Representatives from 1870 to 1878.[28]

Yawkey did have two black players on Minor League contracts by this time: Pumpsie Green and Earl Wilson. Holbrook reported that Red Sox scouts "have been ordered to get the best colored talent available. To date, they have failed to carry out orders."[29] The word had gotten around that the Red Sox had failed to sign either Jackie Robinson or Sam Jethroe back in 1945. Cronin's explanation in 1956: "We didn't have a farm team to send him to. We couldn't send him to Louisville."[30] However, the Sox did have a farm club in Scranton in 1945, and by 1946, though still heavily represented by southern farm teams, they did have a couple of other options—the Lynn Red Sox in Class B and Oneonta in Class C. Had the Red Sox had more foresight or cared enough, they could have established a presence in other cities; they had, after all, as recently as 1938 had their top Minor League team in Minneapolis.

In the summer of 1955 Red Sox scout Ted McGrew had conducted a special tryout in Georgia for Negro players, and five hundred had come to the tryout. McGrew felt that only one was a big league prospect, but "he wanted more money than the Red Sox felt he would be worth and he signed with another club."[31] For a team that had been so aggressive over the years going after bonus babies, it is a little difficult to believe that a similar sum couldn't be raised to help bring the Red Sox into alignment with most of the rest of baseball in regard to desegregation.

Joe Cronin was honored with induction into the National Baseball Hall of Fame on July 23, 1956. The Yawkeys and a party of thirty-two traveled in two special Pullman cars to Utica and then by bus to Cooperstown to represent the Red Sox. As the return bus brought the party back to Utica, those on board—including the driver—sang "When Irish Eyes Are Smiling" as a musical salute to Cronin and then sang "Carolina in the Morning" with Tom Yawkey in mind.[32]

Ted Williams went on a spitting jag over three weeks in the summer, spitting toward the press box after hitting his four hundredth homer on July 17 and repeating the gesture a couple of days later when Commissioner Frick was at the game in Yawkey's box with the Red Sox owner. One informant told the *Boston Record*, "Mr. Yawkey was really mad about it." But he hadn't wanted to say anything at first because he hadn't wanted to detract from Cronin's induction.[33]

Williams wasn't contrite. He told the sportswriters, "That was meant just as much for the fans as for you. Besides when I do that for the press box it isn't meant for everybody up there but just for a few guys."[34]

It happened a third time on August 7 after Williams was walked with the bases loaded in the eleventh inning, the Sox winning a

1–0 game against the Yankees. Yawkey was in his suite at the Hotel Pierre in New York and heard Mel Allen describe the incident on radio. What should have been a happy moment was soured; Williams was upset at himself and at the fans for booing him because he'd dropped a Mickey Mantle fly ball in the top of the eleventh.

Yawkey decided it was finally time to put his foot down and announced that Williams would be fined $5,000. He said he'd warned Ted once before and that he was the one who initiated the discipline. "Why the man does these things is something I can't figure out. I can't. I can't. I can't. O, so many times I've tried to figure it all out, but I can't," he said, continuing, "I can't put myself in his spot out on that field. If I could, I might have the answer. . . . It's too bad, I know that."[35] Kaese suggested that it was obvious Williams was unable to control himself and that he should quit before he did something he would regret even more.[36] Williams apologized, somewhat, saying he was "especially sorry about the $5,000 it was going to cost me" and that he was still angry, but he admitted he'd probably do it again.[37] Some, such as the *Boston Post*'s Gerry Hern, wrote with absurd hyperbole that "[Yawkey's fining of Williams] is the most notable move ever made by Tom Yawkey during his ownership of the Boston franchise."[38]

The next night, in front of a family night crowd, Ted hit another home run, and this time demonstrably—and good humoredly—he clasped his hand firmly over his mouth as he headed into the dugout. The fans had cheered him throughout the game. Some even took up a collection to pay the fine, taking in a few hundred dollars.

It was said the Sox got a million dollars' worth of publicity out of the situation, but Ed Rumill wrote that Yawkey was so straightforward a man that it never would have occurred to him to assess a fine for any reason other than that he thought it was the right thing to do. Still Rumill wondered if Yawkey might restore the money to Ted's account after the season was over.[39] Indeed, Ted wrote later, Yawkey had done just that: "He kept me hanging for a while, then he said, 'Aw, Ted, we don't want your money.'"[40]

It was around this very time—on August 14—that Cleveland Indians slugger Rocky Colavito credited Williams with helping him, an opposing batter. When the Indians visited Fenway, Colavito said,

"[Ted] came out and stood with me by the backstop for about half an hour. . . . He kept firing things at me that he thought would be helpful. . . . Imagine him giving me all that time and taking such an interest in me. I doubt if there is any other player in baseball who would have done that."[41]

Ted helped Al Kaline. He helped Harvey Kuenn. Moose Skowron said, "He's helped every young kid who ever went to him. He has the respect of all the players. I learned more about hitting by talking to Ted for ten minutes than I'd learned in my entire career."[42]

Yawkey had complained to Ted about his tutoring, and Ted purportedly told him, "Come on, T. A., the more hitters we have in this game, the better it is for the game. Listen, when you're coming towards the park and you're two blocks away, and you hear a tremendous cheer, that isn't because someone had thrown a strike. That's became someone has hit the ball."[43] Ted's logic won the day with an owner who cared deeply about the game as an institution.

Yawkey's last day in Boston was September 8. The Red Sox spent almost the whole season in either third or fourth place. They finished in fourth, with the identical 84-70 record they had had in 1955. They were thirteen games behind the Yankees. There had been a number of disappointments. Bob Porterfield's 3-13 season (5.14 ERA) was high among them; he'd come to Boston from Washington in a November 1955 trade, along with Mickey Vernon. Though Vernon hit well and the Red Sox hadn't given up much in the trade, Porterfield had led the league in wins in 1953 and the Sox had hoped for more than they got.

In October it was announced that Bucky Harris, who had managed the Red Sox in 1934, was being brought back in a special assignments position. Predictably rumors followed—one of which was that Harris and Cronin were going to go to San Francisco and pave the way for the team to relocate and that they would take Higgins with them. "Cronin and Higgins going to San Francisco? That's a harebrained thing if I ever heard one," Yawkey had said to Sam Cohen of the *Boston Record* a couple of weeks earlier.[44]

Rumors swirled all over the place: Cronin had been named to head a group that was buying out Yawkey; Cronin was going to be part of the move of the Washington club to the West Coast; Will

Harridge was retiring, and Cronin was going to become AL president.[45] Regarding the recurring rumor that the Red Sox were moving to San Francisco, Yawkey expressed some frustration. "How many times do I have to deny this story? What am I supposed to do? Write an open letter to the public? So long as the Red Sox are under my ownership, they will never move to San Francisco."[46]

The Red Sox installed a new infield after hosting Boston College football for the last time in the fall of 1956. (From that point on, the BC Eagles played their games at Alumni Field.) Tom Yawkey had decided he wanted Fenway Park to be used exclusively by the Red Sox. (John Gillooly of the *Boston Record* wrote about Yawkey's earlier decision to terminate the boxing bouts that Fenway used to host "because the fight mob ground too many burning cigar stubs into the precious ground of his green acre").[47]

And Yawkey was reelected AL VP.

After four years in fourth place, the 1957 Red Sox bumped up to third—but did so with two fewer wins. Boston still finished 16 games behind the Yankees. The outstanding performance of the year came from Ted Williams, with perhaps the most impressive season of his career. He drove in only 87 runs, playing in 132 games, while Jackie Jensen and Frank Malzone tied with 103 RBIs each. Malzone came in second for Rookie of the Year and won the very first Gold Glove ever awarded for his defense at third base. He was an All-Star for the first of six seasons he was so recognized.

Williams hit for a .388 average. If he had had seven more hits, he would have hit .400 again. He turned thirty-nine in August. He was far from fleet afoot and legged out very few infield hits. He homered 38 times, tied for second-most in his career. He earned his fifth batting championship, and he achieved a .526 on-base percentage with a 1.257 on-base plus slugging average (OPS). He finished second to Mickey Mantle in the MVP voting, 233–209. There were once again two writers who listed Williams as only ninth or tenth on their ballots. Yawkey called the unknown voters "incompetent and unqualified to vote."[48]

Jackie Robinson had completed his career in 1956. He was in Boston on February 2, 1957, to kick off a local fund-raising campaign for the NAACP, and he was a breakfast guest of Mayor John B. Hynes. At a postbreakfast press conference, Robinson said, "I can't understand why 13 major-league clubs have Negro players and the other three clubs can't come up with any. I don't know if it's their scouting systems or what. As for Mr. Yawkey of the Red Sox, I don't know him, and I can't say that he is personally against having Negro players on his team." That the Sox had a couple of prospects in the system didn't mollify Robinson much. "That doesn't mean a thing; they don't have any on the Red Sox roster."[49]

Yawkey's first direct comment on the subject came in 1958. "My Red Sox scouts don't have to consider the color line so far as I'm concerned. They never had any instructions of that sort. I've told them I want the best men they can get for every position. We have Negroes on our farm teams. They're being given their opportunities. I'm just as eager as anybody to see if they can make the big team."[50] He went on to name Pumpsie Green, Zeke King, and Earl Wilson.

In spring training the Red Sox offered $1 million to the Cleveland Indians for pitcher Herb Score. Rather than the typical denial, Cronin was quoted as saying, "I finally said to Greenberg, 'I am offering you $1 million for Herb Score,' and I said, 'Take that to your board of directors.'"[51]

The year had reportedly started with several holdouts—Sammy White, Jimmy Piersall, Billy Klaus, and Gene Stephens. Bill Cunningham of the *Boston Herald* said they were the first holdouts in all Yawkey's years.[52]

The Variety Club of New England (one of the leading groups that raised funds for the Jimmy Fund) planned to honor Yawkey in Boston on April 14, and Ted Williams—who hardly ever accepted an invitation to any such event—even agreed to wear a necktie to help honor his boss. Governor Foster Furcolo proclaimed "Thomas Yawkey Day."

In the meantime, as he passed through New Orleans, Ted Williams encountered a reporter and unloaded to him about his recall to the Marines in 1952. "I got a raw deal from the Marines and I said before I've got no use for them." He complained that he'd been used for publicity and blamed it on "phony politicians"—spitting on the ground as he griped.[53] Predictably a national furor erupted, an embarrassment for all concerned. Williams apologized for being misconstrued and said that his four years in the Marine Corps were "the proudest of my life."[54] Williams did attend the April 14 dinner, and with his usual humor praised Boston Mayor Hynes as "one of the few politicians I do like."[55]

Yawkey truly knew his baseball—in detail—and sportswriter Bob Holbrook added, "Yawkey can tell you what every team in the league has for personnel, how its key men are hitting, and how pitchers are pitching."[56] Veteran sports editor L. H. Gregory of Portland's *Oregonian* wrote that "Yawkey is the only club owner in the league who can qualify as a baseball man and a sportsman. The other seven clubs are controlled by individuals who have little knowledge of baseball."[57]

A few years later, J. G. Taylor Spink of *The Sporting News* wrote a lengthy piece starting with the sentence, "It wouldn't be stretching a point to call Tom Yawkey, the American League's elder statesman, the last of the great sportsmen."[58] From becoming an owner at age thirty, Yawkey had become the elder statesman of the league.

Sportsman or otherwise, a minor controversy erupted in May. On May 23, an off day at the end of an eleven-game home stand, Ted Williams took his 20-gauge shotgun and "sat in a chair near the Boston bullpen . . . and sharpened his hitting eye by shooting at every pigeon which cruised within range."[59] Ted may have killed thirty or forty pigeons. It was said the ball club "had a permit to protect the park and assigned the job to Williams," but Herman Dean, the chief prosecuting officer of the Massachusetts Society for the Prevention of Cruelty to Animals, said he could find no record of such a permit. Dean said he would conduct a full investigation. In his autobiography, Williams wrote that the groundskeeper used to "flock shoot" the pigeons more or less routinely. "Mr. Yawkey came out, too, and he's an excellent shot. Together, we knocked off 70 or 80 pigeons. We had a hell of a time. Bang, boom, bang." The next day in Washington, a writer told Ted that the Humane Society had made a complaint against him and him alone. "He didn't say anything about *Mr. Yawkey* shooting pigeons, old Teddy Ballgame is the guy they're after."[60]

July was a momentous month. On July 8 it was announced that

Julia Yawkey would marry Frederick Gaston III in the autumn. He had attended Yale and worked in the insurance field. On July 15 Tom Yawkey was named to chair the board of trustees of the Jimmy Fund. On July 18 the New York Giants announced they would be moving to San Francisco for the 1958 season—a move that could only occur with Yawkey's permission, given his ownership of the Seals and the territorial rights that came with ownership. On July 22 Joe McCarthy and Sam Crawford were inducted into the Hall of Fame. And on July 26 fire destroyed the "winter plantation home" of the Yawkeys near Georgetown, South Carolina.

Given that their New York and Boston residences were hotel suites, the home on South Island was the only true home the Yawkeys had. They divided their time "about equally" among the three locales.[61] Destroyed in the fire was all that Tom had collected since 1915—original paintings, autographed books, sports memorabilia, and other mementos that he said brought back fond memories every time he returned home. What he may have felt inside, of course we can never know. He was philosophical about the loss in his public statement. Paintings were lost that he could never again see, but, he said, "At least I read the books." A little more seriously, he added, "It could have been a lot worse. Nobody was hurt and I still have the memories."[62]

The house itself had been built in 1915 by Tom Yawkey's parents. There had been thirteen rooms and a one-story bungalow with a 25-by-35-foot living-dining area. During my 2012 visit to the property, several long-term residents of the area agreed in describing it as a "rambling beach house." Yawkey himself said, "It was a substantial frame residence with four master chambers. It had a 35-by-55-foot living room, library, servants' quarters, and all modern conveniences. But I won't rebuild it as a frame house. We'll use modern fireproof materials. What we'll miss most is a magnificent collection of books and trophies gathered through the years. At least I'll retain memories of my pleasant years down there."[63]

The fire was an accident, inadvertently ignited by one of the workmen. "No one was living in the home at the time of the fire," reported the *Georgetown Times,* which dubbed the structure a "plantation home."[64] Phil Wilkinson explained:

They were doing the floors. It was hard pine—the heart of the pine that has a lot of resin in it. Beautiful floors. Apparently, a spark was set into the bag of sawdust from a nail on the floor or something. The sander was put away after [the workers] were finished, unknown to the operator of the sander that there might have been a smoldering spark in there. The bag was put away in a closet until the next day. It slowly ignited in the middle part of the night, and that set the whole house on fire, and it just burned to the ground during the night. There wasn't any means of doing anything about a fire like that. This was on an island, with a ferry, and no firefighting equipment on the island except water hoses and things like that. It was hard to actually blame anybody. The people on the island were all in bed. It was an outside contractor. They did their best to try and save some stuff, running into the house while it was still on fire. [Yawkey] was just floored by it. It completely burned down.[65]

In a later interview, Wilkinson said, "The burning of that house was a very severe blow to him. He had a lot of memorabilia . . . that represented the first fish he ever caught in his life and the first shotgun anybody gave him, that sort of thing, all over the house. They all burned up. He had a pretty good gun collection. It burned up."[66]

The isolation and inaccessibility of the Yawkey property was no guarantee that forces of nature would not adversely affect it either. In 1954, when Hurricane Hazel struck the Carolinas with full force, Ted Williams wrote to Jean Yawkey. "He wanted to know if we had been hit hard and had much damage from the hurricane."[67]

In September there was a report that Yawkey had returned to Georgetown "to see how construction is progressing on his South Carolina place. The builders are replacing the mansion recently destroyed by fire."[68] The newspaper misunderstood. As it happens, the "mansion" never was replaced.

In fact, many people would find it strange—eccentric, if nothing else—that Tom and Jean Yawkey lived ever after in a pair of mobile homes built in Elkhart, Indiana, each with their own trailer. "They started looking at building something back in the same place," recalls Wilkinson. "There was another very nice house there that they had built for the manager. [It was a] two-story house, and it had four bedrooms and three baths upstairs. It was built by the first Mrs. Yawkey. She was the one that supervised its construction and design. It was built for Jim Gibson, who was the manager then. He had a large family. Five children, I think."[69] (It had been designed by architect William H. Bottomley of New York City.)

The current (in 2016) resident of the house built for Gibson is Jamie Dozier, the resident biologist for the Tom Yawkey Wildlife Center. Dozier says, "[Yawkey] built this house for Elise Yawkey, his first wife. The house was built in 1932. The story . . . [is] that after they divorced and Jean Yawkey came down, she refused to live in it because she said it was the first wife's house, and they moved into the lodge. And then it became the manager's residence."[70]

After the fire, Wilkinson adds,

Ms. Yawkey thought about fixing up [the manager's house] and living there, and he [Tom] said, "No, that was built for the manager, and that's where it's going to stay." They started looking at plans—this is him telling me about it over time. He wanted something very much like what had been there, a rustic, rambling beach house with porches all around and that sort of thing. Ms. Yawkey had something more elaborate in mind, like something you might find in the nicest part of Boston. She said they just never could compromise to a point where either one of them was happy, so they said, "Well, hell, let's just stay in these trailers then." They had these trailers they were staying in while they were trying to work out building a new house. They had two trailers there, so they stayed in those.[71]

For nearly twenty years, until Tom Yawkey's death, they stayed in the trailers.

Eddie Kasko, who became the Red Sox manager in 1970, hadn't heard about the mobile homes, but he wasn't surprised. "Knowing him [Yawkey], it didn't take much. He could live in a tent, I think, and be happy."[72] Judge Alex Sanders of South Carolina put it succinctly: "Yes! He lived in a house trailer! While his caretaker lived in a mansion. The house trailer's still there."[73]

Sanders noted the exception to many of the other exceptionally wealthy Northerners who had come south:

They had accumulated wealth just untold. But they were not able to acquire one thing, and that was respectability. They were respectable in this country, but they were not recognized among the nobility of Europe because they were essentially common people who had scored big wealth during the last half, particularly, of the nineteenth century.

So . . . they came to places like South Carolina—and I think probably more came to South Carolina than to the other Southern states—and they acquired the old [rice] plantations which were in ruins after the Civil War and established, to the extent that they could, baronies like the great tracts of land owned by European royalty, and attempted to duplicate that life style as best they could. Because that's what they didn't have. They weren't landed gentry, so to speak. They acquired these old plantations. They then constructed mansions on the plantations which were entirely fictitious. No houses like these houses ever existed on Southern plantations. Southern plantations had a farm house; they didn't have a house like in *Gone with the Wind*. As a matter of fact, the house in *Gone with the Wind* was entirely fictitious. There was never a plantation like *that*, with Grecian columns and so forth—although you can see those kind of houses *now*, on plantations in South Carolina, but they basically are reproductions of something that never existed.[74]

Neither Yawkey aspired to that form of ostentation.

Tom Yawkey used to rise exceptionally early, said Jamie Dozier:

> He liked to get up about four or four thirty in the morning. She [Jean Yawkey] didn't like to get up quite that early. He'd meet with his managers. They'd show up about five or five thirty, and they'd come in and talk about the day and what was going to go on. Yeah, they had their separate trailers. Sometimes I think that might be the key to being married that long. Sometimes my wife says, "We need separate trailers." He lived in a suite up in Boston, but he lived in a trailer down here.[75]

Did the separate trailers indicate any degree of estrangement between the Yawkeys? No one contacted seems to have thought so. Jim Sargent, who drove Jean Yawkey around the area and would pick up Tom Yawkey when he came back to town, simply said, "The two of them? Yeah, they seemed happy to me. As much as I could tell. . . . You don't know what would happen when they left. When the house burned down, they did most of the cooking [in one of the trailers]. Then he goes over to what we call the game room; that's where he would handle all the business transactions. . . . It seemed just like [how] me and my wife would talk. Riding with them in the car, they seemed pretty joyful, happy people to me, yeah."[76]

A final note: The tale of the Yawkey's "mobile chateaux" is indeed unusual. Of course, if they wanted to spend a little time in more comfortable surroundings, there was always Mt. Pleasant Plantation to which they could repair. Tom Yawkey had helped his attorney, Frederick DeFoe, buy the land for that (just under three thousand acres, with three miles of frontage on the Black River) back in 1934. (The main residence was designed by William L. Bottomley.) Quail hunting was good there, but a dairy and beef cattle operation had expanded on the grounds. The Yawkeys bought it from the DeFoe estate in 1960 and owned it until after Tom Yawkey's death; it was sold in 1986. It was a much more elegant place than any the Yawkeys had on South Island, inside and out, with manicured grounds. But Tom Yawkey truly loved living on South Island.

There seem to be a few instances of fire throughout the Yawkey years. (One could note a bit of coincidence, given that Elise Sparrow had been the assistant fire chief's daughter in Birmingham.) There were the fires at Fenway Park during the 1934 reconstruction. And there was the destructive fire on South Island. About a year and a half after Jean Yawkey died in 1992, a fire destroyed the former Sunset Lodge brothel in Georgetown. There was a Tom Yawkey connection there too. (See chapter 24 below.)

A "feel good" story emerged in 1957. A youngster of thirteen from New Brunswick, Canada, named Ian Joyce ran away from home, hoping to see a big league ball game, and he made it all the way to Fenway Park, dragging a little suitcase along. Ian said, "I sat on the steps at 24 Jersey Street for a rest. Tom Yawkey and Joe Cronin came along, and I told them I came to see the Sox." Unfortunately the team was on a road trip to Chicago, so Ian was out of luck. But he had caught the eye of the two Red Sox executives.

That is when they took me inside and showed me around. [Tom Yawkey] asked me if I wanted him to autograph a ball, and I didn't want it autographed; I just wanted the ball to play with. I went merrily on my way downtown. At night I crawled into some bushes in the Common, and the police found me—and [they took me] off to the station. I told them my story that I was a runaway, and one of the policemen called a friend at the *Globe*, and a friend of my mother who lived in Boston got wind of it and put me on a plane and sent me home. I got a nice letter from Tom Yawkey's secretary a short time later that invited me back, but [it said] to bring my mother with me the next time.[77]

Ian had enjoyed a private tour of the ballpark and reportedly been treated to lunch. The following year, he returned with his mother during a Red Sox home stand. His story was memorialized in the *Boston Globe* along with a photo showing him with Jimmy Piersall.[78] He had an opportunity to visit the Red Sox clubhouse.

Joyce reports that he was supplied with tickets on request well into his twenties, and as late as 1975 he was provided tickets to the first two games of that year's World Series. It wasn't so much a personal connection with the Red Sox owner; he explained, "I was always looked after, probably more by his secretary [Barbara Tyler] than him, as she was my contact for many years, [as was] her replacement [Mary Trank] after her retirement."[79] (Trank also helped out in another way, helping filter the fan mail sent to Ted Williams. "He [Yawkey] used to give me all the girls' letters to read," she said. "I don't know if I was supposed to OK them or veto them.")[80]

For the first time, rumors began to surface that Yawkey was considering another ballpark in the Boston area. The September 26, 1957, *Boston Traveler* mentioned "a suburban spot out near the new Mass. Turnpike," but columnist George C. Carens said he didn't believe it. In December Joe Cronin said that Yawkey wasn't going to build a new ballpark, but that should the city or the Commonwealth of Massachusetts construct one, he would rent the facility for Red Sox games.[81] There was the possibility of a new ballpark in Auburndale, and a site for a sports center in Norwood came under discussion, but the feeling was that Yawkey would not be interested simply because he enjoyed owning his own park and didn't like to share with anyone.

A 1958 story reported that his sister Emma had wanted to build her own house on South Island, but he hadn't wanted to share the land.[82] In the end, it was simple, wrote the *Record*'s Bill McSweeny: "He is not against progress. . . . He just wants to play in his own park, generally considered the best kept and most beautiful in the nation."[83]

Julia Yawkey married Frederick Gaston in New York City on November 2, 1957.

At the December 5 meeting of the AL, the league voted to require protective headgear (batting helmets) for batters, joining the NL in such a determination. The vote was 7–1, with Yawkey voting against it.[84] At the same meeting, Yawkey resigned from the executive council, and Joe Cronin was named in his place. The resignation was prompted by "business pressures"—a reminder that Yawkey had another life and that, at least from time to time, the needs of his active businesses impinged on his baseball interests.[85]

In packing the equipment truck for spring training in 1958, clubhouse manager Johnny Orlando paused for a moment to praise Tom Yawkey for not stinting. It was nothing but the best, he said. The uniforms, for one thing, were the finest available. "It wasn't always this way, though. I can remember going to spring training 26 years ago when we didn't have quite as many baseballs. In fact, we used to wash them after one day's play, and use them the next."[86]

Orlando had worked in the clubhouse since Yawkey bought the ball club. Yawkey had only had two GMs—Eddie Collins and Joe Cronin (currently serving)—and he had had only seven managers—Cronin for thirteen seasons, with Pinky Higgins starting his fourth.

A whole new infield had been installed at a cost of over $100,000, and the park was newly painted throughout.

The *Record*'s Dave Egan had a suggestion. Yawkey had never asked anything of the city; perhaps it was time for the city to do something for him. Egan suggested constructing a one-thousand-car parking facility nearby since "Yawkey has the nicest ballpark in the majors here but he has the worst parking of any club and this could eventually strangle him and his ball team."[87]

On May 18 there was a reunion of the twenty-five outstanding players of the quarter-century that Yawkey had owned the Red Sox, with ceremonies before the game and a dinner organized by the Boston Sports Lodge, B'nai B'rith.

"Stop Worrying about Yawkey" read a headline in the May 28, 1958, *Globe*. The Sox owner hadn't been to Boston yet in 1958. He'd issued a mimeographed announcement on Opening Day saying that personal business prevented him from attending but that he was as interested as ever. It was personal business that involved "not only myself, but a lot of other people."[88] He remained in daily touch with Cronin about all the details with the Red Sox. The notion that his absence indicated indifference was misplaced.

In early June the Massachusetts Department of Commerce announced its first special achievement award to Tom Yawkey.

On June 20 Yawkey made his first 1958 appearance in Boston. The team had gotten off to a slow start but gradually climbed in the standings and was in second place, albeit nine games behind the Yankees. The first game Yawkey actually saw was on July 1. He saw both Ted and Jackie Jensen homer, and the Red Sox beat Washington, 10-5. Writers assumed he had been supervising the building of a new house on South Island, but, as noted above, he never had one built. At this remove, we don't know what businesses demanded his time.

Also on July 1 Yawkey watched former BC catcher Larry Plenty—newly signed to the Red Sox—take batting practice from Boo Ferriss. "He hit that well," said the boss.[89] Plenty was African American; as it happened, he never played professionally.

The very next day, the Red Sox announced that they would train at Scottsdale, Arizona, beginning in the spring of 1959. Three clubs were already out there—the Giants, Cubs, and Indians. Baltimore had been there as well but had decided to move back east. At that point Yawkey's friend Horace Stoneham of the Giants asked his fellow club owner to take the Sox to Scottsdale so that there would be four teams out west. Yawkey agreed. So-called magnates could decide such matters in those days. Scottsdale was described as a "frontier town" at the time or a "cactus cow town."[90]

There may have been another side to the decision to go to Scottsdale. Joe Cronin had apparently worked in vain to get the city fathers in Sarasota to upgrade the spring training facilities there, so he made the arrangements to go to Scottsdale, "but this was not intended to be permanent. Cronin figured that Sarasota would fix up the park, and the team could return the following year."[91] But new GM Bucky Harris signed a multiyear deal once they were in Scottsdale. That wouldn't have happened without T. A. Yawkey's okay.

How Bucky Harris came to be named GM after Cronin left was another example of what could be called misplaced friendship; it came about because of a promise Yawkey had made to Harris, whom he liked, way back in 1935, when Cronin was first brought to Boston. Yawkey worked out a deal with Clark Griffith to take Harris back to Washington as manager of the Senators, and Yawkey told Harris the Red Sox would always have a job for him if he ever needed one. Fired by the Tigers after the 1956 season, Harris needed a job. Ergo, he became Red Sox special assistant. Fair enough, but when Cronin moved on to head up the AL, Yawkey made Harris GM. "Sentimentality [was] Yawkey's biggest weakness," wrote Al Hirshberg. "Too many of his appointments were made with his heart, not his head. His loyalty to Mike Higgins, who twice served as manager and was O'Connell's immediate predecessor as general manager, cost Yawkey years of progress in his everlasting quest for pennants."[92]

Sox infielder Ted Lepcio (1952–59) remained in the area after his playing career, an observer of the scene. He remarked:

> They made one brutal error. To give a guy like Bucky Harris the general manager's job was just terrible. Terrible at the time that it happened. The guy was an alcoholic, and the rest is history. But he was bad for our organization. I mention his name; I'm not going any further, but that's what was happening then. He was bad for the organization. We heard from the grapevine that [Yawkey] had promised him a job way back somewhere. But what job? A GM job? There's a million jobs he could have had.[93]

The most notorious drinker in the group was Pinky Higgins, often found after games at a local bar named the Dugout and reportedly sometimes found on the floor after he'd fallen off his barstool. As Dick Flavin said about the culture of alcohol that was not uncommon at the time in business generally, "I don't know how the hell anybody got any work done after lunch."[94]

Columnist Bud Collins suggests that there was something of a reverence around Yawkey. Collins started as a reporter in 1956, and he picked up on this. "I was a young reporter and I wrote a critical column—I don't know what year it was—and the people at Fenway Park did not like it. They thought we should only laud Yawkey."[95]

A movement to relocate the Washington franchise to Minneapolis was reportedly blocked by Yawkey during a league meeting in July.

In mid-July the *Record* ran a four-part series in which Yawkey talked baseball with Joe Cashman. There weren't any revelations. Yawkey did say that he considered Frank Malzone the best player the Sox had developed through their farm system rather than purchased or acquired through trade.

Being back in his ballpark gave Yawkey the chance to work out on the field, some of the time with Haywood Sullivan, who was out injured all of 1958. Batboy Jackie McLeod enthused about working with Ted Williams in the clubhouse, adding, "Mr. Yawkey is tops, too. He works out with us bat boys and the clubhouse boys whenever the team's on the road. He jokes and kids with us and is a wonderful guy."[96]

After "two dry years" (when Ted did no expectorating) there was another incident, in Kansas City, involving the "Splendid Spitter." This time he was given a league fine of $250 and made a quick apology to President Harridge.

On August 9 there was another old-timers' day at Fenway, this time reuniting the 1946 team. Rogers Hornsby, George Sisler, and Bill Terry—.400 hitters all—came and posed for photos with Ted Williams.

Was it a trial balloon or what? It wasn't clear at the time how it cropped up, and it isn't clear today, but in mid-August a story surfaced that suggested the Red Sox were seeking "a larger left field, a lower fence, and new stands" for Fenway, with the buildings on Lansdowne Street condemned and a "huge parking area over the toll road" now known as the Mass Pike.[97]

Questions arose as to whether Higgins would be managing in 1959. When the team lost nine of ten on the road in August, many thought his days were numbered. The team seemed to be coming unglued, and there were some stories along the lines of "Maybe

Manager Higgins Is Too Easy with Them."[98] But Yawkey seemed to be personally fond of him. Better pitching might have made the difference. After a September 21 phone call from Yawkey to Cronin, Higgins was rehired but only on a one-year contract, not the three-year term he was completing.

Red Sox fandom was displeased. John Gillooly wrote a full column anticipating that—since Yawkey seemed so satisfied with his team's executives—he must be about ready to go on a spending binge to acquire ballplayers. The season, after all, "never did get off the ground." Yawkey, "naïve but no numbskull, must realize that Higgins is not going to turn stern taskmaster now." But Gillooly blamed Yawkey as "culpable, too, because he wasn't around often enough to spot the clock watchers and the water-cooler malingerers on his payroll. He might have ordered changes months ago. That the Red Sox were dolts was obvious as early as June. . . . He must [now] know that wholesale changes are mandatory."[99]

It is hard to fathom Yawkey's ongoing tolerance of Pinky Higgins, which lasted for a full decade of Red Sox torpor. There have been intimations by those who couldn't know that the two were drinking buddies. It was well known that Higgins imbibed (as noted above), but he was more often a solitary drinker. He was, of course, a former ballplayer, and Yawkey must have found something about him congenial. Their friendship went back to the 1930s, when Higgins joined the Yawkey party in hunting expeditions. Sox pitcher Jerry Casale was pretty blunt about Higgins: "I don't like to say things like this, but the son of a bitch was always drunk. And he'd never talk to you. He seemed like a nice guy, but I don't think he wanted to talk to anybody, because half the time he was bombed. . . . I'll tell you: if I'd known what I learned later, I never would have signed with the Red Sox. I'd have signed with anybody but."[100]

During the September 21 game, Williams became so angry at himself that he flung his bat without regard for where he flung it—and it struck a woman in the stands on her head. Bud Collins went downstairs to learn more about the incident and ran into Joe Cronin, who said the woman had been treated in the Red Cross room and was all right. "Are you sure she's all right?" Collins asked. "There could be a lawsuit, Joe." Cronin said, "There'll be no lawsuit." Collins asked, "How can you say that?" Cronin said, "I'll tell you how I can say that. Gladys Heffernan [the woman in question] is my housekeeper."[101]

Those were less litigious times, but the Red Sox were nonetheless extremely fortunate that the woman was Gladys Heffernan, who indeed happened to be Joe Cronin's housekeeper and a big Ted Williams admirer too. She was hospitalized overnight. Williams was stricken with remorse, and the game was delayed slightly because he was crying in the dugout.[102]

The season ended with the Red Sox in third place (79-75), thirteen games out of first, but nonetheless one of their better showings in the 1950s.

As noted above and despite local gossip, rather few ballplayers seem to have visited Yawkey in South Carolina since the 1930s. One exception was Frank Sullivan, who paid a visit in 1958. He and Sox catcher Sammy White were delivering a forty-two-foot Convertible Flying Bridge Chris Craft to Fort Lauderdale for a man named George Page. Sullivan recalls the visit:

> I was told when we left New England that Tom Yawkey owned an island off the South Carolina coast. Just south of Georgetown are a number of islands, and, sure enough, one of them is called Cat Island, and, yes, Tom Yawkey was the owner. Nothing to do but stop and see our boss, right? After a quick stop, we called, and damn if we weren't invited. I pulled the boat up to a very long pier, and out came two WWII Jeeps. Mrs. Yawkey was with them and warmly greeted us. We were taken to the main complex for drinks and dinner but not before Mr. Yawkey himself showed us his island game reserve.
>
> After a great dinner with much wine and many laughs, we retired into the trophy room and settled around some superior brandy. One drink led to another, and the conversation somehow settled around hitting, and the next thing I knew, Mr. Yawkey had a broom in his hands and was showing Sam what he thought was wrong with Sam's swing. Honestly, fearing the worst, I did everything in my power to get them off the subject, but to no avail. I heard Sam tell our host, "You may be right Tom, but if I was that fat I'd never get around to the ball."
>
> I have never been in a room where people sobered more quickly.[103]

It was, Sullivan recalls, the only time he ever spoke to Tom Yawkey.[104]

Sam's wife Sally recalls the evening too, and she recalls sleeping overnight in one of the Yawkeys' trailers before departing the next morning.[105] The Whites' daughter Deborah says her mother told her that Yawkey was "a complete gentleman ... no airs or pretense" and that they "felt really welcome, especially since they gave him no advance notice of their arrival."[106]

At the winter meetings, Yawkey personally traded Jimmy Piersall to the Indians for Vic Wertz and Gary Geiger. The Red Sox owner had been exercised at the start of the meetings, complaining about excessive player demands; the players were asking for 20 percent of the gross. He again asked whether the players would want to share the losses or just the proceeds. Yawkey said he might quit baseball.[107] He acknowledged, "I have lost some money in baseball; I did it voluntarily. But nobody is going to force me to lose money." He added that he saw three choices for himself: "I can sit back and do nothing. I can fight. I can withdraw."[108] There remained the ongoing notion that his "suffering is of his own making because he becomes too fond of some employees and will not disturb their reveries."[109]

Will Harridge did quit; though not directly in response to labor-management matters, he resigned as president of the AL. It seemed that Joe Cronin had the inside track to take Harridge's place. Yawkey was reelected once again to the executive council. Had he been less of a hands-on owner, simply content to own his club as a plaything, it might have been another matter, but he clearly enjoyed being involved in leadership (or felt responsible enough) that he continued to be elected year after year.

The usual rumors, of course, ensued, including one that had Cronin becoming president, Ted Williams retiring, and Tom Yawkey selling the Red Sox to Lou Perini, who would in turn sell the Milwaukee Braves.

On December 5 Frederick DeFoe died at the age of ninety. He had been secretary of the Red Sox from the day Tom Yawkey purchased the team, though he remained resident in New York. DeFoe had come to New York in 1915 to work as a personal representative of William H. Yawkey and served as financial and business adviser to Tom Yawkey and Tom's sister Emma. As noted above,

DeFoe's Mt. Pleasant Plantation at Andrews, South Carolina, later became home to Tom and Jean Yawkey—essentially their mainland home when they were not on South Island.[110] In early 1959 Joseph LaCour of New York, a longtime Yawkey employee, was named to take DeFoe's place.

A couple of days later, Julia Yawkey Gaston gave birth to her first child, named Frederick Gaston, after her husband. For whatever reasons, the Gastons had their world, and the Yawkeys had theirs. Phil Wilkinson said of Julia, "I never met her. Mr. Yawkey would talk about her to me but not around Mrs. Yawkey. He would talk about her past. He didn't talk about her present too much."[111]

Trustee Bill Gutfarb of the Yawkey Foundations made a similar remark:

> I never met [Julia]. I did talk to her on the phone a few years ago. It was a very bizarre situation. We get phone calls from all over the place. A woman called and said she met Mr. Yawkey's daughter Julia with Barbara Bush at a luncheon at the Four Seasons Hotel in Boston, and she was trying to get a hold of her. She asked if I could give her the phone number or address in Connecticut. I said, "I'm sorry, I can't, but I will let her know that you're looking for her." I sent a note to Julia, and then she called me back and said, "I've never met Barbara Bush, and I was never at a luncheon at the Four Seasons in Boston." That was the end of it.[112]

In league affairs, Tom Yawkey was head of the screening committee to find a replacement for Harridge. The committee ultimately selected Cronin and moved the American League office to Boston.

In December the Sox traded Jimmy Piersall to the Indians for Vic Wertz and a center fielder with upside, Gary Geiger. GM Frank Lane of Cleveland later paid Yawkey a compliment, noting that it was Yawkey who'd made the deal on behalf of the Red Sox and saying, "I'll never deal with that Yawkey again—he's a horse-trader."[113] That was genuine praise coming from a man who had earned the moniker "Trader Lane."

The screening committee to select the next AL president set January 14, 1959, as the date to meet with candidates and make their recommendation. Since Cronin was the only one invited to appear before the committee, it was no surprise who the committee recommended: Joe Cronin. When the meeting convened, its chairman (Yawkey) was absent—perhaps due to the press of personal business, with the loss of Fred DeFoe, or simply to recuse himself. He was represented by Red Sox attorney Jack Hayes.

Tim Horgan of the *Herald* suggested that Yawkey was suffering some ennui about the Sox. That he didn't attend the screening committee meeting and appointed Harris GM by sending Cronin a telegram from South Carolina and telling him to make the announcement, Horgan said, reflected a lack of interest in the multi-million-dollar investment he had in the business enterprise that was the Red Sox. Was Harris even ready for the job? Horgan quoted him as saying, "I didn't get too thoroughly acquainted with the (general manager's) job the past two years. I'll need help from Cronin for a while." Cronin, of course, was going to have his hands full running the American League—though with the league offices moving to Boston, at least there would be proximity. "Shooting birds in Georgetown, S.C. is a fierce way to show interest in the future of one's ball team," Horgan wrote.[114] If Yawkey were indeed not as uninterested as Horgan hypothesized, he seemed to be relying on a kind of chummy cronyism to see the Red Sox through.

George Carens of the *Boston Traveler* wrote that he had once asked Yawkey what he found the most distasteful aspect of owning the ball club. Without a moment's hesitation, Yawkey replied, "Changing personnel in key positions."[115]

The perception of Yawkey's lack of interest became so bad in Greater Boston that—of all things—the Massachusetts branch of the veterans organization AMVETS passed a resolution at its annual convention calling for Yawkey to give up the team. It read as follows:

WHEREAS members of our AMVETS organization have time and again demonstrated their interest in our national pastime, the game of baseball, and

WHEREAS it is apparent to even the least educated baseball fan that the Boston American League franchise has been allowed through mis-management and disinterest to fall to a low estate, the lowest in a quarter of a century, and

WHEREAS the responsibility for this unhappy state of affairs rests on the shoulders of the absent owner, Mr. Thomas A. Yawkey, whose team has been investigated by State authorities because of its obvious segregation policies and

WHEREAS the cause of big league baseball in New England would be greatly improved if the Sox franchise could be purchased by Massachusetts citizens, genuinely interested in providing competent, on-the-spot leadership,

THEREFORE, Be It Resolved that this convention urge Mr. Thomas A. Yawkey to sell his interest in the Red Sox to a syndicate of local businessmen who will not practice segregation but will instead revitalize this franchise and restore Boston to its rightful place in the sun in the junior circuit.[116]

Yawkey never enjoyed public scrutiny, and he enjoyed Georgetown precisely because people there were not rabid Red Sox fans. Jamie Dozier agrees: "My uncle worked for Mr. Yawkey a little bit, and my other uncle was the sheriff of Georgetown County for many, many years, and they were close friends. He said he thought one of the reasons [Yawkey] liked it here was that people around here weren't fanatical Boston Red Sox fans. They could talk about hunting and fishing and dogs and things like that, whereas when he was in Boston, everybody wanted to talk about the Red Sox. I'm sure it was draining."[117]

Fandom was far-reaching in New England. Boston's Roman Catholic prelate Richard Cardinal Cushing was a speaker at the annual baseball writers' dinner and praised Yawkey (who was not present) as "Mr. Baseball Himself. . . . Mr. Yawkey is truly Boston's indispensable baseball man."[118] Reporters covering the January 31 meeting in which Cronin was officially elected to head the AL commented on how engaged and even "sparkling" Yawkey was and noted how it irritated him to have his passion for the game brought into question.[119] Yawkey did play an active role in his other business interests. Alex MacLean, writing in the *Boston Record*, noted that he had "multiplied his fortune several times by his sound business manipulations."[120]

Both Mayor Hynes and the Boston Park Commission approved a plan to pave over the public Victory Gardens in the Fens and turn the community garden into a 1,200-car parking facility to serve Red Sox fans.[121] The cost was estimated at $189,000. Only Boston City Council approval was required to seal the deal.

Early in the year Jackie Robinson again accused the Red Sox of racial prejudice. While in Boston on business for Chock Full O' Nuts coffee, he remarked:

> Fifteen major-league teams had Negroes playing for them. The only exception is the Boston Red Sox. You can quote me on this: They are prejudiced. It is unfortunate, in a way, because the Negro ballplayer got his best reception in Boston. The fairest fans in the world are here. I played major ball for ten years and whenever I came to Braves Field I knew I would get a fair reception. The Red Sox are hurting their own fans more than they are the Negro race by denying Negro players a chance to play for them.[122]

Joe Cronin quickly shot back in the same story: "Just let the Yankees offer Elston Howard or Chicago offer Minnie Minoso and see how quickly we'll make a deal. We're interested in ballplayers, not their color." Once again, one might wonder how hard Red Sox scouts were trying to sign players of color since every other Major League team had now done so and had produced an array of All-Stars and even MVPs in the process.

Since Jackie Robinson broke into the big leagues in 1947, there had been 8 Rookies of the Year (of a total of 22) and 60 All-Stars (out of 623) who were "black," defined by Mark Armour as "any player who would have been prohibited from playing major-league baseball before 1947." In 1955, 20 percent of the players in that year's All-Star Game were black.[123] And still the Red Sox had not yet fielded a black ballplayer, even as a bench player.

Pumpsie Green was a standout during spring training in Scottsdale—though segregation in Scottsdale itself prevented him from staying in the same quarters as the rest of his teammates. He had to be outside the city limits by nightfall and stay in quarters the Red Sox found for him at a motel in nearby Phoenix. (He ended up moving into the same Phoenix hotel as the San Francisco Giants.)

The Red Sox organization tolerated this situation rather than picking up and leaving Scottsdale in solidarity with Green.

Pumpsie himself reported a time when Red Sox coach Del Baker, though talking about a player on another team, was "saying some things one night . . . using these words—I don't ever want to repeat them, they were derogatory words—and he knew I was there. I just looked at him, wondering what I should do and Bill Monbouquette just got up, walked over to him, and said, 'Del, Pumpsie's here now. You can't talk that way anymore.'"[124] Monbouquette had told writer Danny Peary, "Pumpsie Green was an amiable, quiet guy, and I think the media made it uncomfortable for him by making what was happening bigger than it should have been. The fans were warm to Pumpsie and Earl Wilson. I never saw them have trouble."[125]

Bill Monbouquette remembered the incident with Baker well:

He used the "n" word, and Mike [Pinky] Higgins used the "n" word, and I told them, "I don't want to hear that." And then he [Baker] started to give me a bunch of crap, and I said, "I'm going to tell you something. I'll knock you right on your ass. I don't care if you're the coach or not." I said, "You don't do things like that!" I grew up in a black neighborhood. West Medford. They were in our house. We were in their houses. There was none of that. To me, there was no sense to that whatsoever.

Monbo remembered being at a banquet in San Antonio during a stint in the service, and Del Baker was at the same event. "He never even said hello to me. That didn't bother me. I told Ted during spring training, "I thought this was supposed to be a team." He said, "You're right."[126]

Although Pumpsie seemed to shine with the Red Sox in spring training, manager Higgins sent him to Minneapolis for what was said to be more seasoning. There was a firestorm when Pumpsie was sent to Triple A because it looked to many like racial discrimination. Good arguments could be made that he wasn't ready for prime time in the Majors, but the 1958 Sox had finished only four games over .500 and had a team batting average of just .256. And, as noted, they had become the only team in the Majors to have never fielded a black player. The situation, already on the brink of untenable, was aggravated when Green was not brought up to the big leagues in the spring of 1959.[127]

Yawkey was not in Scottsdale and not in Boston, but he could have spoken up at any time—in fact, at any time in the previous twenty years. He did not. The *Globe*'s Jerry Nason depicted a side of Yawkey that was less pleasant than that of the genial sportsman in an article titled "Will Yawkey Quit Boston?" "Yawkey is an owner who has always bridled at outside interference," Nason wrote, referring to moves that might be made to pressure the Red Sox to finally field a black ballplayer. Nason recalled that a few years earlier, regarding another issue, Yawkey had asked him what it would be like in Boston if the Red Sox left town. Nason's response at the time: "As a sports town, it would probably break Boston's back." "Exactly," said Yawkey, snapping his fingers, "and I could do it like that!"[128]

On April 14 the Massachusetts Committee against Discrimination announced that it had invited Tom Yawkey to appear before the committee "to answer charges of racial discrimination made by the Boston branch of the National Association for the Advancement of Colored People."[129] GM Bucky Harris was asked to appear as well. The story was carried nationally. A Tufts pre-med student, Alvan Levenson, picketed outside Fenway Park on Opening Day and was attacked by a couple of people who snatched his signs away from him. One sign read, "We want a pennant, not a white team," and the other, "Race hate is killing baseball in Boston." MCAD chair Mildred Mahoney said, "There is enough here to warrant action of some type," and local NAACP president Herbert Tucker alleged that the Red Sox had a pattern of anti-Negro discrimination going back at least a dozen or more years, citing the Jackie Robinson "tryout" that had been forced on them by city councilor Isidore Muchnick.[130] The only employee of color the ball club had ever hired was a cook whose service lasted only three weeks.[131]

Yawkey was out of town. Representing the Red Sox before the committee was business manager (and later GM) Dick O'Connell, who declared, "The Boston Red Sox are entirely American. We have no discrimination against race, color, or creed." He added, "We have a right to manage our own ball club. People from City Hall and the State House don't hire people for us. We hire them." He then asserted and acknowledged, "We're not antagonistic, but we will be accused of it until we have a Negro on our roster."[132] O'Connell said that there had been black employees at the park working in concessions (he may not have explained that concessions were run by a company that contracted with the team as concessionaire) and that one had worked there for ten years. He said there were seven black players in the Red Sox farm system.

The *Record*'s Gillooly suggested that Higgins—whatever his prejudices—was on a one-year contract and had to perform, so he couldn't afford to let racism get in the way. Therefore, perhaps it truly was the case that Higgins felt Green needed more seasoning. (Others, including those who demonstrated friendship with Pumpsie, agreed that could be a reasonable baseball assessment.) But appearances were important too. Gillooly wrote that Yawkey was clearly a prudent man and "would not permit himself to be placed in the predicament he is today—accused of Jim Crowism." He noted that boycotts of the Red Sox were in the air.[133]

On April 12 Bucky Harris issued a formal denial of discrimination in a letter to MCAD, adding that the Red Sox admired players like Howard, Minoso, and Larry Doby and that they were hoping that Green, Earl Wilson, Larry Plenty, and others in their own organization would soon be ready to come to the Majors. Their goal, he wrote, was a winning ball club, and "when capable players are available, they will be used, regardless of race, color, or creed."[134]

The Red Sox were not adept at public relations, or they might have foreseen and forestalled the problem—were it one of perception or practice—sooner than they did. That they did not left a stain on the organization that influenced perceptions more than fifty years later.

There may have been some hesitancy then at one Boston newspaper in addressing the issue more forcefully. Bud Collins was working for the *Boston Herald* at the time, and he'd had some say but felt he was being reined in. Speaking of Higgins in late 2014, Collins assessed, "He was a petty little figure, really. He was certainly racist, and he certainly didn't like me. I'd written a few things. We weren't able to be too tough on him. I'm sure the newspapers covered it up. . . . I was told to lay off because the ball club was on WHDH, which the *Herald* owned at the time, and the *Herald* wasn't going to criticize Higgins very much."[135] At the World Series in 1963, Higgins finally snapped (see below).

In late May, John Gillooly wrote that Yawkey had been "absent so long that some have presumed him lost."[136] Five days later, citing a reader who had written in, Gillooly titled his column "Wants Yawkey to Mind Store." Yawkey didn't even turn up when the Sox played two games in New York on May 26 and 27.

The Sox owner arrived in Boston in early June and held a lengthy baseball conference with reporters on June 2. The Red Sox were in last place at the time. Ted Williams was batting just .194 that morning; in 1959 he had by far the worst start of his career, hampered as he was by a horrific pinched nerve in his neck that he had suffered during spring training and that troubled him all season. Yawkey said he'd never discussed Ted's future with him but that if he were interested, there would always be a job of some sort for him with the Red Sox.[137] For about a week in early April, both Williams and Jean Yawkey were in Baptist Hospital at the same time, for different reasons.

Yawkey told reporters he was against interleague play; he didn't see any excitement in the seventh-place team of one league playing the eighth-place team of the other. He mentioned the stories that continued to circulate about a new, possibly multisport, stadium in Greater Boston, but he wondered aloud where the money would come from.[138]

We see Yawkey wax hot and cold in his public statements regarding replacing Fenway. Jackie Jensen probably got it right as to where Yawkey's heart was. He told of talking to the boss about Fenway's unique size and shape. "There was a lot of talk then: Why don't they make another park outside the city limits or something where there was more room? And he [Yawkey] said he loved this old place. He said this is the only ball park that was a part of him as far as he was concerned, and that everything he wanted to do was here and to keep it right in the middle of the city it retains a certain charm. . . . Tom was kind of a voice in the wilderness at the time."[139]

With the team still in last place (31-40) when June ended, Yawkey did something he'd never done before: he asked his general manager to investigate and bring him the answer to the age-old question, "What's the matter with the Red Sox?" He asked Harris to go to Washington to observe the team and report back.[140] Yawkey seemed to have finally lost his patience with Higgins as field manager: "Whether Mike Higgins is to continue as manager of the Red Sox is a decision Bucky Harris will have to make." Harris, for his part, said that he would submit his report to Yawkey; though he believed he had the authority to fire Higgins and that Yawkey "isn't very happy," in the end, Harris concluded, "What he does with [the report] is his business. He is the owner of the baseball team."[141]

On July 3 Higgins was fired, and Billy Jurges was named to take his place. The firing may have been difficult for Yawkey in that Higgins was "his only personal managerial appointment during the 26 years he has owned the ball club."[142] He called a press conference to express his regrets at the release of Higgins and then expressed surprise that Jurges had been hired, the news breaking during his press conference. He said he hadn't expected Harris to fire Higgins but hoped that a Harris visit to the team while it was in Washington would "pep up" the club. He himself took the final step, however.[143] It was with all the usual expressions of regret, the feeling that this would be better for the ball club, and the comment that "the press probably helped hasten Higgins' departure."[144] Higgins would take some time off but would be offered another position with the team.

According to Tom Shaer, switchboard operator Helen Robinson was "tight with Mrs. Yawkey":

They used to go to the theater together and everything. When Mr. Yawkey went on a bender, obviously Mrs. Yawkey was not happy. So Helen was not happy with Mr. Y. [In the case of the Jurges hiring] Yawkey didn't know anything about it; he didn't know who the new manager was. The owner of the team did not know who the new manager was! So he calls the ballpark. Now, keep in mind, this was in the days when there was no direct dial. Everything went through the switchboard. He called, and Helen answers the phone, and he asked, "Hey, who's the new manager?" And she wouldn't tell him. She wouldn't tell him because she was so pissed—like, where have you been? According to Dick [O'Connell]—and it's a great story—she would not tell him who the new manager was, and she wouldn't transfer him in to anybody who would know.[145]

Jim Rice broke out laughing when Helen Robinson's name came up in an interview inside the Red Sox clubhouse.

> Don't get talking about Helen Robinson! Helen was a spy. Helen was good. She was good. She was some kind of lady, boy. Helen used to treat him [Yawkey] like he was one of the players. If he did something she didn't like, she let him know! Yeah! I'd say, "Helen, this man owns the ball club." "I don't care! We have rules. He made the rules, and we're gonna stick by the rules. Those are the rules." "OK, Helen."
>
> Lunch time, you couldn't make no phone calls from down here. Anything. Helen would say, "No! Go outside. There's a payphone outside. Go outside." She was a beauty.[146]

Yawkey didn't cut his ties to Higgins. They had a long history, he liked him, and he felt some sense of obligation. The *Globe* foresaw the likelihood that Higgins would be groomed to become GM. In keeping Higgins on board, it could be argued that Yawkey's loyalty and companionship may have cost him another six years of Red Sox teams playing below .500. Higgins as manager was said not to have been at all demanding,

> not strong on instruction. . . . Players liked him, of course. Why not? He did not fine them, harry them, or put detectives on them. He was an easy manager to play for, with the kind of good nature it is natural to take advantage of, even without meaning to. If he did not like a player, he simply sat him on the bench and forgot about him. He knew baseball but was sometimes slow to make obvious moves—a base-runner for a slow-molasses, or a nimble fielder for a shoemaker. And he was not the type to fire up a team.[147]

Not everyone felt a connection with the manager. More than one player tells of being on an elevator with Higgins and Higgins not even saying hello to them. We will see that just a few years later (1963–64), Higgins as GM routinely refused to even talk to his field manager, Johnny Pesky.

A countervailing view in the *Record* was that of John Gillooly, who spent three weeks observing Higgins in spring training and then called him "a genuine brain, a true talent . . . as keen a manager as I've encountered . . . the manager most respected in the AL today."[148] Gillooly didn't present any evidence to back up his point of view.

Dom DiMaggio didn't mince any words about Higgins's style, which was not unlike that of earlier Sox managers but was quite unlike the way Lefty O'Doul had managed when Dom was on the way up and playing with the San Francisco Seals: "A manager should have control of the game and the players all the time. It is bad when the players are running the manager, a situation which existed most of the time while I was with the Red Sox."[149] Clearly DiMaggio's comment embraced Joe Cronin as well. He said the players were basically on their own most of the time and that the managers never did much to try and confuse the opposition; he felt it was one reason that Yawkey had only the one pennant to show for all this years of ownership. DiMaggio believed that the candor of his remarks could have cost him a chance to buy the team after Tom Yawkey's death.

The team turned around under Jurges, sweeping a rare five-game home stand against the Yankees (July 9–13) and playing 44-36 for him. On July 21, with Higgins gone, Pumpsie Green was called up to the Boston club. He played his first nine games on the road and was hitting .292 when he reached Fenway Park, where he tripled in his first at-bat. Fans were loud in their support for Green. Earl Wilson joined the club as a pitcher just days later.

Yawkey and Harris were determined to give younger players a shot. They didn't have a lot to lose. It was a far less passive Yawkey who said, "We'll bring 'em in and we'll throw 'em out. If the players we have aren't doing the job, we'll get rid of 'em. We'll give everyone an opportunity. It's up to them to make good. We can't run, throw, hit, or field for them. They've got to do that for themselves, and if they do it well, they'll stay around here."[150]

Pumpsie felt welcomed by the Red Sox owner. He was asked to come in to Yawkey's office and was naturally nervous. "He made me feel like I belonged. He didn't even mention the fact that I was the Red Sox's first black."[151] Recalling the day fifty years after the fact, he said, "When I first got there, he invited me up to his office, and I went up and sat down and talked to him for a while. I found him to be a very interesting person. I had a nice conversation with him, and he treated me with respect, as I treated him, and he wished me good luck, and if I ever needed anything, he was there and give him a call."[152]

There was talk of organizing a third major league, the Continental League, and Commissioner Frick appointed a committee of seven executives, including Yawkey and Cronin, to look into perhaps aiding the promoters of the new league.

In early August, Jackie Jensen talked about retiring. He didn't like flying, and he wanted to be around his family more, a family he feared he was losing. He stuck it out through 1959 but retired after that season.

Williams hit only .254 on the season, by far his worst year in baseball. The lowest he'd ever hit was .317, and he was just coming off back-to-back batting championships. Most people thought he'd come back for one last try because he was eight homers shy of five hundred and he no doubt wanted to go out in a year in which he hit over .300. But Ted heard from Yawkey that maybe Dick O'Connell didn't want him back. Williams visited O'Connell over the winter, when in town for the Sportsman's Show, in which Ted appeared annually. O'Connell said, "Don't be silly" and pulled Ted's contract out of a pile; it was for the same $125,000 he'd been paid in 1959. Williams says he told O'Connell, "I don't deserve what I made last year. I've had the biggest raises a player ever had. I've gone up from nothing on this club to $125,000 a year. I want to take the biggest cut ever given a player." They settled on $90,000, a 28 percent paycut.[153] "I was surprised at first and later I wasn't," Yawkey said when told. "You have to know Ted. He's an unusual person. He does what he wants and doesn't give a damn what other people think."[154] Yawkey was an unusual person too. Roy Mumpton of the *Worcester Telegram* said that Yawkey later gave Ted a $50,000 going-away present.[155]

Jurges was a hustling manager, the opposite of Higgins. The Red Sox pulled themselves up and were able to finish in fifth place. Jurges was even out there on the field during some of Yawkey's sessions with the clubhouse crew.[156]

Seemingly inexplicable was the sacking of Johnny Orlando, who'd worked in the Fenway clubhouse since 1925. He was particularly close to Ted Williams and was one of the favored few who shagged balls during Yawkey's sessions on the field. "Orlando was sort of a court jester for years for Yawkey," wrote Gillooly. "He spent hours jabbering with the owner in his plush office up on the roof. Yawkey was always partial to the lesser people in his organization, preferring their company to that of the personages."[157] One wonders what went wrong. Not all was well in the clubhouse, but that was learned only years later, when Don Fitzpatrick was accused of sexually molesting a considerable number of youths over two decades at the spring training home of the Red Sox.

In December the Red Sox hired Pinky Higgins as a special assistant to GM Harris. "Yawkey's feelings toward Higgins as a genuine person have not changed. Tom admitted that one of the main reasons for removing Higgins as field manager was 'you can't buck public opinion.' He had nothing but praise for Mike as a person."[158] Higgins would remain based in his hometown of Dallas but was the heir apparent to Harris.

Billy Sullivan was spokesperson for a new and as-yet-unnamed American Football League franchise based in Boston. The team—which became known as the Patriots—also lacked a place to play, and even though Dick O'Connell had turned down their request to play at Fenway, Sullivan planned a direct appeal to Tom Yawkey. "Marse Tom"—as some of the press enjoyed calling him—wanted his park to be baseball-only and would not make it available for football, explained Dick O'Connell. When they'd redone the field a few years ago, they had removed the supports that had previously helped anchor the sideline seating that was brought out for the various high school and college football games, and they had given it away.[159]

16

From Ted to Yaz, the First Sox
Seasons of the 1960s

WOULD TED WILLIAMS play again in 1960 after experiencing such a dropoff in 1959? Tom Yawkey reportedly recommended he retire but left the decision entirely up to Ted and agreed to pay him the same amount he had been making. At the same time, in January 1960 Yawkey announced that—rumors to the contrary—he was not selling the Red Sox. As for the ongoing stadium question, he said he would not permit the Boston Patriots to play in Fenway Park—even temporarily—but that the Red Sox would listen to ideas regarding themselves playing in another stadium. He discounted the idea of a domed stadium, though, due to the expected cost.[1]

It was just before the 1960 season that the Yankees' former executive Larry MacPhail told in more detail about the almost-was 1947 trade of Ted Williams for Joe DiMaggio. "I thought we had the deal all made," he said. "I had made the original proposal. The Red Sox had won the pennant in 1946 and then laid a big egg the next season." He got a call from Eddie Collins to come to Boston, only to arrive and find the deal was off. He said he never learned why, but he thought New York GM Ed Barrow may have talked Tom Yawkey out of it. "Ed was a good friend of Tom's. They used to hunt together down in Yawkey's plantation and I feel sure Ed persuaded Yawkey not to make it." MacPhail thought the deal would have helped all concerned but that on balance the Yankees would have come out well ahead.[2]

Regardless of how much time he spent in South Carolina, Tom Yawkey was in constant contact with the team in Boston, even during January. He called the office frequently; he "telephones almost daily."[3]

With Jackie Jensen retiring, Ted Williams about to retire, and Sammy White refusing a trade to Cleveland—thereby retiring—rumors surfaced, reported by even such respected reporters as Gordon Cobbledick of the *Cleveland Plain Dealer*, that Yawkey himself might retire.[4] He was said to have suspected that White was trying to frustrate the trade so he'd be returned to the Red Sox; Yawkey let it be known, very privately, that should White succeed and be returned to Boston, he would not play for the Red Sox again.[5]

In 1960 Yawkey came to Boston on May 2 and, in a reversal of his usual practice, planned to spend more time in Boston than New York, in hopes of bolstering the ball club. Deals tended to happen more when Yawkey was around and active. He was perhaps worried, with good cause, about the direction the team had taken in recent years. When he arrived, the Sox were in third place and only percentage points from second. He was pleased that many of the pitchers were ones the Sox system had developed—Frank Sullivan, Tom Brewer, Bill Monbouquette, and Jerry Casale. The catchers were all home grown (Haywood Sullivan, Ed Sadowski, Don Gile), and there were others among the position players. A ten-game losing streak in May put a damper on his optimism.

"Want Rumors? Stick with Sox" was the headline of an Arthur Siegel *Globe* column on Memorial Day. One of the latest was that Billy Jurges would be fired and Ted Williams named manager, despite Williams's never having shown the least interest in managing. Siegel mocked some of the rumors, pointing out their impossibility, such as purported huddles in hotel rooms between Yawkey and Williams on days that they were in completely different cities. He joked about equipment manager Don Fitzpatrick's being named manager since he was so often seen pitching to Yawkey at the park when the owner took his workouts.

The team was 14-21 at the end of May when Yawkey finally exploded at the Boston press. "I know we have a lousy ball club," he said on the last day of the month. But he boiled over at all the criticism of the team under Billy Jurges. It was Jurges's first full season, and Yawkey thought he should be given a fair chance, particularly given that he'd turned the season around in 1959. "We need human dignity in this world."[6]

Yawkey was caustic: "I can take any one of your stories and find 30 mistakes in it every day. People who couldn't run trolley cars are telling me how to run a $6,000,000 business."[7] He didn't pull any punches and seemed to warn the writers in postgame remarks in the press room that he could pull the Red Sox out of Boston. "I hold the last card. I have the last ace. I won't hesitate to use it. It's as simple as that. Take it or leave it. . . . I don't bluff. I may be talking in innuendoes, but the meaning is clear. Right?"[8] Every news account took it as a threat to move the team.

It wasn't the first time Yawkey's temper had flared, but it was the first time it had been widely reported. At one point in 1948, he'd almost come to blows with a member of the press.[9]

What Yawkey may not have fully grasped was that the writers hadn't blamed Jurges. It was the team itself that was lackluster from the start—"a bloodless crew" in the words of Red Smith—even while the team was still in Scottsdale.[10] And Jurges seemed in over his head from the start. There had even been stories that several of the Red Sox players had advised Yawkey of this situation near the end of spring training.[11]

The strain took its toll on Jurges. With Vic Wertz out with an injury and Ray Boone ailing on June 7, Jurges put veteran outfielder Bobby Thomson at first base for the one and only time in his career. Thomson committed two of the four errors the Sox made in the fourth inning. The Sox infield was charged with five errors, and the Sox lost to the Indians, 12–3. (Thomson hit a solo homer in the game.) John Powers recounts a story that Curt Gowdy told him. "[Thomson] didn't have a mitt, and he made like three errors, so Gowdy goes up after the game [when] Yawkey's had a couple of drinks. Yawkey says, 'Want to buy a ball club? Seven million. Seven million will take it.' Gowdy says, 'Come on, T. A. You're not going to sell this thing.' Yawkey said, 'I saw something tonight I've never seen. A finger glove at first base. This is the Major Leagues! Take it off my hands. Seven million.'"[12]

On June 8 the Red Sox manager announced that on the recommendation of doctors he needed to take a three-week vacation. Two days later, in a move that seemed to legitimately surprise Jurges, he was released (but with full pay). Del Baker was named interim manager and ran the club for seven games (he was 2-5). And then, guess who came back like a bad penny? Pinky Higgins. Harold Kaese's June 13, 1960, column had a headline that summed up the sentiment outside the Sox front office: "Sox Save Money by Naming Higgins; Only Fans Unhappy."

Larry Claflin later wrote that Jurges was fired because of Yawkey's ire over the Bobby Thomson episode (among other reasons). "Jurges told him to play first base one night and Bobby played there with an outfielder's glove. When Tom Yawkey saw Thomson, he cringed in horror, and Jurges soon was an ex-manager."[13]

Managing in Boston was no plum position. Reacting to the recurring rumors that Yawkey wanted Ted Williams to become the manager, Williams replied, "Mr. Yawkey is the greatest owner in the world, without question. I'd do anything in the world for Mr. Yawkey, but he knows how I feel about this. A guy would have to be a sap to manage here unless he's the greatest politician in the world."[14] Cleveland's Cobbledick had a different take on it: "Tom Yawkey, owner of the Red Sox, is a hero worshipper and Williams is his hero. He would not willingly stick Teddy with the managership of a 'lousy ball club.'"[15] A couple of days later, Yawkey said he'd never used the word "lousy" to describe his club but admitted he may have said some things he shouldn't have—though he felt better for having gotten some things off his chest. He said he was not telling the writers what to write.[16]

Some of the criticism was bitter. Milton Gross wrote of "this masquerade for a major-league outfit . . . with an affinity for last place" and how "ridiculous" it was that Yawkey would rehire Higgins, whom he'd fired just a year earlier. Gross hardly got going, given the limitations of space, but he reminded readers that the Sox had paid $100,000 for Les Moss only to let him go for the $10,000 waiver price just a year later. Someone had to take responsibility for hiring the GMs, the managers, and the scouts. He castigated Yawkey for twenty-seven years of "benevolent fumbling."[17] The image of "Baseball Santa" was long gone.

John Gillooly wrote a column in the June 15, 1960, *Record* that characterized the clubbiness of the Red Sox administration and left little hope that the "managerial musical chairs" of bringing in Higgins was going to make any difference at all.

The Sox made a move or two. They traded to acquire outfielder Carroll Hardy and catcher Russ Nixon. The search for a catcher had been long-standing. Indeed Joe Cashman wrote that "Tom Yawkey has spent more money in bonuses for catchers than some owners have spent for an entire big league ball club."[18]

Ted Williams hit his five hundredth home run on June 17. He was only the fourth player in history to reach that mark; Babe Ruth, Jimmie Foxx, and Mel Ott had preceded him. One Red Sox batboy, Paul Needham, will never forget the experience: "I was the Red Sox batboy in 1959 and 1960. It was [Yawkey's] treat for the batboy each year to go on a Western trip. Normally it would have been toward the end of the season, but I was going to the Coast Guard Academy in early July 1960. Mr. Yawkey sent me on a two-week Western trip with the team in June, and Ted wound up hitting his five hundredth home run on that trip, in Cleveland. That was a thrill."[19]

Both Yawkeys reached out to Needham when he left the team. "I remember Mrs. Yawkey sending a cutting down from the *New York Times* that featured the Coast Guard cutter *Eagle*, where we did our training. I got a nice check from [Yawkey] when I left for the Coast Guard Academy, a nice generous 'tip' if you will, a thank you."

As if to show that Ted Williams was not alone in popping off on the field, pitcher Ike Delock got himself suspended by the league for three days for obscene gestures after being removed from the mound.[20]

There was good news on the charitable front. On June 27 the Jimmy Fund elected Tom Yawkey as president of the Children's Cancer Research Foundation. In August he and Ted Williams helped launch a drive to raise a million dollars (more than double the prior fund-raising totals) to help the organization burn the mortgage for a new Jimmy Fund building, which would be burned at home plate prior to the September 24 game against the Yankees.[21] They fell short of the $1 million goal, but in less than two months they still raised over $750,000.

Yawkey often rallied to the side of his players when they were struck with medical adversities. Gary Geiger, the team's twenty-three-year-old outfielder, suddenly suffered a collapsed lung and was rushed to the hospital. For three days in a row, Yawkey spent considerable time at Sancta Maria Hospital visiting the young player. Jean Yawkey visited as well. Tom Yawkey had a very strong benevolent feeling toward many of his players; the man he'd traded to acquire Geiger—Jim Piersall—once called him his "second father" and related how Yawkey had given him $5,000 at a time when he was short that much and hoping to buy a house for his family.[22] The day Geiger was released, he had dinner with Yawkey and watched the ballgame from the owner's roof box. Shortstop Don Buddin was beaned near the end of August and spent several days in the hospital; the Yawkeys visited him as well.

The climactic moment of the 1960 season—which ended with the Red Sox in seventh place—came on September 28, the last home game of the season. Three days earlier, Tom Yawkey had announced that Ted Williams was retiring from baseball. In his last at-bat in the Major Leagues, Ted Williams dramatically homered into the Red Sox bullpen. It was homer 521, the last one of a long career that dated back to just six years after Yawkey bought the team. Ted gave the bat to Bobby Sullivan, Red Sox batboy, and asked him to take it upstairs as a gift to Mr. Yawkey. The Sox owner had watched the game with Jackie Jensen and Dick O'Connell.

The last-minute round of rumors—that Williams would be given stock in the club and brought back as a pinch hitter in 1961—had no basis in fact.

New York Yankees manager Casey Stengel retired as well. "That Tom Yawkey is as fine a man as you'll ever want to meet," he said. "I'll never forget all the help he gave me when I started out in Boston (with the Braves)."[23]

Fortunately for the Red Sox offense, Jackie Jensen agreed to return to the Sox in 1961. A new left fielder—Carl Yastrzemski—was expected to take over, and the team's Minneapolis farm club had a number of other good players waiting in the wings.

The team recorded the worst won/lost mark (65-89) of any Red Sox team since Tom Yawkey had purchased the ball club. Attendance reflected the torpor on the field; the team had drawn over a million but only because of a major promotion Dick O'Connell had arranged with grocery chain First National Stores that added almost three hundred thousand fans coming through the turnstiles.

Near the end of the year, it looked to some that Yawkey's interest in the Red Sox had revived a bit compared to the year before. He'd taken action in late September, relieving both Bucky Harris and farm director Johnny Murphy (he'd held the post for twelve years) of their positions. Dick O'Connell became executive VP, in effect running the business. The "superfluous" position of general manager was eliminated. Neil Mahoney took over the farm system, which would include the Seattle Rainiers, a team that Yawkey had recently purchased. It was the biggest shakeup of Yawkey's ownership. "Sox No Longer Toy for Yawkey" wrote Tom Monahan of the *Traveler*. No one was untouchable any longer. "Today sentiment has no part in his thinking of the Red Sox."[24] But Higgins was given a three-year contract.

Baseball itself was undergoing tremendous change, with expansion on the horizon. Yawkey favored expansion: "I have been for it for the last six years. My fellow club owners of the American League know my sentiments. We missed the boat out in California and now we have to be careful not to miss it again. I did everything I could to further expansion. I acquired the San Francisco club and gave the American League a foot in the door. But my associates felt that the time was not ripe for moving to the Pacific. Well, while we were dawdling, the National League seized the opportunity."[25] Yawkey wasn't as active in league affairs at this time. He was in South Carolina and did not attend the October AL meetings in New York, nor the winter meetings in St. Louis—the only club owner not present. He was nonetheless reelected league VP.

The television show *Lawman*, starring John Russell, featured an episode titled "Yawkey" on October 23. TV listings described it: "A stranger threatens to kill Marshall Troop but refuses to give any reason for the murder attempt." The marshall kills Yawkey in a shootout on the street; Yawkey's gun was unloaded. He had chosen suicide by marshall. The show had nothing to do with Tom Yawkey of the Red Sox, but such an uncommon surname makes one wonder why screenwriter Richard Matheson (a New Jersey native) selected the name.

Something astonishing occurred early in the 1961 season. For the first time since 1933, Tom Yawkey's ball club cut compensation to some of its players. Executive VP Dick O'Connell—effectively the GM—made the announcement in early February. Prior to the announcement, Red Sox policy had been as enunciated by Yawkey just a couple of years earlier: "We'd trade a player, rather than cut his pay." "There have been a few exceptions," he added. "If a player had a bad year and we felt he could make a comeback, we'd promise to restore him to his regular pay if he were worthy of it. But generally speaking, we've never cut a player's salary."[26]

And yet for all that, there had always been change in the club. In all his years as owner, only once (1947-48) had Yawkey seen even the three starting Opening Day outfielders remain the same from one year to the next. In those two years, it was Ted Williams, Dom DiMaggio, and Sam Mele. The most consistency had been in the infield from 1939 through 1941: Foxx (1B), Doerr (2B), Cronin (SS), and Tabor (3B), with Gene Desautels behind the plate all three years.

Yawkey arrived in Scottsdale even before the team. Milt Bolling and Mel Parnell were given new positions with the Red Sox in a conscious effort to bring in younger and more energetic personnel. Higgins was given a bit of a pass by some in the press; Joe Cashman wrote that the Sox had made a mistake in letting Higgins go during the 1959 season but had "rectified" that by bringing him back in 1960.[27]

Without Ted Williams, though, attendance at Scottsdale dropped dramatically. The largely unknown new guy was taking over in left field—Carl Yastrzemski. Ned Martin joined Curt Gowdy in the broadcast booth. But some things did not change; Tom Yawkey still invited five thousand high school and Boys Club youths from around Greater Boston to come to Fenway Park on April 18 for the eleventh annual baseball clinic. Over the years, over two hundred thousand teenagers had seen baseball for free as guests of Mr. Yawkey.[28]

The Sox were 7-7 through April 30—and Jackie Jensen had gone

AWOL the day before. He hopped on a midnight train out of Cleveland without telling anyone. Interviewed as he passed through Ogden, Utah, Jensen said, "I've had it. I know when my reflexes are gone."[29] He was cajoled back after a week and finished out the season but with stats that were nothing special. Between Sammy White and Jensen, Yawkey was having his problems with player personnel. (And in 1962 Gene Conley and Pumpsie Green hopped off the team bus while it was stuck in New York City traffic and decided that they would fly to Israel; see below.)

Yawkey was very sympathetic to Jensen: "Think of Jackie as a member of the family who is harassed by problems and confusions and who needs the sympathy and consideration of everybody. You do everything to help him. You're patient and you encourage him. Jackie is a member of the family, a wonderful member. He's a gentleman. He's a great athlete. He's a great person all around. He deserves every chance to help himself and, I mean this, with the Red Sox coming second."[30]

Yawkey arrived in Boston on May 8 and watched his first game on May 15. On June 9 he paid the biggest bonus he'd ever paid out to seventeen-year-old Boston English High School student and first baseman Bobby Guindon. The bonus was understood to be about $135,000.[31]

Later in June another high school prospect, Rico Petrocelli, paid his first visit to Fenway Park.

> I came into Boston after graduating high school in '61. I came in to work out. I worked out Friday night and Saturday, and on Sunday we got a call to go up to the office. The Red Sox farm director and the general manager and a couple of other people were there, and Mr. and Mrs. Yawkey came in. They said hello and welcome to us—my mother and father and my brother were there. And they offered us a contract. [Yawkey] kind of directed it at my mother and father.
>
> Wow, great! I was supposed to go work out at other places, but we talked about it for a little while and then said, "Yes, we'll sign with Boston." . . .
>
> [It was interesting that Jean Yawkey came in with Tom Yawkey.] Yeah. I didn't expect to see her. I didn't expect to see Mr. Yawkey,

either. They told me later that Mrs. Yawkey liked me. She told me, "You look like Perry Como." I don't know if she had her glasses on.[32]

Track aficionados at Balmoral on June 18 could have put money on one of the greyhounds in the first race of the day—"Yawkey."[33]

Major League Baseball had two All-Star games in 1961. The second was at Fenway Park on July 31. Ted Williams threw out the first ball. The game was tied 1–1 after nine innings, and then rain came. After thirty minutes without a letup, the game was called. Apparently the score amused Tom Yawkey, who had "grumbled" to Curt Gowdy about all the pregame talk that Fenway Park was an easy park to hit in. Gowdy later said he'd run into Yawkey in the press dining room after the game. "He raised a glass as a toast. 'Here's to little ol' Fenway,' Yawkey said. 'They didn't score all the runs they thought they would. We did pretty good today.'"[34]

When the annual Hall of Fame game was played at Doubleday Field, Cooperstown, the capacity was increased by three thousand new bleacher seats thanks to the generosity of Tom Yawkey.[35] The seats had been used at Fenway Park for Boston Patriots games, but with the Patriots having left to play elsewhere, they were no longer needed and were transported from Boston to Cooperstown.

There was another beneficiary of Yawkey largesse during the summer of 1961 (if donating a dozen baseballs could be considered largesse). Thirteen-year-old Jim Prime played first base for a rag-tag team called the Freeport Schooners in the village of Freeport (population 420) on Long Island, Nova Scotia. The team had no equipment to speak of—three bats, cracked and with screws holding them together, and a few balls that had been so taped and retaped that there was no satisfying sound when bat and ball made contact. Jim followed the Red Sox on radio, the signal coming across the water from New England. He heard Curt Gowdy talking about Tom Yawkey, and he wrote to "Tom Yawkey, Owner, Boston Red Sox," asking if he could spare a few baseballs.

Here young Jim was on an isolated island in a small province, in a different country, but, he says, "Two weeks later, to my astonishment and delight, a dozen gleaming American League balls arrived at the local Canada customs office. Most sported green stains. Fenway Park grass. Others had traces of reddish clay. Fenway Park base-path soil. Inexplicably, one bore the signature of Harmon Killebrew, the future Hall of Famer of the Minnesota Twins. I confess that I can still recall the smell of those balls. It was the smell of baseball." A second letter, in 1962, brought the Schooners another dozen base-balls. Prime says today, "Tom Yawkey was no doubt a man of his time and a man with many faults, but I will always remember him fondly as the man who brightened the lives of a group of young boys on a fog-bound island in the Bay of Fundy."[36]

In August Yawkey took in the annual Hearst Sandlot Game at Yankee Stadium. It was a game Yawkey always enjoyed and one he took seriously. Watching Yawkey watch the game, wrote the *Record*'s Bill McSweeny, "it is obvious that he would make as good a talent scout as anyone in this tricky business." He quoted the Red Sox owner: "Look, this is part of the business. I'll give you a few good reasons—Joe Cammarato, Mike Ryan, Russ Gibson, Bill McLeod. Ever hear of them? Those are four kids I first saw in this game. We've got them in our system now. They're great prospects. I'll give you a few more—Bob Guindon, Wilbur Wood, Bill Monbou-quette, Chuck Schilling, Carl Yastrzemski. We took them all out of your big game in New York."[37] In 1962 Yawkey canceled the tradi-tional Red Sox tryout camps in favor of scouting the Hearst game.[38]

In early September Ted Williams was Yawkey's guest in his box at Fenway. Williams was in town to work with, and generally encour-age, Carl Yastrzemski with his hitting.

In the first year after league expansion from eight teams to ten and with the new 162-game schedule, the Red Sox finished sixth, with a record of 76-86 (33 games behind the first-place Yankees). Frank Malzone's 87 RBIs led the team (Yaz was second with 80). Pete Runnels led the team with a .317 average. No pitcher won more than Don Schwall (15-7, 3.22 ERA). The home-versus-away figures were remarkable. The Sox played .617 ball at home and .321 on the road.

As a back story to expansion, Arthur Sampson outlined the moves Joe Cronin and Yawkey had made to pave the way. In 1955, as we have seen, Cronin had undertaken a study of San Francisco as a West Coast location. To "hold" the area on behalf of the American League and the Red Sox, Yawkey purchased the San Francisco Seals and moved his Triple A team there from Louisville. The AL wasn't prepared to place a team on the West Coast but began to think of the Twin Cities for a new franchise, so Yawkey made another move, leaving San Francisco and installing his Triple A club in Minneapolis. The Washington Senators wished to relocate there, so in 1961 Yawkey moved to situate the team's top club in Seattle—not exactly proximate to Boston.[39] The National League snapped up San Francisco, but Yawkey's willingness to continually shift club locations had held three locations for the American League. All three ultimately hosted an AL team, though it was not until 1969 in the case of Seattle. In 1968 the Kansas City club moved its franchise to the Bay Area, becoming the Oakland Athletics.

For the first time in three years, Yawkey attended the winter meetings, in Miami. Again, though they had little to show for it in the standings, the Red Sox were said to have outspent all the other teams in baseball.[40]

In the twenty-first century, the idea of a baseball preseason "fan fair" or caravan tour is almost de rigueur. In 1962 several members of the Red Sox went on a seventeen-day, seventeen-city caravan. Yaz, Pesky, Monbo, Malzone, Schwall, Wilbur Wood, Tracy Stallard, and executives like Dick O'Connell and publicity man Bill Crowley were all part of the tour.

"What's wrong with the Red Sox?" The age-old question was raised again during spring training, with even National League teams asking the question. In the days before interleague play, it was only during the preseason that a team other than a pennant-winner would face a team from the other league. "Where have they been all these years? Why haven't they been right up there with the best?" Those were the kinds of questions baseball people were asking.

Everyone knew how passionate Tom Yawkey was and that he was one of the wealthiest men in America and (with Phil Wrigley of the Cubs) one of the few individuals to own 100 percent of a Major League team. Money was almost no object. Harold Kaese remarked, "That the Red Sox have lacked leadership and good organization is agreed, but why? That is the puzzler." Kaese didn't have any answers.[41]

One hint might have followed a couple of weeks later, when Kaese quoted former farm director Johnny Murphy: "It's one of the hazards of the game. You can like players too much."[42] In Yawkey's case, he may indeed have fallen too much in love with a Gary Geiger, but his bigger failing was probably coming under the spell of some of his staff, with Pinky Higgins perhaps foremost among them. Some even felt, at least in retrospect, that Higgins had something of a Svengali-like influence on Yawkey. It may be difficult from a later perspective to believe that a Pinky Higgins could enthrall someone like Tom Yawkey. The confusion implies rational thought. There was seemingly something else—one suspects it was not just sentiment and not just having a drinking buddy—that made the Red Sox owner something of a captive of so many of his employees. The amateur psychologist could have a field day.

The 1962 Sox were picked to inch up a bit in the standings and to finish fifth. They did not. They sank to eighth place, though winning the same number of games as in 1961. Attendance was down from the start, with only 8,011 coming out for a nice Easter Sunday game. And only 4,937 came to "Couples Night" on May 21 (with 913 ladies); it may have been the first night game at Fenway that drew fewer than five thousand. The game after that only drew 1,424. By year's end, total attendance was only 733,080—in a year when the league average was over 1 million. Turnout at Fenway was down more than 35 percent over what it had been just two years before, in 1960.

Maybe poor attendance wasn't due to inept leadership and a dull team. Maybe one could blame it on the ballpark. Attendance had already fallen off in 1961, and now there was a bit of a drumbeat to reconsider Fenway Park. If the Sox were to stay there, perhaps the parking problem would need to be addressed. If the city of Boston saw the ballpark as an asset, the mayor and some city development officials could sit down with Yawkey and O'Connell and figure out ways to help. Other locations were bruited about—Norwood or Peabody or Saugus or somewhere. The Mass Turnpike was being built, and it was going to pass more or less right behind Fenway's left-field wall, but there was nothing in the way of planned construction of, say, a large municipal parking garage adjacent to the Pike. The buildings on Lansdowne could be demolished, the fence in left field (which some pitchers at the time called the "Green Death") could be moved back a bit, a larger-capacity park could be built, and the area could be enhanced with parking and other modern urban amenities.[43] No one at the time foresaw that Fenway Park could exist, more or less unspoiled, well into the twenty-first century.

Politicians acted. The Massachusetts Senate approved funding for a $50 million stadium for Boston on July 25. Governor John A. Volpe signed the bill into law the next day. Yawkey suggested he might be open to having the Red Sox play in a multisport stadium, though he would want to study the situation thoroughly; however, no one had even yet asked for his thoughts on the subject.[44]

It was at this very time that Pumpsie Green and Gene Conley walked off the team bus while it was stuck in traffic in Manhattan. AWOL for twenty-seven hours, Green showed up in Washington, a little sheepish. Conley took another couple of days before he turned up. He had tried to board a plane for Israel ("I'm going to the Promised Land. I'm gonna get everything straightened out between me and my Savior").[45] But without a passport, that wasn't possible. Green was fined $1,000 and Conley more than that.

Again, though, these were fines for public consumption. While Conley was waiting to talk to the boss in Yawkey's office, Dick Johnson of the Sports Museum of New England relates, "he could see Yawkey in the bathroom shaving. Wearing a t-shirt and shaving. And he could see that Yawkey was smiling or grinning. I am sure Yawkey knew exactly how Gene Conley felt after he'd drunk most of a six-pack of beer and then went off the bus looking for some more. There was something about it that was so amusing, outlandish, and colorful that once he came in for his punishment, he saw that Yawkey was sort of bemused. He wasn't as angry as he was bemused."[46]

Conley told of his meeting with the boss. "Do you really want to know the truth?" Yawkey asked him. "There are times I'd like to do the same thing. But I can't do it because of who I am. When you're in the limelight, you can't do things like this because the publicity's bad, and it's just not done. And you probably don't understand what kind of influence you really have on the public and the kids." Yawkey told Conley he was fining him $1,500 and would take it out of his paycheck as the season progressed, but he added, "If you behave yourself and not pull any more antics like you did and straighten yourself out and show me that you really are concerned about your pitching and your welfare and your family, I'll give it back to you at the end of the season."[47] Dick Johnson's summary: "The fine was a formality. [Yawkey] loved Gene Conley as he loved all of his players and that was that."[48]

"He never stopped loving players," reflected Hall of Fame sportswriter Peter Gammons. "I never thought Tom Yawkey was bitter in any way. He did love the players. He took care of them. When Yaz said he might go to Japan in 1972, he never got mad at Yaz or agent Bob Wolff. I was right in front of his box when Fred Lynn went down in a heap in center field, and Yawkey—you'd think his son had been shot. Before that game was over, he ordered the padding on the center-field wall."[49]

In 1961 pitcher Bill Monbouquette lost his mother to cancer. She was only forty-six at the time. "The first thing he [Yawkey] always said was, 'How is your family?' I wasn't married at that time, but my mother was sick. . . . I remember him saying, 'I'm sorry to hear about your mother.'"[50]

Ted Williams was no longer with the team, and Yaz hadn't yet become the player he would be. The rookie class of 1961 had yet to mature. One player who began to develop in '61 was Jim Pagliaroni. He'd had one plate appearance in 1955 (and got a run batted in with a sacrifice fly) but then didn't get back to the Majors until the last couple of months of 1960. Earlier that year, the Sox had placed him with Spokane, a Dodgers farm club, but Yawkey personally intervened, thinking that Pagliaroni would never get the development he needed while in another team's system. So he told GM Bucky Harris to bring him to Boston, where he had the opportunity to work with Ted Williams the last couple of months that Williams was an active player. It paid off in 1961, with Pagliaroni having a decent season for what was expected of catchers in those days. Had Yawkey not himself perceived the route to pursue, it's possible Pag would never have made it back to the big leagues.

Yawkey arrived in Boston on May 28, prepared to stay for the summer of '62 with occasional trips to New York as needed. He'd tried to make a couple of trades; adding Harvey Kuenn would have been nice, but neither the trade for Kuenn nor Chuck Essegian could be executed.

The well-connected Ed Rumill wrote that Ted Williams was feeling a little underutilized. One wonders if both he and Yawkey were sufficiently self-effacing that an opportunity was lost in the year or two after Ted had retired from the game. "Even though geared most of the time to the minor-league end, Ted is far more absorbed in the operation of the parent club than one would imagine. He finds it difficult, most of the time, to play the 'co-ordinating' role that he understands he is supposed to play with the front office, perhaps because he is basically a shy man and doesn't want to step on anybody's toes," said a close friend of Ted's, according to Rumill. "But I think it's a pity that Tom Yawkey, a fair, wonderful fellow, doesn't know how intensely interested Ted is in building a winner at Fenway Park and that [Ted] would welcome an opportunity to move permanently into an office at Fenway, roll up his sleeves, and plunge into the building of a winning cast." There was a caveat, and a big one: "Ted wouldn't consider it unless Yawkey would give him as much free rein as is possible in a tremendous big-league operation of this sort."[51]

It may have been for the best. Whether Williams could work months on end the way a modern GM does, without going fishing for a fair part of the time, would have been an open question. He wasn't always the most patient of men, and he did have his prejudices (against pitchers) and his blind spots. One might suggest, though, that he'd have tried harder than Higgins.

The 1962 ball club played so poorly that as early as mid-June there were comparisons with the 1933 Red Sox, Yawkey's first ball club—albeit one he had just purchased, not one that had benefitted from twenty-eight years of purported development under the auspices of a wealthy owner for whom baseball was a passion. The 1933 club had a .423 winning percentage. After the June 14 game, the 1962 Red Sox were at .421. They ended at .475. This time the home-versus-away figures were not as marked as in some other years; the Sox were under .500 both home and away. A 3-3 road trip ending in early June wasn't cause to break out champagne, but it was celebrated in the sports cartoon of the June 4 *Record American.*

Yawkey saw his first game of the year on June 6. On June 26 Earl Wilson threw a no-hitter against the White Sox. Making one of his rare visits to the Red Sox clubhouse, Yawkey tore up Wilson's contract on the spot and gave him a new one. It was a typical Yawkey move. In this case, given that Wilson had been the second black player on the team, it perhaps reflected the side of Tom Yawkey that had always argued he had no personal prejudice.

Monbouquette threw a no-hitter on August 1, and he got the same $1,000 raise that Wilson got.

Nobody won more than fifteen games, however. Conley and Monbo each won that many. Wilson won twelve. "The Monster"— Dick Radatz—was stellar in relief, pitching in sixty-two games, earning a 2.24 ERA, and winning nine games. But the team just wasn't drawing.

Newspapers wondered if Higgins would quit. Should he do so, "it will not be all teardrops at Fenway Park, where . . . some people consider him a steady, patient man with too little imagination to wake up a steady outfit," wrote Larry Claflin, who claimed that a number of other managers in baseball—Al Lopez, Paul Richards, John McHale—had all declined tentative offers to come work for the Red Sox.[52]

Austen Lake suggested that Yawkey should put up a portion of the club for public sale. If he did that, he might have "a flock of hardboot investors to satisfy at his annual stockholders' meeting." If he did, "he'd start chasing his pampered pets around Fenway Park, including those 30-odd scouts on his payroll." Lake thought "Yawkey's kind of patient resignation over the years is an admirable trait for a church deacon or a welfare worker or a spouse," but Lake clearly subscribed to Leo Durocher's "nice guys don't win pennants" philosophy.[53]

On October 6 the Red Sox announced that Johnny Pesky would be promoted from skipper of the Triple A Seattle Rainiers to become field manager of the Boston team for 1963. Higgins was bumped upstairs and named "executive vice president in charge of baseball." Yawkey and Higgins called Pesky together, and the next day he joined them in Yawkey's box at the World Series between the Yankees and Giants. Hiring Pesky was seen as a move to give the club more vitality and increase ticket sales in the year to come.

The search for a right-handed slugger let the team to a pair of November trades. They picked up Dick Stuart (and pitcher Jack Lamabe) from the Pirates on November 20 for Don Schwall and Jim Pagliaroni. And on November 26 the Sox traded the 1962 AL batting champion, Pete Runnels (who'd also won the crown in 1960), to the Houston Colt .45's for Roman Mejias. By spring training 1963, Mejias's family had been brought to the United States from Cuba, and there were suggestions that Yawkey had worked some quiet diplomacy to reunite the player with his family.[54] Indeed after acquiring Mejias, Yawkey instructed his front office to spare no expense in reuniting the ballplayer with his family. Red Sox management worked with the State Department and the Red Cross to, in the overwrought Cold War rhetoric of reporter Hy Hurwitz, "ransom the outfielder's brood from the clutches of Castroism."[55]

Higgins represented the Red Sox at the 1962 winter meetings in New York, where it was decided to revert back to having just one All-Star game during the season.

The Red Sox took in the homeless. There was a change of mind early in January, and the Red Sox agreed to permit the American Football League's Boston Patriots to play their 1963 and 1964 home games at Fenway Park. The agreement followed two months of negotiations between Dick O'Connell of the Red Sox and Billy Sullivan of the Patriots. Playing at old Braves Field had limited the Patriots' crowd size to about twenty-two thousand, so the opportunity to play in much larger Fenway offered them a chance to better establish themselves in Boston. (Fenway had hosted the Boston Redskins for four years beginning in Yawkey's first year of ownership, 1933, as well as the Boston Bears [1940] and the Boston Yanks [1944–48].) "Yawkey Saves Pats for Boston" read the January 7, 1963, headline in the *Boston Globe.* The headline in *The Sporting News* was "Red Sox Agree to Shelter Homeless Patriots."[56]

New manager Johnny Pesky brought some fresh air to the Red Sox. He determined to build a little more discipline. Early in spring

Portrait of a younger Tom Yawkey.
Courtesy of the Yawkey Foundations.

William Clyman
Yawkey, Tom Yawkey's
grandfather. Courtesy of
the Yawkey Foundations.

William Hoover Yawkey,
Tom Yawkey's adoptive
father. Courtesy of the
Yawkey Foundations.

Tom Yawkey as a baby.
Courtesy of the Yawkey
Foundations.

Tom Yawkey as a child.
Courtesy of the Yawkey
Foundations.

Young Tom Yawkey at the Irving School.
Tom is in the second row on the far left.
Courtesy of the Yawkey Foundations.

Tom Yawkey in the Red Sox dugout with slugger Jimmie Foxx, ca. 1936–41.
Leslie Jones photograph, courtesy of the Boston Public Library.

Boston Red Sox owner Tom Yawkey with American League president Will
Harridge near the dugout at Fenway Park. Leslie Jones photograph, courtesy
of the Boston Public Library.

Tom and Jean Yawkey on South Island during the earlier years of their marriage. Courtesy of the Yawkey Foundations.

Ted Williams signing his contract at the desk of Red Sox general manager Eddie Collins at Fenway Park. Leslie Jones photograph, courtesy of Boston Public Library.

Red Sox manager Pinky Higgins, owner Tom Yawkey, and general manager Joe Cronin, ca. 1956. Leslie Jones photograph, courtesy of Boston Public Library.

Tom and Jean Yawkey in their separate but adjoining boxes above and behind home plate at Fenway Park. Courtesy of the Yawkey Foundations.

An original oil painting by Jean Yawkey, now gracing a wall at Tara Hall. Her choice of subject matter demonstrates how deeply she came to care about baseball and the Red Sox. Photograph by Bill Nowlin.

Tom Yawkey and Dr. Sidney Farber of the Jimmy Fund, the official charity of the Boston Red Sox since 1953. Courtesy of the Yawkey Foundations.

A younger Tom Yawkey, with a hat full of puppies in South Carolina. Courtesy of the Yawkey Foundations.

Sunset Lodge. Courtesy of Keta Forrest.

Tom Yawkey all dressed up—for comfort. Courtesy of the Yawkey Foundations

Phil Wilkinson and Tom Yawkey.
This is the way almost all Yawkey's
employees in South Carolina saw
him. Courtesy of Phil Wilkinson.

Tom Yawkey catching a ball at Fenway Park during one of his many workouts on the field with the clubhouse crew. Courtesy of the Yawkey Foundations.

Tom and Jean Yawkey in later years. Courtesy of the Yawkey Foundations.

Tom Yawkey watching a
ballgame—one that may have
been going well. Courtesy of the
Yawkey Foundations.

Tom Yawkey's principal residence: Tom's trailer, South Island, South Carolina. Photograph by Bill Nowlin.

Interior, Tom Yawkey's trailer, South Island, South Carolina. Photograph by Bill Nowlin.

Jean Yawkey, New England Woman
of the Year, May 1988. Courtesy of
the Yawkey Foundations.

Four employees at the Yawkey Wildlife Center, 2013. (*From left*) Joseph "Tiny" Collington, Jim Sargent, Phil Wilkinson, Jamie Dozier. Photograph by Bill Nowlin.

General view of part of the Yawkey Wildlife Center. Photograph by Bill Nowlin.

Earthen dam at the Yawkey Wildlife Center. It illustrates one of the ways that the land and waters were managed in the interests of wildlife and not run as a preserve. Photograph by Bill Nowlin.

Ted Williams and Tom Yawkey.
National Baseball Hall of Fame
Library, Cooperstown, New York.

training, he imposed a midnight curfew. Touring the winter dinner circuit, he said he was going to require more hustle. Incoming managers always say that, but early in spring training, one of the players said, "Johnny really means it. Furthermore, he makes you like it."[57] He took an active role himself, even to the point of holding teaching sessions where he instructed his men in sliding. Pesky had been Yawkey's personal choice for manager, the owner overruling some of his advisers who had recommended someone with more experience.[58]

Pesky was fiery enough that he even managed to get himself ejected from a spring training game. Higgins—sometimes called "Mr. Stand Pat"—was never ejected from a game, not as a player, coach, or manager. Pesky was certainly a hit with the fan base.

The Red Sox opened the 1963 season in Los Angeles, playing the Angels in a night game that was broadcast in Boston beginning at 11:00 p.m.—not the way any East Coast team would want to try to kick-start a season. Given newspaper deadlines of the day, the final results wouldn't even make the morning papers. The Sox lost, 4–1.

For the first five to six weeks of the season, the Sox played much better than in the prior couple of years. They won the fifteen-inning game on April 20—with Tom Yawkey listening to Higgins giving him a pitch-by-pitch account over the telephone.[59]

The Sox were tied for first place as late as May 19. Yawkey arrived for the summer on June 10. The team was only five games out on that date, and he saw them win six games in a row. Yaz was beginning to make his mark; on June 19 he hit two homers—both into the center-field bleachers. As the season developed, though, the Red Sox fell progressively further and further behind the league-leading Yankees. They had made a brief appearance in second place as late as July 23, though they were nine games behind at the time, more or less tied with the Twins, White Sox, and Orioles. A nine-game losing streak to kick off August did not help, part of a 3-18 stretch from July 23 to August 11. It was one of the worst stretches any Yawkey club had suffered.

One would never see a thousand nuns at a Red Sox game in the twenty-first century, but that's how many turned out for the annual

Nuns' Day at Fenway on July 25, all eating complimentary ice cream and peanuts.

Yawkey expressed regret that in thirty years his teams had won only one pennant. "There have been so many wonderful people coming to this park through the years and it had bothered me very much that they have often gone away disappointed. This is a great baseball area and it is deserving of much, much more than I have been able to give it." Baseball humbles people, and Yawkey said that the game had taught him patience, adding, "The game is bigger than any club or any individual."[60]

In each year of the early 1960s, Yawkey was less visible in the papers than in the year before. When he gave an interview to the *Globe* at the end of August, he seemed oddly upbeat. "This club made the summer lively around Boston. It's too bad the club went into a slump where nothing seemed to work for victories. The finish of the season could be exciting, although this time it's a matter of how high it can finish instead of being a pennant contender."[61] The team was twenty-one games out of first place and there was a possibility of finishing in fifth place, but perhaps fans could be forgiven for not seeing such a finish as "exciting."

The team finished 76-85, in seventh place, twenty-eight games behind New York. It drew 209,000 more fans than the year before, though, a 28.5 percent increase. Near the end of the year, however, attendance dropped; only 674 paying customers came to the September 24 game. The overall boost in ticket sales took the team to profitability. Pesky was given another one-year deal.

Bill Monbouquette was a twenty-game winner (20-10), and Dick Radatz had been superb out of the bullpen, 15-6 (with a 1.97 ERA). No one else won more than eleven games, and the two who did (Earl Wilson and Dave Morehead) both had losing records. Yaz led the league with a .321 batting average and a .418 on-base percentage. Dick Stuart homered 42 times (second in the league) and drove in a league-leading 118 runs. But standout stars alone don't guarantee success.

The *Boston Herald* held a contest during the season to come up with a nickname for Dick Radatz, who reportedly hadn't liked being called "the Monster." Neither Yawkey voted, but Tom said he thought "the Moose" was good because that's what Radatz had been called in college. Jean favored "Smokey" since Willie Mays had characterized Radatz's pitching after the All-Star Game as "Smoke—just smoke." The paper's readers settled on "Smokey," but it never caught on.[62] "The Monster" he remained.

There were still ongoing issues regarding race and the Red Sox. The NAACP wrote to the team in September, asking it to reconsider its use of Ocala, Florida, for one of its farm clubs due to segregation there. Hundreds had been jailed in anti-segregation protests over the summertime.[63]

GM Pinky Higgins still hadn't changed his personal views, as became evident during the World Series between the Yankees and Dodgers. There, Bud Collins recounted, he had a memorable encounter with Higgins and a plate of beef stroganoff:

All the writers were in a larger room, and I was seated at a table with seven or eight guys. One was Danny Murtaugh, the manager of the Pirates at the time. I was sitting with Larry Claflin. Higgins sort of staggered into the room. Claflin said to me, "Mike has had a few too many." I was just eating and trying to ignore Higgins as he staggered around the table, and suddenly he reached out when he got behind me, and all of a sudden I found myself in a plate of beef stroganoff. He was mumbling, "doesn't know anything about baseball"—directed at me—and the other guys at the table were shocked. Something was wrong. Everybody quieted. And there I was in the beef stroganoff. I didn't have any recourse; I wasn't going to chase him. And he staggered out of the room and went on.

Higgins had "very strong racial views," as Collins put it. The beef stroganoff incident was no accident. "He wanted to get even or think he was getting even about something I had written." Collins had been served seconds before finishing his own meal. "I like beef stroganoff. It was fine. I had a drip-dry suit on so I could straighten myself out."[64]

Yawkey was again elected chairman of the Jimmy Fund and as VP of the American League.

On December 12 Tom Yawkey lost his sister Emma at the age of sixty-nine. She had been the owner of the Daneshall Stables in Louisville. It is not clear how close the two were, though the Yawkey business interests later passed to her son, Robert Gardner.[65]

Looking ahead to 1964, Higgins seemed to acknowledge that the team didn't have the pieces they needed to make trades. "I think I proved a year ago that I am willing to make trades, and trade good players," he said. "But the situation is different this winter. We can't afford to trade a player if we have no one to take his place." Larry Claflin wrote, "If that isn't a clear admission of a lack of talent on Tom Yawkey's team, then what is?"[66]

Frank Sullivan offered some gallows humor just as the new year broke. He'd heard how much the payoff would be if an airline crash killed the whole team and asked, "Which way do you think Yawkey is rooting?"[67]

Some minor flare-ups occurred during the first month or two of 1964. Charles Finley of the Athletics talked about moving the franchise out of Kansas City to Louisville, Kentucky. That didn't go over well with the other owners. Carl Yastrzemski made some remarks at the writers' dinner that were critical of his manager, Johnny Pesky. In early March, Pesky even felt compelled to deny there was a plot against him. Dick Stuart and Higgins were known to have their differences with him as well. "I probably did too much expounding last year, and that may have bothered some of the boys," Pesky said.[68] The team made almost no moves over the winter and was described by Bud Collins as "Inertia, Inc."; he wrote that "even Aladdin's genie would get a hernia trying to pull them into the first division."[69]

Higgins seemed to be content to sit on the sidelines and do little or nothing to help Pesky, perhaps hoping that Pesky would fail. Johnny himself told of times when he walked into Higgins's office and the GM kept his back to him, reading the newspaper and ignoring his appeals to make some moves to build up the ball club.[70] As John Gillooly wrote, "[Higgins] acted most of the time as though he didn't even know Pesky was around Fenway Park."[71]

President John F. Kennedy had been shot and killed in Dallas in November 1963. Tom Yawkey and the Red Sox decided to take all the receipts from Opening Day 1964 and donate them to the John F. Kennedy Memorial Library. "This was Mr. Yawkey's own decision," said Dick O'Connell.[72] Among those attending the game was John S. Dooley, 91, who was there for his seventy-first consecutive opener, along with his daughter Lib.

In Scottsdale, Tony Conigliaro—who had turned nineteen only in January—showed talent with the bat that hadn't been seen in a Boston ballplayer since Ted Williams.

Yankees co-owner Del Webb attended a meeting of the Greater Boston Real Estate Board at the end of April. He said he was disappointed that he hadn't heard much more about a multisport stadium in Boston. "I'm sure Tom Yawkey would welcome one," he said. "If you don't get one, Fenway Park will be an antiquated part of the New Boston."[73] For his part, O'Connell was explicit, "Yes. Mr. Yawkey would like to see a new stadium in Boston."[74] Whether he would leave Fenway was yet to be determined since no details regarding how the Red Sox might fit into any new stadium plans had been forthcoming.

Greater Boston Stadium Commission chair Billy Sullivan said he thought they were getting very close. Even though they'd not talked with Yawkey himself, they had met with Dick O'Connell and others with the Red Sox. The Sox didn't know what it would cost to be a tenant in a new stadium, with whom else they might be sharing the facility, nothing.

Yawkey came to town at least sixty pounds lighter. He first appeared at his Fenway Park desk on May 26. He was looking forward to seeing Tony Conigliaro and hearing good things about Tony Horton of the Reading Red Sox. Gary Geiger was gone by then; he'd played five games and then had to be hospitalized for an ulcer and then had an operation for a urinary obstruction. He was out for the rest of the year.

Another of those classic Tom Yawkey stories cropped up during the 1964 season. Right-hander Pete Charton was with the Red Sox for what proved to be his only season in the Majors. He'd debuted on April 19 and worked exclusively in relief until he was given five starts in September; he lost his only two decisions. At one point not long after Yawkey arrived in town, Charton had decided to wash his new Corvette under the stands at Fenway. Charton tells the tale:

An older, plain-looking gentleman in scruffy crepe-soled shoes appeared and asked if I needed any help. Glad to have some help, I carefully explained to the man how to wash and wax, giving him some blunt tips about not scratching paint with his belt buckle and watchband. I explained that since we were using Red Sox towels, we needed to be quiet to avoid the wrath of the clubhouse manager.

He nodded sagely and said he could handle the assignment. As we worked, the man asked me many questions, mostly about me. When we finished, I thanked him and tried to pay him and even offered him an autographed baseball. He declined and I told him to call on me if he ever needed help. I then asked him his name and he replied, "Tom Yawkey," with a twinkle in his eye. He assured me of how much he had enjoyed assisting me and talking, and said in the future I could have all the towels I needed! [75]

Charton says that several other times that summer Yawkey helped him clean and wax the car. "We had some wonderful talks, and I began to appreciate what Bostonians had known about him long before I arrived. His humility and concern for other people stood out. He spoke with such pride and admiration for the history and tradition of the Red Sox, and he had such confidence in the future."

The season's first half ended at 38-41, after a July 5 win in which the Sox scored three times in the bottom of the eighth to take a 9-6 win. After the game, Pesky's phone rang and reporters heard him say, "Thank you, sir" several times. Apparently Yawkey had called and been pleased that Pesky had shown some fire, arguing with the umpire that Radatz had been thrown at intentionally by the Angels pitcher.[76] After Radatz was hit by the pitch, a walk followed and then a Tony Conigliaro home run, his fifteenth of the season.

Conigliaro's arm was broken in the second game on July 26, struck by a Pedro Ramos fastball. He was out until September 4. (Tony had a habit of crowding the plate; a bone in his hand had been broken by a Moe Drabowsky pitch on May 24.) Pesky had taken a big chance promoting a teenager to the big leagues, but Conigliaro had quite a rookie year, despite missing over fifty games; he still hit 24 homers (batting .290) and drove in 52.

The sale of the Yankees to a group in which CBS held a majority stake was approved in August by an 8–2 vote. A couple of weeks later, Yawkey said that, regardless of what the public liked to think, baseball was a business and needed to be run like one. The Red Sox had voted for the sale. He didn't see a conflict of interest.[77]

The Red Sox continued to slip as the season wore on, and losing twelve out of thirteen games starting on August 1 sank the team into eighth place. That's where it ended up—72-90, twenty-seven games behind. After the seventieth win (total attendance: 306), Johnny Pesky was fired, and Pinky Higgins named Billy Herman as interim manager for the final two games. Yawkey absented himself, leaving town just before the press conference at which the announcement was made by Higgins, whom the *Traveler* called the "chief executioner."[78] Even though Pesky managed in the Pirates system over the following four seasons, he was back with the Red Sox as a broadcaster in 1969 and remained on the Red Sox payroll until his death in 2012. His understanding was that on his return, Yawkey had ensured he would be with the Red Sox for life, a pledge honored by the team even after it passed from Yawkey hands.

As 1965 opened, the Red Sox views about the proposed new stadium had become clarified; Dick O'Connell announced in January:

> We want a new stadium, but only if we are designated the principal tenant. That means we would want to make all the big decisions concerning the stadium. We would want control of the concessions, and in general, we would want to be in charge. To date, the Red Sox have not been offered anything concrete. For example, we haven't any idea how much our rent would be in the [proposed] new stadium. So until we're given something definite that would make it feasible for us to move we will only say that we hope it works out.[79]

For a team that would play a minimum of eighty-one dates in the facility—more than any other tenant—control no doubt seemed reasonable. Chairman of the Stadium Commission Sullivan (who happened to be president of the Boston Patriots) said the commission could not abdicate the responsibility invested in it by the state legislature.

In a bit of a rebuke to Red Sox management, the biggest applause of the night at the Writers' Dinner on January 28, 1965, was for Johnny Pesky, seated in the audience. The conventional wisdom became that Higgins had had it in for Pesky since Yawkey installed Pesky and kicked Higgins upstairs; but Higgins preferred being on the field, and "instead of being able to work closely with the general manager as any successful manager, Pesky was forced to work with one eye on his players and the other over his shoulder. He was a marked man from the start. Higgins resented [Pesky's] succession to the job, and was determined to get rid of him as soon as possible."[80] It was Yawkey again who reappointed Pesky for 1964. Whatever Pesky's shortcomings may have been, "his direct boss [Higgins] hardly spoke to him, and then only to make snide remarks about the failure of the ball club to do better."[81]

Billy Herman became the manager for 1965 and 1966. The team lost ten more games than under Pesky in '64, finishing with 62 wins and exactly 100 losses. It was the first time since Yawkey had purchased the team that the Red Sox lost as many as 100 games. The only pitcher to win more games than he lost was Bob Duliba (4-2). Earl Wilson (13-14) had the most wins. Radatz's ERA worsened by a full run, and he was 9-11. Yaz led batters in average, his .312 the only one over .300, but he drove in only 72 runs. Felix Mantilla led the team with 92 RBIs. Tony Conigliaro's 32 homers ranked him first on the Red Sox. By July 5 the team was in ninth place, and it never got any higher. The Red Sox finished 40 games behind the Minnesota Twins. Things weren't getting better; they were getting worse.

Al Hirshberg wrote that Billy Herman "was more interested in golf than in baseball. . . . All Herman had in his favor was Higgins's blessing. . . . Herman lasted two years, and the Red Sox finished ninth both times."[82] It was cronyism at its worst. Clark Booth said, "It was like a lodge. It wasn't a company. It wasn't a team. It wasn't an operation. It was a lodge; it was a club in the other sense. A social club."[83]

The 1965 season may have been the nadir of the Yawkey years. As the *Herald*'s Steve Buckley said nearly fifty years later, "It wasn't a curse that kept the Red Sox from winning a World Series. It was 'isms'—it was alcoholism, it was cronyism, and it was racism. . . . Yawkey liked hiring drinking buddies, because they weren't just club executives and foot-soldiers; they were people he could drink with. And that's not a good way to run a business."[84]

Neil Mahoney was farm director at the time. His assistant, Ed Kenney, somewhat bluntly told Jack Mann of *Sports Illustrated*, "We don't fire many people." Mann noted at the time that "all Red Sox officials except Personnel Vice-President Mike Higgins, Executive Assistant Ted Williams, and Yawkey himself are Massachusetts products."[85] Of course, this closed system of hiring was one of the reasons that the team later found itself forced into a settlement with the Massachusetts Commission against Discrimination because friends hiring friends typically resulted in no employees of color being hired.

Most of the players on the team were home grown too. Of the thirty-nine men on the Sox spring roster that year, twenty-seven were farm products, Mann noted. As mentioned above, Yawkey hardly ever cut a player's salary from year to year. "They say there's no sentiment in baseball," he says almost sheepishly, "but I guess I have more than most."[86]

Yawkey also took the time to comment on race, albeit a little clumsily. Mann wrote, "It is easy now for Bostonian critics, seeking a policy man behind such a self-defeating pattern, to point fingers at Mike Higgins, an unreconstructed Texan with classically Confederate views on Negroes, but it is too easy. Higgins, who did not become field manager until 1955 and did not take a desk in the front office until 1962, could hardly have become the Caucasian in the woodpile." Mann continued:

"They blame me," Yawkey says, "and I'm not even a Southerner. I'm from Detroit." Yawkey remains on his South Carolina fief until May because Boston weather before then is too much for his sensitive sinuses. "I have no feeling against colored people," he says. "I employ a lot of them in the South. But they are clannish, and when that story got around that we didn't want Negroes they all decided to sign with some other club. Actually, we scouted them right along, but we didn't want one because he was a Negro. We wanted a ballplayer."[87]

Needless to say, it strains credibility to believe that the Red Sox were simply victims of bad luck in scouting, and stories passed around among black players. And it begs the question of whether Tom Yawkey felt he was so powerless that he and his staff couldn't have managed to sign black ballplayers to the team until after every other team in baseball had done so.

During the baseball season, Yawkey arrived early—for him—on May 18. The team was already in seventh place. The first game he saw was a 17–5 drubbing at the hands of the Twins.

Bud Collins wrote a scathingly sarcastic column a couple of days after the June 15 trading deadline had passed: "Would they try to break up an eighth place ball club? Although many people were fearful of what might happen to Our Dear Old Town Team when Uncle Tom and Patient Mike and Brave Billy got through thinking (in that order), their fears were unfounded. Red Sox loyalists were not disappointed. Because what the three did was in the great Red Sox tradition, the tradition we have learned to love and respect. The Red Sox Triumvirate reached the decision to do: Nothing."[88] To be fair, some teams saw the situation the Sox were in and tried to take advantage by asking for too much in exchange.

The only trade the Sox had made in preparation for 1965 was to swap their leading home run and RBI man—Dick Stuart—to the Phillies in November 1964 for left-handed pitcher Dennis Bennett. Bennett's record in 1965 was 5-7. He had a sore arm; before the season began, Bob Carpenter of the Phillies assured Yawkey that his team would adjust the terms of the trade to compensate the Red Sox after they saw how Bennett performed.[89]

After a 3-14 stretch, Herman decided to do a bed check and see if his unusually liberal curfew was being observed. Nope. Six players were still out after 2:00 a.m. That he fined the players in question was "a bit of a bomb hurled into . . . Yawkey's traveling country club."[90] Ed Rumill's next-day column was titled "Yawkey, Boston Deserve Better." He suggested that if fines didn't do the trick, dumping a couple of players might make the point. Al Hirshberg added, "I don't know why other clubs get good general managers and we get Mike Higginses. I don't know why Tom Yawkey, a class guy who always refused to settle for anything less than the best, has had such a tough time finding a top man to run his ball club. There are plenty of good ones in the two leagues."[91]

The letters-to-the-editor columns of the various Boston papers reflected criticism of Yawkey himself. Richard Perkins of Needham wrote the *Traveler*, "To my mind, what's wrong is owner Tom Yawkey. The club is too much of a plaything and too little a serious venture with him. He relies more on friendly relations than on efficiency, both in players and executive positions."[92] Dick Brown of Wenham wrote, "A more demanding owner would, it seems to me, require a more productive business."[93] One wonders how the New York office handling the Yawkey lumber and mining interests was run.

Ed Linn was bemused by the reverence accorded Yawkey: "Because he loved his players, he spoiled them rotten. And because he spoiled them rotten, they praised him to the skies. Yet there was always the sense that the praise was so unreserved ('the greatest owner in baseball' was practically engraved on his forehead) that it was being overdone. There was always the whiff of something obligatory about it."[94]

Peter Golenbock was a little harsh, writing about slugging first baseman Dick Stuart: "Stuart fit the Tom Yawkey player prototype: he hit home runs, packed the stadium, was overpaid, and lost more ballgames than he won. And worst of all, he invested everyone around him with his negative attitude."[95]

Glenn Stout and Richard Johnson quote a former associate as saying that Yawkey did little more than "act like a rich guy and pretend to work."[96] They continue:

> The front office was usually indifferent, making few trades and apparently satisfied with a group of chronic underachievers. . . . [Yawkey's] familiar old cronies still ran the organization, chief among them Pinky Higgins, protecting the status quo, demanding little from his team, virtually guaranteeing mediocrity. . . . It was said of Yawkey that he never met a big league player he didn't like and never met a Red Sox player he didn't love like a member of the family. [For the Sox players] he was the perfect boss—he paid well and didn't expect much in return.[97]

It sounds like the reputation William Yawkey had with the Tigers. Tom Yawkey himself was going through another phase of being discouraged: "I am not planning to sell the Red Sox. I am not soliciting potential buyers. But I have been thinking about selling the team and I would sell the Red Sox if I thought the 'right' people want to buy it." He was very clear that he wouldn't sell to "peculiar" people or to those seeking a fast buck. But he was sixty-two years old and didn't want to see the team caught up in estate issues. He said he was well aware of the criticism, "and in most instances I think it has been just."[98]

Seeing the turmoil team ownership would go through after Yawkey's death in 1976, one wonders if he had taken his own advice sufficiently to heart. Talking on the subject in 1965, he said the following:

> No one has come forth with a concrete dollars-and-cents offer for the franchise in the past few years. I have been asked if I ever considered selling the club, and the honest answer is yes. Anybody who gets past 60 thinks of such things as setting up an inheritance.
>
> A ball club is a poor thing to have in an estate. A probate court wants liquid assets. In many cases, the courts have insisted a ball club be sold immediately. I know it caused a lot of havoc in the Briggs case in Detroit. I have given this question a lot of thought. I'm not worrying, but I like to plan things out in advance. I feel better than I have in 15 or 20 years, but I'm a fatalist. When your time comes, that's it.[99]

Bob Holbrook wrote that Yawkey "has made mistakes, plenty of them, and admits it. One of them was the lamentable situation when Jackie Robinson, Sam Jethroe, and another Negro got the brush off at Fenway Park in 1945. The sale of Pee Wee Reese was another."[100]

Player-manager Joe Cronin had resisted Reese's advancement in the Red Sox system—quite possibly because Reese, as a shortstop, threatened him at his own position. When the Dodgers' Larry MacPhail realized there was an opportunity, he offered Yawkey $75,000 for Reese and bought the future Hall of Famer's contract. David Halberstam later wrote, "Yawkey, who did not need the money, had virtually given away a diamond of a player without even giving him a shot at the major leagues."[101]

The veteran Harold Kaese wrote, "The Red Sox are dead." He'd been covering Boston baseball since Yawkey's first year, 1933, when he worked for the *Boston Transcript*. Kaese was led to the conclusion that "ever since Tom Yawkey bought the Red Sox from Bob Quinn, they have been weak on organization. The only thing in which the Red Sox have excelled as an organization is arrogance. . . . On the Sox, the brass blames the scouts for not digging up prospects. The scouts blame the managers for misusing their prospects. And the managers blame the brass for not giving them moral support. What the Sox have always lacked is thoroughness, attention to detail."[102]

After Kaese's remarks appeared, Billy Herman made an announcement that was hardly likely to boost morale: he said that the club would rid itself of ten players by year's end, four of them before the end of the season. "We're going to get rid of the dead wood we've been carrying, all of the dead wood."[103]

There might have been a shakeup coming, but Kaese correctly predicted it wouldn't include Higgins or Herman. He later suggested the team employ a detective agency to check up on the players because it was clear that Herman would never do it effectively. On September 5 Kaese's column was headed "Boston's Decline Traced to Yawkey." There was no personal animosity in the air, and everyone acknowledged Yawkey's humility and his commitment to charitable works. A big part of the problem, Kaese argued, was "Green Death"—the left-field wall. The Sox had never led the league in ERA and even in 1946 ranked only fourth of eight teams. The wall bore blame, yes, but, Kaese continued,

[the park] cannot be blamed for the complacency, disorganization, over-confidence, and poor judgment that have beset the Red Sox. The fault here lies with the owner and his executives. The closest the Sox have come to a keen, lively, efficient general manager was Eddie Collins, who held office TAY's first 15 years and was responsible for the most successful teams. . . . Yawkey picked Cronin after Collins because he liked him. When Cronin became league president, Yawkey picked Bucky Harris because he liked him and owed him something for having fired him as manager in 1934. . . . When Harris was released, Yawkey gave the GM job to another man he liked—Mike Higgins.[104]

Some thought Yawkey's impulse to charity may have also included keeping on less than fully competent scouts and other front office people simply because he couldn't bring himself to let them go. In a nationally syndicated column, Jim Murray—later awarded a Pulitzer Prize for his commentary—noted that Yawkey "has remained as unconcerned as the skipper of the Titanic."[105]

Yawkey let it be known during the summer that the shedding of 60–80 pounds over the winter was deliberate. He hadn't been feeling well during the summer of 1963, when he turned sixty, and doctors had advised him to lose weight. Trainer Jack Fadden convinced him to have a physical, and it was found he had diabetes.[106] It was the first checkup he'd had in many years. He gave up drinking almost entirely. He had a more thorough workup at the Lahey Clinic.[107] There may have been much more involved than a routine checkup, though the newspapers took no note at the time. Ted Lepcio, who played eight seasons for the Red Sox, alluded to a hospital stay: "I think when Yawkey spent those thirty days in the hospital, the doctors told him, 'You either quit or you're going to die.'"[108] The treatment and abstinence may well have saved his life. Television reporter Clark Booth, who began covering the team for WBZ-TV in 1967 and was friends with Dick O'Connell, says of Yawkey, "He went through a drying-out period in the mid-sixties, when he got the riot act read to him."[109]

Addressing the idea that he was seen as something of a phantom in Boston, Yawkey said, "I have never tried to be a mysterious type of character. I just like to do things my own way and keep to myself. I don't like to ask favors. In my position if someone does you a favor they'll be looking for 12 in return."[110] He had earlier said he'd only asked one favor of the powers-that-be in all his years in Boston—and that he'd been turned down. Yawkey's wishes for the city to help provide more parking in the area never bore fruit. "I don't know who was advising him from a local standpoint," said Dick Johnson. "It doesn't seem that he had a real brain trust. That is almost fatal in Boston. It's not enough to just be the Red Sox. You've got to have some political skills to do things."[111] But that wasn't the kind of guy Tom Yawkey was, nor did he seem to have what it took to hire people with such skills.

Dick Flavin served as Boston mayor Kevin White's press secretary at City Hall from 1967 to 1970. In contrast to the early twenty-first-century Red Sox, Flavin didn't recall any interaction between the ball club and the mayor to speak of. "I don't remember there being much contact at all. The Red Sox just weren't set up that way. Dick O'Connell was a baseball guy. He didn't get involved in the politics of things, and I don't remember reading anything about Yawkey having any political leanings." Today it's a different story. "Kevin liked baseball and all that, but he wasn't into it the way [Mayor Thomas] Menino was. It's one of [Red Sox President Larry] Lucchino's great, great strengths that he knows how to work the political system. It's because of the years he spent in Washington at Edward Bennett Williams's law firm. Edward Bennett Williams was *the* great fixer in Washington for all those years, and Larry was his prized pupil."[112]

Longtime sports cartoonist Eddie Germano offers, "To this day, I think Yawkey was a little afraid of putting lights in because the two stanchions for the lights in left field are not on Red Sox property. That's City of Boston property. They had to get a variance to put the stanchions outside the ballpark. Otherwise, they would have had to put them in front of the left-field wall. Yawkey didn't want that. He said, 'I'm not going to kiss any politician's ass to put lights in here.' He didn't want to have anything to do with City Hall."[113]

On September 16 Dave Morehead pitched a no-hitter at Fenway, 2–0, over the Indians. He got the now traditional $1,000 increase in pay—and Yawkey even paid the extra taxes on it, so it netted out at $1,000.[114] The big news that day came only forty-five minutes after the game: the announcement was made that Pinky Higgins had been fired. The firing had apparently come during the fifth inning. "Yawkey Finally Gets Message," wrote Bud Collins; it had only taken him seven or eight years, the columnist muttered.[115] "Maybe what this club needs is a resident SOB," Yawkey was said to have said; Dick O'Connell became "the new boss man of the Yawkey operation."[116] Five years later, the *Boston Record*'s sports editor Sam Cohen declared the firing "the greatest move Yawkey ever made."[117]

The hundred-loss season was ten games worse than the ninety

losses the year before, which itself had been the worst of the Yawkey years. Attendance plummeted from 883,276 in 1964 to 652,201—a decline of over 26 percent in just one year. The two games played on September 28 and 29, 1965, represented the full home stand against the visiting Angels. Total attendance for them came to 870—461 for the first game and 409 for the second. These games came less than two weeks after the September 16, 1965, Morehead no-hitter, which was attended by just 1,247 fans (including the author of this book). The games featured Yaz, Tony Conigliaro, Dick Radatz, and other Red Sox stars but still failed to draw.

Bob Holbrook said it only in passing, but he called Yawkey a "meddling owner." The Red Sox needed a true baseball man at the helm, not an "apathetic intrigue-riddled front office operation" charged with overseeing an "apathetic, lack luster, phlegmatic collection of pampered performers."[118]

If Yawkey was sometimes a meddler, he wasn't on October 4, when the Red Sox traded Bill Monbouquette to Detroit for George Smith, George Thomas, and a player to be named later. Billy Herman admitted that Yawkey was "told about the trade after we made it."[119] Yawkey was not at all pleased, and Herman quickly understood he was not to make further trades without approval. "What was the rush?" asked Arthur Daley of the New York Times, wondering about trading a twenty-game winner from 1963 for "a couple of strangers of little distinction."[120]

Yawkey may have read Holbrook's column and may have had it in mind a couple of years later when he said, "I know some people claim I have meddled with my managers. That's not true. Why doesn't someone ask Joe McCarthy if I ever meddled when he managed here? I have not spoken to Dick Williams [who became manager in 1967] in person or by phone since the season started. . . . I reserve the right to pick my managers as I always have, but they are on their own."[121]

Trainer Jack Fadden retired in November, and Edward G. "Buddy" LeRoux took over. Haywood Sullivan was named VP in charge of player personnel. Sullivan said he had no contract with the club; "I've known Mr. Yawkey too long for that."[122]

In June 1965 came the first free-agent draft in baseball history.

It was approved by a unanimous vote of the owners, but Yawkey had spoken out against it and let it be known he'd been opposed to it. "I'm against this free-agent draft because it deprives a boy of his freedom of choice." Of course as the owner with perhaps the deepest pockets in baseball, Yawkey had an advantage in going after players. When the vote had been taken, Yawkey had voted against it, but when the "ayes" carried the day, "I voted 'yes' when it was moved that the vote be unanimous. You see, while I believe in freedom of choice, I also believe in majority rule."[123]

Yawkey attended the winter meetings for the first time in several years. His attendance was read to presage trade activity. He held a ninety-minute gathering of the press and said he was not going to sell the Red Sox. Larry Claflin wrote that "the writers were seldom allowed to get near enough to him to know him."[124] At the press meeting Yawkey said he'd hold weekly press conferences during the season. Bruce McCabe murmured sarcastically, "Now we know what's wrong with the Red Sox. Tom Yawkey hasn't been holding enough press conferences."[125]

Three Red Sox were untouchable: Tony Conigliaro, Dick Radatz, and Carl Yastrzemski. It was later written that Yawkey himself had "interfered . . . and blocked" a trade for Radatz over the winter.[126] In Yaz and Conig, the Sox had a great one-two punch in the outfield, Yaz batting left and Conig batting right. Yawkey also said that the team needed a new stadium and that it would embark upon a youth movement in 1966.[127] Rico Petrocelli, Tony Horton, Joe Foy, and the newly acquired George Smith were meant to be the infield. A mid-December trade secured them two right-handers—Dan Osinski and Bob Sadowski for Arnold Earley and Lee Thomas.

Finally the Greater Boston Stadium Commission determined what it would seek from the Red Sox for rent in the proposed new facility: 17 percent of revenues. Yawkey let it be known that the figure was way out of line. "We have investigated the rentals paid by other major league clubs for the use of municipal stadiums. The average rental was 7%. We certainly couldn't afford to pay 17%."[128] At one point, it seemed that the stadium might have been a go if the Red Sox had agreed to a facility with a retractable roof, but that did not interest them.

In January 1966 Ted Williams was voted into the Hall of Fame on the first ballot with 93.3 percent of the first-place votes (282 of 302). At the time, only Ty Cobb had ever registered a higher percentage.

After fifteen years of broadcasting in Boston, Curt Gowdy gave notice to take a position as NBC-TV's top baseball announcer. He expressed gratitude to Tom Yawkey for giving him his break in the business. "Next to my late father, no man in my life has had any more influence on me and my family. I talked this all over with Mr. Yawkey. He said I should do what I thought best. And he wished me luck and would always have the same thought for me. He is a great, great man."[129]

Yawkey and Gowdy had had an unusual arrangement, at least by current standards. According to John Powers, Gowdy "said he had a handshake agreement with Yawkey. He was almost a little nervous about it because Yawkey was getting up in years; one time he asked him about it, and Yawkey was stunned that he would even ask. He almost seemed hurt. Once you were hired, you were in." Finally Yawkey—just to humor Gowdy—had written something out.[130] In fact, Gowdy said Yawkey had told him straight out: "What do you need a contract for? You've got a job here for life."[131]

The Red Sox returned to Florida for 1966 spring training, based in Winter Haven. Yastrzemski and Radatz called a closed-door team meeting and spoke up about the lack of hustle on recent Red Sox clubs. "I have a lot of professional pride," Yaz said. "I must admit that many times during the past five years I've been ashamed to wear a Red Sox uniform. If we didn't have the talent, I wouldn't say anything. We have too much talent to waste it."[132]

There had been this group and that group, but word came out that a syndicate fronted by Dom DiMaggio was half way toward raising the money that might be enough to buy the Red Sox. (Dom was one of ten owners of the Boston Patriots.)

In early June, not long after his arrival, Yawkey watched college baseball at Fenway as Northeastern beat Colby, 5-4.

In less than a year, the Sox had begun to shake things up under Haywood Sullivan. They traded away eighteen players, including eight of the eleven pitchers they'd had at the end of 1965. Only Lonborg, Morehead, and Jerry Stephenson remained among the pitchers, and Yawkey had ever seen only nine of the players in a Red Sox uniform. There had been a good deal or two mixed in, first among them perhaps being the purchase of right-hander Jose Santiago for $45,000 in October 1965, though that deal had been done before Sullivan had joined Boston management.

The team lost its first five games; it was 3-10 at the end of April and 7-20 in mid-May—the worst start the team had ever had in the Yawkey years. The team was hustling, but it was losing. On June 2 one of the "untouchables" was traded: Radatz went to Cleveland for Don McMahon and Lee Stange. It was a smart move in retrospect. Radatz only ever won three more games, one in 1967 and two in 1969. It was likely overuse that had worn him out. Sullivan made the trade on his own account but let Yawkey know before he heard it on the radio. In mid-July the *Record-American* ran a series by Larry Claflin titled "The New Boston Red Sox." Claflin credited O'Connell, Sullivan, and Herman as not being sycophants who would mislead Yawkey.

A noticeably thinner Yawkey chatted with the press on June 15. The team was in tenth place. No, he didn't have any thought of selling the team. Yes, he always heard about trades before they happened, but he preferred to leave the details to others. He said that a number of baseball executives spoke highly of Haywood Sullivan, and that he—Yawkey—was well aware of the criticism that the Red Sox hadn't done enough. "I suppose now we'll get blamed for having done too much," he remarked.[133] He was touched that Earl Wilson, though traded to the Tigers the day before, had paid a personal visit to him earlier in the afternoon. (The Sox sent Wilson and Joe Christopher to the Tigers for Don Demeter and Julio Navarro. There were suggestions later that it was Yawkey and O'Connell who had pulled the trigger on the trade and that Sullivan had not wanted to trade Wilson.)[134]

When Boston took both halves of a July 10 doubleheader from the visiting White Sox, Yawkey phoned down to the clubhouse and announced that the beers were on him.[135]

Jackie Robinson spoke up again about the Red Sox early in 1966, saying that Yawkey "has always been content with the status quo. . . .

As soon as he overcomes his sense of bigotry and hires some fine Negro ballplayers he will join the ranks of the winners."[136] With George Scott joining the Red Sox in 1966 (he played all 162 games in his rookie year), the *Pittsburgh Courier*—the newspaper that had sponsored the Jackie Robinson/Sam Jethroe/Marvin Williams tryout back in 1945—was pleased to write, "The team of Millionaire Thomas A. Yawkey is building anew, with the best talent available, regardless of race."[137] Scott made the AL All-Star team and came in third in Rookie of the Year voting.

In late July Yawkey appraised the Red Sox: "This team is determined. They feel they can win." And he singled out Scott for attention. "Writers did their jobs when they devoted a lot of attention to Scott as the exciting and new face of the club. . . . Remember he's only 21 and it's still a long jump from Double-A ball to the majors. At 21 in the face of the publicity and all, Scott has to make the adjustment. He will make it, I'm confident."[138] To hear Yawkey pleased with a black ballplayer as the "exciting and new face of the club" perhaps signaled a new day.

Will McDonough compared Yawkey to an elk hunter, one still gunning for a world championship more than a third of a century after buying the Red Sox. Yawkey was a little philosophical: "When a man loses so much at something continually . . . he'd have to love it. I love baseball. For me there's still the challenge to build the best team in the game. I'd like someday to see that world championship flag flying in center field in Boston. . . . In baseball . . . just like hunting you have to be patient and take the good with the bad. There's a lot of luck involved. When the chance comes you have to make the most of it." (Cynics would say it's easier to blame luck than one's own hiring policies.) With the Sox in tenth place at the time, Yawkey added, "I don't like being in last place. No one likes to lose. But despite our present situation I see elements of good for the future. We've got some good players and they are giving it everything they've got. In time, we should have a fine team."[139] It would happen sooner than he probably could have hoped.

Yawkey was extremely pleased to see Ted Williams inducted into the Hall of Fame at Cooperstown on July 25. He could still remember hearing Eddie Collins talk about Ted and Bobby Doerr after a scouting trip to the West Coast. Yawkey heard Ted call for Satchel Paige and Josh Gibson to be named to the Hall of Fame "as symbols of the great Negro players who are not here because they were not given the chance." Williams also paid tribute to the Red Sox owner: "I have said it before and I repeat it now—Tom Yawkey is the greatest owner in baseball. I was lucky I played for the club he owned and I am happy that he is here on this day."[140]

On August 10 the owners of the Red Sox, Bruins, Celtics, and Patriots all met with Governor John A. Volpe regarding the stadium issue.

The team played better in the second half of the '66 season, though not *that* much better. The Sox played .365 ball from April through June and .511 ball from July through September. Regardless, Billy Herman was told on September 9 that his contract would not be renewed. Coach Pete Runnels became interim manager. Yawkey admitted he'd been thinking about changing managers as far back as May. He said he hadn't settled on a replacement, but "I want a younger man."[141] The *Globe*'s Clif Keane mentioned Dick Williams as an example of the sort of man Yawkey might have in mind; Williams had very successfully managed the team's Triple A farm club in Toronto.

The day after Yawkey left for South Carolina, the Red Sox named Dick Williams as manager for 1967. He became the eleventh field manager in the Yawkey era; he was given a one-year contract. Williams's first act was to remove the "captain" status of Carl Yastrzemski. He remarked, "This club has become a cruise ship overrun with captains and players thinking they are captain. The cruise is over and you don't need a captain anymore. You have a new boss now—me. Eliminating the club captaincy is my way of letting you know that things will be done one way—my way."[142]

Williams was asked what he thought about players being asked to play pepper with Yawkey on off-days during the season and answered obliquely but nonetheless rather bluntly: "No one on the Toronto club played pepper with the owner."[143]

The hiring of Williams may have been a result of O'Connell's being granted more free rein. Stout and Johnson write: "Yawkey's abject neglect left the club almost entirely in Dick O'Connell's hands, leaving him free to hire Williams and make other moves without interference or worrying about offending any of Yawkey's cronies. That was the best thing that could have happened. In 1967, Yawkey didn't even speak to Williams until July. And under O'Connell and Neil Mahoney, Boston's increasingly colorblind farm system had never been more productive."[144]

"Neglect"—and particularly "abject neglect"—may have been too strong a term. Yawkey respected O'Connell's leadership and may have learned a lesson or may at least have been willing to give O'Connell more autonomy. He had approved the hiring of Williams before leaving for Georgetown. His philosophy—for better or worse—was to give his executives free reign. "I have never interfered with my managers or general managers," he said a few years later. "I may not always agree with what they do, but I've never stopped them from doing it. Why should I pay these people good salaries, and then do their jobs for them? If they can't do the job, I fire them and get somebody else."[145] Of course it could be argued that at times it took Yawkey far too long to conclude their inability to do the job. And we have seen how soft he typically was with former ballplayers in his employ, seemingly unable to pull the trigger with a firing despite years of underperformance.

The American League was without divisions at the time, a ten-team league. The Red Sox (72-90) finished twenty-six games out of first place, deep in ninth place, and only a half game separated them from tenth place. The Red Sox fans, and their owner, might have found that only one thing offered a little comfort: the Yankees were the team that held last place.

17

The Impossible Dream

THE YEAR 1967 was about the "Impossible Dream" Red Sox. For a team that finished a half game out of last place in 1966 to win the pennant and come within one game of winning the World Series the following year would indeed have seemed an impossible dream before the season began. The turnout for Fenway's Opening Day in 1967 was fewer than 8,500 people (figures differ, depending on the newspaper). Regardless of the precise number, the fact remains that the park was 75 percent empty on Opening Day.[1] A ticket to a Red Sox game (reserved grandstand seats cost $2.25) was not a hot commodity. Years later Tom Yawkey's secretary, Mary Trank, had a colorful way of describing the largely empty park: "Oh my God, you could go out behind home and whistle and somebody in center field can hear you. It was terrible."[2]

Dick O'Connell predicted that Yawkey would like new manager Dick Williams. "Yawkey wants an aggressive manager on the ballfield," he said. He wanted a manager with the autonomy to levy fines on players and follow through and implement the fines, but he also wanted one who could communicate with players young and old. Clif Keane averred that Lou Boudreau had gotten his job because of his readiness to play pepper with Yawkey and to butter him up. "The less that happens, the better," said O'Connell. "Just because Yawkey walks down to have a workout doesn't mean a manager is to drop everything he's doing and spend an hour with Tom Yawkey."[3]

Eddie Germano recalled that Keane was caustic on the subject of sycophancy: "Clif Keane used to ride the shit out of Haywood Sullivan. Keane would be on the first-base side of the press box, between first base and home plate, and Yawkey's box was on the third-base side. Keane would go, 'Haaay-wood! Hey, Sully, go get him another one. He's dry!' And then he'd say, 'I think he wants some more popcorn.' He'd call Sullivan [Yawkey's] prattboy. Someone who caters to someone of influence. Sully would just laugh."[4] Clark Booth said of Keane, "There were a couple of really good old reporters. Jake Liston. Good guy. He and Clif were pretty much plugged in. Clif could go up and say, 'How're you doing, you old bastard?' and get away with it. . . . Jake was more of a gentleman. But they were the last of that generation as we get into the late sixties and early seventies."[5]

The *Boston Herald* ran a sizable feature on O'Connell in which Al Hirshberg said the team had been on a "treadmill to nowhere for years" until Yawkey finally fired Higgins and replaced him with O'Connell.[6]

Dick Williams was thirty-seven, just two years out of baseball himself, but with two consecutive International League playoff championships to his credit. He brought a number of young players with him either from Toronto or ones he had managed in 1965. The Red Sox had been twenty-two games under .500 at one point in 1966 but were 44-40 in the second half of the season and truly believed the team was coming around. One notable aspect of the 1967 season was the inclusion of significant numbers of players of color; it seemed in some respects the first truly integrated and "color-blind" team the Red Sox had ever fielded.

Dom DiMaggio featured in stories both for his important role in helping found the BoSox Club and for being turned down as a potential purchaser of the Red Sox. Yawkey just wasn't interested in selling the Sox, and he enjoyed quite a ride before the '67 season was done.

Yawkey arrived in Boston on June 9. The Red Sox were in fourth place—heady territory—and only 5½ games out of first. Yawkey hadn't spoken with Dick Williams since the previous fall. Rather than taking it as a vote of confidence, Williams was apparently bothered that Yawkey hadn't called him even once all season: "I was the first manager in several years who wasn't his drinking buddy or bobo, and this made him uncomfortable. . . . Yawkey tolerated my presence only because his new general manager, Dick O'Connell, wanted me." Williams said that the only time he ever saw Yawkey in his two years as a Red Sox player (1964–65) was when the team won. They were winning in 1967, and Williams continues,

> Suddenly I couldn't get him out of my face. In the second half of the 1967 season you'd have thought he was one of the damn players. He was in the clubhouse, on the field until the last possible minute, chatting and kibitzing and being about as fake as an owner could be. . . . Didn't he know that being friendly with players would soon make them think they were in good with the owner and didn't have to listen to Williams? Didn't he understand how players worked? His presence in our domain late in 1967 wasn't just a distraction, it was an insult.[7]

Moreover, Williams's wife, Norma, was a little irritated that Jean Yawkey seemed to "keep track of" how often Norma came to Fenway. "As if all Norma had to do was cheer for a team."[8]

Outfielder Joe Lahoud talked about how Yawkey would always approach Yaz, not Dick Williams, to talk about the games. "He loved his players. He loved Yastrzemski more than any of them. And he loved his players more than he loved his managers. Always. He would side with the players before he would side with Williams."[9]

Just a few days after Yawkey arrived, the game of June 15, at Fenway, really woke up the fan base. The park was half full (at the time, quite a good crowd), and the fans saw the White Sox and Red Sox go scoreless through ten innings. In the top of the eleventh, Chicago scored the first run of the game and took a 1–0 lead, but with two outs in the bottom of the inning, Joe Foy singled, and then Tony Conigliaro (after swinging and missing at two pitches) hit a two-run homer for the win. The team soon acquired a nickname—the "Cardiac Kids"—for their late-inning heroics.

White Sox manager Eddie Stanky was known to bluster a bit from time to time. On June 26 he complained about "inadequate protection" at Fenway, saying that he would sue for $3 million if he were injured by fans throwing cans and other debris at him. "I might have been killed or maimed because of the inadequate protection here. Mr. Yawkey thinks more of the deer and the pheasants on his farm in Carolina than he does of human flesh here on his ball field."[10]

On the ongoing matter of a new stadium, Yawkey made his most pointed statement to date, declaring the team would not be playing at Fenway Park five years from now. Unless a new stadium was built, he'd be gone. He explained:

> This is not a threat. This is a mere statement of fact. I cannot continue indefinitely under present circumstances. I am losing money with the Red Sox and no one—unless he's a damn fool—likes to lose money. . . . I don't care who you are or how much money you have—you can't lose a million or so each year. . . . I have come to this realization and I hope that Boston does before it's too late. . . . With a new stadium, this club would be a financial success. There's no doubt in my mind. Without one, it cannot be.[11]

He added, reflecting the five years of discussions, "While others build stadiums, Boston talks."[12]

Yawkey's comments rekindled a fire at the state level, and Governor Volpe said he agreed on the need for a new stadium. Discussions were under way regarding a new facility to be built near Suffolk Downs and using private funds. The lack of parking at Fenway was the biggest problem. It was, in 1967, the only single-deck Major League park. Yawkey told the *Globe*'s Will McDonough that Fenway Park was deteriorating badly and that Milwaukee was appealing to him to move the Red Sox there. (The Braves had left Milwaukee for Atlanta.) McDonough asked, "Can you see the Red Sox playing in Fenway in five years?" Yawkey said, "No. I don't intend to bankrupt myself."[13]

But then the Red Sox started winning. A ten-game winning streak July 14–23, with the last six games on the road, had the Red Sox in second place. When they returned home to Boston, a large crowd, estimated at five thousand or more, spontaneously turned out to greet them at the airport, many spilling over onto the tarmac. The last time the team had won ten in a row was in May 1951. Pennant fever gripped the Hub. In retrospect, many believe that this was the birth of what is called "Red Sox Nation" today; the ball club had reached its nadir and was quickly climbing out of a hole. Clearly the area was still primed for baseball. All people needed was a winning team.

On July 27, a Thursday night, the team (then 53-41 and in second place, one game out of first) drew over thirty-four thousand for a game against the Angels. Trailing 5–2, the Sox scored three times in the bottom of the ninth thanks to a two-run homer by Joe Foy and a solo home run from Tony C, and then they won it in the tenth after Reggie Smith tripled to lead off the inning. The next day, Clif Keane's *Boston Globe* column was headlined "The Impossible Dream?" and he dared lead, "If the Red Sox can finish the season in the same fantastic manner that they finished Thursday's ball game, they will be in the World Series for sure."

The team continued to appeal across New England, and on July 31 governors from five of the six New England states watched the game from Yawkey's rooftop box. The only one absent was Governor John Chafee of Rhode Island.[14]

Attendance had already begun to rise sharply. By season's end, it had more than doubled from 1966, from 811,172 to a new team-record 1,727,832. Other than 1981, a year that was interrupted by a strike, the team never drew fewer than 1,400,000 fans again, and despite remaining in Fenway Park, it saw attendance grow such that there was more or less no looking back.

More fans meant more revenue, and the losses turned to profits. Quite unexpectedly, fans found their way to Fenway Park, even without any resolution of the parking problem. A winning team cures many ills. Clif Keane wondered if Yawkey would be comfortable in a park that wasn't his, sharing the facility in a multisport stadium. At Fenway one could reach his office only if one was buzzed through. "The place is gorgeous once you get through to it. If you've just left the shoe store, you still want to wipe your feet. He has a private stairway to the roof and a walk to his private box. Tom Yawkey can be so aloof half the employees in the place might not know he's there."[15] His roof box was between home plate and third base.[16] It was, perhaps, something of a cocoon. Tom and Jean sat in separate boxes, Mrs. Yawkey usually behind glass. It just worked better for the two of them that way. Tom could, if he wished, invite in a friend or two, and Jean could entertain her own friends while letting Tom cuss as much as he wanted. She faithfully kept score while he was sometimes high-strung.

An observer from *Boston* magazine watched Yawkey during a

game in 1975 through a pair of binoculars: "Yawkey takes it all in, expressionless, his eyes riveted on the field. Chain-smoking, he occasionally bites his fingers. After a particularly bad play, he stubs out a cigarette he has just lit, only to light another. During the seventh-inning stretch, Mrs. Yawkey gets up and goes into Yawkey's box. They talk. She returns promptly for the first pitch of the eighth."[17] At one point, Yawkey himself told Pete Farley of the *Brockton Enterprise*, "My wife says I cuss too much. My doctor tells me I smoke too much. When I was younger, I know damn well I drank too much. Hell, though, if I had my life to live over, I'd do all those things a little harder than I did them the first time."[18]

To bolster the team, a deal was done on August 3—with the Yankees no less—to bring catcher Elston Howard to Boston. He'd been the first African American ballplayer on the Yankees, in 1955, and had always thought he'd retire as a Yankee. "I admit it," he said. "I wanted to finish my career with the Yankees. But I talked to Mr. Yawkey. When you talk to somebody like that it makes a difference. He made everything all right. He wanted my services."[19] Howard noted that the Yankees, owned by CBS, were essentially a corporate club at that point. Clearly Yawkey's personal charm and interest played a role in landing an important veteran backup on what was otherwise a very young Boston ball club. (The average age among the position players was 25.2 years. Among the regulars—those who played in ninety or more games—only Yaz and Tartabull were older than twenty five. They were twenty-seven and twenty-eight respectively.)

Bud Collins saw a side of Tom Yawkey that surprised him a little.

The year they won the pennant—'67, I think—he had stopped drinking, and he was not too bad. At one of the games, the clubhouse man came up to me and said, "Mr. Yawkey wants to see you." I was rather startled, and I figured it was something negative that I had written. I went into the clubhouse, and I shook hands with him, and he said, "Tell me about Rosie Casals." I was really startled because I didn't think he cared anything for tennis. He had obviously been pleased by Casals's play in the U.S. Doubles Championships that were going on at Longwood Cricket Club at the time. [Later] everybody was really curious about what he had wanted, and I said, "He wanted to talk tennis."[20]

One of the first references to Fenway's famed left-field wall as a "monster" came in a John Hall column in the *Los Angeles Times*, "Boston's Monster."[21] Rather than Fenway's being decried as antiquated, there was perhaps the beginning of a new appreciation for some of the quirks of the old park, at this point in its fifty-sixth year.

On August 18, the day Ted Williams had sent a message to Tony Conigliaro to warn him to back off the plate and not stand so aggressively close, Tony was beaned by a Jack Hamilton fastball. Those who heard the ball hit his head (this was before batting helmets offered protection) said the sound was sickening. There was immediate concern that Tony had in fact been struck a fatal blow. Tony did recover, but never fully, and there is every reason to believe that the injury did some permanent damage that shortened his life despite a later determined comeback. It was a tremendous loss of baseball talent. Tony had hit 104 home runs in his career to date, and he wasn't even twenty-three years old.

When Tony woke up in Sancta Maria Hospital the next morning, his eyes were bandaged, but he said he felt someone holding his hand. "A voice said, 'It's me, Tony. Tom Yawkey.'"[22] Conigliaro was not allowed visitors in the hospital for some days, but an exception was made for Tom Yawkey, who brought the best wishes of the whole organization.

On August 22 the Red Sox reached first place—tied with the White Sox. Both the Twins and the Tigers were one game behind. It wasn't just the Red Sox that were doing well; this was a true four-team pennant race and remained so until the final days, and it was a three-team race right to the very last game on the schedule.

Even more than a month before the end of the '67 season, Yawkey was like a "youngster with a new toy."[23] Ed Rumill wrote, "Mrs. Yawkey shares her husband's enthusiasm. She, too, is at the park in the late afternoon before a night game and stays through until the end. She admits, though, that these close come-from-behind games 'are like being put through a wringer.'"[24]

Tom Yawkey changed his tune about the stadium. He said a new facility was "still a necessity. . . . Boston needs it," but any threat he would move the Red Sox out of the city of Boston was no longer on the table.[25]

Jackie Robinson spoke up as the American League season went into its final week with four teams jostling for first place. He predicted the Minnesota Twins would win, but in any event, he said, "Because of Boston owner Tom Yawkey, I'd like to see them [the Red Sox] lose." Yawkey, he said, "is probably one of the most bigoted guys in organized baseball."[26] The "probably" was Robinson hedging a bit, appropriately. After all, he had admitted that he didn't know Yawkey and couldn't say that Yawkey personally had ever been against Negroes on the ball club. Yawkey wisely declined to comment, though a Red Sox spokesman noted that the team had six nonwhite players on its active roster: Joe Foy, Elston Howard, Reggie Smith, George Scott, Jose Tartabull, and John Wyatt.

Much has been made of that one Robinson quotation. He certainly didn't pull any punches. Having previously said that he'd never met Tom Yawkey, he seemed to be relying on circumstantial evidence to come to his conclusion. Admittedly a good case can be made in that regard.

Things had arguably changed by 1967. Indeed once Higgins was gone as GM, Dick O'Connell had turned things around rapidly regarding race. Clark Booth points out:

> What he did has never been fully recognized. He changed that team instantly. Instantly. With an amazing series of moves. And he was taking on complicated black players [such as] the old statesman [Elston] Howard. And a guy who was thought to have been a very bad guy but was fine when he was in Boston, Johnny Wyatt. He came with a bad reputation. He took on Reggie [Smith]. Reggie had some problems in his youth. He came out of Watts, and Reggie had had a brother who was killed or badly hurt during the rioting in '63 or '64. Why do you think the Twins let Reggie go? The Red Sox picked him, and Joe Foy, in the Rule 5 draft or whatever they called it then. Foy was another guy, a kid out of the Bronx, a tough kid. Here's Dick O'Connell—only a year or two after Higgins had finally been banished. He's throwing off all these moves. Within months, he got Smith and Foy.[27]

In their history of the Red Sox, Glenn Stout and Richard Johnson write, "The 1967 team was the most integrated and cohesive unit in modern history."[28]

Some, like Tom Shaer, believe that Yawkey should get some credit for what may have been an evolution in his views on race. "It was my privilege," Shaer wrote, "to spend much private, off-the-record time with O'Connell when I worked for his trusted friend, Associated Press New England sports editor Dave O'Hara. O'Connell detailed to me his criticism of Yawkey on many topics. But O'Connell never so much as hinted that Yawkey stood in his way when it came to black players. O'Connell's effort to truly acquire players without regard to race led to two World Series. Does Yawkey's growth as a human being and owner mean nothing?"[29]

It was Rico Petrocelli's third year with the ball club, and he had heard that there had been issues in the past. "I heard that when Mr. Yawkey was a lot younger, there were problems in his outlook on race. The time I was there and the guys who were my teammates . . . never had a problem. When he came down to the clubhouse, he talked to all the guys. Joe Foy. George Scott. Reggie Smith. 'How're you doing?' He'd talk to me—same thing. 'How's everything?' He gave us his private number—all of us—and he said, 'Anything's bothering you guys, give me a call, and I'll talk.' That was great."[30]

Reggie Smith had a locker near Yaz's—and Tom Yawkey's locker was in between. "He kept his things in there," recalled Smith in 2015. "His old glove and everything. Sometimes he would be there when I would get there, and sometimes we would have conversations. Later on, when he realized that I was saving money to buy and build a house, he asked me if I needed anything. He took care of the players, and he was friendly." (As we recall, Tom Yawkey had loaned John Kennedy funds to help him buy his home, and Kennedy wasn't the only one.) Reggie continued:

He [Yawkey] said it's something he had always done, that he helped players get their first homes and things like that. I just said, "Mr. Yawkey, I really appreciate everything that you've done and your willingness to do that, but that's something my wife and I wanted to do, and we've saved for it." He said, "No worries. If you ever need anything, just let me know." Actually, he kind of got mad at me—teasingly—because I saved the money for our first house that we built in Sharon. He said, "What's the matter? My money's not good enough for you?" He did it for several players that I know of. It was a security blanket, knowing that that was there. There were other conversations that we had with him. If there were something that he knew that we needed, he would help us out with it.[31]

And Reggie said, yes, Tom Yawkey had given him his private number too. "It was the number to his suite at the hotel there."[32]

Tom Yawkey was around the ballpark more than usual—and who could blame him? A very exciting team was seemingly coming out of nowhere (ninth place is pretty close to nowhere) to contend for the pennant. Stout and Johnson say Yawkey was maybe around the park too much; we've already seen that the manager felt that way. "Yawkey, who had kept his distance from the clubhouse for more than a decade, now became a near-constant presence. He wasn't altogether welcome. While some players, like Yaz, basked in the attention of the wealthiest man they'd ever met, Dick Williams, who disliked Yawkey, grated against the intrusion, which he considered 'an insult.'"[33]

In a later column, the *Herald*'s Tim Horgan underscored the point about Yawkey keeping his distance. He was "always in the clubhouse from the time he bought the Sox in 1933 until he hired Joe McCarthy as manager in 1948. Then a friend in New York advised him that McCarthy believed a club-owner should not mingle with his players, so Tom next [*sic*] visited the clubhouse until the day the Sox won the pennant in 1967." Horgan also wrote that Yawkey was careful not to undermine the manager: "Yawkey freely admits he's invited players to visit his office, but only after he'd gotten the manager's consent, and only to discuss their personal problems, not their professional gripes. He's acutely aware of the difference, and also very sensitive about what his presence in the clubhouse before a game might do to the manager's authority."[34]

Later Sox players, such as Dwight Evans and Bob Montgomery, stressed the same—that Yawkey's conversations were about them and their families more than play on the field. His presence none-theless grated on Dick Williams.

As noted above, the 1967 pennant fight went right down to the final day, and Yaz was a huge part of it, as was right-hander Jim Lonborg. Before pitching on the final day, Lonborg stayed over-night at a Boston hotel; his home record had been only 7-5 while his road record was 15-4, so he decided to act as though he was on the road.[35] Yawkey laughed at the suggestion that he offer Lonborg the $12-per-day meal money and said he'd be more than glad to if it helped him win the game.[36]

Yaz had put on one of the most superlative stretch drives one could imagine. "In the final 12 games of the season—crunch time—Carl Yastrzemski had 23 hits in 44 at-bats, driving in 16 runs and scoring 14. He hit 10 homers in his final 100 at-bats of 1967. He had 10 hits in his last 13 at-bats. And when it came to the last two games with the Twins—with the Sox needing to win both games to help avert a tie for the pennant—Yaz went 7-for-8 and drove in six runs."[37]

After the Sox beat the Twins, 5–3, on October 1 and won the flag for the first time since 1946, there was "pandemonium on the field" (in Ned Martin's famous phrase), and Tom Yawkey visited the club-house for the celebration. So did Tony C. No one drenched Yawkey with champagne, but he was handed a cup of it. "I haven't had one of these in four years," he said, having given up drinking, but he offered a toast to Dick Williams, who responded in kind, "Here's to you, sir, for giving me the opportunity." Yawkey responded, "And here's to you, Dick, for making the most of it. This is the happiest moment of my life."[38]

It probably remained so.

Yawkey said he'd gotten a greater thrill out of the 1967 pennant than the one in 1946, simply because the earlier team had been more or less expected to win, and this one had not.[39] The final two games of the season and the back-to-back, do-or-die games against Minnesota were, he said, his brightest moments in the game. In 1967 "we had to fight all the way, and winning it then has to be my greatest thrill."[40]

A headline in *The Sporting News* read, "Tears of Joy in Yawkey's Eyes as Players and Fans Went Wild." The accompanying story reported that Tony Conigliaro plaintively wished he could have been a pinch runner or something in the game, just to have contributed, to which Yawkey responded, "Tony got what I believe was the biggest hit of the year when he beat the White Sox, 2–1, with a home run with a man on in the eleventh inning one night."[41] Eddie Germano saw those tears. "I was down in the dressing room waiting for the score to come in from the Tigers game. I remember he cried almost uncontrollably. He was so emotional. All he did was wipe tears [from his face.]"[42]

Winning the pennant may have been one of the happier moments in Jean Yawkey's life too. Haywood Sullivan said his fondest memory of Jean came from the night they won. That Sunday night, "everybody was up in the office. There was such a feeling of jubilation and satisfaction. It was a small office. The players and their wives were there. I watched people mingle. Both she and Tom were there. It was like you were dreaming. Jean was running up and down the hall feeling as young as the rest of the team. It's my favorite memory."[43]

Tom Yawkey later revealed that he had torn up the contracts of some of the players during the course of the season. "We had some younger fellows make the team this year who were just getting the minimum salary. The rules don't allow for a bonus clause in the contract, so what you do is tear up the old one and make out a new one. We did it for a few of the boys because they were doing such a good job for us."[44] The rule prohibiting bonuses had, of course, been passed in the wake of Yawkey's generosity back in 1946. But it seems that it was pretty tough to prevent Tom Yawkey from lavishing monetary gifts on his players.

John Powers recalls the following:

Lonborg told me in '67, when they beat the Twins but had to wait for the final game, that Yawkey came down and was walking around and was very emotional. Some guys were drinking beer. I think Stange might have been one of them. I think he was supposed to pitch the playoff if there was one. Dick Williams said, "Lay off that stuff, because we might be playing again." I think they were listening to the radio broadcast, and after it was over and they won it . . . the ballpark had been shut down for hours. And Lonborg said, "I'm going to go up and give Mr. Yawkey the ball."[45]

Jim Lonborg remembers the moment vividly:

Probably my biggest memory would have been the night we clinched the pennant in 1967. We were waiting around to find out the results from Detroit. After we were assured we'd won the championship, the clubhouse had started to clear out, and guys were starting to go wherever they were going. I was headed down to Kenmore Square to a friend of mine's establishment—Smoky Joe's.

Rico Petrocelli had saved the baseball that he caught for the final out and then given it to me. I was just sitting there at my locker looking at the ball and thinking, "There's one person who would truly love to have this baseball." After all he had been through with the team. And so I asked the clubhouse guy how to get up to Mr. Yawkey's office. Fenway is staircases and hallways. I found out Mr. Yawkey was still here. I took the baseball up, the way they told me to get up there. I went into this dark. . . . Everybody was gone. . . . It reminded me of that scene in *The Natural* when he walked into that drab office in the back of the stadium. I just walked in and told Mr. Yawkey I'd like to present him with the game ball.

He was *so* emotional. If you see some of the pictures, he was such a happy man after we had won that thing. He graciously accepted and gave me a big hug. He was just overwrought with good emotion.

In those days, I never saved anything because it didn't seem like that big a deal. It seemed like we were always going to be moving forward and probably have more of these opportunities.

I just thought it was important that he have the ball, because it was his team and his hard work and patience. There was nobody there but him and me, and that made it even more special.[46]

The Red Sox took the World Series to Game Seven, once again losing the final game to the Cardinals, just as they had in 1946. But this was one of those rare years when it seemed almost okay to have lost the final prize because of all the thrills that had led to so unexpectedly winning the pennant. The Yawkeys went to the games in St. Louis—Tom's first road trip with the team in seventeen years.

During the flight, both Yawkeys went through the team plane, shaking hands with all the players and with all the wives, who had been invited to join the traveling party.

Coming back from a three-games-to-one deficit in the Series and winning Games Five and Six, the Sox took it to the wire but came up short in the end. After the Game Seven loss, 7–2 at Fenway, on October 12, Yawkey walked into a gloomy clubhouse and "wandered around personally thanking each of his players for what they had done for his Red Sox this season."[47] He made a point of telling Elston Howard that he wanted him back in 1968. In fact Howard had told the *Herald*'s Larry Claflin as they were on a plane to play the Cardinals in October 1967, "In all my years of playing in the World Series for the Yankees not once did they invite my wife to go to the games as guest of management. I've been with the Red Sox only a few weeks and the Yawkeys invited my wife to St. Louis as their guest and gave me free tickets for the games for her."[48]

"Any time you play, you want to win," Yawkey told the media. "When you don't, you're disappointed. But—we had a great year and I have a lot of wonderful memories."[49] He credited Cardinals ace Bob Gibson (who'd won three of the Series games—all complete games—and had given up just three earned runs in twenty-seven innings), and he no doubt wondered what might have been had Tony C been able to play out the full 1967 season.

Naturally the Sox felt they would contend for years to come. Yaz even said so in a newspaper column he wrote. He wrote that he had wanted badly to win the World Series, and particularly so for Mr. and Mrs. Yawkey, but he believed the team would be a contender for the next five to ten years.[50]

Just after the World Series Jackie Robinson visited Boston and didn't let up. He came to speak just down the street from Fenway Park, at Boston University, on October 24. Yawkey had already left town. Robinson talked about the 1945 tryout and chuckled, saying it was too bad that he'd not been signed then. "We could have helped them a little bit. With all the money Yawkey was spending we'd have been tickled to take a little bit of that home. We're not prejudiced. . . . If Yawkey has seen the light, it's only because the fans want a winner and couldn't care less what color a player's skin is. You can't find better fans than the ones in Boston. But you know Yawkey is prejudiced. Everyone knows he's prejudiced."[51] He added that he was happy to see the Red Sox crowds cheering for George Scott and Reggie Smith—and that he hoped Yawkey had taken note too. "It was nice. I always felt a bigot who sees the light is our best friend."[52] The *Pittsburgh Courier* noted that Yawkey had "defied the enemies of major league jim crow longer than any other major league club" but was now "grey haired and mellowing."[53]

Perhaps Robinson hadn't given Yawkey sufficient credit. Reggie Smith said that Yawkey himself introduced the subject of race and Jackie Robinson when they talked: "I had several interesting conversations with him. . . . Everyone knew what had happened with Jackie Robinson and everything. He talked about that, and it was reassuring. He wanted to make sure that we felt welcome on that ball club and that he would take care of us. [He said that] it was a sign of those times, and it wasn't something that he was particularly proud of." Smith was asked, "He [Yawkey] brought that subject up?" "Oh, yeah! Yeah, he did. That's what I'm saying. . . . An open and frank discussion. . . . One time I can remember, in the Minor Leagues, there was a total of maybe six of us African Americans in the [Sox] organization, and three of us played the same position. But we all got to the big leagues."[54]

On October 14 Dick Williams was rewarded for his leadership with a contract for $150,000 and three more years. He posed signing the contract with a smiling Yawkey and O'Connell. It was the second-longest contract that Yawkey had ever offered a manager (Joe Cronin had had a five-year deal). He said he liked the way Williams had handled the players and had them hustling, and he liked the way he delegated authority to coaches Popowski and Doerr, and he liked the way he worked with the media. Shirley Povich of the *Washington Post* wrote that Yawkey was disappointed Ted Williams had not come to see the World Series games but instead stayed in Maine, fishing.[55]

Yaz got himself a six-figure contract, propelling himself into Ted Williams territory. Ted was a better hitter, Yawkey said, but Yaz was a better fielder and thus more versatile. Lonborg was resigned at a much higher amount; Jim won the 1967 Cy Young Award. Yaz was the MVP. It was hardly a surprise—he'd won the Triple Crown, leading the league with 44 homers, 121 RBIs, and a .326 batting average. On November 14 UPI named Dick O'Connell the Major League executive of the year.

The Red Sox had won the pennant with a .568 winning percentage—the lowest of any team in league history. They were prepared to trade almost anyone in an effort to improve. They made a December trade, sending Mike Ryan to the Phillies for lefty Dick Ellsworth and versatile catcher-first baseman-outfielder Gene Oliver. Some Yawkey cash was added in to balance the scales.

18

After the Dream

PLEASANT MEMORIES FROM 1967 helped Yawkey (and the rest of Red Sox fandom) through the winter months. Going into the 1968 season, Yawkey told the *Globe*'s Will McDonough, "I guess last season knocked a lot of other years out of my head." After reminding McDonough that he got up at 4:30 every morning and had his work done in time to go quail hunting in the afternoon, he said he was sorry the stadium supporters had fallen short of the necessary two-thirds vote in the legislature and that he was also sorry when he had learned that Jim Lonborg had broken his leg in a skiing accident at Christmastime. Any hopes for the stadium rested on public pressure; it was in the hands of the people. Yawkey himself had stayed in Boston longer than usual in the fall and so had a lot more work to do on his twenty thousand–plus acres in South Carolina; he said he hadn't been to spring training since 1941 and didn't think he could make it in 1968. He also said he hadn't heard from Ted Williams for months.[1]

"He's Just a Shirt-Sleeved Fan at Heart"—Jerry Nason's column in the April 7, 1968, *Globe* offered a light-hearted portrait of the Red Sox owner, a man who embodied some of the same paradoxes as the rest of us. The Red Sox were still far from a ball club run by lawyers who had to parse words in every agreement. Another glimpse into the world of Red Sox decision making of the day comes from sports cartoonist Eddie Germano:

> I did a series of posters of the '67 team the following year. Some of them are still around. The deal was with the D'Angelo brothers across

the street. They asked me. I was delighted to pick up a few bucks, but I would have to get permission from the Red Sox. I said OK. I talked to Dick O'Connell, and he said, "Give me a couple of days. Let me talk to some people." So I went back and I told Henry [D'Angelo]. Then John Harrington said to me, "I did some checking. Go ahead. Do what you want. Whatever you want, go ahead and do it." He said, "You're not going to draw dirty pictures." I said, "No, I'm not." I understand Yawkey had to OK it. I don't know whether he did or didn't. That's the way they used to do things. If they liked you, OK and so be it. That's the way they were.[2]

There was no contract, no written agreement. Germano said that he understood Yawkey liked sports cartoons and had asked him for the originals on a few occasions.

Still suffering serious vision problems, Tony C decided not to attempt to play at all in 1968 and to take more time to try to recover from the blow to his head.

Before the rained-out game on April 15, the 1967 pennant winners were presented their championship rings, a gift from Tom Yawkey.

Yawkey had recognized his own mortality and had begun to plan for the future. In mid-April Dick O'Connell told the Gridiron Club of Greater Boston that Yawkey had set up a trust fund. "When Yawkey dies, the club ownership will go into a trust fund which may or may not choose to keep the club in operation."[3] O'Connell was there to receive the club's Man of the Year award.

Yawkey's investments brought him to New York earlier than usual in 1968. When he joined up with the team, in New York, just before the middle of May, it was the first time he'd been to Yankee Stadium since the final game in 1949. He even rode the team bus back and forth from the game. Yawkey said of Boston, "I've given up thinking about a new stadium in Boston."[4] He said when he'd talked about moving the team if no new facility was built, he'd done so hoping it would spur movement, but despite several meetings he'd gone to during the summer of '67, "nothing happened." He added, "We definitely do need a new stadium but I don't know how we are going to get one."[5] A month and a half later, when the issue was rekindled, Yawkey said the Sox were "vitally interested in a new stadium" and said he backed a publicly funded multipurpose stadium in Boston, pledging the team's "complete cooperation."[6]

During the off-season, there had been talk of trading the Hawk—Ken Harrelson, who'd come to the Red Sox at the end of August 1967. He'd helped fill the gap created by the loss of Tony Conigliaro, but he hit only .200 in what remained of the season and was just 1-for-13 in the World Series. But Hawk got off to a great start in 1968, leading the league in RBIs with sixteen after the season's first thirty-four games. Yawkey said, "Often the best deals are the ones you don't make. I'm happy we didn't trade him."[7]

After the Sox owner settled into Boston, he was prompted to answer whether or not he'd ever offered Ted Williams the job of managing the Red Sox. Never directly, he said. "Looking ahead to when [Ted] was through playing, I sounded him out a few times on how he felt about managing, and learned he wasn't interested. I never offered him the job and I'm quite sure nobody in the organization offered it to him, either."[8]

There was often some speculation as to why Ted Williams hadn't been brought more definitively into the Red Sox fold; Yawkey had taken such care of so many others over the years that it surprised many he hadn't brought Ted on board. The answer may have rested more with Williams than Yawkey; he always pretty much went his own way. "Like everyone else in Boston," Ed Linn wrote, "Ted Williams genuflected toward Tom Yawkey in public. There was nothing Yawkey could ask of him, for as long as Yawkey was alive, that Ted wouldn't do. There was also a kind of pretense to a closer relationship than actually existed."[9]

Despite their mutual love of fishing and hunting, Ted visited Yawkey only once in South Carolina. He told Linn, "It was not a father-son relationship. I felt Yawkey liked me, but I never pursued trying to get extra close to him. He was there. He was a simple man. He knew how lucky he had been in his life and he tried to do everything he could to be a good guy. He had an open heart for charity, an open heart for a sad story. He was just a nice easy man, really and truly." Linn asked, "But, when you think about it, why should Ted have wanted to get close to him? Yawkey wasn't really bright. There was nothing Ted could learn from him. Yawkey did two things: he drank and he played bridge. Ted did not drink, and he did not play cards."[10] Linn seems not to have known Yawkey at all well and bought into a one-dimensional view of him, almost certainly underestimating the Red Sox owner.

Baseball planned to expand in 1969 and to create two twelve-team leagues, each divided into an East and a West division. For his part, Yawkey saw that as a stopgap measure on the road to a future with three major leagues.[11] He favored expansion but declared himself against the designated hitter and any attempt to move the mound back a little farther from home plate to help out the offense.[12]

The Red Sox were unable to repeat as pennant winners in 1968. They finished in fourth place. Losing their Cy Young Award winner (Lonborg, out for the season) didn't help. Tony Conigliaro was out too. There was bickering on the ball club. George Scott was again having difficulties with Dick Williams and said he was going to go straight to Yawkey with his complaints. At one point Elston Howard said Williams hadn't talked to him in two weeks, and Rico Petrocelli said he'd not talked with Dick Williams for at least a month.[13] A few days later, Yaz and the manager were seen to exchange words.

An amusing anecdote referring to Yawkey's Boston residence at the Ritz Carlton was recounted in July: "In the years when the Red Sox were consistent losers, a sign in the Ritz kitchen said, 'See that Mr. (Tom) Yawkey's order is filled promptly and that the food is hot.' Below it was scribbled, 'And don't mention the Red Sox.'"[14]

Author Leigh Montville later found it ironic that Yawkey "lived in the Ritz for so many years, and he was a plantation owner, and then Manny Ramirez lived in the Ritz. That's the victory of the workers over the employer."[15] Red Sox slugger Manny Ramirez (with the Red Sox from 2001 to 2008 and World Series MVP in 2004) indeed lived in the Ritz-Carlton during his time in Boston, but it was at the Ritz-Carlton condominiums on Avery Street.[16]

Another story emerged when Carl Yastrzemski told of the time he'd suffered an injury in 1965 that placed him in the hospital for nine days, "nine days in which I would have gone nuts if it hadn't been for Tom Yawkey. He came to see me every day, spending hours with me, talking about everything under the sun."[17]

Yaz felt a strong personal loyalty to Tom Yawkey and shared a story with sportswriter Joe Giuliotti in 1989. In 1976 there was an expansion draft, and teams had to determine which players to protect, leaving the rest exposed to the draft, which would supply talent to stock the Toronto Blue Jays and Seattle Mariners. The Blue Jays were understood to have hatched a plan whereby they'd draft Yaz, give him whatever it took to sign him, and then trade him to the Yankees for five players. But Yaz told a very ill Tom Yawkey not to bother to protect him and to protect one of the team's other players or prospects instead.[18] His point was that he (Yaz) wasn't going to sign with any other team.

A great deal of press attention was devoted to Yawkey's support of amateur baseball in New England. He joined with the *Lynn Item* in funding the Harry Agganis Schoolboy Scholarship Fund.[19] The winner was honored with, among other things, dinner with Tom Yawkey himself in his "penthouse" atop Fenway Park. Yawkey's interest also extended to following semipro ball such as the Boston Park League.[20]

On December 4, 1968, the Massachusetts Turnpike Authority filed a stadium bill with the legislature calling for a new facility to be built in Boston's Back Bay; it proposed that Tom Yawkey gift Fenway Park to the cause and have the new stadium named after him.[21] It was presumptuous, but that was the proposal.

Marvin Miller had been hired as executive director of the Major League Baseball Players Association (MLBPA) in 1966 and had negotiated the first collective bargaining agreement (CBA) in 1968. By the spring of 1969, there was already talk of the possibility of a players' strike in spring training. Writer Ed Rumill was very sympathetic to Yawkey, who he knew had lost several million dollars over the years through generous salaries. A new television contract provided more revenue for owners, and there could thus be more to share, but, Rumill argued, it would be unwise to kill the goose that laid the golden eggs. Ballplayers were already much better off than 99 percent of the fans who came to see them, and any prolonged strike would simply reduce interest in baseball and likely lead to increases in the fan base of other sports.[22] Dick O'Connell, asked how Yawkey felt about the possibility of a strike, said, "It is difficult in a way to say. Tom is wondering if we have treated our players incorrectly. We think we have been more than fair to them in the past."[23]

Jim Lonborg was the player representative for the Red Sox. He said that Mr. Yawkey had always been good to him but that many of the other teams were owned by trusts or corporations, and his concern was for the principle of the thing.[24] A few months later, Yawkey himself said, "I wasn't bitter because I realized they weren't striking against me. They were striking for what they believed was a principle." He added that he hadn't thought that most of the players had their hearts in it but went along to be loyal to their mates and to stick together.[25]

Meanwhile, about four hundred miles to the south of Boston, Ted Williams had taken a position as manager of a rival team—the Washington Senators. The team's owner, Bob Short, signed him to a five-year contract. Williams revealed that as the negotiations toward the agreement had become more serious, he had telephoned Tom Yawkey to ask two questions: would he have Yawkey's blessing, and did Yawkey think he could perform the job well?[26] The deal paid Ted well, and after eight years out of the game, it was a challenge to which he looked forward, though not without ambivalence. And because Williams still had time remaining on his contract with the Red Sox as a VP, Yawkey had had to give permission for Short to talk with Ted in the first place.[27]

Williams could have had the same salary from Tom Yawkey to work with the Red Sox but not as much as might have convinced him to take an executive position with Boston. Williams was given a share in the Senators as part of the deal; he had a stake in the Washington ball club, something Yawkey had never offered and, according to Al Hirshberg, never would have.[28] There had always been something about owning 100 percent of the team that meant a lot to Tom Yawkey. Before he bought the Red Sox, a half-interest in the Brooklyn Dodgers had been available, "but Mr. Yawkey didn't want a half."[29]

Hirshberg once asked Yawkey a hypothetical question: if he had to give up all of his possessions one by one, what was the last one he would hold onto? The choices came down to his place in South Carolina and the Boston Red Sox. "I think it would be a tie," he finally said. From 1933 it had been his club, "all his to do with as he pleased, when he pleased, without advice from anyone but people he had selected himself."[30]

On March 21, 1969, Mike Higgins died in Dallas of a heart attack. Just the day before, he had been released from prison on parole. He had been incarcerated after serving two months of a four-year sentence that followed a February 1968 incident in which he had driven his car into a road crew in Louisiana, killing one and wounding three others. Higgins had pleaded guilty to drunk driving.

Yawkey's nephew, sister Emma's son William A. Gardner, took over ownership of the Louisville Colonels farm team in the International League. Gardner was described as a shopping center developer in Louisville.[31] Gardner's new position presented an interesting coincidence at the end of 1969. Former Red Sox infielder Billy Gardner (1962–63) had gone on to manage in the Red Sox Minor League system, working at Double A in Pittsfield in 1967–69, but he was ready to be promoted to Triple A, and that meant Louisville. The *New London Day* noted, "Billy Gardner is going to manage Louisville . . . next summer, and his boss is going to be Bill Gardner."[32]

Tom Yawkey introduced his nephew to Reggie Smith, and Gardner invited Smith to go fishing at his place in Florida. Reggie and Carl Yastrzemski took him up on the offer later, though Gardner wasn't there at the time.[33]

After the 1970 season, the franchise moved its Triple A team to Pawtucket, Rhode Island, where it remains today. Billy Gardner managed there again in 1971, but Joe Buzas replaced William Gardner as the owner. "[Gardner's] widow stayed fairly close to Mrs. Yawkey over the years," said Bill Gutfarb in 2014. "Marea Gardner. She would come up with one of her sons or daughter and visit every so often. Go to a Red Sox game or two. Very nice woman."[34]

Tom Yawkey himself enjoyed his first day taking in baseball at Fenway Park in 1969, seeing the Sox win both halves of the May 21 doubleheader, with 5–2 and 8–3 wins over the Angels. Lonborg improved to 2–0, his comeback seeming a success, and Sonny Siebert (acquired in an April 19 six-player deal that sent Ken Harrelson to the Indians) won the second game. Harrelson had threatened to quit rather than accept the trade, but it seems that additional inducements were offered.

Tony Conigliaro mounted a comeback too, and there was a modification at Fenway to accommodate him after he'd threatened to quit because of the white shirts in the "batter's eye" of section 34 in the bleachers. The background made it difficult for him to see the ball. It had been dubbed "Conig's Corner," and fans there pledged to wear dark clothing. Fans attending twenty-first-century day games at Fenway will note that the section is unpopulated and bears a large dark covering. Conigliaro had a good season, with 20 homers and 82 RBIs in his first season back.

The team had a good start, reaching 35-19 at the one-third point of the season. Only in 1946 had they had such a good first third.

The Red Sox had clearly begun to cool on the idea of a new stadium. The 1967 season had proven that the lack of parking was not an obstacle; fans would come if winning baseball was on offer. Tom Yawkey owned the park outright and liked it that way. He did not need to consult or cooperate with anyone. It was an intimate facility as ballparks go. At one time public funding might have produced a new multipurpose stadium, but the political will had faltered, and the time appeared to have passed.[35]

Harold Kaese took a moment at the end of June and looked back at the history of trades under Tom Yawkey. The Harrelson trade had been a good one, he said, noting "Hawk's" poor performance for the Indians. ("At no time last season, when he was voted the most valuable member of the [Red Sox] team, did he help the Sox any more than he did in five games the past week when he was wearing a Cleveland uniform.") Yawkey was no Frazee and no Bob Quinn, Kaese decided. There had been many good trades; the worst was the 1966 one that sent off Earl Wilson (48-29 for the Tigers since the swap) for Don Demeter and Julio Navarro.[36] Kaese only mentioned in passing the November 1967 trade that brought Ray Culp from the Cubs for Bill Schlesinger and cash. Culp was 16-6 in 1968 and 17-8 in 1969.

In pregame ceremonies on July 5, the Red Sox welcomed the seven living members of the "all-time all-star Red Sox team" as voted by the fans. And Ted Williams doffed his cap. The other six

present were Cronin, Doerr, Grove, Malzone, Tebbetts, and Yastrzemski. The deceased players on the Sox all-star team were Jimmie Foxx, Tris Speaker, and Cy Young. Babe Ruth didn't make the
final list. Yawkey had been asked whom he would have voted for,
and his answer was interesting: "I didn't submit a team because I
find it hard to let my mind dwell in the past. I live in the present. I
think in terms of today, tomorrow, next month, next year. Rarely
do I think of yesteryears.[37]

Was Yawkey losing his faith in Dick Williams? In July he was
asked how he thought Williams was doing, and he answered, "Dick
is a good manager." It didn't sound like a ringing endorsement.
If there were any criticism to be made, it might be that Williams
held himself remote from the players and was not the best com-
municator.[38] His contract ran through 1971, and Boston was in
second place at the time, almost tied with the Tigers, trailing only
the Baltimore Orioles, who were twelve games ahead and running away with everything. The O's were on their way to a 109-
win season (but would face a comeuppance from the Mets in a
4–1 World Series).

Williams maybe wanted to light a fire under the team; he pulled
Carl Yastrzemski out of the August 1 game with Oakland "for not
hustling" and fined him $500. "I fined him in front of the whole ball
club," Williams told the press. "I've warned all the players about this
and it has finally come to a head."[39] The fine didn't sit well with Yaz,
but he didn't say much about it. On another matter, Billy Conigliaro
said of Williams, "I don't think he's an honest manager."[40] Billy was
defending his brother Tony, who he felt had been mistreated. Billy
was in Louisville at the time but said he wasn't unhappy to be there
because it meant he wasn't around Dick Williams. Joe Lahoud was
an unhappy camper too.

The Red Sox drew more than any team in the now twelve-team
league, with 1,833,246 tickets sold, but Yawkey said he was nonetheless losing about $1 million a year.[41] As to the "other Williams"—Ted,
who was in his first year managing—Yawkey said in early September that he'd vote him Manager of the Year for the success he was
having with the Senators. Yawkey proved prescient. Washington finished in fourth place but ahead of the Yankees and Indians. Owners

didn't have a vote, but after the season was over, Ted was indeed named Manager of the Year.

Dick Williams didn't make it to the end of the season. With nine games left to go on the Red Sox schedule, he was fired (Tim Horgan of the *Boston Herald* wrote that Williams had said it was due to a "personality clash" with Yawkey).[42] Louisville manager Eddie Kasko was named to the job for 1970. Eddie Popowski managed the team to season's end, winning five of the nine remaining games. Boston ended up in third place. It was the lack of communication with the players ("the players are Mr. Yawkey's pets"), wrote Clif Keane. Yawkey had already left for Georgetown after several days in New York; it was O'Connell who delivered the news. Larry Claflin wrote, "Yawkey will get no croix de guerre for that performance."[43]

Yawkey later said that it was clear in July that there was a problem. He denied that any players had approached him but said, "I've been around 37 years. I walk into that clubhouse and look around. If you can't sense things, there's something wrong with you."[44] Dick Williams's wife, Norma, said it was the lingering "country club atmosphere" on the ball club and that "Yastrzemski has been a major headache since Dick took over the ball club. . . . Yastrzemski is a real favorite with Mr. Yawkey. And he takes advantage of every opportunity to promote himself with the owner."[45] A month after the season, Reggie Smith spoke up and said that Dick Williams really did have to go for the morale of the team; he singled out times that the manager had left in pitchers "who were getting hit very hard, to humiliate them."[46] Smith said he knew that Yawkey had been criticized for visiting the clubhouse too often, "but he mingled with the players to show concern, and the players appreciated this."[47]

There were some who perhaps envied the closer bonds between Yaz and Yawkey, but infielder John Kennedy remarked:

> "[Yawkey] was always in the clubhouse wanting to know how your family was, how everybody was doing. I think he got a bad rap from some people who said that when he went in, he only talked to Yaz. They would make it sound like he'd walk by everybody, ignore everybody, and go right to Yaz. That was not true. My locker was probably three down from the door that he would come in. He would come in,

and he would stop and talk to the first person he saw. He might eventually get to Yaz, but he would stop and talk to everybody on the way. He'd want to know how the kids were, how everybody was doing.

It was the players with whom Yawkey visited, not the manager. Kennedy allowed that Yawkey might have visited Kasko or Darrell Johnson, but he added, "I don't remember him ever going in [the manager's office]."[48]

PR man Dick Bresciani, who joined the Red Sox in 1972, offered another perspective on Yawkey's visits to the clubhouse:

> He was just down to earth, no matter what job you had in the organization. When I was there, he'd go down to the clubhouse, but he wasn't talking about strategies. When he'd see those guys, he'd be talking about families and what they did in the offseason, things like that. He liked to know about them personally and if they had problems. He was that kind of person. He wasn't down there to interfere. He was in there as a friend to those guys. He saw them as part of his family. That's how he was with those guys, and that's how he was with all of the employees.[49]

"If you had to describe him," said Ted Lepcio, of earlier days, "I think, in retrospect, that he was a little self-conscious. He didn't like a crowd to be in. As soon as three or four of us got in the clubhouse, he left. None of us really sat down and chatted with him except [Ted] Williams."[50]

When Yawkey was a young man, his father had seen to it that he spent some time each summer working in the logging camps. Haywood Sullivan was among those who believed this experience taught him how to relate to people who had had a less privileged life and helped breed in him an honest compassion, not just one engendered through obligation.[51] Yawkey truly preferred to be out playing pepper with the clubhouse kids than hobnobbing at country clubs with financiers. Jean would often simply sit in the stands and watch Tom.

Perhaps Dick Williams had been too outspoken in criticizing his players. "Candor is good press-wise, but it is not good player-wise," said O'Connell.[52] Williams, for his part, said that O'Connell "has been great to me ever since I came to Boston. I still respect and admire him." He chose not to say anything about Tom Yawkey, though the AP story reported that he made reference to a "personality conflict" between him and the owner.[53]

Williams later wrote, "Mr. Yawkey didn't want a professional baseball man, he wanted a politician." And he believed that Haywood Sullivan was "constantly ripping me to Mrs. Yawkey." Sullivan was, he thought, "perhaps feeling I was getting too much recognition for a lousy manager." Williams added a note to Sullivan in his autobiography: "Hey, Haywood, if you're reading this: I never wanted your power. I never wanted your office. I only wanted to win with your baseball team. I only wish you could have gotten off Mr. Yawkey's lap long enough to see that."[54]

Incoming manager Eddie Kasko—fresh off three years of managing the Red Sox Triple A clubs at Toronto and then Louisville—had a different understanding of what had gotten Dick Williams fired:

[Williams] didn't think Mr. Yawkey appreciated him as a manager. Well, Mr. Yawkey is not going to say a whole lot in appreciation, and I think Dick got all bent out of shape just at the time, and this had a big thing to do with his firing. While the club was away, there was a writer, Clif Keane, who stayed back from the trip; he went into the ballpark, and he saw Mr. Yawkey there, so he thought he'd sit down and do a story. Well, he asked Mr. Yawkey, "What kind of a manager do you think Dick Williams is?"

You've got to know Mr. Yawkey because if you put it in print and just read it, it would sound like "Dick Williams is a good manager." But the choices were great manager, good manager, fair manager, poor manager. [Williams] won the pennant for [Yawkey] in '67, so Dick figured he should be considered a great manager. Well, if you know Mr. Yawkey and the way he talks, when he was asked the question... I can just see him: "Well, goddamn it, Dick's a good manager. Dick's a *good* manager!" I don't know what more you could say, but when you read it in print, it doesn't sound as great.

Dick got off the road trip. He read the paper, or his wife kept the paper for him or whatever, and he went into the ballpark and went up to see Mr. Yawkey and put the paper on the desk and said, "I'll put my record up against any manager you had here."

Well, if you own a ball club, you don't have to sit there and listen to that. Dick left. He said his piece and left, and Mr. Yawkey just said to Dick O'Connell, "Have him fired at the end of the year." As simple as that. You don't challenge the guy who owns the ball club.[55]

Yawkey had heard the "country club" charge for years—the "Gold Sox," the "Yawkey Millionaires," and all that. In October 1975 he finally said, "The 1927 Yankees was one of the best clubs ever put together. I knew all the guys on that club—Babe Ruth and the rest. There was never a club more 'country club' that that team. As far as I'm concerned, we always had pretty good discipline on this team. We haven't been any worse behaved off the field than a lot of others."[56] Frank Malzone thought a lot of the "country club" remarks were exaggerated:

Tom Yawkey was known to be fair with salaries, but he didn't mingle with players as much as was made out. I saw very little of him. Once in a while he'd come in and ask how guys were doing, but that's the extent of it. He didn't throw any parties or anything for his players. The "country club" label they placed on the Red Sox was bullshit. Someone just trumped that up. After I'd been with the club a few years I wondered what the hell they were talking about. We worked as hard as any team.[57]

Dick Williams had a contract that paid him through 1970. He then managed Oakland in 1971–73, winning the AL West the first year and the World Series in the next two.

A few days after the death of Joseph P. Kennedy, an AP story came out at the end of November that Kennedy had tried to buy the Red Sox right after the war, in 1946, saying at the time, "I'd like to get Jack, Bobby and Teddy interested." He was reportedly very disappointed that Yawkey wouldn't sell him the team.[58]

In December the Red Sox acquired left-hander Gary Peters from the White Sox. Three other players were involved, but it was understood that cash to Chicago was a major consideration.

On December 23 the Izaak Walton League of America—a leading conservationist group—filed suit in Minneapolis to prevent Yawkey and associates from opening a mine in a wilderness area in Superior

National Forest. The area offered iron, cooper, and nickel deposits but had been protected even against motor vehicles as a true wilderness area.[59] Yawkey's attorney asked that he be dropped from the suit, stating that he had made no claim to any mining rights in the wilderness area.

Construction began early in 1970 on a $10 million cancer center under the aegis of the Children's Cancer Research Foundation (Tom Yawkey, chairman), with $5 million of the money having been donated by lawyer and industrialist Charles A. Dana. It became the Dana-Farber Cancer Institute.

The Curt Flood case was a major story in 1970, with Flood's challenge to baseball's reserve clause threatening to give every player the right to earn free agency. One would expect Tom Yawkey to have been dead set against changes to the reserve clause, but it didn't seem that he was. He said such changes wouldn't mean the end of baseball, that something would be worked out. He talked about how much was invested in developing a player over the years—he specified $250,000 at the time—and for teams to continue to invest in that way, they needed to have some control over players, but "I don't say a club has to control a player for life."[60]

The Patriots decided to move to Foxboro, pretty much ending talk of a new stadium in Boston that would host both football and Red Sox baseball. That decision didn't stop entrepreneurs from coming up with ideas for a new home for the Red Sox. Thomas Wheeler hatched a plan by which the Sox would move to Readville (part of Boston's Hyde Park) and a new fifty-five-thousand-seat stadium, which they could use rent free for thirty years. The only catch was that Yawkey would have to give Wheeler's group all the real estate at Fenway, on which the group would build a very large high-rise apartment complex.[61]

Labor negotiations continued into the season, and in mid-May the Red Sox voted 21-4 not to accept the owners' most recent offer. Lonborg stressed, "There are certainly no militants on the team," and he said there had been no talk of any strike.[62]

Racial issues with the Red Sox seemed to have finally taken a back seat. Perhaps it was O'Connell's influence, perhaps more than that. In 1970 George Scott talked about his time with the Red Sox, remembering quite a number of black players in 1966 and 1967: "I joined this organization when I was 18 years old, and just out of high school. And I can honestly say I've always been treated fair by everyone in it—Mr. Yawkey, Dick O'Connell, Haywood Sullivan, Neil Mahoney, Ed Kenney, everybody. My only beef was a personal one with Dick Williams."[63]

In his first visit of the year to Fenway, at the end of May, Yawkey saw a team that was in fifth place and faring poorly, with a terrible road record (5-17). Even Yastrzemski was getting booed at home, "the object of frustration which poured from the stands with the subtlety of a hard-hat construction worker at a peace rally."[64] Yawkey confessed he wasn't sure why the Sox were struggling but that he had complete confidence in new manager Eddie Kasko. Rather than experience a September swoon, the team finished the season on an upswing, pushing into third place on September 9 and finishing the season securely in third (87-75), twenty-one games behind the Orioles (and six behind the Yankees) but eight games ahead of the fourth-place Tigers.

Yawkey's generosity cropped up once more in a story that emerged only in 2014. Red Sox infielder John Kennedy remembered it as follows:

George Scott got hurt—this was the first year I was here—and I had to go in and play for about a month. That's when he was playing third base. So I went in and played third. Kasko said to me, "You know, when he's ready, he's going to have to come back in." And I was playing pretty well. I understood that, that he had to come back in and play. The day George came back, Eddie came out in the dugout and he said, "Dick [O'Connell] wants to see you in my office." I thought, "Oh, no. Here I go." I thought I was gone. I went up there and he handed me a check for $2,000, and he said, "You did a good job while you were in there." I'm sure he had some leeway to do certain things on his own, but I would think something like that would have to come from Mr. Yawkey.[65]

Ray Culp again led the team in victories with a 17-14 record (3.04 ERA). Gary Peters won 16, and Sonny Siebert won 15. Yaz led the team in batting average (.326) and homers (40), but it was Tony Conigliaro who batted in the most runs (116). Petrocelli had 103 RBIs and Yaz, 102. The most remarkable offensive accomplishment of the year was probably the home run production of the Conigliaro brothers: Tony hit 36, and Billy hit 18. Tony's comeback was impressive, so it was all the more shocking when a trade was executed on October 11. Tony Conigliaro, the hometown hero who'd grown up in the shadow of Fenway Park, was sent to the California Angels (with Ray Jarvis and Jerry Moses). In exchange the Red Sox received Doug Griffin and two unrelated Tatums: Jarvis Tatum and Ken Tatum.

Many Sox fans were outraged. It was, however, a trade that took advantage of Tony Conigliaro's post-beaning value at the time it had peaked. Yawkey was reportedly told of the trade after it had happened, but he had approved the idea of Tony C's being dealt.[66] The Sox needed pitching. They'd led both leagues in home runs and had come in second in AL runs scored, only six behind Baltimore, but they had still finished twenty-one games behind in the standings. In December they traded for Luis Aparicio from the White Sox, sending Chicago the popular Mike Andrews and Luis Alvarado. Before the '70 season began, Andrews had been one of the very few to ever hold out before signing his contract.

It is not clear when it first appeared, but a story circulated that while Joe Cronin was still Sox manager and Cardinal Cushing was still a bishop, Cushing once asked Michael Cronin, Joe's young boy, "Who made the world?" "God made the world" was Michael's response. "Who made the Red Sox?" "Tom Yawkey."[67]

With a year under his belt, Eddie Kasko was no longer a rookie manager. Early in 1971 spring training he credited Yastrzemski for his willingness to shift to first base; he was making the point that he didn't believe the stories that Yaz got managers fired through his close relationship with Yawkey. Yaz had played ninety-four games at first base in 1970.

With free agency a possibility as the Curt Flood case made its way through the courts, the Red Sox signed Yaz to a three-year deal, estimated to be worth more than $500,000. It was, to that time, the largest contract a player had been offered. Money was becoming a factor in deals once more, Yawkey told reporters.[68] Yaz was fiercely loyal to Tom Yawkey, a stance that put him at odds with Flood and the players pressing to get rid of the reserve clause. Many years later, in a 2005 interview with author Brad Snyder, Yastrzemski "confessed that his loyalty to Tom Yawkey clouded his judgment about the reserve clause." Yaz told Snyder, "We played for a great owner. The players on the Red Sox didn't understand the conditions on the other teams."[69]

The Sox had decided to go for more balance, willing to give up some offense in exchange for better defense. That quest for balance had been part of the reason for trading Tony C. Yawkey looked back on 1970 and said, "We were last in double plays, last in fielding. What do you do, go along with stuff like that? No sir, not this man. We had to do something—help the defense, right? Tony went and Mike [Andrews] went."[70]

Something was working. By the time Yawkey first came to Fenway at the end of May, the Red Sox had been in first place for a full month. It was the first time since 1946 that they'd been atop the standings when he arrived.

When Tony Conigliaro announced his retirement in July—he was hitting only .222 with only fifteen RBIs after seventy-four games—brother Billy alleged a conspiracy on the Red Sox. Still upset over Tony's being traded away, he said, "Tony was traded because of one guy—over there." He pointed to Yaz on the other side of the clubhouse. "You can quote me because I don't care. I know I'm next. It's about time they—owner Tom Yawkey and everybody—woke up."[71] Reggie Smith had something to say: "I don't want to play with Billy Conigliaro anymore."[72]

Red Sox player rep Gary Peters said, "Billy is very emotional. I was sorry to hear about [Billy's statement]. I don't think it was very nice. I'm sorry that it happened."[73] The other players said pretty much the same—Billy was emotional, and it was unfortunate that he'd said what he'd said. Yaz, however, said that Billy was "just alibiing for his lack of ability," and he said that he didn't want to play with Billy. He added that the belief that he was the one who orchestrated any trades was "an insult to Tom Yawkey and all the other officials of the club."[74]

Yawkey, for his part, was known to be resentful of the notion that he "shouldn't" spend time with the players any time he might feel like it. These were his employees, playing in his park. He was the one who paid all the bills.[75] The man who paid the salaries said, "The whole thing is a lot of bull. . . . It makes me sick every time I read one of those stories that say Yaz conspires with me to get rid of managers. . . . I've never discussed a manager with Yaz." It was more than just one player popping off. "It involves team attitude that could affect our performance the rest of the year."[76] A day later he suggested that all the players "shut their mouths." He included Yastrzemski in that suggestion. "Yaz has talked too much, too. It's all got to be stopped."[77]

The press had a field day. Bud Collins suggested that maybe Yaz would fire Yawkey. Billy Conigliaro said he had no plans to apologize. Yaz joked with Brooks Robinson at the All-Star Game: "When I signed, my father sold his potato farm and bought the Red Sox. We agreed to keep Mr. Yawkey on as a front man."[78] Ultimately, of course, the buck stopped at Tom Yawkey's desk, and some, such as Neil Singelais and Harold Kaese of the *Globe*, suggested that maybe the owner spent too much time making a beeline for Yaz's locker instead of talking with the players who weren't household names. A couple of days later, the Conigliaro brothers and Yaz agreed to a mutual truce.

The Sox were in second place as all this spewed out. Yawkey indicated that he'd be open to the idea of realignment, instead of expansion, creating three eight-team leagues.[79]

Yawkey wanted to "clear the air," wrote Singelais, in more ways than one. The *Globe* writer devoted a lengthy article to another Tom Yawkey initiative, that of conservation. For years Yawkey had devoted time and resources to wildlife preservation and soil conservation on his land in South Carolina. "We must be doing something right," he told Singelais. "We're often visited by these biologists in conjunction with the U.S. Fish and Wildlife Service. We're glad to give them the benefit of the things we've discovered in the control of water level and water salinity and in our marsh land expansion. We have our own laboratory and testing facilities for upland soil." Chances are that most baseball aficionados never knew a thing about this side of Tom Yawkey. Yet he had, Singelais wrote, "played a major role in the passage by Congress of a law forbidding interstate shipment of alligators and killing them for hides." South Carolina's senator Eugene Hollings had shepherded the legislation, Yawkey told Singelais. Yawkey funded a study of alligators that, almost fifty years later (as of 2017), was still ongoing. Yawkey estimated he had as many as fifty thousand ducks on his land. "I've been interested in ecology for a long time. The existence of man can be determined by his health. Everybody gets stirred up, and worried about it. Certain animals and birds were becoming extinct, and nobody paid attention to it."[80]

One might say Yawkey's consciousness had evolved. In 1919, when he was sixteen and had fond memories of hunting with his father in South Carolina, he talked about taking tennis at his prep school, but he added, "I would leave tennis at any time to go duck shooting or fishing. That is one of my ambitions. I want to equal my father's record, popping ducks down at South Island. I haven't been able to do that yet, but I have scored fifty-two at a round."[81] In 1975 he told Bill Liston, "I haven't shot a duck for about 20 years. I just shoot quail and dove now. The waterfowl population went down considerably and I just figured I'd killed enough and now I want to help them out."[82] He created such a successful sanctuary for ducks that neighbors in South Carolina found many of their ducks flocking to Yawkey's place in preference to their own. Phil Wilkinson agreed: "This Goose Pasture actually wound up drawing the mallards out of the Waccamaw Delta, where the Vanderbilts were, and some responded that all the damn ducks had gone to the Yawkey place. And I just said, 'Well, you can either like it or you could lump it.'"[83]

Freddie Cumbee, who worked for the Yawkeys in South Carolina and often fished with Tom, told a story about how he and Yawkey were fishing once and a big snake was very close to their little boat. Freddie asked, "Do you want me to get him?" and Mr. Yawkey said, "No, this is his territory."[84]

Yawkey was also worried about pollution and overpopulation. He wouldn't recommend eating a fish out of Boston's Charles River, he said, and he didn't allow oystering on his land because of the mercury content. It was because he loved hunting and fishing so much that he cared as much as he did. Some may find it a paradox that he loved to kill quail and doves on his properties but drew the line well short of extinction. "I've used a shotgun all my life, and I've never hurt anything in regard to the extinction of wildlife. I never cut down the coveys below six."[85] How he knew the numbers that were well short of extinction was not explained. Yawkey also had staff working to thin out long-leaf and short-leaf pine timber in South Island. He believed not just in keeping humans off the land to let it be but also in the proper management of land, water, and growth.

Very serious discussions appeared in the newspapers about even Yaz being on the trading block.[86] The *Record American* ran a story quoting Tom Yawkey as saying that every player on the club, including Yaz, was available for trade. "I never talked to the person who was supposed to have quoted me," Yawkey said the next day. Yes, Yaz was having a poor year, but Yaz was "the most complete player in the American League, and it would take one hell of a deal for any club to acquire him. . . . I doubt there's a club that could make an offer attractive enough to get him."[87]

Phil Elderkin of the *Christian Science Monitor* suggested that Yawkey hire Frank Robinson as manager, a bold move that would give the Red Sox the first black manager in the Major Leagues. Elderkin said Kasko had lost control of the team.[88] Two days later Rico Petrocelli jumped in, saying that the club "had the potential to win the pennant, but that Kasko helped blow it."[89] Three days after that O'Connell announced a one-year extension on Kasko's contract, with a raise, and said the Sox would "get rid of any player who doesn't want to play."[90] Rico, chastised, apologized. Red Smith's column was headed "Loudmouthed Ballplayers Breed Nothing but Trouble."[91] Yawkey said he'd been talking with O'Connell, and he expected there would be some changes over the winter. Yawkey stayed in Boston until the end of the season; it was the first time he'd done so since 1967. The *Herald*'s Tim Horgan wrote that if he waited around until he figured out all that was puzzling about Yawkey's dysfunctional club (Horgan didn't use that word), he'd be at Fenway for New Year's Eve.[92]

As to what remained an ongoing question regarding race and the

Red Sox, Yawkey himself said on September 2, "We have made a concentrated effort to get black players. We judge players on their ability, not their color. We don't care if a player is black or white, or Chinese or Indian. If he has good potential, we'll go after him."[93] Chief scout Neil Mahoney said that Yawkey had specifically asked him—it sounded as though it had been several times—if he'd seen any good black players and added, "Be sure you do." GM O'Connell said, "The Red Sox have four black scouts. Stan Johnson in California, [Lou] Dials in Los Angeles, Ed Scott in the central-South, and Felix Maldonado in Puerto Rico. We also have a scout in Venezuela." Mahoney said 34 of the 150 players in their system were black.[94]

It wasn't surprising to see Billy Conigliaro go. Back in July, Yawkey—in a rare moment of public pique with a player—had muttered, "The Conigliaros have called more press conferences in one year than I have called in all the years I have owned this team."[95] On October 10, after just the first game of the World Series, Billy C was traded to the Milwaukee Brewers with Ken Brett, Joe Lahoud, Jim Lonborg, Don Pavletich, and George Scott. The Sox got Tommy Harper, Lew Krausse, Marty Pattin, and Minor Leaguer Pat Skrable. "The Red Sox brass told Tom Yawkey about the big Milwaukee trade *after* it was made," wrote the *Herald*.[96]

The Sox finished in third place, three games ahead of the Yankees but eighteen games behind the first-place Orioles.

Times were changing. The Red Sox scheduled forty-three night games for 1972. It is interesting to note that—in contrast to twenty-first-century practice—the average ticket price at Fenway was the lowest in the Majors. The average price was $2.32 in Boston, but it was $3.00 throughout the big leagues.[97]

Just as he had resisted night games originally, Yawkey's attitude toward certain promotions was perhaps predictable. "I've been in baseball long enough," he had said in the late 1950s, "to know that when you try to stimulate interest and attendance with giveaways and premiums you're merely kidding yourself. When you have to lure fans to the park with a band concert, fireworks and stuff like that you're admitting that your product is not adequate. I feel it's much better in the long run to improve your team with that money."[98] To

Curt Gowdy he put it as follows: "I get criticized for not promoting. I don't put on shows. I don't have exploding scoreboards. Well, the best promotion you can have is eight skilled players on the field and some good pitchers. Win. Just win. That's the best promotion."[99]

A New Year's Eve 1972 jewel heist "at the luxurious Pierre Hotel"— the Yawkeys' residence in New York—resulted in a number of people losing valuables. The wife of a Swiss banker was thought to have lost $500,000 worth of jewels.[100] Five men were arrested just over a week later.

During spring training, Marvin Miller of the players' association visited the various camps asking for a vote to authorize a strike, to have that in his arsenal as he went into collective bargaining. Almost every team voted unanimously to give him the authorization (the total for the first thirteen teams [not counting the Sox] was 338-0, with one abstention), but on the Red Sox it was 19-4. Actually it was announced at 19-3, but then Rico Petrocelli turned in his ballot. Sox player rep Gary Peters said he'd already announced the vote, but Rico said, "I don't give a damn." It was thought that Yaz and Reggie Smith were two of the other dissenters.[101] Peters said, "The reason it wasn't unanimous here is our owner."[102] Some players had a very strong sense of loyalty to Tom Yawkey. Some players may have crossed the line, though, and Bill Lee says that's what got Sparky Lyle sent out of town, traded to the Yankees for Danny Cater. Lyle saved a league-leading thirty-five games for the Yankees in 1972 and went on to win the Cy Young Award in 1977.

Not all the owners engendered affection. They fell short of what the players were seeking in health and pension benefits, and when the players rejected their offer of an additional $400,000 (about a 7.4 percent increase), the owners were unanimous in their stance against further increases. August Busch of the Cardinals declared, "We're not going to give them another damn cent. If they want to strike, let 'em."[103]

The players across baseball did strike, the first strike in Major League history. Some may have been in shock that they'd actually done it. The *Herald* observed, "The Red Sox clubhouse was eerie and silent." Bill Lee had something to say: "I don't know what the players are so stunned for. They voted for the strike."[104] A couple of days later, Claflin wrote, "Some of the players admit openly they have no idea how it all came about. They are shocked that they are on strike after voting to strike. . . . The players he [Yawkey] coddled have responded by striking his baseball club."[105] Greed was on first base and avarice on second, and the pigeons had Fenway to themselves on the day the season would have opened, wrote Harold Kaese, not taking sides in the dispute.[106]

The strike was resolved, and the season started on April 15 for the Red Sox. It was agreed to simply pick up the schedule as originally constituted and not to make up the games that had been lost—regardless of whether some clubs played a different number of games from others.

Yawkey was pleased looking back on the big trade with the Brewers. "We should have more harmony on this team," he said.[107]

A news story in June reported that Yawkey had helped raise enough money to save Tara Hall, a shelter run by Father Owen O'Sullivan for homeless and abused boys near Georgetown, South Carolina. Yawkey had "obtained contributions from baseball people and other sports figures."[108] A July 9, 1972, story in the *Boston Herald* was about the mutual devotion between the fifteen boys at Tara Hall and Father O'Sullivan and Jim Dumm, who ran the place, and it reported that Jean Yawkey found it sad that on the one day a month families were allowed to visit, some of them never did. It was said to be the first time in the thirty-nine years that Tom Yawkey had owned the Red Sox that he had permitted publicity regarding one of his charitable enterprises; it was because the need for additional funds was considerable. Tara Hall had been ready to close, but Jean Yawkey had responded to an appeal from Father O'Sullivan. The Yawkeys had done so much in Georgetown, the priest said. He continued:

Nobody knows how much because they never want anyone to know what they're doing. . . . We were ready to close last Christmas and the Yawkeys saved us. They gave us the land, the building, financial aid. But just as important, they've given the boys their love. They are indeed the boys' adopted parents. They know all the youngsters by their first names and spend time talking with each boy and are deeply interested in each one. The boys aren't awed by them either. They simply consider the Yawkeys their friends.

The thought was expressed that Jean Yawkey may have been "inspired in part by Tom's childhood experience of being tossed from one family branch to another" and thus took a special interest in Tara Hall.[109]

Yawkey's reaction to the player strike, expressed after he had made the trek north to Boston in June, was to call it "an unfortunate incident" but to say it was all one-sided, with the players asking for more of this, that, and another thing while turning a deaf ear to whatever owners might ask. Fans wanted to see baseball played on the field and didn't at all want to hear about disagreements between players and owners. He said that most people didn't realize how many teams truly lost money, and he worried that teams would be hurt in the box office when they inevitably would need to raise ticket prices. He concluded, "I've taken the attitude that from every bad situation, something good has to come. I hope from the strike comes the realization that we can't go through something like this again."[110] He let the players off the hook a little by saying that he didn't think most of them had known just what they were voting for.[111] The Red Sox were 18-23, in fourth place, at the time Yawkey turned up in Boston.

Rico and Reggie were off to slow starts, and Yaz was struggling to mount a comeback, but new catcher Carlton Fisk was enjoying a good start. Yawkey reflected on the idea that the Red Sox system had developed a number of malcontents, that many of those who expressed the most unhappiness were those who had come up through the Sox system. He didn't think it was true, but he remarked:

All right, I spoil them. But tell me how? I'd like to know how I spoil them. I don't sign them to their contracts. I don't tell them how to hit or field or play the game. The only thing I do, I make it a point to tell a young player, "Nice going," if he does something well. . . . When any player is in a slump, I'll talk to him a little, too. I know he's mentally down. Ballplayers have pride. They want to do well. So I just try to give them a little mental boost. If trying to treat a player like a human being is spoiling them, then I spoil my players. But I was brought up to treat every human being as a human being until he proves unworthy of it. And I'll never change in that respect.[112]

In the same article Yawkey admitted he was a little soft when it came to providing jobs for former players in the organization.

At one point, Yawkey may have also acknowledged that his paternalism had a down side. "Players are the most helpless people in the world," he said in the days before every player had an agent. "If you told them to go to San Francisco by themselves, they might wind up in Mexico City. I guess we could have really used a resident s.o.b. in the organization. There hasn't been one since Eddie [Collins], and he wasn't one really."[113]

Hall of Famer George Kell felt not only that Yawkey spoiled his players, but that it also had a negative effect: "Outside of Detroit, I loved playing in Boston the best. I loved the city and the people, and I sure loved Fenway Park. But I was disappointed in my experience there. What was wrong with the team was what was always wrong with them: Tom Yawkey was too good. He wanted a winner so bad but thought he had to pamper everybody and be every player's friend. He should have kicked some ass because the players never gave him his money's worth."[114]

Yawkey didn't expect the strike to have a lasting impact, but he also said of the ballplayers, "They don't seem to have any idea of what it takes to pay the bills. Someone should tell them that the bills have to be paid and that it takes an awful lot of money to break even for a season. I'm sure the players would be shocked like everyone else if they actually knew how many teams are not breaking even."[115]

By July 18 the Red Sox had passed the .500 mark, and with a 20-12 July they began to make a little headway. They were 17-12 in August and then had an excellent 20-9 in September.

There was a little discord on the team but nothing like the year before. Reggie Smith and Luis Tiant tangled in the runway behind the dugout at one point, but the dispute passed quickly. There had been criticism that Eddie Kasko was too passive or indecisive a manager, but as team performance improved as the season unfolded, such criticism stopped. Luis Aparicio suffered a broken finger during the season, and Yawkey spent some time with him in the trainer's room, then had Luis up to his box for a couple of days. Former Sox player Ken Harrelson (who had turned golf pro and missed qualifying for the British Open by just one stroke) also spent a game in Yawkey's box, as had Red Auerbach of the Boston Celtics. In mid-August Carlton Fisk was reported to have said that some of the veterans on the club weren't showing enough in the way of leadership, perhaps being a little too content with their large multiyear contracts. There were closed-door meetings with Kasko, Reggie Smith, Yaz, and Fisk. Yawkey liked the attitude of players like Tiant and Fisk and wasn't about to criticize Yastrzemski.

On August 26 Jean Yawkey threw a surprise party at Fenway after the day's game with the Texas Rangers. Jean had taken advantage of Ted Williams's being in town as Texas Rangers manager. "T. A." had been told it was a reception for retiring sports reporter Ed Rumill, but in fact about 125 people celebrated Tom Yawkey's fortieth year of owning the Red Sox. No other man had owned a big league team for as many years.

As it happens, Williams had played a role in helping Bob Short engineer the shift of the Washington Senators franchise to Texas, where they became the Rangers after the 1971 season. Longtime Senators broadcaster Shelby Whitfield was there when Williams, at Short's behest, asked Yawkey to approve the move.[116]

Yawkey didn't run as tight ship in terms of personal grooming as the New York Yankees; a good percentage of the team had a mustache and longer hair.

Five years before Melissa Ludtke filed suit against commissioner Bowie Kuhn to secure equal access for women as sports reporters, two female baseball writers were working in the Red Sox clubhouse in mid-September, and there was a little controversy. Yawkey's response was all one would want: "What was all the uproar about? Much ado about nothing. It was perfectly simple: they've got the credentials, they've got the right to be here."[117] This comment came at a time when, according to journalist Lesley Visser, "a media credential actually said that no women or children were allowed in the press box."[118]

In "Sharing the Beat," writer Diane K. Shah recalled being assigned to cover some games at Fenway Park for the *National*

Observer in September 1972. Red Sox PR man Bill Crowley was hesitant about providing credentials, mentioning "We don't let women on the field, and the Baseball Writers Association runs the press box." The head of the Boston chapter of the BBWAA "sort of stuttered and put me [Shah] on hold for a long time, and then he said he couldn't do it." After the publication's attorney called the Red Sox, there was a little more compliance. "When I got up there all I'd heard was 'Well, that girl can come in if she behaves herself,' and I didn't know what that meant. Bill Crowley had told me he'd get me a box seat and said he'd bring players there for me to interview. I said, 'You mean you'll bring Carl Yastrzemski to see me in the stands right after a game?' and he said, 'Well, I'll try.'" Shah got a field pass but found that none of the players would talk to her. There had apparently been a team meeting, and the players were told to "watch their language"—a quaint notion that most of them took to mean they shouldn't talk to her at all. She later got in a word with Carlton Fisk and pitcher John Curtis.[119]

Dick Bresciani could laugh about it forty years later, but it was clearly an awkward time.[120] Shah remembers the following:

> Before the game, Dick Bresciani, the assistant public-relations man, took me up on the roof, where the press box and the pressroom are. I could see he was terribly uncomfortable about something, and when we got there he explained that I could come into the press box but that the pressroom was a social place, for eating and drinking, and no women were allowed in there. I saw that they'd set up a little ice-cream table outside the pressroom, with one chair and one place setting, and there was a little folder on it with 'Ladies' Pavilion' written across it. I didn't eat at all that night. I just ignored it.

Bresciani himself remembered a little picnic table set with a white tablecloth and a small vase with a red rose in it. The Red Sox were trying, in their own way, with gallantry and pleasantries, though a separate but not quite equal approach wasn't going to work in the long run. The next night, the pressroom was open, and seeing no one sitting with Shah, Tom Yawkey invited her over to his table. Shah summed up the experience: "The strangest thing of all, when I look back on it, is that none of this seemed to have been done with any malice. They were all polite, in a distant sort of way. They just didn't know what to do about me."

Donna Mountain had worked in Crowley's office for a few years in the late 1960s, and she remembered the days:

> Women were not allowed in the press box upstairs back in those days. The men went up for dinner when we had night games, but they brought the dinners down for the gals in the office. We had a little kitchen off the ladies room. . . . Whether they had lobster night or swordfish or hot dog night or whatever, that's where we had our dinner. And Jean Yawkey would come in and sit with us. Not most nights, but often. I was getting married that first summer, and I remember Mrs. Yawkey saying a couple of times—when something would come in on a nice platter—"Leave the platter for the bride. She needs it more than we do." She was just a very nice person.[121]

It was, Mountain said, "definitely a man's world in the office. When the Red Sox wives had a fashion show, I sat in on the planning of it a couple of times. Mrs. Yawkey came in and sat in on that as well. She helped make some arrangements and probably took care of the financial part of it as well."[122]

With a 15-6 season and a 1.91 ERA, the thirty-one-year-old Tiant—originally acquired just to help out Louisville—was the surprise of the season. Fisk led the team in homers (22) and batting average (.293) and was fourth in RBIs (61) behind Rico, Reggie, and Yaz. The team played 155 games, 7 games short of a full season due to the strike. It was still far from an offensive juggernaut, with a .248 team batting average and just 594 RBIs. The team ERA of 3.47 ranked the Sox eleventh of the twelve AL teams, but they put together a superb season, falling just a half game short of winning the AL East. The half game deficiency resulted from the Detroit Tigers playing one more game (and winning it) since, as noted, it had been decided to play out the schedule as originally constituted and not play the full 162 games. Happenstance gave the Tigers one more game, and they took advantage.

When it came down to the final week of the season, with the Red Sox very much in the race, columnist Tim Horgan mused that criticism of Yawkey's "benevolent despotism" and his habit of working crossword puzzles in his office was now seen as the "genius of a clubowner" but, truly, it was "only because he had the perspicacity to retain Dick O'Connell as his VP in charge of the whole shebang."[123]

Unlike the magical 1967 season, however, the park was not packed in the final weeks. The team had taken first place on September 7 and held it for most of the rest of the month—all but one day—though never with a lead of more than a game and a half. The last six games of the season were on the road—three each in Baltimore and Detroit—and Yawkey traveled with the team.[124] The Sox lost the first two games to the Tigers, 4–1 and 3–1, and those losses ultimately did them in. (They'd lost one to the Orioles, 2–1.) There was good pitching but no offense, with only one run in each of three crucial games. The October 5 *Globe* ran a photograph that became famous; it showed Yawkey in the clubhouse, his hand on Carlton Fisk's back as Fisk had his face buried in his hands, the team owner consoling the catcher, the 1972 AL Rookie of the Year.

Such compassion wasn't unusual for Yawkey. Jim Lonborg, who'd pitched for the Sox from 1965 to 1971, said, "I remember having pitched a tough game one night and coming into the locker room the next morning. It was way before game time. I was over in one of the corner lockers next to Earl Wilson, and Mr. Yawkey came over and sat down next to me. He just wanted to tell me what a heroic effort I had performed the night before and to just keep my spirits up. He was wonderful like that."[125]

Current *Boston Herald* sports columnist Steve Buckley met Yawkey just one time. His uncle, Bill Fitzgerald, was an usher at Fenway, and Buck often went to Fenway in his formative years.

> When the Red Sox lost that second-to-last game to the Detroit Tigers in '72, me and my friend Greg Mattos thought it would be cool to go and meet the Red Sox because we heard that their flight was coming in at such-and-such a time at Logan Airport. We expected hundreds of thousands of fans to be there, but nobody was there. They had lost. The players were waiting for their luggage at a carousel. There were only maybe one hundred or so fans there, and the players were all standing there. I remember talking to Bob Veale. And Yawkey was

there. I talked to Yawkey—in fact, I got his autograph, and I still have it in an old autograph book I had as a kid. I was sixteen.

He [Yawkey] was an old man but not as old as he looked. He was certainly an icon then. If you go back and listen to the 1967 *Impossible Dream* record album . . . I can do it off the top of my head:

Thomas Austin Yawkey
Owner, sportsman, fan
Baseball lives in Boston
Through the efforts of this man.

That blurb, narrated by Ken Coleman, encapsulated all that I knew about Tom Yawkey at that point in my life.[126]

After the now meaningless final game of the season, Eddie Kasko was rehired for two more years. He'd helped bring the team as close as one could—a half game—but had still fallen short because of the vagaries of the strike and the schedule. "Naturally, you hate to lose," said Yawkey, "but we showed plenty. I think we have a lot to look forward to in the future."[127]

For whatever reason, 1972 is often overlooked when one lists the near misses the Sox have suffered—1946, 1967, 1975, 1978, 1986, 2003(among others)—but there they were at the finish, with a record of 85-70 to Detroit's 86-70.

Former Red Sox manager Dick Williams led the Oakland Athletics to the 1972 World Championship.

For a sixteenth season, Yawkey was again voted VP of the American League.

On Christmas, Tom and Jean Yawkey visited the boys at Tara Hall who had no family to welcome them home.

On January 10, 1973, the Red Sox held the traditional showing of the official World Series film at Fenway Park. It was bittersweet because not only had the Sox fallen that half game short of a playoff spot, but also the manager of the world champion Oakland A's was their prior manager, Dick Williams. At the showing, Dick O'Connell told the media that increased labor costs under the new deal with the players would probably result in pay cuts for about half a dozen players.

With the criticisms about Yawkey coddling ballplayers, one might expect iconoclast southpaw Bill Lee, "the Spaceman," to rag on Yawkey. He did not. "Mr. Yawkey was a simple compassionate man who cared about his players more than winning," he wrote. "He didn't mind winning; he just never crucified you if you lost."[128] Lee added, "Mr. Yawkey and I weren't particularly close, but whatever relationship we did have was a good one. We had a common bond, solidified by our mutual interest in the *National Geographic*. I had a subscription to the magazine, and I would bring it into the clubhouse, leaving it at my locker while I did my running. One afternoon I returned to the clubhouse to find that my latest issue was missing." When it went missing again the following week, the Spaceman knew something was up, and he was determined to catch the culprit. While Lee was meeting with Dick O'Connell in his office, "Mr. Yawkey popped in and handed me a brown paper bag, saying, 'I think these are yours.' Inside the sack were the purloined magazines." The two ended up in a discussion about ivory-billed woodpeckers and how they had become extinct in Yawkey's part of South Carolina. Lee found out that pesticides had been used to deal with a soft pine beetle problem and informed Yawkey that the ivory-billed woodpecker was the natural predator of the soft pine beetle, so the pesticides had secondarily deprived the woodpecker of its food. "He admitted he had never thought of that. He should have," wrote Lee.[129] It was another lesson in ecology and conservation, this time courtesy of the left-hander who won seventeen games for the Red Sox three years in succession (1973-75).

Lee's phrase "he didn't mind winning" seems a little jarring in that clearly Yawkey wanted to win. It may be that Yaz understood Yawkey's demeanor a little better:

A misconception grew about him and the club. Because he liked ballplayers and was in the clubhouse, some people thought he spoiled us, that he wasn't demanding. Nothing could be further from the way it really was. . . . No one wanted to win more than he did. Mr. Yawkey controlled that anxiety, though. He hated losing, but he rarely got on a player. I was one of the exceptions. Maybe Ted was, too. Who knows why? Maybe it's because I was so honest with him. I never misled him when he asked a question. And since he never second-guessed his managers, at least to their face, I was the guy he could air his frustrations to. The thing is, he'd never bother you if you were going bad. That's when he'd pat you on the back. He waited until you were going well, and then he'd jump down your throat and rake you over the coals pretty good.[130]

At least, perhaps, if you were Yaz. None of the other players report that kind of experience.

Yaz recounted one specific time when Yawkey fulminated after a game, "Dammit, I'm tired of this, finishing thirty games out.... I'm going to fire everyone in here. I'm going to trade the whole goddam ball club ... including you." Yaz wrote, "That was a lot of crap about him being calm and promoting a country club atmosphere and how losing didn't matter."[131]

Another skirmish in labor talks came when the owners announced what might in effect be interpreted as a lockout—that is, they would not open spring training camps while contract negotiations remained unresolved. Yawkey, from Georgetown, remarked, "I don't know whether I want to stay in baseball much longer. Last year's players' strike made me stop and think what the future holds in this game, and here we go again. If this stuff is going to continue every spring, I have to ask myself it it's all worthwhile." He continued, noting the Red Sox had about broken even in 1972. He particularly didn't like what he knew of Marvin Miller. "I've never met the man personally, so I don't know him or what his aims are. But he keeps saying all owners are s.o.b.'s and that really bothers me. I don't think my players feel this way about me, or at least they've never said so to my face, so what right does Miller have to say it?"[132]

On February 25 the two sides came to terms, and they agreed on a three-year deal. There was no delay in the 1973 season.

There was a big change on the field in 1973: American League teams featured a designated hitter (DH) for the first time. The first Red Sox DH was Orlando Cepeda. He produced, coming in second on the team in RBIs (86), third in batting average (.289), and third in homers (20). As a baseball traditionalist, Yawkey had originally voted against implementing the DH (as had the Detroit Tigers), in part because the NL was fairly solidly against the concept, and he didn't think that the leagues should have different sets of rules. "But when we found that the majority of clubs in our league still wanted it, we voted to go along."[133] Yawkey later acknowledged it had resulted in more run scoring and provided opportunities for players like Cepeda and Tony Oliva to stay in the game a little longer, but there was also a down side: it would prevent some younger players from making it to the Majors.[134]

The Sox won the first four games of the season, but a six-game losing streak set them under .500, and it took them until June 10 just to get back to it. Yawkey hadn't wanted another slow start; before he'd left Boston at the end of the 1972 season, he had said, "I don't want to come back next year and find the club under .500 and out of contention." He'd timed his return well. He arrived on June 12, the day the Sox went over .500; they were only a game and a half out of first place. "Now if only they can stay well," added Jean Yawkey.[135] That was the closest they came to the lead for most of another month, but the pack was tightly bunched, and they were in contention into at least the first week of September.

Joe Giuliotti had started his career as an office boy at the old *Boston Record-American* in 1954 while still a student at Boston College High. He covered the Red Sox for twenty-seven years, retiring after the 1999 season. The arrival of the Yawkeys made an impression on him: "The Red Sox treated him [Yawkey] like he was some kind of a king. He would come up from his plantation during June or July, and they would have a big press conference. He would sit there. Everybody was . . . not afraid of him, but . . . what's the word I want to use? . . . It was supposed to be something great to be known by Mr. Yawkey (as everybody called him). It was a big thing when he came up."[136]

Giuliotti had seen Tom Yawkey from time to time, from a distance, and had the impression that the ball club was just a toy for him. "And when I did get to cover him, I was convinced that I was right. It was a toy for him. He cared, but he didn't care, if you know what I mean. He wanted to win, but he spent all his money in the wrong way. He didn't get the right players."[137] Giuliotti was, if anything, a little bemused by how so many others were a little in awe of the Red Sox owner. He was asked if there was something of a mystique. "Yeah, there was, and I don't think he liked it, but like most millionaires he was kowtowed to and everybody went along with it. I called him 'Tom,' and he had to stop and think. 'Goddamn,' he used to say. 'Goddamn it, I *like* that Tom.' Everybody called him Mr. Yawkey, which I couldn't understand. He wasn't God, you know."[138]

Peter Gammons said he understood why people called him "Mr. Yawkey": "I understand that. It was sort of old style. People here now call Bob Kraft "Mr. Kraft." But I never found it to be that Yawkey wanted credit. When he won in '75, he was just happy. He would just get so happy about what was going on. He was truly a fan."[139]

Bud Collins, who started as a reporter in 1956, agreed there was something like reverence around Yawkey. "I was a young reporter, and I wrote a critical column—I don't know what year it was— and the people at Fenway Park did not like it. They thought we should only laud Yawkey."[140] Commenting on the issue almost forty years after Yawkey's passing, Collins added, "There's still a worship there."[141]

In July Rico Petrocelli talked about quitting baseball, but he was talked out of it by Mr. Yawkey. In late 2014 he was asked about that time:

> I was struggling. My wife had contracted cancer of the uterus. I was really distraught. Very down. I just thought, "Maybe I should be with her. Much as I love baseball . . . ." We had four kids. Mr. Yawkey called me up to his office and we talked, and he said, "You know, she'll get as good treatment as possible here in Boston. . . . whatever she needs. Don't worry about that. You don't want to make a decision that you might regret later on. Hopefully, she's going to make it through and things are going to be a lot better." He was just like a grandpa. It did work out. I'm looking at her right now! Elsie. Fifty years in March.[142]

At one point in the season, Reggie Smith soured on Sox fans and asked for a trade after the 1973 campaign. He had nothing against management, only the fans. "They don't deserve an owner like Mr. Yawkey," he said, "or a team like the Red Sox."[143] Asked about his remark in a 2015 interview, Smith replied as follows:

I did make that comment at that time. It was a frustrating time for me, still youthful and a little intolerant of some of the things that had happened. I had gotten hurt and thought that some of the fans were insensitive to the fact that I had gotten hurt, and they started throwing things at me. . . . You know, enough is enough. A kid who was sitting over the dugout threw me a penny and hit me under my eye. Enough was enough. I was being followed home. . . . I felt it when they were doing things like that. . . . A guy pulled up early one morning, and I found him in my driveway and then . . . he took off. It was time to go. My family meant more to me than baseball. . . . Well, it happens [that Boston fans sometimes get a little too intense], but the thing that I do know about the Boston fans and that you learn over time to appreciate is that I learned how to play baseball there, with fans demanding so much, and later on I realized they knew the game.[144]

The Sox reached a high point on July 10, tied for first place for one day, but then spent most of the rest of the season in second, from August 22 until the end. They slid in the standings, however, and finished at 89-73, eight games behind the first-place Orioles.

Eddie Popowski managed the last game of the year. The Red Sox decided not to renew Kasko's contract and promoted Darrell Johnson from Pawtucket to manage Boston in 1974. Johnson had more or less followed Kasko's path: he had managed at Triple A and then graduated to the big leagues. Harold Kaese pointed out that the garter snake had a life expectancy of about six years but that the expectancy of the average Red Sox manager—even including Joe Cronin's long tenure—was 3 years, 32 days, 20 hours, 2 minutes, and 2.4 seconds.[145] Kasko was given a position scouting for the Red Sox.

Kasko had enjoyed Red Sox owner Tom Yawkey. "When I was managing, I'd come into my office, and he'd be sitting there and just want to talk," he recalled. "In the four years that I managed, he never once said, 'Why don't you think about playing this guy in left field or batting this guy in the sixth position,' or something like that. He never did it. He never interfered."[146] Kasko had told O'Connell that when the time came, just let him know that his time was up. That day came just a day before the end of the 1973 season. O'Connell told him, "We're going to make a change." Kasko perhaps knew it because Tom Yawkey hadn't been around to the office for several days. "Mr. Yawkey hated that end of it, the firing of people. He would almost go into hiding for four or five days before it happened." Kasko asked who would replace him, and he offered to be at the press conference for the announcement, indicating his approval of the choice of Johnson. He then said, "And tell Mr. Yawkey to come on out of the closet. Come on back around." He said he'd finish the season, and then O'Connell said, "We were wondering what you wanted to do." I said, "What I'm going to do is go out and look for a job." He said, "No, no, we want you to stay with us. I want you to be an executive scout." Kasko asked O'Connell, "Does this mean I'm supposed to scout executives?"[147] But he didn't manage that last day in 1973:

> The next day, Sunday, I came into the office, and Mr. Yawkey was sitting in the office. I said, "Well, good to see you again." He said, "Yeah, yeah, yeah. Come on in. Close the door." This is about 9:30. We just talked. We talked about everything. We talked about the past years; we talked about family; we talked about everything. It got to be about twelve o'clock, and I got up and I started getting dressed. He said, "What are you doing?" I said, "I'm getting dressed. I told Dick I'd finish out the season." "No, no, no, goddamnit, give the ball club to Pop. You come up in the box and sit with me. We're not through talkin'." So I said, fine, and I gave the ball club to Popowski for the last day, and we went upstairs, and I sat with him in his box for the whole game and we just talked again.[148]

In effect, the team created a new position for Kasko, and he scouted Major League teams (and headed up Red Sox scouting of Cincinnati for the 1975 World Series). He became the scouting director for the Red Sox and VP in charge of player personnel. He retired in 1994.

At the 1973 league meeting in Houston in December, Tom Yawkey was named VP emeritus, and Calvin Griffith took over as actual VP.

As winter approached, Carl Yastrzemski took a trip to the Orient and talked about taking a sabbatical to play baseball in Japan, but it never came to pass.

Tara Hall had expanded to care for twenty-eight boys with the construction of a dormitory provided by the Yawkeys, and Jean

Yawkey herself had given each of the boys $35 at Christmastime to spend on new clothing in Georgetown.[149] Tom had been a "baseball Santa" back in the early 1930s. Forty years later he and Jean would load up a truck on Christmas morning and deliver presents to Tara Hall.

In 1974 the Massachusetts Commission against Discrimination was back. It had no complaint regarding Red Sox players but instead "initiated complaints against the Boston Red Sox for the baseball club's alleged exclusion of blacks from such jobs as coaches, managers, front-office workers, ushers, ticket-takers, and refreshment vendors."[150] Tom Yawkey was in South Carolina, and people at his home on South Island said he was literally unreachable there by phone; it was an unlisted number and he called people when he wanted to talk to them, but they were supposedly unable to phone him.

Team spokesman Bill Crowley said that the team had twenty-six front-office people, but most of them had been there for many years, and there hadn't been any openings for a long time. He said he knew of only three or four black people working in baseball front offices around the country. Three of the team's twenty-six scouts were black, and the Sox had had more in the past.[151] Work with a state legislator to bring in more black employees as ticket takers, ushers, and vendor personnel had drawn some recruits, but none of them wanted to work the hours stipulated at the pay offered. Larry Whiteside, a black sportswriter for the *Boston Globe* (the paper's first), said that the Sox probably would have hired Elston Howard as a coach had he stuck around, but the Yankees had lured him back to New York.[152]

In spring training Darrell Johnson let go both Orlando Cepeda (who was bitter) and Luis Aparicio (who was more philosophical). Yawkey approved the cuts, though he'd become quite friendly with Aparicio—more than with any other player on the 1973 team other than Yaz. Johnson had decided to go more with youth and speed, and Yawkey endorsed his approach. The team added three good pitchers in Reggie Cleveland, Juan Marichal, and Rick Wise.

Right around the time Tom Yawkey arrived in Boston—on June 18—there was talk with the Angels about bringing Frank Robinson to Boston. The Sox were under .500 (28-31, in fifth place, five games out of first). Then they put together a run. From July 14 to September 3, the Sox were in first place and as much as seven games ahead of the pack as late as August 23, with just thirty-eight games to play. They collapsed at the end of the month, losing eight games in a row from August 30 through September 6, but they were still in it, tied for first place on September 8. A record of 11-18 in September did them in, and they finished third, seven games behind the Orioles (who won sixteen of their last eighteen games) and five behind the Yankees. It was a substantial stumble, a deeply discouraging one. Yawkey said, "If you can't hold a lead like we had, you don't deserve it."[153]

Luis Tiant had been 20-13 in 1973 and improved to 22-13 in 1974, with a 2.92 ERA. Bill Lee was second in wins (17-15, 3.91 ERA). Yaz led the offense, batting .301 with 15 homers and 79 RBIs—tops on the team in all three stats but stats that weren't saying much for run production. The Sox did show more speed, with left-fielder Tommy Harper stealing 28 bases and Juan Beniquez, 19.

Carlton Fisk had been badly hurt on June 28 and required season-ending knee surgery. Yawkey almost got himself hurt. Though he was seventy-one, he would still work out daily at the ballpark. He admitted to Tim Horgan, though, "I can't move around like I used to. I was playing third base the other day and Pete Cerrone [the Red Sox clubhouse man] must have thought I was Rico Petrocelli. He hit some shots that almost tore my head off. So I guess I must be getting old."[154]

On August 7 and—two weeks later to the day—August 21, Roger Moret had flirted with no-hitters, pitching a total of 16⅔ innings and giving up a total of two hits. Yawkey tore up his contract and gave him a new one with a modest raise. Whether that memory stuck with him or not, some forty-plus years later, Moret's memory of Tom Yawkey was nothing but positive.[155]

Yawkey, ever optimistic, admitted disappointment but felt that Darrell Johnson would benefit from working with the team in 1974 and that the Sox would be better in 1975. Yawkey had continued to work out in uniform every day, even while the team was on the road and the park was his own, batting and fielding grounders. Asked how he himself did in the workouts, he said, "The stats won't be out for a few days."[156]

Johnny Pesky had been working as a color man on Channel 38 TV broadcasts. Late in 1974, he was hired as Red Sox first base coach. Ken Coleman was out, though, as Red Sox broadcaster. He'd been with the Red Sox from 1966, but after 1974 he was let go. The day he learned, he encountered Tom Yawkey in a hallway at Fenway. Tom Shaer tells the story: "Yawkey said, 'Hi, Kenny. How are you?' Ken said, 'Well, not too good, Mr. Yawkey. I just found out that I'm no longer the TV announcer for the Red Sox.' Yawkey was genuinely surprised. He had no idea." A day or two later, Yawkey called Coleman and said, "I'm really sorry about this. Let me know if there's anything I can do; I'll do anything I possibly can." Coleman confided, "Look, I knew what he meant—that if my kids were sick or if I was going to lose my house to foreclosure because I was unemployed, he would definitely take care of me. I knew that. He did that for so many people. But what I wanted to say to him was, 'Mr. Yawkey, what you could do was get me my fuckin' job back. It's your team.'"[157] Of course Yawkey wasn't going to interfere with Dick O'Connell (who had some say in the matter), and Dick O'Connell was not going to interfere with VP Gene Kirby.

19

Another Game Seven

"HE IS THE last of a vanishing breed—a true sportsman." So began Will McDonough's profile of Tom Yawkey in the March 23, 1975, *Globe*. When he's gone, McDonough wrote, that's when Red Sox fans will truly appreciate what he'd done for the franchise. He estimated Yawkey had lost $7 million while owning the team, making money in only nine of the twenty-seven years from 1933 through 1959, when the team had been required to file profit and loss statements with the state. As the 1975 season opened, the average Red Sox player was paid about 25 percent more than the average player on any other team, and that had pretty much always been the case under Yawkey. There was a value to ownership of the team that Yawkey had originally purchased for $250,000, and McDonough thought it to be about $20 million, so Yawkey was definitely well ahead on his investment.

Aside from McDonough's profile, Tom Yawkey wasn't mentioned in the news that much anymore and hadn't been for the last few years. Charles Maher of the *Los Angeles Times* wrote that he was "publicity-shy. . . . He is rarely seen at social functions. He thirsts to be interviewed like Howard Hughes." Maher added that the players liked Yawkey not just because they were well treated, but simply because he was a "nice guy."[1] Former Sox shortstop Rick Burleson was among many who appreciated the way Tom Yawkey kept to himself: "He never was a guy who was going to make himself the main attraction. He wanted the spotlight to be on the players."[2]

David Halberstam saw Yawkey's shyness in another light. Writing about a much earlier era, before Yawkey had quit drinking, he noted the following:

> Yawkey's shyness, almost pathological, had profound organizational consequences. He drank quietly but steadily in his solitude. He had very few friends, and those with whom he was truly close were such men as Eddie Collins, Joe Cronin, Haywood Sullivan, and Mike Higgins, all of whom worked for him. Obviously, this situation was unhealthy. There was a constant blurring between professional matters and friendship. Yawkey's management staff became small and incestuous. . . . Some of them became expert at playing to him, at knowing what he wanted to hear, what subjects were forbidden, and how to get what they wanted from him. He liked, for instance, to arm wrestle with Mike Higgins, and Higgins knew when to lose and when to win. It was a matter of instinct and survival.[3]

Morris Siegel of the *Washington Star* offered a different view from McDonough's. In October 1975, after the Red Sox had won the American League pennant, Siegel wrote that Yawkey's team had averaged winning a pennant every seventeen years: "Sportsman or not, Yawkey is an absentee owner. He had been conspicuous by his absence from spring training for more than 30 years. His luxury perch above Fenway also goes unoccupied until about June 1 when the Buddah [*sic*] comes north. He has been honored several times for his 'contributions to baseball.' As far as Yawkey watchers can ascertain, his 'contributions' have been mainly money."[4]

In 1975 there was a bidding war for pitcher Catfish Hunter, Cy Young Award winner with Oakland in 1974. Yawkey's negotiators dropped out when the price reached $3 million. Hunter won a league-leading twenty-three games for the winning bidders, the Yankees. Early in the year both Bucky Harris and Billy Herman were named to the Baseball Hall of Fame. They joined Cronin, McCarthy, and Boudreau as five former managers who had worked for Tom Yawkey and later found themselves in the Hall. (In 2008 Dick Williams was so honored as well.)

Why wasn't Yawkey himself in the Hall of Fame? He is now, voted in by the Veterans Committee in 1980. During the summer of 1975, when the Red Sox and Giants were scheduled to play the annual Hall of Fame exhibition game on August 18 in Cooperstown, there were plans to honor Yawkey at the same time, with induction. A problem cropped up and someone blew the whistle, even as plans were under way: he was still active, and under Hall rules one had to be out of baseball for five years before one was eligible. "If that's the case," Yawkey said, "then I'll be six feet under before I'm put in."[5]

After the 1974 season outfielder Bernie Carbo filed for arbitration. He had been a holdout in the spring after the Sox had tried to peddle him all the previous winter. Under the new collective bargaining agreement between organized baseball and the MLBPA (the CBA had just been adopted in 1973 after the 1972 work stoppage), the reserve clause remained in effect, but players with more than two years of continuous Major League service were eligible for salary arbitration. One might expect that the generously paid Red Sox would be among the last to go the route of arbitration, but Carbo did so, becoming, he said, "the first player in history to take the Red Sox to arbitration" and asking for another $10,000.[6] He lost.

It had taken some courage to file, given the possibility of retaliation. O'Connell reportedly told Carbo not to worry about having filed: "It's a non-issue. Everything's fine." O'Connell told the AP's Dave O'Hara that he believed Bernie had gotten some bad advice from his agent. After the season was under way and Yawkey was in town, he talked with Carbo. "Why did you take us to arbitration? Weren't you happy with what you were making?" Carbo replied, "Well, yes, sir, but my wife's pregnant. I'm having a baby. I need to buy a new house. I needed that $10,000." Yawkey said, "Well, you just play good baseball, and everything will work out for everybody around here. We've got a real good team." Not long afterward, there was an envelope in his locker with a check from Thomas A. Yawkey Enterprises for $10,000.[7]

Tony Conigliaro tried a comeback in 1975 but lasted only twenty-one games, batting .173, before he retired. The 1975 team was sparked by two rookie outfielders dubbed the "Gold Dust Twins": Fred Lynn, voted as both AL MVP and Rookie of the Year, and Jim Rice, who was a close second in the Sox offense (and a future Hall of Famer). Lynn batted .331 (the same average as the fully healed Carlton Fisk, who rejoined the team on June 23), with 21 homers and 105 RBIs. Rice hit 1 more homer, drove in 3 fewer runs, and hit .309. Lynn scored 103 runs to Rice's 92. Rice's totals would have been a bit higher, but his wrist had been broken by a Vern Ruhle pitch on September 21, causing him to miss the playoffs entirely. There was some criticism of Darrell Johnson's playing Yastrzemski as if Yaz had tenure, batting .269 with only 60 RBIs.

Yawkey's first day in Boston was June 9. His late arrivals were simply climate-related: "Can't stand the cold. Never could."[8] After he came to town, he expressed interest in holding on to the team's younger players: "I feel we have traded young players for older ones and it hasn't worked out. So I say let's keep the young ones and see how they do."[9] He remarked that the player he most regretted trading, over all his years, was pitcher Lynn McGlothen, then pitching for the Cardinals.[10]

Yawkey still showed a personal interest in his players and made an impression on utility infielder Bob Heise, who had come to Boston over the winter in a trade from the Angels. The Red Sox were Heise's sixth big league team. As had been the case with so many other players, his first meeting with the Red Sox owner was a surprise:

When I first came to the Boston Red Sox, he [Yawkey] was down in the clubhouse with Pete, the clubhouse man. I didn't know who he was. I think I asked him to get me a shirt or something. After he got it for me and I was in the trainer's room, Bob Montgomery came over to me and said, "Do you know you just asked Tom Yawkey to get you a shirt?" I was embarrassed. When I saw him again, I said, "Mr. Yawkey, I'm sorry." He made you feel very comfortable. He didn't have any overpowering "I'm the owner of the club" [attitude]. . . . He was really down to earth and just a good guy. He just looked like one of the clubhouse guys, and I said, "Wow."

He was really different from the other owners. I remember I was told [on another club] to sign a contract or "I'll bury your ass in the Minor Leagues." Tom Yawkey wasn't like that. He treated his players with respect. When I came over in '75, he tore up my contract in spring training; then I got some key base hits, we won some games, we went back into first place, and he called me back in. It doesn't sound like much now, but back then in '75 it was a lot; he gave me a $5,000 raise. He was one of the owners who treated his players well. [Heise's salary at the time was just $30,000.][11]

Jim Rice appreciated Yawkey's interest in the players: "The only two owners I saw that ever came down and talked to a club were Thomas Yawkey and Gene Autry. When we went to Anaheim, Gene Autry came into the clubhouse and said, 'You guys need anything? Is your family here? Let us know.' That's how Mr. Yawkey was too. And he was that way every day. And Mrs. Yawkey was the same way." Rice added, perceptively (he said he hadn't known of Yawkey's days on the team at Yale), "Mr. Yawkey, I think in the back of his mind, he once thought he was a player."[12]

Catcher Bob Montgomery, reflecting on Yawkey's clubhouse visits, observed the following:

> He really admired baseball players, whether they played for his team or whether they played for an opposing team. He made a point—maybe to a fault—of coming into the clubhouse, every day, and going to each one of the players and saying something to them. He found out what your interests were, and he would bring up something about your interests. Now, he wouldn't spend as much time at my locker as he would maybe at Yaz's locker or one of the other players' lockers, but every day when he came into the clubhouse, he would make a point of going by each player's locker and having something to say to the player. On a personal basis, he found out that I collected model trains. Once he found that out, he would ask me about how I got involved with it, what it involved, and from then on it was maybe something about model railroading or maybe about something else—a game two or three days ago—but he always made a point of talking to a player. He didn't come into the clubhouse and go to one end of it and stay there and ignore everybody else.[13]

Pitcher Jim Willoughby came over from the Cardinals in a July 4, 1975, trade. His first impression of Tom Yawkey was about how much he loved the game: "When I first walked into the clubhouse after joining the Red Sox, Yaz was the first player to come up to me. He was there early and he welcomed me, and then Tom Yawkey was in the office talking to the manager. He came out, and we all were talking; it was just like back when I was a kid and playing ball [just for fun]. His presence gave that kind of feeling. You could definitely pick that up."[14]

Bob Montgomery added another memory:

He [Yawkey] didn't only like *his* players. He liked all players. Brooks Robinson told me this story, so it's fairly safe that it's true. Mr. Yawkey invited Brooks Robinson up for dinner in his private press room after a Saturday afternoon game. During the dinner or toward the end of the dinner, he asked Brooks if there was anything they could do for [the Orioles] while they were in Boston. Brooks said, "Mr. Yawkey, the visiting clubhouse gets awfully hot. We could use air conditioning in there." Monday they were putting air conditioning in that locker room.[15]

Dwight Evans remembers the deep personal interest Yawkey took in his players: "He loved his players. He'd come to the clubhouse every day, and he'd sit next to everybody. 'Hi, how are you doing? How's your family?' He didn't want to know about baseball. If you were struggling, he'd still sit by you and talk to you." It was a sincere interest. Evans continued: "I had a lot of issues with my boys, and I remember when Tim, my oldest, had surgery. It was raining, but Mr. Yawkey got out of his car, and he came over and wanted to know how Tim was. A very special guy."[16]

Except for a brief four days near the end of June, the Red Sox were in first place from May 24 to the end of the year, with a lead as large as 9½ games at one point and 7 games as late as September 7.

The team and the city of Boston—and particularly Luis Tiant— all enjoyed a heart-warming moment when the Red Sox pitcher was reunited with his father, Luis Sr., and his mother, Isabel, on August 26. Because of the mutually hostile relationship between Cuba's Castro and the American political leadership, Tiant had not seen his father since 1960 or his mother since 1968. During a visit to Cuba, Senator Edward W. Brooke of Massachusetts prevailed upon the Cuban regime to grant visas to the Tiants. It was the first time Luis's parents had ever seen him pitch in a Major League game. Luis Sr. had been a superb pitcher in his day, many older players feeling he'd been at least as good as his son became.

Before the game Tom Yawkey asked if the elder Luis would throw out the first pitch. Reluctant at first, he did so, wearing a Red Sox cap and throwing the ball to Tim Blackwell behind the plate. Luis Sr. asked to have the ball back but not as a souvenir. "'What's wrong, Papa?' asked Luis. 'It wasn't a strike.' He said. 'Give me the ball.'" He threw a second pitch, "right down the heart of the plate."[17]

The Red Sox finished in first place, 4½ games ahead of the Orioles and 12 ahead of the third-place Yankees. Tom Yawkey said, "I'm thrilled, but not so much for myself as these guys in the clubhouse. They did the battling, they did the playing, they did the hard work and they earned it."[18]

On the eve of the American League Championship Series (ALCS), Jean Yawkey said, "I've never seen Tom so nervous and excited. He hasn't slept a wink at night since we won the pennant. I told him this is the time we should really be enjoying ourselves, after all the years we've waited, but to tell you the truth, I feel awful about Jim Rice. After the wonderful season he had, I think it's terrible that he has to miss the playoffs. It just doesn't seem fair, does it?"[19]

Yawkey was actually quite ill, and he wasn't around the clubhouse much in 1975, not as he had been in 1967. Fred Lynn was a rookie then, of course, but he observed: "I met him one time in '75, but he wasn't one of those guys who came in every so often. He was not feeling rather well; I knew that. He didn't hang around much. He wasn't like Gene Autry; anytime *he* was in town, he was in. Even when we went to play the A's, I don't remember him being there. He could have been, but I don't remember him."[20]

The Red Sox swept the ALCS, beating Al Dark's Oakland A's in three games. Tiant threw a three-hitter in Game One. After the Sox clinched a World Series berth with the final game of the ALCS, Yawkey declared, "This is the most exciting team I've ever had. Look at what everyone did this year. Lynn, Rice, Yaz, Burley. Please print the names of everyone."[21]

Yaz played well in the postseason, batting .455 in the ALCS and .310 in the World Series. Yawkey had watched the Sox win the third and final game of the ALCS in Oakland, from seats on the first base side. Rarely taking in road games, he was seeing the game from the vantage point of the fans, not from his aerie above Fenway. "I must say that it was bedlam. But I enjoyed it—for a night." He said that Yaz was the greatest all-around player he'd ever had.[22]

In the World Series, the Red Sox faced Cincinnati's formidable Big Red Machine. The Reds had won 108 games, finishing a full 20 games ahead of the Dodgers in the NL West. Years later Cincinnati manager Sparky Anderson recalled his first meeting with the Red Sox owner: "It remains one of my greatest thrills meeting Mr. Yawkey. He was so down-to-earth. Why, he had on a Red Sox jacket that must have been 10 years old. But he was comfortable. And oh so nice a man."[23]

Oddsmakers picked the Reds to win the World Series, but a lot of popular sentiment was on the side of the Red Sox. They hadn't won a World Series since 1918, after all—fifty-seven long years—and Tom Yawkey was liked by most, including the Boston sportswriters.

At one point during the Series, on October 20, as the Sox waited out three consecutive days of rain delays in Boston before they could play Game Six, Yawkey strolled over to the visitors' clubhouse and chatted with Pete Rose and Joe Morgan and Johnny Bench (who said to Yawkey, "I heard you can really pick it. They tell me that you're still good with that glove. You've done a great deal for baseball").[24] Yawkey replied, "I hope I haven't done too much to harm it."[25] Many of the players on the Red Sox were suffering from a virus, and Yawkey was too, though he was actually suffering from quite a bit more.

Before Game Six, the Red Sox honored Red Sox legend Duffy Lewis—who had played for the team in the 1912, 1915, and 1916 World Series—by asking him to throw out the ceremonial first pitch. Tom Yawkey escorted him down to the field, through the stands. For the opening ceremonies, Yawkey sat next to Commissioner Bowie Kuhn before heading back upstairs to his private box.[26]

The Red Sox took it to the seventh game, thanks to a spectacular Game Six, which remains one of the greatest World Series games ever played. The Sox were facing sudden death at Fenway, down by three runs in the bottom of the eighth, when Bernie Carbo pinch-hit for Roger Moret and homered into the bleacher seats in straight-away center to tie the game. Then Carlton Fisk won it in the bottom of the twelfth with a home run to the left-field foul pole—one of the most replayed TV moments in baseball history.

Yawkey was very ill with leukemia at the time. The Fisk home run produced what Curt Gowdy said was his "most enduring memory of T. A." Right after the game-winning home run that sent all of New England into euphoria, Gowdy noticed, "Yawkey didn't jump up and down or clench his fist and cheer. No emotion whatever. He just sat there and stared at the left-field wall and shook his head. Then T. A. got up and walked out of his box. Nine months later he was dead."[27]

The Sox were hurt by the loss of Jim Rice prior to the postseason, though. It's not unlikely that the Sox could have taken the Series had they had Rice. Rice was a South Carolinian by birth, but Yawkey and Rice never talked about that. There was, of course, the distance inherent between owner and player, particularly by the time the twenty-one-year-old Rice joined the team.[28]

Game Seven (at Fenway) was tied, 3–3, going into the ninth inning, the Reds having climbed back after Boston had taken a 3–0 lead in the bottom of the third on two singles and four walks. In the top of the ninth—on two walks and a Joe Morgan single—Cincinnati took a 4–3 lead. The Sox were retired 1-2-3 in the bottom of the inning, Yaz popping up to center for the final out. "The season's last movement was in adagio," wrote Peter Gammons, "and so dolorous. Thomas A. Yawkey folded his arms, wrapped in the sleeves of his tan windbreaker, on the table in front of him and into them sank his head."[29]

He sat there for eight minutes and then left his box. "I guess it just wasn't meant to be. But we gave them a helluva battle. For a team that was supposed to blow us out of the series."[30] Yawkey did take time to phone Sparky Anderson and congratulate him. Sparky said, "With a series like this, we didn't win. Baseball did."[31]

Ted Williams later remarked about Yawkey, "He'd tell you it didn't bother him, but you knew it was eating him up inside. He said very little, but he always had that little pat on the shoulder for you." Carl Yastrzemski chimed in, "He hated to lose, but he never showed it. I never saw him chew out a player when things were going bad. He'd always wait until you were going good. He'd always pat you on the back. A bad situation, a loss, and he'd be there. And he did it knowing there was no one to pat him on the back."[32] Yaz gave an example of Yawkey's waiting until a player was "going good" rather than getting on him when he was down:

I remember one time he really got on me. I was in the middle of a real hot streak, after struggling for a couple of weeks. Out of nowhere he comes up to me and asks me, "Why the hell did you take that big swing against Wilbur Wood a couple of weeks ago?" It had been a game that I ended with a fly ball in the ninth inning with two men on base. "You shouldn't have that big of a swing with a knuckleballer like Wood. Just try for the base hit, that's all. Contact." That's what a lot of people didn't know about Mr. Yawkey. He knew the game so well. He was really an expert. He knew it and he loved to talk about it.[33]

"He knew everything," Yastrzemski added. "For years, I knew about every player in the Red Sox minor-league system. It was because he'd stand there [next to Yaz's locker] and recite all these little facts about these minor leaguers. Some obscure pitcher in Double-A, he'd know if the kid was having control problems. 'That's not like him,' he'd say. I knew about [Joe] Foy and [Reggie] Smith two years before they came up to the club because of Mr. Yawkey."[34] (Apparently Yawkey used to enjoy pronouncing Yaz's name as "Yamstramski.")[35]

Yaz also recounted a story that spoke volumes: "He had the most humility of any person I ever knew. He had a soft heart. My mother was dying of cancer and for a month Mr. and Mrs. Yawkey went every day to the hospital to visit her. Then he went out of his way so she could see the World Series before she died." Yawkey himself was feeling the effects of his own leukemia. People knew he wasn't in good shape, but that he had leukemia was not known outside a very small circle who was aware of his ongoing treatment at New England Baptist Hospital. Yaz continues: "He was feeling bad at the time, but he even gave up his box seat in Cincinnati so my mother would be warm while she watched the game. After the fifth game when I went into the clubhouse I found Mr. Yawkey. He had watched the entire game there on television."[36] Yastrzemski's mother died in January 1978. Carl himself dedicated his 1990 autobiography *Yaz: Baseball, the Wall, and Me* to two people: his mother, Hedwig, and Tom Yawkey.

Because Fred Lynn had hurt himself banging into the wall in center, padding was added over the winter. An electronic scoreboard was installed, to be ready in 1976. Darrell Johnson was given a new two-year contract. Yawkey had not favored such dramatic changes to the ballpark, but, consistent with his habitual approach to management of the Red Sox, he let O'Connell have his way. O'Connell found it kind of amusing that Yawkey so often came around once a change had been implemented. With regard to the scoreboard, O'Connell said that when they demonstrated it for the Yawkeys, they were fascinated, so, according to Tom Shaer, Yawkey "had started to soften a little bit, and then he saw the reaction on Opening Day. . . . The first play on that board was Jim Rice sliding into home. He went in to see Jim Healey and said, 'You're right, and I was wrong. It's good for the fans.'" Shaer continued: "The scoreboard was one thing. The other was the red seats. I don't want to make Mr. Yawkey look bad, but Dick said that after Yawkey saw the red seats in there, he thought it made the park look so much nicer, and he started telling people that it was his idea. O'Connell told me that with a chuckle. It wasn't said with disdain."[37]

Yawkey himself was less active in New York business. He told Bill Liston, "The business handles itself pretty well now because I have a wonderful organization there. We have turned over a lot of the natural resources things to my nephews and niece. The main thing we have now is securities."[38] And the Red Sox.

Though Yawkey had once again been gracious in defeat, he may not have been so in private. And there were those in the press who were not—and they blamed Bill Lee. Clark Booth offers a look into how a couple of veteran reporters, who felt for Tom Yawkey, saw things:

When the Red Sox lost the seventh game, Yawkey was all bundled up. It was kind of a rough evening all the way around. Bill [Liston] and Clif [Keane] saw him; they were the only ones that did. One *Globe*, one *Herald*, and they each got a line on him which they did share with everyone else. Jake [Liston] was actually near tears. Clif was really pissed. They were absolutely bullshit at Lee. They were calling him a "cocksucking son of a bitch, California motherfucker" . . . all this.

Because they blamed him. . . . Yawkey apparently was very upset. This has never been reported, really, but Yawkey apparently was devastated by losing that last game. Everyone blamed Lee. It was stupid, that pitch he threw to Perez. Perez was waiting for the goddamn ball. It was an arrogant act. Irresponsible. Immature. Selfish.

Lee was a jerk. Everyone's canonized him over the last thirty, thirty-five years. Don't misunderstand; I ran with Bill a little bit in the old days. We all did—Kimball and Gammons and me and others. But he was an asshole. He was capable of the most monstrous incivilities you ever saw. He'd walk into a roomful of women and say something gauche.

They were really upset with him. "That son of a bitch, he cost the old man this, etc." They knew that Yawkey was on his last legs at that point. Kind of sad. That was kind of the coda to the 1975 World Series. Not reported . . . out of respect. . . . It was a different time. You didn't have some hotshot in the press box mouthing off about Yawkey's dying. It would have been considered inappropriate." [Yawkey hadn't said a thing about Bill Lee.] "He didn't speak to anybody. He apparently shared this with O'Connell, who shared this with Liston and Clif. But they quoted him after he said that, that very night.[39]

The last time George Sullivan saw Tom Yawkey—whom he'd known since he was visiting team batboy in 1949—was at Game Seven:

I got a call from Bill Crowley. He said he'd talked to the commissioner, and he offered me the job of being in charge of credentials for the Boston games in the World Series. I was sitting in the press box. The Red Sox had a 3–0 lead. I was getting fidgety. The innings were going by. I would get up occasionally and stretch my legs. I went out to walk on the back of the roof; I was walking down in the direction of the left-field line, and all of a sudden the door to Mr. Yawkey's box opens up. His box was right to the left of the working press. He had two small boxes. He'd be in one, and Mrs. Yawkey would be in the other, and they had a thing—it was like a confessional thing—in between them, where they could talk. He's coming down the three stairs and running across in front of me. He spotted me. It was just him and me on the roof at that particular time. "Sully," he says—these were his last words to me—"this may be it." He said this on the trot—he was going to the men's room. He had to come out of his box and run about fif-teen or twenty steps to get to the john.

"Sully, this may be it." Those were the last words. He skipped by me. He was all smiles and happy. If he was Fred Astaire, he would have danced over there.

Not long after I got back in my seat, we weren't winning any more.[40]

20

Tom Yawkey's Final Campaign

THERE WAS EVERY hope that the Red Sox could build on their so-close finish of 1975 and perhaps, in the nation's Bicentennial Year, finally win the World Series for Tom Yawkey in 1976.

Soon after the year began, Tom Yawkey was admitted to Boston's New England Baptist Hospital. The hospital had no listing for him, and it was assumed he'd registered under an assumed name, wrote Will McDonough. "He has been in good health in recent years, although he was bothered last fall by what was described at the time as a heavy cold."[1] The day after McDonough's comments appeared, UPI mentioned a "routine checkup," though a checkup could have been done in South Carolina at the Georgetown Hospital, a well-equipped institution that Yawkey had helped establish.

Yawkey was still in Boston in March, and he joined O'Connell and Treasurer John Harrington to help negotiate a contract extension with Luis Tiant and get him to spring training before the exhibition season was over.[2]

Three players (Rick Burleson, Carlton Fisk, and Fred Lynn), all represented by attorney Jeremy Kapstein, opened the season without having signed their contracts. It was the first time that such holdouts had occurred in the Yawkey years.[3] Were they to play out the year without signing, the reserve clause would no longer apply to them, and each would become a free agent. Kapstein was later described as "the Scott Boras of his time."[4]

Carl Yastrzemski had always taken a different approach to contract negotiations with the Yawkeys. Yaz typically signed one-year contracts, and, he writes, "from the 1970s on, all my contracts were done on handshakes, first with O'Connell and then Sullivan, as I did with Mr. Yawkey." Yaz would have lunch with (say) O'Connell, and maybe they'd haggle, but Yaz would never quite get around to signing a deal until Opening Day, when someone would have to fly in and get his signature before he could be permitted to play. He had understandings with the executives, "such as bonuses and deferred payments," he writes, that were never in the printed contract itself. "I signed a lot of blank contracts over the years, deals that never had any figures in them," he adds. When the contracts started getting up past a half-million dollars or so, he'd call agent Bob Woolf for advice. "But I'd still go in myself to make the final deal. You know where else I got advice from? Mr. Yawkey's man in New York, Joe LaCour. And John Harrington, who ran the Yawkey affairs in Boston. Talk about how different it is now. I was using Mr. Yawkey's people for advice on writing my own contract—that *he'd* have to pay for."[5]

It was a quiet spring, generally, though the team got off to a poor start. Reigning pennant winners they were, but they were 6-15 after the May 11 game.

A week later there were rumors that Tom Yawkey had been confined to his room at the Ritz. Paul Sullivan of the *Herald* reported that Yawkey was being treated in his room for a serious blood disease and that he'd been undergoing treatment in Boston since January.[6] A *Globe* story reported he'd been a regular visitor to his office at Fenway Park and quoted his doctor, Russell S. Boles Jr., as saying, "He's doing well. I can tell you he's not seriously ill."[7]

Seriously ill? "Where do they come up with bull like that?" asked an irate Yawkey. He said he'd had an intestinal problem in South Carolina but that all his doctors and records were in Boston. When he'd arrived, he'd been hit by a series of bugs and then some chest congestion. He expressed irritation that reporters were calling around to hospitals and wasting the time of medical personnel.[8] He dubbed it an ordinary flu bug—though on May 26 he let it be known through a statement issued by the Red Sox that he had just been hospitalized for anemia.[9] Assistant PR man Dick Bresciani notes that Yawkey called him into his office and said, "Please tell the writers to stop bothering the doctors about my condition. The doctors are busy people doing important work and don't need to be bothered. Tell the writers I've had a bad cold and will be all right."[10]

Yawkey attended Opening Day at Fenway, and it was said to be the first home opener he'd attended in forty years. The day before, he had gone "through the Red Sox clubhouse and introduced himself to all of the new players."[11]

A lawsuit was filed against the Red Sox in March by Thomas Zamagni, twenty, who said he was on the way to see Game Seven of the 1975 World Series when someone fell some forty feet off the left-field wall and landed on his head, breaking his (Zamagni's) neck. The suit claimed it was the ball club's responsibility to prevent injury to people walking on a public way from people sitting illegally on the ballpark's walls.[12]

In June Charlie Finley's Oakland A's sold three star players for cash—Vida Blue and Joe Rudi to the Red Sox for $1 million apiece and Rollie Fingers to the Yankees for $1.5 million. It was one of the few Yawkey-era deals involving nothing but cash. Understandably Yawkey hadn't been pleased with the Burleson/Fisk/Lynn situation. Peter Gammons writes that Haywood Sullivan (later) stated the following about the two issues:

> Mr. Yawkey was undergoing chemotherapy at the time the club left for the Coast and he was so sick and tired of the way things were going—the way [Burleson, Fisk, and Lynn had] refused to negotiate early, then the way the agent used the three as a package—that he told O'Connell to trade Lynn and Burleson before the deadline; he figured that Fisk, being a local guy, could eventually have things work out. They'd talked to some people, too. But not only did Dick not trade them, he went and bought these other two Kapstein clients. Yawkey called me up at home at 7:30 the next morning. "Do you know anything about this?" he bellowed. I told him I didn't. He was outraged, and O'Connell was gone from that point on.[13]

Gammons adds his own take: "A lot of people said Yawkey wouldn't be too happy when he became aware of what O'Connell did. He was very happy with it. They went to the hospital—John Harrington and Dick O'Connell and Haywood Sullivan. They told him what they were trying to do, and Yawkey said, 'Why don't you get Sal Bando? He's the guy that I want.'"[14]

Almost immediately Commissioner Bowie Kuhn stepped in to block Finley's fire sale to the Red Sox. Tim Horgan wrote that Yawkey had tried to buy a pennant before—back in the 1930s—and had "struck out."[15] Finley said he would file a lawsuit against Kuhn. Yawkey's initial response? "I don't know what the hell the commissioner is basing his ruling on, but it doesn't surprise me one bit." He added, "I hate lawsuits. There are too many lawsuits in sports already. I've had my stomach full of them and I think the public has had enough, also. You'll get no lawsuits against the commissioner from this organization."[16]

Kuhn called Tom Yawkey to say that he thought the sales were bad for the game. Gammons understands that Kuhn explained, "I think it's not in the best interests of the game to have big-market teams buying up small-market players," and that Yawkey replied, "Well, then, we'll accept that." Gammons adds, "Finley initially sued and George Steinbrenner (owner of the Yankees since 1973) threatened to sue, but the fact that Tom Yawkey went along with it [the commissioner's ruling] made it possible for Kuhn to void the three sales. I saw Kuhn in Cooperstown a few years ago, and he said that that was one of the best moments when he was commissioner. He knew that Yawkey wanted to keep the players, but at the same time he put the Red Sox interests below those of the rest of the game."[17]

John Harrington concurred with the end result: "He [Yawkey] just didn't think it was good for baseball to have Finley dismembering a team piece by piece."[18] Clark Booth wrote in the *Pilot* that Yawkey may even have been "rather relieved" when the commissioner stepped in and may have gone along with the deal in part because he feared that the Yankees might just buy up all of Finley's players and do even more damage.[19]

Decades later Gammons commented:

One of the things I loved about Yawkey—and I really thought it told a lot about his respect for other teams—was that for years, whenever they played a day-night doubleheader, he would always have a steak and lobster dinner for both the Red Sox and the opposing team. They would all go upstairs, and everyone dined together. It was very gentlemanly. It reminded me of a tea after a Harvard-Yale game or a Groton-St. Mark's game. Both teams would get together and have tea and sandwiches. [It was OK to fraternize between games in the privacy of the dining room?] Absolutely, because if you're going to stay around and fill that ballpark for two games, we're going to feed you.[20]

Jim Rice agreed, from a player's perspective, saying Yawkey was the owner who started the dinner practice. "During a doubleheader, they'd have food upstairs. He [Yawkey] made sure that you were in a first-class ball club. We were flying charter when no one else was flying charter. He and his wife made sure that this was more like a family than anything else. You see how long Yaz stayed here. You see how long I stayed here. It was more of a family thing."[21]

Then the news broke: Tom Yawkey was dead. He had died at 4:20 in the afternoon of July 9, 1976, at New England Baptist Hospital, of leukemia, a serious blood disease. Ironically it was leukemia in children that had been the scourge against which Dr. Sidney Farber had fought for so many years through his work supported by the Jimmy Fund. Farber and his colleagues had made great strides, but people still succumbed—including Tom Yawkey, since 1953 one of the leading supporters of Farber's efforts and chairman of the Jimmy Fund for so many years.

Yawkey Foundations trustee Bill Gutfarb says, "Will McDonough told me he talked to Tom Yawkey about a week before he passed, at the Baptist, and Tom told him, 'I'm fighting this. I'm going to get out of here.'"[22] Red Sox PR employee Mary Jane Ryan remembers a visit in March:

Before he died—it was so sad—he kind of came by the office during spring training and kind of said goodbye to us. I hadn't realized he was really that sick. It was March of '76. Everybody was at spring training, but he came by to see us. The two of them [Tom and Jean] came over. I was so stupid; I didn't realize he was that sick. He spent quite a bit of time with me. He went around all of the offices to see the girls. Just chatting with them. He looked fine. Then he died in July.[23]

The tributes poured in. "No One Had More Fun" was the headline of Ray Fitzgerald's eulogy in the *Globe*. After forty-three years of Yawkey ownership, half the people in New England had never known another Red Sox owner. Yawkey had never won a World Series, "but he had 43 years of fun trying. A lot of us would take that for an epitaph."[24] Bill Liston wrote in the *Herald*, "The world of baseball lost its best friend late yesterday afternoon." The official Red Sox statement listed him as "sports executive, conservationist"—an indication of how much Yawkey had adopted the cause of conservation.[25]

The players learned of his death as they were preparing for that evening's game. Manager Darrell Johnson made the announcement but then asked the media to leave the clubhouse. "I think the players want to be alone now. There's nothing they want to talk about," he said. The UPI story noted, "The shocked silence blanketing the dull-colored room as the players stared at their own lockers contrasted sharply with the filtered traces of the cheerful din of fans filing in."[26]

The game went on, starting less than three hours after Yawkey's death. Personnel at the ballpark, from ushers on up, all wore black armbands. Dick O'Connell admitted, "We knew he was seriously ill, but it was his wish that we didn't make it public. So I kept his secret and did exactly what he asked. I told the players first and said to them that it was Mr. Yawkey's wish that the games be continued." Accolades poured in. Ted Williams said, "I loved the man for all the years I played with his team and have always admired him from the bottom of my heart for his love of the game, his unselfishness, his fairness, his sincerity, his honesty with everyone. Mr. Yawkey had a heart the size of a watermelon. He was generous. His wonderful work with the Jimmy Fund is something which cannot be measured. He was a champion of all champions."[27] "He walked the outfield just a week before he died," wrote Clark Booth, "and even tossed the ball around a little. It was during one of those curious lulls the brutal disease that killed him sometimes allows."[28]

There was no funeral, per Yawkey's wishes. His body was cremated. He had been "a private man in life, and he remained a private man in death."[29] City Councilor Christopher Iannella filed a measure to rename Jersey Street in Yawkey's honor; a stretch of the street running past the ballpark has since been named Yawkey Way.

As to the future of the Red Sox, Yawkey had planned that out, just as he had planned for the conservation efforts in South Carolina. The team was placed in a voluntary trust. Indeed ultimately two trusts were created, Yawkey I and Yawkey II, the latter set up by Jean Yawkey in 1982. When the Boston Red Sox were finally sold in 2002, the sale fetched a price of over $700 million—more than half of which would go to charity. It's no stretch to believe that as the portion of that money that is invested earns additional money, a total in excess of $1 billion in charitable donations will be distributed over the years.

Old friend Ed Rumill, who'd retired four years earlier but had otherwise covered the Red Sox beat for all of Yawkey's years, first mentioned in print what he called the "Yawkey Forum." It was what he said he missed most about not covering the Red Sox.

> [The forum was a] small group of friends and associates who sat down in the rear of the Fenway Park grandstand, just opposite an office door, before the gates had been opened to the public on a game day or evening. Tom and his wife Jean were always there and sort of presided, though anyone could express an opinion and the subjects reached in many directions. When baseball was the topic, everything was "off the record," unless otherwise indicated. But you can be sure that a mere occupant of the press box like myself usually walked away much smarter than when he arrived.[30]

Tom Yawkey never won a world championship, Rumill wrote, but Yawkey had once asked him, "How can you ever think failure when you've called men like Ted Williams and Carl Yastrzemski your friends?"

There is no reason to think they were close friends, nor that Tom Yawkey ever had any truly close friends. He had hunting companions. He had those who would visit in his box at Fenway. But a very brief sentence in *Red Sox Century* spoke volumes: "He had many acquaintances but few friends."[31] Curt Gowdy offered one nice thought. The Red Sox were reigning American League champions after 1975. "The greatest owner baseball ever had died with the pennant flying above his ballpark."[32]

When Yawkey's will (dated June 8, 1973) was read at Manhattan Surrogate's Court, it was reported that he had left $10 million to establish a charitable trust, a half-million to be distributed in bequests to various employees, and annuities for adopted daughter Julia Gaston.[33] Jean Yawkey inherited half the remaining estate outright, with the other half set up in a trust fund to provide for her for the rest of her life. GM Dick O'Connell said, "The ball club is in a trust to continue operating as it is indefinitely. This is the way he wanted it so that it would continue in good hands."[34]

Longtime sports editor of the *Hartford Courant* Bill Lee wrote the following in his column:

> One of these days, I imagine, some eager beaver will want to write a book about Tom Yawkey. He may find it difficult. Most biographers research through a score of tomes to dig out pertinent information about the man whose life they are putting between the pages of a book.
>
> In Mr. Yawkey's background, rich and useful though it was, comparatively little was printed. Tom Yawkey took fewer bows than any baseball owner I can remember. He refused to allow anyone to pull him out of the background in which he preferred to work.
>
> It is even a little difficult to write a column about him. . . . I don't even remember seeing a biographical sketch of Yawkey in a Red Sox press book. . . . Tom Yawkey was a simply towering figure of straightforward common sense and baseball integrity. Baseball will find it very difficult to get along without him.[35]

Of course baseball did get along without him, and so did the Red Sox. Yawkey had provided for continuity for the Sox as far back as 1959, the year the club was first put in trust, more than sixteen years before he died. The two surviving trustees were Jean R. Yawkey and James A. Curran of New York. Curran had been an accountant in Yawkey's New York office, but his duties there had more or less been taken over by Joe LaCour. The two trustees issued a statement that Tom Yawkey's will had asked the trustees to "continue the management of the Boston Red Sox organization pursuant to the general policies and principles followed during my lifetime."

They added, "There seems, therefore, little more to be said than 'steady as she goes.'"[36]

Easier said than done, as far as on-field play was concerned. The team, coming off from winning the pennant, barely finished over .500. Manager Darrell Johnson was fired midway through the season (when the Sox were in first place, 41-45) after a loss on July 18, just nine days after Yawkey's death. Don Zimmer was named the new manager. "Good luck, skipper. I'm with you all the way," read a telegram from Jean Yawkey.[37] The club was 42-34 under Zimmer's leadership in 1976. But it finished in third place.

Julia Yawkey Gaston has taken rather few bows herself. She has remained steadfastly reticent on the subject of her upbringing, a stance that is frustrating to writers or others who have contacted her over the years wishing to get more of a sense of the very private Yawkey family. In response to a letter from this author in January 2013, she wrote simply, "I have been asked many times to give an interview about my parents and I have chosen not to." Another appeal for some information regarding her adoptive mother Elise elicited a few sentences: "She was a beautiful and very charming lady, born in Birmingham, Alabama. She was instrumental in having the little church built on South Island so the African American community could attend and have weddings. She was very outgoing and had a wide circle of friends. One of her great loves was bird shooting and she was invited to participate everywhere, including Georgia, Scotland, and Hungary. Her generosity was legendary. I hope this helps."[38]

Yes, it helped, but one wishes to know so much more—about Elise as a person, about Julia's life growing up as a child of the Yawkeys, and about her relationship with Tom Yawkey. She had once told a reporter about her dad in the early 1970s: "He's a strange man." She had written Glenn Stout in the 1990s: "As you know my parents separated shortly after I was born. I had very little contact with my father after that."[39]

Tom and Elise Yawkey had not only helped build the small AME church on South Island, but Tom Yawkey had also arranged to have a house built for each family among the 125 residents on the island, "and when a young couple gets married, he presents them with a house of their own."[40] Jim Sargent recalled that on Christmas, the first Mrs. Yawkey would always arrange to have delivered "a truck-load of groceries—all type of groceries, with food, clothing, and all of that stuff."[41] As part of Yawkey's will, the State of South Carolina's Wildlife and Marine Resources Commission was bequeathed over twenty thousand acres of Yawkey land near Georgetown. (The church, which still stands, is featured on a tour that visitors to the wildlife sanctuary are offered.)

In August 1976 Jean Yawkey was named president of the Red Sox. Peter Gammons wrote in the *Globe* that the Red Sox would be run as a business, not so much as a family-owned club.[42] A six-member advisory board was appointed to assist her. Among the board members were Dick O'Connell, John Harrington, and Haywood Sullivan.

The team drew well at the gate. Advance ticket sales prior to the '76 season had been the best ever, and the year-end attendance figures placed second in franchise history. The excess cash that was generated had something to do with the largesse lavished on a player like reliever Bill Campbell ($1 million) after the season since the tax bite would have taken half that money. Even though Campbell said, "I'm not worth this kind of money," the club preferred to invest profits in players rather than just give them to the government. Will McDonough wrote that the front office was "years ahead of their competitors" in taking advantage of such matters.[43]

Though it didn't come to pass for more than a quarter century, rumors already began to circulate that Jean Yawkey would sell the team "within the next year." She had reportedly already told friends that she "[did] not plan to hold onto the team for a long time."[44] The first game she attended after her husband's death was on August 20; once she resumed going, she rarely missed another game until her own death in 1992. Her "interest in baseball has been nearly as great as her husband's over the years," observed the *Herald*.[45]

The Hall of Fame appointed Bud Selig of Milwaukee as a director of the Hall, filling the vacancy created by Yawkey's death.

Within baseball Tom Yawkey had perhaps represented an earlier era. Red Smith of the *New York Times* wrote the following:

In his late years he [Yawkey] hardly ever attended either the business meetings or the boozy revels of the baseball hierarchy at All-Star games, the World Series or the winter convention. He had little in common with the other club owners and they were mystified by him, if not downright suspicious, because he was a strange fish who was in baseball not to make a buck or feed his ego but because he happened to love the game. Not many of the others could understand this, and it embarrassed them.

Smith had a more elegant way of putting the idea that Yawkey had tried to buy a championship: "To the extent that this has a slightly pejorative or unsportsmanlike connotation, it is a bad rap. Tom Yawkey wanted to win and he wasn't disposed to count the costs."[46]

Jean Yawkey spent very little time in South Carolina after Tom's death. She did not care to live there by herself, without Tom. Of course Tom Yawkey's will provided for the property to be turned over to the State of South Carolina; such time as Jean did spend in the Georgetown area, she spent at the Mt. Pleasant estate.

That holiday season, Jean Yawkey again hosted an event for fifteen boys from Tara Hall—the boys who had no homes to which they could return. From the beginning and despite some local criticism, the home had welcomed boys in need regardless of race, color, or creed.

21

Jean Yawkey in the Late 1970s

EARLY IN THE 1977 baseball season, there was a surprise. Dick O'Connell announced on behalf of the trustees who owned the team that "consideration will be given to offers to buy the Red Sox." He added there was no urgency, that "[the team] could be sold in the near future or sold years from now. There is no desire to sell the club, but the executors had to make a decision on the future of the club and they did."[1] It was the fiduciary duty of the executors to do the best they could on behalf of the beneficiaries named in Yawkey's will. They would require 60 percent of the purchase price to come in liquid assets, and any prospective buyer would be asked to have $2 million in operating capital. O'Connell said the ball club had made money for ten consecutive years.

Some unresolved matters needed to be addressed. For one thing, Luis Tiant said he'd been promised a certain deal by Tom Yawkey before he died, but it wasn't in writing. Tiant said he'd been offered a $25,000 bonus and an additional year's salary (encompassing 1978) if his work in 1976 was good. He'd been 21-12 and lopped almost a full run off his 1975 ERA. It had been more than a good year. The bonus was paid, but Tiant (and his agent Bob Woolf) believed that he'd also earned the extra year, and he wanted to be guaranteed for 1978. His salary was $200,000 at the time. Several other players—Fisk, Lynn, and Bill Campbell among them—were getting more, with more years of security in these early days of longer-term contracts. The Red Sox leadership said it didn't want to renegotiate Tiant's contract. It complicated matters to have no one as clearly in charge as Tom Yawkey had been.[2]

In 1977 the team was in contention all year long and in first place for much of June and August and part of July. The Sox won 97 games, though so did the Orioles. Both finished tied for second, 2½ games behind the Yankees. Four Sox players had over 100 RBIs, and three hit 30 or more home runs. Fans set an all-time attendance record, surpassing the two-million mark for the first time: 2,074,549.

The odd announcement that the team was for sale earned a headline in the *Chicago Tribune*: "For Sale, Kind Of." According to Jean Yawkey, the paper reported, "No price has been given and, according to the seller, no buyer is being sought." Jean's statement was quoted, with some of the same language as O'Connell had used: "Consideration will be given to offers to buy the Red Sox. Offers are not being sought, nor will they be sought. A time limit is not in mind, nor will one be fixed."[3]

Later in the year, the trustees invited bids and set September 1 as the deadline for accepting them. Dom DiMaggio still hoped to purchase the team. So did Edward J. DeBartolo of Ohio, the "father of the American shopping mall." He'd been invited to submit an offer, but when his offer of $14 million and his interest became public, the trustees withdrew the invitation, writing him, "The inordinate amount of publicity surrounding your interest in the Red Sox has distressed us."[4] The trustees apparently wanted to keep the process a little more private.

DiMaggio's good friend Dick Flavin reflected on his own understanding of the process: "After Tom died and they announced that the team was going to be for sale, Dom—who, of course, had been very successful in business—took them at their word and put together a whole group; he had tentatively hired Dick O'Connell to come back and be the general manager. And then he discovered that the team wasn't really for sale and that Jean wanted Haywood Sullivan to have it." DiMaggio felt some resentment but largely kept it to himself. "He felt that he had been used as a pawn, that the team wasn't really for sale anyhow. It was just a sham. He never made any public statements to that effect because he wasn't that way, but for some years Dom and Jean didn't speak."[5]

There were later intimations that Mrs. Yawkey hadn't wanted to sell the team to Italians, perhaps belied by the fact that there were those of Italian ancestry in the group to which she later did sell. New York sportswriter Dick Young wrote that Jean Yawkey, hearing that DiMaggio might head the Sox in the future, exclaimed, "Over my dead body." Dom's reaction: "I was really upset by that. When I went into my interview with them [executors of the estate] I asked them about the quote. They just tried to dismiss it without much of an explanation. Everyone knows I didn't get the club, and since then I have not heard anything from Fenway Park until this invitation [to a 1982 old-timers' game]. I haven't been to a game since this new ownership took over, and I don't intend to go to any."[6]

There had been a time in the 1950s when some of the team's Italian ballplayers felt discriminated against, as well as allegations that Higgins and Joe Cronin were part of an "Irish mafia" that held back Italian players like Frank Malzone, Bob Aspromonte, and Jerry Casale. "I'm sure prejudice came into the thing," Casale told author Peter Golenbock.[7] DiMaggio told Leigh Montville he believed Malzone could have come up to the big leagues several years earlier. "He said they [the Red Sox executives] didn't want anybody that wasn't along their lines."[8]

There was a period of estrangement between Dom DiMaggio and Jean Yawkey, but Flavin says it had something of a satisfactory ending. "It [the estrangement] ended at Joe Cronin's funeral. They were standing near each other outside the church after the mass. They hadn't spoken to each other. Dom sort of said, 'Life is too short to go on this way,' and she sort of ran up and hugged him. From that point, John Harrington in particular went way out of his way to bring Dom back into the family."[9]

It may simply have been that Jean Yawkey wanted Haywood Sullivan to have the team. "She essentially gave the team to Haywood," said Peter Gammons. "I think he put $22,000 into the deal and got $34 million out. But what can I say? He was a really good guy."[10]

There was a lot of drama before Sullivan cashed out. First he had to get in. Haywood Sullivan initially tried to purchase the team with a group that included Sox trainer Buddy LeRoux and, reportedly, Ted Williams.[11] Williams said he wasn't interested in being an investor, "but if there is something I could do to maintain the dignity and respect which Mr. Yawkey built into the operation through more than 40 years, I would listen."[12]

Four groups filed bids; they were said to average $13 million, with the high bid $18.75 million. Concern was expressed that with employees worried about job security, the enterprise could not run smoothly until the matter was resolved.

On September 29, 1977, the trustees announced the sale of the Sox to the Haywood Sullivan–Buddy LeRoux group for $15 million.[13] Jean Yawkey and ten others were limited partners. Among them were Thomas DiBenedetto, a partner in the John W. Henry–led group, which later bought the Red Sox in 2002, and Harold Alfond, whose sons remain partners in that group. Sullivan was described as a "close friend and protégé" of Tom Yawkey. It was expected that Dick O'Connell, VP of administration Gene Kirby, and assistant GM John Claiborne would all be asked to resign. In other words, the new owners would bring in their own front office staff. At least ten of the fourteen AL clubs had to approve the new ownership.

Among the players, Bernie Carbo said he was happy for LeRoux, whom he'd known as team trainer, and was glad Mrs. Yawkey would remain involved. "If she went with Sullivan," he said, "then he must be a hell of a man, although I don't know him very well. It's just like keeping the club in the family, because Sullivan was almost family to Mrs. Yawkey."[14]

Sullivan himself said, "There's no question I have personal feelings for them [the Yawkeys] and learned to love them both. You might say they treated me like a son they never had."[15] He later told the AP, "Yes, it was a father-son thing."[16] Essentially Sullivan was the only one of the prospective purchasers that Jean Yawkey trusted to run the club the way Tom Yawkey had. "Sullivan," Tim Horgan wrote, "was more than Yawkey's friend and confidante. He's very much like Yawkey, a shy, friendly, unassuming and candid man who also happens to understand baseball."[17]

Dom DiMaggio felt he'd been treated poorly in the process and that afterward, "All of a sudden, I was not invited back [to spring training], and not invited to other things. That rubbed me the wrong way."[18] He was another who felt that after Tom Yawkey's passing there was less of the kind of family atmosphere to which so many had become accustomed.

On the exterior of Fenway Park, there is affixed a plaque reading as follows:

THOMAS AUSTIN YAWKEY

1903–1976

IN MEMORY

FROM THOSE WHO

KNEW HIM BEST

HIS RED SOX EMPLOYEES

It would be easy to skeptically dismiss such sentiment as artificial but for the fact that for nearly forty years after Yawkey's death, so many former employees have said—and continue to say—that there was very much a sense of family in the Red Sox offices.

Mary Jane Ryan worked at Fenway Park for thirty-one years, from December 7, 1970, until she retired in 2001. She fondly remembers the Yawkeys: "They were such wonderful people. They were like family to us girls. I was probably the youngest one when I went to work—and the oldest one when I left. All those girls had been there for years and years—Helen Robinson, Mae Fitzpatrick, Barbara Tyler, Mary Walsh, Evelyn McDonald, Elinor Mossman, Ruth O'Neil. They were all there umpteen years."[19] It is interesting that Ruth O'Neil's sister Eleanor had worked at the Ritz since 1948, ultimately serving as the assistant manager. The concierge as of 2014, Tom Carroll, recalls of the O'Neil sisters, "They would drive in together, and then Ruth would go on to the ballpark." Carroll has a copy of an in-house newsletter of the hotel from 1978 that shows Eleanor at her desk with a Boston Red Sox pennant on the wall behind her.[20]

Mary Jane Ryan came from Bellows Falls, Vermont, and still remembers coming home from school and hearing her father listen to Curt Gowdy broadcast Red Sox games. After working for some time in the former Braves Field administrative offices and in Boston University's athletics department, she thought, "I always wanted to work for the Red Sox." As it happened, Red Sox PR director Bill Crowley's secretary was having a baby, so there was an opening.

It wasn't until May 1971 that Ryan first met the Yawkeys. There was an annual flurry of anticipation, no one knowing quite when they would show up, and she was advised to be sure to keep a ship-shape desk.

The girls always used to say, "Keep your desk neat." That was one pet peeve of his [Tom's]. He liked a nice, straightened-out desk. Every time it might be time for him to come back, they'd get the word out. "He could be coming back. He might come in on the weekend." But when you'd meet him, he was just like somebody you'd known all your life. Both of them. Terrific people. Family-type.

They were interested in you. They cared about you. You weren't a number; you were a person. There's one cute story I have—that I think is interesting—about how caring he was. During the All-Star break, in the early years, the men all took off to play golf. The women all showed up for work. Nobody told us to take off to play golf or go shopping. But he [Tom] showed up during the All-Star break. . . . He liked to run the show. He just got a kick out of it. When Helen got back to work at the switchboard after lunch, he called her up. "Helen, I want to close the office at two o'clock. Get the word out to everybody—go home at two o'clock." That's what he loved to do. The first time he did it, Helen called me, and I was the first one out the door. I was gone.

All of a sudden, he was in another part of the ballpark, and he thought to himself, "I wonder if anybody told Mary Jane. I wonder if they got over there to tell Mary Jane. She might be over there all by herself." He calls Ruth O'Neil. She was laughing her head off. She says, "Mr. Yawkey, she was the first one out of here." That's what he wanted you to do. He didn't want you to say, "Oh, I can't go. I've got to do this. . . ." He was just so cute about it. That was him.

Helen sewed like mad. You go out and you buy something, and you just bring it to Helen; Helen would shorten it for you. . . . That was the family-type atmosphere."[21]

Ryan's immediate predecessor in PR was Donna Mountain. When Mountain first started, she was naturally nervous, "but he [Yawkey] made everybody feel at ease." There was, though, one moment when she recalls being apprehensive:

It was in the off-season. He [Tom] was off the property. I used to cover for Helen at the switchboard when she would go for lunch or when she was out for vacation. Back in those days, Mr. Yawkey used to have two buttons. If those buttons lit up, you were to answer those. That was priority. You could mute the buzzing, and I had it muted because I was doing some sidework. . . . But one day I turned around and looked, and *both* of those lights were lit up. I went, "Oh, my God." I was expecting to get yelled at, but he was real nice, saying, "You must be very busy there" or something to that effect.[22]

Jean Yawkey and Dick O'Connell were not at all close, and indeed O'Connell was replaced at the end of October, Haywood Sullivan himself taking over as GM. This despite O'Connell's having served thirty-one years with the Sox and having presided over a near-tripling of attendance during his twelve years as the top officer and despite Gene Kirby's having negotiated the richest broadcast deal in team history.

Far from close would be a better assessment of the Yawkey-O'Connell relationship; some even referred to it as a relationship of bitterness. Described as "one of her blood enemies," O'Connell once said, "I never knew Mrs. Yawkey to like anyone for very long." The *Globe*'s Curtis Wilkie wrote that Jean Yawkey had become "the most formidable woman in professional sports."[23] "He [O'Connell] used to call Mrs. Yawkey an old whore and things like that," said one of her associates. "She hated O'Connell. She heard these things. They got back to her."[24]

"O'Connell loved that stuff," recalls Peter Gammons. "He was a Boston politician, a brilliant guy in a lot of ways. He loved the tension. He had no problem with being the archenemy of Jean Yawkey. Of course, as soon as the estate was settled in '76, Dick was out the door."[25] Mrs. Yawkey insisted on firing him personally, and she did so during a twenty-minute tirade in O'Connell's office, LeRoux said. "It was obvious she took specific delight in it."[26]

When media representatives got word of the firing, naturally they wanted to talk to O'Connell. Tom Shaer was working under Dave O'Hara as a stringer for the AP. He, O'Hara, and O'Connell had spent many an evening together in the press room after games in 1977, but it took Shaer a while to locate O'Connell:

> The day O'Connell was relieved of his duties, nobody could find him. It turned out that he was over at TV-38. I found out he was there, and I remembered he was good friends with Mary Trank [executive secretary at Fenway Park from May 1947 to 1976], so I called her. I did an interview with her, and she said it had to be all background stuff, not for attribution. She was very critical. It wasn't about how Mrs. Yawkey had treated her but how Dick was treated. She was very down on Buddy and Sully, as you could imagine. She described Buddy as a guy who used to put on Band-Aids and Sully as a catcher who couldn't find home plate with a seeing-eye dog.[27]

O'Connell was not entirely out in the cold, however, Shaer explained. "O'Connell spoke well of Tom Yawkey. He never said anything disparaging. It's a fact on the record—Clark Booth did a story on this in November or December of '77—that Mr. Yawkey knew that Mrs. Yawkey was not going to retain Dick O'Connell or that the chances were slim that she would do so because Mrs. Yawkey didn't have a good relationship with him. Mr. Yawkey gave O'Connell a new contract when he knew he was terminally ill. Dick was very well taken care of."[28]

There were changes in the broadcast team too. Ned Martin and Jim Woods were fired by radio station WITS. Martin found a home with WSBK (TV-38); Woods moved on. They weren't fired with any finesse. Tom Shaer overheard a conversation between Joe Scanlan of WITS and Woods on the runway between the press box and the press room. "Scanlan said to Woods, 'Look, I'll let you know what I'm going to do, but remember this: I could get King Kong or Mickey Mouse to broadcast the Red Sox, and people would still listen.' Without skipping a beat, Woodsie said, 'Well, Joe, I don't know about King Kong, but Mickey Mouse is under contract in Anaheim and Orlando.'"[29]

Sullivan and LeRoux reportedly put up only $100,000 each and were due to get 52 percent ownership, while the limited partners each had to kick in half a million. In addition, Sullivan and LeRoux were to be paid annual salaries of $75,000. Jean Yawkey had reportedly put in $3 million.[30] Whether there would be any money for operating capital was a good question. A *Globe* article questioning undercapitalization was titled "Some Experts See Too Much Red in Sox Purchase."[31] An editorial in the *Globe* about a month later decried the deal as "Buying the Sox with Beans."[32] Another publication stated that Sullivan's and LeRoux's financial commitment was along the lines of a "48-month car loan."[33]

The trustees had not taken the highest bid. Red Smith wrote that the bid accepted was actually the lowest one offered.[34] Larry Claflin wrote that Jean Yawkey's "singular, overwhelming interest is to pass the ballclub on to Sullivan, no matter what."[35] Larry Whiteside asked the obvious question: if Jean just wanted to get rid of O'Connell and associates and let Sullivan run the club, why sell it? Why not just fire the ones she didn't want and hire the ones she did?[36] By announcing a sale and then seeing it unfold the way it did, Jean put herself through all sorts of turmoil and heartache.

Adding to the controversy, O'Connell let it be known that LeRoux had been fired in 1974 at Tom Yawkey's request. (LeRoux said he'd resigned, not that he'd been fired.) Moreover, some of the AL owners appeared to be uneasy about the financing. And then rival bidder A-T-O (the owner of Rawlings Sporting Goods) filed for an injunction to block the sale, pointing out that it had made the highest bid—by far—and that the trustees' taking a dramatically lower offer was manifestly not in the best interests of the estate. But since Mrs. Yawkey was the sole heir and had voted for the sale, A-T-O had a high hurdle to overcome.

With less than twenty-four hours before the scheduled vote by the other owners, the Yawkey estate requested a postponement. The new owners requested that the A-T-O injunction be dismissed, but Suffolk Probate Court declined to expedite their request. A couple of weeks later, the court denied an injunction.

On December 8 the AL owners overwhelmingly rejected the sale, 10–4.[37] The Red Sox were one of the four. League president Lee MacPhail declined to give any specifics of what went on in the closed-door session but offered, "Obviously, they [AL owners] were not satisfied with the financial, economic long-term viability of each of the partners."[38] Bud Selig, at the time the chair of the league's finance committee, said, "This is the most important franchise in the American League, and we can't afford to let it be underfinanced or second rate. The situation is a mess. It seems inconceivable that what Tom Yawkey built could come to this."[39] Someone in Boston printed up "Save Our Sox" bumper stickers. Peter Gammons reported that both the *Herald* and the *Globe* had investigative teams competing to turn up dirt on some of the general partners. Gammons quoted Red Sox publicist Bill Crowley as saying, "If nuclear war were to break out, it would only make page two in Boston."[40]

LeRoux talked about "dirty pool." There were reports of anonymously mailed packages of derogatory clippings being sent to the owners of the other teams and postmarked Boston. Did Dick O'Connell act vindictively? It's possible that he called Speaker of the House Tip O'Neill and that O'Neill called Commissioner Bowie Kuhn. Joe Fitzgerald of the *Herald* suggested that O'Connell might not have been entirely innocent; his behavior may have been, in Joe Fitz's words, "something less than honorable."[41]

California Angels GM Buzzy Bavasi said that if Jean Yawkey were to become one of the general partners instead of just a limited partner, it might make all the difference.[42] That's just what began to happen in 1978. One of the proposed limited partners—Earle Groper—had meanwhile gone bankrupt, and Mrs. Yawkey was now to retain 20 percent ownership. *Globe* columnist Bob Ryan said that the owners' vote had really been "Haywood, si. Buddy, no" and that LeRoux should depart the ownership group. (Ryan commented that LeRoux mocked Jean Yawkey as "forever intent on doing her female impersonation of Howard Hughes.") Ryan further questioned the implicit cronyism in firing team doctor Thomas Tierney and hiring Arthur Pappas, one of the prospective limited partners, in his place.[43]

With a restructured deal, by which the team would be held by the JRY Corporation, league president MacPhail expected approval to be merely a formality. The team hadn't been inactive, despite the unsettled ownership; it had swung a sizable deal to sign pitcher

Mike Torrez in the off-season and had landed Dick Drago too. Fans lined up before the season to buy tickets; two thousand fans were in line when tickets first went on sale.

The sale was approved unanimously on May 23, 1978. Bud Selig and George Steinbrenner had both seconded the proposal for the restructured deal. The final price was $20.5 million—at the time the highest price ever paid for a sports franchise. Jean Yawkey would be president and a general partner along with Sullivan and LeRoux. Courtroom testimony in 1983 stated that Jean Yawkey had given Sullivan a million-dollar interest-free loan to enable him to boost his portion of the revamped offering.[44]

The Sox were in first place at the time, claiming the spot on May 13, 1978, and—except for one day—holding it until September 13. They had built up a big early lead, and were ten games over the second-place Yankees as of July 8. But then the lead began to erode over the weeks that followed. The Sox were four games ahead of the Yanks on September 6, but then they were swept at Fenway in a four-game series against New York; it was dubbed the "Boston Massacre" because they were outscored by the Yankees, 40-9.

There was internal discord on the team, with some of the counterculture players (who took on the name the "Buffalo heads") simply not in synch with straitlaced skipper Don Zimmer. When Bernie Carbo was sold to Cleveland on June 16, lefty Bill Lee cleaned out his locker and quit the team in protest. He'd already seen all his other friends dealt to other teams—Rick Wise, Reggie Cleveland, Ferguson Jenkins, and Jim Willoughby. "They trade away all the genuine personalities," Lee exclaimed. "Gutless. If Tom Yawkey were still running this club, it wouldn't be like this. I just wish he could return from the grave and breathe some life into this organization."[45]

At the end of June, treasurer John Harrington resigned to seek other business opportunities in the Boston area. He was the last front-office man left from the O'Connell era; he left despite Jean Yawkey's urging him to stay.[46]

Zimmer's team nonetheless won ninety-nine games. It finished the 162-game schedule tied with the Yankees, necessitating a one-game playoff at Fenway Park on October 2. This was the game of the famous and improbable Bucky Dent home run off Mike Torrez, which won the game for New York. (The Yankees scored four times in the top of the seventh.) "I feel so sorry for Mrs. Yawkey," said Carl Yastrzemski, who was then told she had said the same about him.[47] It was almost the first time she'd been mentioned in the *Boston Globe* for months. She'd kept a low profile. One could hardly blame her.

The playoff game was a crushing loss, made worse because it was directly at the hands of the rival Yankees. The Sox had had a huge lead, had seen it evaporate, and then had fought back into contention, only to lose the playoff. The Red Sox season was over.

Jim Lonborg flew up to Boston to see the game:

In 1978 I was with the Phillies, and we had just clinched against Pittsburgh. My manager gave me permission, so my wife and I flew up just to watch the playoff game in Boston. We got to sit with Mrs. Yawkey and Mr. Harrington. We watched the game and were there for six innings, but then we had to catch our plane back down to Philadelphia. We had a two-run lead and I said to Mrs. Yawkey as we were leaving, "I got you two runs. That should be enough."

We got in a cab, and by the time we got to the airport, it was like a pall had hit the airport bar. We asked, "What's going on?" Bucky Dent had just hit a home run.[48]

Later that fall, Jean Yawkey lost her brother George. He had been eastern-district sales manager for the Union Camp Company of Wayne, New Jersey. A mass was held for him on December 3 in Freeport, New York.

Some changes were made after the season. For one thing, starting in 1979, bleacher seats would be reserved rather than exclusively held for day-of-game sale (as Tom Yawkey had preferred).[49]

Bill Lee was traded in December—for Montreal's Stan Papi. A look at their respective records makes it clear that the only purpose of the trade could have been to dispose of Lee. Lee wrote a column in the December 10, 1978, *Globe* offering his thoughts on departure. He said he'd enjoyed a good rapport with Tom Yawkey, but "a dark cloud" had descended on Fenway Park the day Yawkey died. He asked, "Whaddya suppose would happen if we tried to get in touch with Mr. Yawkey? Like we could have a séance out in the players' parking lot. Get Dick O'Connell, maybe Luis Tiant and Bernie (Carbo) . . . start chanting out there by the service gate, or better yet, out in the bullpen."[50]

The new owners invested in the players they wanted. Although they hadn't made any moves to bolster the team in the last couple of months of 1978, they ponied up $5.4 million in January 1979 to resign Jim Rice, at the time the largest player contract ever signed.[51] Meanwhile, they let Luis Tiant go to free agency (and sign with the Yankees), and they brought in Dennis Eckersley and Jerry Remy. They retained the scouting staff under Eddie Kasko, one of the largest in the game.

Ed Kenney was another executive who was retained. His father, Tom, had worked on the grounds crew and then assisted Tom Yawkey, doing some driving for him and Eddie Collins and just generally helping out as needed. "He was more or less like a personal assistant. I don't know if there was an exact title. He was just around the ballpark," said Ed in a 1999 interview.[52] Keeping it in the family—a long-standing Fenway tradition—Kenney rose in the organization to become VP of player development, while Tom's grandson, Edward P. Kenney, became assistant GM. (In September 2000 Edward P. Kenney was courted and hired by the Baltimore Orioles to become their VP of baseball operations.) The Kenneys are a fine example of the Yawkey hiring history of holding onto employees (through three generations in this instance), a position that naturally inhibited diversity in hiring.

Another employee befriended by Tom Yawkey was Jim Gately. He worked at Fenway for fifty-four years. His nephew, Brian Aitchison, was working at Fenway in 1999. Brian remembers his uncle: "He bled Red Sox. When we lived in Jamaica Plain, Tom Yawkey would drive him home after the game. They'd sit out front and have a few Black Labels."[53]

Yawkey's driver in his later years was Bill Souris. He started working for Harry M. Stevens Concessions in 1967, cooking hamburgers or chicken or whatever the clubhouse man Vince Orlando ordered for the players in the days before the Sox hired a caterer. When the previous driver retired, Orlando suggested to Souris that he take over driving for Mr. Yawkey. "He was at the Ritz," says Souris. "I would pick him up and bring him to the park, then maybe go and pick his wife up and bring her to the game. Sometimes I went up. Not often. Usually they would come down because they knew what time we were coming." It was a Chevy station wagon that Souris used, a car that belonged to the Red Sox—a "woody" (with wooden trim on the outside—maybe a little rustic, certainly nothing special). "Basically it was back and forth. He [Yawkey] was a very low-key guy." Souris doesn't recall ever being asked to take Yawkey to a restaurant or any other event around town. "I could be wrong, but I think that was his life. Going back and forth. Having dinner at the park, speaking to the players or whoever else he would see at the park, and that was his enjoyment in life."[54]

Did Souris wear a uniform, or a cap like a regular limo driver?

Oh, no, no, no, no. They were the most low-key people that you'd ever meet. They didn't flaunt things. Today you rent a limousine [and] you have these guys dressed up. You could come the way you came to work. If you wore a tie, you wore a tie. If you had casual clothes, you had casual clothes. Out of respect for them, 99.9 percent of the time I'd probably have a tie on. Or a suit, out of respect for who they were, but no one ever said[a suit or tie was necessary]. You just did what you felt was right.

He respected you, and you could do what you wanted. He was just a fantastic guy. He and his wife. Great people.[55]

All of a sudden, there was talk of relocation again. The Red Sox wanted some tax breaks to stay in Boston and to be given one or two adjacent streets—Jersey Street and Van Ness Streets—to enable them to add another 5,000–6,000 seats. Fenway was the oldest park in the Major Leagues.

The '79 Red Sox finished third, behind Baltimore and Milwaukee, 11½ games out of first. Attendance had increased in both 1978 and, slightly, in 1979. After the third-place finish in '79, the team didn't draw as well in 1980. "Red Sox chic" was gone, wrote Bob Ryan, and the undercapitalized Sullivan and LeRoux found themselves "presiding over the systematic destruction of a franchise and a mythology that has uplifted us all for the past decade. We would have liked the tradition to be maintained."[56]

A little paranoia emerged. Sullivan claimed the media were out to get him, out to drive a wedge between him and Buddy LeRoux. He thought it was due to jealousy of the fact that a former player and former trainer had become owners of a big league ball club. He noted that he'd been named to a four-year term on the executive council of Major League baseball. As the first ex-player to be on the executive council, it was a significant honor, but he remarked that his achievement earned only a "passing note" in the Boston papers.[57]

Over the winter Jean Yawkey took a completely unpublicized three-week trip to China. There was an adventurous side to her personality that only those in her inner circle may have known about or appreciated.

22

Tom Yawkey Remembered and the
Jean Yawkey Years, 1980–1985

IN EARLY 1980 the Veterans Committee of the National Baseball Hall of Fame elected Tom Yawkey and Chuck Klein to the Hall. Yawkey was only the sixth executive named to the Hall of Fame. He was, however, the only person in the Hall who hadn't been either a GM, a manager, or a player. He was inducted on August 3. Commissioner Bowie Kuhn presented his plaque to Jean Yawkey. Ted Williams made his first appearance in Cooperstown in fourteen years, since his own induction in 1966, and called Tom Yawkey "a great sportsman and humanitarian, and a man I loved . . . the humblest, most down-to-earth man I ever met."[1] Tommy McCarthy, the press room steward at Fenway since 1946, said Yawkey had urged him not to feel the need to rush in his work. "You're just as important as anybody else around here, just as good as anyone else."[2]

Red Sox PR director Bill Crowley said, "He [Yawkey] never looked for headlines. Was completely sincere. He could be tough, but fair. You could argue with him. Let me give you an anecdote. I was overruled on something. The next day he said, 'You don't like it, huh?' I said I was in the Army and I can take orders. But he said, 'I don't want that kind of relationship. We'll discuss it.' He was completely sincere."[3]

Yawkey and Crowley did have their disagreements. Art Keefe, who worked as Crowley's assistant, recalled,

> Bill and I had a good working relationship. We were both very candid, and he told me one time they [Yawkey and Crowley] both got very looped up in Yawkey's office, and Crowley decked Yawkey! And

Yawkey fired him. Then the next day, Bill came in to work and went up to Yawkey's office and said, "So am I still fired?" [Yawkey] said, "Oh, no. No. You got your job, but don't be such a pain in the ass in the future." What prompted the punch? It's called drunkenness. I'll bet that neither of them recalled the issue the morning after.

[Yawkey] was a wonderful guy, but I think that a lot of what you might have heard about him over the years may have been true. He had a narrow focus. Nice man. Good guy to work for, but he wasn't a businessman. He hired cronies, and Pinky Higgins was one of the biggest examples of a drinking buddy, whom he hired a couple of times, and he was an atrocious manager."[4]

Crowley's punching the boss wasn't the only time that physical violence broke out in Yawkey's office. Curt Gowdy writes that there was a time that he heard Cronin and Yawkey arguing in the office. "I walked in and there they were, wrestling on the floor. 'I think Cronin's going to lose his job,' I told my wife when I got home. But the next day, Yawkey and Cronin were back together. No problem."[5]

Veteran Boston sportscaster Don Gillis echoed Williams's comment years later: "Tom was a most unusual man; probably one of the shiest and humblest men I've ever met; and what a great straight shooter and admirer of great talent. I asked him at one time, 'Tom, I would like you and I to sit down with the camera and do something.' He said, 'Don, I would like to do that, too, but I'm getting awfully wrinkled and I don't look that good anymore.'"[6] Perhaps it was a touch of vanity or perhaps just a bit of dissembling.

Yawkey was, some like Gillis said, shy. Others felt he was simply humble. He once told a sportswriter, "I really don't want to be noticed. I don't come to the ball park to attract attention. I come here to see baseball, just like the fan. All I want is to be left alone and watch my team in action." He dressed for comfort, perhaps dressing down. Gerry Finn of the *Springfield Union* wrote, "Everyone knew he looked as though he just walked off a barge, but it didn't bother him."[7] Jim Lonborg's comment was an understatement: "He was not ostentatious at all."[8] Chas Scoggins wrote in the *Lowell Sun*, "Clad in the baggy, bargain-basement tan trousers and an unpressed white shirt, and perhaps if the weather was chilly a tan windbreaker, all of which comprised his simple utilitarian daily wardrobe [Yawkey] gave the uninitiated the impression that he was the clubhouse boy instead of the benevolent, wealthy owner so often criticized for being over-generous with his ballplayers."[9]

Indeed at least one player had that very impression—Bernie Carbo:

> One day I walked into the clubhouse and there was an old man shining some of the players' shoes. Well, Pete Cerrone, our clubhouse manager, always seemed to have lots of older people working in the clubhouse so I didn't think much of it. So I went over to this guy and gave him $20 to get me a cheeseburger and some fries. No problem as he took the money and left the clubhouse. Next thing I knew, Tommy Cremens, our batboy, came in with my food. He looked at me kind of funny and said, "Do you know who you gave that money to? . . . That's Mr. Yawkey. He owns the team." "You've got to be kidding me," I gasped, adding a few more words that I try not to use anymore.
>
> When Mr. Yawkey came back in the clubhouse I said, "Mr. Yawkey, I'm really sorry. I didn't know that you owned the team." He just smiled and said, "Bernardo, just win the game."[10]

It wasn't the first time by any means that the impression had been wrong. Back in 1940, when pitcher Earl Johnson arrived for his first Red Sox spring training, he saw a "heavy-set man dressing at the locker next to him" and wondered to himself, "How can that fat guy play baseball? That's disgraceful—he's way out of shape." Just then, Tom Yawkey offered his hand and introduced himself. When Johnson said, "Nice to meet you, Mr. Yawkey," the predictable response came: "Cut out that Mister stuff, my name's Tom."[11]

Buddy Hunter, who played in a total of twenty-two games over three seasons in the early 1970s, tells a similar story. When Hunter had first arrived in Boston, he checked into the Fenway Motor Lodge (later the Howard Johnson's on Boylston Street, and in 2015 the Verb Hotel) and had then gone over to the ballpark three hours before he was due to report, just to meet the batboys and clubhouse kids.

> So I go over there and I meet them, and there's this old guy who picked up this towel. He's got this white shirt on, a real thin white shirt, and

in his pocket he's got this yellow card. You could see the yellow color; … that's how thin his shirt was. The next day, same old man picking up the towels. I went to the clubhouse kid, and I asked, "Hey, who's the old man over there, picking up the towels?" He says, "That's Mr. Yawkey. He owns the team." So I went up to Mr. Yawkey, and he had the same white shirt on, the same yellow card in his pocket. I couldn't believe it. I said, "Mr. Yawkey, I heard so many nice things about you. I just want to introduce myself. I'm Buddy Hunter from South Omaha, Nebraska." He said, "Well, Buddy, congratulations on making the Boston Red Sox. I hope you have a great career." Two months later, I get called down to Louisville, and Dick O'Connell—he was the general manager—calls me into the office, and he says, "Buddy, we've got to send you down. Doug Griffin's coming off the disabled list. We've got to send you down to Louisville. I don't know what you said to Mr. Yawkey, but he wanted you to keep your Major League money." And he said, "That's the first time this has ever been done." I was making more than the managers were down there. It was only like $20,000 a year, but still . . . [it was a lot when you were] playing Minor League baseball. Those guys were only making around $1,200 a month, you know, at the most.[12]

Ronald Jones, the caretaker of the Yawkeys' Mt. Pleasant Plantation in South Carolina said, "Mr. Yawkey would walk around here in khaki pants and a frayed jacket. You'd never know he was the boss and we were the employees."[13] Jones was perhaps Yawkey's closest friend down south; Freddie Cumbee was his constant fishing and quail-hunting companion; he was involved with the dairy operation, and he also drove Mrs. Yawkey when she was going somewhere that Tom Yawkey was not going. Tom always preferred to drive himself.[14]

Freddie's son Mark Cumbee said his father had worked at Mt. Pleasant for the DeFoes, but after Tom Yawkey bought Mt. Pleasant from the DeFoe estate, he transitioned to working for the new owners, the Yawkeys. Freddie would be the one who would drive Jean Yawkey "from A to Z. He did chauffeuring and other odd jobs. When other things needed to be done, he would do them. Trimming azaleas. Odd jobs of painting. He helped with the Black Angus cows. . . . He did a lot of the hauling of the cows to fairgrounds."[15]

The Cumbees lived a couple of miles from Mt. Pleasant. They were described by an area resident as part white, part Negro, part Indian.[16] Tom would often go over to Freddie's house and pick him up to take him back to the plantation so they could fish or hunt. "Mr. Yawkey, he would come to my dad's house all the time. They would leave there and go out to the fish pond; the fish pond was on the plantation, but he would come and pick my dad up, and they'd go fishing."[17]

Had there been any racial undertones that were uncomfortable? (Just my asking the question was uncomfortable.) Mark replied unhesitantly:

> No, no. Not at all. He never showed any racial . . . intent or any racial thought. He'd always been very down to earth. . . . I mean, I've heard that question before, but with my siblings and my dad, I'd never seen any type of racial [undertones]. . . .
>
> I've heard people talk about that, about the Red Sox not being integrated over a period of time, but I don't think it was a racial thing. Being around him and seeing how he and my father communicated, it was just like he took my father under his umbrella, like he was a part of his family, you know?
>
> They got along just like they were two people doing a normal thing. He would come and drink coffee with my dad at my dad's house before they went out.[18]

In Boston two of the people Yawkey spent more time with than any others may have been clubhouse attendant Vince Orlando and press steward Tommy McCarthy—not bankers or financiers or anyone on the social scene. Longtime employees of the Red Sox often say they didn't recall ever seeing Tom Yawkey in a suit. He had a jacket and tie in the office but typically just wore khakis and a light shirt. Catcher Bob Montgomery observed, "He struck me as kind of odd, as a guy who was really quite wealthy but who bought the same color pair of pants and the same color shirt and the same pair of penny loafer shoes from which he knocked the backs down and tried them on as slippers. Every day when he came in the ballpark, he had on a khaki pair of slacks and a blue shirt. I never saw him dressed any other way."[19] "He wore his khakis," recalled Jim Rice.

And then he added succinctly, "Maybe he believed this: clothes never made the man."[20]

Ritz concierge Tom Carroll has a favorite story about Tom Yawkey and his accommodation to dress codes:

> Back in those days, you couldn't come into the Ritz Carlton lobby without a coat and tie. Mr. Yawkey would come out of the elevator, and there was a driver waiting [outside the Newbury Street door] to take him to the ballpark. He'd walk through the lobby and through the revolving door. As soon as he got through the door, off came the coat. Off came the tie. Just to walk that forty feet, he'd put the coat and tie on and then immediately take it off. He wanted to keep with the rules.[21]

There was the occasional social event in Georgetown County, Phil Wilkinson noted. "He would try to conform somewhat in situations like that, but . . . he was very reticent to do that sort of thing. We would have what we'd call 'suppers' down there. It would always be local-type food, and he would come to those. Everybody would be extremely casually dressed, including him and Mrs. Yawkey."[22]

Some of Yawkey's clothing may not truly have been off the rack. Grant Southward of the American fashion trade journal *Daily News Record* wrote, "Admittedly no clothes horse, Tom Yawkey takes an interest in lightweight and comfortable clothes. He has always had his clothes made by Joe Cippola who custom-made his suits when he was in New Haven, and later when he went to New York." Yawkey seemed to chuckle in telling Southward what a bonanza it had been for Cippola when he lost 70 pounds around 1963—dropping from 252 to 178. "When I lost weight, I had to get a whole new outfit. Everything I had fitted me like a tent." He was 5-foot-9½ and wore a size 43 regular but sometimes bought a 44 "because I like 'em a little looser—I like comfort in my clothes, even in my Dixbak hunting pants, which I don't want to bind me every time I step across a log."[23]

Carl Yastrzemski wrote, "He was probably the most affluent man I've ever known, and also the simplest and most direct. 'Don't you have anything else except those old brown pants?' I would tease him. He'd get insulted and when I saw him the next day he'd bring in pictures from his days at Yale, showing me what a fancy dresser he had been."[24]

Dick O'Connell told Tom Shaer that Yawkey had "lost all this weight, and he never got his pants taken in. Here's this guy walking around with baggy pants. It was because of two things. He was unpretentious, and he also didn't care to spend money. He would spend a lot of money on other people, O'Connell said; he was very generous with other people, but with himself, he doesn't care."[25]

Art Keefe, Dick Bresciani's predecessor as assistant public relations director, recalled, "He wore the same brown suit all the time; it was kind of funny. I made a comment to Bill Crowley one time that the ballplayers were taking a collection. John Kennedy, one of the reserve players at that time, wanted to take a collection to buy Mr. Yawkey a suit. Bill Crowley told me he probably had thirty suits that were all the same."[26] Kennedy doesn't recall the story, but he remembered Yawkey's look: "You didn't see him in a suit too often. He did have brown pants on all the time and always a short-sleeved white shirt."[27]

A *Globe* columnist in Yawkey's later years, Leigh Montville, recalled, "He was always in the press room. He had his little coterie of people after games. He was always smoking. He dressed like my father—these kind of short-sleeve shirts and dress pants. Always smoking. He would always have that table in the press room but he never really seemed to be saying much. He was always with his wife. They were all over there in the corner and nobody bothered him." (Montville added as an aside, "They had very good food. The Culinary Institute of America sent people over—students—to cook food. Then they had that open bar with Walter Underhill, the bartender, and they were open late after games. There was really very little interaction.")[28]

Keefe added, "The thing that most impressed me about Tom Yawkey was that he was easy to talk to, he was down to earth, he was never aloof, and he would just as easily be seen talking to an usher, a ticket seller, or a grounds crew person in the ballpark as anybody else. He never acted like he was above anyone."[29] Sports cartoonist Eddie Germano told a story about his son from around 1972 or 1973:

My son Eddie Jr. worked here at the ballpark for Joe Mooney, scraping and painting the poles in the grandstand. Tom Yawkey came out of the office from the door behind third base and said, "There's something wrong here, boys." He says, "Oh, yeah. Where's your music?" My kid was in high school. Rock and roll. "Oh, somebody told us we shouldn't be playing that—that you wouldn't like it." He said, "Someone told you to turn off the radio because I wouldn't like the music you're playing?" Yawkey went into a tirade. He said, "Put the radio back on and who-ever it is, if they come back out again, you tell them to see me." He says, "I want you to put the radio on twice as loud as what you had it."[30]

As a junior at Boston University, Bill Gutfarb had worked on the grounds crew for a year under Joe Mooney, starting as a part-timer by sweeping out the skybox seats and coming in on Saturdays to help install the new red plastic seats in the offseason of 1973-74. He remembers the first time as an employee that he saw Tom Yawkey:

I was sweeping peanut shells on the first base side skybox seats. For some reason, I happened to look down on the field, and just as I did that, Tom Yawkey came out of the Red Sox dugout. He was wearing what he normally did—khaki pants and a khaki windbreaker. He was walking double-time, straight out to the mound. On the mound was the mound-and-plate man, Jim McCarthy. Mac. Mac didn't see him because Mac was working on his hands and knees with the clay around the pitching rubber. As Tom Yawkey got to maybe within ten feet of him, he must have said something because Mac looked up, and then he stood up straight and started wiping off his hands. Mr. Yawkey was walking toward him with his arm outstretched and I thought, "Gee, isn't that nice? Here's a very wealthy person who owns the whole place and he goes to one of the lower-echelon employees and he knew him." I couldn't hear them but you could tell it was like, "How are you? How's the family? How was your winter?" It was a very nice and warm greeting that I witnessed.

That's how I'd always heard of Tom Yawkey, as a friendly person and very comfortable with working people.[31]

Jean Yawkey also was humble. A *Globe* story reported, "Though she was worth millions, she would never show it. Yawkey did all her own shopping and banking locally. One day when she went to her local bank, there was a long line, and when the manager spotted her at the rear, he wanted to bring her to the front. She refused. She would wait her turn."[32]

Of course there was some benefit in keeping out of the limelight. Anyone with wealth becomes a target for supplicants. Bill Gutfarb remembers Jean Yawkey saying that in South Carolina "Tom had to have the barber come out to the house because every time Tom would go to the barber shop, someone would come in and say, 'I need a new fishing rod. I need a new gun. I need a new this. . . .' He was a very kind-hearted guy, but if you want to get a haircut, you don't want to have someone badgering you all the time." Gutfarb recalled a time with Jean Yawkey: "The charitable nature of the Yawkeys is something that . . . you don't hear about that much. In South Carolina, driving out from Mt. Pleasant to Tara Hall, we made a turn. There's a church, and she said, 'Oh, that's the church. They had just bought a new organ, and someone poured paint all over it. Ruined it. So Tom bought them a new organ.' Very generous."[33]

All that said, Yawkey's 1980 induction into the Hall of Fame may well have reflected his generosity to the Hall as well as his service to the game. Steve Buckley wondered out loud in 2007 why Jake Ruppert of the Yankees had never been named to the Hall. His teams, after all, had had quite a lot more success on the field of play. (Ruppert was finally inducted in 2013.)[34]

Jean Yawkey was almost never in the newspaper, but at the end of August 1980, Will McDonough wrote that she had begun to assert herself in her role as president of the club. At a meeting apparently held in July, she had vetoed a plan presented by Buddy LeRoux to expand Fenway Park's capacity to forty thousand. She also determined to live in Boston year round, taking up permanent residence in the apartment at the Ritz and not returning to South Carolina in the wintertime except perhaps for an occasional visit. All the Yawkey estate business had been conducted out of New York, but now that office was closed, and Joe LaCour had moved to Westwood, Massachusetts. Jean and Haywood Sullivan had asked John Harrington to return to the Red Sox. On February 1, 1981, Harrington took Joe

LaCour's place as executor of the Yawkey estate and Mrs. Yawkey's right-hand man.[35]

The Sox on the field were desultory. Attendance was off in 1980 by more than 350,000. The team finished in fourth place, sixteen games out of first. During a September series against Cleveland, disaffected fans at Fenway booed Don Zimmer when he came out to the mound to replace his pitcher. In her private box, Jean Yawkey stood up and applauded Zimmer. He was clearly someone she liked, and she didn't think the struggles of the Red Sox were his fault.[36] Her support wasn't enough to save him, however. Zimmer was let go, and Johnny Pesky was asked to manage the final five games of the year. In announcing the firing, Sullivan said that the termination vote was not unanimous. Jean Yawkey was said to be "too sad to stay in Boston that day."[37] For that matter, perhaps no one truly blamed Zimmer. It was just one of those times when a new manager seemed needed to offer a fresh start, but if Zimmer had just been the fall guy, that surely hadn't made Jean Yawkey any less upset.

Ralph Houk got the call. He was a "baseball optimist" and a "comfortable choice" where a Frank Robinson or Pawtucket manager Joe Morgan would have been a bolder choice.[38] Houk had the image of a tough disciplinarian (he was known as "the Major"), but that was from his service days and did not suit his demeanor in baseball. Dick O'Connell, asked for his thoughts, let it be known that the Sox had tried to hire Houk (and Earl Weaver and Dallas Green) in earlier years but had been denied permission to talk to any of the three.[39]

Bud Collins mocked the choice of Houk as a "historical monument," a relic of decades past.[40] Ray Fitzgerald was more sarcastic, referring to "Wayward and Muddy" rather than Haywood and Buddy, and writing, "Through a series of beautifully crafted moves, the dynamic duo has succeeded in changing what had been one of the more stable rosters in the American League into baseball's version of a garage sale."[41]

Tom Boswell wrote a *Washington Post* column headlined "Funeral for a Friend: Franchise Crumbles behind Fenway Façade."[42] Only Dwight Evans remained on the field for a team that as recently as October 1978 had seemed like a dynasty. Yaz was in his final season, playing it out as a DH. The Sullivan-LeRoux leadership group had fumbled free agency, allowing both Carlton Fisk and Fred Lynn to become free agents by failing to mail them their new contracts until two days after the deadline. Rick Burleson and Butch Hobson were allowed to depart as well, via trades that never seemed to bring back equal value. After nearly a decade with his next team, the White Sox, Fisk said of the Red Sox, "I never wanted to leave [Boston]. The trouble was, a couple of people just didn't believe that." It was clear to the *Springfield Union*'s Garry Brown that he was obliquely referring to Sullivan and Jean Yawkey.[43]

The Sox seemed to have neither the competence nor the will to hold onto their most spirited players, or they had developed a misguided notion that it was a privilege to play for the Red Sox and ingrate players who had agents just weren't wanted. Key agent Jerry Kapstein was reportedly banned from the ballpark.[44] Management was seen as "bumbling and inept" in player relations, and it had turned formerly friendly Fenway fans into ones embodying antagonism and even hostility.[45] Ken Harrelson, one of the team's broadcasters, said the Sox had become "the laughing stock of the American League."[46] Peter Gammons wrote measured articles in the *New York Times* summarizing the situation. His April 4, 1981, column reported that the Sox were a whole new team under Sullivan and that they might prove to be a better team than the worrywarts feared, that Sullivan could prove to be a baseball man who knew when to hold 'em and when to fold 'em.[47]

In some regards, the Tom Yawkey legend may have been fortunate never to have been sullied by the new era in baseball. Arbitrator Peter Seitz's decision establishing free agency in baseball had come on December 23, 1975. Just a few days over six months later, Tom Yawkey died.

Among the new owners, Buddy LeRoux in particular stood out far from the baseball purists that the Yawkeys were, and LeRoux's sentiments were shared by Haywood Sullivan. Peter Gammons remembers that this was around the time one could find Haywood Sullivan and his people on one side of the press room and Jean Yawkey on the other.[48] LeRoux was busy investing in Florida real estate, around Winter Haven, taking advantage of opportunities accorded him at the time, including the purchase of the team headquarters, the Winter Haven Holiday Inn.[49] And testimony came out later that LeRoux had also been negotiating behind the scenes to buy the Cleveland Indians and move them to Tampa-St. Petersburg.[50] If nothing else, that had the look of a conflict of interest.

A *Globe* poll of season ticket holders found that almost 25 percent of them had not renewed for 1981.[51]

This was another strike year, and no Major League ball was played from June 12 to August 9—in other words, more than one-third of the season was lost to the work stoppage. It was determined to split the season into two halves. In the first half, the Red Sox had been 30-26, and in the second half, 29-23. They finished in fifth place overall in the seven-team AL East. As it happens, both Fisk and Lynn had true "off" years, while some of the players Sullivan had imported via trade—Mark Clear, Carney Lansford, and Rick Miller—played very well. A number of homegrown players seemed to be starting to come into their own—among them Rich Gedman, Bruce Hurst, and Glenn Hoffman.

After the 1981 season, George Sullivan took over as PR director of the Red Sox. There could hardly have been a worse time to assume the role:

> I couldn't believe it, when I got a call from Buddy LeRoux to be PR director. He asked, "What would you like to have?" Financially and conditions. I was walking into a hornet's nest, and I didn't know it. Ironically, the first thing on my list was that all three owners be unanimous. This wasn't because I knew they were fighting with each other. It's just that I knew things could happen when you have an ownership with three people or more; usually there's stuff going on behind the scenes. If IBM were calling, I would have asked the same. I didn't know that they were feuding.[52]

Houk's 1982 edition of the Red Sox improved to 89-73, in third place and only six games out of first. This despite Mark Clear's fourteen wins (all in relief), the most of anyone on the team.

After the season, LeRoux announced the Fenway Park expansion plan, which would add four thousand more seats with the erection of a double deck along both the first and third base sides.

There was discussion during the off-season that supermarket

millionaire David Mugar would buy out a group of limited partners headed by LeRoux; one of Mugar's group was Carl Yastrzemski. The idea didn't get far, reportedly in part because Jean Yawkey didn't want Mugar as a partner.[53]

By early 1983, a true feud had broken out between LeRoux and his two partners, Sullivan and Yawkey. But LeRoux wasn't leaving, he said, and he wouldn't be bought out. Under the partnership agreement, he'd have to offer his shares to the two partners, and he said he'd rather stay than sell them his shares.[54] The problem seemed to be Jean Yawkey against Buddy LeRoux, perhaps dating back to the Zimmer firing. One of the limited partners—Rodgers Badgett, a LeRoux ally—accused Jean Yawkey of charging her personal travel expenses to the Red Sox, as though she had remained sole owner of the team.[55] The feud broke out into the public eye in the worst of ways—on June 6, 1983, when the team hosted a "Tony C Night" benefit to raise funds for Tony Conigliaro, who had been felled by a stroke in January 1982. It was a "feel-good" affair, bringing together many of Tony's teammates from the "Impossible Dream" year. It was, however, marred by the tone-deaf Buddy LeRoux, who held a press conference minutes before the festivities began, announcing that he and a group of the Red Sox partners had assumed control of the team, taking over from Haywood Sullivan and Jean Yawkey. The press immediately dubbed it "Coup LeRoux," by which name it's been known ever since.

George Sullivan, who had been on duty for a year and a half by then, said the following of the ownership wrangle:

> I walked into that hornet's nest. And it was fine for the first year because it was fairly subtle. I didn't start seeing it as a major thing until '83....
> Tony Conigliaro Night was the worst nightmare of my professional life. It would be good for a public relations work-study thing.
>
> I knew Haywood before I knew Buddy. There was a situation in the front office that you're either with one or you're against him. I treated them equally. If anything, I gave Mrs. Yawkey a little favoritism. I don't think I did, but if I did, it was in her direction. I was friendly toward all

three of them. Mrs. Yawkey gave me a big bear hug when I got hired and said, "I'm so happy." But somebody turned her against me.[56]

The coup set off a firestorm that backfired badly on Buddy. Peter Gammons remembers:

Leadership in the front office was always divided. It was always O'Connell against Mrs. Yawkey, O'Connell against Haywood. . . . That famous day when they had the Coup LeRoux in 1983, the whole '67 team was standing in the back of the press room about to have their press conference, and all of a sudden Buddy came in with Dick O'Connell and George Sullivan to announce they had taken over the team. About forty minutes later, Haywood came in with Dick Bresciani and his team. It was one of the most amazing nights in Red Sox history. It sort of defined the whole era, how divided they were.[57]

Even with all this going on, the Red Sox farm system kept adding new players. In the 1983 amateur draft, the team's first choice was a pitcher from the University of Texas named Roger Clemens.

Regarding the ownership issues, Jean Yawkey didn't say anything for public consumption until July 13, and when she spoke, it was in courtroom testimony. Asked about LeRoux, she said, "I have lost a great deal of respect for him in the last couple of years." She preferred not to speak with him and had not done so since October 1982. Indeed if she had business to conduct with someone at Fenway, her driver would pull up to the curb and fetch the person. She would explain, "I will not come into this ballpark again until he [LeRoux] is gone. I want nothing to do with him ever again." Will McDonough explained the reason: "The rift in the ownership came to light a week ago when it was revealed that Jean Yawkey had moved to prevent LeRoux and his pals from tapping the till too often to pay their notes. In recent years she had been disheartened by all the maneuvering to make money. It wasn't in the Yawkey tradition to jack up ticket prices, buy parking lots, open souvenir shops and, most of all, go to the city for help in getting a loan to build luxury boxes. She objected to that, but they walked right over her and kept on going."[58]

Then came Coup LeRoux. LeRoux said that a majority of the team's limited partners had designated him as "managing general partner," and in his first act he appointed Dick O'Connell as GM. The "coup" was seen as illegal and was immediately challenged. "Couldn't it have waited a day?" asked Joe Foy, one of Tony C's teammates who had come in for the benefit. The sentiment was shared by all.[59] Indeed there was ongoing wonder that Tom Yawkey, a man of nearly unlimited resources and aware that he was battling leukemia, hadn't planned better for his own passing.

LeRoux's move was blocked by Jean Yawkey and Sullivan, who were granted a preliminary injunction to prevent changes. Another minor point of conflict was Mrs. Yawkey's desire to leave her one limited partner share (which she held in addition to her general partnership) to John Harrington in her will; LeRoux objected, thinking that Harrington had been leaking confidential team information to the press. Jean took some responsibility for letting Lynn and Fisk go, saying that the two had been "asking for exorbitant salaries and had to go. They were way out of line."[60]

The seven-day trial and the 113-page decision rendered afterward resulted in LeRoux's coup being judged invalid. *Globe* writer John Powers told a fellow reporter that at the trial Jean was "the most brilliant witness I'd ever seen—couldn't remember a damned thing." Powers remembered that she was in a "$29.95 Zayre's pantsuit and looked as though she belonged in Tuesday night bingo somewhere."[61] Years later, he said, "It was as though he [LeRoux] didn't exist. I remember writing somewhere, 'Buddy is short, but he's not yet invisible.' She was either the most forgetful person or someone who had been coached brilliantly. She didn't remember anything. 'I loaned him one or two million, I don't remember which. . . .' She was apparently very loyal to the people that she was with—Yaz, Haywood, Harrington, those guys . . . but just loathed Buddy."[62]

After the trial was over, WBZ-TV sports reporter Bob Lobel thought he had a scoop, the first television interview with Jean Yawkey. "I asked what her reaction was and she said, 'I'm very happy.' That was the end of the interview." He talked to her off-camera, and she said she didn't ever want the spotlight on her. He marveled, "She's the first lady of Boston baseball, but nobody knows a thing about her."[63]

LeRoux was not disfranchised as a general partner, however.

The Yawkey group had wanted him to be forced to sell, but Superior Court justice James P. Lynch Jr. wrote in the 113-page civil suit decision, "Litigation is no panacea for all the ills of a troubled partnership." Yawkey and Sullivan were still stuck with LeRoux. LeRoux had become, in Leigh Montville's words, like "the house guest who will not leave, the visiting second cousin who sits in the living room and eats the chips and drinks the drinks and won't budge."[64]

Buddy LeRoux was aware of his isolation, and reveled in it to some extent. He was said to have thought about writing his autobiography and titling it *The Skunk at the Garden Party*.[65]

The relationship among the partners was far more than frosty. When LeRoux had raised objections to Jean's plan to vest voting power in John Harrington as trustee after her death, he said she stalked out of one Fenway Park meeting with the threat, "You'll be sorry for this. I'll get even." "She just about called me everything in the book," LeRoux said. "She referred to me as 'it.'" He said she often cursed him. "She was a love-hate kind of person, and if you were on her bad list, she could be as nasty as they come." Finally she quit speaking to him altogether.[66]

John and Maureen Harrington had become Jean Yawkey's best friends, Maureen very often sitting with Jean at Fenway Park. Yawkey Foundation vice president Bill Gutfarb and his wife Nancy often joined them. Susan Trausch of the *Globe* reported, "She doesn't like a lot of chitchatting, though. A game is not a social event. She concentrates as she chain-smokes, missing nothing down on the field, and 'scores the game like a medieval scribe,' according to Dick Johnson, curator of the New England Sports Museum." Johnson said that as the Sports Museum was starting out, Jean was one of the most generous donors. Lou Gorman (who became Red Sox GM in 1984) said the same thing. Jean followed games intently and didn't like chatter in her box.[67]

Johnson has a vivid recollection of first meeting Jean:

At one point, she made a six-figure donation, payable over a number of years. She loved [Celtics basketball player] Dave Cowens. Dave and she really hit it off. I'll never forget; one time we held a fundraiser at Fenway Park. I think Shawmut Bank let us use their luxury suite, maybe around 1987. We got over there a little early, and Dave asked to see Mrs. Yawkey. He knew where her suite was. He went to the gentleman—the security guard—who was outside, and he went in and spoke with her. I was with Dave at the time. And [the guard] comes out and silently gives a nod—like we were going in to see the Pope or something. She was sitting there—I loved it—she had several packs of cigarettes laid out on a table top and a scorebook—the kind of scorebook that you bought at a sporting goods store, the kind of scorebook that you'd have if you were a high school or college coach. She had it laid out on the table. You could have painted that as a still life—as "Jean Yawkey, Fan." There was her scorebook, her cigarettes, her seat looking out at the ballpark. She was ready for her team to play.

She was incredibly frail looking in person, I thought. You wanted to hand her a box of cannolis or something. But she was very pleasant. You could tell immediately just from eye contact that she was very sharp and with it.

She talked in a very reserved, soft, quiet way to Dave. She said hello to me.[68]

The Harringtons and Jean Yawkey traveled rather extensively in her later years—an around-the-world trip in 1989 and then another in 1990 to China, Hong Kong, Australia, and New Zealand, along with Jean's friend Ellie Armstrong, the Gutfarbs, and (on one trip) attorney Justin Morreale.[69] Bill Gutfarb remembers the trips:

We went from here and overnighted in San Francisco and then went to Tokyo, Hong Kong, Paris, Amsterdam, and then came back on the Concorde. That was 1989. We flew in separate planes, just in case. Justin, my former wife, and I in one and John and the others in another.

The second trip we went to New Zealand, Australia, and Hong Kong again. Mrs. Yawkey liked Hong Kong. We also went to Guangzhou by hydroplane up the Pearl River and came back by train. The next year, we went to Hawaii for three weeks. First we stayed in Oahu and then we went to Maui and then we went to the Big Island.

She [Jean] had gone to Russia after Tom had passed away. She liked to travel, liked to see things.[70]

Not only did Jean travel with the inner circle, but she also treated the front office employees to a trip to Hawaii in 1983. "The whole front office. In December. If you were married, you could bring your husband or wife. They told us in July, so we had all that time to plan it. We were talking about it constantly. We were there at Pearl Harbor Day. We were there about nine days. . . . It was wonderful. There were two planeloads of us. We all went first class. It was great. We stayed at the Sheraton, right on Waikiki."[71]

In the summer of 1974, Bill Gutfarb went to work in the ticket office and worked there for several summers while working in the accounting department during the winters as he progressed toward his MBA at Babson College. He worked in accounting through the end of June 1982. "I did the Red Sox financial statements, players' payroll, tax stuff with some of the agents, and also kept the books for the Winter Haven team," Gutfarb recalls. "I had a pretty good handle on the financial operations of the franchise." Then he decided to seek another position elsewhere. He had sent a letter to John Harrington at the Yawkey Foundation. Gutfarb had a desk in the computer room, but the constant humming there prompted him to set a desk out in the hall too. (The buildings at Fenway are old and lacked a lot of office space.) "I would sit out in the hall a lot, and Mrs. Yawkey would come and have dinner with Helen Robinson or one of the other women that were working through the game. She'd say hello to me in the hallway; I don't know whether she knew my name or not." He interviewed a couple of times at the Yawkey Foundation office in Dedham. Then one day he got the idea he was about to be hired. "Mrs. Yawkey was walking down to go to dinner, and she looked at me and she winked. I figured, 'Hmm. I guess it's going to work out.'"[72] Offered the job at the foundation, he gave notice to the Red Sox and made the move.

An article in the *Boston Globe* in 2001 remarked on Harrington and his family:

The closeness of the Harringtons and Jean Yawkey is perhaps best illustrated by her 80th birthday party, when John Harrington arranged to take Yawkey and a few of her intimates to New York to see *The Phantom of the Opera*. When the group gathered for cocktails in her suite afterward, Harrington ducked into his room and donned a costume and mask modeled after the Phantom's. Bursting into the suite, Harrington acted out a scene from the play, casting Yawkey as his muse. Failing to recognize Harrington beneath the mask, Yawkey recoiled in horror. "Once she discovered it was John, she couldn't stop laughing," Yawkey's lifelong friend Ellie Armstrong, a guest at the party, recalls. "He gave her a lot of joy, and there were precious few people who could do that for her."[73]

The idea of Jean Yawkey's laughing may seem unlikely for those who only saw her looking down on Fenway from her box, seemingly sternly. Joan M. Thomas wrote in her SABR biography of Jean Yawkey that "her acquaintances attributed that demeanor to shyness. Some said that she had a great sense of humor and a loud, hearty laugh. She was also known to engage in warm conversation with fans, ballplayers, and Red Sox staff members. But when approached by the media, she would clam up." She also had a bit of a hearing deficiency, Thomas explained, and it "undoubtedly contributed to her seeming reticence."[74] A longtime associate, Jim Healey described Jean as follows:

She liked her privacy. She did not want to be out in public. She was nervous when she was out in different ceremonies. Getting to do that was hard. A lot of people think Jean was aloof, but Jean had a hearing problem. You had to speak loudly, and she had to look at you to be able to hear you. This was in her later years of course. A lot of people took that as her being aloof but, knowing her, I knew that wasn't the case. She was very down to earth, a not at all pretentious person.[75]

Maureen Cronin had a view from the inside too:

When you got to know her, she was wonderfully funny. She had a great wit. She would pretend that she couldn't hear things when she really could. After somebody would say something, she'd pretend she didn't hear, and then she'd say to me later, "Did you hear . . . ?"

She had very strong likes and very strong dislikes. For the most part, she was very discerning. There were usually reasons for it. I don't think she was judgmental. . . . I think because she didn't hear all that well, she was a great observer. She would watch people a little more closely than other people do, I think, especially when she was older.[76]

Red Sox announcer Sherm Feller said he'd never been one of Jean's favorite people. She wasn't really a conversationalist, but it was more a matter of shyness than aloofness. Both Tom and Jean were quiet people who believed one should be judged by what they did, not what they said. Jean would go to the team Christmas party, though, and she would stay—not just make an appearance. She'd stay and talk with everybody.[77] Frank Malzone added that she was quiet but had a presence: "She lights up a room."[78]

At the end of July, Jean Yawkey was added to the board of directors of the Baseball Hall of Fame.

When Yaz played his last game on October 1, 1983, he asked for a moment of silence for two people who had meant so much to him—his mother and Tom Yawkey.

The club hadn't played well at all on the field since the Coup LeRoux. The Sox had been in first place on the date of LeRoux's announcement; over a season's worth of games since, they had been 72-90. They finished 1983 in sixth place. And attendance had dropped to 1,782,285 after three years (1977–79) above 2 million.

On May 30, 1984, the Massachusetts Appeals Court reaffirmed the decision against LeRoux's attempted takeover of the Red Sox, with strong language indicating that LeRoux had gone "substantially beyond accepted behavior" and that he had failed in his fiduciary duty to his two general partners by allying with some of the limited partners to attempt to strip Sullivan and Yawkey of their powers.[79] The prevailing partners immediately appointed Lou Gorman as GM, made Sullivan CEO, and prepared to loosen the purse strings LeRoux had held more tightly. They then voted to buy out the sixteen limited partners' shares held by LeRoux's allies and instructed them to surrender any keys or passes to the park they may have had.

LeRoux found it hard to accept the verdict. He also offered gratuitous and demeaning comments such as, "On the recommendation of Joe LaCour, we brought her [Jean Yawkey] in for window dressing and she's been pulling the shade up and down ever since."[80] LeRoux tried to reappeal, but at the end of June the Massachusetts Supreme Judicial Court denied his application to do so. Still LeRoux wouldn't let go. He was, Michael Madden of the *Globe* wrote, like a husband who loses his case in divorce court but won't leave the house.[81]

On July 2 Mrs. Yawkey and Haywood Sullivan exercised their option to terminate the rights and privileges of the limited partners. LeRoux remained as a general partner, but the May 30 court order declared that he was not to participate in any votes or even in deliberations.[82] There were uninformed concerns that Jean Yawkey might not be able to afford to buy out the limited partners or to re-sign Jim Rice to another contract, but it all worked out.

Joe Cronin died on September 7, 1984. The "jut-jawed son of Irish immigrants" had been acquired by Yawkey at great expense in October 1934 and had served as manager, GM, and AL president.[83] It was at his funeral that Jean Yawkey and Dom DiMaggio reconciled.

Ralph Houk announced his retirement as manager; he'd served four years, 1981–84.

By 1985 there were three female owners among the twenty-six Major League clubs—Jean Yawkey, Joan Kroc of the Padres, and (as of December 1984) Marge Schott of the Cincinnati Reds. Previously only Grace Comiskey (White Sox) and Joan Payson (Mets) had been women owners of big league ball clubs.

In July Buddy LeRoux and others filed a suit against the Red Sox claiming that they were being taxed on profits they had never received and more or less alleging accounting shenanigans. Appraisers valued the club at $55 million. Finally, on December 4, 1985, LeRoux and the limited partners were bought out—the day before a court-ordered deadline. It wasn't the end of LeRoux's running commentary, however. In fact, he sued again on January 31, 1986, asking that the team be placed in receivership and for the court to declare null and void the manner in which buyout had taken place. The suit even targeted his fellow limited partners who had already been paid.[84]

In February 1986 LeRoux talked about Haywood Sullivan: "He appointed himself CEO. . . . I was never invited to attend a meeting on the baseball end. The only time I said something was 1978 when he screwed up with Fisk and Lynn. . . . They want to retain Yawkey tradition? What's that, 67 years of losing?" LeRoux said they fired

Tommy Harper in December 1985 because Harper and he had been friends. He did call Jean Yawkey "a very strong woman" and said she hadn't always automatically disagreed with his ideas.[85]

LeRoux's assessment of Sullivan received some support from others. As Curtis Wilkie wrote in the *Globe* several years later, "Sullivan is a popular figure in baseball circles, but even his friends admit he has presided over some dubious decisions. 'Haywood is a nice guy,' said one National League executive. 'But for making basic deals involving baseball, he's not too bright, to be frank about it.'"[86] There have been snarky suggestions that Sullivan was a "surrogate son" to the Yawkeys, a description that Sullivan himself later suggested may have applied to John Harrington. But it was Dick O'Connell who had first appointed Sullivan. At least one veteran sportswriter reflected on the appointment a few years later: "A sharp observer of youthful talent, and with far more than the average dose of common sense, Haywood Sullivan was thoroughly qualified to handle the job O'Connell had hired him for."[87] Sullivan himself said he never saw Jean Yawkey socially. It was only at the ballpark. "She doesn't go to an awful lot of places. She goes to the games. A driver picks her up and takes her to the park. It's a normal company car."[88]

The mention of Tommy Harper bore extra significance because Harper himself never thought he'd been fired because of any personal friendships or alliances with the feuding ownership group. He thought he'd been fired because of a Michael Madden story that ran in the *Boston Globe* back in March 1985.[89] The lengthy title of the article pretty much said it all: "Tacit Complicity? For over a Decade, the Red Sox Have Helped the Winter Haven, Fla., Elks Club Distribute Membership Cards to White Players and Officials While Blacks Were Excluded." The story embarrassed the team. It had been thirty-eight years since Jackie Robinson desegregated Major League baseball and twenty years since the Voting Rights Act of 1965. Tommy Harper was quoted in the story as saying that he'd been aware of the practice since spring training in 1972, and he had talked with Reggie Smith about it back then, but the Red Sox had done nothing about it for all those years.

Rico Petrocelli remembered the Winter Haven membership card

issue from the early '70s: "Everybody got a ticket to go to the Elks Club. They put these passes on top of our lockers. We went there, but we weren't thinking, 'Where's Tommy Harper? Where's George Scott?' because nobody said anything right away. When we found out about it, none of us would go back."[90] Indeed Petrocelli remembered when Earl Wilson had been turned away from a local bar in Lakeland (named Cloud Nine) because of the color of his skin. He'd gone with teammates Dennis Bennett and Dave Morehead. Bennett recalled the incident: "The bartender asked Dave what he wanted and asked me what I wanted and looked at Earl and said, 'We ain't serving you. We don't serve niggers in here.' That was the first time I had ever run into any of that. So we got up and left the place."[91]

Howard Bryant writes, "Wilson went to Red Sox management, expecting to be backed by the organization." That's not what happened. "Billy Herman, his manager, coldly rebuffed him. Forget the incident. It never happened, he was told. Also, should any members of the press ask, Wilson was told in no uncertain terms to tell them nothing."[92] The Sox were primarily concerned about negative publicity.

A bit of the problem came out, but the lid was kept on well enough. When Harper experienced the Elks thing all over again a decade later, it was too much to take. "It is the principle of the matter," said Harper. "They still got those passes on team property, and they still hand them out, and some people still go there, even if the players don't go like they used to. The Red Sox should have cut their ties with this place a long time ago; to me, they're still condoning racism. . . . Here it was in the 1980s, and the ballclub's allowing this kind of membership card in our clubhouse. I thought enough was enough. . . . I wasn't angry; I just said it was wrong."[93] Harper had gone to Haywood Sullivan beforehand—maybe years earlier—and asked that Sullivan put an end to the Elks Club situation, but nothing had happened.

Credit Sox GM Lou Gorman for acting quickly when Madden asked him about the practice while working on the story. Gorman, Madden wrote, "said that the Red Sox will have no further connection with the Elks Lodge and that he would personally rip up all the Elks passes on the team's premises."[94]

The story resonated, of course, and cropped up from time to time during the year. Harper recalled the reaction in Winter Haven: "I went through hell in spring training after that story came out. Phone calls in the middle of the night. Tires slashed. But it had gone on for years. Everyone knew it, but it had never been reported before."[95]

Harper said at the time—it was in Madden's story—"I'm going to get fired for talking about this. I know I'm going to get fired, but I don't care because this has been going on for too long." When Harper was indeed fired—a few days before Christmas, after fourteen years with the Red Sox—Madden reprinted Harper's words. Asked for comment, Lou Gorman said, "This whole story is being blown up out of proportion," and he used the word "loyalty" several times: "The Red Sox have been loyal to people who have been loyal to them. . . . You judge people on their job performance and how loyal they have been to you." Madden added, "But do not come down too hard on Lou Gorman because he works for Haywood Sullivan and the Boston Red Sox; Gorman does what he is told."[96]

The story didn't end with Harper's dismissal. In January 1986 Harper filed a discrimination lawsuit with the Massachusetts Commission against Discrimination (MCAD), jointly with the Equal Employment Opportunity Commission (EEOC), a federal agency then headed by future Supreme Court justice Clarence Thomas.[97] This was the same MCAD to which Harper had gone the first time the Red Sox fired him, in 1979. It was, wrote Bob Hohler in a September 2014 *Globe* feature, "the second time the Sox stripped him of a job for blowing a whistle on racial intolerance. . . . He was dismissed from a front-office position in 1979 after he informed the MCAD that the Sox had violated their pledge to improve the franchise's racial diversity."[98]

The Red Sox, of course, protested their innocence. There was a surprise compliance visit as investigators looked into the broader question of race and the Red Sox in 1985. The EEOC found "probable cause" that the Sox had unlawfully fired Harper, that his firing was retaliation for the Elks Club episode. The commission also ruled that "sufficient evidence" supported Harper's allegation that team executives had "created and perpetuated a working environment hostile to minorities.[99] There was a settlement that remains confidential.

Had Harper any impressions of Tom Yawkey?

I didn't know the man. I don't think I had two words of conversation with Tom Yawkey. When he came down to the clubhouse, it was always to go right to Yaz's locker, and then he'd disappear. Reggie Smith knew Tom Yawkey a lot better than I did. He was standing right over there next to Yaz. Other than that, he was up in his office and never really came down. I signed my contract with Dick O'Connell. Never really had any real conversation with Tom Yawkey. I knew Jean Yawkey a little better. I used to have conversations with Jean Yawkey.

Jean Yawkey treated me OK. We used to have conversations in the lunchroom at Fenway Park. . . . My wife [Bonnie] talked to her, and she didn't seem to know that my lawsuit was going on . . . and I can believe that because Tom Yawkey and she never really got involved with the everyday running of the Red Sox. But Jean Yawkey was the one who said, "Let's stop this lawsuit and get this thing settled." That's what I understood happened. I don't really know for sure."[100]

It was nice that Jean Yawkey made Harper feel somewhat more comfortable. "Yeah, and I believe Tom would have been [friendly] too," Harper added. "I never heard anything negative."

On Mr. Yawkey, Harper added the following:

People [who] have a grudge against Tom Yawkey are going to say what they say. I didn't know the man. All I know is that he has to take the responsibility for whatever happened at Fenway Park. The "gentleman's agreement" wasn't a written policy, so if you're looking for a smoking gun, you're never going to find anything. It's an exercise in futility to say, "Well, who is the racist person? Show me the written policy that they didn't want any black players." If you just use your common sense, you're going to say, "Twelve years? Come on."[101]

23

The 1986 World Series and the Years That Followed

IN 1986 THE Red Sox played their way into the postseason again and were in first place from May 13 on. Twins Enterprises, a store selling Red Sox items across Yawkey Way, said it could hardly keep Red Sox items in stock. The Red Sox started to put the squeeze on the street vendors who sold peanuts and the like outside the park, withholding the requisite permission that abutters must grant for licensed vendors. Every time there had been such a conflict before, the vendors pretty much prevailed. At the same time, there were individual acts of charity, with Jean Yawkey giving $250,000 to fund a home that would serve as temporary residence for the families of very young children undergoing transplant operations.[1]

Ten years after his death, "Yawkey's presence is missed," wrote Joe Fitzgerald in the *Boston Herald*'s Opening Day edition. He quoted Tom Yawkey from some of his interview notes. One quote summarized Yawkey's outlook on life:

> If a man starts out with a good financial nucleus, as I did, he's got to decide what he wants to do with it. Some men are obsessed with compiling massive fortunes; they want to make all the money they possibly can. Personally, I never saw the sense in that. I just wanted to make sure I had enough, so that if certain things went sour I wouldn't wind up broke.
>
> I never looked upon baseball as an investment. There are a lot of markets which offer better security and I have investments that are secure. If I didn't, I wouldn't stay in the game. If I had to keep running to the bank for loans, operating on a shoestring, I'd get out. The

worry would be too great. But I've enjoyed being in baseball, and I figure I've been doing something that's brought enjoyment to a lot of other people, too. . . .

As you get older you get more selfish with your time. You become more cognizant of your health; without it, you have nothing. . . . Eddie Collins once said of baseball: "If you don't enjoy it, get out, because you'll only make yourself miserable." That's been the case with me. I've never stopped enjoying it.[2]

Yawkey was very knowledgeable about baseball but perhaps a trifle casual about some of his holdings. Eddie Kasko relates the following:

He [Yawkey] was funny. I remember the one year that I got my contract extended for the last two years and he made the road trip. We were close. We were playing Detroit and Baltimore, and we were fighting Detroit. [It was near the end of] '72. So he made the last road trip, and they called me up to his suite at the Pontchartrain Hotel. He said, "We'd like to extend your contract for another couple of years." I said, "Great." He looked out the window and he said, "Yeah, yeah, yeah, yeah. Yeah, you see that power station up there?" On the Detroit River. He said, "Yeah, from that power station coming down here to the bend in the river where that road comes in there, we used to own that property up there. I wonder if we've still got it."[3]

Though he saw the Red Sox get to the seventh game of the World Series three times (1946, 1967, and 1975), Tom Yawkey never got to see them win a world championship. It looked as though Jean Yawkey might have that opportunity in 1986.

When the Sox clinched the AL East on September 28, the team celebrated in the usual fashion. Haywood Sullivan said that he and Mrs. Yawkey had some "private" words after the final out. "As you know," he said, "she's a private person. We spoke briefly. She's thrilled and celebrated with the players' wives that we had in a private box upstairs for the game."[4]

The Sox lost three of the first four ALCS games against the California Angels and seemed about to lose the fourth when Dave Henderson hit one of the biggest home runs in Red Sox history, a two-run come-from-behind blast in the top of the ninth in Anaheim. The Sox won the game, in the eleventh, and won the ALCS in seven games. Jean Yawkey toasted Tom Yawkey's memory and then walked to the private box of Angels owner Gene Autry. She told Autry that "if the Red Sox had lost, she would have wanted it to be to the Angels because she felt Autry deserved a chance to have his team in the World Series."[5]

The Red Sox played the New York Mets in the World Series, winning the first two games (on the road), losing the next two (at home), then coming within one strike of winning the World Series in Game Six. The Sox were up three games to two and had a 3-2 lead in the top of the seventh in Game Six at Shea. Calvin Schiraldi relieved Roger Clemens in the bottom of the eighth but saw a runner reach third base on a single, a bunt single, and a sacrifice bunt. Gary Carter hit a sacrifice fly to left field to tie the game. It went into extra innings, but in the top of the tenth, the Red Sox's Dave Henderson—the hero of the ALCS—homered to lead off, and then Boston also scored a bonus run when Wade Boggs doubled and Marty Barrett singled. The score was now 5-3, Red Sox. It looked like the long sixty-eight-year drought might be over and the Sox might win—particularly when Schiraldi got the first two batters to fly out in the bottom of the tenth. There was nobody on and only one out to get. The champagne was already being organized in the Red Sox dressing room; Larry Cancro had to run over to the Mets' dressing room to borrow from their supply.

The Shea Stadium message board operator goofed. He inadvertently flashed on the screen the message he had just prepared: "Congratulations to the Boston Red Sox, World Champions." It was gone a moment later.

But Gary Carter singled to left off Schiraldi, and then pinch hitter Kevin Mitchell singled to center. Schiraldi got two strikes on Ray Knight. The Red Sox were truly just one strike away. As Sox GM Lou Gorman put it (it was the title of his book), they were "one pitch from glory": "Looking over at Mrs. Yawkey, I could see for the first time the faintest traces of a smile of long, long awaited satisfaction."[6] She was not in the clubhouse, as some accounts have had it, but was about to be, having left her seat along with Gorman, John Harrington, and Haywood Sullivan.

Knight singled to center too, scoring Carter and making it a 5–4 game, with runners on first and third. Still all the Sox needed to do was get that final out. Manager John McNamara called to the bullpen for Bob Stanley. Mookie Wilson was the batter, and a pitch went astray—officially a wild pitch, though catcher Rich Gedman kindly said, "The ball grazed my glove and anything that hits my glove I should catch."[7] Wild pitch or passed ball, Mitchell scored from third with the tying run.

Jean Yawkey and party "trudged back to our seats," wrote Gorman. He later commented, "To tell you the truth, I never did care for champagne that much, and liked it less after that night."[8]

And then Mookie hit an easy chopper to first base. Bill Buckner, unaccountably and perhaps unforgivably still in the game (though one understands McNamara's sentimental reasons) let the ball skid through his legs, and Knight scored the winning run.

Bill Livingston of the *Cleveland Plain Dealer* wrote, "Tom Yawkey could have picked up the grounder." Not all agreed. Red Sox pitcher Oil Can Boyd said, "Even if he caught it—from what I was looking at—it would be a footrace to the base, and it looked like Mookie Wilson was beating the pitcher to the bag anyway."[9] Gorman wrote, "Mrs. Yawkey simply stared out onto the field in stunned silence, a thousand lost hopes playing across her face."[10]

Sportscaster Bob Costas reported in detail that Jean Yawkey was actually in the visitors' clubhouse at Shea in the bottom of the ninth, with Commissioner Peter Ueberroth, with protective plastic sheeting covering all the lockers and the trophy itself on a table right in front of her, when all went wrong and workers hastily packed up the trophy and tore down the plastic.[11] The story was specious, reports Sox vp Larry Cancro. "Anybody who knows Mrs. Yawkey knows she never left her seat or stopped scoring before the last out. Anybody knows that that story's false because she would have never left her seat until after the last out. She was rabid about scoring." Costas was in the visitors' clubhouse, as were Cancro and Jackie MacMullan of the *Boston Globe*. Some years later, Cancro asked Costas, "Why do you tell the story that you were in there with Mrs.

Yawkey?" And he says, 'Because nobody wants to hear that I was in there with you!'"[12]

Jean Yawkey was smart about baseball, and not that many minutes later, as she and her GM were waiting in a room, with some others talking about how, yes, the Sox could still come back and win Game Seven, she motioned for Gorman to sit next to her. "She looked me straight in the eye and said, 'You know, your manager just cost us the world championship. Do you understand what I'm telling you? Your manager cost us the world championship.'"[13]

There was a Game Seven. And the Red Sox scored three runs in the first inning, holding a 3-0 lead through five innings. Bruce Hurst was pitching a shutout. But then he wasn't. In the bottom of the sixth, a single, another single, a walk, another single, and then a run-producing groundout tied the game, 3-3. In the bottom of the seventh, Schiraldi came back in—and gave up a leadoff homer to Ray Knight. Before the inning was over, the Mets had scored three more runs—enough to win the game, all the runs charged to Schiraldi. They were up, 6-3. Each team scored twice in the eighth, but the Mets were the world champions with an 8-5 victory.

Oddly Lou Gorman had been VP of player personnel for the Mets from 1980 through 1983 and had played a large part in building the team that became the 1986 Mets before he moved to become Red Sox GM in 1984. Jean Yawkey, on the other hand, had been a Red Sox devotee at least since she and Tom married in 1944. She'd lived through 1946 and 1967 and 1975 and now 1986. Gorman wrote in his memoir, "I was afraid to even look at her, knowing the pain she must have been feeling."[14] But Rico Picardi, of Harry M. Stevens, the Fenway Park concessionaire and a Red Sox limited partner, "recalled that at the time she was consoling everyone else. He said that with tears rolling down her face she said, 'We got beat fair and square and there was nothing to be ashamed of.'"[15]

After it was all over, the New York Times' George Vecsey wrote a column under the headline "Babe Ruth Curse Strikes Again" on October 29, 1986. He never posited an actual curse but claimed that "the ghosts and demons and curses of the past 68 years" provided "haunted memories in this franchise," noting that once Harry Frazee had sold Babe Ruth to the Yankees, "it has never been the same."

Boston Globe columnist Dan Shaughnessy picked up and expanded on the idea and published his famous book *The Curse of the Bambino* in 1990. The book itself never suggested that any curse was uttered or that it was real, but snakebitten Red Sox fans everywhere intuitively understood the notion. There had been such a streak of misfortune experienced by the team over the decades that it seemed to cry out for an explanation, however fanciful.

On March 30, 1987, the Red Sox finally rid themselves of Buddy LeRoux. He sold his general partnership share to the JRY Corporation, an entity bearing Jean Yawkey's initials and of which she was sole owner. She now owned two of the three votes; full control of the Red Sox was finally and uncontestably back in Yawkey hands.

Five years after the drama had ended, editor George Whitney of *Diehard* wrote that the Yawkeys had saved the Red Sox three times: once when Tom bought the team after the disastrous 111-game-loss season of 1932 during the depths of the Depression, a second time when Jean Yawkey joined with Sullivan and LeRoux to take control of the Red Sox in 1978, and this third time, to spare the Sox from LeRoux, who Whitney believed had planned to enrich himself by trading away players as soon as they started making more than the Major League minimum.[16]

A sign of changing times was the prolonged drama over coming to terms on a new contract with pitcher Roger Clemens (24-4, AL Cy Young winner and MVP in 1986). The *Boston Herald* took to counting the days, and on Day 30 it quoted Dwight Evans: "I don't think management's handled it right. If (late Red Sox owner Tom) Yawkey was still around, he would have had the kid signed and signed for less—and still had the kid smiling."[17] Jean Yawkey insisted that she had faith in GM Lou Gorman. She was, however, consolidating her position at the same time. Operational control of the New England Sports Network (NESN, owned 48 percent by the Red Sox) was assigned to John Claiborne, who reported to John Harrington, who was, in effect, Jean Yawkey's proxy.[18] When the *New York Times* wrote Jean Yawkey's obituary, it noted that Sullivan had become "little more than a figurehead." For his part, John Harrington was "merely the prime minister and Mrs. Yawkey was always the queen."[19] Haywood Sullivan later acknowledged, "I was closer to Tom. John was closer to Jean, especially after Tom's death. And as the years passed, he became a kind of surrogate son. Certainly she depended on him more and more . . . and when he talked, you knew he was speaking for Jean."[20]

Rich Gedman was a hard sign in the off-season too, turning down a large offer in January. Neither side budged until after the season was under way. A meeting in which Mrs. Yawkey took part may have helped break the impasse, though the calendar itself may have accomplished that. Jean is said to have told Gedman, "You're going to be back, my friend."[21] He didn't get into a game until May 2 and distinctly underperformed when he did.

Jean Yawkey continued to keep a very low profile. As one writer put it, Yawkey "brings a little Garbo to the game."[22] Writer Joe Murphy later called her "Greta Garbo in a baseball cap."[23] Dan Shaughnessy once confided to a colleague, "I think she's right out of a Tennessee Williams novel."[24]

On April 29 Jean attended the dedication of a new Massachusetts Bay Transportation Authority (MBTA) commuter rail stop named Yawkey Station. (The station was renovated and expanded in 2014.) She had missed most of the early part of the season because of a fall she suffered but typically could be spotted in her box, looking down on the games, although she generally was "so shy she never shows her face in public," in the words of the *Herald*'s Norma Nathan.[25] She had to show herself on May 15, however, when there was a Symphony Hall tribute to her at the Boston Pops to help raise money for the Massachusetts Association for Mental Health and the Colonel Marr Boys and Girls Clubs.[26] Ted Williams was the honorary chairperson. Cohosts were her reported favorite author, Robert B. Parker, and Joan Parker.

The team had instituted two alcohol-free sections (32 and 33) in the grandstand, but when some bleacher fans requested that two sections near the flagpole be designated areas where marijuana could be smoked, the request went nowhere. That smoking pot was illegal was not mentioned in a news story that reported that Mrs. Yawkey had turned down the request as (in the newspaper's words, not hers) "highly un-American and just a little decadent."[27]

There was still concern about the affirmative action goals of the Red Sox, but the concern this time was prompted by an unrelated development: Dodgers GM Al Campanis was saying that blacks "lack[ed] the necessities" to handle managerial and upper management jobs. The Boston NAACP requested a meeting with the Red Sox. It resulted in a "productive discussion," reported NAACP director Robert Hayden, who said the Red Sox were willing to continue talks to find "ways to shore up their weaknesses."[28] The Reverend Jesse Jackson also noted the lack of women executives in the game.[29] Scrutiny was on all of baseball.

John McNamara may have cost the Red Sox a world championship in 1986, but he didn't lose his job until July 14, 1988. He saw the Sox through a losing season in 1987 (78-84, fifth place), but the natives were getting restless, and with the team just one game over .500 (43-42) at the All-Star break in 1988, he was fired, replaced by third-base coach Joe Morgan as interim manager. It was understood that Jean Yawkey had outvoted Haywood Sullivan, overrode Lou Gorman's advice, and ousted McNamara.[30]

Someplace along the way, Jean Yawkey began to rely on John Harrington's counsel more and on Sullivan's less. A source in ownership told the *Globe*'s Nick Cafardo, "Nobody really knows what happened between Mrs. Yawkey and Sullivan."[31] Of course there are any number of possible reasons for a change in interpersonal dynamics between people.

While Sullivan could legitimately feel he had had a sort of "father-son" relationship with Tom Yawkey, Tom was gone now. And wags shifted some of their attention to the Jean Yawkey–John Harrington tie. Radio host Eddie Andelman came up with a fantasy of a "rumor that Sox co-owner Jean Yawkey may adopt John Harrington in order to ensure that he gets club control when she passes away." Andelman was reportedly very close to LeRoux and may have been doing his bidding here. He said his understanding was, nonetheless, that Tom Yawkey's will had specified the ball club would go to Sullivan after Jean died.[32] One had to have a hard skin to survive the sarcasm and supposition in the Boston market. The purported filial relationships even received note at the level of a *Boston Globe* editorial in 2002, which referred to "two surrogate sons, Haywood Sullivan and then John Harrington."[33]

For a week, Jean Yawkey declined interviews regarding the firing of McNamara but then spoke in the press room on July 22. She said, "There are times when being a woman can be a disadvantage, because people try to put you down, but not this time. I decided that something had to be done. Because our fans have been so supportive, I felt they deserve better, that it was time to make a decision."[34] She had apparently been swayed not just by the team's mediocre performance on the field but also by complaints from fans who wrote the club about the shabby treatment accorded them when McNamara was approached for autographs outside the park.[35] On the same day MacNamara was fired, the team announced the hiring of Elaine Weddington to the Red Sox front office as associate counsel. Her race was not noted in the newspapers, but the NAACP was no doubt reassured. (In January 1990 Weddington was promoted to assistant GM, the first woman to hold that high a position in baseball.) Jean Yawkey had always been more active than people may have perceived, explained John Harrington, noting that over the winter she left her residence at the Four Seasons and came to the ballpark several times a week for lunch and meetings.[36]

After Tom's passing, Jean had sold the New York apartment at the Pierre. Mt. Pleasant Plantation was sold in 1986. Bill Gutfarb recalls the following:

> She'd go there [Mt. Pleasant] after the season and then come back up here probably in March. I remember her saying that she and Tom would always experience three springs—[first in] South Carolina, then they'd go to New York for a month or two, and then they'd come to Boston in early June. In October or September, they'd go back to New York for a month or two, and then they'd go to Mt. Pleasant, and then they'd go out to South Island.
>
> They ended up with Mt. Pleasant Plantation. The way I understand it, it was a Black Angus cattle farm owned by Fred "Pop" DeFoe, who was Tom's guardian following Tom's uncle's passing. When Mr. DeFoe passed in the mid-'50s, his family didn't want it and so—the

way Jean Yawkey explained it—Tom said, "OK, all right. I'll buy it." After she sold Mt. Pleasant, she bought a larger apartment up here.

When they built the other building next to the Ritz, she got a little apartment there with a porch. If you look at it, just below the penthouses there's a porch. That was her apartment. Then when Mt. Pleasant was sold, she wanted something bigger. There were various negotiations with other owners at the Ritz, but she ended up going to the Four Seasons one day, and they showed her something that was available, and she liked it so she bought that. I don't remember the floor, but she had a porch that she could walk out on from her kitchen. If you look at the building, it goes up maybe eight or ten stories, and then it goes back and goes up again. She was on the first. . . . She liked the access to the outdoors.

[In South Carolina] she bought a condo at DeBordieu Colony. She would be here well before Opening Day.[37]

There may have been another reason Jean went to the Four Seasons rather than remaining at the Carlton Condominiums, the "new building" next door to the Ritz-Carlton. "I think she had a dislike for Buddy LeRoux, and he had a condo there at the Carlton House," said retired Ritz-Carlton door attendant Norman Pashoian. "I think she disliked him."[38] That was an understatement, one not intended to be clever.

Hotelier Robin Brown arrived in Boston in 1988 as the third-general manager of the Four Seasons. He got to know Jean Yawkey well.

At 11:45 every morning she came down in the same beige knit dress. She was there, in the Bristol Lounge. With her one gold, very humble, low-key necklace. Maybe it wasn't even gold. And her little flat shoes and her gray hair and her glasses, and she strolled through the lobby and she came in. In those days, you could smoke. She was smoking her cigarette, and she would order a glass of chardonnay, and then she would order—almost every day—the same dish, chicken stir fry. It was one of the specials on the menu, and she had the chicken stir fry with rice. She didn't want any limelight. None. She came in and sat at the same table and tried to lie low.

She'd sit there, and within five minutes, John Harrington would come through the lobby. John would carry a leather satchel full of all the mail and paperwork and all the correspondence for their business world, and they would sit. That meeting occurred, I would say, four days a week, with John at the Bristol.

I got to know them both and chatted sociably. As time went by, I'd walk through, general manager wandering around, particularly at lunch in the Bristol; everybody was there. Jean would invariably say, "Robin, come, join us." And I would say, "Oh, no, no, no." But certainly every two weeks, I would say, "OK, a quick bite."

I sat through lunches, one in particular when she was extremely elevated about the contract with Roger Clemens. She was talking to John, and she got into all the details of the financial package and all the negotiations and basically just said, "Robin, cover your ears."

[Did she seem to be fully conversant with the business details?] "Fully conversant? Oh my God, she was completely on top of all of those details.[39]

After bringing in Joe Morgan, the Red Sox won twelve games in a row and nineteen of their first twenty games under the new manager. It was called "Morgan Magic," and the team turned its season around. The Sox were in first place from September 4 on. As a result, they were back in the postseason for the second time in three years, but they were swept in four games by Oakland in the ALCS.

After the 1988 season ended, significant renovations were made to the ballpark. The roof was literally blown off. Since the grandstand roof needed to be replaced, extra seating was put atop the new roof, and a three-story structure was added behind home plate that would include luxury seating and the press box, including rooms for radio and TV broadcasters. (The luxury seating was initially named the 600 Club and was behind heavy glass that walled out the sound and ambience of the game, so these had to be brought in by audio speakers.)

Jean Yawkey had been listed as "president of the Red Sox" since Tom's death, but the 1989 edition of the *Media Guide* did away with executive titles for her and Haywood Sullivan. John Harrington was not listed. "A lot of people ask me about that," Harrington told Mike

Shalin of the *Herald* in 1991. "But I'm not ownership and I don't work for the Red Sox; I work for one of the owners of the Red Sox."[40]

Jean Yawkey was an exceptionally private woman. But she did make friendships. Robin Brown of the Four Seasons said he had arrived in July 1988. Come September, he had an experience he's never forgotten:

> I'm from England, and Jean found out I'd never been to a baseball game in my entire life. Jean asked me to go with her to my first game. I sat in her box. She had the sliding glass window, and she had her glass of wine and her cigarettes. The entire game, she marked score. She kept score but gave me the entire blow-by-blow. We had our lunch and drink, and she walked me through, nonstop, the entire game. Everything that was going on. So my first-ever baseball game and my first baseball lesson was from Jean. You cannot make this up.[41]

There was an ongoing brouhaha occasioned by the affair between Wade Boggs and Margo Adams; it became a national news story when Adams sued Boggs for breach of contract and went public with embarrassing details about the affair (including her allegations that most of Boggs's teammates knew all about it). Adams planned to give a tell-all interview with *Penthouse* magazine that would reveal even more. For his part, Boggs said that he'd suffered for four years from "sex addiction." There were repeated rumors that Jean Yawkey was extremely upset with the whole sordid episode and even that she'd ordered that Boggs be traded.

Rumors are frequently untrue. Jean Yawkey may have surprised a few people—including some GMs from opposing teams, who may have thought they would have leverage in any trade—when she issued a brief statement in February: "I like Wade Boggs, and what he does off the field is his own business."[42]

Indeed Maureen Cronin recalls, "There was a time when Debbie [Boggs] was leaving the ballpark and Jean was leaving at the same time, and they ran into each other. This was when [news of the affair] had just come out in the papers. It was so difficult for Debbie, and Jean just put her arms around her and she said, 'As long as I'm here with the ball club, Wade has got a job.' Everybody wanted him to be traded, and there was a lot of pressure put on Jean to move him. So she was reassuring to Debbie, and she was very helpful to her."[43]

Numerous ballplayers have commented on the interest Jean took in them and their families. Bob Stanley said, "She is very caring to families. She knows everybody, knows all the wives' names and the kids' names. A lot of people wouldn't know that."[44]

Rico Petrocelli, then a Red Sox alumnus, remembered Jean Yawkey fondly. "We had things in the off-season and she was always there, and she was always very nice. One of the things about Mrs. Yawkey [was] her concern with the wives. The wives and the kids. She'd get a kick out of seeing the kids. She'd watch them during the game from upstairs with her binoculars. She'd crack up. She'd tell us later. And she'd remember all the names of all the kids. She'd be at all the games."[45]

In August Carl Yastrzemski was inducted into the National Baseball Hall of Fame. Seated in the front row were Carl Sr. and Jean Yawkey.

In May 1990 the Jimmy Fund research labs were named in honor of Tom Yawkey. Permission to honor the Yawkey name began to become possible in a way it never had been when Tom Yawkey was still alive.

Jean Yawkey donated $1.5 million to the National Baseball Hall of Fame to expand the library in Cooperstown.

There had been fear of yet another work stoppage before the 1990 season. Fans were getting tired of the recurring uncertainty, and Peter Canellos of the *Boston Globe* even published an article about nationalizing baseball teams or perhaps having each team owned by a local municipal corporation and operated like a utility company, like the Green Bay Packers in football, a publicly owned nonprofit. Canellos concluded, "Magic this potent and this deep ought not have any keeper but the public. Baseball is simply too important to too many people to be left to the stewardship of the Steinbrenners, Seligs and Schotts."[46]

It was in 1990 that Dick Williams published his autobiography, *No More Mr. Nice Guy*, an amusing title since he had never been known to make nice with people. Williams talked to Gerry Callahan of the *Boston Herald* about how much he had loved Boston and how "devastated" he had been when Tom Yawkey "decided on another steam-bath buddy for the job." He also had some unkind things to say about Haywood Sullivan, calling him an "office flunky," "head rat," and "Yawkey's bobo." Dick O'Connell, on the other hand, was "the best general manager I ever worked for." It was O'Connell who was left to fire him, not Yawkey. "I guess he had a full schedule and had to be somewhere sometime," he said to Callahan with heavy sarcasm. "The team was his little toy. Mr. Yawkey was playing with his toy and it broke. And that was it."[47]

The 1990 Red Sox made the postseason once again, finishing in first place again as they had in 1986 and 1988. The Sox had been swept in four games in the ALCS by Oakland in 1988. History repeated itself; the same thing happened again in 1990: the Sox were swept by Oakland. This time the Red Sox scored only four runs in four games, one run in each of the four.

After the ALCS, the Red Sox released Dwight Evans. In a way, it marked the end of the Tom Yawkey era, since Evans was the last player who had been on a Tom Yawkey–owned team.

By a 12–0 vote, the board of directors for the Hall of Fame voted in February 1991 that anyone on baseball's ineligible list would be excluded from the Hall; the vote kept Pete Rose from being considered for inclusion. Jean Yawkey had been a director since 1984; she was one of four directors not present and thus not voting. A display, *Women in Baseball,* that opened that year featured her. She donated two wings to the Hall, and was also the one to finance and present a large wooden statue of Ted Williams by Armand LaMontagne; visitors pass it on their way into the Hall.[48]

The amateur baseball Boston Junior Park League changed its name in February with Jean Yawkey's permission; it was henceforth the Thomas A. Yawkey Baseball League. She was no doubt pleased. She had always remained loyal to the memory of Tom Yawkey.

Senior vice president for Fenway affairs Larry Cancro began working for the Red Sox in 1985, so he never knew Tom Yawkey.

She [Jean] was devoted to him [Tom] from the time I met her to the end of her life, and I would imagine, based on the stories she told, that she was devoted to him from the time of their marriage to the end of her life. She was one of the most wonderful people I've ever met. I was twenty-nine. She was like this wonderful woman that you didn't want to let down. She'd come by and pat you and tell you she loved something that you were doing; it was sort of like working for your grandmother.[49]

Cancro was in sales and marketing, and one of the first things Jean Yawkey asked him to do was organize an event to thank those employees who had worked for the Red Sox for thirty years or more. "What became clear was that the thirty-year employees were half the staff! And she wanted to have a different gift for the people who were thirty years or more, forty years or more, fifty years or more, and sixty years or more. And we actually had those! It was kind of amazing." And then she told him, "My one worry is that you're going to work too hard, and I want you and your wife to have a good time."[50]

On February 8, 1991, Roger Clemens signed a $21.5 million four-year contract extension, making him at the time the highest-paid player in baseball history. The negotiations had taken time but wrapped up before spring training began. As the best pitcher the Red Sox had had for at least a generation, Clemens seemed to have leverage, and some resented it. Gerry Callahan of the *Herald* wrote, "The Red Sox treated him as if he were holding Jean Yawkey for ransom. Some of Clemens' more devout supporters pleaded with the Sox to give the Rocket a blank check, and it seems they did just that."[51]

Jean Yawkey herself retained some humor about the astronomical salaries being paid in baseball. Sportswriter Bob Holbrook wrote about 1991:

We were at the park last summer. We took a group of about 30–40 kids from the Yawkey League out onto the field. We asked her [Jean] to throw out the first ball. She said there was no way she could reach home plate. We told her just put the ball into this pitching machine and it will throw it up to the plate. Someone revved the machine up to about 90 miles an hour and it goes like a bullet to home plate. Mrs.

Yawkey turned around and said, "If I could throw like that, it would cost the Red Sox about $29 million a year."[52]

In March John Harrington—in Fort Myers—let it be known the city was the front-runner for the next spring training home of the Red Sox. Winter Haven hadn't stepped up to try and hold onto the team. Its eleventh-hour effort was "too little, too late."[53] The Sox spent lavishly during the 1990–91 off-season, to the point they apparently angered other teams in the league. There was a sense that Jean Yawkey quite understandably wanted to see the Red Sox win it all while she was still around.

One might think that by 1991 racial issues would have subsided substantially, but the 1991 Red Sox drew a few raised eyebrows with Mo Vaughn and Ellis Burks the only black players on the team. The ball club was indeed making progress in hiring, but for black fans going to the ballpark, it could still be an uncomfortable experience, as a three-part *Boston Globe* series in August pointed out.[54]

The 1991 team finished in second place, tied with the Tigers at 84-78, both of them behind the Blue Jays by seven games. There was no wild card at the time, so when they played the last game of the regular schedule on October 6, that was that. Joe Morgan was fired as manager, replaced by Butch Hobson. Morgan had brought them in first two times, third in 1987, and second in 1991, but that wasn't good enough. Haywood Sullivan said that the owners were united on the change and that they felt they had to promote Hobson to prevent another team from snapping him up. And there had been disagreements between Morgan and Lou Gorman.

24

The Passing of Jean Yawkey

THOUGH IN FAILING health, Jean Yawkey had faithfully attended games right through the 1991 season. Her last reported act of charity was to donate a new van to Boston Food Bank's Second Helping program to deliver leftover food from area restaurants to organizations feeding the homeless.[1] On February 20, 1992, the eighty-three-year-old Mrs. Yawkey had not picked up the newspaper outside the door to her condominium at the Four Seasons. Hotel security checked on her; she had suffered a stroke and was rushed to Massachusetts General Hospital (MGH). She arrived at MGH at 5:36 p.m. in a semiconscious state.

It was Robin Brown of the Four Seasons who found Jean in her residence.

> I had a visit from the director of security at the hotel. He said to me, "Jean Yawkey's newspaper is still outside her apartment, from this morning and from the morning before. What should we do?" I said, "Let's go. We'll just go up." So we went up, and we found her there in the unit. . . . She was breathing but not in good shape at all. And her home was very humble, by the way. She was in the kitchen. Clearly she had been up and dressed. It looked like she may have been getting breakfast and had had some sort of stroke or heart attack.
>
> I had my phone and I called John [Harrington]'s cell. He picked up, and I said, "John, it's important. Where are you?" He said, "I'm just in front of Mugar Way. I just came from the airport. Just landed and I'm in my car. I'm on Storrow." I'm in her unit, looking out the window to where he is. I said, "John, there's an ambulance on the way. Come

to the Four Seasons and pull into the loading dock." He got there as we came down with Jean. He and I rode in the front seat together to Mass General. She never recovered.[2]

Jean was "conscious and partially alert" when John Harrington visited her the next day, though with some "partial paralysis" on her left side, but her condition rather quickly worsened over the next few days. She died at 2:30 in the afternoon on February 26.

Tributes, of course, flowed in. Among them was one from Yaz in which he remembered the care Jean had shown when his own mother was dying of cancer. "It was never a player-owner relationship," he said.[3] Longtime Red Sox pitcher and scout Charlie Wagner said, "Mr. Yawkey and Mrs. Yawkey were both born out of the same clip. The heart of the man and the heart of the woman were the same."[4]

Jean had "cut a quiet, mysterious and almost fragile presence at the ballpark that belied her position as one of the most powerful women in baseball history. By no means a figurehead, she had closely watched her ballclub from behind tinted glasses, and kept a strong hand in its operation."[5] Since she had arrived in Boston, she never granted an interview to the press, according to the *Herald*. She attended almost every game; she "chain-smoked, sipped martinis, kept a scorebook and without a trace of flamboyance kept alive an aura that her husband had started in 1933." As David Cataneo put it, the Yawkeys had run the Red Sox since the early days of FDR's administration.[6] Indeed Jean Yawkey truly loved the game. She religiously kept a scorebook at Red Sox games. She kept her focus on the play on the field. "There was no conversation," said Mary Jane Ryan.[7]

To while away the time at home, Jean often did needlepoint. When she had sold Mt. Pleasant, "all her furniture, all her needlepoint, she just left it behind. She gave a few things to a few people but just left everything else behind. Material things weren't important to her. And I don't think they were important to Tom, either."[8] "Beautiful needlepoint," says Bill Gutfarb. "She made a big one for my children; it was like a big Pinocchio-type scene. She made Christmas stockings for them too."[9]

Jean gave Mary Jane Ryan several pillows she'd made and even a pocketbook or two. "She loved pocketbooks. She loved to buy pocketbooks." Ryan showed the author a necklace she had on at the time of the interview. "Mrs. Yawkey gave me this when the pope came. He came here in 1979. Boston Common. He said a Mass. Wasn't that thoughtful? She was a very thoughtful woman. There are so many things they did that you will never know."[10] When Ryan purchased a condo in Arlington, Jean Yawkey asked if she was "okay" to buy the place, basically asking if she would be strapped financially. "She probably would have loaned me the money," Ryan says, but her response was simply to say, yes, she was okay.

Jean Yawkey also painted, and at Tara Hall today one of her paintings graces a wall. It depicts a Red Sox cap and a baseball on a field of green grass. Her choice of subject matter attests to her love of baseball.

Red Sox backup catcher John Marzano may have offered one of the nicer appreciations, he being a bit player and not a star. "It's really sad, she was such a good person. . . . Everybody on the team will miss her. Here I am a guy who plays once a week, and every time she'd see me she'd say, 'John, you're doing a great job keep up the good work.' She was always nice to me."[11]

Contrary to remarks that suggested Jean had left matters in disarray and uncertainty regarding the ongoing state of the ball club and the ultimate sale, Will McDonough of the *Boston Globe* said she was a very organized woman who had made the arrangements years earlier; they included a living will and advance league approval to permit a trust to operate the team until such time as a sale would be deemed beneficial.[12]

There was a private ceremony in Boston. Jean's ashes were spread over Winyah Bay in Georgetown.

What kind of woman had Jean been? Robin Brown says, "I saw a tremendous, humble, hilariously funny, direct, sharp, genuine, caring individual. And I saw an amazing relationship with her and John and Bill [Gutfarb] and a trust factor and a level of integrity. [In regard to] a lot of the press and a lot of the stories that came after, I would say to myself, 'This is all sort of nonsense.'" Hilariously funny? To many who saw her from the seats at Fenway, she seemed aloof and austere. Brown responds, "She said some things that I just couldn't believe. Off the record. . . . Some things that just made me howl."[13]

Former VP and team historian Dick Bresciani started working for the Red Sox in 1972, so he knew both Yawkeys.

> Tom was much more outgoing. "He would talk to everyone every day. He was never one to put on airs. Mrs. Yawkey was much more of a private person, but she had a great sense of humor. She really knew baseball. She would come to every home game unless she was very sick. And she would score the games; she didn't just watch the games. It took her longer than Tom to get to know you, but she was very concerned about everyone that worked for or was associated with the Red Sox. She knew that baseball was a business, but she also considered the Red Sox to be a family.[14]

Bresh (as he was widely known, though Tom Yawkey enjoyed calling him "Brush") recalled how kind and generous Jean had been when he and his wife were involved in a very serious accident on Cape Cod in 1987.

The only extensive profile ever published about Jean Yawkey was written in 1989 by Susan Trausch for the *Boston Globe.* Jean had never granted interviews, though she did talk with the media from time to time. In 1991 at one point she had reportedly "thought about doing a story, or writing a book, but in the end said, 'If I did it, I'd want to tell the truth. And If I did that, I would hurt some feelings and it might be upsetting to the organization, and I don't want that to happen.'"[15] Susan Trausch's 1989 article was the closest to a portrait of Jean Yawkey that we have.

Mary Jane Ryan felt that it wasn't that Mrs. Yawkey frequently fended off calls for interviews. Ryan doesn't recall anyone directly asking for an interview with Jean Yawkey, though Trausch has copies of her requests. Ryan allowed that perhaps those who wished to speak to Jean and were around the ballpark simply spoke to Bill Crowley or Dick Bresciani. "She'd shun all that stuff," Ryan said. "I think she was just shy. She probably just didn't think it was her place. But she knew what she wanted. She kept stuff to herself, but she let you know who was on her team. Of course she loved Haywood. Loved Sully."[16]

The Trausch article was a rather full 4,831-word portrait that twenty-five years later still holds up very well and seems to offer no false notes. It contrasts Jean Yawkey's reluctance to speak for public consumption ("She has hardly said a word on the record to anyone in 44 years") with her readiness to speak one-on-one with people when the occasion merited it. Bernard Carey, the executive director of the Massachusetts Association for Mental Health (the beneficiary of the May 1988 tribute to Jean Yawkey at Symphony Hall) said of her, "She was the first person there [at the benefit] and the last one to leave. She didn't care if you were the owner of a team or a little kid. The fact that you came was important to her. After it was over she was out talking to people on the sidewalk. She's known as reserved but her reserve has nothing to do with not caring about people. You touch the right chord in her and she lights up."[17]

Jean Yawkey's will was filed with the Suffolk County probate court on March 20. Her shares of the JRY Corporation were placed in the Jean R. Yawkey Trust, and votes would be in the hands of its sole remaining trustee, John Harrington. But it wasn't going to be that simple.

Within a couple of months after Jean's death, the drama regarding succession made it into the national news. "Red Sox Are the Subject of a Custody Battle" was the headline in the April 26, 1992, *New York Times*, which reported that "two of the many surrogate sons of the childless Mrs. Yawkey" were pitted against each other: Haywood Sullivan and John Harrington. Sullivan believed he had first option to buy the team, but he had said, "There's a hell of a lot of things we disagree on."[18] Harrington said he had no desire to buy the team but would sell it within two or three years on behalf of the charities it was intended to benefit. It was thought it might fetch $150 million. In November 1993 the JRY Corporation and Harrington bought out Sullivan for a reported $12 million.

In October 1993 Sunset Lodge, the former brothel in Georgetown County, South Carolina, burned to the ground. The story of Sunset Lodge is a fascinating one. Yawkey's connection to it may only have been the stuff of legend but is widely understood to be true. It is not likely to ever be documented.

Former Georgetown mayor Tom Rubillo said, "There doesn't seem to be any dispute that it was Yawkey who started it. He brought the madam, Hazel Weisse, up from Florence, and she set up the operation. She bought it. It was financed by Yawkey, and it was financed by Yawkey because he wanted a place to go. He had appetites."[19] The supposition as to motive is, of course, only that.

"Its story began in the mid-1930s when Tom Yawkey began wintering at this South Island Estate outside of Georgetown," wrote Bob Bestler in the *Myrtle Beach Sun News*. "He would take the train from Boston to Florence, then an automobile to South Beach. During his Florence stays, he became friendly with a Florence madam named Hazel Weiss."[20]

That there was a house of prostitution just outside the city limits on Highway 17 south of Georgetown is beyond dispute. The madam was Hazel Weisse, née Bennett, originally from Greenfield, Indiana. She had been born near Paoli on October 28, 1900. What her parents, John and Elizabeth, had done for a living was a question—literally; a "?" was entered on the 1900 census form in that column. It appears that she grew up near Sterling and lived in 1920 with her sister Leona and her husband, Thomas Grimes, a produce merchant.

Weisse had run a brothel in Florence, South Carolina, but it was closed in 1935 when new mayor D. E. Ellerbe was elected. (The 1930 U.S. census lists her as "proprietor, lodging house" on Commander Street in Florence. She had three lodgers—women between the ages of nineteen and twenty-one, no occupations stated.)

Charleston historian Jack Leland explained in a *Georgetown Times* column that when the International Paper Company began building a wharf in the mid-1930s to serve its paper mill, "a number of hunky steel workers from Pittsburgh were brought in to do all the steel work." They were a rowdy bunch, and on Saturdays women could not walk down Front Street "because these guys were propositioning women right in public."[21]

Weisse had been a schoolteacher and worked in a department store but found her way into other work, keeping a house. The timing was fortuitous. The city fathers in Georgetown were seeking a solution to channel the energies of some of the men on the city streets, and—perhaps reflecting the time and place—it was suggested they recruit a good madam. "Yawkey said he knew just the one," wrote Zane Wilson in the *Coastal Observer*.[22] How Yawkey may have come to know Hazel Weisse would be speculation, but the word was that he was impressed with her business acumen. It was also said that the house she took over had been owned by Annie B. Sisson, from whom Weisse bought it in 1936 for $2,700. Sisson was "the main bootlegger in the area in those Prohibition days," and she was pressured to sell to Weisse under threat of foreclosure of her property by some of the powers that were.[23]

Georgetown's Ralph M. Ford Jr. (whose parents hosted the Tom and Jean Yawkey wedding) wrote in 1989 that "Tom Yawkey did establish Sunset Lodge, but he certainly didn't finance it. Hazel was a shrewd business woman and made a fortune with the business. Sometimes a couple of the girls would visit him at South Island when the wives were away, and . . . he did take Jean there once, and it infuriated her."[24] Mr. Ford may have been prone to some exaggeration or fantasy.

The 1940 census described Weisse as "manager, tourist camp" on the Coastal Highway in Santee, Georgetown County. She had her sister Margaret Brown and two lodgers as helpers in the camp, as well as the Simmons family—Willie, a servant and laborer; his wife Rena as cook; and their three children.

Sunset Lodge became, according to the *Charleston Evening Post* in 1969, "perhaps the most widely known site in South Carolina, with the exception of Fort Sumter."[25] Indeed it was so well known that it was mentioned on late-night national network television. "When it closed, Johnny Carson made a comment about the sheriff at the time. The sheriff went over and raided the place and closed it down. He was shocked after forty years or so to hear that there was a brothel running in town." Carson reportedly called Sheriff Woodrow Carter "the meanest man in America."[26] Tom Rubillo blames the brothel for corruption in the area. Though it was outside the city limits, the sheriff had countywide jurisdiction, and Sheriff Carter no doubt benefited one way or another from tolerating the establishment. The main reason it closed was quite possibly because, as the sheriff explained at the time, Miss Hazel was getting too old to run it and simply asked him to shut it down.[27] Carter said that he had tolerated the business because "it was the common will of the people of Georgetown County to leave the business uninterrupted."[28]

Judge Alex Sanders provides a little more colorful story: "The political pressures of the religious zealots in the area caused the sheriff to have to close it. Nobody wanted to close it. He went out to Mr. Yawkey's plantation and sat with him and patiently explained to him why it had to be closed. That was the kind of deference he [Yawkey] was shown—[the sheriff] apologizing for closing his whorehouse."[29]

"Miss Hazel is our own United Way," said a nurse in the area, who worked to help with the abortions that inevitably proved necessary. "Mrs. Fogel of Fogels Department Store said of the business brought by the lodge and its workers, 'Oh, yes, them shopping with us. Miss Hazel and the girls shopping with us; why, they kept us in the black because they bought so many sheets.'"[30]

Mayor Rubillo adds:

People talk openly about how generous Hazel was, that she gave regularly to the hospital, and [there are] many stories about different individuals from the Sheriff's Office—her showing up with what was called the Christmas money for the deputies. And an employee of the Sheriff's Department was the one who was carrying the biological samples that they were taking on a regular basis up to the Health Department to have them checked so that they could come back with certificates from the Health Department saying that they had no sexually transmitted diseases. . . . It was very, very open and public. That cannot happen in the absence of official involvement. It cannot. It's impossible.[31]

Ralph Ford volunteered in 1989 that he was among the community leaders who used to exchange Christmas cards with Miss Hazel.[32]

One week each spring, Jack Leland recounted, "Hazel would close Sunset Lodge to the public and put a chain across the driveway. During that week, Sunset Lodge was available only to the members of the South Carolina General Assembly and to the Judiciary."[33]

Mary Julia S. Sargent wrote a letter to the editor of the *George-*

town Times explaining, "My aunts worked at the Sunset Lodge as their maids. The thing about it is that the family saw no wrong in it, or I never heard them say. They seemed to accept this way of life. I can remember going for a visit and the chauffeur who drove a yellow wood panel station wagon would pick them up and return them back home later that afternoon. I never heard the churches criticize this way of life or the job they had or the Sunset Lodge itself."[34]

Susan Trausch wrote, "This wasn't a case of a millionaire setting up his girlfriend [recalled one resident who asked not to be identified]. This was a well-run business, respected, if that's the right word. It was a lot like the place in the play 'Best Little Whorehouse in Texas.'" Trausch added, "Who knows what Elise must have thought about the place or what Jean Yawkey thought. 'I heard Tom Yawkey drove Jean there once and she was furious,' said one man. But he also said that Jean Yawkey was with her husband in whatever he did. Hard-drinking, known as 'a man's man,' tough . . . not the easiest guy to live with, but a person with the proverbial heart of gold. She understood all that."[35]

Jean Yawkey definitely knew about Sunset Lodge, said John Harrington in a 2013 interview:

> The whorehouse. We did talk about that with Jean and Ellie [Armstrong], and it was sort of humorous. Tom was a leader down in that community. He helped build a hospital. He wasn't aggressive. He didn't want to be a leader. These other guys were the leaders, and they would bring Tom in because he had the resources and the willingness to work on something.
>
> Back in the old days, they were building the steel mill and the paper mill. The police chief and everyone was concerned with all the construction workers coming into this little Georgetown village. What're we going to do? We're going to have all kinds of drunkenness and whatever. So somebody came up with the idea, well, what the town needs is a whorehouse to take care of the guys, the construction workers, for the couple of years that they are here. I think Tom was part of the collaboration to get a whorehouse going in Georgetown. I don't think Tom was the leader of a group, but I think he might have participated

in this effort while they were dealing with a lot of things regarding this influx of construction workers and keeping them out of trouble after work hours. It was as simple as that.

I would listen to Jean and Ellie talk about it. I've given you my version of it. Jean and Ellie would talk about it, and they referred to her [Hazel Weisse] somewhat respectfully as the leader of this business enterprise.[36]

An associate of Harrington's chipped in: "I remember she [Weisse] was generous with the local charities. Ellie's always said something about her being generous." Harrington concluded, "Knowing Cronin and those guys, I don't think women or parties were any part of their activity on the road in the old days. I think they did a man thing—cigars, alcohol, rough talk—but I don't think it was one of these things like 'Let's bring the girls up now' or anything."[37]

Phil Wilkinson said Yawkey had loaned Weisse the money to effect the move to Georgetown, and she had rapidly repaid it with interest. Was Yawkey himself just helping out a businesswoman he admired? Bettye Marsh Roberts and her first husband, Jack Marsh, came to know Weisse because Jack ran a taxi service and sometimes was asked to pick up the Sunset girls from South Island or even from Columbia. At Weisse's request, the Marshes purchased the Sunset Lodge property from Weisse and let her live in a garage apartment on the property for a couple of years.[38] Weisse died on July 22, 1974.[39]

Sunset Lodge was indeed at least as well known throughout Georgetown as it was elsewhere. The grandmother of Phil Wilkinson's wife, Libby, once told her something along the lines that it was useful to have a place like that because otherwise the men would be raping young girls. Libby thought that was a little far-fetched of course, but it is an indication of how the women spoke among themselves about the place. Everybody knew that it was there. That's perhaps how they rationalized the existence of something they couldn't do much about anyhow.[40]

Could it have been more complex? Ralph Ford Jr. told Ben Bradlee Jr. regarding Miss Hazel's birthday party each year, when everything was on the house, "There were doctors, lawyers, politicians.

The Social Register of Georgetown. Most of the men's wives knew. They were right proud to have their husbands invited, as I recall."[41]

Even as late as 2012, when this author visited Georgetown, people volunteered stories about Sunset Lodge without any prompting at all. Some of the stories were fanciful—for instance, one claimed that the entire Red Sox team would stop in as it traveled to or from spring training in Florida. It's conceivable that a player or two might have visited on the way to Florida, as individuals made their separate ways to spring training, but there was no possibility on the way back since the team had a schedule and barnstormed north.[42] It's unlikely that many happened in while heading to Florida. So far as we can determine, Tom Yawkey almost never entertained ballplayers in South Carolina after the 1930s.

Tom Rubillo acknowledged the following:

> There are interesting stories to hear. He [Yawkey] lived an interesting life. Like, we would hope, all human beings, one that was complicated. If all he did was go to church and sing psalms, you wouldn't be writing about him. I was a lawyer and used to tell people that if everybody behaved themselves, I'd actually have to do some work.
>
> [Even today] area moralists, public officials, and law enforcement have looked the other way as so-called "gentlemen's clubs" have littered the landscape, many being little more than brothels. Radio advertisements for them promise patron satisfaction.
>
> One of the questions that I have is what effect did those women—coming into town, parading around—what kind of role model was that for the young girls that were growing up here and what kind of message did that give the men around here about women and the role of women?

Balancing the scale, Rubillo added regarding Tom Yawkey:

> Yawkey did great stuff. I have a foster son whose name is Jonathan. Jonathan came from Tara Hall when he was six. Did Yawkey do good? He saved that child. He saved that child! Terrific.
>
> He saved all that land. I'll bet you if somebody took you out there in a helicopter blindfolded, took off in Boston and flew around forever and dropped you there, you would have no idea where on the

face of the earth you were. And you'd have to wait for sunrise or sunset to know which was east or west and whether that was the Atlantic or Pacific.

Those are great things.[43]

Rebecca T. Godwin, formerly from the Georgetown area and as of 2014 a professor of literature at Bennington College in Vermont, wrote a novel based on Sunset Lodge, *Keeper of the House.* In it a man from the north, given the name Waldo Carnelian, helped set up the madam, Miss Addie, at the fictional "sporting house" Hazelhedge in the fictional Jameston. Miss Addie, like Miss Hazel, had a background in French Lick, Indiana. Hazelhedge, like Sunset Lodge, closed in 1969. Had Godwin modeled Carnelian after Yawkey? She replied to an email:

> We all knew the stories about Yawkey, and I did interview a fishing and hunting guide who told me a few stories (he has since died). Other Georgetown folks—those who would have truly been in the know, including Sheriff Woodrow Carter, attorney James B. Moore, and banker Arthur Parsons . . .—simply would not speak to me about Sunset and how it was connected to the city and county and state. They have all since died. . . . My Yankee industrialist/Sunset benefactor [Carnelian] was a composite of stories I'd heard in my family. As with most of the novel, he came almost entirely from my imagination.[44]

Former sheriff Carter told a reporter from the *Boston Globe* in 1989, "I knew Tom Yawkey. He was one of the finest Yankees in this town."[45]

25

The Estate, 1994, and Beyond

AFTER JEAN YAWKEY'S estate went through probate, there was complaint from "two fuming nieces" of hers, Patricia Hollander and Jane Esopa. The *New York Post* reported their feeling that "John Harrington pulled a fast one in the final days of their aunt's life, isolating her from her family so that he could cut them out of her will."[1] Hollander suffered from Crohn's disease and said that in her final days, Jean Yawkey had sent her checks totaling $85,000 to cover her medical expenses, "but no more money came as Yawkey's millions went into a private trust under Harrington's control."[2]

Trustee Bill Gutfarb says, "We went by the terms of Mrs. Yawkey's estate plan. It was as simple as that. Mrs. Yawkey considered her wealth that of Tom's, in effect saying, 'This is Tom's money.' So it wasn't unusual that a great deal of Mrs. Yawkey's wealth would not have gone to her nieces. I recall her telling her future executors— John Harrington and me—'that [her] family knows that.'"[3]

In 1994 a players' strike didn't cause just a brief delay or interruption of the season, as it had in 1972 and in 1981. It brought about a sudden end to the season; no games at all were played after August 11. The season just ended. The strike accomplished something that even the Axis nations (Japan, Germany, and Italy) could not do during World War II: it prevented a World Series. The loss of the season may have finally prompted an end to work stoppages, but it was especially painful for the Montreal Expos, who had a solid lead in the NL East and were a good bet to get to their only postseason. It may have done in the franchise.

The start of the season was delayed in 1995. The Red Sox played their first game on April 26. They played only 144 games, not a full 162-game schedule. But Boston won 86 and finished in first place in the AL East, 7 games over the Yankees. For their third postseason in a row (after 1988 and 1990), though, the Red Sox were swept, failing to win even one game, this time thanks to the Cleveland Indians. The last game the Red Sox had won in postseason play was Game Five of the 1986 World Series. Since that time they had lost 13 consecutive postseason games.

In 1995 the Yawkey name rarely came up in the press. A flurry of Yawkey mentions appeared when, in September 1995, Jean R. Yawkey was inducted into the Red Sox Hall of Fame. Most of the press release announcing the induction was devoted to noting her charitable efforts, including her service as chairwoman of the board of the Jimmy Fund. She had been the only woman to serve as a director of the National Baseball Hall of Fame.

Like her husband, Jean Yawkey never sought publicity. An executive at the Yawkey Foundations notes that the Yawkeys did many things privately to help individuals. "The foundations as a whole don't send out press releases because they're private. They're not seeking publicity or extra attention. [For example,] one boy grew up on the Wildlife Center [in South Carolina], went to the navy, and then worked for the fire department in the area after he returned. He had a son who was deaf, and when Jean Yawkey heard about it, she got his son into a special needs school, paying for his education."[4]

After the season, GM Lou Gorman left his position and was replaced by Dan Duquette. (An aside: John Harrington had been very gracious to former GM Dick O'Connell. Tom Shaer says, "I thought it was very typical of John Harrington that he tried to right some wrongs, and he put Dick O'Connell into the Red Sox Hall of Fame after Mrs. Yawkey passed away. I remember O'Connell was a guest of the club at the '99 All-Star Game, and that was the first that I had seen him for sixteen years. I thought that was great, that they were bringing him back.")[5]

In April 1998 to help set the groundwork for a more lucrative transition from Yawkey Trust ownership to the sale of the team, there was the announcement that plans were under way to build a new Fenway Park nearby and replace the old 1912 structure. In response, an ardent group of preservationists coalesced in opposition and in August 1998 formed Save Fenway Park! The plans for the new park—across the street from Fenway—were announced on May 14, 1999, and John Harrington wrote an article for the *Boston Globe* that ran the very next day.

As it happened, the ball club was not sold for ten years after Jean Yawkey's death, provoking charges that Harrington enjoyed running it so much that he was reluctant to sell. In early 1999 the criticism (including a very extensive *Boston Herald* article) had reached a point that Harrington felt he needed to respond, and he did so in a six-page statement in which he strongly denied he had favored personal causes of his own in the Yawkey Foundations' charitable giving.[6] Will McDonough suggested that the negative stories were intended to torpedo Harrington's plans for a replacement Fenway Park.

The office of Massachusetts attorney general Thomas Reilly looked into the allegations and on June 4 concluded, "We looked into the Yawkey trusts very carefully and Mr. Harrington and the other trustees have not done anything wrong at all. We found they were acting in accordance with the wishes of Mr. and Mrs. Yawkey and have operated well within the legal parameters. We found absolutely nothing inappropriate."[7]

The ballpark was expected to cost around $545 million, and the Red Sox selected Fleet Bank to try and line up private financing to build the new facility. The sense was that Harrington wanted to either get the ballpark built or get planning and funds secured and then sell the team for maximum revenue. It was understood he would be looking for up to $200 million in public funds for improvements in the Fenway area (such as a new exit ramp from the Mass Pike) but that the money for the park itself would be raised privately. Some of the public money would be used for better mass transit, including an upgrade to Yawkey Station. The idea was not without precedent. The New England Patriots had received $70 million for infrastructure improvements for their forthcoming new stadium in Foxborough (now Gillette Stadium). The Red Sox planned to get revenue from two new parking garages in the area, an increase of ten thousand seats in the new facility, many more luxury suites, seat licenses, and naming rights. The new park might well be named "Fleet Bank Field" or something other than "Fenway Park."

The Red Sox were proving to be a winning team in 1999. They had finished second in 1998 and finally won a game in the playoffs. They had faced the Cleveland Indians and won the first game with ease (11–3, behind Pedro Martinez) but then lost the next three. In 1999 they faced off against the Indians once more in the best-of-five division series and dropped the first two. They'd started another streak of five consecutive losses in the playoffs (making it seventeen losses in eighteen games), but they rallied and won three games in a row to send them into the ALCS. They had scored forty-four runs in the three wins.

Unfortunately when the Sox hit the ALCS, it was against the Yankees, and they won just one of the five games, a 13–1 win at Fenway, Pedro Martinez beating ex-Sox star Roger Clemens, now with New York. Boston scored only a combined eight runs in the other four games.

Most of the media seemed not to question the need for a new park, many buying the line that the current Fenway Park could not possibly be upgraded or saved.[8] But local political figures, such as House Speaker Thomas Finneran, weren't too forthcoming with public funds. State legislation to provide for infrastructure improvements in the area was contingent on the ball club itself taking care of land acquisition and cleanup. The Kenmore-Fenway area was already showing signs of revival, which would tend to drive up land costs. By the end of 2000, some of the limited partners began to suggest alternative sites in Greater Boston, such as two different sites in Somerville and possibly the area of Suffolk Downs, where land acquisition would be far cheaper. Higher costs would naturally produce a greater burden of debt. And, as Meg Vaillancourt noted in the *Globe*, "Financial analysts have said that the Yawkey Trust cannot place all its assets at risk to guarantee payment of cost overruns."[9]

On October 6, 2000, John Harrington announced that the Yawkey Trust was selling its 53 percent controlling interest in the ball club.

"The team is in strong financial shape; we've had record-breaking attendance this year; we got a ballpark bill passed on Beacon Hill with $312 million in public aid; and the economy is booming," Harrington said. "It's the right time to sell."[10]

Some felt that Harrington's decision to sell reflected uncertainty on the prospects for building the New Fenway, that there were too many obstacles for him to want to overcome them on his own. Dan Wilson, one of the leaders of Save Fenway Park!, called it "an admission that this ball park project is an awful lot more difficult than the Red Sox had initially anticipated." Likewise, Philip Cronin, described as an eminent domain attorney and valuation specialist at Peabody and Arnold, called Harrington's announcement "an admission of defeat" regarding the new park. "The requirement that the owners pay for any overruns on site costs represents 'a huge uncertainty,' Cronin said, that makes securing financing difficult if not impossible."[11]

The next day, Harrington said, his phone immediately started ringing off the hook with potential buyers. One group looking to purchase included Tom Werner and Les Otten, who said in June 2000 that they were studying the possibility of rebuilding Fenway in place, obviating the need for the acquisition of ten or more acres of land.

Unfortunately a number of discouraging things happened to the team late in the 2001 season—even aside from the national trauma provoked by the terror attacks on 9/11. The ballclub fell apart, manager Jimy Williams was fired, interim manager Joe Kerrigan seemed unable to control his players or inspire anything approaching confidence, and in early November the team and former Sox clubhouse manager Donald J. Fitzpatrick were sued by seven former "clubhouse aides" claiming sexual abuse over a twenty-year period. The suit alleged the Sox knew that Fitzpatrick "was committing improper sexual acts on male black children" while he was with the team but did nothing to stop him. "This represents the epitome of corporate irresponsibility," said the suing attorney. The suit was settled on May 28, 2003. Another man, not a party to the lawsuit, later wrote a book regarding his own experiences with Fitzpatrick, *Predator on the Diamond*.[12] And in 2012, ten more people claiming they had been victimized came forward.[13]

The bidding for the rights to the Red Sox continued, a lengthy process that we don't wish to dwell on here. A local group headed by Joe O'Donnell seemed to be the sentimental favorite; Major League Baseball seemed to favor a group headed by John W. Henry of the Florida Marlins. An effort to combine the two groups faltered and then failed over the matter of who would be in control, and on December 20, 2001, O'Donnell and his group withdrew their offer. Tom Werner had joined forces with John W. Henry and late that same night, the Henry-Werner group, with Larry Lucchino, emerged as the winners, with a bid said to be $700 million, more than twice the amount ever paid for any other team. When the notion of a sale was first announced in 1992, it was thought the club might attract offers of around $150 million, so one would be hard-pressed to argue that Harrington's stewardship in the interim had not resulted in tremendous benefit to the Yawkey Foundations and the charities they help fund. The amount going to the Yawkey Foundations was understood to be $420 million.[14]

The Yawkey Foundations hold some interests in land as well. In West Virginia there is even a town called Yawkey, an unincorporated community in eastern Lincoln County. The foundations benefit from income accruing from a number of leases of land in West Virginia—for coal and gas, for mineral rights and the like, on thousands of acres. Some of the leases go back decades. "They [the foundations] didn't think they had the expertise to manage it, so they leased the land out. We have an engineering firm in West Virginia that acts as our consultant. Some [leases] go back to the earlier part of the twentieth century. They've been passed from company to company through mergers and acquisitions and sales. That's the extent of it. To my knowledge, there have been no actual operating companies."[15] There used to be lands in Canada, Georgia, Minnesota, and elsewhere, and as we have seen, the family had land when Tom was a child in northern Michigan, Wisconsin, and Oregon. Another branch of the Yawkey family is reflected in the Leigh Yawkey Woodson Art Museum in Wausau, Wisconsin. One assumes that various properties were sold or otherwise disposed of over the years. As we have seen, Tom Yawkey had given some of the holdings to the Gardners: "Before he died, much of it he shared with his sister's children," says Gutfarb.[16]

The New York office had been staffed with mining experts or lumber experts, not just land managers.

> Yes, [says Gutfarb], "and [the office] also had people who were bond analysts and stock analysts. They had an office manual that said what days they did what. They went to the vault in the . . . bank . . . and . . . they clipped coupons. Everything was within their control; it wasn't sent out to custodians or money managers until the early 1970s. Then relationships with money management firms were established at that point, and I guess the coupon clipping stopped.
>
> The Yawkeys—from what we were told by a fellow named Sigfus Olefson, who was their land man in the late '20s until he retired, probably in the '60s—would invest one-third in stocks, one-third in bonds, and one-third in natural resources. You notice I didn't mention the Red Sox. Apparently the Red Sox at the time—as with almost any sports franchise in those days—were more or less like a yacht. Nowadays things are different. Now it would really be an equity.[17]

Clipping coupons was reflective of an earlier style, what Gutfarb called "accounting by hand."

Although the limited partners accepted the Henry-Werner-Lucchino bid for the Red Sox, it wasn't that simple. Cablevision magnate Charles Dolan presented a somewhat higher late bid. New York attorney Miles Prentice said he would pay even more—$790 million.[18] Massachusetts attorney general Reilly believed the limited partners (and MLB) had accepted a lower bid and that it was his duty to ensure that charitable entities in the Commonwealth of Massachusetts benefited as much as possible from the sale. He said it was "clear that Major League Baseball, and particularly the commissioner's office, played a major role in deciding who the next owner of the Red Sox would be. It's just another example of how they operate. It's a club. That's what it is. They get the benefit of the exemption from antitrust. When you see how they operate, it's not a pretty sight."[19] It was also understood that Reilly was quite close to a locally based group that had been hoping to buy the team, so his public stance may have both looked good politically and reflected some personal allegiances.

Dolan's late bid was reportedly for $750 million, but both MLB and Commissioner Bud Selig were satisfied with the Henry-Werner-Lucchino bid, and they gave their final approval on January 16, 2002. It is bizarre that for a period of time, because the transactions were not affected simultaneously, John Henry continued to own parts of three clubs—the Sox, the Florida Marlins, and a 1 percent share of the New York Yankees. The Yankees abstained from the January 2002 vote of approval because of the minor conflict. All the deals were intended to be consummated before the final closing.

John Henry called Fenway "the Mecca of baseball," adding, "When I think of Paris, I think of the Eiffel Tower. When I think of Boston, I think of Fenway." Larry Lucchino said the Sox planned to renovate and expand Fenway Park. John Harrington said the Yawkeys would have been "very pleased" with the new ownership.[20] Dick Johnson mused: "I think he [Yawkey] and John Henry would have really hit it off because I think in his own way Yawkey was a pretty intelligent guy, as low-key as he was; he went to Yale and everything. He was not someone whose ego was out of check. And he was passionate about owning the team. The story about him and Jean sitting on a blanket in the outfield listening to road games on the radio and having a picnic is quite charming. You could almost see that as the start of a movie about him."[21]

There were cries of "foul," intimating that Commissioner Selig had prevailed upon Harrington and steered the sale to a couple of Selig's cronies. Attorney General Reilly promised to scrutinize the sale, to see if the charities would receive the maximum amount.[22] On January 2, 2002, Reilly said it was clear to him that MLB had played a part in steering the sale, that some people were going to be acceptable to the organization and others would not. On January 10 he told Brian McGrory of the *Globe*, "This was a bag job. I don't care who the next owner is. I don't care. I do care whether the charities were treated fairly and received full value, and I don't believe they did."[23]

The attorney general himself essentially got into negotiations with the Red Sox, and on January 16 he "reached a last-minute deal giving the Yawkey Trust $10 million more for its controlling stake in the team. As a result, the trust and its charitable foundation will receive a total of $420 million. The agreement also calls for Henry's group to fund a separate charity, which will be called The New Boston Red Sox Foundation, that will grow over 10 years to at least $20 million."[24] Reilly may have been grandstanding, but in the end it appeared that negotiations may have resulted in some extra millions going to charities. Reilly claimed he had also insisted on expanding the size of the board so that it would become more inclusive of other voices from the community.

As it happens, the Henry-led ownership group went far beyond the minimums called for in the agreement. The Red Sox Foundation blew past the $20 million figure; through 2015 the foundation had already raised—and distributed—more than $80 million.

On February 27, 2002, the final sale occurred, and for the first time since 1933, no one named Yawkey was an owner of the Red Sox. The Yawkey name, of course, lives on in many other places and remains honored at Fenway Park and in Red Sox history.

Within one year, both Dick O'Connell (August 2002) and Haywood Sullivan (February 2003) died.

As for the Yawkey Foundations, the $420 million received vaulted them into the major leagues of New England–based foundations.[25]

John Harrington became chairman of the Yawkey Foundations. He had once said, "If I'm ever lucky enough to meet with Jean and Tom again someday, I want to be able to say we did what they wanted. That we passed on to the next owners the Yawkey tradition of a highly competitive team that's inspired the most loyal fans in baseball and over nearly 70 years has generated a unique bond with this community. Tom and Jean set the gold standard that all future owners—as I have—will strive to maintain."[26] Harrington's father had worked repairing buses for what became the MBTA. His mother had worked as a domestic. Boston advertising and civic leader Jack Connors said of Harrington in 2001, "After all he's done already, he gets to spend the rest of his life giving money to needy causes. How's that?"[27]

The giving started within days, and in May the Yawkey Foundations "bestowed the largest gift in [their] history, donating $25 million to Massachusetts General Hospital for a 10-story outpatient treatment center."[28]

It was a little odd, but Attorney General Reilly seemed almost to complain that the Yawkey Foundations were becoming *too* generous. He specifically objected to the Mass General gift, saying, "It was handled in a secretive, clandestine manner, not in the way a foundation of this sort should be handling things. It is undisciplined. They are spending money like drunken sailors. It is unworthy of a foundation to act in this way."[29] He objected that the "gift to such a well-endowed institution went against earlier assurances that the foundation would focus its generosity on grass-roots organizations."[30]

Reilly appeared to be holding the Yawkey Foundations to higher standards than other foundations, but other than John Harrington's terming the "drunken sailors" remark an insult, no one objected publicly. An April 2002 grant of $15 million to Boston College (BC) raised further scrutiny since four of the trustees had ties to BC and Harrington himself had earned two degrees there and seen his children attend the college. Those trustees had recused themselves from the vote, however, and all agreed to tighten conflict-of-interest rules.[31] From that point forward, there had been little indication of any problems until a lengthy feature by Bob Hohler in the February 12, 2017, *Boston Globe* raised questions about the compensation and tenure of foundation trustees and a pattern of grants going to institutions that appeared to have personal connections to trustees.[32]

And all was well on the field of play. The Red Sox barely missed making the World Series in 2003 (we won't go into that here), and then—in historic, even legendary, fashion—won the World Series in 2004 (which we'd be glad to dwell on—but this is not the place).[33] Then they won the World Series again in 2007. And again in 2013.[34] One can be quite sure that if John Harrington were to meet Tom and Jean Yawkey again someday, all three could marvel at the three championships in ten years.

Was it ironic that all the winning began almost immediately after the team entered the post-Yawkey years? Perhaps. Had there been a curse on the Yawkeys, as well as on the team, dating back to Harry Frazee? Unlikely. Things happen or don't happen. GM Dan Duquette played a very large part in building the team that won in 2004, but it was GM Theo Epstein who received all the lionization, including, among other things, a cover story in *Boston* magazine.

The Red Sox not only won championships, but they also saved and preserved Fenway Park, the team owners pouring an estimated $270 million into renovations over their first ten years on the job—endeavors that took them right through the one hundredth anniversary celebration of Fenway's 1912 opening. Tom Yawkey would probably have been disappointed in the signs on the Green Monster—indeed the prevalence of advertising all over the interior of the park—but he was also a businessman and could well have understood the dramatically changed economics of what had now become a baseball industry. He certainly would have instantly recognized Fenway Park and been pleased that the successor owners had lived up to their initial promises to be stewards of what they had acquired, rather than ripping down the ballpark, in part to put their own stamp on things.

Meanwhile, the Yawkey money was being put to work. During October 2004, Mass General opened the facility known as the Yawkey Center for Outpatient Care. The Red Sox Foundation too had by the close of 2004 already disbursed its first $7.5 million.[35]

26

The Yawkey Legacy

IF YOU TRAVEL around Boston, you will see the Yawkey name on a number of buildings or gracing a number of charitable programs. If you spend even a day or two driving around Georgetown, South Carolina, you are likely to come across the Yawkey Medical Park. You would not just run into the Tom Yawkey Wildlife Center, but, of course, that's part of the point: it's reserved for wildlife. "Composed of 31 square miles of marsh, managed wetlands, forest openings, ocean beach, longleaf pine forest and maritime forest, the preserve is principally dedicated as a wildlife preserve, research area and waterfowl refuge."[1]

If you visit a medical facility in the Boston area, there's a good chance you'll spot the Yawkey name. Massachusetts General Hospital has the ten-story Yawkey Center for Outpatient Care, which houses the MGH Cancer Center, the Cardiovascular Program, the Mass General Hospital for Children, the Musculoskeletal Program, and the MGH Women's Health Program. A $25 million commitment from the Yawkey Foundations provided the beginnings of the $180 million center, which opened in 2004. Boston Medical Center has the Yawkey Ambulatory Care Center, a multistory structure on Harrison Avenue. And at the Dana-Farber Cancer Institute, there is the fourteen-story Yawkey Center for Cancer Care.

Also in the city, one finds the Yawkey Center for Children and Learning at Boston's Children's Museum. Boston College has the Yawkey Athletics Center, a large $27 million, seventy-two-thousand-square-foot facility. In Dorchester there is the Yawkey Konbit Kreyol Head Start Center, a preschool based in one of Boston's disadvantaged neighborhoods. Less than a mile from Fenway Park, Emmanuel College has the Jean Yawkey Center—a student center, dining hall, and gym and fitness center all rolled into one facility. In Marlborough there is the Yawkey Sports Training Center, the official headquarters of Special Olympics Massachusetts.

The Yawkey name does not appear in these institutions by accident or as a sentimental tribute, as is the case with the renaming of seemingly at least one street in every Massachusetts city and town after assassinated president John F. Kennedy. The naming reflects Yawkey largesse, the tens of millions of dollars that are being dispensed on an ongoing basis by the Yawkey Foundations. Massachusetts law requires any foundation to disburse five percent of its assets each year.

There has been some ongoing negative reaction to the Yawkey name's appearing on public facilities such as Yawkey Station on the MBTA commuter rail line and Yawkey Way itself. In late 2015 Adrian Walker wrote a column in the *Boston Globe* in which he suggested that Yawkey Way be renamed. "It's past time for that ill-fitting tribute to go," he claimed, adding that it would be fun to consider others for whom the street could be named—perhaps Pumpsie Green or Pedro Martinez. He settled on naming it after Ted Williams, apparently unaware that the more or less parallel street known as Lansdowne Street is already officially named Ted Williams Way.[2] A flurry of other articles followed over the next several weeks.[3] The *Globe* itself had not been the first business in Boston to integrate. When it hired Larry Whiteside in 1973, he was the first African American beat writer in its sports department. The matter keeps cropping up because race remains a subject of great concern in America. We need to recognize that for some, the Yawkey name will never be unsullied. Though the Yawkeys themselves the trustees of the Yawkey Foundations have worked hard to build another legacy and continued that mission, forgiving and forgetting may never be possible for those most incensed by the fact that the Red Sox were the last team to desegregate.

In September 2014 another building began to bear the Yawkey name: Boston University's Yawkey Center for Student Services, at 100 Bay State Road, a few blocks from Fenway Park. The Yawkey

Foundations had awarded BU $10 million, enabling the university to endow a program that would, beginning in the spring of 2016, provide about one hundred students, or "Yawkey Scholars," with paid internships each year at nonprofit organizations that lacked the resources to compensate interns themselves. Should each of these students intern at a different nonprofit, one hundred nonprofits each year would reap the benefits.[4]

Tom Yawkey himself was personally generous, as we have seen in, for instance, his helping endow Georgetown Hospital and paying for the education and the medical and dental care of his employees. Jean Yawkey joined in the effort, taking more of a leading role with Tara Hall and other charities.[5] Even in the last full year of her life, 1991, when the Atlanta Braves had made it to the National League Championship Series for the first time in nearly a decade, Jean Yawkey made arrangements to have the forty boys at Tara Hall bused to Atlanta for one of the playoff games and then—with her typical touch—gave them each $25 in spending money to use at the stadium. Later that year she came to visit them over Christmastime.[6] When Tom Yawkey was alive, only one place was known to bear the Yawkey name: the Tara Hall dormitory named Yawkey House. Father O'Sullivan later said, "When I said I wanted to name it after him, he protested something fierce. He didn't want anyone to know what he had done. I never knew a man who did so much for others and wanted so little in return. . . . He took a real interest in all the boys here, all 28 of them. He knew their names, every one, and he talked to them and was interested in them."[7] Tom Yawkey said, "Even if only four or five out of twenty boys go straight because of what we're doing, it's worth all the work and money. This is the only chance these boys have. If we fail them, they'll have nothing. Their lives will be ruined before they even grow up."[8]

Donating these vast sums may have all been a matter of noblesse oblige, but the donations were very real nonetheless and of great benefit over the years to many thousands of direct and indirect recipients.

Yawkey Foundations grants awarded from July 1, 2002, through December 31, 2015, totaled $418 million. The donations break down into several broad categories:

Health care—25 percent

Education—24 percent

Human services—18 percent

Youth and amateur athletics—17 percent

Arts and culture—8 percent

Conservation and wildlife—8 percent

A look at the recipients and the amounts donated leaves one certain that many of the recipients could not adequately fulfill their mission without the generous support of the Yawkey Foundations.[9]

The young Tom Yawkey carried the idea of giving back from his childhood. One of the numerous stories published in 1919, when the young Yawkey inherited the bulk of his wealth from his adoptive father (William Hoover Yawkey), ran in the *New York Tribune*: "Lad of 16, Heir to a Fortune of $20,000,000, Happy on $1 a Week." Young Tom was quoted as saying, "There is something I am interested in. Father mentioned it in his will. He spoke of some permanent charity—some living memorial under the Yawkey name."[10]

The Yawkey Foundations endeavor to further causes they believe Tom and Jean Yawkey would have wanted to support. After the announcement of a recurring $25,000 grant to the American Red Cross of the Cape, Islands and Southeast Massachusetts, Judy Walden Scarafile, trustee with the Yawkey Foundations, said in December 2015, "As a volunteer with the Red Cross I have seen firsthand how important it is to support the work of the volunteers who aid in disasters, especially local devastating events that affect our community. The Yawkey Foundations' grant supports this mission. It is always nice to remember that strong connection since Jean Yawkey was a Red Cross volunteer in the 1940s. So ultimately this grant further supports her good work."[11]

The *Globe*'s Bob Hohler started a 2005 article, "The 2002 sale of the Red Sox turned into the greatest boon for charities in the history of New England sports philanthropy."[12]

Though the Yawkeys often made wholly anonymous donations and eschewed having their names on edifices during Tom's lifetime, Jean reluctantly began to allow Tom's name to appear on a Jimmy Fund building and one or two other places. Former Red Sox employee Mary Jane Ryan was certain her old boss would have been pleased: "I think he'd get a kick out of Yawkey Way. I know he would. And now Yawkey Station. He'd like that. Definitely."[13]

The Yawkeys' insistence on anonymity resulted in some amusing experiences for Larry Cancro: "When I first got here in '85, I would go and talk to different charities about the charitable component in marketing deals, and I would say something nice about the team so that they would know we would be a good partner for their charity. And they would say, 'Oh, we know. The Yawkeys have been our largest contributor for many years. But it's with the condition that we not mention it. I'm just telling you because I presume you would know.' Cancro found it difficult to get Jean Yawkey to take any public credit. She told him, "Larry, you do the right thing because it's the right thing. You don't do the right thing to publicize it. You never wear your pride on your sleeve. It's just not becoming."[14]

All the philanthropy couldn't heal some wounds, however. The Yawkey Foundations gave $3 million to the Boys and Girls Clubs of Boston to help renovate a facility in Roxbury, a Boston community with a large percentage of African Americans. Some local political leaders objected, asking for a meeting "to discuss ways to honor the Yawkeys' generosity while being sensitive to the pain associated with the Yawkey name in the neighborhood." Others in the community took another view: "As a child, I hated the Red Sox because of the racism that was going on," said Brad Howard, an administrator at a local high school and a lifelong Bostonian whose two children used the center. "Tom Yawkey may have been a racist, but his family has made strides in terms of trying to clear up their name. . . . I'm not saying things are great, just that times have changed and people are holding on to things they don't need to hold on to."[15]

27

Tom Yawkey and Race

IN AN APPRAISAL of Tom Yawkey's life, it seems unavoidable that we revisit the question of Yawkey and race. This issue keeps cropping up, turning up like the proverbial bad penny. Had Tom Yawkey been a racist? There appears to be no conclusive evidence one way or another. It remains an inescapable fact that the Red Sox were the last Major League team to field a black ballplayer. As sole owner of the Red Sox, Yawkey had the opportunity—for many years—to take even a symbolic step toward desegregation. He could have done so during World War II, building on the fact that black soldiers were giving their lives to defend America. He could have brought in one, two, or more talented black ballplayers and forged a historic pioneering role for himself and the Red Sox.

Boston was, after all, where the American Revolution began, with the Boston Massacre, the Boston Tea Party, and the battles of Lexington and Concord. It was also, thanks to Frederick Douglass and William Lloyd Garrison, in the forefront of the abolitionist movement. It's not as though Yawkey couldn't have said the "right" things and reaped credit. The Sox could have become a magnet for other African American talent. Instead star ballplayers as recent as Tim Raines have said they'd never sign with the Red Sox because of their racist past. Mo Vaughn played for the Red Sox for years, but in 1991 he told Leigh Montville of *Sports Illustrated*, "'The most racist city in America,' is what you hear before you come here. Sure. I heard that a lot when I signed."[1] Had Yawkey decided to be the first, rather than the last, he could have made a major difference, both in Boston and also on a grander stage. From things he said on other issues, we also know that Tom Yawkey subscribed to "the buck stops here" philosophy as to where ultimate responsibility rested with the Red Sox.

The impact could have been almost immediate. Jackie Robinson, for instance, was the Rookie of the Year in 1947. Sam Jethroe, at the "sham tryout" with Robinson in 1945 (the phrase has become universally used, though Doc Kountze uses the somewhat more polite "insincere tryout"),[2] became the National League Rookie of the Year in 1950. There were black All Stars and MVPs galore in the years between the end of World War II and Pumpsie Green's Red Sox debut in 1959. But does the fact that his team was the last to desegregate prove that Yawkey was a racist? It proves that—for whatever reason—he didn't take the lead. But that's different. We know that several of his fellow owners made explicitly racist statements; Yawkey never did.

Though Tom Yawkey had numerous employees of color in South Carolina and one of his closest fishing and hunting companions— Freddie Cumbee—was of mixed racial ancestry, as late as 1958 the Red Sox themselves not had even one black employee—in Howard Bryant's words, "not with the grounds crew, custodians, concessionaires, or office staff." Bryant doesn't declare Yawkey a racist; instead he writes of the owner's "indifference to integration."[3] GM Dick O'Connell had somewhat cluelessly told the Massachusetts Commission against Discrimination in 1959, "For some reason Negroes do not apply for these jobs."[4]

Dick O'Connell apparently later told Stout and Johnson that by 1950, Yawkey "would have accepted African-Americans [as] players and occasionally wondered aloud why his Boston scouts hadn't. But the topic didn't really concern him. When Sox scouts gave the lame excuse that they couldn't find any black players, Yawkey and Cronin, both of whom had to know better, simply shrugged, sat comfortably on tradition, and accepted it."[5] Stout wrote, "Yawkey took pains to avoid addressing the question at all. . . . At every opportunity, Yawkey foisted the issue off on the collection of sycophants, yes-men, and cronies he employed."[6] Yawkey shied from the issue in public rather than addressing it head on.

In 2006 the *Boston Globe* editorialized, "The Yawkey-era Red Sox shunned black players in the post–World War II years. Tom Yawkey was not overtly racist, but some members of his inner circle were."[7]

Yawkey clearly wasn't any pioneer. He enjoyed the company of ballplayers and of men in the game. As the youngest of the owners when he first bought the club, he wanted to fit in. There is no indication that he ever took the lead on any of the issues of the day, but if he did, it was behind the scenes on the league's executive committee. He was a traditionalist in some areas (his opposition to night baseball, for example) but willing to experiment in others (league expansion to the West Coast). He didn't seem to be one to rock the boat. If any of the men around him—Collins, Cronin, Higgins, O'Connell—had any inclinations toward rocking boats, we don't see the evidence.

Higgins was an unreconstructed racist, but as far as we have found, the others never said anything explicit on the matter of race. When Higgins got quoted with racist remarks, there is no indication he was called to task by his boss. There's a good chance that Yawkey simply wished the issue didn't exist. The issue wasn't going to go away, but that realization still didn't prompt him to act. He had a stubborn streak, more than once saying, in effect, "This is my ball club, and nobody's going to tell me what I can or should do with it." To the extent he took such a stance regarding matters of race, it doesn't necessarily evidence racism, but it does countenance it.

One could argue that Yawkey was never going to take the lead, particularly not while Kenesaw Mountain Landis was commissioner (1921–44), but there was an opening when Happy Chandler was unanimously selected to succeed Landis in April 1945. It was Chandler who supported Brooklyn Dodgers GM Branch Rickey's plan to sign Jackie Robinson and, should he make good with the Montreal Royals in 1946, break the "color barrier" in Major League baseball. These plans fit with the notion that the decision to desegregate was made at a higher level—involving the commissioner—mitigating blame for any one owner. Not long after the Sox were sold, John Harrington told Ben Bradlee Jr., "Cronin told me the American League thought Boston wasn't a good fit, knowing how tribal we are here, and that the Dodgers would be the best fit. They had Montreal as their Triple-A farm team, and there was less racism in Canada. Boston's farm team was in Louisville and that was a problem. So according to Joe, this was being orchestrated by the league."[8]

If Yawkey hadn't the temperament to be first—to take the lead—or if he'd been asked to let another team break the barrier, he could instead have been the second to do so. Or the third. Or the fourth. Instead he was sixteenth—of sixteen. The Red Sox were the last team to integrate, and therein lies the best case for Yawkey's being considered a racist. It is a case built on circumstantial evidence. It was his team. He owned 100 percent of the Boston Red Sox. He didn't report to any board of directors. He owned the team outright. One could argue that the proof was in the pudding. After the 1945 Robinson-Jethroe-Williams tryout at Fenway Park, it was not until Pumpsie Green's debut on July 21, 1959, that the Red Sox had a black ballplayer at the Major League level. Jackie Robinson had played out his entire ten-year career between the two dates—he debuted in 1947 and retired after the 1956 season, winning one MVP award, one batting title, six seasons in the World Series, and six appearances in the All-Star Game. His was a Hall of Fame career on baseball merit alone. After he'd played out his career and retired, another couple of years had passed, and the Red Sox still hadn't fielded a black ballplayer.

Robinson phoned Green in the Red Sox clubhouse and told him, according to Howard Bryant, that Pumpsie's breaking in was no less historic than his own because "the last team to integrate likely suffered from an ingrained, deeply entrenched form of racism that was possibly worse than anything Robinson himself ever endured."[9] It is notable that Ted Williams made his own statement, in deed and not in words, by asking Green to be his throwing partner before the games in Boston as the two warmed up their arms in full view of the media and early-arriving fans.

The April 1945 Robinson-Jethroe-Williams tryout was prompted by local political pressure, not because the Red Sox were genuinely interested in seeking out black ballplayers.[10] The Red Sox bowed to the pressure at the time so that they could secure their City of Boston license to host Sunday games at Fenway Park. Not one of the three players ever heard from them again—not even a "thanks for coming in" card. And for whatever reason, city councilor Isadore Muchnick chose not to keep up the pressure come 1946.

The memory rankled. When Jackie Robinson was asked in 1967 about that year's pennant race, he said he was rooting against the Red Sox, and he made it personal. "Because of Boston owner Tom Yawkey, I'd like to see them lose, because he is probably one of the most bigoted guys in organized baseball."[11]

As previously noted, Boston sportswriter Clif Keane said he'd been at the 1945 tryout and heard someone shout out, "Get those niggers off the field!" The shout supposedly came from the area of the door opening into the park from the Red Sox front office. Did Robinson come to believe it was Yawkey who had shouted this? As noted above, no one other than Keane ever reported hearing the shout, leading many to question whether it had ever occurred. Keane, improbably, said, "I can't recall who yelled it. People used to say it was Collins. But I really don't know."[12] Keane didn't think it had been Yawkey: "It wasn't Yawkey. Yawkey wouldn't do that."[13] Keane's use of the word "recall" implies he once did know who had yelled it. If it happened and if he did recall, he never said. Stout presents the plausible argument that Keane may even have "invented the comment he claimed to overhear at Fenway Park to deflect attention away from his own bigotry."[14] Keane said, "I just couldn't identify who said it. He said it good and loud. It happened. That absolutely happened. I was there. I talked to Yawkey several times about black athletes after that and he said, 'Get me a good one and I'll sign him. I don't want to get a black guy simply because he's black.'"[15] Years later Dick Bresciani confided to another staff member that Keane had once admitted he wasn't even at Fenway Park that day.[16]

Clark Booth said,

> "It's convoluted, but not that complex. There was a certain antebellum tinge and paternalistic thing. And [Yawkey] could be gracious and charming. It really is pretty simple. Pretty basic. This was the attitude they had. Higgins was frightful, as we all know. But it wasn't just Higgins. It was Collins; he was part of it. And certainly Yawkey. Certainly all the blame has to start with him. He has to bear most of

it. You are known by who you run with. No matter what the thing is, whether it's baseball or whatever else it is."[17]

Yawkey maintained residences in Boston and New York (his legal residence), but his principal residence—the only one that was truly his, rather than a suite in a hotel—was in South Carolina. As noted, many mistakenly assumed this meant he hailed from there.

By all accounts, Yawkey seems to have gotten along well with those who worked for him in South Carolina, both black and white, though his was a paternalism that was in line with earlier times. Jim Sargent worked for Tom Yawkey, as had his father before him. Jim joined Jamie Dozier and Phil Wilkinson in showing this author around the Yawkey Wildlife Center in November 2012, and Jim was wearing a baseball cap honoring the Reverend Martin Luther King. Working for the Yawkeys from 1954 through the days of the Civil Rights Movement, Jim clearly would have had his antennae up for indications of racism. And, indeed, around 1965 or 1966, there was an incident that prompted him to take a stand.

I used to pick up the school kids from the ferry. They had a bus for black kids and a bus for white kids. This particular day, all the kids came at the same time. [Superintendent Baron Cooper] had two kids—a boy and a girl; they rode inside the cab with me. The black kids were in the back of the truck—it was a nice sunny day—and they [the Cooper kids] got insulted because the black kids were on the back of the truck.

I got offended. "I'm a black person driving the truck, and you're in the front with me!" I'm trying to see how they draw that distinction. (They were probably ten to fourteen.) So I just told Mrs. Yawkey I didn't want to pick up the kids any more. I said if I'm a black person driving the truck and they're inside with me, and if they can't handle the kids on the back of the truck, then they don't want me inside with them either. So I said before things escalated, they'd be better off having somebody else picking the kids up.

"She said, "Well . . . you have to get adjusted." I said, "I don't see the adjustment. I'm still the same person. My skin hasn't changed, and they're riding with me all the time."[18]

Sargent felt free to raise the subject with Jean Yawkey and free to take the position he did. He had never even overheard her or Tom say anything of a racist nature. Did he have any reason to think either of them might have harbored racist attitudes? "Actually, no, I didn't think so, but then you know . . . um . . . who knows? I don't think so, personally, no. He's number one as far as I'm concerned. He was just a super person. Black or white, I think anybody would tell you the same."[19]

Bill Gutfarb said, "I know of no one who actually knew Tom Yawkey who ever stated that they had ever heard him make a racially disparaging remark or got the impression that he harbored any ill feelings. Plenty of inaccurate accusations have been made, but never have I heard a single one come from someone who ever knew or even met him."[20] Dick Johnson of the Sports Museum of New England concurred. Any suggestions of personal racism attributed to Yawkey were "completely second-hand." Johnson put it in the perspective of Yawkey's relationship with the men around him: "As an owner, he went from being the kid brother to his heroes—like Lefty Grove and people like that; his dream was to go hunting with them in the offseason and to get to know them and everything—to then being a father figure to the next generation of players. Some of the first-generation players that he hung out with, like Pinky Higgins, sort of continued to be brothers, and he—out of personal loyalty, I think—made the mistake of bringing in bad people." Those people created what Johnson dubbed a "Crony Island" culture in the Red Sox front office. Johnson added, "I don't think there was a deliberate hateful bone in his [Yawkey's] body. I seriously believe that. I think he was loyal to the wrong people at the wrong time. Pinky Higgins was a really good player. And Joe Cronin was a really good player. I don't think Joe Cronin had any animus either. I never had the idea that Joe Cronin was a bad guy. But Higgins *was* a guy whose racial views and upbringing and everything were toxic, and he [Yawkey] paid a real price for that."[21]

Phil Wilkinson, who worked for Tom Yawkey for ten years, saw a paternalism and perhaps an unconscious racism, one of circumstance and position:

He considered himself not a racist. I don't think he was, but his basic attitudes were such that he was more sort of a . . . patron parent or something. Taking care of them because they couldn't. . . . They needed him. . . . You know what I mean. I think he was a product of his era and his time, as many people were. I think that he had that growing up with the situation where whites were considered to be a little more advanced than blacks were in this part of the world. That rubbed off on him somewhat, but he never acted like he believed that. He didn't realize he was doing it.[22]

Economic problems cropped up more than any racial ones. Wilkinson observes:

I would say that the stuff that we had to deal with was bringing him [Yawkey] up to date on things. The crew would be working at wages that were way below what everybody else was making, and he wouldn't be aware of that. It wasn't something he thought about. They'd all be grumbling about wanting a raise, and he'd get mad about it. . . . I'd say, "Well, Mr. Yawkey, let me just check and see what everybody else is paying." He'd say, "OK. Check it out." And I'd go back to him when I found out and say, "You know, we are probably the lowest paying outfit around here." And he'd say, "What would it take to fix it?" And I'd give him some ideas about that, and he'd say, "OK, let's do it." He wouldn't think of it himself. It would have to come to his attention.

He used to laugh and say when he had to sign his taxes that he had them cover the numbers. All he needed to see was the line where he put his name. He didn't want to see the numbers.[23]

Maybe not seeing the final figure, Yawkey could pretend to escape a reality that would be upsetting. He could afford that luxury with regard to taxation. The rest of the world was looking at the racial composition of the Red Sox, though. Covering up the numbers—wishing the problem didn't exist—wasn't going to work in the public arena. Perhaps he knew better but somehow couldn't bring himself to act.

Wilkinson enjoyed trying to talk with Yawkey about baseball, though Yawkey preferred to talk about Wilkinson's areas of expertise. As to the Red Sox being the last team to integrate, Wilkinson indicated that Yawkey was aware of the charge but said, "He never talked about that particularly. I think he was sensitive about it."[24]

Years later Dick O'Connell told Tom Shaer that when Red Auerbach of the Boston Celtics asked the Red Sox GM about the team's pension plan for non-uniformed personnel, O'Connell commissioned a study that found that the Red Sox plan was one of the best in the Commonwealth.[25]

Prior to the 1945 tryout, Sox GM Eddie Collins disingenuously declared, "We [the Red Sox] have never had a single request for a tryout by a colored applicant."[26]

In 1946 Yawkey was on a committee of four owners (and the two league presidents) who submitted a report to new commissioner Chandler on the major issues in baseball. The August 27 report started by saying that baseball had "just growed" and that there had been no systematic look at it for thirty-five years. The report touched on a number of issues, one of which was the "Race Question." Apparently that section of the report was removed before the report was made public, but Chandler kept a copy in his personal files. The section began with a grumble:

> Certain groups in this country, including political and social-minded drum-beaters, are conducting [a] pressure campaign in an attempt to force Major League clubs to sign Negro players. Members of these groups are not primarily interested in professional baseball. They are not campaigning to provide a better opportunity for thousands of Negro boys who want to play baseball. They are not even particularly interested in improving the lot of Negro players who are already employed. They know little about baseball and nothing about the business end of its operation. They single out professional baseball for attack because it offers a good publicity medium. [27]

There was recognition of the interest of "the Negro" in baseball, and note was taken that when one Negro played on one Triple A club in 1946, attendance at ballparks in Newark and Baltimore was sometimes more than 50 percent Negro when that ball club came to visit. (The unnamed player was of course Jackie Robinson on the Triple A Montreal Royals.) The 1946 experience suggested that "the preponderance of Negro attendance in parks such as the

Yankee Stadium, the Polo Grounds and Comiskey Park could conceivably threaten the value of the Major League franchises owned by these Clubs."[28] The report argued that to be good enough for the Majors, a player needed years of seasoning (on average seven years) in the Minor Leagues and that Negro players were not getting that experience. Besides, the Negro Leagues themselves needed good-quality players to survive.[29]

The report itself came to no hard and fast conclusions but seemed to suggest that all the owners should stick together rather than that one individual owner act on his own. It did specifically say that it would not question that any given owner might sincerely oppose segregation and that an owner might believe that maintaining segregation would itself be detrimental to baseball.

It's not our goal here to delve more deeply into this question other than to note that Yawkey was involved in formulating policy for organized baseball on this and many other subjects. He couldn't pretend the subject didn't exist. And the conclusion of the report was consistent with the clubbiness of the owners at the time. Everything we know about him indicates that Yawkey always wanted to "fit in" and not take uncomfortable positions on his own. We have no way to know what he may or may not have said behind closed doors. It's possible that his was more of a voice for change, though there is nothing to indicate such a stance, and the hiring record of the Red Sox doesn't indicate anything approaching leadership by example.

In the late 1940s and into the 1950s, the Red Sox used Southern geography as something of an excuse, saying that it would be unfair to sign black ballplayers because the team's two main farm teams were in Louisville and Birmingham, and the players wouldn't have a chance to develop properly. In fact the Red Sox added Birmingham only in 1948. In 1947 their two Triple A teams had been in Louisville and Toronto. Yawkey had the wherewithal to buy and sell Minor League teams almost at will, and indeed he reshuffled the list of farm teams to some degree almost every year. We have even seen how he bought the San Francisco Seals in 1955 to help give the American League a foothold in California.

The particular geography in 1948 could actually have helped the

Red Sox. That very year the Birmingham Black Barons of the Negro Leagues had a ballplayer named Willie Mays. The Barons played in the same ballpark—Rickwood Field—as the American Association's all-white Birmingham Barons, Boston's farm club, so the Red Sox had an "in" with the Black Barons. Stout and Johnson note that the Black Barons "promised Boston first crack at their players." It was, reported Howard Bryant, one of the conditions of the lease.[30]

The seventeen-year-old Mays attracted enough attention that Joe Cronin asked scout Larry Woodall to look him over. Rain prevented Woodall from seeing Mays for three days, and Woodall was alleged to have griped, "I'm not going to waste my time waiting for a bunch of niggers."[31] Woodall did submit a report, but it was unenthusiastic, and Al Hirshberg wrote, "Without ever watching Mays play, Woodall gave the front office a more accurate report on the weather than on Mays and, as I heard the story, when he came home he still hadn't seen Mays in action. Everyone I asked around Fenway Park denied this ever happened. But I would have denied it, too, if I had had let a Willie Mays slip away right from under my nose. Imagine what the Red Sox would have done to the American League with Jackie Robinson and Willie Mays joining Ted Williams at Fenway Park."[32]

Another Red Sox scout, George Digby, said he had seen Mays and had highly recommended him.[33] Indeed he considered Mays "the single greatest talent I have ever seen."[34] But the Red Sox response was cool. In a January 1997 interview with Howard Bryant, Mays said, "There's no telling what I would have been able to do in Boston. To be honest, I really thought I was going to Boston." And he added, "But for that Yawkey. Everyone knew he was racist. He didn't want me."[35] Fair or not, accurate or not, both Robinson and Mays pinned the racist tag on Tom Yawkey. They both knew where the buck stopped.

Before Pumpsie Green was hired, Boston journalist Doc Kountze once asked Red Sox secretary Phil Troy why the Red Sox wouldn't sign any black players. Kountze found the Sox secretary hospitable, but "Troy pointed upstairs," writes Glenn Stout, "which Kountze interpreted as an unmistakable reference to Yawkey."[36]

Perhaps that was a sufficient explanation in the mid-1940s. It didn't wash too well by the mid-1950s. Dick Johnson allows for some understanding, at least in the earlier period, because of Yawkey's isolation or insulation:

> I think he was very much a product of, and to a certain extent a prisoner of, his position in society, his wealth, and his upbringing. He led a very sheltered existence. Not necessarily a pleasant one because his parents both died. But his uncle took great care of him, and the money that he inherited certainly allowed him to buy the Red Sox during the depths of the Depression. Here you have someone who was very much like gentlemen of his station and position at the time. He just didn't happen to be progressive on an issue that is attached to him.[37]

That tag—racist—has had a lasting impact and has been difficult to shake. As noted above, even thirty years after Tom Yawkey's death, there was controversy in 2006, when the Boys and Girls Clubs of Boston named its new center the Yawkey Center.[38]

In 2007 the day after the Red Sox and all of baseball wore number 42 on their uniforms to honor Jackie Robinson on the sixtieth anniversary of his debut, Steve Buckley wrote, "The next time the league chooses to celebrate the life and times of Robinson, I have an idea that's far more symbolic than having a collection of players and coaches wear No. 42 on their backs: Kick Tom Yawkey out of the Hall of Fame. . . . Somewhere on that plaque, it should be noted that Yawkey was the last owner to integrate. Either that, or it should be taken down."[39]

Al Hirshberg was a Red Sox beat reporter for the *Boston Post* and the *Boston Traveler* during the Yawkey years. It was he who wrote that manager Pinky Higgins had told him directly, "There'll be no niggers on this ball club as long as I have anything to do with it."[40] But Hirshberg did not think Yawkey was personally racist. In fact he wrote, "Yawkey wanted a black ballplayer almost from the beginning."[41] How could this be, then, that he couldn't get one, when Yawkey owned the team lock, stock, and barrel? Because of misplaced trust and loyalty, wrote Hirshberg:

> He never made a big deal of it because he trusted his farm system to sign promising ballplayers, regardless of their color. Cronin made the

same mistake. It's possible that even John Murphy, the farm director, was not aware of what was happening within his own department. Murphy, who had no more personal prejudices than Cronin or Yawkey, would have signed a good black ballplayer as soon as his scouts dug one up. But his scouts never seemed able to find one. When they did find one, his so-called superscouts would come back with a poor report on the player.[42]

Murphy should have appointed a black scout, wrote Hirshberg, but he didn't. He relied on the old-school superscouts, and they let him down. It was not until 1960, under Neil Mahoney, that the Red Sox even appointed a Caribbean scout, Pedro Vazquez. The failure came down to Yawkey's long-lasting cronyism and his seeming inability to fire the men who so often let him down. Maybe Cronin suffered from a similar problem. Indeed Hirshberg wrote, "Whether it was Murphy's fault or Cronin's, the club at one point had the biggest collection of useless scouts in baseball. . . . I doubt if a single scout was fired during Cronin's tenure as general manager."[43]

We noted above that Pumpsie Green felt that Yawkey had treated him respectfully. Two writers who studied the subject conclude, "No one has ever reported hearing Yawkey make a racist comment throughout his ownership of the Red Sox." They amplify a bit: "Yawkey was generally considered a gentleman and one of the nicest people to be found in organized baseball at the time; however, he may have been too nice for his own good. Yawkey was devoted to his friends and routinely mixed his personal and professional lives by hiring friends to work for the Red Sox organization. The cronyism that developed was very detrimental to the club, as hiring and firing decisions were not always made on the issue of ability."[44] They note Hirshberg's observation: "If it is a question of hurting a friend or hurting the ball club, Yawkey has usually hurt the club."[45]

Yawkey interacted with African Americans on the Red Sox in 1967 and in later years, and all seemed well. Indeed as Yastrzemski pointed out, the locker reserved for Tom Yawkey in the clubhouse was in between Yaz's and both Reggie Smith's and Joe Foy's. "He spent more time talking with us than with any of the other players," Yaz wrote. And he added that newspaper reports about the lack of black ballplayers on the team had truly bothered Yawkey, who Yastrzemski recalled saying, "Yaz, don't you think I'd rather have signed a Willie Mays instead of a Gary Geiger?"[46]

What might Jean Yawkey have thought about the situation? It had come up in 1979, just three years after Tom died, in a private conversation with George Sullivan. Sullivan had just published *Picture History of the Boston Red Sox*. He didn't care for the title, but the Red Sox ordered one hundred copies or so, and he got a call from Mary Jane Ryan: "Guess who wants to take you out to lunch? Mrs. Yawkey." Sullivan continues:

> I had never met her [Jean] before. I had seen her upstairs, but we had never met. Mary Jane said, "She absolutely loves the book and wants you to come and have dinner with her." The Yawkeys' box seated about eight people. She was going to be there, and it was going to be catered by the regular kitchen help on the roof. We had a very nice dinner, just her and me in the box.
>
> I remember her talking about the Jackie Robinson thing. I don't know what the hell brought it up. Maybe I said something to the effect that it's interesting how he [Tom Yawkey] had taken a share of the blame for this thing on Jackie Robinson, and she sort of stiffened a little and she said—words to this effect—"Well, you know who did that, don't you?" And I said, "No, I don't." In other words, who was the one behind giving him a "How do you do?" and "See you later. Don't call us; we'll call you." She said, "He had nothing . . . you know. . . ." I said, "No, I don't." And she said, "I'm not going to tell, but you can figure it out." Or words to that effect. And that was the end of that.
>
> She was giving me more credit than I [deserved]. . . . I assume she generally thought that I would know. . . . I don't know if she was talking about Collins or Cronin. That was my guess."[47]

Who might have been behind the notorious racist shout that came out of the shadows during the Robinson-Jethroe-Williams tryout? Sullivan responds:

> I certainly cannot see him [Yawkey] doing it, or Cronin. I didn't know Mr. Collins. I knew Cronin pretty well. In fact, he wrote my letter of recommendation into the Marine Corps.

When I say she [Jean] stiffened, that may be a little too strong. I think it irritated her—not that I would bring it up, not irritated with me—but it hit a nerve with her. She didn't throw a tantrum or start yelling or anything, but she said firmly, "You know who it was," and I said, "[Gulp], no, I don't." "You know." "I'm sorry, I don't." She said something like, "I don't want to go into it," but the idea was it was not Mr. Yawkey.

[Had Sullivan ever heard Yawkey say anything at all that could be attributed as racist?] "Not in the least. I would doubt that he ever did."[48]

"Race relations in the clubhouse actually weren't that bad," said Red Sox pitcher John Curtis. "It was the front office where all the bigotry was festering. I don't recall any of my teammates making a racist remark about Reggie while I was in Boston."[49]

The year after Pumpsie Green's debut, the Boston Red Sox became the team that desegregated professional baseball in New Orleans in 1960.[50]

In August 2017, John W. Henry of the Red Sox said he was "haunted" by the team's legacy of racism and said the team wanted to lead the effort to have the city rename Yawkey Way. Henry's statement kicked off a round of columns and controversy. A letter to the editor in the *Boston Globe* by Susan Hammond of Cambridge suggested that whatever Yawkey's attitudes may have been in the 1940s and the 1950s, there is considerable evidence that he changed. She wrote, in part, "If our contry is to deal with our history of racism and move forward, we must encourage people to be willing to change and embrace new views. Otherwise we're saying that because a person took a racist action earlier in their life, they must be a racist forevermore. . . . People grow and learn. . . . We shouldn't hide his 1950s actions, but we also should not take away the recognition of the person he was by the end of his life."[51]

Epilogue

The Red Sox and Race

IN SUMMING UP, we could suggest that there were three points in time we could look at the Red Sox and race: 1945, 1950, and 1955.

1945

It may not be fair to assign a great deal of blame for shortcomings in 1945, given the tenor of the times. While it's easy to look back in retrospect and say the Red Sox should have paved the way, should have taken advantage of the historic opportunity presented them at the Robinson-Jethroe-Williams tryout in April 1945, it may be unfair to hold the team to standards that other leading institutions in Boston did not hold. Yes, today one could argue that baseball more or less led the way toward desegregation in American society and that the Red Sox could have led baseball. Equally, though, the world of journalism could have led the way. Were there any African American newspaper publishers in Boston or any African American editors other than in the *Boston Chronicle*, Boston's black newspaper? Were there any African American reporters? In 1973 the *Boston Globe* hired Larry Whiteside (fourteen years after the Red Sox fielded Pumpsie Green); Whiteside was the only black reporter covering Major League baseball for a major U.S. daily.[1]

How many African American figures served in elected positions in the Commonwealth of Massachusetts? Seventeen years after the Jackie Robinson tryout, in 1962, Edward W. Brooke was elected attorney general of Massachusetts; four years later, he was elected to the U.S. Senate. In 1971 Harry J. Elam became the first African American judge appointed in Massachusetts. It wasn't until 2012 that U.S. District Court judge Denise J. Casper became the first black female judge on the federal bench in Massachusetts.

How many physicians of color were there at Massachusetts General Hospital or at Boston's other medical institutions? How many people of color were in academia? How many black bankers were there?

How fair is it for other institutions in the region to blame the Red Sox for not taking the lead? As Dick Johnson suggests, "Looking at history with progressive-tinted glasses, we can all say, 'Wasn't it horrible?' But you have to look at the broad canvas in Boston at that point in time in order to honestly appraise the Red Sox and Tom Yawkey's culpability. How much blame should be assigned to them? But I think it's only fair to [look at the bigger picture], and I think the Red Sox come out looking as good or bad as everybody else."[2]

Tom Shaer asked, "Could Tom Yawkey have prevented his team's monumental disaster in equal-opportunity hiring? Of course, because he owned the company, but the owner was known back then to often be disengaged from operations. Yawkey's negligence hardly constituted blatant individual racism; rather, he was a detached, typical non-disruptor of social mores of the time—as were most executives and politicians."[3]

1950

Sam Jethroe became the first African American to play for a Major League team in Boston—the Boston Braves. His reception was without notable incident. Jethroe was not only accepted by fans at Braves Field—situated less than a mile from Fenway Park—but he also excited them, particularly with his speed on the base paths. By the time Jethroe signed with the Braves, Jackie Robinson had already played three years at Braves Field with the Dodgers. So had Larry Doby played at Fenway Park (with the Indians). The Braves weren't the first National League team to desegregate, but they were third of the eight teams in the league.

Had the Red Sox been worried about negative fan reaction in Boston to a black player on a Boston baseball team, Jethroe's reception could only have been reassuring. He won the NL Rookie of the Year award in 1950 and played with the Boston Braves for three years, until the Braves decamped and moved to Milwaukee.[4]

Why had the Red Sox still not made a move to build up their farm systems with black ballplayers? One might excuse the Red Sox for not being first in 1945. But after Jethroe's successful season in 1950, what was the excuse? Moreover, as they delayed, the Red Sox lost prospects such as Willie Mays, on whom they purportedly held an effective option.[5]

1955

By 1955 one could posit a third point. The New York Yankees fielded catcher Elston Howard that April. Of the sixteen teams in the Majors, now only three had never deigned to include a black ballplayer—the Phillies (who brought John Kennedy on board in 1957), the Tigers (who brought on Ozzie Virgil in 1958), and—last of all—the Red Sox, who still had never fielded a black ballplayer when the 1959 season began.

It was becoming an embarrassment even by 1955, and the drums began to beat louder for the Red Sox to provide the opportunity to a broader spectrum of talent, an openness that had paid off so well for numerous other teams. Tom Yawkey still owned 100 percent of the team. Whereas one might have given him a pass for not pioneering, it became increasingly difficult to rationalize his being the last.

For that matter, even the Boston Bruins of the National Hockey League (NHL) had a black player—Willie O'Ree, who debuted with the Bruins at the Forum in Montreal on January 18, 1958. He tried out with the Bruins before the season and was assigned to Springfield but was brought up to Boston to replace an ailing player, Leo LaBine. In his debut the Bruins beat the Canadiens, 3–0, and O'Ree, a native of New Brunswick, called it "the biggest thrill of my life."[6] His first game on home ice was the next evening, January 19, and the *Boston American* reported that he "made a hit with the fans with his speed and hustle," also noting that he spoke some French.[7] O'Ree played in just those two games in 1958 but returned to NHL action with the Bruins for forty-three games in the 1960–61 season, scoring four goals and recording ten assists.

By 1959 the pressure had intensified. The NAACP became involved and asked the Massachusetts Commission against Discrimination to look into the Red Sox's overall hiring practices. A spokesman for the ball club who wisely wished to remain anonymous said, "No Negroes had applied for jobs as grounds-keepers or maintenance workers in several years."[8] (Presumably they had not applied for positions as corporate executives either.) Addressing an agenda item advanced by the Red Sox, the NAACP urged that no public land be made available to the Red Sox for parking purposes.

Before spring training got under way, Sox GM Bucky Harris said, "Let somebody offer us a Minnie Minoso or a Larry Doby and see how prejudiced we are."[9] On April 12, 1959, Harris wrote the MCAD that players were used by the Red Sox "regardless of race, color, or creed" and that they were, in effect, doing Green a favor: "The truth is that Pumpsie was optioned [to Minneapolis] to give him an opportunity to play regularly and to develop in his profession."[10] Despite the outcry, the decision to option Green might well have been the correct one from a strict baseball perspective. Harold Kaese said the Sox were guilty of "incredibly poor public relations."[11] Hy Hurwitz wrote in *The Sporting News* that "all of the writers traveling with the team when the announcement was made of Green's departure for Minneapolis thought the matter was unwisely handled. However, nobody questioned the fact that Green needed more experience to become a major leaguer."[12]

On June 3, 1959, MCAD issued its report, noting that it accepted a letter from Harris as "evidence of good faith" that the Red Sox had pledged to "pursue a policy of nondiscrimination in hiring Negro ball players." The Red Sox also promised to make sure that nonsegregated accommodations were available for all players in future spring trainings.[13]

When Pumpsie Green debuted on July 21, and Earl Wilson debuted seven days later, pressure naturally abated.

Even after these debuts, though, and even after what seemed like the "colorblind" leadership at the time of the 1967 Impossible Dream team, the Red Sox as an organization lagged behind in off-field hiring. Al Green was the first black usher at Fenway Park—in 1974. Some of the other ushers shunned him, but the organization was ready to make use of him. The most junior ushers were assigned positions further from the home plate area, but not long after he began, Green was asked to be one of the ushers who would go out on the field in between innings. Green relates the events:

> I know what the story was. I played the game. I was no stupid idiot. They wanted me on the field so that people could see that they had a black guy there. So I did it. Then the next thing after that, the guy came to me and said, "The vice president wants you to work in the information booth." They had a white guy in there. He was about seventy or eighty. He was old. His wife was sick, so he went home to take care of his wife. They told me they wanted me to work in the box there. I said, "Why do you want me? I don't know anything." He said, "Well, they want you."
>
> People would come up to me. People would pass and show one another, "Hey, look, they got a black guy there." They never said that to me, but I could tell that [was] the reaction. They would touch one another to get them to see me, showing them. I plainly saw that.[14]

Green remains customer service representative as of this writing, having served through the 2015 season.

Times change, and organizations change as well. It is worth noting, by way of a postscript of sorts, that the twenty-first-century Red Sox have taken a leading role in honoring Jackie Robinson, hosting an annual educational event. The Red Sox Foundation's contribution to the Jackie Robinson Foundation is perhaps the largest within Major League Baseball. And one can credit the Red Sox with also acting in support of another minority, inviting Jason Collins to throw out the first pitch at Fenway. In May 2013 in *Sports Illustrated*, Collins said, "I'm a 34-year-old NBA center. I'm black. And I'm gay."[15] On June 6 "the first active athlete to come out as being gay in one of the four U.S. major professional sports leagues" was invited to throw out the ceremonial first pitch at Fenway Park.[16]

It is sad to recall this history of the Red Sox and sad to think of what could have been had Tom Yawkey taken actions that were readily available to him. Fortunately other elements of the Yawkey legacy live on today and will for generations to come. For instance, there is the charitable work funded by the Yawkey Foundations. We have discussed much of it above, but let us look at two beneficiaries of longtime funding commitments: Tara Hall and the Tom Yawkey Wildlife Center in South Carolina. Both provide refuge.

Yawkey Foundations and Charitable Work

Tara Hall

We have noted Tom and Jean Yawkey's many years of support of Tara Hall, a long-term residential home and school that accepts neglected, troubled, and abused boys between the ages of six and thirteen. Situated on eleven wooded acres in Georgetown County, it is a cluster of dorms, school buildings, and recreational facilities along Black Mingo Creek. It serves 15–30 boys at a time; over the years its staff has served more than six hundred boys. Most come from within 60–70 miles of the home.

Some of the boys have been effectively freed from neglect and abuse; others have been sent away from their homes for being unmanageable. The boys typically stay eighteen months to three years. The program's website explains, "Many of the boys have faced emotional or behavioral problems so severe that it often takes at least six months to begin building a new foundation of trust."[17]

Tara Hall was begun by Irish priest Owen O'Sullivan in 1969 with one lost boy living on the street. There was such a need that within three years "we turned around one day and had twenty-four kids and $300 in the bank. Father O'Sullivan was actively calling other agencies or the families of the kids to begin to start to place them. He was about ready to hang it up. That's when Mrs. Ellie Armstrong, who was a good friend of Mrs. Jean Yawkey and also knew Father O'Sullivan, put the two of them together. They hit it off, and Mrs. Yawkey bailed Tara Hall out at the time."[18]

In what has to be one of the most successful results of the VISTA (Volunteers in Service to America) program, Jim Dumm arrived as a graduate from Penn State in 1970—and stayed. He has now more than forty-five years of service, all of which grew out of his volunteering for VISTA, which hoped for one or two years of service. Once the immediate financial crisis was solved, Tom Yawkey told O'Sullivan and Dumm, "You'll never get anywhere until you have your own property." He sent out a man to scout around and bought two pieces of adjacent property to house Tara Hall. Father O'Sullivan resigned in December 1978, and Jim Dumm has been the executive director ever since. In late 2012 he worked with a dedicated staff of twelve full-time and four part-time employees. It's a very good ratio; there were seventeen boys at the time of this author's October 2012 visit, four in public school and the others taught on site.

Naturally the program has had its successes and failures. Two members of the current staff are graduates of Tara Hall who came back and serve as wonderful role models for the current boys. Another boy was placed in a job at Wal-Mart during his junior year of high school, graduated, got married, and eventually became a deputy sheriff in Kenesaw, Georgia. Dumm remarks:

> There's lots of good stories and then some not so good. Periodically we'll get collect calls from various prisons throughout the state. That tells me that at least the kids are connected to us, and they still stay in touch. We learned a long, long time ago that all we can really do for these kids is give them opportunities. We don't pretend to think that we're going to change their lives and they're going to live happily ever after. We give them opportunities.
>
> We also give them opportunities to be kids. So many of these kids are coming from situations that are so dysfunctional, they just haven't had opportunities for music lessons. . . . We've even had some kids from Myrtle Beach that haven't set their big toe in the ocean. We do a lot of beach trips. We give them opportunities to be kids, as well as teaching them structure and discipline and reading and writing.

The home has never discriminated on the basis of race. "There's times when we've been two-thirds white and one-third black, and vice versa," Dumm says. "Sometimes it's been two-thirds black and one-third white. Usually it's right around 50/50. . . . In the very beginning, we probably didn't get some support from some quarters because we . . . didn't discriminate. That probably limited some of our funding in those early years, to be honest with you."

The Yawkey Foundation supplies 30–35 percent of Tara Hall's funding. Before her death, Jean Yawkey would visit once or twice a year. Dumm recalls Jean:

One thing Mrs. Yawkey would always do, and the foundation has continued, was to send the kids shopping for Christmas. For a long, long time, there was a particular store she liked and would say let them go in and for a particular amount—I forget the amount—get some clothes and send her the bill. The foundation continues to send us some money at Christmastime for the kids to go shopping. The intent primarily is to make sure they get the clothes that they need. That's a tradition they've wanted to maintain. She was just a neat lady.

Tom Yawkey Wildlife Center

The Tom Yawkey Wildlife Center is a refuge of another sort. Willed to the South Carolina Wildlife and Marine Resources Department on Tom Yawkey's death in 1976, it comprises around thirty-one square miles on the three coastal islands at the mouth of Winyah Bay. North Island was designated a barrier island wilderness where no activities detrimental to its primitive character are permitted. South Island is held for the protection of waterfowl, and no duck hunting is permitted. The remainder of the property, which includes most of Cat Island, is held as a wildlife management area for migratory birds, native game, and other wild species.[19]

Yawkey left not only the land but also a $10 million perpetual trust fund, the income from which funds the management of the property. Other than North Island, the land is managed rather than left as wilderness so as to ensure that it remains welcoming to waterfowl and other birds—and alligators—rather than to perhaps become less hospitable with the incursion of sea water, which intruded into the area of the former rice plantations once the river had been dammed. The South Carolina Department of Natural Resources (DNR) staff, for instance, maintains some causeways that Yawkey had installed and some pastures he had created to help grow grains and grasses that would attract ducks and geese.

Yawkey's determination to manage the land well is reflected in an amusing story from the early 1970s, during Eddie Kasko's tenure as manager.

I was sitting in the office one day when he [Yawkey] came down—I think it was a Sunday morning—and we were just talking before the ballgame, when Helen Robinson—the phone operator—called down. She said, "Is Mr. Yawkey with you?" I said, "Yeah, he's sitting right here. Hold on." I gave him the phone, and he said, "Yeah. Yeah. Mmm. Well. Well, goddamnit it, do it again!" I said, "Now don't get in an uproar. It's a Sunday morning, and you ought to be nice and calm." "Well, goddamnit. Nobody can make a decision!" I said, "What's wrong?" He said, "The storm just came through. We just planted five hundred acres, I think, of seedlings for the Canadian geese. The storm came through and wiped it out." His farm manager said, "What do you want to do?" He said, "Goddamnit, do it again! Plant it again!"[20]

The general public is not permitted access to the property other than through twice-weekly tours of fourteen people per tour. "It is not meant for us, but for the animals, the vegetation, the water-fowl and the shorebirds," explained Yawkey trustee Bill Gutfarb.[21]

(It may be of some interest that in days long gone by, back in 1777, the Marquis de Lafayette—so key to winning the American Revolution—first set foot on American soil when he landed and vis-ited the North Island home of Major Benjamin Huger of the South Carolina Militia.[22] The North Island Light was built in 1811, and the eighty-seven-foot lighthouse remains today at the entry to Winyah Bay. British troops were stationed on North Island for a while during the War of 1812, and Confederate fortifications were set up on all three islands during the Civil War. Today North Island is the most peaceful of all the islands, with no public visitation.)

The property is accessible to the mainland by private ferry to Cat Island. Around 1908 William Yawkey was part of a group of fifteen who named themselves the South Island Gun Club and purchased the property to use as a winter retreat for hunting. Tom Yawkey ultimately bought out all the other owners. It was as he grew older that Tom Yawkey came to appreciate the importance of conserva-tion, and what had been a hunting domain owned by a gun club was converted into a refuge.

The conversion didn't necessarily set well with other wealthy Northerners who had bought up other former rice plantations and properties in the area around the same time in the late nineteenth and early twentieth centuries. "Right in his [Yawkey's] neighborhood, there were plantations owned by DuPont and Astor and Baruch. He adjoined the Baruchs to the north," explained Alex Sanders, a young South Carolina attorney with an expertise in environmental law who met Tom Yawkey at a hearing regarding the discharge of factory waste into the Sampit River waters that flowed to the sea in Winyah Bay. Sanders said Yawkey had already hired Phil Wilkinson, who held an advanced degree in wildlife biology from Auburn. "Mr. Yawkey was serious about taking care of his place. He didn't want just a duck manager. He wanted somebody who was familiar with the whole spectrum of the environment." Sanders continues:

> In any event, time went on, and Mr. Yawkey became opposed to hunting, to all forms of hunting. He became the most rabid environmentalist you'd ever meet. He thought that all this land that he had for duck hunting should be used to propagate ducks but not kill them. Under any circumstances. That, believe it or not, became controversial among his peers. Ducks are pretty smart. If they know they've got a sanctuary they can go to, where nobody's going to threaten them, they'll go there. [Before too long] Mr. DuPont didn't have any ducks. They were all over at Mr. Yawkey's place.[23]

Recall that Yawkey lived in hotel suites in New York and Boston. South Island was where he made his real home, that and—in time—Mount Pleasant Plantation near Andrews. He was typically in South Carolina from October through May.

Other than North Island, which is left as wilderness, the land is managed, explained resident biologist Jamie Dozier when asked about the causeways and dikes on the property: "This is managed. Wading birds, shorebirds, waterfowl. During different times of the year, you manipulate the water. Different depths for different things. Right now we're getting ready for the waterfowl that are going to be coming in here. We provide winter habitat; that's what we're doing. And food. For them to spend the winter."[24]

In other words, the DNR improves the property in service to the waterfowl that come there, as opposed to leaving it be. There are approximately fifty miles of dikes and twelve managed wetlands on South Island and perhaps the only salt-marsh weir system on the East Coast. The bald eagle and red-cockaded woodpecker are among endangered species that have found refuge at the Yawkey Center. Dozier amplifies:

> The Department of Natural Resources' goal is to manage it for maximum diversity of wildlife. If this was a typical privately owned plantation that was managed for duck hunting, they would manage these ponds specifically for ducks, and then when the ducks weren't here, most of them [would] drain the water off and manage it for something different. We manage it for ducks, and then we also manage it for shore birds and wading birds and alligators. The typical private land[owners] . . . care about but they don't really care about shore birds as much. We have a much more holistic approach. Luckily we don't have the typical user group that we have to cater to, such as duck hunters, since Mr. Yawkey set this up as a preserve. He wanted it to be a sanctuary for ducks. That's what this is. We don't have any hunting in here. The ducks winter here. That's the way he envisioned it. And that's the way he had it during his life. He didn't hunt ducks down here after . . . what, the fifties?
>
> [Phil Wilkinson interjects:] Right after World War II.
>
> [Dozier continues:] He quit duck hunting because he already saw the decline in waterfowl numbers. So he made it a sanctuary. He spent a *lot* of money improving these ponds, not to hunt in but just to have the ducks around.[25]

Indeed Yawkey had inherited some dikes from the property's prior owner, but by the late 1930s he began work to improve the property, and in the 1940s in particular he created a series of managed marshes.

Wilkinson talked about how Yawkey enjoyed the solitude. "He wasn't very much of a socialite at all. When we had gatherings, he liked socializing with the folks that worked on the place. They were there because he liked them to start with. If he didn't like you, you wouldn't be over there—if you know what I mean." Several hundred people were living on the property when the Yawkeys were there, and before it was dedicated as a refuge, they provided for themselves with a working dairy and by growing crops. By the time Wilkinson lived on the land, "We still had a pretty good-sized crew that worked over there when I was there. We had about fifteen people, and all of them had their own specialty. There were carpenters and mechanics. That sort of thing. Drivers like Jim [Sargent]. When he wasn't doing that, he was working in the mechanic shop helping keep up all the equipment." There was always a mixture of white people and black people:

Yeah. We had both. Because you lived on an island together, it was a very family feeling about everybody. Tiny [Joseph Collington] grew up with my children, and they all played together and all that sort of thing, so there wasn't all that big divide you might find out in the world, where everybody could go their own way. You didn't have anywhere to go but through each other. It was quite a different mentality that you had to have to live on an island together. You had to watch each other's back real well and all that kind of stuff.[26]

Wilkinson continues:

He [Yawkey] was a fairly shy man, anyway. Around people he was comfortable with, he was anything but shy. He was very open and talkative and full of opinions around folks he knew. He was close to the folks that worked there. I felt he was close to all of them. And felt very at home around them and very secure around them, like nobody was there to get between him and his money; I think that was something that he'd learned earlier in life, somewhere way back down the line, that people did that. Tried to get between you and your money. Once he knew that that wasn't your game, he warmed up to you much better. I think he was leery of that sort of thing. Because he wasn't very social in South Carolina either, except on the island; when the workers would have a cookout of some sort, he would always go.[27]

Wilkinson emphasized one point:

Be mindful of the fact that he [Yawkey] came here, and his world up there and his world here didn't mix much. In other words, when he was down here, it was about things to do here. We talked about baseball some, and if he had concerns, he might sit around and bounce them off of people who knew nothing about baseball—like me. I was a fan, of course, and knew a lot of players from reputation only.

"Ted [Williams] was the only one that came in the roughly eleven years that I was around, the only one who came to the island. Mr. Yawkey said the reason was he did baseball when he did baseball, and he didn't do baseball when he wasn't doing baseball. I wouldn't be able to contribute a great deal about baseball except through casual conversations that would come up sometime when he was chewing his fingernails about something. The other side I can talk about because we were together every day.[28]

Former Red Sox PR director George Sullivan remarked that in certain situations, Yawkey would open up. "He worked a crowd great. If he was among people he knew and was comfortable with, he just was terrific. But I do think there was maybe some shyness in his makeup."[29]

The area embraced by the Wildlife Center also serves as, in effect, a large, twenty-thousand-acre field laboratory for research. There are fourteen miles of pristine beachfront, a real estate magnate's dream for development but now preserved for the ages by Tom Yawkey's will. "It's a very important loggerhead sea turtle nesting area," notes Dozier. "We have about five hundred nests on the Yawkey Center each year. Even when Mr. Yawkey was alive, they were doing sea turtle work here. At the medical university we're looking at how you can use alligators as sentinel species for human health. We're providing some funding for that."[30]

In early 2013 Phil Wilkinson was given the Order of the Silver Crescent, the state of South Carolina's highest award for community service. He was honored for his work with alligators. Part of the credit might be shared with "Big Bertha," a 9-foot-8-inch-long alligator he first captured over thirty years ago on South Island, at that time the largest female alligator to be captured. Wilkinson, retired in the last years of the twentieth century, was still working in the summers a decade and a half later so he could help add to data he had collected while in the Yawkey employ, research done now in coordination with the Medical University of South Carolina.[31]

Wilkinson began working for Tom Yawkey on January 1, 1966, and stayed on for a year after Yawkey's death to assist with the transition to DNR management. It's a bizarre story how Wilkinson and

Yawkey first met, not reflecting the sort of thing one might expect from a wildlife biologist.

> He [Yawkey] used to go over to the Kinlaw Plantation, which belonged to the DuPonts at that time, and fish. I would go in and out of there because I was helping the manager that I'd known all my life practically. I grew up with his children and all that. I would go over there and help him with problems he was having with management. I'd run into Mr. Yawkey while he was over there fishing. He didn't go to these other plantations almost ever. If he went to these other plantations like the Kinlaw Plantation, he went over there to fish at the invitation of the manager. The DuPonts might not even know he went or came. We'd chat, and one day I was with one of the game wardens. I don't even remember why we were there. He and [Yawkey friend Baron] Cooper were fishing on the bridge, and we stopped to chat; we always did. We asked how was the fishing, and he said, "Well, we can't catch anything. These damn garfish keep bothering us." We looked over the railing, and you could see these big garfish just waiting on him to put his line in the water. The game warden said, "Here, Phil. Take this .38 and get rid of that damn garfish." He knew that I had been on a pistol team in the army. So I leaned over the edge and popped that garfish. Mr. Yawkey looked over at Cooper and said, "Did you see that shit?" Cooper said, "Well, I got one over here. See if you could do that again." And I shot that one too. Two shots and two garfish. Then I handed the pistol back and said, "Now let them care of themselves. They need to figure out how to get rid of their own fish." That sort of made Mr. Yawkey take a second look at me. We went on our own way. He called me up a day or two later and said, "How would you like a job?" And I said, "My Yawkey, I've got a job."[32]

Yawkey persisted and prevailed.

Alligators were Wilkinson's special field of study. He took blood samples from captured alligators; he says of the creatures, "They are like the canary in the coal mine, monitoring the contaminants in the environment, and they're looking at those contaminants." Wilkinson stayed on a year or so after Tom Yawkey's death but then departed. He was candid about the change: "Mrs. Yawkey was different from Mr. Yawkey in a lot of ways; she did not trust very many people. She quickly let you know that she was watching you and what was going on. So she was a lot harder for me to get along with."[33] The two Yawkeys had different personalities.

An executive secretary at Fenway Park from May 1947 to 1976, Mary Trank had her own opinions and minced no words about Jean Yawkey. "She was an absolute horror," she says. "She was the biggest nothing. She just wanted his money. I didn't like her at all."[34] Clearly there was no love lost there. Bill Souris, who drove for the Yawkeys, said, "There was a little division there in the office at the time. . . . There was the O'Connell crew and Mary Trank versus the Yawkey crew, or that's what the perception was with maybe Mrs. Yawkey. She would take Mary Jane Ryan, Helen Robinson, a couple of ladies, and go to lunch once in a while. Those were the people she trusted. I think she felt they protected her husband."[35]

O'Connell and Jean Yawkey did not get along. "He hated her," said Clark Booth. "He just *hated* her. And she hated him." And Mary Trank was close to O'Connell. "When Jean took over the team, she ordered [Trank] out. . . . John Claiborne told me it was her first act, to order Mary Trank to leave the premises."[36] (Trank landed a good job at TV-38, says Tom Shaer, a former Boston and Chicago sportscaster and now a Chicago media consultant: "Dick O'Connell and Bill Flynn, who was the general manager at TV-38, were really tight. Bill Flynn got Mary Trank a job, a good job, executive assistant to the head guy or something.")[37]

On the other hand, Maureen Cronin was lavish in her appreciation of Jean and at one point wrote, "I can go on forever about how wonderful she was to me."[38] Obviously many people found Jean a pleasing personality, and her dedication to the Red Sox and to the charitable causes both Tom and Jean had supported over the years remained resolute. In the years after Tom's death, she could have made any number of changes in how she chose to live her life. She stayed on the same course she had set with her husband.

Maureen Cronin offers some elaboration on her own relationship with Jean and perhaps a bit of insight into Tom Yawkey's relationship with women and children. "My memories of Tom Yawkey are not of a personal nature. We were really separate from them. Especially Tom. I can't think of one conversation I ever had with him. He nodded a hello and then would address his comments to the adults in the room, usually to my father. They never saw each other socially, but he demanded a lot of my dad's attention. Was it a case of "Children should be seen and not heard?" "I don't know. Maybe he didn't grow up with siblings and so he felt uncomfortable. I never remember ever seeing him around children. Of course, the most wonderful and ironic thing is that he's done so much for the Jimmy Fund and so much for children."[39]

It was a different world, of course, perhaps also typified by the fact—as we have seen—that Tom and Jean had separate boxes at Fenway Park, just as they had separate trailers on South Island.

The Yawkeys and Cronins never socialized apart from work.[40]

> I would see him [Tom] at the ballpark in the 1950s, but the women shared a box to watch the games, and the men shared a separate one. My parents remained very friendly with Tom's first wife, Elise Yawkey, and I always wondered if that kept them from social meetings.
>
> Elise . . . was just lovely. She was one of the most beautiful people you'd ever want to meet. She wasn't a tall, lanky woman like Jean was. She was shorter—and beautiful blond hair. I think she was a Palmolive hand model; I think my mother told me. She had beautiful jewelry, and she had the hugest rings you ever saw in your whole life. She took her diamond ring off—eight carat or something—and put it on my finger when I was seventeen or eighteen and said, "Now you go out and find someone who can buy you one of these."

Elise remained close to Joe and Mildred Cronin, and she even came to Maureen's wedding. "I don't remember my mother and Jean being particularly friendly."

As a child, Maureen had not really known Jean Yawkey and was maybe a bit in awe of her. At the park she and her mother might sit in Jean's box, but that would make Mildred Cronin nervous, maybe because Jean didn't have children, "and I was young and kind of bratty at the time. I remember spilling a Coke, and I remember my mom being very upset with me for spilling the Coke, a little more upset than she would usually get; I think it was because she was feeling that kids weren't really all that welcome there. I didn't go back to the box for a while. I think we ended up sitting downstairs a little bit more."

Maureen felt that Tom and Jean were more than compatible.

I think they had a good relationship. I think Jean was great for Tom. I loved Jean. She was a wonderful, wonderful woman and a very unique person. But I think personality-wise, they were much more at ease together. She liked going to the ballpark. She kept score at every game. I used to keep score too, so we would sit together after Tom had passed and I had moved to Boston. You wouldn't talk so much, but you'd share opinions about people and situations and keep score. She couldn't have been kinder to me. She was just wonderful.

Jean was always pleasant to me when I was growing up and spending time around the ballpark. It wasn't until she came to my father's funeral that I had a special moment with her. She took my hands in hers and looked me straight in the eyes and said, "Always look for opportunities." . . . That's all that she said. So after thinking about her comment and then becoming a stockbroker, I moved to Boston and wrote her a note telling her what I'd done. She arranged for a dinner for us that included the Harringtons and myself, and we all got along swimmingly that night. So she asked me to join her at the park to see a game, and I quickly became a very frequent guest of hers for the next two years. She was great fun to be with, very smart, didn't waste a lot of words, and had a most generous heart. She also had definite likes and dislikes regarding people, but she had a reason for her opinions that was founded on something specific, not whimsical. We would sit together and keep score for the games, and she would include me in any of the team's social events outside the ballpark. Getting to know her was a special treat for me, and I loved her company.

It didn't seem that Jean had a large number of friends. Maureen agrees: "I don't think she did. I don't think she let very many people in. I was thrilled that she befriended me and was so nice to me, and I was grateful to her for that. I guess it was in the last four years of her life that I got to know her really well." Maureen, too, told of how Jean Yawkey didn't seem to fret the material things:

I was in process of getting divorced, so it was very nice when she took me under her wing when she did. Very, very nice. It was a big step for me to move to the big city by myself. I moved to Boston, and she called me and invited me to dinner. I was kind of nervous about showing up at the restaurant and everything. I remember it was bitterly cold out. She went to a special place for Peking duck that she liked in the North End. It was John Harrington and Jean and myself and Maureen Harrington. [At the dinner with the Harringtons] we had a lovely time together. She [Jean] couldn't have been friendlier.... After we came out, we were all getting our coats, and they came out with this beautiful black ranch mink coat. The maître d' started to put it on Jean's shoulders, and she said, "No, no. That's not mine." Maureen Harrington said, "That's mine." And then he came out with this muskrat coat and went to put it on her, and she said, "That's not mine." It was mine. Then he came out with this scant little cloth coat, and Jean said, "That's mine!"

I looked at her feet, and she kind of had these functional but open-toed shoes. Of course, we were just going from the restaurant to the car, so it wasn't like she was walking for blocks. But I remember thinking how unmaterialistic she was.[41]

In South Carolina, Jean just had a South Island worker cut her hair.[42]

Mary Jane Ryan remembers Jean Yawkey as being down to earth, someone who never carried herself like a celebrity.

I got friendly with Mrs. Yawkey later. I was very friendly with Helen [Robinson]. We did lots of things together. Helen and I were buddy-buddy.... Mrs. Yawkey was staying at the Ritz, but she loved to go grocery shopping. I'd go down and pick her up and take her to the Beacon Market over in Brookline. She loved to do that. And then take us girls for lunch. That was just her thing, you know? She probably didn't get a chance to do those things. She liked to buy things. She liked to cook.

She never really talked about her family. We'd go out to lunch, but we'd just talk about general things. Whatever women talk about at lunch—just whatever's going on. She loved to go to the theater, so we'd get tickets and go to the theater. Downtown, the Schubert. There was a good ticket seller at Fenway who also got tickets to theaters; he took care of us.... She loved to do that.

She was human. She was fun. She was very easy to be around.

[Sometimes "the boss" can be intimidating.] She wasn't. Not at all. We'd go out to lunch a lot. I'd pick her up for lunch and go grocery shopping. There used to be a cute little restaurant right up there near the Beacon Market. We'd just go in there and get a burger or something like that. Or we'd go to TGIF on Newbury Street. She liked to go there.[43]

Ryan's recollection was that no one hopped to attention when Jean Yawkey entered a restaurant. If they even knew who she was, "they didn't make a fuss about it."[44]

Affirmative action at Fenway? Jean Yawkey took a leadership role, quietly, in another area. Larry Cancro relates the following:

The '80s were a different time—the whole ratio of male to female and what women were doing. She [Jean] promoted women and racial ratios in the office. She was very concerned with us being ahead of the curve and not behind. In the years when she was the principal owner of the team, we were ahead of all teams, all the time. Front office. People in the office. And she was proud of that. She was proud that we hired Elaine [Weddington Steward] to be assistant GM. She was the person who was principally responsible for that. Major League Baseball around the 1990s started putting out data on how many teams had women in management roles and minorities of all kinds. From that time on, we were always in the forefront.

She cared about many of the people. . . . I have a disabled daughter. As her disability was coming to light—it was not that long before Mrs. Yawkey's passing—she would express concern to me all the time. "How are things coming along? What are they finding out? Do you need anything?" It was real concern. Not a platitude at all. It made you feel good. That's the way they ran things here.

They [the Yawkeys] would come in, and they'd talk to people. If they found out there was a hardship or a health issue. . . . I heard stories about him from the people who were here for a long time. . . . "My kid was sick, and then we got a note that said, "You're to report here. Mr. Yawkey's taken care of everything."' You never worried about a thing.

The people here were fiercely, fiercely loyal to him and the ball club. When he made a final decision about something, in their minds, it was final forever. We were looking at changing color schemes in the ballpark when he'd been dead about fifteen years, and they were like, "Mr. Yawkey picked that color. We can't change it." And I'm like, … "We can't talk to him anymore." … To them, whatever he decided was the end of the story.[45]

The work of conservation and care for the lands Tom Yawkey willed to the State of South Carolina, of course, never ends. In March 2015 a 475-pound leatherback turtle turned up on a remote beach at the South Island Reserve. The turtle was only ten years old, a juvenile for a species that often lives to over one hundred. It was a big deal; it was only the fifth such sea turtle to ever have been found alive in the United States. This one appeared ill, so it was rescued and taken for treatment at the South Carolina Aquarium. The turtle was given a name: Yawkey.[46] A few days later, it was released back into the wild.

As we have seen, Tom Yawkey was described as "sports executive, conservationist" by the Red Sox in the official team comment on his death. A dozen years later, in 1988, Ernest L. Wiggins visited the three islands that comprise the area Yawkey left to the State of South Carolina and spoke with Bob Joyner, the resident biologist at the Tom Yawkey Wildlife Center. Joyner and his family were among the thirty-two people living on the island, as Jamie Dozier does in 2015. As Joyner was showing Wiggins around, they came upon a six-foot snake stretched across the road, and they simply waited until it chose to move on. This was, Wiggins explained, "a wildlife area, not a people area."[47] To underscore a point made above, the area was managed for the benefit of the wildlife and not simply left untouched. Thus around the beginning of each year, staff members conducted supervised burns of the underbrush of the pine forests on Cat Island. "Joyner said the burning does not harm the pines, but clears the forest floor of the hardwood seedlings, which, if unchecked, would choke out the vegetation that is the natural food of the wild turkeys."[48]

Acknowledgments

SPECIAL THANKS TO those at the Yawkey Foundations—Maureen Bleday, Nancy Brodnicki, Bill Gutfarb, John Harrington, and Jim Healey.

It's a special reporter who preserves her notes from a story printed a full quarter-century earlier, but Susan Trausch had done so, and her notes for her 1989 *Boston Globe* feature on Jean Yawkey were very helpful. Thanks to John Stobierski as well.

Phil Wilkinson was very helpful and patient with interviews before, during, and after my visit to Georgetown in November 2012.

Thanks as well to Chris Wertz, Bijan Bayne, Ben Davis, and many others who helped out in numerous ways.

I wish to express my gratitude for interviews granted by the following: Brian Aitchison, Maureen Bleday, Russell Boles, Clark Booth, Dick Bresciani, Lee Brockington, Robin Brown, Steve Buckley, Rick Burleson, Larry Cancro, Sister Stella Caramitros, Tom Carroll, Bud Collins, Cecil Cooper, Larry Corea, Maureen Cronin, Mark Cumbee, Arthur D'Angelo, Jamie Dozier, Bob Feller, Dick Flavin, Eddie Germano, Joe Giuliotti, Al Green, Pumpsie Green, Bill Gutfarb, Tommy Harper, John Harrington, Jim Healey, Bob Heise, Buddy Hunter, Dick Johnson, Eddie Kasko, Art Keefe, Ed Kenney, Bill Lee, Ted Lepcio, Jim Lonborg, Fred Lynn, Maury McDermott, Bill Monbouquette, Bob Montgomery, Leigh Montville, Roger Moret, Donna Mountain, Paul Needham, Mel Parnell, Norman Pashoian, Johnny Pesky, Rico Petrocelli, Rico Picardi, John Powers, Jim Rice,

Tom Rubillo, Steve Russo, Mary Jane Ryan, Alex Sanders, Jim Sargent, Chaz Scoggins, Tom Shaer, Reggie Smith, Bill Souris, Mary Trank, Susan Trausch, Frank Sullivan, Sally White, Phil Wilkinson, and Jim Willoughby.

Notes

Introduction

1. See http://sabr.org/bioproj/person/6382f9d5. Accessed January 20, 2017. Mark Armour's biography of Tom Yawkey appears in Mark Armour and Bill Nowlin, eds., *Red Sox Baseball in the Days of Ike and Elvis: The Red Sox of the 1950s* (Phoenix: SABR, 2012).

2. The longest article written about Jean Yawkey was Susan Trausch's 4,756-word profile, which ran in the *Boston Globe* on April 6, 1989, just three days into that year's Red Sox season. Tom Yawkey was the subject of two pieces: James S. Kunen, "The Man with the Greatest Job in Boston," *Boston*, September 1975, and Marc Onigman, "Tom Yawkey: Gentleman, Sportsman, and Racist," *The Real Paper*, August 9, 1980.

3. Author interview with Dick Johnson, August 12, 2014.

1. A Baseball Santa

1. *Hartford Courant*, December 17, 1933.

2. By 1933 the *New York Times* had mentioned Yawkey only three times, all in May 1927, and all three mentions referred to his serving as an usher at the wedding of Bertram Work of Oyster Bay. (Mr. Work's father was president of B. F. Goodrich.) The *Boston Herald* did note a Thomas J. Austin who was killed in a Ku Klux Klan shooting in Buffalo in September 1924. That Thomas Austin was called a "K.K.K. investigator" and was killed while in the car of Klan leader George C. Bryant. But our Thomas Austin had already changed his name by that time and was attending Yale as Thomas A. Yawkey.

3. *The Sporting News*, July 19, 1923.

4. The story of Sunday baseball and the Red Sox and of John S. Dooley is told in depth in Bill Nowlin, *Red Sox Threads* (Burlington MA: Rounder Books, 2008), 368, 400, 401.

5. See, for instance, Henry Berry, *Boston Red Sox* (New York: Routledge, 1975), 20.

6. Quoted in *Philadelphia Inquirer*, February 26, 1933.

7. Quoted in Albert Chen, "Mister Fenway," *Sports Illustrated*, November 24, 2011.

2. Yawkey and Collins Buy the Red Sox

1. *Hartford Courant*, February 27, 1933.

2. *New York Times*, February 26, 1933.

3. Quoted in Albert Chen, "Mister Fenway," *Sports Illustrated*, November 24, 2011.

4. *Springfield (MA) Republican*, March 2, 1933.

5. Quoted in *Springfield (MA) Republican*, March 2, 1933.

6. Quoted in *Boston Globe*, March 2, 1933.

7. See Rick Huhn, *Eddie Collins: A Baseball Biography* (Jefferson NC: McFarland, 2008), 272, 273. Huhn's excellent book draws on *The Sporting News* of November 8, 1950, for Collins's account of the first meeting between Yawkey and Collins. See also, for instance, the *Canton (OH) Repository*, December 3, 1934. Norman Macht writes that Collins and Mack had dinner at the Alexandria Room of Schrafft's Restaurant at Fifth Avenue and Forty-Sixth Street. See Norman L. Macht, *Connie Mack: The Grand Old Man of Baseball* (Lincoln: University of Nebraska Press, 2015), 29.

8. *Cleveland Plain Dealer*, November 21, 1949.

9. *Boston Herald*, July 10, 1976.

10. Al Hirshberg, *What's the Matter with the Red Sox?* (New York: Dodd, Mead, 1973), 56, 57. Glenn Stout and Richard A. Johnson, *Red Sox Century* (Boston: Houghton Mifflin, 2000), 182, report that roommate Allan MacMartin won the award twice, in Tom's junior and senior years.

11. Huhn, *Eddie Collins*, 272.

12. *Boston Herald*, September 13, 1948.

13. *Boston Herald*, October 26, 1975.

14. Quoted in *Boston Globe*, October 1, 1967.

15. Quoted in *Boston Globe*, March 2, 1933.

16. *Boston Globe*, February 26, 1933.

17. Huhn, *Eddie Collins*, 274. Huhn cites *The Sporting News* of January 14 and August 5, 1959. The actual share and percentage are both unknown, and we do not know when Collins's share reverted to Yawkey or was purchased back by Yawkey; perhaps Collins's death triggered a buyback provision.

18. Quoted in *Boston Globe*, February 26, 1933. A *New York Times* article of the same date added another Quinn comment: "I haven't the money to stay in Boston baseball and I won't be a hanger-on."

19. *Boston Globe*, February 26, 1933. An odd note: in 1935 the Northeast Merchants, a semipro ball team in Canton, Ohio, featured a lineup including a Yawkey playing left field and batting sixth and a Quinn playing second base and batting seventh. See the box score in the May 26, 1935, issue of the *Canton Repository*.

20. Quoted in *Boston Globe*, February 26, 1933.

21. Quoted in *New York Times*, February 26, 1933.

22. AP in *Washington Post*, February 26, 1933.

23. *The Sporting News*, June 7, 1923.

24. *Boston Herald*, May 9, 1926.

25. Stout and Johnson, *Red Sox Century*, 168.

26. Quoted in *New York Times*, February 26, 1933.

27. *Boston Globe*, February 27, 1933.

28. *Hartford Courant*, February 27, 1933.

29. *Boston Herald*, February 27, 1933.

30. Quoted in *Washington Post*, February 28, 1933.

31. *Boston Herald,* November 16, 1979. Yawkey said this exchange with Ruppert happened during that first year of ownership, in mid-June 1933, when the Red Sox hosted the Yankees for a five-game set and, after dropping the first game, won four straight. See also Berry, *Boston Red Sox*, 22.

3. The First Season

1. *Washington Post*, February 28, 1933.

2. Quoted in *Washington Post*, February 28, 1933.

3. *Boston Herald*, March 18, 1933.

4. Quoted in "From Fifth Avenue to the Fenway," *New York Times*, March 20, 1933.

5. Quoted in "From Fifth Avenue to the Fenway," *New York Times*, March 20, 1933. Kieran was likely mistaken in referring to North Carolina instead of South Carolina. See also *Boston Globe*, July 18, 1961.

6. Quoted in "From Fifth Avenue to the Fenway," *New York Times*, March 20, 1933.

7. Quoted in *Boston Globe*, March 26, 1951. Stout and Johnson, *Red Sox Century*, rightly point out, "Mack's benevolence appears somewhat disingenuous" (177). After all, Mack himself was in financial straits during the Depression, and over the next few years Yawkey purchased several players from Mack's Athletics.

8. The *New York Times* of April 3 printed a photograph of the wreckage and quoted a captain of the Delaware state police as to how helpful and efficient the Red Sox players—in bare feet and pajamas—had been in checking over the passenger list to ensure there were none missing.

9. *Boston Globe*, May 10, 1933.

10. Quoted in *Boston Globe*, May 13, 1933.

11. Quoted in *Boston Globe*, May 10, 1933.

12. *Boston Globe*, May 13, 1933.

13. Quoted in *Boston Globe*, June 10, 1933.

14. *Hartford Courant*, May 13, 1933.

15. *New York Times*, July 4, 1933.

16. AP in, for example, *Augusta (GA) Chronicle*, August 1, 1933.

17. Quoted in AP in *Augusta Chronicle*, August 1, 1933.

18. *Boston Globe*, September 19, 1933.

19. Quoted in F. C. Lane, "A Master Baseball Builder," *Baseball Magazine*, June 1934.

20. Author interview with Dick Johnson, August 12, 2014. See also Stout and Johnson, *Red Sox Century*, 186.

21. *Boston Globe*, September 19, 1933.

22. Author interview with Dick Johnson, August 12, 2014.

4. The First Offseason

1. *Boston Globe*, October 3, 1933.

2. *Boston Globe*, October 13, 1933.

3. *Boston Globe*, October 26, 1933.

4. *Washington Post*, October 27, 1933.

5. *Washington Post*, October 27, 1933.

6. *Hartford Courant*, October 20, 1933.

7. *Hartford Courant*, October 20, 1933.

8. *Boston Globe*, October 29, 1933.

9. *Hartford Courant*, October 30, 1933.

10. Quoted in *Boston Globe*, December 2, 1933.

11. *Boston Globe*, December 6, 1933.

12. *Boston Globe*, December 13, 1933.

13. The article ran in several newspapers, including the *Boston Globe*, December 15, 1933.

14. *Washington Post*, December 15, 1933.

15. Quoted in *Boston Herald*, December 16, 1933.

5. Tom Yawkey's Past

1. *Boston Globe*, February 26, 1933.

2. Richard Bak, *A Place for Summer: A Narrative History of Tiger Stadium* (Detroit: Wayne State University Press, 1998), 75, 80.

3. Bak, *A Place for Summer*, 80.

4. Hugh C. Weir, "The Richest Man in Baseball," *Baseball Magazine* 13, no. 4 (August 1914): 49–54.

5. Bak, *A Place for Summer*, 94.

6. Weir, "The Richest Man in Baseball," 53–54.

7. Bak, *A Place for Summer*, 119, 121.

8. *Daily Register Gazette* (Rockford IL), November 28, 1896.

9. Glenn Stout and Richard A. Johnson, *Red Sox Century* (Boston: Houghton Mifflin, 2000), 180. Stout has researched the Yawkey family background more thoroughly than anyone before.

10. *Chicago Tribune*, June 28, 1935.

11. *Chicago Tribune*, June 28, 1935. It was another newspaper that described the plumbing store and ran a photograph of it. See *San Diego Union*, June 28, 1936.

12. Quoted in *New York Tribune*, March 20, 1919.

13. *New York Tribune*, March 20, 1919.

14. At the time Margaret Yawkey died in 1933, a payment of $250,000 from her estate was made to Elizabeth Carmichael Witherspoon. A handwritten note from Margaret "allegedly acknowledged Elizabeth as her child, and that of Bill Yawkey." The amount paid was in settlement of a claim Elizabeth brought against

the estate upon learning of Margaret's death. See *San Diego Union*, June 28, 1936. Elizabeth had visited Bill and Margaret occasionally but had understood them to be an aunt and uncle.

15. Stout and Johnson, *Red Sox Century*, 179–183, present the most extensive genealogy on the Yawkey family.

16. Stout and Johnson, *Red Sox Century*, 179–183.

17. See "Capitalist Dies at Local Hotel," *Augusta Chronicle*, March 6, 1919.

18. *The Sporting News*, March 9, 1933.

19. The figures come from *New York Times*, March 19, 1918, 6. "My dad" is from *Baltimore Sun*, March 23, 1919.

20. In *San Diego Union*, June 28, 1936.

21. The phrase was used in an exhibit at the time of a visit to the museum by the author in October 2012. George C. Rogers Jr., *The History of Georgetown County, South Carolina* (Spartanburg: Reprint Company, 2002; published for the Georgetown County Historical Society), has "The Rich Yankees" as its penultimate chapter.

22. Rogers, *The History of Georgetown County*, 494.

23. Mary Boyd and James H. Clark with the Georgetown County Historical Society, *Georgetown and Winyah Bay* (Charleston SC: Arcadia, 2010), 11. For a complete history of Hobcaw Barony, see Lee G. Brockington, *Plantation between the Waters* (Charleston SC: History Press, 2006).

24. Carl Yastrzemski and Gerald Eskenazi, *Yaz: Baseball, the Wall, and Me* (New York: Doubleday, 1990), 77, 78.

25. Stout and Johnson, *Red Sox Century*, 182, 193.

26. *New Haven Journal-Courier*, May 20, 1922.

27. *New Haven Journal-Courier*, June 19, 1924.

28. Thomas Yawkey's alumni file at Yale University, form date-stamped October 30, 1924.

29. Given the annual inflation rate of 2.93 percent over the intervening years, $3,000 pocket money in 1924 would total $40,413.12 in 2014, according to the inflation calculator at www.dollartimes.com. Accessed January 20, 2017. Yawkey didn't live too badly.

30. *New York Times*, February 26, 1933.

31. Quoted in *Boston Globe*, October 1, 1967.

32. James R. McKeldin, "Tim Yawkey Buys Boston Red Sox; Youthful Yale Alumnus Enters Ranks of Magnates by Purchasing American League Baseball Club," *Phi Gamma Delta*, April 1933. McKeldin, a 1925 graduate of the University of Virginia, wrote that another "Fiji" (Phi Gamma Delta member) had made overtures for the purchase of the Red Sox: Winfield A. Schuster, Brown '28.

33. Author interview with Jim Sargent, October 19, 2012.

34. Leigh Montville, *Ted Williams* (New York: Doubleday, 2004), 140.

35. Author interview with Maureen Cronin, December 11, 2013, and Maureen Cronin email to author, May 16, 2014.

36. Author interviews with Phil Wilkinson, October 20 and December 12, 2012.

37. Author interview with Bud Collins, September 22, 2014.

38. Author interview with Alex Sanders, June 5, 2012.

39. Quoted in *Baltimore Sun*, March 23, 1919.

40. *Baltimore Sun*, March 23, 1919.

41. Quoted in *New York Tribune*, March 20, 1919.

42. *New York Tribune*, March 20, 1919.

43. Quoted in *Baltimore Sun*, March 23, 1919.

6. Yawkey at Yale

1. *Boston Globe*, February 26, 1933.

2. *Tampa Tribune*, December 16, 1933.

3. *Yale Daily News*, October 9, 1920.

4. *Yale Daily News*, April 30, 1923.

5. Quoted in *Boston Herald*, October 26, 1975.

6. *Boston Globe*, August 4, 1980. There is no mention of the play in the *Yale Daily News*.

7. John Alden North, ed., *History of the Class of Nineteen Hundred Twenty-Five Sheffield Scientific School Yale University* (published under the direction of the Class Secretaries Bureau, 1925). The full names of his roommates were Allan Alderson MacMartin, Lawrence Bogart, Ernst Ohnell Jr., and Frederick Anthony MacDevitt. Though he had his numerals, Tom was not a letter man. One of the ballot questions in the '25 S. Class Book asked the respondent to name the "Honor most to be desired." Tom drew the letter "Y."

8. Nurmi was "the Flying Finn" who won a total of nine gold and three silver medals in the Olympics. The "confidential" ballot, date-stamped February 20, 1925, is included in Thomas Yawkey's alumni file at Yale University.

9. James R. McKeldin, "Tim Yawkey Buys Boston Red Sox; Youthful Yale Alumnus Enters Ranks of Magnates by Purchasing American League Baseball Club," *Phi Gamma Delta*, April 1933.

10. Thomas Yawkey's alumni file at Yale University, date-stamped October 30, 1924.

11. Note included in Thomas Yawkey's alumni file at Yale University, dated November 29, 1932.

12. *Vernon Views*, June 1, 1938.

13. *Boston Globe*, February 26, 1933.

14. *The Mirror*, Phillips High School, Birmingham, Alabama, 1925. Elise is said to have also modeled for artist James Montgomery Flagg, but the only references I could find were to Howard Chandler Christy.

15. Glenn Stout and Richard A. Johnson, *Red Sox Century* (Boston: Houghton Mifflin, 2000), 183.

16. Frederick G. Lieb, undated 1943 newspaper column in Yawkey's file at the National Baseball Hall of Fame.

17. *The Sporting News*, May 4, 1939.

18. *The Sporting News*, March 2, 1933.

19. *New Haven Register*, June 19, 1925.

7. First Season of the Yawkey Era, 1934

1. *Boston Globe*, January 4, 1934.

2. *Boston Globe*, January 4, 1934.

3. *Chicago Tribune*, January 2, 1934. Woodson used a revolver to shoot himself soon after telephoning his mother to wish her a happy new year. An AP story noted that the coroner understood Woodson had done so because he had been denied the use of one of the family's automobiles.

4. Quoted in *Boston Globe*, January 6, 1934.

5. *Boston Globe*, January 7, 1934.

6. *Boston Globe,* January 25, 1934.

7. Quoted in *Hartford Courant*, January 25, 1934.

8. Quoted in *Boston Herald*, January 25, 1934.

9. Mickey McDermott, with Howard Eisenberg, *A Funny Thing Happened on the Way to Cooperstown* (Chicago: Triumph Books, 2003), 65. McDermott states that in the off-seasons, ballplayers could stay at the Commodore for $5 a room.

10. *Boston Globe*, March 1, 1934.

11. *Boston Globe*, March 19, 1934.

12. *Boston Globe* and *Boston Herald*, March 21, 1934.

13. *Boston Herald*, April 7, 1934. The proceeds from the 3,500 who attended went to the athletic fund. Elise lost a wager with Eddie Collins when only 1,000 fans turned out in Birmingham; she'd predicted 3,500 for Birmingham too.

14. *Boston Herald,* June 22, 1934.

15. *Boston Globe*, April 10, 1934.

16. At other times in 1934, the park was dubbed Yawkey Stadium or New Yawkey Yard, but it was never designated as anything other than Fenway Park, and the other monikers were out of use by the end of the year. The April 17 *Boston Herald* said Yawkey had stipulated the name remain the same.

17. *Boston Globe*, April 18, 1934.

18. *Boston Globe*, April 23, 1934.

19. *Christian Science Monitor*, April 24, 1934.

20. *Boston Globe*, April 30, 1934.

21. See, for instance, *New Orleans Times-Picayune* and *San Diego Union*, both on June 18, 1934. Grantland Rice in *Omaha World Herald*, December 17, 1947.

22. Quoted in *Boston Herald,* August 13, 1984.

23. *New York Times*, May 7, 1934. Whether John Kieran's story was tongue in cheek, like a Charles Dryden story would have been a generation earlier, we do not know for sure.

24. *New Orleans Times-Picayune*, September 23, 1934.

25. *New York Times*, August 13, 1934.

26. *Christian Science Monitor*, August 15, 1934.

27. *Boston Herald*, October 20, 1934.

28. *Washington Post*, October 27, 1934.

29. Mark L. Armour and Daniel R. Levitt, *In Pursuit of Pennants* (Lincoln: University of Nebraska Press, 2015), 80. Dr. Michael Haupert of SABR and the University of Wisconsin-LaCrosse cites the House Committee of the Judiciary report on Organized Baseball, 82nd Cong., 1st Sess., 1951, which presents 1933 salaries on page 1610. The figures include salaries not just for players but for coaches and managers as well. Only the Cubs, at $266,431, and the Yankees, at $294,982, had greater aggregate team salaries than the $225,000 cash portion of the Cronin purchase.

30. *Boston Globe*, October 27, 1934.

31. Quoted in *The Sporting News*, July 30, 1952.

32. Quoted in *New York Times*, October 27, 1934.

33. *Hartford Courant*, October 28, 1934.

34. AP in *Richmond Times Dispatch*, June 12, 1938.

35. House Committee of the Judiciary Report on Organized Baseball, 82nd Cong., 1st Sess., 1951, 1610. The total for all sixteen clubs was $3,005,049.

36. Quoted in Minutes of the Annual Meeting of the Board of Directors of the American League of Professional Baseball Clubs, December 11, 1934, 48. The minutes are on file at the National Baseball Hall of Fame.

37. Quoted in *Boston Globe*, December 13, 1934.

38. Quoted in *State Times Advocate* (Baton Rouge LA), December 12, 1934.

39. Quoted in *Chicago Tribune*, December 21, 1934.

8. Settling in as Red Sox Owner, 1935-1938

1. Quoted in *Hartford Courant*, January 16, 1935.

2. Quoted in *Washington Post*, February 9, 1935.

3. Unidentified newspaper clipping dated June 27, 1935; found in Yawkey's Hall of Fame file.

4. Unidentified newspaper clipping dated September 17, 1937; found in Yawkey's Hall of Fame file.

5. *Cleveland Plain Dealer*, March 15, 1935.

6. *Boston Herald*, April 8, 1935.

7. Quoted in *Seattle Daily Times*, April 26, 1935.

8. *Boston Post*, November 12, 1944.

9. Quoted in *Boston Globe*, July 14, 1935.

10. *Boston Globe*, June 28, 1935.

11. A detailed account of the shooting and confessions is in the July 2, 1936, *Chicago Tribune*.

12. Quoted in *Trenton Evening Times*, April 27, 1936. The same day's *Cleveland Plain Dealer* contained a summary of developments.

13. *Boston Herald*, June 16, 1935.

14. Quoted in *Boston Globe*, July 22, 1935.

15. *Boston Globe*, July 24, 1935.

16. *Boston Globe*, September 24, 1935. The Fenway team included Hugh Duffy, Ed Kenney, Johnny Orlando, Phil Troy, and Hi Mason. The writers included Ed Rumill, Jack Malaney, Gerry Moore, Harold Kaese, and pitcher Joe Cashman. Rumill and Kaese were each 3-for-3 in the three-inning affair.

The Tom Yawkey Cup was awarded for amateur baseball in Greater Boston's Suburban Twilight League. Yawkey's encouragement of baseball is part of an ongoing tradition in the region and was reflected in the early twenty-first century by the Yawkey Baseball League, which began under that name in 1990 or 1991.

17. Yawkey quoted in *Boston Globe*, October 2, 1935; *Chicago Tribune*, October 3, 1935.

18. *Literary Digest*, December 21, 1935.

19. Quoted in *Boston Herald*, January 21, 1958.

20. Quoted in Minutes of the Annual Meeting of the Board of Directors of the American League of Professional Baseball Clubs, December 10, 1935, 54.

21. *Boston Herald*, December 20, 1935.

22. Daniel M. Daniel, *The Sporting News*, March 9, 1933.

23. Quoted in *Washington Post*, January 17, 1936.

24. Quoted in *Richmond Times Dispatch*, February 5, 1936.

25. Quoted in *Washington Post*, March 15, 1936.

26. *New York Times*, March 20, 1936.

27. *Boston Globe*, April 8, 1936.

28. *Boston Herald*, March 11, 1936.

29. *Boston Globe*, April 5, 1936.

30. *Christian Science Monitor*, April 9, 1936.

31. *Boston Herald*, January 7, 1936.

32. Quoted in *Hartford Courant*, April 18, 1936.

33. UP in *Washington Post*, June 2, 1936.

34. Susan Trausch interview with Haywood Sullivan, March 10, 1989. Ms. Trausch provided the author with full access to the original notes of her various interviews conducted in preparation for her April 6, 1989, *Boston Globe* article on Jean Yawkey.

35. *Omaha World Herald*, July 9, 1936.

36. See, for instance, the *San Diego Tribune*, January 16, 1936.

37. *Christian Science Monitor*, July 2, 1936.

38. *Christian Science Monitor*, July 2, 1936.

39. Quoted in *Chicago Tribune*, July 8, 1936.

40. *Boston Globe*, July 11, 1936.

41. Quoted in *Boston Herald*, July 11, 1936.

42. *Boston Herald*, February 1, 1936.

43. Quoted in *Chicago Tribune*, July 31, 1936. In 1934 the Cincinnati Reds had flown from Cincinnati to Chicago but in three separate planes.

44. *State Times Advocate* (Baton Rouge LA), February 5, 1936.

45. Quoted in *Cleveland Plain Dealer*, March 6, 1936.

46. Quoted in *New York Times*, August 23, 1936.

47. *Boston Globe*, August 22, 1936, as quoted in Dick Thompson, *The Ferrell Brothers of Baseball* (Jefferson NC: McFarland, 2005), 200.

48. "From the *Sunday Worker*," in *Chicago Defender*, August 29, 1936. On the subject of hot potatoes, Yawkey literally liked his baked potatoes steaming hot. A curious story about this preference and floor waiter Dug Flynn at the Ritz ran in the *Boston Herald* on July 16, 1976. Room service waiter Mario Labadini told Susan Trausch that the Yawkeys loved seafood and that Tom always had a big double scoop of chocolate ice cream. See Susan Trausch interview with Mario Labadini, March 15, 1989. Labadini later became maître-d' at The Café at the Ritz and after that had his own restaurant, the Charles Restaurant on Chestnut Street, where Jean Yawkey frequently dined.

49. *Washington Post*, November 6, 1936.

50. Quoted in Frederick G. Lieb, *The Boston Red Sox* (New York: G. P. Putnam's Sons, 1947), 215.

51. Quoted in *Christian Science Monitor*, November 18, 1936.

52. "We told Wes we didn't want to take his money," Yawkey explained. Quoted in *Boston Herald*, November 19, 1936.

53. *New York Times*, April 28, 1937.

54. *New Haven Register*, December 9, 1936. The article continued, "But the betting is plenty to one he'll not get away with it."

55. *The Sporting News*, December 3, 1936. Yawkey told Ray Trullinger of the *New York World-Telegram* that the only real problem they had on the hunt was Eddie Collins, who kept falling down. "He fell over rocks and when he couldn't find anything else to fall over, he'd trip over his own feet. He practically wore us out." Foxx apparently left his automobile at Yawkey's place in South Carolina, and one of Yawkey's employees brought it out to the railroad station as the Foxx family headed south for spring training in 1937; Jimmie, his wife, and two sons took the car the rest of the way to Sarasota. See W. Harrison Daniel, *Jimmie Foxx* (Jefferson NC: McFarland, 1996), 101.

56. *New York Times*, July 10, 1976.

57. Unidentified newspaper clipping dated September 17, 1937; found in Yawkey's Hall of Fame file.

58. Lew Freedman, "Red Sox Allegiance Never Died," CodyEnterprise.com, December 31, 2014. Accessed on the same date.

59. *Afro-American*, February 15, 1936.

60. See, for instance, the *Boston Globe*'s 1935 All-Scholastic Baseball Team roster in the June 19, 1935, newspaper.

61. *Boston Globe*, June 19, 1935.

62. *Boston Globe*, September 3, 1935. The December 31, 1935, *Globe* ran a photo of Foxx and Zagami. Later in 1935 Jack Wilson of the Red Sox also homered into the center-field seats.

63. Frannie Matthews's story is told in depth by Chris Wertz, "The Frannie Matthews Story," a paper distributed at SABR's Jerry Malloy Conference in 2013.

64. Quoted in *Boston Globe*, January 14, 1937.

65. Quoted in *New York Times*, February 3, 1937.

66. Quoted in *New York Times*, March 25, 1937.

67. *Boston Globe*, April 22, 1937.

68. Lloyd Johnson and Miles Wolff, *Encyclopedia of Minor League Baseball* (Durham NC: Baseball America, 2007).

69. *Springfield (MA) Republican*, July 7, 1937.

70. Freedman, "Red Sox Allegiance Never Died."

71. Quoted in *Greensboro (NC) Daily News*, April 2, 1937.

72. *Cleveland Plain Dealer*, September 20, 1937.

73. Bill Nowlin, "Ted Williams—Hoover High, Before and After" in *The Kid: Ted Williams in San Diego*, ed. Bill Nowlin (Burlington MA: Rounder Books, 2005), 100.

74. *Boston Globe*, January 31, 1938.

75. *Boston Globe*, February 3, 1938.

76. Quoted in *Greensboro Record*, March 25, 1938.

77. Quoted in *Boston Globe*, March 2, 1938. Baseball's "reserve clause" would have prevented the players from signing with another team. Owners were very much in a "take it or leave it" position once they had a player under contract. Some owners abused that advantage. Yawkey was better known for tearing up contracts and offering larger ones than for insisting on pressing his rights under the clause, which allowed him to reserve a player for the following year.

78. Quoted in *Omaha World Herald*, October 19, 1938.

79. Quoted in Michael Blake, *Baseball Chronicles: An Oral History of Baseball through the Decades* (New York: Betterway Books, 1994), 92.

80. *Baton Rouge Advocate*, June 28, 1938.

81. *The Oregonian*, August 4, 1938.

9. The Kid Makes the Big Leagues, 1939

1. Quoted in Ed Linn, *Hitter* (New York: Harcourt, Brace, 1993), 82.

2. *The Sporting News*, August 28, 1976.

3. *Boston Record American,* March 14, 1970.

4. Quoted in *San Diego Union*, April 3, 1939. In terms of never biting at a bad ball, Williams demonstrated excellent plate discipline from his first year. He drew 107 bases on balls, without any of the "help" an umpire might give a veteran player who had earned a reputation. Williams still holds the highest career on-base percentage of any player who ever played the game.

5. *Boston Herald*, May 30, 1939.

6. Unidentified newspaper clipping dated June 15, 1939; found in Yawkey's Hall of Fame file.

7. Al Hirshberg, *The Red Sox, the Bean, and the Cod* (Boston: Waverly House, 1947), 51.

8. Michael Seidel, *Ted Williams: A Baseball Life* (Chicago: Contemporary Books, 1991), 61.

9. *Boston Globe*, July 19, 1939.

10. Quoted in *Chicago Tribune*, July 26, 1939.

11. Associated Press, July 26, 1939.

12. Quoted in *Boston Herald*, July 1, 1939.

13. See, for instance, *Greensboro Record*, August 21, 1939.

14. *Los Angeles Times*, December 31, 1939.

10. Before the War, 1940–1941

1. Quoted in *Boston Traveler*, June 16, 1942.

2. *Christian Science Monitor*, March 26, 1940.

3. *Los Angeles Times*, January 22, 1940.

4. *Los Angeles Times*, February 6, 1940.

5. *Los Angeles Times*, April 14, 1940. A photo ran in some papers in mid-March showing the Yawkeys watching a spring training game together, so Elise may have returned to Florida at least for a while.

6. *Hartford Courant*, February 5, 1940.

7. Quoted in *Washington Post*, March 10, 1940.

8. AP in *Washington Post*, March 10, 1940.

9. *Boston Globe*, March 12 and 15, 1940.

10. *New York Times*, April 26, 1940.

11. Quoted in Ed Linn, *Hitter* (New York: Harcourt, Brace, 1993), 122.

12. *Cleveland Plain Dealer*, August 22, 1940.

13. Quoted in *Christian Science Monitor*, August 14, 1940.

14. Quoted in *Boston Globe*, August 14, 1940. See also the *Boston Record* of the same date.

15. For a comprehensive look at every one of Ted Williams's 521 home runs—and ones he hit in All-Star Games, in the Minor Leagues, in high school even—and some of his thoughts about hitting homers, including why he preferred hitting at Fenway to hitting at Yankee Stadium with its short right-field porch, see Bill Nowlin, *521: The Story of Ted Williams' Home Runs* (Cambridge MA: Rounder Books, 2013).

16. *Boston Globe*, January 14, 1941, and *New York Times*, January 19, 1941.

17. Quoted in *Boston Globe* and *Boston Herald*, January 22, 1941. See also Jim Kaplan, *Lefty Grove: American Original* (Cleveland: SABR, 2000), 234–35.

18. *Boston Globe*, January 21, 1941.

19. See, for instance, *Boston Herald*, January 19, 1941.

20. Letter to the editor from Dick Cunningham of Wellesley Hills in *Boston Globe*, February 26, 1941.

21. *New York Times*, April 2, 1941. Kieran still seemed to have North Carolina, rather than South Carolina, firmly in mind.

22. *Christian Science Monitor*, March 6, 1941.

23. Norman L. Macht, *Connie Mack: The Grand Old Man of Baseball* (Lincoln: University of Nebraska Press, 2015), 132.

24. *Hartford Courant*, March 7, 1941.

25. *Boston Traveler*, March 15 and 16, 1941.

26. *Boston Globe*, May 30, 1954.

27. *Greensboro Daily News,* August 29, 1941.

28. David Halberstam, *Summer of '49* (New York: William Morrow, 1989), 137. None of the various people with whom I talked and who had worked out with Yawkey in later years had a sense that different baseballs were used.

29. Quoted in *Boston Herald*, January 17, 1941. In the early twenty-first century, Ted Williams's photograph still graced the walls of the Hotel Nacional, along with photos of movie stars and other celebrities who had visited the hotel in years gone by.

30. *Boston Herald*, April 6, 1941.

31. Dom DiMaggio with Bill Gilbert, *Real Grass, Real Heroes* (New York: Zebra Books, 1990), 169.

32. The phrase "royal box" was used a few times by the *Boston Herald*—e.g., April 14 and 16, 1941.

33. *Washington Post*, April 17, 1941.

34. Quoted in *Boston Globe*, August 8, 1944. The next day, Foxx said he'd been misquoted.

35. Quoted in *Boston Traveler*, May 2, 1942.

36. Quoted in *Washington Post*, April 22, 1941.

37. Quoted in *Christian Science Monitor*, April 24, 1941.

38. *Boston Globe*, May 21, 1941.

39. Quoted in Leigh Montville, *Ted Williams* (New York: Doubleday, 2004), 86.

40. *Boston Globe*, June 13, 1941.

41. *Washington Post*, July 6, 1941.

42. Williams would have hit .411 in 1941, and there would have been no last-day drama, except for the fact that in 1941 a sacrifice fly counted as an out and a time at bat.

43. Quoted in Montville, *Ted Williams*, 92.

44. Quoted in *Baton Rouge Advocate*, September 1, 1941.

45. Bill Nowlin, *Day by Day with the Boston Red Sox* (Cambridge MA: Rounder Books, 2006), 406.

46. *Washington Post*, December 8, 1941.

47. Wide World syndicated column appearing in (among other newspapers) *Augusta Chronicle*, December 16, 1941. On another occasion, Martin called Yawkey the "chubby baseball merchant" and added, "Everyone hopes he some time will get his picture in the papers as the owner of the new champions. He's tried too hard, and is too nice a guy to deserve anything but the best of luck." *Hartford Courant*, December 16, 1941.

48. *Hartford Courant*, December 24, 1941.

49. Quoted in *Boston Traveler*, August 4, 1954.

11. The War Years, 1942–1945

1. Ted Williams with John Underwood, *My Turn at Bat* (New York: Fireside Books, 1969), 99.

2. Williams with Underwood, *My Turn at Bat*, 99; emphasis in original.

3. See *Boston Globe*, May 2, 1944.

4. The July 15, 1944, *Washington Post* quotes Yawkey as saying, "I never did like night ball; I don't like it now, and I don't believe I ever will."

5. For two such columns, see Harold Kaese, "Deferment of Williams Will Put Him on Hot Spot as He Faces Critical Fans," *Boston Globe*, February 28, 1942, and Vic Stout, "Ted May Face Hostile Fans," *Boston Traveler*, March 6, 1942.

6. A full chapter is devoted to the controversy in Bill Nowlin, *Ted Williams at War* (Burlington MA: Rounder Books, 2007), 17–30.

7. *Boston Traveler*, March 6, 1942.

8. Williams with Underwood, *My Turn at Bat*, 99.

9. Michael Seidel, *Ted Williams: A Baseball Life* (Chicago: Contemporary Books, 1991), 115.

10. See the Kaese column in the March 13, 1942, *Globe*. Yawkey was said to have been relieved that the crowd reaction was favorable when Ted pinch-hit in his first spring game on March 12.

11. Quoted in *Washington Post*, March 14, 1942.

12. For more about Johnny Pesky (born John Paveskovich), see Bill Nowlin, *Mr. Red Sox: The Johnny Pesky Story* (Cambridge MA: Rounder Books, 2004).

13. Quoted in *Boston Globe*, April 14, 1942.

14. *Boston Post*, April 18, 1942.

15. *Rockford (IL) Morning Star*, March 19, 1942.

16. *Washington Post*, June 20, 1942. A photograph of Mrs. Yawkey in her CDVO uniform appears in the June 4, 1943, *New York Times*. A full story of her work starting up the blood drive appears in the March 23, 1943, *Boston Traveler*.

17. *New York Times*, August 17, 1942.

18. *Washington Post*, August 20, 1942.

19. *Washington Post*, January 12, 1942.

20. *Boston Globe*, September 25, 1942.

21. Quoted in *Washington Post*, June 1, 1942.

22. *New York Amsterdam Star-News*, August 1, 1942.

23. Williams placed second in the MVP voting. He led the league only in average, on-base percentage, RBIs, home runs (winning the Triple Crown), slugging, and runs scored. Yankees second baseman Joe Gordon won the MVP. Though Gordon hit .322 and drove in 103 runs and the Yankees won the pennant, the only two categories in which Gordon led the league were striking out and grounding into double plays.

24. *Washington Post*, October 27, 1942.

25. See, for instance, "Yawkey Opposed to Red Sox Trades," *Boston Herald*, December 3, 1942.

26. Quoted in *Boston Globe*, December 4, 1942.

27. Quoted in Nowlin, *Mr. Red Sox*, 62.

28. John Drohan, *Boston Herald*, December 22, 1942. Not that there were any rice fields there that were being actively worked in the twentieth century.

29. *Trenton Evening Times*, April 4, 1943.

30. *Boston Globe*, April 11, 1943.

31. *Boston Globe*, June 27, 1943. Jones's column placed Yawkey in the company of numerous other professional sports teams also owned by "absentee landlords."

32. *Springfield (MA) Republican*, October 7, 1943.

33. UP in *Springfield (MA) Republican*, April 5, 1944.

34. *San Diego Union*, December 11, 1943.

35. *Boston Globe*, April 4, 1944.

36. Quoted in *The Sporting News*, December 21, 1944.

37. Quoted in *Boston Globe*, June 25, 1944.

38. *Christian Science Monitor*, June 28, 1944.

39. *Christian Science Monitor*, July 6, 1944.

40. *Boston Globe*, July 10, 1944.

41. *Boston Globe*, August 9, 1944.

42. Quoted in *Boston Globe*, August 31, 1944.

43. See Duke Goldman, "The 1944 Red Sox: What Could Have Been," in *Who's On First? Replacement Players in World War II*, ed. Marc Z. Aaron and Bill Nowlin (Phoenix: SABR, 2015).

44. *New York Times*, December 13, 1944.

45. Author interview with Phil Wilkinson, December 12, 2012.

46. Glenn Stout and Richard A. Johnson, *Red Sox Century* (Boston: Houghton Mifflin, 2000), 234, 235.

47. Quoted in *Boston Globe*, May 26, 2013.

48. Author interview with Norman Pashoian, October 11, 2014.

49. Author interview with Tom Carroll, October 10, 2014.

50. Author interview with Dick Johnson, August 12, 2014.

51. James S. Kunen, "The Man with the Greatest Job in Boston," *Boston*, September 1975.

52. Author interview with Arthur D'Angelo, September 10, 2014. I also conducted a lengthy interview with D'Angelo on July 13, 2000, a portion of which is printed in Bill Nowlin, *Fenway Lives* (Cambridge MA: Rounder Books, 2004).

53. Author interview with Mel Parnell, December 11, 1999. Ed Linn, *The Great Rivalry* (New York: Ticknor and Fields, 1991), has more on John Donovan's rise from the bottom to the top. See, for example, page 224.

54. Author interview with Larry Corea, July 8, 1999.

55. David Halberstam, *Summer of '49* (New York: William Morrow, 1989), 135.

56. Email from Maureen Cronin, May 16, 2014.

57. Susan Trausch, "The Woman Who Owns the Red Sox Keeps Her Private Life Private," *Boston Globe*, April 6, 1989.

58. *Boston Herald*, February 27, 1992.

59. *Time*, January 8, 1945.

60. Charles Oppenheim's obituary ran in the November 17, 1981, *New York Times*.

61. Susan Trausch interview with William Oppenheim, March 13, 1989.

62. Letter of Ralph M. Ford Jr. to Susan Trausch, April 23, 1989.

63. Trausch, "The Woman Who Owns the Red Sox Keeps Her Private Life Private."

64. All data regarding Freeport High School activities for both Jean Hollander and Charlie Hiller are courtesy of the Freeport Historical Society. Thanks to Regina G. Feeney, librarian/archivist, Freeport Memorial Library.

65. UP in *The Oregonian*, April 2, 1945.

66. Bob Hohler, *Boston Globe*, July 8, 2008.

67. Bob Hohler, *Boston Globe*, July 8, 2008.

68. Bill Nowlin, ed., *Pumpsie and Progress: The Red Sox, Race, and Redemption* (Burlington MA: Rounder Books, 2010).

69. *Boston Globe*, November 26, 2000.

70. Author interview with John Powers, August 12, 2014.

71. Tom Shaer, email to author, December 28, 2015.

72. Author interview with Clark Booth, September 2, 2014. The "Whitey" referred to, in a bit of Booth hyperbole, was Boston mobster Whitey Bulger.

73. Author interview with Clark Booth, September 2, 2014.

74. Author interview with Clark Booth, September 2, 2014. Booth offers a fascinating look at some of the reporters covering the issue: "It wasn't just the ball clubs that were racist back then. But there were reporters who agitated about it. Much to his credit, and he died a very bitter man, Larry Claflin stirred around about it a lot in the early fifties. A lot of the other guys told him to shut up. Higgins called him a nigger lover and stuff like that. Claf was a hard-nosed guy, not a very educated man—a tough kid from Melrose. Hard-drinking guy and all that, but he did [raise the issue of racism], and others did too. Even Clif [Keane], who's been wrongly cast as some kind of Klansman; no way was he that. I knew Clif really well. . . . Clif was a character. He had an odd sense of humor. And he comes from a different time. He was very much a . . . Hyde Park or Dorchester (I think it was Dorchester) kid who came right out of the late twenties and early Depression period. Hard knocks all the way. Not much education. But he had a big heart. I saw it again and again. He really was good with black players. Frank Robinson was one of the toughest guys—up there with [Bill] Russell, [Bob] Gibson, and a couple of others, guys who were really difficult to deal with because they were really strong-minded men, very gifted, able men, and they didn't take any shit from anybody. Frank was in that group. Frank loved Clif. Frank would come with the Orioles and say, 'Where's Keane?' Frank was not a back-slapping guy, but he loved Keane. There were a lot of examples like that."

75. Rick Huhn, *Eddie Collins: A Baseball Biography* (Jefferson NC: McFarland, 2008), 301–7.

76. Bijan Bayne has also done considerable research on the subject of black baseball in Boston.

77. See "Matthews May Play Ball with Tenney's Team," *Boston Traveler*, July 15, 1905.

78. The Matthews story is discussed at length in Karl Lindholm, "Rumors and Facts: William Clarence Matthews' 1905 Challenge to Major League Base-

ball's Color Barrier," NINE: *A Journal of Baseball History and Culture*, 17, no. 1 (Fall 2008): 38–53.

79. Quoted in *Boston Traveler*, August 9, 1905.

80. Lindholm's careful consideration of the question led him to the conclusion, regarding the rumor that the Boston Braves were considering bringing Matthews on board, "that there is reason to doubt the truth of the Matthews rumor." "Rumors and Facts," 51.

81. Mabray "Doc" Kountze, *Fifty Sports Years along Memory Lane* (Medford MA: Mystic Valley Press, 1979), 45.

82. Kountze, *Fifty Sports Years along Memory Lane*, 45. Bing Miller played sixteen seasons in the Majors, the final two (1935–36) for the Red Sox.

83. Quoted in *Chicago Defender*, September 23, 1967.

84. Quoted in *Boston Globe*, May 26, 2013.

85. Kountze, *Fifty Sports Years along Memory Lane*, 24, 25.

86. Kountze, *Fifty Sports Years along Memory Lane*, 25. Bob Quinn Jr. was at the helm when the Boston Braves brought up Sam Jethroe in 1950, the first African American Major League baseball player in Boston—a little more than nine years before the Red Sox brought up Pumpsie Green.

87. Quoted in *Boston Globe*, July 22, 1979.

88. *The Sporting News*, October 9, 1946.

89. *Boston Herald*, February 20, 1988.

90. Bart Fisher, "Speaking of Sports," New England Newsclip, July 12, 1976. Otherwise unidentified column found in Yawkey's Hall of Fame file.

91. Author interview with Dick Johnson, August 12, 2014.

92. *Pittsburgh Courier*, August 2, 1947.

93. Quoted in *Richmond Times Dispatch*, May 2, 1945.

94. Quoted in Rich Cleveland, *Boo: A Life in Baseball, Well-Lived* (Battle Ground WA: Pediment Publishing, 2008), 69.

95. *New York Times*, July 27, 1945.

96. The January 3, 1946, *Christian Science Monitor* devoted a full story to the subject but dismissed any idea that Yawkey would give consideration to such an offer.

97. Author interview with Jim Healey, January 25, 2013.

98. Author interview with Jim Sargent, November 15, 2012.

99. Author interview with Jim Sargent, November 15, 2012. For Yawkey, Jim says he was "just a plain laborer. Cut the grass with bush axes, stuff like that. . . . I drove the tractors. I'd run errands. I took Miz Yawkey and Miss Mary. . . . [Mrs. Yawkey] had a companion, but I don't remember the last name. . . . We used to go shopping, to Georgetown, to Charleston. We'd visit the hospital in Charleston." Miss Mary Burke had been a nurse and is understood to have taken care of Jean's mother before becoming Jean's companion. Miss Mary often sat with Jean during games, and they sometime traveled together. "She used to come all the time. She used to take care of Mrs. Yawkey's mother. That's what I remember. Lovely person. Good-sized gal. Tall gal. . . . Pleasant-looking. White hair.

Very quiet. Probably about the same age [as Jean]." Author interview with Mary Jane Ryan, August 6, 2014.

100. *Georgetown Times*, March 3, 1992.

101. Information provided by the City of Georgetown on its website: www .cityofgeorgetownsc.com/history/history.cfm. Accessed January 20, 2017.

102. The story and quotes, in this paragraph and below, come from author interview with Phil Wilkinson, October 19, 2012.

12. Postwar and the Pennant, 1946

1. *Boston Globe*, July 4, 1946.

2. *Washington Post*, January 15, 1946.

3. Author interview with Bob Feller, May 3, 1997.

4. The story regarding the Pasquels and the Mexican League has been told elsewhere. Recommended reading includes G. Richard McKelvey, *Mexican Raiders in the Major Leagues: The Pasquel Brothers vs. Organized Baseball, 1946* (Jefferson NC: McFarland, 2006), and John Virtue, *South of the Color Barrier: How Jorge Pasquel and the Mexican League Pushed Baseball toward Racial Integration* (Jefferson NC: McFarland, 2007).

5. *Saturday Evening Post*, March 23, 1946, and *Boston Globe*, May 8, 1946.

6. *Boston Globe*, May 8, 1946.

7. *Boston Globe*, May 21, 1946.

8. Email to author from Don Doerr, July 24, 2014.

9. *New York Times*, June 13, 1946.

10. *Boston Globe*, June 14, 1946.

11. Quoted in *Boston Globe*, June 14, 1946.

12. *Boston Globe*, June 14, 1946.

13. *Boston Globe*, June 14, 1946.

14. Quoted in *Boston Traveler*, June 17, 1946.

15. See, for instance, *Greensboro Record*, June 24, 1946.

16. *Cleveland Plain Dealer*, October 9, 1946. Cobbledick may have reflected some of the apparent friction between Yawkey and the Indians organization.

17. *The Oregonian*, October 10, 1946.

18. *Boston Globe*, July 10, 1946.

19. Quoted in *Boston Globe*, July 11, 1946.

20. *Canton Repository*, July 17, 1946.

21. *Cleveland Plain Dealer*, July 16, 1946.

22. *New York Times*, July 19, 1946.

23. *New York Times*, September 17, 1946.

24. See, for instance, *Washington Post* and *Boston Globe*, September 13, 1946. In the September 10 *Boston Herald*, Williams verified the story.

25. Ted Williams with John Underwood, *My Turn at Bat* (New York: Fireside Books, 1969), 122.

26. *Boston Herald*, September 14, 1946.

27. Quoted in *Boston Globe*, September 13, 1946.

28. Al Hirshberg, *What's the Matter with the Red Sox?* (New York: Dodd, Mead, 1973), 24. Hirshberg has a whole chapter on press relations, beginning with his explanation of how cushy the press had it; in effect, writers were bribed or at least compromised by the ball club paying all their traveling expenses, including transportation, hotels, and even food, liquor, and incidentals. It's not surprising that coverage was less critical in the day. Hirshberg doesn't mince words; he calls it "sheer bribery" on page 123.

29. For instance, see the September 14, 1946, *Boston Traveler*.

30. *Boston Herald*, September 24, 1946. Numerous stories told of tickets Yawkey gave gratis to this or that person who had somehow come to his attention and had a good story to tell.

31. See *Boston Globe*, October 6 and 8, 1946. Yawkey urged Ted to ignore the stories, but it was difficult to do, and Yawkey never said anything publicly until October 10, when he stressed, "I wouldn't trade Ted Williams for the entire New York Yankees franchise" (quoted in *Boston Globe*, October 11, 1946).

32. Reprinted in *Washington Post*, October 8, 1946.

33. *Boston Globe*, October 9, 1946. Late in December, Kaese wrote that Yawkey had been irritated enough that he'd said, "Instead of firing Williams, I'll buy a newspaper and fire some baseball writers" (quoted in *Boston Globe*, December 30, 1946).

34. *Christian Science Monitor*, October 9, 1946.

35. AP in *Augusta Chronicle*, October 2, 1946.

36. *Boston Globe*, October 10, 1946.

37. *Boston Globe*, October 8, 1946.

38. Quoted in *Boston Globe*, October 18, 1946.

39. *Boston Globe*, October 16, 1946.

40. *Los Angeles Times*, October 20, 1946.

41. George Carens of the *Boston Traveler* said he'd heard there would be a $5,000 per player bonus if the Sox won the World Series. *Boston Traveler*, October 19, 1946.

42. Quoted in *Boston Globe*, October 18, 1946.

13. Strong Seasons, 1947–1950

1. Quoted in *Boston Globe*, January 26, 1947.

2. Quoted in *Boston Globe*, January 29, 1947.

3. Quoted in Dick Bresciani, "Kind and Caring," *Memories and Dreams*, Opening Day 2012, 35, 36.

4. Quoted in *Washington Post*, February 14, 1947.

5. *Boston Globe*, April 11, 1947. Installing the lighting required some adjustments but was considered to be very well done. See *Christian Science Monitor*, June 13 and 14, 1947.

6. Quoted in *Christian Science Monitor*, May 22, 1948.

7. *Boston Herald*, September 9, 1948.

8. Quoted in *Hartford Courant*, April 30, 1988.

9. Author interview with Maureen Cronin, December 11, 2013. See also *Boston Globe*, February 27, 1992.

10. Susan Trausch interview with Clif Keane, February 28, 1989.

11. Quoted in *Boston Globe*, April 11, 1947.

12. Quoted in *Boston Globe*, August 20, 1947.

13. *Boston Globe*, April 25, 1947.

14. *Boston Globe*, June 13, 1947.

15. *Boston Globe*, May 19, 1948.

16. Quoted in *Boston Globe*, April 4, 1993.

17. *Boston Globe*, July 5, 1947.

18. Quoted in *Boston Globe*, September 9, 1947.

19. Quoted in *Washington Post*, October 3, 1948.

20. Quoted in *New Haven Register*, July 10, 1976.

21. *Chicago Tribune*, November 22, 1947.

22. *Boston Globe*, January 14, 1958. The UP story reported that it was Sam Breadon (of the St. Louis Cardinals) and Wrigley, not Briggs.

23. *Springfield (MA) Union*, December 12, 1947.

24. Ed Linn, *Hitter* (New York: Harcourt, Brace, 1993), 307–8. Linn says Williams's 1948 contract was for $115,000 and that Williams reached $125,000 in 1949.

25. Quoted in *Standard-Times* (New Bedford MA), September 24, 1965. Williams might well have been even better at Yankee Stadium, but the park he preferred most was the one in Detroit. Ted said he heard that Yawkey would have gone through with the Yankee deal later that morning but asked that Topping throw in Yogi Berra. See Ted Williams with John Underwood, *My Turn at Bat* (New York: Fireside Books, 1969), 219.

26. Quoted in *Standard-Times*, September 24, 1965.

27. Quoted in *New Orleans Times-Picayune*, January 22, 1948.

28. *Boston Globe*, April 24, 1948.

29. *Boston Herald*, April 24, 1948.

30. *Christian Science Monitor*, May 26, 1948.

31. Quoted in *Boston Herald*, April 24, 1948.

32. A very nice appreciation of Lynch appears in the July 23, 1948, *Boston Herald*.

33. *Boston Herald*, October 1, 1948.

34. Author interview with Mary Jane Ryan, August 6, 2014.

35. Quoted in Carl Yastrzemski and Gerald Eskenazi, *Yaz: Baseball, the Wall, and Me* (New York: Doubleday, 1990), 79.

36. Quoted in *Boston Herald*, October 5, 1948.

37. *Christian Science Monitor*, April 11, 1949.

38. *Chicago Tribune*, May 12, 1949. See also *Boston Herald*, July 11, 1976. Koney scouted full time for the Red Sox through 1992 and then remained with the Sox as a consultant. He died on October 12, 2015.

39. *Boston Traveler*, January 30, 1959.

40. Al Hirshberg, *What's the Matter with the Red Sox?* (New York: Dodd, Mead, 1973), 114, 115. Hirshberg says that Johnny Murphy "was not a good farm director for the Red Sox. But Cronin wouldn't fire Murphy for the same reason Yawkey wouldn't fire Cronin. Murphy was his friend, a good guy, and Cronin wouldn't fire a friend."

41. *Boston Globe*, July 15, 1949. An article in the August 9, 1949, *Boston Traveler* agreed that Yawkey would miss working out at the park. "He has the Orlando brothers and their gang shagging for him, and the keen enjoyment he takes out of these sweat sessions could be advanced as still another reason why he won't sell the Red Sox." A 1952 article said Yawkey paid a local sandlot pitcher $50 a day to pitch to him and two others $50 each to shag for him. See *Washington Post*, April 28, 1952.

42. *Boston Globe*, January 18, 1950.

43. See, for instance, *Washington Post*, August 24, 1949.

44. Quoted in *Hartford Courant*, September 18, 1949.

45. Quoted in *Boston Herald*, October 3, 1949.

46. *The Sporting News*, August 2, 1961.

47. Quoted in David Halberstam, *Summer of '49* (New York: William Morrow, 1989), 277.

48. *Hartford Courant*, October 4, 1949.

49. Quoted in *Boston Globe*, October 7, 1949.

50. Quoted in *Boston Globe*, December 31, 1949.

51. *Boston Herald*, January 22, 1950.

52. Quoted in *Boston Globe*, December 30, 1949.

53. Author interview with George Sullivan, October 3, 2014.

54. *Boston Globe*, January 1, 1950.

55. AP in *San Diego Union*, January 26, 1950.

56. Quoted in *Boston Herald*, February 8, 1950.

57. *Christian Science Monitor*, April 11, 1950.

58. Quoted in *Boston Traveler*, April 12, 1950.

59. The closest they have come since has been the 961 runs scored in 2003. They scored 949 in the World Series championship season of 2004.

60. *Boston Globe*, May 3, 1950.

61. *Christian Science Monitor*, May 13, 1950.

62. *Boston Globe*, May 13, 1950.

63. *Boston American*, May 13, 1950.

64. *Boston Globe*, May 13, 1950.

65. Quoted in *Boston Herald*, June 2, 1950.

66. Birdie Tebbetts with James Morrison, *Birdie: Confessions of a Baseball Nomad* (Chicago: Triumph Books, 2002), 98-105.

67. *Boston Traveler*, June 10, 1950.

68. Quoted in *Boston Globe*, June 24, 1950.

69. *Boston Traveler*, August 25, 1950.

70. Quoted in *Boston Globe*, September 15, 1950. The portion of the road trip Yawkey was on was said to be his first "western" trip (Chicago and St. Louis) with the team since 1946. One story out of St. Louis had him sitting by himself in the back of the Sportsman's Park grandstand during one game. *Boston Herald,* September 15, 1950.

71. Quoted in *Hartford Courant*, October 3, 1950.

72. Tebbetts with Morrison, *Birdie*, 115.

73. Tebbetts with Morrison, *Birdie*, 115.

74. *Boston Globe*, November 17, 1950.

75. *New York Times*, December 6, 1950.

76. *Chicago Tribune*, December 13, 1950.

77. *Chicago Tribune*, December 22, 1950.

78. *Boston Globe*, December 29, 1950.

79. Howard Bryant, *Shut Out* (New York: Routledge, 2002), 47.

80. A detailed summary of the whole Piper Davis story is told in David Nevard with David Narasco, "Who Was Piper Davis?" in *Pumpsie and Progress: The Red Sox, Race, and Redemption,* ed. Bill Nowlin (Burlington MA: Rounder Books, 2010), 134–47.

81. Tygiel in Bryant, *Shut Out*, 36.

82. Quoted in Peter Golenbock, *Red Sox Nation* (Chicago: Triumph Books, 2005), 225.

83. Curt Gowdy with John Powers, *Seasons to Remember* (New York: Harper-Collins, 1993), 130, 131.

84. Author interview with John Powers, August 12, 2014.

85. Gowdy with Powers, *Seasons to Remember*, 160.

14. The Early 1950s

1. *The Sporting News*, January 10, 1951.

2. *Hartford Courant*, January 17, 1951.

3. David Halberstam, *Summer of '49* (New York: William Morrow, 1989), 89.

4. See remarks in Shirley Povich's *Washington Post* columns on March 4 and 20, 1951.

5. *Boston Globe*, March 19, 1951.

6. *Wall Street Journal*, October 20, 1951.

7. *Boston Globe*, February 15, 1951.

8. *Boston Globe*, March 21, 1951.

9. *Chicago Tribune*, July 10, 1951.

10. Dick Bresciani, "Kind and Caring," *Memories and Dreams*, Opening Day 2012, 36.

11. Quoted in *Hartford Courant*, March 19, 1951.

12. See Doerr's evaluation in the March 28, 1951, *Christian Science Monitor*.

13. *Boston Globe*, March 30, 1951.

14. *Boston Globe*, April 16, 1951.

15. *Washington Post*, March 25, 1951.

16. *New York Times*, May 8, 1951.

17. *Boston Traveler*, October 8, 1951.

18. Quoted in *Boston Herald*, July 15, 1951.

19. See, for instance, *Boston Globe*, September 2, 1951.

20. *Washington Post*, September 4, 1951.

21. *Springfield (MA) Union*, September 2, 1951.

22. Rumill in *Christian Science Monitor*, September 11, 1951. Williams quoted in *Boston Globe*, September 20, 1951.

23. *Boston Globe*, September 30, 1951.

24. Quoted in *New York Times*, October 23, 1951.

25. *Atlanta Daily World*, December 20, 1951.

26. *Boston Traveler*, November 27, 1951.

27. Quoted in *Los Angeles Times*, January 10, 1952.

28. Author interview with Jim Sargent, October 19, 2012.

29. *Boston Globe*, January 21, 1952.

30. Peter Golenbock, *Red Sox Nation* (Chicago: Triumph Books, 2005), 194. The *Saturday Evening Post* article was "I'll Make the Rules for the Red Sox," by Al Hirshberg and Lou Boudreau, February 23, 1952.

31. *Boston Globe*, April 13, 1952.

32. *Boston Herald*, May 1, 1952.

33. Quoted in *Boston Traveler*, May 2, 1952.

34. *Boston Herald*, May 4, 1952.

35. *Boston Record*, March 31, 1952.

36. *Christian Science Monitor*, June 20, 1952. The June 22, 1952, *Washington Post* put the total at $476,000.

37. *Boston Traveler*, September 2, 1952.

38. Quoted in *Boston Traveler*, January 8, 1952.

39. *Boston Record*, July 22, 1952.

40. *Boston Record*, April 6, 1972.

41. Author interview with Tom Shaer, May 17, 2015.

42. *Boston Record*, September 3, 1952.

43. *Boston Record*, September 9, 1952.

44. *Boston Traveler*, September 29, 1952.

45. *Wall Street Journal*, November 10, 1952.

46. *New York Amsterdam News*, December 13, 1952.

47. *Boston Record*, September 16, 1952.

48. *Christian Science Monitor*, February 25, 1953.

49. For a comprehensive study of Williams's Korean War experiences, including detailed descriptions of each of his thirty-nine missions, see Bill Nowlin, *Ted Williams at War* (Burlington MA: Rounder Books, 2007).

50. Quoted in *Boston Herald*, March 15, 1953.

51. Quoted in *Boston Herald*, March 16, 1953.

52. *Boston Record*, March 20, 1953. Egan's April 8 column was full of nothing but praise for Yawkey. His May 8 column ran under the headline "Yawkey Lone Hope to Save Baseball."

53. *Boston Record*, May 28, 1953.

54. *Boston Record*, February 17, 1954.

55. *Boston Globe*, April 13, 1953.

56. Quoted in *Boston Globe*, April 13, 1953.

57. *Boston Globe*, April 17, 1954.

58. Email from Don Doerr, reporting his father's remarks, July 24, 2014.

59. *The Sporting News*, August 2, 1961.

60. *Boston Record*, July 13, 1953.

61. Golenbock, *Red Sox Nation*, 204.

62. *Omaha World Herald*, January 30, 1953.

63. Author interview with George Sullivan, October 3, 2014. See also Leigh Montville, *Ted Williams* (New York: Doubleday, 2004), 172-75.

64. Author interview with George Sullivan, October 3, 2014. The next quote is also from his interview.

65. *Boston Globe*, August 18, 1953.

66. *Boston Globe*, September 3, 1953.

67. Author interview with Jim Healey, January 25, 2013.

68. Quoted in *The Sporting News*, August 2, 1961.

69. Author interview with Dick Johnson, August 12, 2014.

70. Yawkey's explanation of the trade is found in *Boston Globe*, December 10, 1953.

71. One could say that Ted Williams had three .400 seasons—1941, 1952, and 1953—and five seasons where his on-base percentage was .500 or greater.

72. Quoted in *Boston Globe*, December 7, 1953.

73. Quoted in *Boston Globe*, December 7, 1953.

74. Quoted in *Boston Globe*, January 3, 1954.

75. *Boston Globe*, December 5, 1964.

76. *Boston Globe*, April 4, 1954.

77. Quoted in *Boston Globe*, January 28, 1954.

78. Quoted in *Christian Science Monitor*, April 8, 1954.

79. Quoted in *Boston Globe*, April 16, 1954.

80. *Boston Herald*, June 22, 1954.

81. *Boston Traveler*, July 26, 1954.

82. *Boston American–Sunday Advertiser*, June 16, 1965.

83. Quoted in *Baton Rouge Advocate*, May 24, 1954.

84. Quoted in *Boston Globe*, July 13, 1954.

85. *San Diego Union*, July 2, 1954.

86. *Boston Globe*, October 7, 1954.

87. *Boston Globe*, December 7, 1954.

88. *Boston Traveler*, October 11, 1954.

89. Ted Williams with John Underwood, *My Turn at Bat* (New York: Fireside Books, 1969), 191–92. One could say, tongue in cheek, that it was all Ted Williams's fault that the Sox saddled themselves with Pinky Higgins.

90. *Omaha World Herald*, October 12, 1954.

91. *Boston Globe*, October 12, 1954.

92. *Boston Record*, October 12, 1954.

93. *New York Times*, November 18, 1954.

94. Quoted in *Boston Globe*, December 9, 1954. San Francisco was, coincidentally, the city of Cronin's birth.

95. *Washington Post*, December 23, 1954.

96. Quoted in *Boston Record*, July 22, 1954.

97. *Boston Traveler*, December 31, 1954.

98. *Boston Record*, August 17, 1954.

99. *Boston Record*, September 9, 1954.

100. Quoted in *Greensboro Record*, September 27, 1954.

101. *Hartford Courant*, January 16, 1955.

102. *Boston Record*, May 12, 1955.

103. *Boston Record*, February 11, 1955.

104. Ben Bradlee Jr., *The Kid: The Immortal Life of Ted Williams* (New York: Little, Brown, 2013), 406.

105. *Boston Globe*, April 15, 1955.

106. Quoted in *Boston Traveler*, July 7, 1955.

107. *Boston Globe*, April 7, 1955.

108. Author interview with Mel Parnell, December 11, 1999.

109. This and the quoted material in the next couple of paragraphs come from Booth's film. See Clark Booth, *Agganis: The Golden Greek, Excellence to the End* (DVD, Agganis family, 2012).

110. Clark Booth interview with Michael S. Dukakis. Pages 1 and 22 of interview transcript provided to the author on October 29, 2015.

111. Booth, *Agganis*. Yawkey did come to visit Harry's mother, Georgia, later in the summer at the family home in Lynn. Booth says that the Red Sox have continued to make an annual donation to the Harry Agganis Foundation for the past fifty years. Among other things, the money was used to build a bell tower for a church in Langanikos, the Greek village in Sparta from which Harry's parents had come to America.

112. Quoted in *Boston Globe*, July 14, 1955.

113. Quoted in *Boston Traveler*, July 22, 1955.

114. *Boston Globe*, September 13, 1955.

115. Quoted in *Boston Globe*, September 16, 1955.

116. *Boston Herald*, December 5, 1955.

117. *Boston Herald*, October 5, 1956.

118. *Boston Record*, December 6, 1955.

15. Doldrums Descend, the Latter 1950s

1. *New York Times,* February 6, 1956.

2. *Christian Science Monitor,* February 11, 1956.

3. *Boston Globe,* February 2, 1956.

4. Carl Yastrzemski and Gerald Eskenazi, *Yaz: Baseball, the Wall, and Me* (New York: Doubleday, 1990), 75, 76.

5. Yastrzemski and Eskenazi, *Yaz,* 76.

6. Author interview with Donna Mountain, August 10, 2014.

7. Author interview with Paul Needham, August 20, 2014. John Pohlmeyer was said to have been a former Minor League catcher (though his name does not turn up in SABR's Minor League Database) who was with the Red Sox organization after service in World War II, but when his "career was cut short by an injury . . . Yawkey named him manager of the old Lynn Red Sox of the New England League. When the league folded, Pohlmeyer was made a scout for the Red Sox and later was brought into the parent organization as a special assistant to Yawkey." See Pohlmeyer obituary, *Boston Traveler,* March 30, 1964.

8. Author interview with Jim Lonborg, August 22, 2014.

9. Curt Gowdy with John Powers, *Seasons to Remember* (New York: Harper-Collins, 1993), 161.

10. *Boston Globe,* September 15, 1973.

11. *Boston Globe,* August 3, 1958.

12. Author interview with Mary Jane Ryan, August 6, 2014.

13. Gowdy with Powers, *Seasons to Remember,* 159.

14. *Boston Herald,* July 9, 1991.

15. Author interview with Rico Picardi, June 27, 2000. Maureen Cronin said she had been particularly close to Faith Stevens of the Stevens family. Harry M. Stevens Concessions was later bought out by the current concessionaire, Aramark.

16. Quoted in *Boston Globe,* March 21, 1956.

17. *Boston Globe,* March 21, 1956.

18. *Boston Traveler,* April 5, 1956.

19. Quoted in *Boston Record,* May 1, 1956.

20. AP in *San Diego Union,* July 15, 1956.

21. *Chicago Tribune,* July 14, 1956.

22. Author interview with Mel Parnell, December 11, 1999.

23. Author interview with John Kennedy, September 5, 2014.

24. Author interview with Bob Montgomery, May 5, 2015.

25. Author interview with Dick Johnson, August 12, 2014.

26. The July 15, 1956, *Boston Globe* offered some perspective on the problem.

27. Mabray "Doc" Kountze, *Fifty Sports Years along Memory Lane* (Medford MA: Mystic Valley Press, 1979), 47.

28. Mary Boyd and James H. Clark with the Georgetown County Historical Society, *Georgetown and Winyah Bay* (Charleston SC: Arcadia, 2010), 7, 8.

29. *Boston Globe,* July 15, 1956.

30. Quoted in *Boston Globe,* July 15, 1956.

31. *New York Amsterdam News*, August 4, 1956.

32. *Boston Traveler*, July 26, 1956.

33. *Boston Record*, July 27, 1956.

34. Quoted in *Hartford Courant*, July 22, 1956.

35. Quoted in *Boston Globe*, August 8, 1956.

36. *Boston Globe*, August 8, 1956.

37. Ted Williams with John Underwood, *My Turn at Bat* (New York: Fireside Books, 1969), 136.

38. *Boston Post*, August 8, 1956.

39. *Christian Science Monitor*, August 14, 1956.

40. Williams with Underwood, *My Turn at Bat*, 136.

41. Quoted in *Christian Science Monitor*, September 15, 1956.

42. Quoted in Ed Linn, *Ted Williams: The Eternal Kid* (New York: Thomas Nelson and Sons, 1961), 126.

43. David Halberstam, *Summer of '49* (New York: William Morrow, 1989), 175, and Gowdy with Powers, *Seasons to Remember*, 179.

44. *Christian Science Monitor*, October 3, 1956; *Boston Record*, September 20, 1956.

45. *Boston Herald*, October 6, 1956. Harridge was instead elected to a new ten-year term.

46. Quoted in *Boston Herald*, December 11, 1956.

47. *Boston Record*, June 6, 1958.

48. *Boston Globe*, November 23, 1957.

49. Quoted in *Boston Globe*, February 3, 1957.

50. Quoted in *Boston Traveler*, June 27, 1958.

51. Quoted in *Boston Globe*, March 19, 1957. A couple of weeks later, Yawkey claimed the offer had been a joke.

52. *Boston Herald*, March 2, 1957.

53. *Hartford Courant*, April 2, 1957.

54. Quoted in *Boston Herald*, April 6, 1957. The story is told in more detail in Bill Nowlin, *Ted Williams at War* (Burlington MA: Rounder Books, 2007).

55. Quoted in *Boston Globe*, April 15, 1957.

56. *Boston Globe*, May 12, 1957.

57. *The Oregonian*, June 13, 1957.

58. *The Sporting News*, August 2, 1961.

59. *Hartford Courant*, May 24, 1957.

60. Williams with Underwood, *My Turn at Bat*, 79; emphasis in original.

61. *Boston Traveler*, July 29, 1957.

62. Quoted in *Boston Globe*, July 29, 1957.

63. Quoted in *Boston Traveler*, July 29, 1957.

64. *Georgetown Times*, August 1, 1957.

65. Author interviews with Phil Wilkinson, September 12 and October 19, 2012.

66. Author interview with Phil Wilkinson, December 12, 2012.

67. Quoted in *Boston Globe*, December 6, 1954.

68. *Boston Traveler*, September 5, 1957.

69. Author interview with Phil Wilkinson, December 12, 2012. Wilkinson talked about how Jim Gibson came to be replaced. "Jim Gibson was there for quite a while. He raised his children there. Shortly after Mr. Yawkey married the second Mrs. Yawkey, around Christmastime, Jim was going to town anyway, and he [Mr. Yawkey] said, 'I'm expecting a package. Go by and check at the post office and see if it's in.' Jim said OK. He did, and he got the package and put it in the back seat of his car and went on about his business. . . . He didn't come back that day or the day after; I don't remember what [the reason] was. When he got there, he got the package out and went over. It was Mrs. Yawkey's Christmas present, it turned out, which was delivered late. It was a necklace. She was furious. Mr. Yawkey said after that situation—I don't know, maybe there were other things that happened too—but he said, 'I'm going to have to let you go.' That was not acceptable. In firing him . . . he built him a beach house over at Pawley's Island to move to. So it wasn't like *he* was that mad."

70. Author interview with Jamie Dozier, October 19, 2012.

71. Author interviews with Phil Wilkinson, September 12, October 19, and December 12, 2012.

72. Author interview with Eddie Kasko, January 5, 2015.

73. Author interview with Alex Sanders, June 5, 2012.

74. Author interview with Alex Sanders, June 5, 2012.

75. Author interview with Jamie Dozier, October 19, 2012.

76. Author interview with Jim Sargent, November 15, 2012.

77. Email from Ian Joyce, July 14, 2014.

78. *Boston Globe*, August 16, 1958.

79. Email from Ian Joyce, July 14, 2014. Ian's brother was a Red Sox fan at the time, but Ian himself was a Yankees and Mickey Mantle fan, he told Yawkey. After CBS bought the Yankees and as time passed, he converted to the Red Sox cause. Perhaps Yawkey's generosity played a part.

80. Quoted in *Boston Globe*, May 26, 2013.

81. *Boston Record*, December 21, 1957.

82. *Christian Science Monitor* and *Boston Globe*, April 2, 1958. Naturally Mayor Hynes of Boston was opposed to any moves that might take the Red Sox and other sports teams out of the city.

83. *Boston Record*, April 2, 1958.

84. *Boston Record*, March 17, 1958.

85. *Boston Globe*, December 6, 1957.

86. Quoted in *Boston Globe*, February 9, 1958. Orlando went on to describe Williams's bats, the cost of the sunglasses the players used, and more.

87. *Boston Record*, March 7, 1958.

88. *Boston Globe*, June 21, 1958. Yawkey prioritized business. When a reporter mentioned that he was going to vacation on Cape Cod, the Sox owner replied, "That's one place I've never been, although I've heard plenty about it from Joe Cronin." Quoted in *Boston Traveler*, June 24, 1958.

89. Quoted in *Boston Traveler*, July 3, 1959.

90. *Boston Globe*, July 3 and 12, 1958.

91. Al Hirshberg, *What's the Matter with the Red Sox?* (New York: Dodd, Mead, 1973), 117.

92. Hirshberg, *What's the Matter with the Red Sox?*, 51.

93. Author interview with Ted Lepcio, August 20, 2014.

94. Author interview with Dick Flavin, September 5, 2014.

95. Author interview with Bud Collins, September 22, 2014.

96. Quoted in *Boston Herald*, August 31, 1958. During the period Sullivan was hospitalized, he said that Tom Yawkey visited him every day.

97. *Boston Globe*, August 25, 1958. The October 7, 1986, *Hartford Courant* noted that Yawkey had wanted to annex Lansdowne Street but could not get the requisite political support.

98. *Christian Science Monitor*, September 16, 1958. Ed Rumill seemed to agree with the proposition that some players had taken advantage of the manager and not been held to account.

99. *Boston Record*, September 26, 1958.

100. Quoted in Peter Golenbock, *Red Sox Nation* (Chicago: Triumph Books, 2005), 219.

101. Author interview with Bud Collins, September 22, 2014.

102. *Boston Globe*, September 22, 1958.

103. Email from Frank Sullivan, September 15, 2012.

104. Author interview with Frank Sullivan, October 15, 2012.

105. Email from Sally White, via Deborah White, October 9, 2012.

106. Email from Deborah White, October 14, 2012.

107. See, for instance, *Washington Post*, December 3, 1958.

108. Quoted in *Boston Record*, December 3, 1958.

109. *Boston Record*, May 30, 1958.

110. DeFoe obituary, *New York Times*, December 6, 1958.

111. Author interview with Phil Wilkinson, December 12, 2012.

112. Author interview with Bill Gutfarb, July 24, 2014.

113. Quoted in *Boston Record*, August 28, 1959.

114. *Boston Herald*, January 19, 1959.

115. Quoted in *Boston Traveler*, January 30, 1959.

116. Quoted in *Boston American*, July 7, 1959.

117. Author interview with Jamie Dozier, October 19, 2012.

118. Quoted in *Boston Herald*, January 30, 1959.

119. *Boston Herald*, February 2, 1959.

120. *Boston Record*, February 10, 1959.

121. *Boston Globe*, March 20, 1959.

122. AP, quoted in *Seattle Daily Times*, January 23, 1959.

123. Mark Armour, "Integration, 1947–1985," http://sabr.org/bioproj/topic /integration-1947-1986. Accessed January 20, 2017. Armour's article was orig-

inally published as "The Effects of Integration," *Baseball Research Journal* 36 (SABR, 2007).

124. Quoted in Steve Buckley, *Boston Red Sox: Where Have You Gone?* (Chicago: Triumph, 2005), 210, 211. Howard Bryant tells this story in more graphic detail in *Shut Out* (New York: Routledge, 2002), 63.

125. Danny Peary, ed., *We Played the Game* (New York: Black Dog and Leventhal, 2002), 446, 447.

126. Author interview with Bill Monbouquette, April 17, 2009.

127. For a full-length study of the Red Sox and integration, see Bill Nowlin, ed., *Pumpsie and Progress: The Red Sox, Race, and Redemption* (Burlington MA: Rounder Books, 2010).

128. *Boston Globe*, April 12, 1959.

129. *Chicago Tribune*, April 15, 1959.

130. *Washington Post*, April 15, 1959.

131. *Chicago Defender*, April 21, 1959.

132. Quoted in *Chicago Defender*, May 2, 1959.

133. *Boston Record*, April 10, 1959.

134. Quoted in *Boston Herald*, April 14, 1959.

135. Author interview with Bud Collins, September 22, 2014.

136. *Boston Record*, May 20, 1959.

137. *Boston Globe*, June 3, 1959.

138. *Boston Globe*, June 10, 1959.

139. Interview with Jackie Jensen on WSBX, aired July 1, 1983. George I. Martin, *The Golden Boy: A Biography of Jackie Jensen* (Portsmouth NH: Peter E. Randall, 2000), 274.

140. *Boston Globe*, July 2, 1959.

141. Quoted in *Boston Globe*, July 3, 1959.

142. *Boston Globe*, July 4, 1959.

143. *Boston Globe*, July 4, 1959.

144. *San Diego Union*, July 4, 1959.

145. Author interview with Tom Shaer, May 11, 2015.

146. Author interview with Jim Rice, June 7, 2015. Helen Robinson's first year with the Red Sox was 1941. She worked until her death in 2001. Rice's story was reminiscent of one Johnny Pesky told about being a rookie with the Red Sox in 1942 and asking secretary Barbara Tyler if he could have a sheet of Red Sox stationery and an envelope. Tyler told Pesky, "They sell stationery in the drugstore down in Kenmore Square." Quoted in Bill Nowlin, *Mr. Red Sox: The Johnny Pesky Story* (Cambridge MA: Rounder Books, 2004), 52.

147. *Boston Globe*, July 9, 1959.

148. *Boston Record*, March 14, 1959.

149. Quoted in *Boston Globe*, August 16, 1959.

150. Quoted in *Boston Globe*, July 28, 1959.

151. Quoted in *Boston Herald*, July 22, 1979.

152. Author interview with Pumpsie Green, March 27, 2009.

153. Williams with Underwood, *My Turn at Bat*, 207, 208.

154. Quoted in Leigh Montville, *Ted Williams* (New York: Doubleday, 2004), 221.

155. Reported in Golenbock, *Red Sox Nation*, 239.

156. *Boston Record*, September 10, 1959.

157. *Boston Record*, September 30, 1959

158. *Boston Globe*, December 20, 1959.

159. *Boston Record*, December 23, 1959.

16. From Ted to Yaz, Sox Seasons of the 1960s

1. *The Sporting News*, May 18, 1960.

2. *Boston Globe*, April 24, 1960.

3. *New Orleans Times-Picayune*, January 28, 1960.

4. *Cleveland Plain Dealer*, March 30, 1960.

5. *The Sporting News*, August 2, 1961.

6. Quoted in *Boston Record*, June 1, 1960.

7. Quoted in *The Sporting News*, June 8, 1960.

8. Quoted in *Boston Globe*, June 1, 1960.

9. See Bill Cunningham's column, *Boston Herald*, May 28, 1948.

10. *Washington Post*, June 5, 1960.

11. *New Orleans Times-Picayune*, April 12, 1960.

12. Author interview with John Powers, August 12, 2014.

13. *Boston Herald*, February 18, 1972.

14. Quoted in *Boston Record*, June 1, 1960.

15. *Cleveland Plain Dealer*, June 3, 1960.

16. *Boston Record*, June 4, 1960.

17. Gross's column was syndicated; see *Omaha World Herald*, June 14, 1960.

18. *Boston Record*, February 16, 1960.

19. Author interview with Paul Needham, August 20, 2014 (also in following paragraph). Needham remembered, "It was a full two weeks—Detroit, Cleveland, Kansas City, Chicago. Tom Dowd was the traveling secretary at the time. I got the business from the players because everybody else had to double up except Ted Williams. Ted Williams and Stan Musial were supposedly the only players that got single rooms at that time."

20. *Springfield (MA) Union*, June 30, 1960.

21. *The Sporting News*, August 10, 1960.

22. *Boston Record*, July 30, 1960.

23. Quoted in *Omaha World Herald*, September 26, 1960.

24. *Boston Traveler*, September 28, 1960.

25. Quoted in *The Sporting News*, July 27, 1960.

26. Quoted in *Boston Globe*, February 8, 1961.

27. *Boston Record*, March 10, 1961.

28. *Boston Herald*, April 13, 1961.

29. Quoted in *Chicago Tribune*, May 2, 1961.

30. Quoted in *Boston Globe*, May 9, 1961.

31. *Boston American,* June 10, 1961.

32. Author interview with Rico Petrocelli, October 22, 2014.

33. *San Diego Union,* June 18, 1961.

34. Quoted in *Boston Globe,* July 13, 1999.

35. *The Sporting News,* April 5, 1961.

36. Author interview with Jim Prime, January 19, 2015. As with the 1957 story of Ian Joyce (in chapter 15 above), there is a Canadian connection.

37. *Boston Record,* August 16, 1961.

38. *Boston Record American,* June 25, 1962.

39. *Boston Herald,* January 15, 1961.

40. *Boston Globe,* December 3, 1961.

41. *Boston Globe,* March 15, 1962.

42. *Boston Globe,* April 4, 1962.

43. *Boston Globe,* May 13, 1962.

44. *Boston Globe,* July 26, 1962.

45. Quoted in Peter Golenbock, *Red Sox Nation* (Chicago: Triumph Books, 2005), 259.

46. Author interview with Dick Johnson, August 12, 2014.

47. Conley was making $30,000 at the time, so it would have been a painful fine. See Kathryn R. Conley, *One of a Kind: The Gene Conley Story* (Altamonte Springs FL: Advantage Books, 2004), 286ff. At year's end, Yawkey phoned Conley and said, "You got your money back, Gene. Congratulations, you really straightened yourself out." Quotes here and in the text are in Golenbock, *Red Sox Nation* 261–62.

48. Author interview with Dick Johnson, August 12, 2014.

49. Author interview with Peter Gammons, December 1, 2014.

50. Author interview with Bill Monbouquette, August 24, 2014.

51. *Christian Science Monitor,* May 29, 1962.

52. *Boston Record American,* May 26, 1962.

53. *Boston Record American,* May 29, 1962.

54. See the March 17, 1963, *Boston Globe.*

55. Hy Hurwitz, "Red Sox Worked to Rescue Mejias' Family from Cuba," *The Sporting News,* March 30, 1963. Some of the language here is borrowed from the Ron Briley/Rory Costello/Bill Nowlin biography of Mejias that appears on SABR's BioProject site and in Clifton Blue Parker and Bill Nowlin, eds., *Sweet '60: The 1960 Pittsburgh Pirates* (Phoenix: SABR, 2013).

56. *The Sporting News,* January 19, 1963.

57. Quoted in *Christian Science Monitor,* March 9, 1963.

58. *Boston Record American,* June 18, 1963.

59. See the April 23, 1963, *Boston Herald.* In the June 11 *Herald,* Yawkey told Arthur Sampson that he went over the details of each game with Higgins.

60. Quoted in *Christian Science Monitor,* June 26, 1963.

61. Quoted in *Boston Globe,* August 27, 1963.

62. *Boston Herald,* August 4, 1963.

63. *Boston Traveler*, September 25, 1963.

64. Author interview with Bud Collins, September 22, 2014.

65. *New York Times*, December 13, 1963.

66. *Boston Record American*, December 7, 1963.

67. Quoted in *Boston Record American*, January 2, 1964.

68. Quoted in *Boston Globe*, March 4, 1964.

69. *Boston Globe*, March 4, 1964.

70. See a detailed account of the frosty relationship between Higgins and Pesky in Pesky's biography: Bill Nowlin, *Mr. Red Sox: The Johnny Pesky Story* (Cambridge MA: Rounder Books, 2004).

71. *Boston Record American*, October 22, 1964.

72. Quoted in *Boston Herald*, March 18, 1964.

73. Quoted in *Boston Globe*, May 1, 1964.

74. Quoted in *Boston Record American*, May 2, 1964.

75. This and the following quote from Charton are in Dick Bresciani, "Kind and Caring," *Memories and Dreams*, Opening Day 2012, 35.

76. *Boston Globe*, July 6, 1964.

77. *Washington Post*, August 18, 1964.

78. *Boston Traveler*, October 5, 1964.

79. Quoted in *Boston Globe*, January 27, 1965.

80. *Boston Traveler*, March 2, 1965.

81. *Boston Traveler*, March 2, 1965.

82. Al Hirshberg, *What's the Matter with the Red Sox?* (New York: Dodd, Mead, 1973), 109.

83. Author interview with Clark Booth, September 2, 2014.

84. Author interview with Steve Buckley, November 5, 2014.

85. Jack Mann, "The Great Wall of Boston," *Sports Illustrated*, June 28, 1965.

86. Quoted in Mann, "The Great Wall of Boston."

87. Mann, "The Great Wall of Boston."

88. *Boston Globe*, June 17, 1965.

89. *Boston Traveler*, April 2, 1965.

90. *Boston Globe*, June 25, 1965.

91. *Boston Traveler*, June 24, 1965.

92. *Boston Traveler*, June 25, 1965.

93. *Boston Traveler*, June 29, 1965.

94. Ed Linn, *Hitter* (New York: Harcourt, Brace, 1993), 206.

95. Golenbock, *Red Sox Nation*, 273.

96. Glenn Stout and Richard A. Johnson, *Red Sox Century* (Boston: Houghton Mifflin, 2000), 297.

97. Stout and Johnson, *Red Sox Century*, 298.

98. Quoted in *Boston Globe*, July 9, 1965.

99. Quoted in unidentified Larry Claflin newspaper clipping dated July 24, 1965; found in Yawkey's Hall of Fame file.

100. *Boston Globe*, July 11, 1965. The failure to sign future Hall of Famer Reese is another story. One of the best accounts appears in a Joe Williams column in the *Standard-Times*, September 20, 1965.

101. David Halberstam, *Summer of '49* (New York: William Morrow, 1989), 134. Mark Armour, in his biography of Cronin, makes a compelling case that "from the Red Sox's point of view . . . there is no credible evidence that Joe Cronin needed to be replaced then, or would be anytime soon." Mark Armour, *Joe Cronin* (Lincoln: University of Nebraska Press, 2010), 110. Armour notes that Yawkey unreservedly assumed any blame. See *The Sporting News*, May 8, 1941.

102. *Boston Globe*, July 11, 1965.

103. Quoted in *Boston Globe*, July 12, 1965.

104. *Boston Globe*, August 16, August 27, and September 5, 1965.

105. See, for instance, *Greensboro Record*, August 26, 1965.

106. *Boston Globe*, November 11, 1965.

107. Curt Gowdy with John Powers, *Seasons to Remember* (New York: HarperCollins, 1993), 170.

108. Author interview with Ted Lepcio, August 20, 2014.

109. Author interview with Clark Booth, September 2, 2014.

110. Quoted in *Boston Globe*, July 18, 1965.

111. Author interview with Dick Johnson, August 12, 2014.

112. Author interview with Dick Flavin, September 5, 2014.

113. Author interview with Eddie Germano, September 10, 2014.

114. Golenbock, *Red Sox Nation*, 282.

115. *Boston Globe*, September 17, 1965.

116. Quoted in *Boston Herald*, May 10, 1970. The *Herald* story detailed O'Connell's background and hiring and some of his thoughts after five years in the position. *Boston Record American*, September 18, 1965.

117. *Boston Record American*, April 15, 1970.

118. *Boston Globe*, October 3, 1965.

119. Quoted in *Boston Globe*, October 9, 1965.

120. *New York Times*, October 22, 1965.

121. Quoted in *Boston Record*, June 24, 1967.

122. Quoted in *Boston Globe*, November 29, 1965.

123. Quoted in *Boston Record American*, June 9, 1965.

124. *Boston Record American*, December 3, 1965.

125. *Boston Record American*, December 11, 1965.

126. *Boston Record American*, May 7, 1966.

127. *Boston Herald*, December 2 and 3, 1965.

128. Quoted in *Boston Globe*, January 5, 1966.

129. Quoted in *Boston Record American*, February 18, 1966.

130. Author interview with John Powers, August 12, 2014.

131. Gowdy with Powers, *Seasons to Remember*, 162.

132. Quoted in *Christian Science Monitor*, April 13, 1966.

133. *Boston Globe*, June 16, 1966.

134. *Boston Traveler*, May 26, 1967.

135. *Boston Globe*, July 11, 1966.

136. Quoted in *Springfield (MA) Union*, March 28, 1966.

137. *Pittsburgh Courier*, July 16, 1966.

138. Quoted in *Boston Herald*, July 22, 1966.

139. Quoted in *Boston Globe*, July 17, 1966.

140. Ted Williams with John Underwood, *My Turn at Bat* (New York: Fireside Books, 1969), 224, 225.

141. Quoted in *Boston Globe*, September 15, 1966.

142. Quoted in Stout and Johnson, *Red Sox Century*, 317.

143. Quoted in *Boston Record American*, September 30, 1966.

144. Stout and Johnson, *Red Sox Century*, 317–18.

145. Quoted in *Boston Herald*, August 12, 1973.

17. The Impossible Dream

1. Bill Nowlin and Dan Desrochers, *The 1967 Impossible Dream Red Sox* (Burlington MA: Rounder Books, 2007), 332.

2. Quoted in *Boston Globe*, May 26, 2013.

3. *Boston Globe*, January 25, 1967.

4. Author interview with Eddie Germano, September 10, 2014.

5. Author interview with Clark Booth, September 2, 2014.

6. *Boston Herald*, August 13, 1967.

7. Dick Williams and Bill Plaschke, *No More Mr. Nice Guy* (San Diego: Harcourt Brace Jovanovich, 1990), 97–98.

8. Williams and Plaschke, *No More Mr. Nice Guy*, 98.

9. Quoted in Peter Golenbock, *Red Sox Nation* (Chicago: Triumph Books, 2005), 326.

10. Quoted in *Boston Record American*, June 16, 1967.

11. Quoted in *Boston Globe* and *Boston Herald*, June 21, 1967.

12. Quoted in *Boston Record*, July 8, 1967. See also *The Sporting News*, July 8, 1967.

13. *Boston Globe*, June 21, 1967.

14. *Boston Record American*, August 1, 1967.

15. *Boston Globe*, August 2, 1967.

16. *Christian Science Monitor*, August 2, 1967.

17. James S. Kunen, "The Man with the Greatest Job in Boston," *Boston*, September 1975.

18. Quoted in *Brockton Enterprise*, July 12, 1976.

19. Quoted in *Boston Globe*, August 5, 1967.

20. Author interview with Bud Collins, September 22, 2014.

21. *Los Angeles Times*, August 19, 1967.

22. Quoted in *Boston Herald*, August 16, 1970.

23. *Christian Science Monitor*, August 2, 1967.

24. *Christian Science Monitor*, August 2, 1967.

25. Quoted in *Hartford Courant*, September 7, 1967.

26. Quoted in *Chicago Defender*, September 23, 1967.

27. Author interview with Clark Booth, September 2, 2014.

28. Glenn Stout and Richard A. Johnson, *Red Sox Century* (Boston: Houghton Mifflin, 2000), 327.

29. Email from Tom Shaer, December 28, 2015.

30. Author interview with Rico Petrocelli, October 22, 2014. Petrocelli continues: "It took a long time for Pumpsie Green to become the first black player. If you're the owner of a team and you want somebody there, he's going to be there. We heard—in [Yawkey's] early time with the team—he wasn't interested in having any black players. I guess they tried out Jackie Robinson and Willie Mays, to have it look good, but they didn't want them as players. We heard. That's all it was. I know the years when I came up and was with the team, he was wonderful. He and Mrs. Yawkey were great."

31. Author interview with Reggie Smith, February 4, 2015.

32. Author interview with Reggie Smith, February 4, 2015.

33. Stout and Johnson, *Red Sox Century*, 329.

34. Tim Horgan, "The Paradoxical Mr. Yawkey," *Boston Herald*, August 12, 1973.

35. "Lonborg, the night before he pitched against Minnesota, he fell asleep reading *The Fall of Japan*. It was Hawk Harrelson's hotel room, apparently. Hawk got traded in midseason, so he had a room at the Boston Sheraton that he wasn't using most nights. He told Lonny, if you need it. . . ." Author interview with John Powers, August 12, 2014.

36. *Boston Herald*, October 2, 1967.

37. Nowlin and Desrochers, *The 1967 Impossible Dream Red Sox*, 136.

38. Quoted in *Boston Globe*, October 2, 1967.

39. He elaborated on this theme in the December 26, 1967, *Record American*.

40. Quoted in Henry Berry, *Boston Red Sox* (New York: Rutledge, 1975), 24.

41. *The Sporting News* headline ran over a story in the October 14, 1967, edition.

42. Author interview with Eddie Germano, September 10, 2014.

43. Susan Trausch interview with Haywood Sullivan, March 10, 1989.

44. Quoted in *The Sporting News*, November 4, 1967.

45. Author interview with John Powers, August 12, 2014.

46. Author interview with Jim Lonborg, August 22, 2014. Lonborg added, "The sad thing is that in the move from Harrington to the new ownership, the ball has somehow become misplaced. I find that very sad."

47. *Boston Globe*, October 2, 1967.

48. Quoted in *Boston Herald*, July 11, 1976.

49. Quoted in *Boston Herald*, July 11, 1976.

50. *Boston Globe*, October 13, 1967.

51. Quoted in *Boston Herald*, October 25, 1967.

52. Quoted in *Boston Globe*, October 25, 1967.

53. *Pittsburgh Courier*, October 14, 1967.

54. Author interview with Reggie Smith, February 4, 2015.

55. *Washington Post*, October 15, 1967.

18. After the Dream

1. *Boston Globe*, January 30, 1968.

2. Author interview with Eddie Germano, September 10, 2014.

3. Quoted in *Boston Globe*, April 18, 1968. See also *The Sporting News*, May 4, 1968.

4. Quoted in *Boston Record*, May 25, 1968.

5. Quoted in *Boston Globe*, May 11, 1968.

6. Quoted in *Hartford Courant*, June 26, 1968.

7. Quoted in *Boston Record American*, May 22, 1968.

8. Quoted in *Boston Globe*, July 5, 1968.

9. Ed Linn, *Hitter* (New York: Harcourt, Brace, 1993), 305.

10. Linn, *Hitter*, 305.

11. *Washington Post*, August 6, 1968. See also *The Sporting News*, August 24, 1968.

12. *Boston Record American*, May 21, 1968.

13. *Boston Globe*, September 9, 1968.

14. *Boston Record American*, July 10, 1968.

15. Author interview with Leigh Montville, September 4, 2014.

16. Author interview with Tom Carroll, concierge at The Taj (formerly Ritz-Carlton), October 10, 2014.

17. Quoted in *Boston Herald*, August 30, 1968.

18. *Boston Herald*, January 10, 1989.

19. *Boston Herald*, July 28, 1968.

20. *Boston Record American*, August 9, 1968.

21. *Boston Record American*, December 5, 1968.

22. *Christian Science Monitor*, January 29, 1969.

23. Quoted in *Boston Record American*, February 24, 1969.

24. *Boston Herald*, March 10, 1969.

25. *Boston Record American*, June 28, 1969.

26. *Washington Post*, February 22, 1969.

27. *Boston Herald*, February 15, 1969.

28. Al Hirshberg, *What's the Matter with the Red Sox?* (New York: Dodd, Mead, 1973), 53.

29. *New York Times*, February 26, 1933.

30. Hirshberg, *What's the Matter with the Red Sox?* 53, 54.

31. *Washington Post*, April 20, 1969.

32. *New London Day*, November 24, 1969.

33. Author interview with Reggie Smith, February 4, 2015. It may be worth remarking on the friendship between Smith and Yastrzemski here and that Yawkey and Gardner both welcomed the sometimes outspoken Reggie Smith. Smith had occasion to meet Jackie Robinson. "I saw Jackie later on—he was my hero—in the early '70s—'71, '72, around there. He told me, 'I know who you are, and I like what you stand for.' That meant a lot to me."

34. Author interview with Bill Gutfarb, July 24, 2014. Marea Gardner died in March 2014.

35. See, for instance, Bud Collins's column, "Sox Aren't Avid for a Stadium," in *Boston Globe*, June 13, 1969.

36. *Boston Globe*, June 29, 1969.

37. Quoted in *Boston Record American*, June 27, 1969.

38. *Boston Globe*, July 20, 1969.

39. Quoted in *Boston Globe*, August 2, 1969.

40. Quoted in *Boston Globe*, August 11, 1969.

41. *Boston Globe*, August 24, 1969.

42. *Boston Herald*, September 24, 1969.

43. Keane in *Boston Globe*, September 24, 1969; Claflin in *Boston Record American*, September 25, 1969.

44. Quoted in *Boston Globe*, September 25, 1969. O'Connell said it was unfair to criticize Yawkey, that they had planned to tell Williams at the end of the season, but that while Yawkey was in New York, Williams came to ask about hiring a new bullpen coach, and O'Connell felt his hand had been forced.

45. Quoted in *Boston Globe*, September 26, 1969.

46. Quoted in *Boston Globe*, October 30, 1969.

47. Quoted in *Boston Record American*, November 8, 1969.

48. Author interview with John Kennedy, September 5, 2014.

49. Author interview with Dick Bresciani, November 11, 1999.

50. Author interview with Ted Lepcio, August 20, 2014.

51. Sullivan expressed this thought in, for example, his March 10, 1989, interview with Susan Trausch.

52. Quoted in *Boston Herald*, September 24, 1969.

53. *Boston Record American*, September 24, 1969. The AP story ran nationally.

54. Dick Williams and Bill Plaschke, *No More Mr. Nice Guy* (San Diego: Harcourt Brace Jovanovich, 1990), 113-14.

55. Author interview with Eddie Kasko, January 5, 2015.

56. Quoted in *Boston Herald*, October 26, 1975.

57. Quoted in Danny Peary, ed., *We Played the Game* (New York: Black Dog and Leventhal, 2002), 580-81.

58. *Charleston News and Courier*, November 20, 1969.

59. The most detailed initial account appeared a few weeks later in the January 15, 1970, *New York Times*.

60. Quoted in *Boston Herald Traveler*, May 31, 1970.

61. *Boston Herald*, April 12, 1970.

62. Quoted in *Boston Globe*, May 11, 1970.

63. Quoted in *Boston Herald*, August 18, 1970.

64. *Boston Record American*, June 1, 1970. Yaz turned things around, at least for a while and for himself, when he hit a two-run homer later in the same game the newspaper described.

65. Author interview with John Kennedy, September 5, 2014.

66. *Boston Globe*, October 13, 1970.

67. *Boston Record American*, March 6, 1970.

68. *Boston Globe*, May 26, 1971.

69. Brad Snyder, *A Well-Paid Slave*: *Curt Flood's Fight for Free Agency in Professional Sports* (New York: Viking, 2006), 118. Snyder interviewed Yastrzemski on February 25, 2005.

70. Quoted in *Boston Globe*, April 4, 1971.

71. Quoted in *Washington Post*, July 11, 1971.

72. Quoted in *Boston Herald*, July 12, 1971.

73. Quoted in *Boston Globe*, July 12, 1971.

74. Quoted in *Boston Herald*, July 14, 1971.

75. *Boston Record American*, July 31, 1971.

76. Quoted in *Boston Globe*, July 12, 1971.

77. Quoted in *Boston Globe*, July 13, 1971.

78. Quoted in *Boston Globe*, July 14, 1971.

79. *Boston Herald*, June 9, 1971.

80. *Boston Globe*, July 18, 1971.

81. Quoted in *New York Tribune*, March 20, 1919.

82. Quoted in *Boston Herald*, October 26, 1975.

83. Author interview with Phil Wilkinson, October 19, 2012.

84. The story was related by Bill Gutfarb in an interview with the author on July 24, 2014.

85. Quoted in *Boston Globe*, July 18, 1971.

86. See, for instance, Harold Kaese's column in the *Boston Globe* on August 20, 1971.

87. *Record American*, August 30, 1971. Yawkey quoted in *Boston Globe*, August 31, 1971.

88. *Christian Science Monitor*, September 1, 1971.

89. Quoted in *Boston Globe*, September 3, 1971.

90. Quoted in *Hartford Courant*, September 12, 1971.

91. *Hartford Courant*, September 12, 1971.

92. *Boston Herald*, September 28, 1971.

93. Quoted in *Boston Globe*, September 3, 1971.

94. *Boston Globe*, September 3, 1971.

95. Quoted in Larry Claflin, *The Sporting News*, July 31, 1971.

96. *Boston Herald*, October 21, 1971. The emphasis was the newspaper's.

97. *Springfield (MA) Union*, October 5, 1971.

98. Quoted in Harold Rosenthal, "They Belong to Boston," unknown publication, June 1958.

99. Quoted in Curt Gowdy with John Powers, *Seasons to Remember* (New York: HarperCollins, 1993), 157–58.

100. *Trenton Evening Times*, January 9, 1972. A detailed account of the robbery ran in the January 9, 1972, *Boston Record American*.

101. *Boston Record American*, March 17, 1972.

102. Quoted in *Boston Globe*, March 17, 1972.

103. Quoted in *Chicago Tribune*, March 23, 1972.

104. *Boston Herald*, April 2, 1972.

105. *Boston Record American*, April 6, 1972.

106. *Boston Globe*, April 6, 1972.

107. Quoted in *Boston Record American*, March 21, 1972.

108. *New Orleans Times-Picayune*, June 6, 1972.

109. See Meg Vaillancourt's article in *Boston Globe*, August 5, 2001. Of course Yawkey had long served on the board of the Jimmy Fund, so the notion that this was the first time he'd allowed a charitable initiative to be publicized was incorrect.

110. Quoted in *Boston Herald*, June 10, 1972.

111. *Boston Record American*, June 10, 1972. The June 19, 1972, *Christian Science Monitor* contains a good summary of Yawkey's thoughts.

112. Quoted in *Boston Herald*, June 25, 1972. Yawkey was likely responding to the June 21, 1972, *Boston Globe*, which had a long Kaese column, "Sentimental Yawkey: Does He Spoil His Ballclub?," on his sentimentalist streak and the cronyism that resulted.

113. Quoted in Peter Golenbock, *Red Sox Nation* (Chicago: Triumph Books, 2012), 384.

114. Quoted in Danny Peary, ed., *We Played the Game* (New York: Hyperion, 1994), 275-76.

115. Quoted in *The Sporting News*, June 24, 1972.

116. Shelby Whitfield, *Kiss It Goodbye* (New York: Abelard-Schuman, 1973), 236.

117. Quoted in *Boston Globe*, September 17, 1972.

118. *Boston Baseball*, May 2007.

119. Shah quotations here and below come from Roger Angell, *Late Innings* (New York: Simon and Schuster, 1982), 142-43.

120. The following story is as told in Bill Nowlin, *Red Sox Threads* (Burlington MA: Rounder Books, 2008).

121. Author interview with Donna Mountain, August 10, 2014. Donna married former Pawtucket ballplayer Jack Mountain. The Yawkeys sent them regrets after receiving a wedding invitation but gave them some pieces of silver as a wedding present.

122. Author interview with Donna Mountain, August 10, 2014.

123. *Boston Herald*, September 19, 1972.

124. *The Sporting News*, October 14, 1972.

125. Author interview with Jim Lonborg, August 22, 2014.

126. Author interview with Steve Buckley, September 5, 2014.

127. Quoted in *Springfield (MA) Union*, October 5, 1972.

128. Bill Lee with Dick Lally, *The Wrong Stuff* (New York: Viking, 1984), 48.

129. Lee with Lally, *The Wrong Stuff*, 161.

130. Carl Yastrzemski and Gerald Eskenazi, *Yaz: Baseball, The Wall, and Me* (New York: Doubleday, 1990), 78.

131. Yastrzemski and Eskenazi, *Yaz*, 80.

132. Quoted in *Hartford Courant*, February 18, 1973. The *Boston Sunday Herald Advertiser* had an exclusive by Tim Horgan on the same date. See also *Providence Journal-Bulletin*, August 2, 1980.

133. Quoted in *Boston Herald*, June 20 and 21, 1973.

134. *Boston Herald*, June 21, 1973.

135. Tom and Jean quoted in *Boston Globe*, June 14, 1973.

136. Author interview with Joe Giuliotti, September 30, 2014.

137. Author interview with Joe Giuliotti, September 30, 2014.

138. Author interview with Joe Giuliotti, September 30, 2014. For Giuliotti, covering the Red Sox wasn't a dream. It was a job. "Once I quit, I was not one of those guys like Clif Keane who used to go and hang around the ballpark. I haven't been to the ballpark since I quit, and I have no desire to be there. I never liked baseball anyway—which is a tough thing to say. I covered it all those years, but I just didn't like it. It was a job."

139. Author interview with Peter Gammons, December 1, 2014.

140. Author interview with Bud Collins, September 22, 2014.

141. Author interview with Bud Collins, September 22, 2014.

142. Author interview with Rico Petrocelli, October 22, 2014. The 1973 season was definitely a down year statistically for Rico, and he struggled through May, hitting under .200 at the end of the month. He'd begun to climb back by July, but the year was not nearly as productive—in RBIs, for example—as the year before or the year after. He drove in 75 runs in 1972 and 76 in 1974 but only 45 in 1973.

143. Quoted in *Boston Herald*, August 21, 1973.

144. Author interview with Reggie Smith, February 4, 2015.

145. *Boston Globe*, October 3, 1973.

146. Author interview with Eddie Kasko, January 5, 2015.

147. Author interview with Eddie Kasko, January 5, 2015, and *Salem News*, April 1974. Undated clipping found in Kasko's Hall of Fame player file.

148. Author interview with Eddie Kasko, January 5, 2015.

149. *Boston Herald*, January 9, 1974.

150. *Boston Globe*, March 15, 1974.

151. *Boston Globe*, March 15, 1974.

152. *Boston Globe*, March 23, 1974.

153. Quoted in *Boston Herald,* June 10, 1975.

154. Quoted in *Boston Herald*, August 25, 1974.

155. Author interview with Roger Moret, May 5, 2015.

156. Quoted in *Boston Globe*, October 3, 1974.

157. Author interview with Tom Shaer, May 11, 2015.

19. Another Game Seven

1. *Los Angeles Times*, October 14, 1975.

2. Author interview with Rick Burleson, May 5, 1975.

3. David Halberstam, *Summer of '49* (New York: William Morrow, 1989), 135.

4. *Washington Star*, October 4, 1975.

5. Quoted in *Boston Herald*, August 5, 1975.

6. Bernie Carbo and Dr. Peter Hantzis, *Saving Bernie Carbo* (Fort Pierce FL: Diamond Club Publishing, 2013), 131. See also Andrew Blume, "Bernie Carbo," in *'75: The Red Sox Team That Saved Baseball*, ed. Bill Nowlin and Cecilia Tan (Phoenix: SABR, 2015).

7. Tom Shaer recounted the conversations as told to him by Dave O'Hara. The check was not from the Red Sox organization itself. Shaer says that O'Connell "told me it was [from] Yawkey Enterprises." Author interview with Tom Shaer, May 11, 2015.

8. Quoted in *Springfield (MA) Union*, June 15, 1975.

9. Quoted in *Boston Herald*, June 11, 1975.

10. *Boston Herald*, July 29, 1975.

11. Author interview with Bob Heise, January 9, 2015. The $30,000 contract figure is as reported in Peter Gammons, *Beyond the Sixth Game* (Lexington MA: Stephen Greene Press, 1986), 281.

12. Author interview with Jim Rice, June 7, 2015. Of course Jean Yawkey did not visit the clubhouse, but the family feeling endured.

13. Author interview with Bob Montgomery, May 5, 2015.

14. Author interview with Jim Willoughby, May 5, 2015. Willoughby added, "He was just a down-to-earth guy. You could talk to him, and you could talk to him without any fear of losing your job or any paranoia. He was just a regular person. He made it personal and real, and he was a good guy."

15. Author interview with Bob Montgomery, May 5, 2015.

16. Author interview with Dwight Evans, May 5, 2015.

17. Quoted in Mark Frost, *Game Six* (New York: Hyperion, 2009), 163.

18. Quoted in *Boston Herald*, September 29, 1975.

19. Quoted in *Boston Herald*, October 2, 1975.

20. Author interview with Fred Lynn, August 19, 2014.

21. Quoted in *Boston Herald*, October 8, 1975.

22. Quoted in *Boston Globe*, October 9, 1975.

23. Quoted in *Boston Herald*, June 19, 1979.

24. Quoted in *Boston Globe*, October 21, 1975.

25. Quoted in *New York Times*, October 21, 1975.

26. Frost, *Game Six*, 38.

27. Curt Gowdy with John Powers, *Seasons to Remember* (New York: HarperCollins, 1993). 170–71.

28. Author interview with Jim Rice, June 7, 2015.

29. *Boston Globe*, October 26, 1975.

30. Quoted in *Boston Herald*, October 23, 1975.

31. Quoted in *Boston Herald*, June 18, 1989.

32. Quoted in Boston Red Sox scorebook, third edition, 1980, 10, 12.

33. Quoted in *Boston Herald*, March 16, 1981.

34. Quoted in *Boston Herald*, March 16, 1981.

35. Henry Berry, *Boston Red Sox* (New York: Routledge, 1975), 25.

36. Quoted in Boston Red Sox scorebook, third edition, 1980, 12.

37. Author interview with Tom Shaer, May 11, 2015.

38. Quoted in *Boston Sunday Herald Advertiser*, October 26, 1975.

39. Author interview with Clark Booth, September 2, 2014.

40. Author interview with George Sullivan, October 3, 2014.

20. Tom Yawkey's Final Campaign

1. *Boston Globe*, January 28, 1976.

2. *Hartford Courant*, March 20, 1976.

3. *Boston Herald*, April 10, 1976.

4. Author interview with Peter Gammons, December 1, 2014.

5. Carl Yastrzemski and Gerald Eskenazi, *Yaz: Baseball, the Wall, and Me* (New York: Doubleday, 1990), 75; emphasis in original.

6. *Boston Herald*, May 18, 1976.

7. *Boston Globe*, May 18, 1976.

8. *Boston Globe*, May 19, 1976.

9. *Boston Herald*, May 27, 1976.

10. Dick Bresciani, "Kind and Caring," *Memories and Dreams*, Opening Day 2012, 36.

11. *Boston Herald*, May 18, 1976.

12. *Boston Herald*, March 24, 1976. I did not elect to try and determine how the suit played out.

13. Quoted in Peter Gammons, *Beyond the Sixth Game* (Lexington MA: Stephen Greene Press, 1986), 59–60.

14. Author interview with Peter Gammons, December 1, 2014.

15. *Boston Herald*, June 16, 1976.

16. Quoted in *Boston Herald*, June 19, 1976.

17. Author interview with Peter Gammons, December 1, 2014.

18. Quoted in *Boston Globe*, April 4, 1993. Different Red Sox executives have different takes on the whole story. Another version had Yawkey asking O'Connell why he hadn't bought Fingers too. See also *Boston Herald*, June 9, 1976, in which Larry Claflin wrote he suspected that Yawkey admired Commissioner Kuhn for his courage.

19. *The Pilot*, July 16, 1976.

20. Author interview with Peter Gammons, December 1, 2014.

21. Author interview with Jim Rice, June 7, 2015.

22. Author interview with Bill Gutfarb, July 24, 2014.

23. Author interview with Mary Jane Ryan, August 6, 2014.

24. *Boston Globe*, July 10, 1976.

25. *Boston Herald*, July 10, 1976.

26. *New Haven Register*, July 10, 1976.

27. O'Connell and Williams quoted in *Boston Globe*, July 11, 1976.

28. *The Pilot*, July 16, 1976.

29. *Boston Herald*, July 14, 1976. The words were Larry Claflin's.

30. *Christian Science Monitor*, July 12, 1976.

31. Glenn Stout and Richard A. Johnson, *Red Sox Century* (Boston: Houghton Mifflin, 2000), 176.

32. Curt Gowdy with John Powers, *Seasons to Remember* (New York: HarperCollins, 1993), 171.

33. The amount left to Julia Y. Gaston was reported as $10,000 cash and a $5,000 annuity for life. *Boston Globe*, July 17, 1967. Tom was never close to Julia. He had taken care of her education, however, and not only had his first wife Elise married a man of means, but so had Julia. Glenn Stout raised a question in email correspondence: "Some years ago [Julia] sent me a nice note to that effect saying that since her parents divorced when she was so young she didn't really know him. The interesting thing there is that she was adopted, but in the only adult picture I saw of her she was a dead ringer for Yawkey, which makes me think there was a girlfriend." Email from Glenn Stout, April 3, 2007. There was a photograph in the November 26, 1954, *Boston Globe* of Julia's making her debut at the Junior League Debutante Ball, but it did not seem to this author that she resembled Tom Yawkey. Another rumor used to circulate around Georgetown and tied in to Sunset Lodge. "Some people think that might have been his child with Miss Hazel," said Lee Brockington of Hobcaw Barony. Author interview with Lee Brockington, October 18, 2012. If this had been the case, the elaborate travel to Chicago for Julia's adoption might have truly been overkill. Rumors around Georgetown also had the entire Red Sox team coming to Georgetown (and Sunset Lodge) every spring; a comprehensive compilation of Red Sox spring training schedules since 1901 proves this to have been an impossibility.

34. Quoted in *Boston Globe*, July 17, 1976.

35. *Hartford Courant*, July 20, 1976.

36. *Boston Globe*, July 24, 1976.

37. Quoted in *Boston Herald*, July 22, 1976.

38. Letter from Mrs. Frederick K. Gaston III, April 23, 2014.

39. Quoted in Stout and Johnson, *Red Sox Century*, 234.

40. Unidentified newspaper clipping dated March 19, 1936; found in Yawkey's Hall of Fame file.

41. Author interview with Jim Sargent, October 19, 2012.

42. *Boston Globe*, August 22, 1976.

43. *Boston Globe*, November 10, 1976.

44. *Boston Globe*, December 1, 1976.

45. *Boston Herald*, August 25, 1976.

46. Smith comments reprinted in *Cleveland Plain Dealer*, July 13, 1976.

21. Jean Yawkey in the Late 1970s

1. Quoted in *Boston Herald*, April 21, 1977.

2. *New York Times*, March 6, 1977, and *Boston Globe*, March 16, 1977.

3. *Chicago Tribune*, April 22, 1977; *Boston Globe*, April 22, 1977.

4. Letter to Edward DeBartolo reproduced in *Boston Herald*, August 28, 1977.

5. Author interview with Dick Flavin, September 5, 2014.

6. Quoted in *Boston Globe*, April 15, 1982.

7. Quoted in Peter Golenbock, *Red Sox Nation* (Chicago: Triumph Books, 2005), 218.

8. Author interview with Leigh Montville, September 4, 2014. Eddie Germano even said that longtime grounds crew worker Al Forester changed his name so that it wouldn't be known he was Italian. And yet Johnny and Vince Orlando ran the Red Sox clubhouse for years and years. Germano also said, "Pinky Higgins didn't like Malzone. Didn't like Conigliaro. That's how Johnny [Pesky] eventually lost his job as manager. The story that I heard was that Conigliaro hit a ball over the center-field scoreboard at Scottsdale. No one had ever hit a ball over the scoreboard. Close to five hundred feet. He was nineteen at the time. Higgins was checking over the roster about who was going back to Boston and who was going down to Louisville. And he said to Johnny, 'What's this Conigliariario—whatever the heck his name is; what's he doing going back to Fenway Park?' 'Oh,' Mike, this kid's going to be. . . .' 'Oh, no, no, no.' 'I think he's ready right now. I can't believe the bat this kid has.' 'Oh, no, no.' So Neil Mahoney says to Pesky, 'I hope you're right.' Higgins was a very vindictive guy. He never warmed up to Pesky and was almost pissed off that Conigliaro did so well because it made Higgins look bad." Author interview with Eddie Germano, September 10, 2014.

9. Author interview with Dick Flavin, September 5, 2014.

10. Author interview with Peter Gammons, December 1, 2014. Gammons added, "I liked Haywood Sullivan a lot. If there were times I didn't agree with him [in something I had written in the newspaper], he would call me at quarter of seven in the morning, and we'd talk it all out—which I really appreciated. He was terrific about that. He would never yell and scream and so forth. He would laugh, 'Oh, you got me today.' That kind of thing."

11. *Boston Herald*, August 31, 1977.

12. Quoted in *Boston Herald*, September 5, 1977.

13. *Boston Herald*, October 28, 1977.

14. Quoted in *Boston Herald*, September 30, 1977.

15. Quoted in *Boston Herald*, November 1, 1977.

16. See, for instance, Dick Braude's column, which ran in many December 25, 1977, newspapers, including the *Mobile Register*.

17. *Boston Herald*, May 24, 1978.

18. Quoted in *Springfield (MA) Union*, July 26, 1985. As an aside, the inclusion of Thomas DiBenedetto in the ownership group might argue against any anti-Italian sentiment.

19. Author interview with Mary Jane Ryan, August 6, 2014.

20. Author interview with Tom Carroll, October 10, 2014. Eleanor O'Neil told Gloria Negri of the *Boston Globe* about the Ritz: "We were very careful about taking in guests. Mr. Wyner [owner of the Ritz] had three requirements. If they had been there before, they could come again. They were also welcome if they were in the Social Register or Poor's Directory of Executives. If they were not

in any of those, we'd have to use our common sense." It was O'Neil who registered the first black guest at the hotel—Eddie Anderson, who worked as "Rochester" with comedian Jack Benny. "Mr. Wyner told me it was up to me. He said he didn't object to black guests. None ever came." It was also O'Neil who persuaded the Ritz's then general manager, William Ebersol, in the 1960s to ease the hotel's dress codes so that women guests and patrons could wear pantsuits. "But they had to be coordinated. I told him that if I had paid $350 for a pantsuit, I'd be highly insulted if I were a guest and were told I couldn't wear it," she said (quoted in *Boston Globe*, April 26, 1987). Other guests at the Ritz included Winston Churchill, Joan Crawford, Howard Hughes, and even Rin Tin Tin. Another unusual connection of some interest: the son of the Ritz Carlton owner Edward Wyner was George Wyner, who played assistant district attorney Irwin Bernstein in the TV show *Hill Street Blues*.

21. Author interview with Mary Jane Ryan, August 6, 2014.

22. Author interview with Donna Mountain, August 10, 2014.

23. *Boston Globe*, April 4, 1993.

24. Quoted in *Boston Globe*, April 4, 1993.

25. Author interview with Peter Gammons, December 1, 2014.

26. Quoted in *Boston Globe*, April 4, 1993.

27. Author interview with Tom Shaer, May 11, 2015. Shaer added, "Personally, I got along great with Sully and Buddy LeRoux. . . . I never had a problem with them, but she [Mary] did say it."

28. Author interview with Tom Shaer, May 11, 2015.

29. Author interview with Tom Shaer, May 11, 2015.

30. *Boston Globe*, September 30, 1977.

31. *Boston Globe*, October 5, 1977.

32. *Boston Globe*, November 1, 1977.

33. Quoted by Peter Gammons, "There's a Rub in the Hub," *Sports Illustrated*, November 14, 1977.

34. *New York Times*, October 26, 1977.

35. *Boston Herald*, October 26, 1977.

36. *Boston Globe*, October 22, 1977.

37. *Wall Street Journal*, December 12, 1977. Other publications reported votes of 11–3.

38. Quoted in *Boston Herald*, December 9, 1977.

39. Quoted in Gammons, "There's a Rub in the Hub."

40. Gammons, "There's a Rub in the Hub." Gammons noted that of the eleven general partners, one had "been subpoenaed to testify before a grand jury regarding a murder and a bankruptcy and charged another with conflict of interest in the appropriations of state funds for handicapped children. A third partner had previously been accused of another conflict of interest in a kickback scandal."

41. *Boston Herald*, January 7, 1979.

42. *Rockford (IL) Morning Star*, December 11, 1977.

43. *Boston Globe*, February 25, 1978.

44. *Hartford Courant*, July 14, 1983.

45. Quoted in *Boston Globe*, January 17, 1978.

46. *Boston Globe*, June 28, 1978.

47. Quoted in *Boston Globe*, October 3, 1978.

48. Author interview with Jim Lonborg, August 22, 2014.

49. *Boston Globe*, October 11, 1978.

50. *Boston Globe*, December 17, 1978: 73-74. Lee expanded on this notion twenty years later. In a 1999 interview with author Jim Prime, he recalled, "It was weird the day that Tom Yawkey died. There wasn't a cloud in the sky and then he died and right before the game a cloud passed over and delayed the game and it was kind of an homage to him. I was driving to the ballpark that day and a pigeon stopped me going into the parking lot. I tried to pull to the left and he walked to the left; I'd cut my wheels back to the right and he'd move over that way. And he refused to let me go in there. I knew then that Tom Yawkey had come back as a bird because of all the DDT he had sprayed to kill spruce budworms. He'd sprayed his pine forests in South Carolina and in the process killed all the birds there. We'd talked about that when he stole my copies of *National Geographic*. I told him that he would have to do penance and come back as a bird. He was undergoing chemotherapy at the time. We got along great. Someone said that at the end of that ball game there was a pigeon that went up into the air and dove headfirst and committed suicide into the bleachers at Fenway Park. Even today I'm always seeing Tom Yawkey out in the field. He's matriculated up. Now he's a crow." Jim Prime with Bill Nowlin, *Tales from the Red Sox Dugout* (Champaign IL: Sports Publishing, 2000), 161.

51. *Los Angeles Times*, January 30, 1979.

52. Author interview with Edward F. Kenney, July 19, 1999.

53. Author interview with Brian Aitchison, September 22, 1999.

54. Author interview with Bill Souris, September 12, 2014.

55. Author interview with Bill Souris, September 12, 2014. Souris drove for Jean Yawkey after Tom's death, but before too long he was offered a position in the ticket office.

56. *Boston Globe*, November 23, 1979.

57. *Boston Globe*, December 25, 1979.

22. Jean Yawkey Years, 1980-1985

1. Quoted in *Boston Globe*, August 4, 1980.

2. Quoted in *Boston Herald*, March 13, 1980.

3. Quoted by Harold Rich in *Providence Journal-Bulletin*, July 10, 1976.

4. Author interview with Art Keefe, August 12, 2014.

5. Curt Gowdy with John Powers, *Seasons to Remember* (New York: Harper-Collins, 1993), 148.

6. Quoted in *Boston Herald*, May 25, 1986.

7. *Springfield (MA) Union*, July 10, 1976.

8. Author interview with Jim Lonborg, August 22, 2014.

9. *Lowell Sun*, July 10, 1976.

10. Bernie Carbo and Dr. Peter Hantzis, *Saving Bernie Carbo* (Fort Pierce FL: Diamond Club Publishing, 2013), 130–31.

11. David Halberstam, *Summer of '49* (New York: William Morrow, 1989), 136.

12. Author interview with Buddy Hunter, August 24, 2005.

13. Quoted in *Patriot Ledger* (Quincy MA), March 13, 1980.

14. Email from Phil Wilkinson, May 19, 2014.

15. Author interview with Mark Cumbee, July 21, 2014. Jean herself drove a Jeep around on South Island but never drove in town because she hadn't a driver's license (Susan Trausch interview with Ralph M. Ford Jr., February 23, 1989. "She had a nice young man from around the ballpark. [Ticket office employee] Billy Souris used to take her. There was somebody assigned to pick her up and take her back" (author interview with Mary Jane Ryan, August 6, 2014). Jim Healey noted, "In the early '80s another driver was Kevin Harrison." Email from Jim Healey, August 11, 2014.

16. Email to author from Phil Wilkinson, May 19, 2014.

17. Author interview with Mark Cumbee, July 21, 2014.

18. Author interview with Mark Cumbee, July 21, 2014.

19. Author interview with Bob Montgomery, May 5, 2015.

20. Author interview with Jim Rice, June 7, 2015.

21. Author interview with Tom Carroll, October 10, 2014.

22. Author interview with Phil Wilkinson, October 19, 2012.

23. *Daily News Record*, September 22, 1967.

24. Carl Yastrzemski and Gerald Eskenazi, *Yaz: Baseball, the Wall, and Me* (New York: Doubleday, 1990), 75.

25. Author interview with Tom Shaer, May 11, 2015.

26. Author interview with Art Keefe, August 12, 2014.

27. Author interview with John Kennedy, September 5, 2014.

28. Author interview with Leigh Montville, September 4, 2014.

29. Author interview with Art Keefe, August 12, 2014.

30. Author interview with Eddie Germano, September 10, 2014.

31. Author interview with Bill Gutfarb, July 24, 2014.

32. *Boston Globe*, February 27, 1992.

33. Author interview with Bill Gutfarb, July 24, 2014. Jean had her own regular hairdresser on Newbury Street in Boston. Gutfarb himself experienced the problem: "I'd go to a place and they'd ask for tickets all the time, so I'd have to go to a different barber."

34. See Steve Buckley, "Jacob Ruppert Joins (Undeserving) Yawkey in Hall of Fame," *Boston Herald*, December 4, 2012. The reason for Yawkey's election to the Hall, Buckley wrote, was money. He quotes Glenn Stout and Richard A. Johnson: "Yawkey had been a benefactor of the Hall of Fame for years . . . and his enshrinement was a kind of belated thank you" (*Red Sox Century* [Boston: Houghton Mifflin, 2000], 392).

35. *Boston Globe*, August 28, 1980. LaCour came down with cancer and died at the age of sixty-two on April 15, 1981, within a year or so of moving to Boston. He had worked for the Yawkeys for forty years. John Harrington came in shortly before he died and took over. The last former employee of the New York office was a secretary who lived to be around one hundred, still receiving her retirement benefits at a home in New Jersey until she died around 2010.

36. *Boston Globe*, September 25, 1980.

37. *Boston Globe*, October 4, 1980.

38. *Boston Globe*, October 25, 1980.

39. *Boston Globe*, October 30, 1980.

40. *Boston Globe*, October 31, 1980.

41. *Boston Globe*, February 14, 1981.

42. *Washington Post*, February 21, 1981.

43. Quoted in *Springfield (MA) Union*, August 30, 1987.

44. There were those at the time who blamed Jerry Kapstein and his three players "as having driven Tom Yawkey into the grave. Which is a little unfair but was typical Boston." (The quotation comes in an off-the-record interview conducted for this book in 2014.) In August 2014 Kapstein declined a request for an interview, saying that he had never met Tom Yawkey and thus had no comment. A profile of Kapstein by Will McDonough ran in the *Boston Globe*, June 6, 1976.

45. *Washington Post*, February 21, 1981.

46. Quoted in *Chicago Tribune*, March 16, 1981.

47. *New York Times*, February 23 and April 4, 1981.

48. Susan Trausch, contemporary notes.

49. *Boston Globe*, March 4, 1981.

50. *Boston Globe*, July 12, 1983.

51. *Boston Globe*, March 22, 1981.

52. Author interview with George Sullivan, October 3, 2014.

53. *Boston Globe*, May 12, 1983.

54. *New York Times*, February 19, 1983.

55. *Boston Globe*, July 12, 1983. An earlier article in the February 11, 1983, *Globe* by Will McDonough and Peter Gammons outlined the issues well.

56. Author interview with George Sullivan, October 3, 2014.

57. Author interview with Peter Gammons, December 1, 2014.

58. *Boston Globe*, February 17, 1983.

59. *Boston Globe*, June 7, 1983.

60. Quoted in *New York Times,* July 15, 1983.

61. John Powers, internal *Boston Globe* memo to Susan Trausch, February 23, 1989.

62. Author interview with John Powers, August 12, 2014.

63. Susan Trausch interview with Bob Lobel, March 23, 1989.

64. Quoted in *Boston Globe*, August 11, 1983. The *Globe* provided good coverage throughout the trial in July and is a good resource for those wishing to dig more deeply into the details.

65. *Boston Globe*, April 4, 1993. A little over twenty years later, Leigh Montville recalled LeRoux's talking to him about working on the book but said, "He made me nervous." Author interview with Leigh Montville, September 4, 2014.

66. Quoted in *Boston Globe*, April 4, 1993.

67. Susan Trausch, *Boston Globe*, April 6, 1989. Lou Gorman's observation comes from a conversation he had with Trausch.

68. Author interview with Dick Johnson, August 12, 2014.

69. Author interview with John Harrington, April 18, 2013.

70. Author interview with Bill Gutfarb, July 24, 2014.

71. Author interview with Mary Jane Ryan, August 6, 2014.

72. Author interview with Bill Gutfarb, July 24, 2014.

73. *Boston Globe,* August 5, 2001.

74. Joan M. Thomas, "Jean Yawkey," at http://sabr.org/bioproj/person/48ac0f5c. Accessed January 20, 2017.

75. Author interview with Jim Healey, January 25, 2013.

76. Author interview with Maureen Cronin, December 11, 2013.

77. Susan Trausch interview with Sherm Feller, undated, 1989.

78. Susan Trausch interview with Frank Malzone, undated, 1989.

79. *Hartford Courant*, May 31, 1984, and *New York Times*, June 4, 1984.

80. Quoted in *Boston Herald*, May 31, 1984.

81. *Boston Globe*, June 3, 1984.

82. *Boston Herald*, July 3, 1984.

83. *Pittsburgh Post-Gazette*, September 8, 1984.

84. See the February 15, 1986, *Boston Globe* for details on the new suit.

85. Quoted in *Boston Herald*, February 16, 1986.

86. *Boston Globe*, April 4, 1993.

87. Al Hirshberg, *What's the Matter with the Red Sox?*, 167.

88. "A normal company car" meant not a livery service or limousine. Susan Trausch interview with Haywood Sullivan, March 10, 1989.

89. Michael Madden, "Tacit Complicity? For over a Decade, the Red Sox Have Helped the Winter Haven, Fla., Elks Club Distribute Membership Cards to White Players and Officials While Blacks Were Excluded," *Boston Globe*, March 15, 1985.

90. Author interview with Rico Petrocelli, October 22, 2014.

91. Quoted in Peter Golenbock, *Red Sox Nation* (Chicago: Triumph Books, 2005), 229.

92. Howard Bryant, *Shut Out* (New York: Routledge, 2002), 78.

93. Quoted in *Boston Globe*, March 15, 1985.

94. Quoted in *Boston Globe*, March 15, 1985.

95. Quoted in Bill Reynolds, "Harper Exposed the Nation's Divide," *Providence Journal*, October 22, 2014. Madden himself was threatened.

96. Michael Madden, "Harper Fired: Sox Dishonor," *Boston Globe*, December 28, 1985.

97. Howard Bryant devotes several pages to the whole story in *Shut Out*, 147–53.

98. Bob Hohler, "Tommy Harper Still Haunted by Time with Red Sox," *Boston Globe*, September 21, 2014.

99. See Hohler, "Tommy Harper Still Haunted by Time with Red Sox," which draws from documents in Harper's possession.

100. Author interview with Tommy Harper, October 2, 2014.

101. Author interview with Tommy Harper, October 2, 2014.

23. 1986 World Series and Years That Followed

1. *Springfield (MA) Union*, September 18, 1986. A story on the vendors appeared in the July 24, 1988, *Boston Herald*. See the June 27, 1988, *Boston Globe* for more on the temporary children's home, the Family Inn.

2. Quoted in *Boston Herald*, April 14, 1986.

3. Author interview with Eddie Kasko, January 5, 2015.

4. Quoted in *Boston Herald*, September 29, 1986.

5. *Boston Globe*, October 18, 1986.

6. Lou Gorman, *One Pitch from Glory* (Champaign: Sports Publishing, 2005), 10.

7. Quoted in Dan Shaughnessy, *The Curse of the Bambino* (New York: Penguin Books, 1991), 169.

8. Gorman, *One Pitch from Glory*, 11.

9. *Cleveland Plain Dealer*, October 26, 1986. Author interview with Dennis "Oil Can" Boyd, January 6, 2015.

10. Gorman, *One Pitch from Glory*, 12.

11. So wrote Will McDonough in the February 27, 1992, *Globe*.

12. Author interview with Larry Cancro, June 12, 2015. Cancro was in the clubhouse to help with the presentation. "I was the first person in history to think about giving out hats and shirts to the players. The first time we did it was when we clinched the division. And then we sold so much product that MLB wanted to do it again when and if we clinched the league, and we did. Again, it went crazy. So I was in there getting ready to do it again for the World Series. Now every team in every sport—professional and amateur—does this."

13. Quoted in Gorman, *One Pitch from Glory*, 13.

14. Gorman, *One Pitch from Glory*, 26.

15. "A Night to Honor Mrs. Yawkey," *Boston Herald*, May 22, 1988, and Joan M. Thomas, "Jean Yawkey," at http://sabr.org/bioproj/person/48ac0f5c.

16. George Whitney, "Fans' Passion for Team Surpassed Only by Mrs. Jean Yawkey's," *Diehard*, March 1992, 2.

17. *Boston Herald*, April 3, 1987.

18. *Boston Herald*, September 15, 1987.

19. *New York Times*, February 27, 1992.

20. Quoted in *Boston Globe*, August 5, 2001.

21. Quoted in *State Times Advocate* (Baton Rouge), April 30, 1987.

22. Michael Globetti in *Boston Herald*, August 11, 1987.

23. Unidentified clipping dated February 27, 1992; found in Yawkey's Hall of Fame file.

24. Dan Shaughnessy, internal *Boston Globe* memo to Susan Trausch, February 14, 1989.

25. *Boston Herald*, April 29, 1988.

26. A full story covering the event ran in the May 22, 1988, *Boston Herald*.

27. *Springfield (MA) Union-News*, February 9, 1988.

28. *New Pittsburgh Courier*, June 6, 1987.

29. *New York Times*, July 27, 1987.

30. Indeed Sullivan explicitly said that he'd been outvoted. "I was outvoted, two to one. Mrs. Yawkey gets two votes, so it was a majority decision." Quoted in *Springfield (MA) Union-News*, July 15, 1988. Sullivan added that it was a simple difference of opinion, not some rift in management.

31. *Boston Globe*, January 27, 1991.

32. *Boston Herald*, October 9, 1991.

33. *Boston Globe*, February 28, 2002.

34. Quoted in *Springfield (MA) Union-News*, July 23, 1988.

35. *Springfield (MA) Sunday Republican*, October 2, 1988.

36. *Boston Herald,* July 31, 1988.

37. Author interview with Bill Gutfarb, July 24, 2014. DeBordieu Colony is a 2,700-acre oceanfront golf community in Georgetown, South Carolina, near Myrtle Beach and Pawleys Island.

38. Author interview with Norman Pashoian, October 11, 2014. Pashoian added, of the more than thirty years his employment overlapped with the stay of the Yawkeys at the Ritz, "She [Jean] went out practically every day. I don't know where she went. As the years went by, I conversed with her a little. I never talked about the Red Sox. We always talked about the problems of the hotel. She was a very nice person. He [Tom] always kept more to himself."

39. Author interview with Robin Brown, June 17, 2015. Responding to further inquiry, Robin said, "I think she was literally wearing the same dress most of the time. I think it was the same outfit almost every day. I assume she just hand-washed it, probably, based on her lifestyle. She walked down the street to buy groceries, with a bag."

40. Quoted in *Boston Herald*, April 14, 1991.

41. Author interview with Robin Brown, June 17, 2015. About a year later, Prime Minister Kaifu of Japan came to Boston and stayed at the Four Seasons. The Japanese consul general made all the arrangements for him to meet with the heads of various colleges and universities in the area, to walk through the Public Garden to see the ducks and the swanboats. But there was also the need to go to a baseball game. Robin Brown was asked how to arrange it, so he called John Harrington. "I called John, and Jean got all involved and excited. I'll never forget doing the walk-through with the consul general, with lunch in the old 600 Club when it first launched. Jean invited Kaifu to sit in her box. They did a whole lunch for celebrities in the lounge below. It was a big deal having a head of state in her box with her. She loved that story." Prime Minister Kaifu threw out the ceremonial first ball. "When Kaifu threw the ball to Red Sox catcher Rich Gedman,

he became the first Japanese leader to do so at a game in the United States." *Los Angeles Times*, September 4, 1989.

42. Quoted in *Boston Herald*, February 2, 1989.

43. Author interview with Maureen Cronin, December 11, 2013.

44. Quoted in Susan Trausch, *Boston Globe*, April 6, 1989.

45. Author interview with Rico Petrocelli, October 22, 2014.

46. *Boston Globe*, March 18, 1990.

47. *Boston Herald*, September 11, 1990.

48. A nice story about the statue appears at http://mlb.mlb.com/news/article .jsp?ymd=20140613&content_id=79582060&vkey=perspectives&fext=.jsp&c_ id=mlb. Accessed January 20, 2017.

49. Author interview with Larry Cancro, June 12, 2015.

50. Author interview with Larry Cancro, June 12, 2015. Cancro added: "Halfway through the first dinner—the first one of these that we did—she [Jean] came up to me and pinched me on the cheek and said, 'You throw great parties. But you work too hard.' And she pulls out an envelope from her purse and puts it in my inside jacket pocket. 'You go out with Louise and you have fun.' She had gone out, all by herself, to a restaurant and got me a gift certificate to thank me. This is how she was. She was personable. She was nice. She was thoughtful."

51. *Boston Herald*, February 13, 1991.

52. *Boston Globe*, February 27, 1992.

53. *Boston Herald*, March 14, 1991.

54. The series, by Steve Fainaru, began on August 4, 1991.

24. The Passing of Jean Yawkey

1. *Boston Herald*, February 9, 1992.

2. Author interview with Robin Brown, June 17, 2015.

3. Quoted in *Boston Herald*, February 27, 1992.

4. Quoted in *Boston Herald*, February 27, 1992.

5. *Boston Herald*, February 21, 1992.

6. *Boston Herald*, February 27, 1992. *Globe* columnist Will McDonough in an internal memo to Susan Trausch also mentioned that Jean had never granted an interview to the press, adding, "Many from the media have tried, and none have been chosen." McDonough to Trausch, February 14, 1989. McDonough had suggested that Trausch "bump into her [Jean]" as she went for her daily walk from the Ritz up Newbury Street. Trausch had struck out herself, despite valiant efforts. Because of McDonough's closeness to the inner circles at Fenway, though, Trausch did hear back after her profile was published that Jean had been satisfied with the piece.

7. Author interview with Mary Jane Ryan, August 6, 2014.

8. Author interview with Jim Healey, January 25, 2013.

9. Author interview with Bill Gutfarb, July 24, 2014.

10. Author interview with Mary Jane Ryan, August 6, 2014.

11. Quoted in Steven Solomon, "Baseball World Mourns Death of Sox Matriarch," *Boston Herald*, February 27, 1992.

12. The March 7, 1992, *Globe* had a number of articles on the future of the Red Sox.

13. Author interview with Robin Brown, June 17, 2015.

14. Quoted in *Middlesex News*, February 27, 1992.

15. *Boston Globe*, February 27, 1992.

16. Author interview with Mary Jane Ryan, August 6, 2014.

17. Quoted in Susan Trausch, "The Woman Who Owns the Red Sox Keeps Her Private Life Private," *Boston Globe,* April 6, 1989.

18. Quoted in *Boston Globe*, April 4, 1993.

19. Author interview with Tom Rubillo, October 18, 2012.

20. Bob Bestler, "Yawkey's Other Gift to S. C. Wildlife," *Myrtle Beach Sun News*, December 23, 2001. Bestler's sources are unclear, and he misspells Weisse's surname.

21. Leland's article is quote by Elizabeth Scroggins, "Sunset Lodge," *Myrtle Beach Magazine*, date uncertain.

22. Zane Wilson, "Sunset Lodge," *Coastal Observer*, March 19, 1992.

23. Wilson, "Sunset Lodge."

24. Ralph M. Ford Jr. letter of April 23, 1989, to Susan Trausch.

25. *Charleston Evening Post*, December 24, 1969.

26. Author interview with Tom Rubillo, October 18, 2012.

27. Tom Hamrick, "Georgetown 'House' Closed," *The State* (Columbia SC), February 29, 1972.

28. Quoted in *Georgetown Times*, October 21, 1993.

29. Author interview with Alex Sanders, June 5, 2012.

30. Author interview with Lee Brockington, October 18, 2012.

31. Author interview with Tom Rubillo, October 18, 2012.

32. Ralph Ford Jr. letter of February 24, 1989, to Susan Trausch.

33. Quoted in Scroggins, "Sunset Lodge."

34. Letter to the editor, May 25, 2012. Sargent added, "I wonder if they did not see the ugliness in the operation of such a place in Georgetown. I was taught when something is wrong it is the same way for everybody. But we overlooked what we want and crucified what we want."

35. Susan Trausch, "The Woman Who Owns the Red Sox Keeps Her Private Life Private."

36. Author interview with John Harrington, April 18, 2013.

37. Author interview with John Harrington, April 18, 2013. The associate also spoke during this interview but preferred to remain anonymous.

38. Interview with Phil Wilkinson, October 19, 2012, and Wilson, "Sunset Lodge."

39. *Georgetown Times*, July 23, 1974. The newspaper described Weisse as a "former Georgetown resident."

40. Gleaned during conversation with Phil and Libby Wilkinson, October 19, 2012.

41. Ben Bradlee Jr. interview with Ralph Ford Jr., November 1, 2005. See Ben Bradlee Jr., *The Kid: The Immortal Life of Ted Williams* (New York: Little, Brown, 2013), 123.

42. There was one time that a team visit may have been possible—on April 6, 1939, when the Red Sox played a game in Florence as they headed north—but that was the one and only time, and Sunset Lodge had been well established in Georgetown by that point.

43. Author interview with Tom Rubillo, October 18, 2012, and Tom Rubillo, *The Waccamaw Times*, December 17, 2010. Though he was fully appreciative of the complexities of human beings and of the good that Tom Yawkey had done in life and though he never personally knew Yawkey, Rubillo was nonetheless convinced that Yawkey could have done more. His final thought in the interview: "All that potential was just wasted away in womanizing and debauchery of one kind or another."

44. Email from Rebecca Godwin, July 6, 2012. The novel *Keeper of the House* was published in New York by St. Martin's Press in October 1994.

45. Susan Trausch interview with Woodrow Carter, February 23, 1989, in *Boston Globe*, April 6, 1989.

25. The Estate, 1994, and Beyond

1. *New York Post*, March 19, 1999.

2. Quoted in *New York Post*, March 19, 1999.

3. Author interview with Bill Gutfarb, July 24, 2014.

4. Author interview with Yawkey Foundations executive, October 15, 2012.

5. Author interview with Tom Shaer, May 11, 2015.

6. *Boston Globe*, March 21, 1999. The *Herald* article ran on March 17, 1999, subtitled "Sox CEO Reaps Windfall from Yawkey Estate." It was suggested that Harrington was steering Yawkey Foundations money to his alma mater, Boston College, as though that was improper. Harrington was also said to be raking in $700,000 a year from the foundations and $2 million a year as CEO of the Red Sox, on top of additional fees paid to companies he owned such as Boston Trust Management Corporation, which had received over $2.2 million in fees at the time. An attorney who was asked to review information provided by the *Herald* concluded, "Is it legal? Yes. But is it moral and ethical? That's questionable."

7. Quoted in *Boston Globe*, June 5, 1999.

8. Dick Bresciani was perhaps the ultimate Red Sox staff loyalist. When John Harrington announced plans for a new Fenway Park in 1999 and in anticipation of opposition from preservationists (the group Save Fenway Park! coalesced on the issue), Bresciani published a color brochure on behalf of the Sox titled "Preserving the Red Sox Experience." It contained quotes about how a new ballpark would be wonderful. Among those quoted were Ted Williams, longtime

fan Lib Dooley, Bill Brooks of the BoSox Club, Doris Kearns Goodwin, Nomar Garciaparra, Bud Selig, and George Will.

One name intrigued this author: Sister Stella Caramitros, a nun of the Sisters of St. Joseph. Under the heading "A New Ballpark Is Just the Ticket," she was described as a "Boston Red Sox ticket holder" and purportedly said, "I've enjoyed going to Fenway Park to root for the Red Sox for 40 years. I want to see them win the World Series in a wonderful new ballpark."

Reached by telephone in June 1999, Sister Stella spoke with me from Framingham for a good thirty minutes. She was quite a character; she had grown up in Roxbury and followed the Red Sox all her life. She talked about the techniques she used to use at age ten to sneak into Fenway Park and fondly remembered later Nuns' Days at Fenway when Cardinal Cushing would take nuns to the park. Talking about the 1995 Red Sox, she noted they'd led the league pretty much all season long, but she added, "Then when they came to the playoff, they flubbed wicked." Asked about her endorsement of the new Fenway, she said, "Dick Bresciani is a personal friend of mine, and he said to me, 'Stel, can I use your name for a little advertisement?' I said, 'Sure, go ahead.' I didn't know what was going to happen. And so he put Sister Stella, csj (Congregation of Saint Joseph), season ticket holder. I never held a [season] ticket in my life!" Author interview with Sister Stella Caramitros, June 17, 1999. She added, in a follow-up interview on June 24, "I hate to tell you how many people were calling up and asking me if they could use the season ticket while I was in the hospital." Thanks to Erika Tarlin of Save Fenway Park! for preserving a copy of the brochure and supplying details about it in email on April 10, 2015.

9. *Boston Globe*, September 28, 2000.

10. Quoted in *Boston Globe*, October 7, 2000. The $312 million figure included the city's proposed investment in the deal—$140 million in site acquisition and cleanup, $72 million for a parking garage, and the state's commitment to spending $100 million for infrastructure for the new park.

11. *Boston Globe*, October 7, 2000.

12. *Boston Globe*, November 8, 2001. The book was written by Gary G. Tavares. *Predator on the Diamond: The Boston Red Sox Youth Molestation Story* (Smyrna GA: Tavares Entertainment LLC, 2012). The settlement was described in the May 28, 2003, *Globe*.

13. *Boston Globe*, March 5, 2012.

14. *New York Times*, January 17, 2002.

15. Author interview with Bill Gutfarb, July 24, 2014. "I do know a lumber story that might be of interest," Gutfarb offered. "When I came here in '82, one of the ways to learn about the operation was to go through the files. One of the money managers had a position in Masonite that was way out of line with what a single stock would be allocated. You might look for 2 percent at most of some securities, and this was like 18 percent. This was after Tom had passed away. Then the manager scaled it back. I later learned from one of the Gardners that

[a businessman named] Mason would take the woodchips from the Yawkey saw-mills, and he figured out a way to glue them together and make this particle-board called Masonite. And apparently in return for the sawdust and woodchips, Mason gave shares of his company. That's how that huge chunk of Masonite ended up in the portfolio."

16. Author interview with Bill Gutfarb, July 24, 2014.

17. Author interview with Bill Gutfarb, July 24, 2014.

18. See, for instance, *Boston Globe*, December 22, 2001.

19. Quoted in *New York Times*, January 3, 2002.

20. Quoted in *Boston Globe*, December 22, 2001.

21. Author interview with Dick Johnson, August 12, 2014.

22. See *Boston Globe*, December 28, 2001.

23. Quoted in *Boston Globe*, January 11, 2002.

24. *Boston Globe*, January 17, 2001. The initial $10 million came from the part-ners, not the purchasers. Harrington's share was said to be $500,000. Of course nearly every ball club has its own foundation these days.

25. See *Boston Globe*, January 13, 2002, for a sense of where the Yawkey Foun-dations stood relative to others in New England.

26. Quoted in *Boston Globe*, August 5, 2001.

27. Quoted in *Boston Globe*, December 6, 2001.

28. *Boston Globe*, May 7, 2002.

29. Quoted in *Boston Globe*, May 9, 2002.

30. *Boston Globe*, May 31, 2002.

31. An article outlining the issues appeared in the May 8, 2003, *Boston Globe*. Twelve days later, one of the trustees indicated that Harrington himself and one other had recused themselves from the vote. See a letter to the editor by trustee Charles Clough in *Boston Globe*, May 20, 2003. Regarding the Mass General grant, "He [Reilly] said the funding violated the foundation's state-ment to him that it would not funnel money to well-endowed institutions, but rather to grass-roots organizations. Harrington heatedly denied he made any such commitment and said the donations are in line with the Yawkeys' wishes" (*Boston Globe*, May 9, 2003). The tightening of the rules was reported in the September 6, 2003, *Globe*.

32. Hohler also raised the question of nepotism. Bob Hohler, "Good Works and Insider Culture, the Twin Legacies of Yawkey Charity," *Boston Globe*, Feb-ruary 12, 2017, A1.

33. Interested readers are urged to peruse Allan Wood and Bill Nowlin, *Don't Let Us Win Tonight! An Oral History of the 2004 Boston Red Sox's Impossible Play-off Run* (Chicago: Triumph Books, 2014).

34. Readers are further recommended Bill Nowlin and Jim Prime, *From the Babe to the Beards: The Boston Red Sox in the World Series* (New York: Sports Pub-lishing, 2014).

35. *Boston Globe*, January 2, 2005.

26. The Yawkey Legacy

1. South Carolina Department of Natural Resources website at https://www .dnr.sc.gov/mlands/managedland?p_id=64. Accessed January 20, 2017.

2. Adrian Walker, "Banish the Racist Legacy of Tom Yawkey," *Boston Globe*, December 7, 2015. An earlier comment is Ron Chimelis, "Rooting for Boston Red Sox Still a Challenge for African-Americans: Viewpoint," masslive.com; accessed July 24, 2015.

3. See, for instance, Marc Normandin at http://www.overthemonster .com/2016/2/1/10885892/red-sox-david-ortiz-yawkey-way. Accessed January 20, 2017. Earlier Bill Dain of Newtonville had written a letter to the editor, published in the *Boston Globe* in September 28, 2014, noting that he was angered by encountering the name each day he commuted to work: "I have known for years about the racism endemic under Yawkey and his minions and have often wondered why the city would have allowed such names on its public facilities." Frederick Hurst, publisher of *Point of View*, a Springfield (Massachusetts) news-magazine aimed at the African American community, said he was discouraged each time he went to a ballgame at Fenway Park and saw the Yawkey Way signs: "Every time I go there, I have to see that. In some ways, it's more significant than the Confederate flag because 'Yawkey Way' was established in modern times. What compelled otherwise good people to do something so painful and offensive to so many people?" See "Time to Take Yawkey's Name off the Signs," *Boston Globe*, September 28, 2014.

4. Drew Schwartz, "$10 Million Endowment Creates Non-Profit Internship Program," *Daily Free Press*, September 19, 2014.

5. A nice appreciation of Tara Hall as of 1984 appeared in the December 23, 1984, *Boston Herald*.

6. *Georgetown Times*, March 3, 1992.

7. Quoted in *Boston Herald*, July 11, 1976.

8. Quoted in *Boston Herald*, August 25, 1974.

9. See a complete listing at www.yawkey.org.

10. *New York Tribune*, March 20, 1919.

11. Quoted in Jeff Hall, "The Enduring Legacy of the Yawkey Foundation," American Red Cross, posted December 11, 2015. at http://www.redcross.org /news/article/The-Enduring-legacy-of-the-Yawkey-Foundation.

12. *Boston Globe*, October 24, 2005.

13. Author interview with Mary Jane Ryan, August 6, 2014.

14. Author interview with Larry Cancro, June 12, 2015.

15. Quoted in *Boston Globe*, September 16, 2006.

27. Tom Yawkey and Race

1. Quoted in *Sports Illustrated*, August 19, 1991.

2. See Ken Krause at http://medford.wickedlocal.com/x2082692166 /Historian-recounts-Medford-African-American-journalists-role-in -integration-of-baseball. Accessed February 15, 2013.

3. Howard Bryant, *Shut Out* (New York: Routledge, 2002), 7, 8.

4. Quoted in Bill Nowlin, ed., *Pumpsie and Progress: The Red Sox, Race, and Redemption* (Burlington MA: Rounder Books, 2010), 151.

5. Glenn Stout and Richard A. Johnson, *Red Sox Century* (Boston: Houghton Mifflin, 2000), 279.

6. Glenn Stout, "Tryout and Fallout: Race, Jackie Robinson, and the Red Sox," originally published in *Massachusetts Historical Review* and reprinted in Nowlin, *Pumpsie and Progress*, 77.

7. *Boston Globe*, September 16, 2006.

8. Quoted in Ben Bradlee Jr., *The Kid: The Immortal Life of Ted Williams* (New York: Little, Brown, 2013), 284.

9. The words were Bryant's. See Bryant, *Shut Out*, 53.

10. For a full book devoted to the question of the Robinson tryout and the years through Pumpsie Green's debut, see Nowlin, *Pumpsie and Progress*.

11. Quoted in *Chicago Defender*, September 23, 1967.

12. Quoted in Stout and Johnson, *Red Sox Century*, 242.

13. Quoted in Dan Shaughnessy, *The Curse of the Bambino* (New York: Penguin Books, 1991), 56.

14. Stout, "Tryout and Fallout," 82.

15. Quoted in Shaughnessy, *The Curse of the Bambino*, 56.

16. Author interview with Jim Healey, March 16, 2016.

17. Author interview with Clark Booth, September 2, 2014.

18. Author interview with Jim Sargent, November 15, 2012.

19. Author interview with Jim Sargent, November 15, 2012.

20. Author interview with Bill Gutfarb, July 24, 2014.

21. Author interview with Dick Johnson, August 12, 2914.

22. Author interview with Phil Wilkinson, December 12, 2012.

23. Author interview with Phil Wilkinson, December 12, 2012.

24. Author interview with Phil Wilkinson, December 12, 2012.

25. Author interview with Tom Shaer, May 17, 2015.

26. Quoted in Dave Egan, "What about Trio Seeking Sox Tryout?" *Boston Record*, April 16, 1945.

27. Reported by Marc Onigman, "Tom Yawkey: Gentleman, Sportsman, and Racist," *The Real Paper*, August 9, 1980. As noted, the report itself is dated August 27, 1946—in other words, more than sixteen months after the Robinson-Jethroe-Williams tryout at Fenway Park. It wasn't meant to be an unbiased investigation. The purpose of the report, according to the summary at its beginning, was to look at "methods to protect Baseball from charges that it is fostering unfair discrimination against the Negro by reason of his race and color." Thanks to Steven Wisensale of the University of Connecticut for providing a copy of the report.

28. See p. 18 of the August 27, 1946, report.

29. The Major League owners in general "were saying that, in effect, there had not been any blacks in baseball because they were not . . . good enough for the Majors, but that they couldn't very well sign them to *make* them good enough

because if they did, then they would have ruined the Negro Leagues. And if the Negro Leagues kept hogging all the good black players, how were the white owners supposed to get any? The prototype of Catch-22." Onigman, "Tom Yawkey."

30. Stout and Johnson, *Red Sox Century*, 276; Bryant, *Shut Out*, 45.

31. Quoted in Bryant, *Shut Out*, 45. Al Hirshberg offers a bit more on the shortcomings in scouting for the Red Sox in *What's the Matter with the Red Sox?* (New York: Dodd, Mead, 1973), 141–53.

32. Hirshberg, *What's the Matter with the Red Sox?*, 146.

33. Among other sources, see Ron Anderson's interview with George Digby, January 18–20, 2007, in Jim Sandoval and Bill Nowlin, eds., *Can He Play? A Look at Baseball Scouts and Their Profession* (Phoenix: SABR, 2011), 52–59.

34. Quoted in Bryant, *Shut Out*, 46.

35. Quoted in Bryant, *Shut Out*, 46.

36. Stout, who interviewed Kountze at length, refers readers to Kountze, *Fifty Sports Years along Memory Lane*, 24.

37. Author interview with Dick Johnson, August 12, 2014.

38. See *Boston Globe*, September 16, 2006.

39. *Boston Herald*, April 16, 2007.

40. Hirshberg, *What's the Matter with the Red Sox?*, 143.

41. Hirshberg, *What's the Matter with the Red Sox?*, 141.

42. Hirshberg, *What's the Matter with the Red Sox?*, 141–42.

43. Hirshberg, *What's the Matter with the Red Sox?*, 115.

44. Craig E. Urch and Sydney Finkelstein, "The Boston Red Sox and the Integration of African American Players," in *The Northern Game—and Beyond*, ed. Mark Kanter (Cleveland: SABR, 2002), 7.

45. Hirshberg, *What's the Matter with the Red Sox?*, 112.

46. Carl Yastrzemski and Gerald Eskenazi, *Yaz: Baseball, the Wall, and Me* (New York: Doubleday, 1990), 80.

47. Author interview with George Sullivan, October 3, 2014.

48. Author interview with George Sullivan, October 3, 2014.

49. John Curtis email to Jeff Angus in 2003. See Angus's biography of Reggie Smith for SABR's BioProject at http://sabr.org/bioproj/person/29bb796b. Accessed January 20, 2017.

50. See Bill Nowlin, "When the Red Sox Desegregated New Orleans Baseball," in Nowlin, *Pumpsie and Progress*, 54–56.

51. Susan Hammond, letter to the editor, *Boston Globe*, September 2, 2017: 12. Hammond quoted George Scott as saying, "If he was prejudiced in any way towards the black ballplayer, I did not detect it." See Lary Whiteside, "Sox' Children of the 60's Look Back . . . ," *Boston Globe*, July 29, 1978: 78. Scott added, "I think if you ask Reggie [Smith] and some of the other guys, they'd tell you the same thing."

Epilogue

1. See "Larry Whiteside, 69, Black Sports Journalist," *Houston Chronicle*, June 15, 2007.

2. Author interview with Dick Johnson, August 12, 2014.

3. Tom Shaer email to author, December 28, 2015.

4. For more information, see Bill Nowlin, "How Sam Jethroe Was Received in Boston," http://www.thenationalpastimemuseum.com/article/how-sam -jethroe-was-received-boston. Accessed January 20, 2017.

5. See, for instance, UPI, "Mass. Commission to Open Red Sox Quiz," *Chicago Defender*, April 25, 1959, 24; Glenn Stout and Richard A. Johnson, *Red Sox Century* (Boston: Houghton Mifflin, 2000), 276. Mays is quoted as telling Ted Williams, "I always thought I was supposed to play with you in Boston."

6. Quoted in *Boston Herald*, January 19, 1958.

7. *Boston American*, January 20, 1958.

8. Quoted in *Chicago Defender*, April 13, 1959. The executive was probably Dick O'Connell, as indicated above. See Bill Nowlin, ed., *Pumpsie and Progress: The Red Sox, Race, and Redemption* (Burlington MA: Rounder Books, 2010), 151.

9. Quoted in *Chicago Defender*, March 2, 1959.

10. *New York Times*, April 13, 1959.

11. *Boston Globe*, April 9, 1959.

12. *The Sporting News*, April 22, 1959.

13. *Boston Globe*, June 4, 1959.

14. Author interview with Al Green, September 26, 1999.

15. Jason Collins, "Coming Out," *Sports Illustrated*, May 6, 2013.

16. AP, "Jason Collins Throws Out First Pitch at Fenway Park," http:// boston.cbslocal.com/2013/06/06/jason-collins-throws-out-first-pitch-at-fenway -park/. Accessed October 19, 2015.

17. See http://tarahall.org. Accessed January 20, 2017.

18. Author interview with Jim Dumm at Tara Hall, October 18, 2012. All quotations from Jim Dumm come from this interview. Ellie Armstrong had been a nurse anaesthetist, wife of Bill Armstrong, the first surgeon at Georgetown Memorial Hospital. She worked not at the hospital but at the Baskerville Free Clinic, now known as the Smith Medical Clinic at Pawley's Island, South Carolina.

19. Much of the language here comes from a booklet titled *Tom Yawkey Wildlife Center*, first published by the South Carolina Department of Natural Resources in 1979 (2004 edition).

20. Author interview with Eddie Kasko, January 5, 2015.

21. Quoted in *The State* (Columbia SC), October 8, 2006.

22. *Tom Yawkey Wildlife Center*, p. 11.

23. Author interview with Alex Sanders, June 5, 2012.

24. Author interview with Jamie Dozier, October 19, 2012. For more on Dozier's background and his predecessor Bob Joyner, see Zane Wilson, "Wildlife Refuge Changes Leaders," *Myrtle Beach Sun News*, December 4, 2006.

25. Author interview with Jamie Dozier and Phil Wilkinson, October 19, 2012.

26. Author interview with Phil Wilkinson, October 19, 2012.

27. Author interviews with Phil Wilkinson, September 12 and December 12, 2012.

28. Author interview with Phil Wilkinson, September 12, 2012.

29. Author interview with George Sullivan, October 3, 2014.

30. Author interview with Jamie Dozier, October 19, 2012.

31. *Post and Courier* (Charleston SC), January 13, 2013.

32. Author interview with Phil Wilkinson, October 19, 2012.

33. Author interview with Phil Wilkinson, October 19, 2012.

34. Quoted in *Boston Globe*, May 26, 2013. An earlier profile of Trank on the job ran in the August 10, 1958, *Boston Globe*, part of a series on the women who worked at Fenway Park. Mary Lynch, Elinor Mossman, Helen Robinson, Ruth Stewart, and Barbara Tyler were the other women profiled. Barbara Tyler said that taking dictation from Tom Yawkey was like being pelted by Ryne Duren's fastball.

35. Author interview with Bill Souris, September 12, 2014.

36. Author interview with Clark Booth, September 2, 2014. Booth liked O'Connell: "Dick was the real deal. There was no guile. There was nothing of that in him. I liked him a lot. He was not an easy guy. He was a tough son of a bitch in a lot of ways, but I loved him."

37. Author interview with Tom Shaer, May 11, 2015.

38. Maureen Cronin email to author, May 16, 2014.

39. Author interview with Maureen Cronin, December 11, 2013.

40. The quotes in the next several paragraphs are from Maureen Cronin email to author, May 16, 2014. Cronin had earlier said, "When I became a stockbroker, she [Jean] gave me the Red Sox account. Which is what I thought she was trying to tell me when I was at my dad's funeral. She set me up with a nice account at Shearson. It was a big help to me, getting started in Boston as a stockbroker." Author interview with Maureen Cronin, December 11, 2013.

41. Author interview with Maureen Cronin, December 11, 2013.

42. Susan Trausch, *Boston Globe*, April 6, 1989.

43. Author interview with Mary Jane Ryan, August 6, 2014.

44. Author interview with Mary Jane Ryan, August 6, 2014.

45. Author interview with Larry Cancro, June 12, 2015.

46. Http://www.inquisitr.com/1912159/leatherback-sea-turtle-rescued -from-lonely-beach-christened-yawkey/#vuquJIZCpm2HEFu6.99. January 20, 2017.

47. Ernest L. Wiggins, "Yawkey's Island a Walk on Wild Side," *New Orleans Times-Picayune*, January 3, 1988, 3.

48. Wiggins, "Yawkey's Island a Walk on Wild Side," 3.

Index